PILGRIMAGE

A HISTORY OF WESTERN CIVILIZATION

VOLUME 1

FROM ANTIQUITY TO THE HIGH MIDDLE AGES

PILGRIMAGE

A HISTORY OF WESTERN CIVILIZATION

VOLUME 1

FROM ANTIQUITY TO THE HIGH MIDDLE AGES

by
Richard Allington, PhD and Joseph J. Reidy, PhD

TAN Books
Gastonia, North Carolina

Cover design by Caroline Green
Typesetting by David Ferris, www.davidferrisdesign.com

Front cover image: Appian Way towards the Colosseum, photo by Luca Saraceni/ Shutterstock
Back cover image: Alexander Mosaic (detail), House of the Faun, Pompeii, circa 100 BC, public domain via Wikimedia Commons

ISBN: 978-1-5051-2648-8
Kindle ISBN: 978-1-5051-3299-1
ePUB ISBN: 978-15051-3298-4

Published in the United States by
TAN Books
PO Box 269
Gastonia, NC 28053
www.TANBooks.com

Printed in India

In memory of Dr. Brendan McGuire (1983–2020)
Classmate, mentor, and noble pilgrim, with prayers for a happy homecoming.
Requiescat in pace.

Acknowledgements

The authors would like to thank all those who supported this project with their prayers, advice, and feedback, especially Sarah and Mary Wieneke, John Forbes, Sebastian Garren, the Keys family, Peter Carter, Dennis Reidy, George Capps, Dr. Vaughn Griesbauer, and Dr. Jared Goff. We would like to express particular gratitude to Isabel Nolan for her excellent, insightful comments. This work is much stronger due to her willingness to review and critique multiple drafts. We also thank our editorial team—Brian Kennelly, Jason Gale, Thomas O'Sullivan, and Dr. Daniel Davy—for their professional feedback and patience throughout the writing process. This book's beautiful design and excellent maps are the fruit of the respective labors of David Ferris and Jordan Avery. We are grateful for their tremendous contributions to this project. Our wives and children deserve our special gratitude for their patience, love, and support, which helped make this project a reality. Finally, the authors wish to thank the Most Blessed Trinity, the Virgin Mary, and all those heavenly patrons who aided us as we sought to share our love for history with the next generation of historians. May this work give glory to God and lead its readers into greater unity with Him.

June 16, 2023
Feast of the Sacred Heart

CONTENTS

UNIT V: Gain and Loss

UNIT VI: The Rise of Christendom

UNIT VII: The Flowering of Christendom

A NOTE TO PARENTS

Pilgrimage can be a demanding text. It both offers much content for students to learn and expects them to wrestle with challenging material. While we have tried to introduce all topics with decorum and respect for the students' age, we also felt it would be useful for parents if we highlighted different points of the narrative where some students may have more questions and need further guidance as they navigate the text. Below is a brief list of topics that may require further discussion together.

Chapter 1: This chapter defines many important concepts and explains some of the philosophical thought behind studying history. Students may initially feel overwhelmed and need more time to consider the material, especially since there is no easy narrative to follow.

Chapter 2: We introduce Enkidu and Shamhat in our discussion about *The Epic of Gilgamesh* and use their relationship to convey important social developments. While there is nothing explicit in our discussion, the *Epic* as a whole contains themes and episodes that may be too mature for most high schoolers.

Chapter 11: This chapter highlights the myth of Lucretia, in which a Roman noblewoman is assaulted by a tyrannical prince.

Chapter 18: The narratives of ecumenical councils, particularly those of the fifth century, can be distressing, especially for those unfamiliar with their events. We have tried to prepare students by providing an insert in chapter 16 that discusses the reality of human limitations and divine grace at ecumenical councils.

Chapter 22: The formal condemnation of Pope Honorius I as a heretic may be difficult to understand for students with only a basic familiarity with the Church's teachings on papal infallibility.

Chapter 24: Many of the moral shortcomings of the Early Medieval papacy are included here. The pontificates of John XII and Benedict IX may be especially troubling to students not familiar with papal history.

Chapter 27: This includes a discussion on the abuse of annulments by medieval nobility and royalty. This discussion reaches its conclusion in chapter 29 with the pontificate of Innocent III.

A NOTE TO STUDENTS ON ABBREVIATIONS AND SPELLINGS

Historians often identify the time period for a given individual (or dynasty) when introducing that person. Typically, these years indicate when a person was born and died or when a given dynasty began and ended. Sometimes, however, historians use abbreviations to clarify how they are using these dates or to provide some additional information about an individual. Below is a brief guide to the abbreviations used in this text.

AD = "*Anno Domini*" (Latin for "Year of the Lord"); this designates that a given year or range of years took place after the estimated birth of Jesus of Nazareth. Unlike BC, AD is placed before the number it references. Secular texts typically use the designation "CE" ("Common Era"). This is an attempt to be more inclusive of non-Christian societies, but there is no difference in the reckoning of the year.

BC = "Before Christ"; this indicates that a given year or range of years took place before the estimated birth of Jesus of Nazareth. Secular texts typically use the designation "BCE" ("Before the Common Era"). This is an attempt to be more inclusive of non-Christian societies, but there is no difference in the reckoning of the year. Most historians believe that our current reckoning of Jesus's birth is off by four years and thus date the birth of Christ to 4 BC rather than AD 1. This adjustment takes into account modern estimates for when Herod the Great died.

c. = "circa" or "around"; this indicates that we are uncertain of the precise year.

d. = "died"; this refers to the year that a given individual died.

fl. = "flourished"; we use this for individuals of whom we know very little except for the fact that they lived, or "flourished," at a given period.

r. = "ruled"; this indicates when a given individual ruled or held power. This is typically used for monarchs, but in this text, we will also use this designation for papal reigns.

St. = "Saint"; this designates those individuals who have been recognized by an Apostolic Church (e.g., the Catholic Church, the Orthodox Church, etc.) for their lives of holiness. In this text, we do not use the title "St." when referring to an individual within the chronological narrative. This title was often applied years, if not centuries, after a person's lifetime, and contemporaries did not always know who was saintly and who was not. In fact, saints could be on opposing sides of a given (theological) debate. Therefore, it helps students engage more directly with a given period if they do not rely on the title "saint" as a convenient shorthand for "good guy."

Regarding spelling, there is no single best way to write words which originate in languages that use different characters from those of the English alphabet—a process known as transliteration. We have attempted to choose spellings that would either be familiar to students or reflective of modern scholarship. Since our goal is to facilitate learning, we have made such choices on an individual basis. Please note that multiple spellings exist for certain terms and that students will likely encounter alternate spellings in other history texts.

UNIT I

Lands of the Fertile Crescent

CHAPTER 1

A Catholic Approach to History

When artists paint on panels and on walls the events of ancient history, they alike delight the eye, and keep bright for many a year the memory of the past. Historians substitute books for panels, bright descriptions for pigments, and thus render the memory of past events both stronger and more permanent, for the painter's art is ruined by time.

Theodoret of Cyrrhus, *Ecclesiastical History*[1]

The fifth-century bishop Theodoret wrote these words at the beginning of his ecclesiastical, or Church, history. Despite the passage of many centuries, his comparison between the painter and the historian remains a fitting one and inspired our own efforts as we wrote this book. Like Theodoret, we realize that vivid paintings are more memorable than uninteresting ones, and we have attempted to include as many details as space permits so that your encounters with the individuals and societies of earlier eras will be as rewarding as possible. Furthermore, while our primary audience is Catholic high school students, we hope that this volume will be of value to all those who are interested in deepening their understanding of history from a Catholic perspective.

This is not a simple task. It is all too easy to reduce history to an oversimplified narrative that encourages a given political or ideological position. In such cases, it is as though Theodoret's painter had produced a caricature rather than an accurate portrait. Such cartoons distort and exaggerate the features of their subjects, and a poor history does something similar to the past. Instead, like those producing

1 Theodoret of Cyrrhus, *Ecclesiastical History*, trans. Blomfield Jackson, vol. 3 of *Nicene and Post-Nicene Fathers: Theodoret, Jerome, Gennadius, Rufinus: Historical Writings*, Second Series, eds. Philip Scaff and Henry Wace (1892; repr., New York: Cosimo, 2007), 33.

The Last Chapter by James Doyle Penrose. Oil on canvas c. 1902. Property of the Cambridge University Library, Cambridge, England. In this painting, the dying Bede the Venerable, patron saint of historians, dictates a translation of the Gospel of John to a young scribe.

a realistic portrait, historians attempt to recreate the decisions and events of the past as accurately as possible. Achieving this goal requires an understanding of the tools available to the historian and their limitations. We therefore begin our journey through the past by defining and explaining the subject of history and the role it plays in the formation of a Catholic.

What is History?

History is more than a "simple" list of what happened. It incorporates and references all other human endeavors and their methods of gaining knowledge. The literature, education, and philosophy of a civilization are as much a part of its history as are its medicine, architecture, and theology.

We usually divide branches of learning into "arts" and "sciences." While different fields can employ these words in different ways, for our purposes here, we define "science" as an *objective* discipline whose goal is to gain knowledge and an "art" as a *subjective* one that seeks to express knowledge. Scientific studies, such as biology, mathematics, and physics, require evidence and proof and strive to find and understand abstract, universal laws. In contrast, arts such as painting, poetry, and music are subjective. That is, the individual, or "subject," is central to its origin. Whereas a science's laws exist whether or not one discovers them, an individual must produce a work of art for it to be real. While an art may follow a set of rules, the final product is always the fruit of the artist's intellect and imagination. Art can reflect the truth of the world about us, but we do not seek to "prove" whether art is true or untrue—it simply exists.

Where, then, does history fall in these categories? Theodoret's comparison above implies that history is an art, but that is only part of the picture. History is also based on scientific principles. Its study, like that of a science, requires evidence. We use, for example, the objective reality of buildings constructed, tools forged, and, most importantly, the words written and spoken by previous generations to develop theories about the past. We call such evidence **primary sources** because these words and artifacts left behind serve as our "primary," or first, way of understanding the past. Primary sources form the foundation for any historical inquiry since they offer us the best opportunity to "hear" the voices of earlier generations. We can never simply ignore such sources when attempting to understand the past. In this way, historians act like scientists. Their work incorporates the evidence related to the topic about which they are writing. If a historian rejects a source out of a preconceived interpretation or ideological preference, he is no longer practicing history but instead has become a storyteller with a particular ending already in mind.

Nonetheless, no historical narrative is fully objective or scientific. The past, by its very nature, is inaccessible to our observation. Unlike the sciences, no universal laws await our discovery through experimentation. Moreover, primary sources possess limitations. Some are external: Is a source still extant, that is, existing, or has it been (partially) lost or destroyed? Can we decipher its language or interpret its symbolism? What information was not included because an author considered it unimportant at the time? Other limitations are embedded in the sources themselves: What details might ancient authors have chosen to emphasize or obscure because of their own perspectives or biases? How should historians balance conflicting evidence from different types of sources and from sources that represent opposing "sides"? We may choose to favor one source over another, but such a decision must weigh factors such as a given source's trustworthiness and the confirmation of its details through other pieces of evidence. There is no mathematical equation that lets us know which of two sources is more trustworthy. Instead, we carefully consider alternatives and deduce what we believe to be the best interpretation in a way that is not purely scientific.

History's "artistic" nature extends even deeper. We can frequently narrate important events in their correct order with confidence, but as historians, we also seek to explain *why* an incident happened or *what* motivated a given individual.

Exploring such questions is inherently subjective. We seldom understand our own motivations entirely, so we cannot assume that we comprehend all the factors that shaped someone's life or inspired a given decision. Careful historians frequently admit that their deductions are, in the end, only theories. In this way, two good historians can draw different, yet valid, interpretations from the same evidence.

Historians' theories are known as **secondary sources**. History books, such as this one, offer conclusions and interpretations, but these explanations, no matter how accurate or satisfying, should not be confused with the primary sources left behind by a given society. A diligent historian consults both primary and secondary sources to learn what evidence the past has left for us and how others have used that evidence in an attempt to understand that past. The "historiography" of a given topic is the study of its related secondary sources and the methods and interpretations that historians have developed to explain that topic.

So, what can we conclude about history from this discussion about arts and sciences? History is both the science of organizing and presenting evidence from the human past *and* the art of unraveling human motivations. In short, history does nothing less than study human thoughts and actions—some of the most complex and mysterious processes in the universe.

What is History for the Catholic?

Our examination of what the study of history is likely inspires a second question: What role does this "scientific art" have in our formation as Catholics? Some may suggest that Catholics should limit their study to "what happened." From this perspective, the Catholic historian simply recounts the ordering of events and links these together in a seemingly straightforward chain of cause-and-effect. While it may be tempting to embrace a "facts only" approach, this easily leads to the cartoon caricatures we mentioned earlier. Whether or not we realize it, we are *constantly* interpreting the past for ourselves and others. (Just think of the last time you were explaining a decision to someone. The narrative you provided involved more than a series of factual statements; it included your interpretation of people's motives—including your own—and how those interacted.) Every historical narrative presents its own interpretation. As Catholics, our understanding of history's value derives from an interpretation rooted in our Faith. This interpretation asserts that God Himself, though unconstrained by time and space, chose to become part of our history and gave it supernatural significance through His very presence. For this reason, the Incarnation of Christ and His mission to redeem humanity from sin and lead all souls to Heaven is the central core of history and the event that gives meaning to every age, society, and individual.

The Annunciation by Philippe de Champaigne. Oil on canvas c. 1648. Property of the Wallace Collection, Westminster, England. The painting shows the moment of the Incarnation, when the Holy Spirit came upon the Virgin Mary during the Annunciation (see Lk 1:35–38).

Building upon this perspective, some saints and doctors of the Church have embraced a doctrine known as the **Absolute Primacy of Christ**. This belief, typically associated with Franciscan spirituality, proposes that God did not become man as a consequence of Adam and Eve's sin, but that He intended the Incarnation from before time, regardless of the Fall. According to this reading of St. Paul, God willed the Son's human nature—"the first-born of all creation" (Col 1:15)—before the creation of the world and intended that union of divine and human natures in Jesus to be the summit, the climax, of human history. In other words, human history was intimately tied to the Incarnation even before humanity existed! That is why elsewhere Paul joyfully declares, "He chose us in him [Jesus] before the foundation of the world . . . [and] destined us in love to be his sons through Jesus Christ" (Eph 1:4–5). St. Peter deepens our understanding of the significance of this adoption in his own epistle when he declares that God desires us to "become partakers of the divine nature" (2 Pt 1:4). If you are not astounded by those words, please read them again. God desires us to share the *divine nature* through the coming of His Son. Of course, we remain creatures, but through adoption, we become God's children and "partake" in His very essence, and God intended this "before the foundation of the world"!

Not every saint has agreed with the Absolute Primacy of Christ; both St. Thomas Aquinas and St. Alphonsus Liguori, for example, rejected the premise that God the Son would have become man without Adam's sin. Others, such as St. Albert the Great and St. Francis de Sales, did hold to the Absolute Primacy and declared that Original Sin did not motivate the Incarnation but rather added a redemptive character. Due to our first parents' disobedience, they argued that Jesus's coming now not only involved enabling our "partaking of the divine nature" but also required our redemption from sin through His passion. For this reason, we sing at the Easter

Vigil about "the happy fault" that gave us a Redeemer still willing to bring us into His own divine life, even though He now suffered in order to do so. Regardless of whether we personally hold the doctrine of the Absolute Primacy of Christ, the debate about whether Jesus would have become man if Adam had not sinned helps illustrate the profound value of history for a Catholic. History is, at its core, tied to God's desire to unite us with His own divine life. Put simply, history is the epic story of the preparation for Jesus's coming, His redemptive sacrifice, and His commission to baptize all nations in order to incorporate everyone into the "divine nature." The Catholic historian Christopher Dawson went so far as to call history "the greatest work of God."[2]

While the Church features large in a Catholic understanding of history, the Catholic historian realizes that those societies that never knew of Jesus or that have hitherto rejected His message also form an integral part of the Incarnational narrative. After all, Christ commissioned His Church to bring all peoples into His sheepfold. A global history is, therefore, inherently valuable to Catholics. Nonetheless, there is also a place for more limited and manageable studies, and this text focuses its narrative on **Western Civilization**. This term can be used in multiple ways, but we employ it here to designate those societies that influenced the culture into which Jesus was born as well as those subsequent, predominately European societies that embraced the teachings of the Gospel.

A Catholic understanding of history not only directs us to the importance of the Incarnation but also leads us to contemplate the four marks of the Church: one, holy, catholic, and apostolic. According to the *Catechism of the Catholic Church*, the four marks are both the Church's attributes and her mission (see *CCC* §811). They are *attributes* insofar as the Church is the Mystical Body of Christ and therefore possesses all perfections in Him. They are her *mission* insofar as every generation, and every individual within that generation, must strive to live out the four marks. History helps us trace out that mission, its successes, and its setbacks throughout the centuries.

For example, while faith sees the *oneness* of the Church in her teachings, her sacraments, and her fidelity to Jesus, history teaches us how each era has confronted, more or less successfully, the tensions that frequently threaten to divide the Church's community. Catholics of each generation are called to do their part through prayer and work to deepen the unity that Jesus so ardently prayed for during the Last Supper (see Jn 17:21–23). History aids us in this task by informing us how each tragic division among Christians has arisen and by offering us, its students, lessons for healing those divides.

---

2 Donald J. D'Elia, "The Catholic as Historian: Witness in Every Age to Christ's Presence among Us," in Donald J. D'Elia and Patrick Foley, eds., *The Catholic as Historian* (Naples, FL: Sapientia Press, 2006), 3.

The study of history also offers us a nuanced perspective regarding the Church's *holiness*. The Church is both divine and human. In her divine Head, her sacraments, and her liturgy, she is always holy; in her humanity, the failings and vices of her members are seen in every generation. The distinction between the divine and human is crucial if we are to understand how the Church can remain holy despite the significant sins of individual Catholics. This awareness will also help us emulate those heroic Catholics of past ages who used their historical circumstances as an opportunity to seek holiness.

In addition, history enables us to observe the *universality* of the Catholic Church, whose saving Baptism is intended for all peoples, at all times, and in every region of the world. We learn through the investigation of the past how the same Faith can be embraced by different cultures, which are then inspired to highlight different facets of that same Truth. Furthermore, the historical narrative features numerous intrepid missionaries whose selfless example inspires us to evangelize the world today.

Lastly, history gives us a deeper context for how Catholicism is *apostolic* in its origin, its teachings, and its structure. The historical narrative connects the present to the Church's past through an unbroken transmission of Catholic leadership and teaching, stretching back to the twelve apostles. This, however, does not imply that Catholicism has never experienced developments. Its teachings have been enriched through further study and debate, and its organization has evolved during its two-thousand-year journey. History informs us what motivated these developments and helps us to discern how our shared Faith unites us to those of previous centuries.

All this is good, you may say, but formation is more than intellectual development. What virtues can the study of history foster? The first is the natural virtue of empathy. As noted previously, we cannot know the motivations of others with certainty. We can deduce and theorize, but God alone sees within. Empathy builds upon this awareness and motivates us to exercise compassion in our dealings with others. Our study helps us to develop this charitable attitude because in history we frequently realize the limitations of our knowledge. It is hard to pretend to know what truly motivates someone when many basic questions remain unanswered. History, therefore, encourages us to withhold judgment of others, especially those who oppose what we most value. "To withhold judgment" does not mean accepting or agreeing with sinful views and actions. Rather, it means that we acknowledge that God alone knows each person's motives. Certain beliefs and actions may be wrong and need to be condemned, but as the Gospel commands, we refrain from judging the individuals themselves (see Mt 7:1).

A second virtue is the theological virtue of hope. We learn from the Old Testament that God never abandoned His people despite the Israelites' repeated sinfulness. We see His solicitude, too, in the centuries after the Incarnation. Even though Christians grievously sinned, God still inspired saints and popular movements to help reform society and to bring His children back to Him. History thus encourages confidence that God will not allow evil to prevail in the end.

Finally, history can instill a deeper patience, which is closely connected to the virtue of hope. As we journey through the centuries, we will encounter many injustices and wrongs, and we will likely wonder why it is that God did not intervene immediately to correct the situation. History helps us to ponder our shortsightedness and how what may seem like an obvious solution from our limited perspective may actually contribute to further turmoil and suffering. Of course, God's ways are not our ways, and historians should not pretend to know God's providence by assuming that a given situation was "providential." Nonetheless, there are some events that clearly do indicate the hand of God in time, and these should inspire our hope and patience since God continues to work in history even when we do not discern it.

To return to the introduction of this chapter: Our aim is to provide Catholics, particularly high school students, with an accurate "painting" of Western Civilization's history. Some well-intentioned Catholic history texts present a universally favorable or "triumphalist" account: these narratives generally avoid many troubling details or explain them away. For example, individuals who are Catholic are given the benefit of the doubt, while those who are not Catholic or who opposed a given saint implicitly assume "villain" status. Many times this triumphalist perspective comes from a desire to highlight the achievements of Catholics and Catholic society, but the danger of distorting the past is very great. History is messy. Individuals can simultaneously be a hero and a villain depending on what aspect of their lives you study. Unless students realize that even pious Catholics have done ignoble acts, they will be unprepared when they encounter a more accurate historical narrative that undermines a triumphalist account. We stress again: the Church is both divine and human. While her teachings, sacraments, and liturgies are resplendent in their beauty, the ugliness and distortion of sin are also present in the lives of her members. Therefore, in *Pilgrimage*, our goal has been to offer a nuanced text that shows both the beautiful and the unsightly in the story of Western Civilization. We do this neither to glory in the bad nor to scandalize the reader but rather to prepare you for when your friends, classmates, and coworkers mention some less-than-edifying event in the past as evidence against Catholicism or the value of Western Civilization.

We hope this approach strengthens your Catholic faith and prepares you to engage with and respond to explicitly anti-Catholic historical narratives, particularly those regularly taught at modern universities. It is important to be familiar with these perspectives. To know, for example, the standard account of humanity's earliest years can prepare you for secular theories that attempt to use history to reject the existence of God or His involvement with creation. We have therefore chosen to incorporate many aspects of contemporary academic scholarship, such as the established chronology of humanity's earliest centuries, while simultaneously providing a Catholic context for interacting with these ideas. Some questions have no easy answers, such as the dating of the Exodus, but we hope that our own faith-infused discussion helps you conclude that even matters whose solutions are elusive are no reason to doubt God's perpetual presence and guidance throughout history.

We, the authors of this book, are convinced by our faith, reason, and historical training that the Catholic Church is the institution established by Jesus to lead as many as possible to supernatural beatitude. Yet, we also believe it is important for you to remember that there have been Catholics, including monarchs, popes, and even saints, who committed grave errors and wrongs. Recognizing these faults does not denigrate Catholic men and women of the past; rather, it acknowledges their humanity and helps us remember that they, too, were wounded by Original Sin. Understanding the faults they struggled to overcome can give us greater respect for the victories in virtue that they achieved.

Our "Pilgrimage" Begins

Spiritual writers sometimes describe our individual lives on Earth as acts of pilgrimage aimed towards reaching our final home in Heaven. The pilgrim's journey is a fitting symbol for the narrative you will encounter in this book. Just as a pilgrim attempts to reach a distant sacred destination through physical travel and spiritual growth, humanity has been isolated from God by Original Sin but yearns for the happiness that can only be attained through communion with Him.

You dear reader, are beginning your own pilgrimage through the pages of this book. You may have taken on this journey for love of history, casual interest, an obligation to your studies, or some combination of all these reasons. The end of this book and the knowledge we hope you will gain from its study may seem far distant, but we encourage you to persevere and grow through the challenges ahead. Along the way, we wish you all the joys and benefits that we ourselves have experienced from the study of history and which we have endeavored to share with you here.

CATHOLIC HISTORIANS

Catholics throughout the centuries have embraced the historian's vocation, but two in particular have inspired the approach of this present volume. The first is Bede the Venerable (c. 673–735), the patron saint of historians. In the fourth and fifth centuries, Christians developed and refined a new type of history, known as Church history, which focused on the Church itself and only touched upon secular events insofar as they affected the ecclesiastical. One of the most respected examples of this genre is Bede's *Ecclesiastical History of the English People*. Bede's style and commitment to historical accuracy are exemplary. Furthermore, Bede's narrative never reduces the people he discusses to mere names or curiosities. In his history, every individual soul has an eternal destiny that weighs in the balance, and though he decries their sins, he never loses sight of the common humanity and vocation to holiness we all share.

The second historian is more recent. Christopher Dawson (1889–1970) converted to Catholicism as a young man and combined a lively faith with profound historical insight. Bede lived in Early Medieval Europe, and he could assume that his readers both understood and shared his religious worldview. Dawson, on the other hand, lived in the modern world. Ecclesiastical history, while important, needed to be understood within a broader context of secular events and ideas if Catholic historians were to influence the worldview of their peers. Thus, Dawson's writing took a "big picture" approach. He did not focus exclusively on the Church or even on one era but rather wrote comprehensively about civilization and its roots. He particularly emphasized the importance of religious belief. Religion, he argued, was a fundamental component of human culture, and Christianity in particular has played a critical historical role in inspiring many of the greatest developments in human thought. Notable Christian contemporaries such as the poet T.S. Eliot and the author J.R.R. Tolkien incorporated elements of Dawson's thought in their literary works, and future generations will, no doubt, continue to draw upon his insights and his faith as they seek to deepen their own understanding of history.

Christopher Dawson sitting in his study at Harvard campus c. 1958–62.

In *Pilgrimage*, we hope to combine the strengths of both historians into a single narrative so that our readers may finish this work with Bede's empathy and Dawson's ability to engage with modern society. Both lead us back to the Catholic Church and to the firm belief that God has intervened in history and has made it sacred by His Presence.

CHAPTER 2

The Neolithic Revolution

You are wise, Enkidu, and now you have become like a god.

Shamhat, *The Epic of Gilgamesh*[1]

The Epic of Gilgamesh is the oldest fictional narrative of heroic deeds that survives from antiquity. It was written in its present form around the year 2000 BC and tells the tale of Gilgamesh, the selfish king of Uruk. When the people cried to the gods to save them from Gilgamesh's abuses, the deities responded by sending a wild man of nature, Enkidu, to stop the king. After fighting, the two men became friends and sought glory through adventure together. The *Epic* describes their battles against various foes, but the chief quest of the story was Gilgamesh's attempt to learn the secrets of immortality. This adventure took him to the ends of the earth and ultimately taught the king—and the audience—the inevitably of death and how to find joy despite our mortality.

While there are many reasons that *The Epic of Gilgamesh* remains a fascinating and rewarding read thousands of years later, this chapter's opening quotation, known as an epigraph, highlights a particular theme. Before Enkidu met Gilgamesh, he lived alone in nature. The animals accepted him as one of their own, and he thrived in this wild environment. This situation changed when he met the woman Shamhat. She befriended him and "tamed" his uncivilized ways.

1 *The Epic of Gilgamesh*, ed. N. K. Saunders (New York: Penguin Classics, 1996), Tablet 1.

At first, Enkidu regretted this change since the animals now fled from him, but Shamhat consoled him with the words above. He had, as it were, lost the innocence of childhood but gained the wisdom and ability to shape his destiny like a god. This fictional transformation, which is portrayed as both tragic and beneficial, is a fitting symbol for a development that took place many centuries before the composition of the *Epic*. Just as Enkidu came to wisdom by befriending another human, the Neolithic Revolution involved the foundation and expansion of human communities so that many could live and work together and thus form the beginning of human civilization.

Prehistoric Humanity

Technically speaking, the study of humanity's origins is not a historical topic. Since the earliest generations of people did not leave us any written records, the study of prehistoric humanity is chiefly left to the domain of anthropology and archeology. Anthropology, literally "the study of humanity," can include the study of society as well as theories regarding the origin of human life itself. Archeology studies the material remains from human activity, such as pottery, tools, buildings, and monuments. Often anthropologists, archeologists, and historians work together to expand our knowledge of the past. Though many of the topics below are considered "prehistory," we believe it is useful for students to know some of the prevalent modern theories regarding humanity's earliest experiences.

The question of the origins of humanity remains a hotly contested topic, one that is fundamentally linked to a given person's theological worldview. For those with a theistic, Judeo-Christian worldview, the biblical book of Genesis presents a narrative of Adam and Eve's descendants and how their selfishness ultimately led God to send a powerful flood to destroy their society. Only one faithful man, Noah, and his family were spared. (Interestingly, *The Epic of Gilgamesh* and other ancient sources also record a flood as well as a man whom the gods preserved.) After the Flood narrative, Genesis links the origins of various peoples with Noah's descendants.

For those who hold a purely materialistic perspective in which there is no God or spiritual reality, an atheistic form of the **theory of evolution** is used to explain the biological origins of humanity. This holds as a central claim that life developed, or "evolved," gradually over many years from simple organisms to more complex ones and ultimately produced the first *homo sapiens* (the scientific term for humanity) without any divine intervention. While different schools of thought propose different mechanisms for this proposed evolution, all varieties of atheistic evolution are incompatible with Catholicism because they deny God, the individual soul, and other key concepts such as sin.

Theistic versions of evolution affirm divine causality, and the Catholic Church allows Catholics to accept the principle of evolution as a general biological framework as long as they uphold three important principles.[2] First, one must believe in the existence of God and His gift of a soul to each individual human. Second, Catholics are obligated to affirm that Adam and Eve were individual people, not a name for a group or class of early humans, and that all humanity is naturally descended from these first two parents. Third, one must hold that Adam and Eve committed the first human act of disobedience against God and that the consequences of this "original" sin have been passed down to all subsequent human beings, with the exceptions of Jesus and the Virgin Mary.

Turning to archeology, we can outline some of the features of humanity's earliest societies during the so-called **Paleolithic Period** ("old stone"). These were hunter-gatherer communities. Groups of up to sixty members formed what might be called a tribe and provided for themselves by gathering fruits and vegetables and hunting animals. They had no fixed home but were nomads who migrated according

The **Cave of Beasts** is a rock shelter in Wadi Sura in southwest Egypt. It contains paintings of human and animal figures including an elephant, ostriches, gazelles, and giraffes from c. 5000 BC.

2 See *CCC* §327 (creation out of nothing), 360 (origin from one human couple), 376 (original state of innocence), and 389–90 (the historic Fall of our first parents).

INTERPRETING GENESIS

The Church has always held that the book of Genesis is without error, though she leaves open for discussion whether certain details in the biblical account should be interpreted literally or as an analogy for some broader spiritual or historical truth. Creation out of nothing ("*ex nihilo*" in Latin), our common ancestry from a first set of parents, their sin, and their subsequent expulsion from their state of innocence are core beliefs that the Church obliges us to hold.[3] The Church further teaches that the Book of Genesis "pertains to history in a true sense," but she also acknowledges that its account does not conform to the "historical method" developed by Greek, Roman, and modern historians.[4] Rather, as Pope Pius XII wrote, we should be conscious of Genesis's "metaphorical language [that was] adapted to the mentality" of the people at the time.[5] In Genesis chapters 1-11 we encounter, among other details, the creation of the universe, the stories of Cain and Abel, Noah, and the Tower of Babel. How should a Catholic historian interpret these accounts? Where does simple historical fact end and "metaphorical language" begin?

Tradition, as embodied in the commentaries by the Fathers of the Church and the medieval scholastics, strongly favors a literal interpretation of both Genesis's six days of creation and its account of the early history of humanity.[6] In contrast, secular historians reject the possibility of direct interaction between God and humanity and conclude that such episodes are evidence that the text has little historical credibility. For these scholars, Genesis is, at best, garbled echoes of folk memories concerning events like a catastrophic regional flood.

Modern Christian biblical scholars acknowledge the reality that God intervenes in human history, but many also accept the prevailing interpretation of archeological evidence that indicates a much longer epoch of prehistoric activity than that given in the Genesis genealogies. These Christians hold that modern historical disciplines, such as archeology, seek answers to questions that likely do not directly apply to the biblical text. In their opinion, Genesis offers illustrative

---

3 See, for example, CCC §327 (creation out of nothing), 360 (origin from one human couple), 376 (original state of innocence), and 389–90 (the historic Fall of our first parents).

4 Pius XII, *Humani Generis*, 38. See also the Pontifical Biblical Commission's *Concerning the Historical Character of the First Three Chapters of Genesis* in Acta Sedis Sanctae, vol. 1 (1909), quoted in Dennis J Murphy, *The Church and the Bible: Official Documents of the Catholic Church* (St. Paul's: Alba House, 2007), 131-133 and its *Letter to Cardinal Suhard* in Acta Apostolicae Sedis, vol. 40 (1948), 45-8. Interested students should also consult John Bergsma and Brant Pitre, *A Catholic Introduction to the Bible: The Old Testament* (San Francisco: Ignatius Press, 2018), 93-117. While it is true that Genesis does not conform to later Greco-Roman historiographical techniques, we also note that Genesis's style shares more affinity with that later genre—for example, in its genealogical precision—than those accounts of early humanity found in other cultures of the Fertile Crescent.

5 Ibid.

6 A notable exception is St. Augustine, who argued for an instantaneous creation which was symbolically divided into six periods. The designation "(Early) Church Father" refers to those first theologians whose writings and sermons helped to establish Christianity's doctrinal foundations. Many Church Fathers lived in the fourth, fifth, and sixth centuries, though some lists include theologians from later centuries, too. For more, see the insert on the Church Fathers in chapter 18.

stories, or myths, that encapsulate certain historical and spiritual truths but are not the straightforward sequence of factual events that modern readers typically expect in a historical narrative. Rather, they are representative episodes that signify the gradual unfolding of centuries.

A small number of academics offer an alternative to the predominant approaches above. Despite the fact that some of these scholars are agnostic and discount the presence of God in history, their school of thought proposes that the events in Genesis have more factual accuracy than is typically granted by modern scholarship. They claim that archeology actually supports different stories in Genesis, such as the Tower of Babel, and that what is needed is a reevaluation of the *interpretation* of archeological findings. This position offers a number of potential connections between historical figures and the individuals and places of the Bible, but many of their arguments require further research and evidence in order to win more widespread academic support.

In light of this contemporary academic environment and mindful of the Church's teachings, *Pilgrimage* employs the chronology for ancient societies of the Neolithic era that the majority of scholars and students teach and study today. We can take what is valuable for deepening our knowledge and faith and also better follow the admonition of St. Peter to be prepared to offer an answer when we encounter those who challenge our hope in Christ on historical grounds (see 1 Pt 3:15).

In conclusion, we approach these earliest years with a sense of reverence. First and foremost, we firmly uphold the essential historical value of the Biblical account. At the same time, we welcome what our God-given reason can discern through disciplines such as archeology and acknowledge that the "metaphorical language" encountered in Genesis transcends the basic chronological cause-and-effect prose typically found in today's history books. This does not imply that Genesis is somehow inferior to our modern approach; rather, Genesis is both a historical and a theological text, and its account of our most distant past seamlessly integrates great spiritual and historical truths regarding God's providence in a that way goes beyond the limits of our modern academic historical genre.

Creation of Adam by Michelangelo. Fresco c. 1512. Located on the ceiling of the Sistine Chapel in Vatican City.

to the changing seasons of their food supply. They learned how to sharpen stones into knives for hunting and fought one another to gain control of the best hunting grounds. The use of fire is also thought to have become widespread during this period, first as a means of warmth and protection and later as a means to food.

While there are no written sources from this era, the people still displayed a desire to communicate what mattered to them by painting pictures, often of animals, on the walls of the caves where they sheltered. These paintings show us that our earliest ancestors possessed a rational ability to contemplate their situation and a desire to express their thoughts through depiction. Both characteristics distinguish humans from irrational animals and provide us early examples of human culture.

We can, building upon Dawson's insights, understand "culture" as the inheritance a given society has received from its ancestors and then bequeaths, or hands down, to later generations.[7] This includes its language, its learning, and its morals. Culture is related to, but different from, the term "society." Society is the structure or organization of a group. It is not necessarily human. Bees, for example, also have a social structure, but they lack art, education, and the other features of culture. (Animals do have instinct, but this is distinct from education.) In contrast to animals, even the simplest human society has a culture which is passed down from generation to generation and forms a link with the past.

This human connection with those who have gone before can be seen in early burial practices. Burial as a method of sanitation could occur almost anywhere, but some early humans deliberately fashioned cemeteries to create a specific location where people's lives were commemorated by their descendants. By maintaining a cemetery, they created a physical location that linked their society with previous generations and identified the living as part of a larger world that reached beyond their individual lifespans.

The desire to honor and remember the dead points towards a significant aspect of human culture, the widespread belief in a spiritual, or immaterial, reality. Some of the Paleolithic cave paintings depict religious rituals, indicating the belief in supernatural powers who oversaw and influenced the world. The evidence of these early religious practices suggests that some societies also worshipped their ancestors. Many early cultures around the world held that deceased ancestors interceded with the gods to provide for the living, to protect them, and to help them defeat their enemies. The discovery of decorated skulls has led some archaeologists to suggest these objects were the bones of the ancestors who had become objects of worship.

---

7 See, for example, Christopher Dawson, "The Sources of Cultural Change," in Christopher Dawson, *Dynamics of World History*, ed. John J. Mulloy (Wilmington, DE: ISI Books, 2002), 3–11.

Ancient human groups turned to the worship of their ancestors partly out of veneration for the cycle of fertility. The reproduction of humans, animals, and plants formed the very heart of human society. Without more people and the resources to sustain them, humanity would simply disappear. Therefore, they prayed to their ancestors, who had already completed their journey through the cycle of birth and death, to assist the living's efforts to feed themselves and reproduce.

Some of the earliest archeological sites highlight the important role religion played in the formation of ancient societies and their cultures. The **Göbekli Tepe** site in modern-day southeast Turkey—intriguingly, not far from Mount Ararat, the alleged site of Noah's landfall after the Genesis Flood—is considered one of the oldest archeological sites in the world, between nine thousand and twelve thousand years old. It is made up of approximately two hundred T-shaped stone pillars, some as large as twenty feet tall and weighing as much as twenty tons, arranged in twenty circles ranging from thirty to ninety feet in diameter. Each pillar is carved with elaborate animal motifs. Despite the fact that these carvings reveal expert craftsmanship and must have taken many hours to complete, archaeologists have found no records to suggest that any humans settled permanently at the site. Instead, the evidence suggests that Göbekli Tepe was a place where people gathered to carry out religious

The main excavation area of **Göbekli Tepe** in south-eastern Turkey. The site dates from c. 12000–9000 BC. It is a UNESCO World Heritage Site.

rituals and to feast. Though humans were still living a migratory lifestyle, Göbekli Tepe indicates that they returned regularly to specific locations to produce the structures and carvings that survive today.

The Neolithic Revolution

Religious practice and a desire to understand the world men inhabited likely inspired a profound change in human life known as the **Neolithic Revolution**. The word "Neolithic" ("new stone") refers to the production of more efficient stone tools during this period. Historians use this term generally to signify the era when many people adopted fixed homes in specific locations as well as the cultivation of crops and domestication of animals to provide their new stable communities with food. This lifestyle provided the foundation for the subsequent religious, political, educational, and technological achievements that go hand-in-hand with civilization.

"Civilization" is a term that lies at the heart of our pilgrimage through the past, and it is important that we understand what it signifies. A civilization is an advanced form of human society that relies on physical, social, and cultural practices and technologies to support large populations. Some of the common hallmarks of a civilization include stable agricultural networks that support people living together in cities, communal sites dedicated to worship, and specialized skills such as metalwork and writing.

Historians have suggested multiple explanations for why humans first embraced the cultivation of crops and the stability of a farming lifestyle. Some have proposed that, as the climate of the planet warmed, many of the largest animals that humans had hunted, such as woolly mammoths, began to die due to the changing environment. Humans thus needed to develop new sources of food to avoid a similar extinction. Others have suggested the opposite—that the climate began to cool slightly from the highs of the Paleolithic Era. This forced humans to become more creative in their efforts to feed themselves. A third theory proposes that the formation of apparent holy sites like Göbekli Tepe inspired a desire for new lifestyles that enabled people to settle permanently at or near these locations. While none of these theories has been proven, all of them rely on each individual human's unique ability to reflect on a given situation and to solve problems or satisfy desires by conscious change.

The Neolithic Revolution began with farming. The capacity to recognize patterns of growth and reproduction among plants allowed humans to begin growing crops to feed themselves. They formed camps where they could live in the summer to cultivate and harvest the crops they had planted earlier in the year. Gradually these settlements became permanent as the inhabitants developed the shelters and storage facilities necessary for them to live in these locations during the less abundant seasons of the year.

Another important advancement was the domestication of animals. This process began with dogs long before the Neolithic Revolution, but during the revolution itself, domestication focused on those animals whose milk, meat, and hide provided key resources for people. A new lifestyle, "pastoralism," took root as individuals and groups cared for herds of domesticated cattle, sheep, and other animals by rotating them from pasture to pasture. The animals became sources for clothes and food, though presumably the pastoralists also supplemented their diet by gathering plant-based nourishment as they traveled. Eventually, some people established permanent plots of land where they could maintain a small number of animals for themselves. These cultivators learned to use animal droppings to fertilize their fields and thereby increased the health and productivity of their crops. Some herders, especially shepherds, continued to live as pastoralists. While they might be based near a settlement and spend the winter there, they would still leave to find more fertile grazing grounds for their flocks at other times of the year.

The Fertile Crescent

Although the Neolithic Revolution took place at many different sites across the world, the most important area for Western Civilization was in Northeast Africa and West Asia in a region that became known as the Ancient Near East or the **Fertile Crescent**. The Fertile Crescent includes the Nile valley in Egypt and extends up the coast of the Mediterranean through Palestine, Lebanon, and southern Turkey, before curving southeastward through Syria, Iraq, and the western part of Iran to reach the Persian Gulf. (In ancient times Turkey was known as Anatolia or Asia Minor; we will refer to it as "Anatolia" throughout this text.)

One of the earliest groups in the Fertile Crescent to cultivate grain was the **Natufians**, estimated to have lived in Syria and Palestine from about 12000–8000 BC. (The name "Natufian" derives from a local valley near the area where the early twentieth-century archeologist Dorothy Garrod discovered evidence for the society.) The Natufians cultivated local grains to bake a type of pita bread, collected nuts such as almonds and pistachios, and hunted gazelles to complete their diets. They developed permanent villages of about a hundred and fifty people and lived in semi-underground houses with stone foundations and central fireplaces that provided heat for cooking and warmth. Archeological excavations have found stone mortars and pestles used to grind grains into flour, plows and sickles used for planting and harvesting, residue from history's earliest-known brewery, and stone weapons and fishhooks for hunting. The tombs of the Natufians also contain jewelry

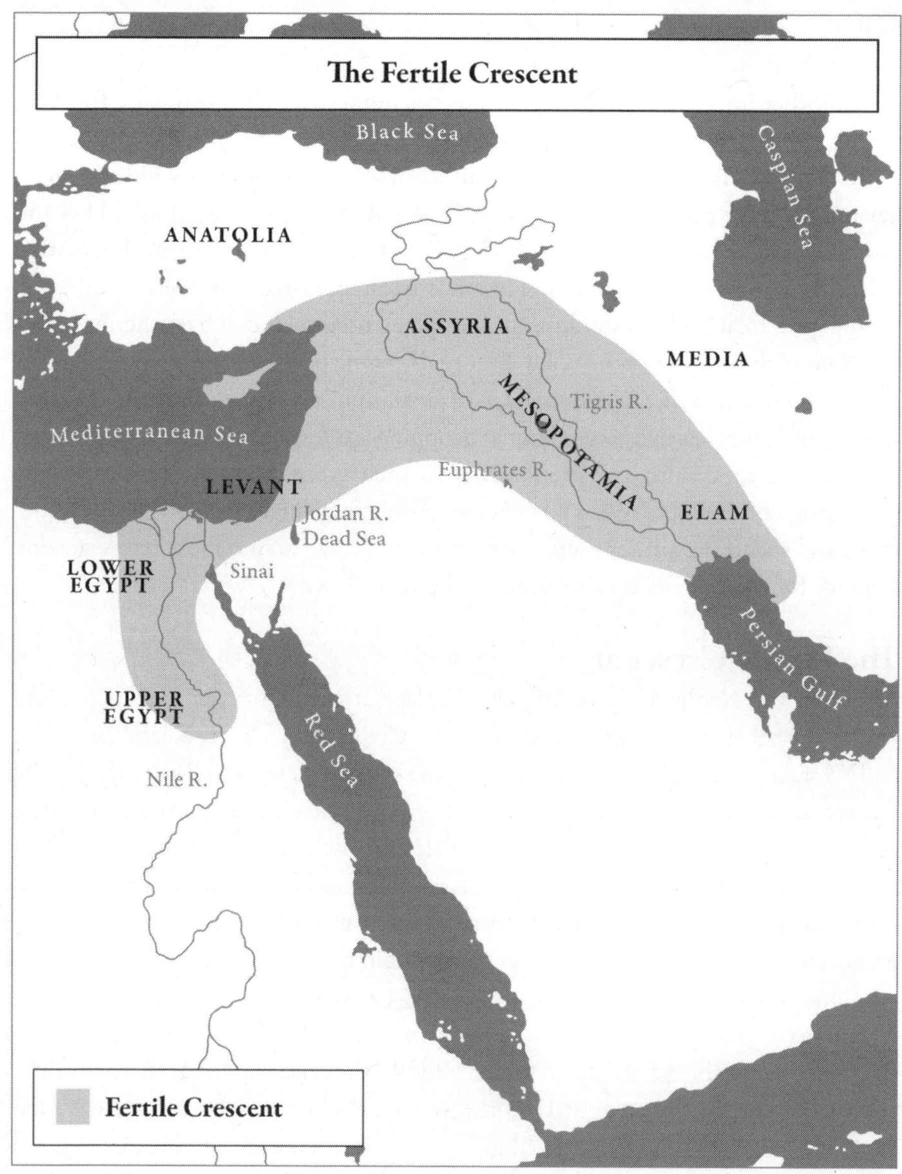

made from shells. The presence of dog skeletons alongside humans in these graves suggests that they domesticated dogs, which likely helped protect the community and hunt for food.

One of the Natufians' settlements was at the site of the biblical city of Jericho. This settlement was founded in approximately 9000 BC around a spring which continues to this day to provide fresh water for the community. Archaeologists estimate

The dwelling foundations discovered in ancient **Jericho** (Tell es-Sultan) are located about one mile north of the modern city of Jericho. It has been called "the oldest town in the world," dating from 10,000 BC. It is a UNESCO World Heritage Site.

that sometime between 8300 and 7300 BC, Jericho experienced dramatic growth and became one of the first cities where people lived in a larger community than tribes and clans, sharing a common identity that transcended biological ties. The population grew to more than two thousand residents, who cultivated barley and wheat and lived in round houses made of hardened mud bricks. Massive stone walls ten feet thick and thirteen feet tall sheltered the city from flooding and enemies. In the center of the city stood an enormous thirty-foot tower that was perhaps used for religious rituals. Such structures indicate that the community could be organized and united in order to complete substantial projects.

Despite the Natufians' achievements, it was further to the east, in modern-day Iraq, that the first civilization flourished. At first glance, this region seems particularly inhospitable. Temperatures can average as high as 120°F in the summer, and the annual rainfall is typically less than ten inches. Furthermore, the two rivers in close proximity, the Tigris and the Euphrates, flood erratically in late spring and early summer. As crops were not yet ready to harvest, the often-violent influx of flood water hampered rather than helped the agricultural foundation necessary for any settled society. Furthermore, the rivers encountered little natural resistance as they approached the Persian Gulf and frequently divided into numerous, shifting branches over the level plain before terminating into extensive marshlands. This made flooding particularly dangerous because the locations affected could shift suddenly.

Despite these difficulties, the area between the two rivers, later known in Greek as **Mesopotamia** ("between rivers"), also had significant advantages. The presence of marshes in the far south enabled extensive fishing, and the plains permitted husbandry (the care, cultivation, and breeding of plants and animals). More importantly, the land was rich and fertile when proper irrigation methods were used, and the rivers—though unpredictable in their flooding—provided not only water for crops but also an efficient means of transportation. Even the clay deposited by the floods could be used as material for building and writing. Through the development and maintenance of irrigation canals, the people of southern Mesopotamia turned desert and marshland into the seedbed for humanity's first civilization.

Advantages and Disadvantages

Neolithic populations across the Fertile Crescent adopted the practices of living in villages and cultivating domesticated crops and animals to provide themselves with food and clothing. In the years that followed, their agricultural production became stable enough to produce surplus goods to exchange with other settlements and to establish a system of trade. Desirable items included obsidian, a type of glass used to produce sharp tools; bitumen, a type of petroleum used for brick mortar and waterproofing boats; and salt, a food preservative. Canoes enabled the first merchants to transport these goods over long distances, while the domestication of oxen and donkeys brought further benefits for travel.

The successes of the Neolithic age contributed to further achievements. The craft of pottery, which is produced by shaping and heating clay, dates from approximately 6000 BC and is an extremely important artifact for historians. It can be broken, but it is almost impossible to destroy completely. Along with providing us with durable evidence from some of the most ancient societies in the world, the various designs produced by different potters help historians differentiate between early societies who are otherwise indistinguishable prior to the survival of written sources. Furthermore, pottery kilns provided enough heat to melt copper to a point where it was flexible and could be forged into weapons, tools, and jewelry. This first metalworking was a significant achievement for humanity.

While the Neolithic Revolution enabled many successes, these achievements were not gained without sacrifice. Leaving behind one's migratory tribe to settle in a permanent location could involve breaking bonds of family and friendship and exposing oneself to the vulnerability of potential starvation if the crops failed. Archeological records of the early Neolithic sites have provided evidence of the hardships faced by those who pioneered this way of life. Skeletons from these sites show that the men and women of these societies developed deformed toes, knees, hips, and backs, probably from kneeling to grind grain into flour for long periods of time. These skeletons also display evidence of increased tooth decay, probably because their diets relied more heavily on carbohydrates, such as oats and bread. Those who lived in these communities were also exposed to higher levels of disease due to primitive sanitation systems in densely populated areas. Neolithic farmers were less healthy, worked harder, and had a shorter average lifespan than their nomadic Paleolithic peers.

When considering these disadvantages, some modern historians go so far as to suggest that the Neolithic Revolution was the greatest mistake in human history. By adopting the Neolithic model of cultivation, human beings set their descendants on a path of ever-increasing human consumption of the planet's resources. In addition, the development of more complex populations meant that some inhabitants enjoyed significantly more wealth and prestige than others. They argue that humans would have been better served if they had learned to limit the increase of the population and to retain the smaller, less established, and more equal societies of the pre-Neolithic eras.

The Epic of Gilgamesh perhaps provides us with the best response to these criticisms as well as the most fundamental explanation of what motivated some Neolithic people to choose a sedentary life. Enkidu learned that friendship with Gilgamesh far outweighed any of the benefits he had enjoyed while running wild and free. The value of human companionship, lived out in a growing community, outweighed the benefits he had enjoyed alone. It may be that a similar desire for enrichment through stable human friendship best explains the decisions of our earliest ancestors to seek a new lifestyle despite its tremendous hardships.

Conclusion

Our earliest evidence of humanity teaches us several important lessons about the dignity of human persons and their centrality to history. First, we see the ability of individual men and women to make choices and to shape the world about them, even to the point of adjusting their way of life. Although geographical and cultural factors certainly exercise important influences in human actions, the Neolithic Revolution is an excellent illustration of the fact that human actions are not predetermined by forces outside their control. Individual humans had the choice to either join the farmers of a developing sedentary society or to remain a part of the nomadic traditions of their ancestors. Their decision had a profound impact on their own lives and those of their descendants.

Second, the centrality of religion and the recognition of the supernatural stands as a clear testament to the elevation of humans above animals. The evidence of sites like Göbekli Tepe indicates that as humans interacted with one another they instinctively developed communal religious practices. Indeed, as we will see throughout this unit, the human desire to understand and interact with the supernatural was a critical factor in encouraging the development of large permanent settlements and the foundation of Western Civilization.

CHAPTER 3

Ancient Mesopotamia

Terah took Abram his son and Lot the son of Haran, his grandson, and Sarai his daughter-in-law, his son Abram's wife, and they went forth together from Ur of the Chaldeans to go into the land of Canaan; but when they came to Haran, they settled there.

Genesis 11:31

With this simple statement, the biblical book of Genesis introduces one of the most influential choices in the early history of humanity. It was while Abram was in Haran that God promised to give him both a special land of his own and numerous descendants if Abram followed Him. Later generations of Hebrews saw Abram's decision to trust in God as the beginning of their own unique history, while Christians consider him an important ancestor of the Messiah. Yet, for all the spiritual richness that the story of Abram provides us, we remain uncertain about its precise historical setting. According to traditional estimates, Abram lived around the year 2000 BC, but Genesis itself provides few details that can be aligned with what we know from nonbiblical sources. Simply put, Genesis is focused on the theological significance of Abram and his family, not the historical context.

In this chapter we explore the earliest societies that have left us written records, their achievements, beliefs, and the birth of empires. At the end, we will return to the question of Abram to see if we can tentatively place him in a historical setting. To do this, we must begin in an age over one thousand years before the traditional date of Abram's birth.

Uruk's Achievement

In literature, the term *in medias res* (Latin for "into the middle of things") describes a storytelling technique of starting in the middle of the tale rather than at its chronological beginning. Our earliest historical records introduced the city of **Uruk** *in medias res*. Historians, like first-time readers of an epic poem, find themselves suddenly thrust into a context which has a long backstory unknown to us. We know little of Uruk's actual foundation or what motivated early residents to leave behind smaller villages and embrace the growing urban environment. Instead, we meet a city that already possessed an established social structure, a large population, specialization in work, and its own writing.

Uruk flourished around 3500–3100 BC, and its territory covered approximately one square mile. While this may seem small in comparison to our modern cities, to its inhabitants the city was massive. Its population swelled to the tens of thousands, and this dense environment provided numerous opportunities for social interaction. These dealings permitted Uruk's inhabitants to specialize in certain crafts or tasks and to exchange what they produced for other things that they still required. Furthermore, the city did not exist in isolation. It was a hub for the hinterland, that is, the neighboring nonurban areas, and drew together both its inhabitants and those in the nearby countryside who brought the fruits of their farming, fishing, hunting, and husbandry to the city for trade. Uruk thus became the first recorded city-state, a politically independent region with a single dominant urban center.

At the core of the city, and closely associated with the exchange of goods, stood a collection of buildings known as Eanna, the "House of Heaven." This temple complex was dedicated to Ianna, the goddess of love and war. Ianna—better known by the later Babylonian name "Ishtar"—held a special role in the life of Uruk. The archeological remains of the temple complex demonstrate this: a perimeter wall within Uruk set apart those buildings dedicated to Ishtar. These structures may have been as high as 240 feet, and historians estimate that the construction of the complex likely required the labor of fifteen thousand men working ten-hour days for five years. The temple priest, called a "priest-king" by historians, was the highest human authority within Uruk and oversaw the city's economic life in the name of the goddess. The temple collected a tribute of resources from those in the city and in the hinterland. This centralized economic activity because workers exchanged the products of their labor for the goods that they needed from the temple's supply.

Such trade required records, and our earliest evidence of these transactions comes in the form of *bullae*. These hollow clay spheres or envelopes preserved within them geometric clay shapes known as tokens that verified the details of a given exchange. If one wanted to know how many cows were involved in a certain transaction, one broke the *bulla* that contained the record and reviewed its contents. Around 3200 BC, scribes began to use symbols *outside* of the sphere to indicate the number and type of token within. These symbols eventually made the *bullae* and their tokens redundant, and later records took the form of clay tablets that used the signs originally appearing on the outside of the *bullae*.

Cuneiform is the name historians use to designate the writing of ancient Mesopotamia. The name is a modern one based on the Latin word *cuneus* ("wedge") and refers to the wedge-shaped imprint that characterizes the symbols. (This shape was caused by the stylus or reed as it was pressed down into the clay.) The first characters were the simple representations found on the *bullae*. A drawing of a cow's head, for example, indicated a cow. Scribes then realized that they could combine symbols to express more complex ideas, such as "to drink" (a human head next to the sign for water) or "stranger" (a human head next to a mountain).

An important breakthrough occurred when scribes began using symbols to indicate a spoken sound. For example, the word for "fish" was *ku* and so the symbol for fish could be used to signify not only a fish but also the sound "ku" in another, more complex, word. Different, unrelated signs or characters could be linked together to express multisyllabic words in a phonetic arrangement.

Writing was no longer limited to its picture-based, or pictogram, origins. Cuneiform now had the flexibility to use its characters to describe abstract or complex thought. In fact, because cuneiform now represented sounds, multiple languages could adopt it as their written script. Just as the characters you are reading now could be rearranged into Latin, German, or French, so, too, cuneiform could be used by people who spoke a different tongue than that of Uruk. Over a dozen languages eventually adopted this writing system. Indeed, cuneiform had a long life ahead of it: The last document we know of to be written in this script dates from AD 75!

As impressive as the ability to develop writing is, it is even more astounding when we consider what it presupposes. 90 percent of our earliest writing involves commerce and accounting. This means that the society of Uruk required standard weights and measures, a common reckoning of time, and, of course, a mathematical basis with which to record all these details. Uruk used the sexagesimal, or base 60, mathematical system, with which they developed a 60-second minute and a 60-minute hour as well as the 360-degree circle—all of which we still use today. The calendar received 12 divisions with equal 30-day months. (An additional month could be added when necessary to realign the calendar with the solar year.) Other measurements included the *talent*, which designated the weight of a given object that a man could carry; they divided this into 60 *minas*, each of which, in turn, was composed of 60 *shekels*. A system of equivalences enabled items of different weights to be traded according to a standard.

Uruk's influence spread throughout the region of southern Mesopotamia and perhaps even as far as Egypt, but the city suffered destruction around 3100 BC. An unknown hand razed the Eanna complex to the ground and signaled the beginning of a new era in Mesopotamian history. Uruk would rebuild and even become strong once more, but it would never again enjoy unrivaled dominance. From now on, there would be competing city-states who desired their share—and more—of power and influence.

The Early Dynastic Period

The term "**Early Dynastic Period**" describes the era that followed Uruk's decline, but no contemporary ever used this designation. Rather, historians invent terms to distinguish different eras more easily, and thus the time from approximately 2900–2350 BC received its current label. These centuries saw numerous city-states rise up as local powers in **Sumer**, the name ancient inhabitants gave to their region of southern Mesopotamia. These city-states were often territorial rivals with one another, but no one city successfully established a lasting supremacy over its competitors.

Despite their political division, the Sumerians shared a common language and religious worldview. They believed in an orderly universe maintained and protected by commonly acknowledged gods and goddesses who lived in the Sumerian cities. They believed these deities had created humanity to serve their wants and needs, and it was in humanity's best interest to do so. Without divine protection, chaos would flood into the cosmos and harm the people of Sumer. The gods, for their part, depended on humanity for basic sustenance. Food, shelter, and even bathing and entertainment were all provided by human communities. Without mortals' help, the gods would become unable to hold back the unraveling of order.

Multiple gods (and temples) might be in one city, but there was always one main deity that was especially reverenced. Uruk, for example, was Ishtar's special dwelling. Sumerian temples could be built on flat ground or elevated by towers and structures so that they dominated the city horizon, as had Uruk's Ianna complex. The temple building itself had three rooms separated from each other by curtains or partitions, and each was richly decorated for the god. The innermost room housed the statue of the deity itself, while the room immediately adjoining the god's chambers held the food and the tub for the god's daily bathing and eating. The priests and priestesses of the city also offered regular entertainment in the form of music and dancing. The rest of the community could see their gods only on days of procession when the statues were taken outside of the inner chamber and paraded through a courtyard or in the city streets.

Despite this worship, the gods were generally neither loving nor sympathetic to humanity. According to myth, these deities could (and did) punish individuals and cities on a whim, often with devastating consequences. We read an example of this in the Sumerian account of the Flood. Unlike the book of Genesis, which described the Flood as a punishment for humanity's sins, the Sumerian account has Enlil, the chief god of Sumer itself, enraged because he can no longer rest well due to people making too much noise. His attempt to destroy humanity was thwarted when Enki, god of wisdom, took pity and warned someone of the coming catastrophe. Though some historians believe that Genesis's account of Noah derived from the Sumerians, there are important differences—particularly in moral emphasis. It seems more likely that both represent independent memories of the same historic event which were then understood according to one's trust (or lack thereof!) in divine power. Nor did Sumerian gods grant happiness in the afterlife to those who faithfully served them. At best, life after death offered an unsatisfying reflection of this world and its happiness. At worst, it was a place of unfulfilled longing for life ruled by demons.

Life *before* death revolved around the city-state, and urban families lived in mud brick houses that lined narrow streets. These homes appear to have been relatively comfortable within and typically had a central open courtyard for cooking. Most education for urban children was informal, though those with talent and resources could become scribes in a memorization-heavy process that required frequent copying of texts in order to learn the numerous characters associated with cuneiform. Society emphasized the community over the individual, and about half of the population lived in varying states of servitude as dependents of wealthy people or the local temple. At the bottom were slaves, who were either captives from war or those whose fortunes had fallen so low that they had been sold into slavery by their parents, husbands, or even themselves. These unfortunates did have limited rights and could possess property.

While trade between areas did exist, powerful city-states such as Uruk, Ur, Umma, and Lagash eventually sought to satisfy the needs of their growing populations by competing for control of Mesopotamia's resources. Increasingly frequent warfare produced a new leader in society: the war chief. This individual and his followers defended the city and added to its wealth through raids and victories. By 2600 BC, warriors had effectively established a parallel authority which rivaled that of the temple's priest-king. The war chief even had his own complex of buildings: the palace. This palace imitated the temple in its significance, for the war chief, like the god of the city, enjoyed servants, wealth, and a large, beautiful home to call his own. He had, in effect, replaced the priest-king's authority and ruled as king.

These kings left behind a new, important type of evidence for us to consult: the royal inscription. Some of these statements simply identify a given ruler who, for example, gave a certain item to a god. Other, more complex, examples recount *why* a king performed a certain action.

Another source for this period is the ***Sumerian King List***. This record of names and dates has mixed historical value, partly because it was composed centuries after the Early Dynastic Period and partly because it includes a mixture of mythical and historical figures. (For example, according to the *King List*, kingship descended from heaven some 200,000 years before the Flood.) Still, if we use it cautiously, it can help us understand the era better. By combining the information from the royal inscriptions and the *King List,* we can begin to trace the broad contours of a historical narrative and even to identify specific individuals and their choices.

Even though cities often fought with one another for dominance, Sumerians saw kingship as a unifying principle. There was an assumption that there existed one overarching king of Sumer. The title "king of Kish" denoted this theoretical sovereignty over the region. Why exactly this designation focused on the independent city of Kish remains a mystery, especially since sometimes there does not appear to be any connection between those who held the title "king of Kish" and that particular city-state. Furthermore, we do not know what exactly enabled someone to claim this title, though military might seems to be a likely component. What we do know is that the king of Kish sometimes acted as a peace-broker between other powers who were at war.

A prolonged conflict between the city-states Umma and Lagash ushered in the last stage of the Early Dynastic Period. This struggle over a common border lasted for approximately two centuries (2500–2300 BC). Toward the end of this struggle, a usurper named Uru'inimgina seized the throne of Lagash and sought to gain support for his kingship by invoking the protection of the city's chief deity, Ningirsu. The new king gave all his personal property, including the royal palace, to the god. Far from diminishing his power and resources, this move increased the king's authority and ideological significance, for Uru'inimgina now became the personal overseer and protector of the god's possessions. In theory, the king gave the god the palace; in practice, the king gained the temple. The distinction between divine and secular was blurred as the temple priests now found themselves under the authority of a king who acted as high priest by administering the god's property. Following Uru'inimgina's example, the status of king-priest (as opposed to the earlier priest-king) soon became a common feature in Sumerian life.

Despite these efforts, it was Uru'inimgina's rival king at Umma who achieved the victory. This king ultimately ruled an impressive array of subjugated cities, but he celebrated his triumph only for a few years. A new era in Mesopotamian history, one of empires, was dawning.

The Rise of Empires

We know little of Mesopotamia's first empire-builder, not even his proper name. His title "Sargon"—which means "the king is legitimate"—is the closest we come to any name. What is more, Sargon's rise to power is shrouded in legend, and historians must sift through accounts written hundreds of years after his lifetime to try to piece together a basic biography.

Sargon the Conqueror (r. 2288–2235 BC) began as a political outsider who first seized power in the northern kingdom of Kish. From there, he took advantage of Umma's weakness after decades of warfare against Lagash and defeated its ruler. Sargon became the new dominant warlord and proceeded to transform Sumer in

The **Mask of Sargon**. Made of bronze c. 2250 BC. Currently in the Roemer- und Pelizaeus-Museum, Hildesheim, Germany. It was discovered in Nineveh, Iraq in 1931 and is thought to depict either Sargon of Akkad or his grandson Naram-Sin.

permanent ways by orienting its focus outside of southern Mesopotamia. He transferred his capital from Kish to Akkad, a city in northern Mesopotamia outside of the traditional boundaries of Sumer. Inscriptions from his era refer exclusively to military matters, and historians often interpret Sargon's boast that he fed 5,400 men every day as evidence that he established history's first standing army. These soldiers helped create an expansive empire that stretched beyond Mesopotamia toward the Mediterranean Sea.

However, acquisition is the "easy" part of creating an empire. In order to establish stability for their rule, aspiring emperors must bring together the different regions of their conquests into a cohesive whole. Sargon understood the importance of this and tried to integrate his new territories with Sumerian society.

For example, he bolstered his position by seizing lands from defeated kings and claiming them for himself as royal territory that could be redistributed to loyal followers. He also selected family members and people he trusted to hold important religious positions in the cities. His daughter Enheduanna became the high priestess and ceremonial wife of the moon god Nanna at Ur. She thus held a position of prestige and influence within the traditional structure of Ur's society. Enheduanna also wrote various hymns and other literary works and is the earliest author we know by name. Subsequent rulers of the Akkadian dynasty expanded this practice by appointing multiple women from their family to the position of high priestess in key cities. In addition to intertwining religious observance with his bloodline, Sargon sought to transcend, or go beyond, local customs by establishing an imperial language, standard imperial taxes, and even an imperial method of reckoning time. (The new common language, Akkadian, still used cuneiform characters.)

The **Victory Stele of Naram-Sin**, King of Akkad. Made of sandstone c. 2230 BC. Currently in the Louvre Museum, Paris, France. The king is shown in the upper portion leading his army and wearing a horned crown to signify his authority. This is one of the best-preserved sculptures from the Akkadian period.

Despite these efforts, most historians agree that Sargon's rule was not uncontested in Sumer. The very title "Sargon" hints at this. If he had to declare that "the king is legitimate," it seems likely that some disagreed. Rebellions broke out after Sargon's death, and the most important of these took place during the lifetime of Sargon's grandson, **Naram-Sin** (r. 2211–2175 BC). Two simultaneous revolts, one in Kish and the other in Uruk, shook his empire. Naram-Sin brutally suppressed both, and he decided to cement his hold over the region by taking a drastic step: he declared that the gods of Sumer had elevated him to share their divine status. He was no longer Naram-Sin, ruler of Sumer and Akkad; he was Naram-Sin, the god. Official records described him as "Naram-Sin, the mighty god of Akkad, king of the four corners of the world."[1] Naram-Sin's new divine status did not end Sumerian resentment, it merely aggravated the situation by adding a religious dimension to the unrest. In the decades after Naram-Sin's death, internal turmoil combined with external invasion to reduce the extent of the Akkadian Empire before ending it entirely in 2111 BC.

Future generations would look upon Naram-Sin as the embodiment of impiety. Interestingly, this was *not* because he claimed to be divine, but because Naram-Sin destroyed the temple of Enlil, the chief god of Sumer. Perhaps the opportunity to claim divinity was too tempting to later rulers for them to deny Naram-Sin's assertion outright. Indeed, as we will continue to see throughout the ancient world, divine status often accompanied the possession of temporal power.

The *Sumerian King List* succinctly conveys the confusion in Sumer after the Akkadian Empire: "Who was king? Who was *not* king?" Turmoil gave way to a

1 Hugo Radau, *Early Babylonian History: Down to the End of the Fourth Dynasty of Ur* (Eugene, Oregon: Wipf & Stock, 2005), 7.

The **Sumerian King List**. Made of clay c. 1800 BC. Currently in the Ashmolean Museum, Oxford, England. It was found in Larsa, Iraq in 1922 and was translated by Stephen Herbert Langdon in 1923.

new power when Ur-Namma (r. 2110–2093 BC) successfully subdued the foreign invaders that had attacked Sargon's realm. He established a new empire in southern Mesopotamia, with the city of Ur as its capital. Historians reckon Ur-Namma's dynasty as the third to rule Ur, and his empire is commonly designated the Third Dynasty of Ur, or **Ur III** (c. 2110–c. 2004 BC).

This empire lasted about a century and has left behind a multitude of sources. Unfortunately, the vast majority of these texts focus on the economic life of the state. While these sources are informative in their own right, they offer an incomplete picture of Ur III as a whole. Historians are forced to reconstruct this society's beliefs and practices as best they can, but if you imagine trying to tell the history of the United States through its grocery store receipts, you will begin to see how limited our knowledge can be! For example, while historians agree that Ur III had a highly centralized government, some propose that it was a totalitarian government which had absolute authority and used its subjects as slaves. Others argue that we only derive such a picture because surviving documents focus on those workers owned or employed by the ruler; they maintain that if we had different sources, we would see more evidence of private property and non-slave labor. Accounts from later generations do not clarify much. Ur III seems to have been relatively uninteresting to later peoples, who, even when they did refer to the empire, usually composed poetry about its destruction rather than writing about its achievements or social structures. Regardless of what we do or do not know about Ur III's own history, the dynasty sponsored literary activity. This included our earliest form of the *Sumerian King List* as well as *The Epic of Gilgamesh*, which we introduced in the previous chapter as the first known literary epic in history.

In addition to these written sources, one of the best-preserved ziggurats from ancient Sumer is located at Ur and dates from the period of Ur III. The term **ziggurat** derives from the Akkadian word "to protrude" or "to build high" and refers to the massive step-like pyramids that the people of Mesopotamia built for their gods. These structures consisted of multiple levels formed out of clay bricks. Each story was smaller than the story immediately below it, and they terminated in a high platform that housed the shrine for that ziggurat's deity. These places of worship likely received their inspiration from the temple complexes of earlier centuries.

We know little regarding Ur III's decline. It involved famine and the breakdown of its centralized tax system. Without the necessary goods being offered by surrounding territories, the famine was especially difficult to bear at the city of Ur itself, and the cost of food rose dramatically. This was compounded by a foreign invasion from the east, leading to the destruction of Sumer's second empire in 2003 BC.

Abraham and the Patriarchs

The biblical book of Genesis mentions nothing that indisputably connects its narrative with the historical eras we have just described. Uruk and Sargon, for example, are not present in Genesis's account of early humanity. Historians even debate whether Abram's former home at "Ur of the Chaldeans" can be associated with the city of Ur, the capital of Ur III's empire. This leaves Christian historians who believe that Abram was an actual historical figure with an exciting puzzle. When did he live, and what events were happening in the wider world when he and his descendants were chosen by God to become His people?

We will return to this question in a moment, but first it is worthwhile to highlight several important differences that separate Abram's life of faith as described in Genesis from the religious worldview sketched out above. First, the gods of Sumer were *immanent*; that is, each was a *part* of the universe rather than "outside" or "above" it. Enlil, for example, was Sumer's chief deity, but his realm was the wind and earth; other gods and goddesses had authority over other phenomena, such as the sea. Furthermore, these gods worked to maintain order in the cosmos and required the services of humanity to do so. In contrast, Abram's God *transcended*, or went beyond, this world. He did not reside in one particular city, and He certainly did not need to be bathed or entertained by priests. All authority in the natural world was His—not just one part of it. God showcased this authority when He renamed Abram as Abraham—thereby indicating a fundamental transformation—and when He defied nature by granting Abraham a son in his old age.

Second, God established a covenant, or permanent relationship, with Abraham. This mutual agreement ultimately bound together the worship of God, the ritual of circumcision, and the promise of a land set aside for Abraham's family. In contrast to the fickle and limited deities of Sumer, Abraham's God offered a stable relationship rooted in trust. This covenantal relationship cannot be overemphasized as one of the defining elements of Hebrew religious belief. Abraham's God had entered into an agreement with him and his descendants, and its clear stipulations enabled Hebrew society to measure its behavior against their God's expectations.

It was belief in this one God's total, transcendent authority as well as His perpetual covenant with Abraham's family that defined the Hebrew people and formed the foundation of their history. But this, of course, begs the question *when* that history began. Several biblical books offer chronological reference points which, when taken at face value, suggest that the era of the patriarchs—that is, the era of Abraham, his son Isaac, his grandson Jacob, and his great-grandson Joseph—took place in the centuries immediately *after* the collapse of Ur III. Unfortunately, the Genesis record is imprecise at those moments when specificity would help confirm (or refute) this traditional estimate. For example, both Abraham and Joseph interact with Egyptian kings, but these rulers are never named.

While conclusive evidence is lacking, a careful reading of Genesis does provide subtle clues that may align its account with other, nonbiblical sources. Genesis

WHO "WRITES" HISTORY?

The idea that the victors write the history of their time is a popular one. After all, those who triumph on the battlefield usually have more opportunities and resources to craft a narrative of events that favors their own cause and villainizes their enemies. Nonetheless, this situation is not as universal as you might expect. Many sources survive that tell history from the perspective of the "losers." For example, much of what we know about the Peloponnesian War in Greece (see chapter 9) comes to us from Thucydides, a historian who fought for the defeated side. Perhaps the best example of the losing side writing its own history is the ancient Hebrews. As we will see, the descendants of Abraham enjoyed only brief periods of stability and political success. For much of their history, they were engaged in desperate struggles against outside forces, and they ultimately suffered two catastrophes that brought a humiliating end to their territorial realms. Nonetheless, their account of their successes, their failings, and even the destruction of their temporal power remains a narrative that helps inform our understanding of this period. The Hebrews–rather than those who conquered their lands–wrote the history that many know today.

describes an era when nomads moved freely through Canaan and could easily enter Egypt. Egypt, in turn, did not yet exercise consistent political influence in Canaan. In contrast, Mesopotamia did intervene in Canaanite affairs, as the story of the war against Sodom and Gomorrah indicates (see Gn 14). Other clues include the apparent lack of Baal worship in Canaan—a god whom we discuss in chapter 5—and the amount paid to Joseph's brothers when they sold him into slavery. In fact, according to arguments from scholar Kenneth Kitchen, the situation described in the Genesis account could only describe a situation that existed for several centuries in the first half of the second millennium, that is from c. 2000–1600 BC.[2] After this period, Mesopotamian influence was replaced by the Egyptians, who had by this time become far less tolerant of foreigners. If correct, this reckoning would coincide with the traditional estimate derived from biblical evidence.

Scholars continue to debate about the proper interpretation of these and other details, and the Church permits a range of opinions regarding the historical chronology of the Book of Genesis. It may be that in the years to come, some future historian—maybe you!—will put the puzzle together in a manner that best solves the riddle of Abraham's era.

Conclusion

Since the age of Uruk and its writing, historians have been able to use the documents of the past not only to describe items and places but to trace a narrative of events and individuals. As we have seen, that narrative primarily concerns the rise and fall of temporal powers as kings and emperors strove against one another for dominance. Already we see how the world of religious belief and political structure could be intertwined, often to the detriment of the spiritual. We have only to think of the divine pride of Naram-Sin to see the logical conclusion of the ideology of king-priests in Sumer. Genesis's story of Abraham's faith stands in stark contrast to this ambition. There, we met not a powerful ruler grasping for more but a single family struggling to survive and trusting in the promises of one God. Abraham's descendants would change world history, but the world was too busy with its empires to notice this humble beginning. In truth, it would be many years before it took any notice of Abraham's descendants. Most histories riveted their attention on the ambition and grandeur of the mighty, and in the world after Sumer, none were mightier than the god-kings of Egypt. To them, we now turn.

---

2 Kenneth A. Kitchen, *On the Reliability of the Old Testament* (Grand Rapids, MI: Eerdmans, 2003), 313–372. See also Bergsma and Pitre, *A Catholic Introduction to the Bible*, 150–2.

Conclusion

CHAPTER 4

Gift of the Nile

About Egypt I shall have a great deal more to relate because of the number of remarkable things which the country contains, and because of the fact that more monuments which beggar description are to be found there than anywhere else in the world.

Herodotus, *The Histories*[1]

Other ancient peoples held Egyptian civilization in awe. The Greek historian Herodotus (c. 484–c. 425 BC) conveyed the sense of wonder that characterized the Greek attitude in his lengthy description of Egyptian history and customs. To him and others, Egypt seemed as though it were a timeless monolith—a civilization that predated their earliest memories and which enjoyed an unrivaled constancy in the ancient world. Yet what natural, religious, and political factors enabled this society to enjoy such stability? How did these shape its history? In this chapter we explore this powerful kingdom and learn about a very different civilization from Sumer and its empires.

The Land of the God-Kings

The Egyptian and Mesopotamian civilizations developed at opposite ends of the Fertile Crescent, and it is hard to imagine more different experiences than those of the Sumerians and the Egyptians. As we discussed earlier, the Tigris and Euphrates Rivers offered dangers as well as benefits to the people of Sumer; the irregular flooding and the necessity of irrigation networks made life difficult and uncertain.

1 Herodotus, *The Histories*, trans. by Aubrey de Sélincourt (New York: Penguin Books, 2003), 109.

Egypt's **Nile** River, in contrast, flooded annually in early June after their first harvest. This inundation left behind dark, rich topsoil and prepared the land for a second planting season in late autumn. The Egyptians recognized the importance of this phenomenon for their society and called their country "Kemet" (literally, "black land"). The floods also caused silt buildup, which formed natural reservoirs of water that were used to irrigate crops during dry periods. Another benefit came from the extensive marshlands in the north where the papyrus plant grew. This plant served as food, matting, material for construction, and as a medium for writing.

Perhaps Herodotus stated it best when he described Egypt as "the gift of the river,"[2] for it was in the Nile that the foundations of Egyptian greatness were laid. Firstly, fertile soil was limited to a narrow stretch of land on either side of the Nile as it snaked its way through an otherwise arid region; inhabitable areas seldom stretched more than fifteen miles from the river and could be easily accessed from the water. Secondly, movement on the Nile was convenient—regardless of which direction one traveled. If you journeyed northward towards Lower Egypt (the delta and surrounding lands) you could take advantage of the river current; if your destination was Upper Egypt in the south, you had the advantage of northerly winds that helped you move upstream. (Upper Egypt was called "upper" because of its elevated terrain.) This natural highway for people, resources, and ideas literally ran through the middle of the Egyptian Kingdom and encouraged its social and political cohesion. Lastly, Egypt enjoyed relative isolation from potential enemies. Deserts limited invasion routes from the east and west to a strip of coastland which could be defended by fortifications. Cataracts protected Upper Egypt from sudden invasion from beyond its southern border since these waterfalls made swift navigation at these points impossible.

Nonetheless, these geographical advantages also came with drawbacks. Egyptian kings eventually ruled a realm that stretched some 750 miles in length along the Nile. This vast distance enabled ambitious regional governors to use their respective zones of influence to challenge the distant authority of their rulers, and Egypt's kings realized that geography alone did not ensure their hold on power. It provided a good foundation, but more was needed to bring about lasting social and political unity. That "more" came with the Egyptian people's spirituality and its accompanying political ideology of the god-king.

Egyptians perceived the spiritual world as one of permanence and order. Just as they could predict that the Nile's annual flooding would last from June to October, so they understood the cosmos itself as an ongoing, predictable cycle. The unifying

2 Ibid., 97.

This satellite image of the **Nile** dramatically shows the difference between the fertile lands immediately adjacent to the river and the arid lands beyond.

principle was known as *maʿat*, a term that incorporated concepts such as order, justice, and truth. *Maʿat* was the underlying force that guided the stars, oversaw the flooding of the Nile, and regulated the lives of gods and men; sometimes *maʿat* was even personified as a goddess.

The key daily event was the rising of the sun-god Re, which set in motion the rituals of Egyptian worship. The sun's journey from dawn to dawn was interpreted in light of the gods' struggle against the chaotic forces that threatened *maʿat*. The gods entered Re's boat each evening to help restrain chaos during the night. When the sun rose triumphant in the morning, priests and priestesses prepared to welcome the return of the various deities to their respective temples. These temples had a floor plan that led to increasingly darkened areas. The darkest room housed the statue of the deity. Such images received divine honors, for it was thought that the gods came to dwell in their effigies during the daylight hours. The priests anointed and clothed the statues and provided food for the indwelling gods. Twice more during the day, the gods received meals and entertainment before they departed their statues to resume the nightly journey to the underworld.

Nearly fifteen hundred deities received homage in Egypt. Sometimes two or more gods were melded to emphasize some shared power or significance. For example, devotion to the hidden god Amun arose in the important city of Thebes and spread to the rest of Egypt. As he gained prominence, Amun became associated with other deities, such as the sun-god Re and the fertility god Min, and received worship under names that combined the deities (Amun-Re and Amun-Min, respectively). Such synthesis united different regional traditions and offered local deities an opportunity to be associated with more prominent gods and their worship. For example, Re, the most famous of all Egyptian gods, not only shared his identity with Amun but also with over seventy other gods and goddesses. To make things even more confusing, images of a given god could vary in form, from anthropomorphic (human form) to zoomorphic (animal form) to hybrid (half human, half animal). In terms of its mythology, Egyptian religion was no less convoluted: there was no single creation story that Egyptians accepted; instead, there were multiple origin stories that arose in different cities and varied significantly from each other.

Despite this diversity, Egyptians saw themselves as belonging to a single civilization and emphasized certain gods whose stories contributed to their sense of social cohesion. An important myth involved a royal family of gods: the king Osiris, his wife Isis, and their son Horus. According to the legend, Seth, Osiris's brother, murdered him and usurped control of Egypt. Isis miraculously revived her husband, who then became the king of the dead. In the meantime, their son Horus successfully drove his uncle from the throne and assumed control over Egypt as the ruler of the living.

This story had profound significance for the human rulers of Egypt. The kings identified themselves with the god-king Horus and even took an additional "Horus name" upon receiving the throne to emphasize this relationship. Royal decisions and acts therefore possessed a divine quality, and the symbols of the human god-king's authority—the flail and the shepherd's crook—revealed the extent of his power. The flail represented his control of the crops, while the crook displayed his role as the shepherd of his people. This close association with the divine continued after death: a deceased god-king became identified with Horus's father Osiris and continued to rule as king of the dead.

Egyptian god-kings oversaw a centralized administration that enabled Egypt to avoid the political fragmentation and rivalry that characterized the land of Sumer. While there is much that remains unknown, historians believe that the formation of the Egyptian Kingdom likely took place before urban areas established a tradition of political independence. This would explain why, unlike the cities of Sumer, Egyptian cities had no defensive walls. They were not competitors or rivals for land but rather administrative components of a unified country that was the personal possession of a single ruler. Bureaucrats made known the king's will to the people and oversaw irrigation, an important task for the growing Egyptian population. The king also had control over trade with those outside Egyptian lands. This monopoly was particularly important. Egypt's economy did not involve currency. Instead, foreign goods marked one's wealth and status. As only the king could bestow such items, it was in one's best interests to provide loyal service to the god-king in order to receive foreign luxuries. Not only did these items benefit you during your life, they also accompanied you to the tomb and assisted in the afterlife. The Egyptian practice of burying items with the dead helped cement the king's authority since each new generation needed to accrue its own exotic goods by currying the god-king's favor.

In many ways, Egypt was the gift of the Nile. The natural abundance that resulted from its annual flooding inspired the Egyptians' understanding of the cosmos as a stable, consistent cycle. Their religious beliefs clothed their political ruler with divine authority, which fostered a common social identity. The result was a kingdom that frequently enjoyed stability, wealth, and great power. Yet, it was not always so. Despite external impressions, Egyptian history was far from static.

Egyptian Kingdoms, from Old to New

Egyptian history presents a unique problem. The available sources are overwhelming. The nearby desert environment helped preserve many papyrus rolls, while other texts are literally written in stone. Consequently, we know more about the daily life and practices of the common Egyptian than we do for any other people of antiquity. However, unlike our modern calendars, the Egyptian understanding of time did not involve an absolute chronology. Their "calendars," like those of other ancients, reset with every new king's reign. Whereas a modern historian writes that Christopher Columbus sailed the Atlantic in 1492, an Egyptian would express the same event by referencing the year of the reigning king. For example, Christopher Columbus sailed in the thirteenth year of King Ferdinand II of Aragon. Both accurately describe the timing of the event, but if you do not know when Ferdinand lived, you are at a loss as to when precisely Christopher Columbus sailed.

In regard to Egypt, we possess many records that indicate how long a given king ruled, but we are not certain *when* that king lived. To make matters worse, historians remain uncertain if some kings should be seen as sequential (ruling one after the other) or simultaneous (with both kings ruling at the same time, albeit in different places, either as rivals or corulers). Unfortunately, a source that would likely answer many questions is largely lost to us: only fragments of Manetho's *History of Egypt* survive. We know that this third-century BC Egyptian historian—note how we just used absolute chronology!—divided his country's narrative into thirty dynasties, a system we still use today. However, without his full narrative, we remain ignorant of the precise relationship among these different groups of monarchs, some of whom we know coruled simultaneously. Modern historians have therefore constructed a tentative absolute chronology from two astronomical phenomena recorded by the Egyptians. They use these to coordinate two Egyptian reckonings—the seventh year of Senusret III and the ninth year of Amenhotep I—with our years 1872 BC and 1541 BC. These "absolute" dates, while still debated, serve as linchpins for identifying when events occurred in ancient Egypt according to our modern calendar. While scholars attempt to corroborate, or confirm, this syncretization through archeology and other dating methods, the fact remains that our absolute chronology for Egypt remains subject to revision. We trace out below the major epochs of Egyptian history as well as important turning points in its social development, but remember that the specific years (and even centuries) are still debated by historians.

The Old Kingdom (c. 2686–2160 BC)

Archeological evidence suggests that the unification of the Egyptian world began in Upper Egypt and spread northward towards the delta. By around 3000 BC, many sites in both Upper and Lower Egypt were unified under a single state that collected surplus crops as tax and possessed a political ideology that emphasized the authority of the god-king. To signify the unity of both Upper and Lower Egypt, subsequent Egyptian kings wore a double crown: The tall white crown of Upper Egypt and the red crown of Lower Egypt. Early royal burial rituals included both human sacrifice and treasures for the deceased king's use in the afterlife. The tombs of these kings were earthen mounds, but techniques gradually evolved until they climaxed in the massive stone structures we know today as pyramids.

Nineteenth-century scholars introduced the designation "**Old Kingdom**" to describe this first period of massive pyramid building. Such projects required a strong, centralized government that could mandate the production and transportation of the necessary provisions as well as implement large-scale compulsory labor among the people. The most famous pyramid is King Khufu's (r. 2589–2566 BC) in Giza. This gigantic structure took twenty-seven years to build and involved the hewing, transportation, and positioning of over two million stone blocks. The estimated weight of the structure is six million tons. It originally stood almost five hundred feet high and was the tallest man-made structure for almost four thousand years. (The pyramid as we see it today is about thirty feet shorter because its outer limestone casing has disappeared.) Incredibly, this and other Old Kingdom pyramids were built without knowledge of the wheel.

If we consider the countless hours of labor involved as well as the resources dedicated to one man's tomb, we may be tempted to agree with the Greek historian Herodotus when he described Cheops (the Greek name for Khufu) as a tyrant. The people of the Old Kingdom viewed the situation differently. The god-king was an absolute ruler and oversaw the proper worship of the gods who brought prosperity and stability to Egypt. What was more, he alone was immortal, though he might bestow this great gift on those who were buried near him. They believed that the worship of the god-king, this crucial link between gods and men, must continue after death. Only elaborate funeral complexes would suffice, and these required a worthy tomb, complete with priests, administrators, and regular upkeep. Many, no doubt, grumbled at the periods of compulsory labor involved, but there was also a sense that the stability and prosperity of the Old Kingdom resulted from their devotion. After all, trade with Mesopotamia flourished and exotic goods flowed into the kingdom. It may even be that the cuneiform of Mesopotamia inspired the Egyptian script, known as hieroglyphics and discussed below.

Ironically, the piety represented by the pyramids ultimately undermined rather than promoted the Old Kingdom's long-term stability. Rulers rewarded their loyal followers with gifts or the (temporary) use of land and its resources. As each subsequent king built temples and burial complexes and devoted more territories and treasures to their upkeep, they drained their own resources and limited their ability to ensure loyalty among their administrators. Fewer treasures and less land as gifts led bureaucrats and local governors to become more independent, and authority decentralized. Famine contributed to the central government's weakening: the Nile experienced low flooding over a series of years, resulting in poor harvests and food

PHOTO BY: NINA ALDIN THUNE

The **Pyramid of Giza**. The term "pyramid" comes from the Greek word *puramis*, a type of wheat cake. Greeks apparently used the term to describe the god-kings' tombs because the shapes of the cakes and the tombs were similar.

shortages. Just as people had looked to the kings as the source of their prosperity, so now they regarded these same god-kings as having failed in their role. The dynasties technically continued, but the authority of the Old Kingdom had effectively dissolved into a number of independent regions.

The Middle Kingdom (c. 2055–1650 BC)

This time of decentralization, known as the "First Intermediate Period" (2160–2055 BC), ended when rulers from Upper Egypt reunited the land. The first dynasty of the "Middle Kingdom" originally came from Thebes, but the new kings moved their residence northward in order to be close to Memphis, the former capital of the Old

The **Great Sphinx of Giza**. This structure from the Old Kingdom period was probably built by one of Khufu's sons, but what precisely inspired it remains unknown to us. Greeks later identified its combination of a lion and human form with the sphinx, a winged woman-lion from their own mythology.

Kingdom. They hoped to continue the grandeur of their predecessors and even built (smaller) pyramids, but much had changed since the breakdown of centralized rule.

The *Tale of the Eloquent Peasant*, a story that dates from the First Intermediate Period, conveys just how different things were. It tells of a covetous royal official who plots to seize a peasant's donkey through deceit. He lays a piece of his clothing on the road and orders the peasant to avoid walking on it. When the farmer dutifully goes off the road so as not to step on the tunic, his donkey eats some of the grain from the nearby field. The official immediately denounces the peasant as a thief and demands the donkey as recompense. The despoiled farmer begs for justice in such eloquent terms that his plea ultimately reaches the king himself, who intervenes on behalf of the innocent man. No god-king of the Old Kingdom would have troubled himself over a peasant's plea for his donkey, but a new sense of judgment permeated the Middle Kingdom: even god-kings needed to practice justice and to rule well. No wonder that statutes now depicted kings as thoughtful and even concerned over their responsibilities.

Common people now saw immortality as available to all—provided that the dead underwent mummification and were buried with the right spells and prayers that would guide them to the afterlife. Mummification had already been practiced for centuries, but with the Middle Kingdom it became commonplace. Egyptians believed that the body needed to be preserved for the soul to continue, and proper technique was important. For society's elite, the process took weeks and preserved as many organs as possible. The poor received a "bargain" mummification that was swift and not as meticulous in preserving one's innards. In addition to the body itself, one needed to provide for basic necessities by burying possessions and treasures alongside the mummified corpse. Families often sought to be buried together, and a replica family home was created in the tomb.

The god-kings continued to build elaborate burial complexes, but they no longer consumed as much of their country's resources in those projects. War and conquest had become more attractive ways to ensure the legacy of an ambitious monarch. Multitudes of slaves became a new part of Egyptian society as thousands of captives were brought back from triumphant campaigns in Africa and those Asian lands along the eastern Mediterranean, collectively known as the Levant. Senusret III (r. 1870–1831 BC), the self-described "throat-slitter of Asia," exemplified this new military might. His campaigns devastated the people of Nubia, while his hatred toward those in the Levant produced special talismans designed to curse his enemies through magic. He and his son brought about a golden age of strength and culture in Egypt, but the Middle Kingdom ultimately went into decline and fragmented in the centuries after their rule. This time, there was a foreign twist: pastoralists from West Asia, known as the **Hyksos** ("foreign kings"), established their own dynasty and ruled the Nile delta for over one hundred years.

The New Kingdom (c. 1550–1069 BC)

How the Hyksos dynasty (Egypt's fifteenth according to Manetho's reckoning) came to power remains mysterious. This era of foreign rule—known today as the "Second Intermediate Period" (c. 1650–1550 BC)—was considered shameful by the Egyptians, and they did not preserve many records of it. Scholars who incorporate the biblical account into their narratives are divided: Some believe that this era coincides with the migration of Abraham's descendants *into* Egypt, while others argue that the Hyksos came to power immediately *after* the Exodus (see chapter insert on the Exodus). The Hyksos ultimately fell when Egyptians from Upper Egypt drove the "foreign kings" from the delta and established what historians now call the "**New Kingdom**."

The New Kingdom sought to undo the humiliation of Hyksos rule through an aggressive foreign policy. Militant rulers expanded their borders and influence across the ancient world. Chariots proliferated, and soldiers returned from campaign with slaves and treasures. Egyptian trade grew to include even Minoan

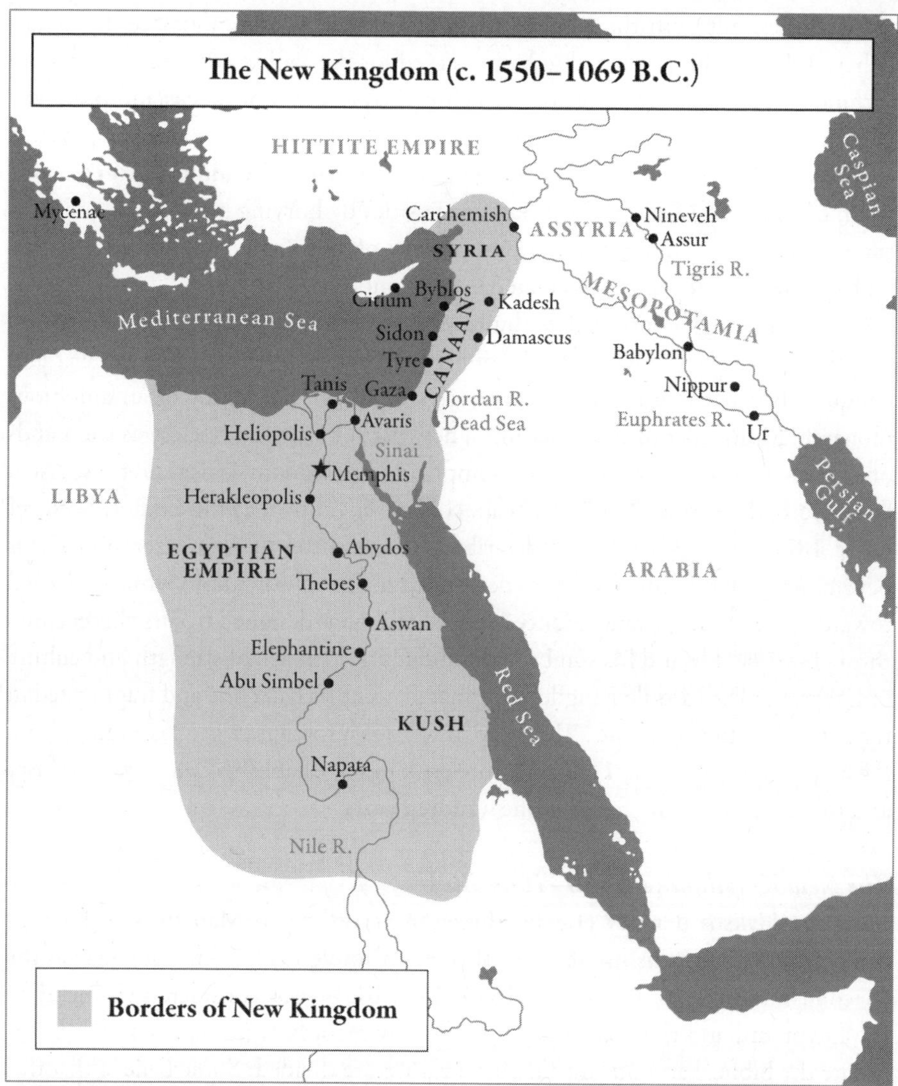

Crete (see chapter 7). The monarchs of the New Kingdom basked in their restored glory and received a new title, "pharaoh." (Though it is common nowadays to use "pharaoh" to designate any Egyptian king, it did not arise as a common title until the New Kingdom. It literally references the king's "great house" and became identified with the ruler himself, similar to the way that we associate "the White House" with the current president of the United States.) God-kings once again built massive monuments, and a large portion of Egyptian labor and resources went into the construction of obelisks, stone temples, and elaborate burial complexes. One of the

THE EXODUS

The conclusion of Genesis describes how the descendants of Abraham migrated into Egypt. The central figure in this transition was Abraham's great-grandson, Joseph, who was sold into slavery by his jealous half-brothers and yet rose to great authority within Egypt itself. Joseph later used his position as vizier to help his family during a severe famine, and thus Abraham's descendants, called Hebrews or Israelites, migrated to the rich land of Goshen within the Nile delta. Their protected status did not last and, as recorded in the book of Exodus, later rulers of Egypt enslaved them. This situation segues to the biblical narrative of Moses and the triumphant exodus of the Israelites from Egypt.

The revelation of God's name, the Ten Plagues, the departure from Egypt, the covenant with God at Mount Sinai, and the giving of the Mosaic Law—each of these events provides riches for theological consideration, but many historians doubt the historicity of this narrative. For some, the Exodus saga, including the person of Moses, was an elaborate myth designed to fashion a national identity for the Hebrew people as they rose to prominence in Canaan. According to this interpretation, there may have been Hebrews who, like Joseph, found themselves enslaved in Egypt. These individuals, or perhaps even small bands of slaves, escaped to freedom and told stories of their journeys that grew in the telling until they had ultimately become a foundational epic for the Hebrew people.

This view enjoys popularity among many contemporary academics, but it fails to address why the Exodus story became integral to the Hebrew identity. Why would people in Canaan emphasize captivity, especially since, according to the very historians who hold this position, most Hebrews' experience did not include enslavement in Egypt? The Hebrew Scriptures abound with references to Moses and the events of the Exodus. Their liturgical life focused on the festival of the Passover, the annual remembrance of their deliverance from slavery through God's power. Why take stories of escaped slaves and use *those* as an argument for your special relationship with God if it was the experience of only a few or something that did not really happen? Such deep traditions do not just arise from a loose collection of stories. It seems far more likely that the story of bondage followed by liberation became a prominent theme for the Hebrews because it reflected historical reality.

Yet challenges do remain for historians who accept the historicity of the book of Exodus. At issue is a question of chronology. Different books of the Bible seem to indicate different eras for Moses. The book of Exodus implies that Hebrew slaves built Piramesse for Rameses II, while 1 [3] Kings 6:1 dates the Exodus to a period several centuries prior to Rameses's reign. Some try to reconcile the situation by interpreting the Book of Kings' reference to the 480 years between the Exodus and King Solomon as signifying the number of generations rather than actual years. (Generations are traditionally reckoned as forty years long, so in this theory the 480 years equals twelve generations. If we then calculate each generation as approximately twenty years, which is closer to an actual biological generation, we end up with a span of years that coincides with the era of Rameses.) This bending of the explicit Biblical dating does not convince everyone, and it does not help that, as we saw, Egyptian chronology offers its own difficulties.

As a result, some historians argue for a "late Exodus" during the thirteenth-century reign of Rameses II; others use the chronology of 1 Kings and various biblical genealogies to contend for an "early Exodus" that occurred in the fifteenth century. This is not merely an academic argument. When the Exodus happened has profound ramifications, at the very least in how you understand the books of Joshua and Judges. For example, if you hold that the Exodus occurred in the thirteenth century BC, you must explain why the ruins of Jericho date from several centuries earlier. (Secular historians frequently cite this situation to discredit the historicity of the Exodus event.) Furthermore, there is the problem of Egyptian strength. Within our current chronological framework for Egypt, both the early and the late Exodus options occurred during a time of Egyptian flourishing, and there is no indication that Egyptian society suffered any setback from, for example, the destruction of its army or deaths of its firstborn children during the Ten Plagues.

Efforts to respond to these challenges have contributed to the formation of a third position—by far the smallest. These scholars, including the agnostic archeologist David Rohl, support a fifteenth-century Exodus but also maintain that our understanding of Egyptian chronology is flawed. They argue for a "New Chronology" that would fundamentally restructure our current nineteenth-century system for dating Egyptian history. In the process, they believe it would reconcile Egyptian history with the events described in Genesis and Exodus. This theory holds that the decline in power we expect from the plagues and destruction of Pharaoh's army *did* occur and even facilitated the Hyksos occupation, which, according to this theory, happened shortly after the Hebrews' departure. This "New Chronology" would radically alter our understanding of the ancient world, and it has received much criticism from those who hold the other interpretations. Nonetheless, even hostile academics admit that our current chronology is tentative and subject to revision. Whether the "New Chronology" is more accurate remains to be seen, but it does seemingly reconcile a number of problems that arise from our current perspective and is worthy of further exploration.

most extensive building programs occurred during the reign of Queen Hatshepsut (r. 1473–1458 BC), the second woman to rule Egypt. She used these structures as opportunities to record her military victories against remaining Hyksos forces.

During this period, an important religious shift was taking place: gods from other societies were now identified with Egyptian ones. Melding gods, as we have seen, was not a new practice, but Egyptians had not previously associated foreign deities with their own. Now Ishtar blended with Isis, while Baal, a Canaanite god whom we will encounter in the next chapter, became the murderous Seth and was particularly honored by Rameses II.

The most enigmatic pharaoh of the New Kingdom was **Akhenaten** (r. 1352–1336 BC). He originally came to the throne as Amenhotep IV, but he abandoned that name in favor of one that honored Aten, the sun disk god. He believed Aten was the purest manifestation of the god Re and forbade the worship of other gods. This was not monotheism. Akhenaten did not deny that other gods existed, and he did not suppress his own cult: people still worshipped the god-king, while he praised Aten. Temples to other gods closed and traditional festivals ceased. Akhenaten even moved his capital to a new city, Akhetaten ("horizon of Aten"), and constructed open-air shrines to Aten to contrast with the traditional temples that had darkened interiors. Even art and language changed. Royal decrees replaced their complex, formal style with simpler prose, and images of the pharaoh were surprisingly realistic, candidly depicting Akhenaten's sloping shoulders and protruding belly. These changes troubled many Egyptians, especially since their society emphasized the importance of continuity. It seems likely that Akhenaten had to rely upon military support for his reforms.

Statue of Akhenaten and Nefertiti. Made of painted limestone c. 1345 BC. Currently in the Louvre Museum, Paris, France. This depiction is significant since most images of Akhenaten and Nefertiti were intentionally destroyed once their religious reforms were rejected after their deaths.

Traditional Egyptian society reasserted itself after Akhenaten's death. The temples reopened and popular festivals resumed. Akhenaten himself became the object of hate. Egyptians destroyed his statues, desecrated his mummified body, and tried to purge all memory of his rule, going so far as to erase his name and to assign the years he reigned to another pharaoh. Furthermore, a shift took place in the ideology of the god-king. Though the traditional titles remained, the intimate identification between the god Horus and the current king became weaker.

Such a trend did not stop the most powerful and famous pharaoh of the New Kingdom from asserting his own divinity. **Rameses II** (r. 1279–1213 BC) knew about propaganda. He had used it well after he fought at Qadesh in Syria in 1274. This battle, the first engagement in history for which we have tactical information, involved as many as six thousand chariots. Rameses almost lost the battle and his life, but we would not know that from the Egyptian account. Official records tell us it was a glorious victory (it was a stalemate) and that Rameses essentially slew the enemy single-handedly (he walked into an ambush). Nonetheless, even when we see through his self-glorification, there is no denying that Rameses II ruled Egypt at its pinnacle. He engaged in extensive building projects, notably at the city of Piramesse, which is mentioned in the Book of Exodus, and his authority stretched far into Syria. It seemed as though the New Kingdom was on the verge of even greater expansion and domination.

Fortunately, we have many sources which bring to life this triumphant period of Egyptian history. Many Egyptians were literate and used a script known as **hieroglyphs** (literally "sacred carving" in Greek) to engrave their records and accomplishments into stone. By the fourth century AD, the meaning of these numerous hieroglyphs had faded from memory. It was not until 1822 that the Frenchman Jean-François Champollion deciphered the language through the famous Rosetta Stone, an inscription that included the same text in hieroglyphic, Greek, and demotic (a more modern Egyptian language). His discovery enabled historians to unlock a treasure trove of personal accounts, love poems, business transactions, and prayers from the ordinary people of Egypt.

We learned, for example, that girls typically married around the age of thirteen in a simple ceremony that involved the spouses and, if living, their parents. Their love poetry suggests that couples highly valued emotional connection, though this did not automatically protect their marriage from divorce, which was common.

A young bride from the New Kingdom had many advantages that her peers in later times and other societies did not. She possessed her own property, could inherit land, and might know how to read. Her new husband, probably a farmer who was slightly older, welcomed her into his mudbrick—not stone—house. Here, the newly married couple eagerly anticipated children, in part because the future generation had an important role to play in the parents' burials. The girl knew that many dangers confronted her during childbirth, and many young women had amulets about themselves to invoke the gods during labor. These magical items honored local household deities—like the dwarf-god Bes—rather than important state gods like Amun-Re. Those major deities focused on the maintenance of society as a whole and were not so involved in the daily life of the common people. For their part, most people did not participate in the daily worship of the gods or regard priests as moral guides. The priesthood functioned to help the pharaoh and the gods maintain *ma'at* in the kingdom; the personal failings or piety of a given priest were of no concern to the average Egyptian.

Hieroglyphic fragment from the tomb of Seti I (r. c. 1290–1279 BC). Currently in the British Museum, London, England. Egyptian hieroglyphs included both ideographic representations and phonetic characters. Phonetic symbols, like our alphabet, told the reader the sounds to make in order to form a word; ideographs offered a figurative depiction of a specific concept or thing. (For example, a red octagon in modern society conveys the concept of "stop.") These characters were intermixed so that one might encounter both types in a single phrase. Furthermore, written ideas could be expressed from left to right, right to left, and top to bottom.

Children quickly learned to contribute to the family. Boys worked in the fields while young girls tended the animals and helped around the house. Whereas, as we will see, Greeks and Romans developed public games and entertainments, Egyptian society centered on home life. Families passed quiet evenings playing board games and drinking beer, the most common Egyptian beverage.

Outside their homes, dangers awaited: scorpions, crocodiles, and hippopotami could turn a happy family gathering into a tragedy. Cats and dogs became trusted companions, and beds were designed to protect the sleeper from the perils of invaders such as rats. Other dangers were easier to avoid: both men and women kept their hair short to avoid head lice, though the wealthy did wear wigs on formal occasions.

Unfortunately, the lifespan of the average Egyptian was short—as low as the early thirties. Parents needed to teach their children, especially their eldest son, to care for them after their deaths. Egyptians believed that the individual consisted of five different parts, including the *ka* and the *ba*. The *ka* was physical, though distinct from the body. This required the food that mourners left for the deceased at the tomb. The *ba* was a spiritual component that could leave the tomb each day and return at nightfall. One's name was another integral part of one's personhood. This is why Egyptians wrote their names as frequently as possible in their tombs so that this fundamental part of their identity would not be forgotten.

Works abounded about how to successfully navigate the dangerous time between death and judgment. The *Book of the Dead*, like mummification, became a necessary part of one's burial. It provided instructions, spells, and hymns that led one to Osiris. This god of the dead judged the deceased Egyptian: The heart was placed in a scale alongside a feather, which represented *ma'at*. The Great Devourer, a crocodile-lion-hippopotamus, ate those whose wrongdoings outweighed the feather. What awaited those who passed the test remained debated, though one had obvious incentives to avoid being eaten.

One important event that an Egyptian family celebrated was the *sed* festival. This occurred on the thirtieth anniversary of the current pharaoh's rule and every three to four years after that. It involved various rituals, such as running, that showcased the pharaoh's physical vigor and ability to rule. Such events may have reflected the early Egyptian monarchy when successfully commanding armies and being personally fit were necessary components for ensuring the loyalty of one's soldiers. Rameses II celebrated thirteen or fourteen *sed* festivals—the most ever achieved by a single pharaoh.

Rameses's reign must have tempted some to think that Egyptian glory and power would never fade, but it was not to be. New threats lay on the horizon, and in the century after Rameses II, Egyptian leadership failed to rise to the challenge.

The **Stele of Intef and Shenetsetji**. Made of limestone c. 2150-2040 B.C. Property of the Boston Museum of Fine Arts, currently in the Carlos Museum, Atlanta, Georgia. This stone was placed at the entrance of the tomb of Intef and his wife Shenetsetji. The hieroglyphic inscription follows the standard offering formula for gifts for the dead.

Egypt entered its third "intermediate period," or age of fragmentation. Though it reunited once more, the glory of the New Kingdom had faded forever.

Conclusion

Egypt rightly fascinated the ancient world. The pyramids bespoke of the might of the god-kings and gave physical form to the belief that Egyptian society was permanent and even timeless. Its geography encouraged this perception because the Nile's cyclical flooding provided a fertile foundation, while natural barriers limited hostile invasion. However, as we have seen, its society was neither invincible nor static. The intermediate periods heralded great changes, and the New Kingdom pursued a policy of foreign expansion that would have been unthinkable in previous centuries. In the next chapter, we explore the wider world which the New Kingdom influenced and encounter the empire that replaced Egypt as the dominant power of its age.

CHAPTER 5

In the Shadow of Assyria

I cut off of some their arms (and) hands; I cut off of others their noses, ears, (and) extremities. I gouged out the eyes of many troops. I made one pile of the living (and) one of heads. I hung their heads on trees around the city. I burnt their adolescent boys (and) girls. I razed, destroyed, and burnt (and) consumed the city.

Monument of Ashurnarsipal II[1]

Violence has been the tool of conquerors since Sargon, but sheer terror was the weapon of choice for the Assyrian Empire. From mutilations and public executions to the deportation of entire populations, the Assyrians understood the power of dread and intimidation. In spite of this harshness, these conquerors were more than fierce brutes. They believed their acts of terror were building a world that upheld honor and honesty.

As Assyria laid its imperial foundations, Abraham's descendants established their own kingdom in Canaan. These Israelites even achieved a brief period of prosperity and unity—until disaster struck. What society did the Israelites establish in their new land and how did it develop? What events and ideas transformed Assyria into the ancient world's most notorious empire? To answer these questions, we return to Mesopotamia in the aftermath of Ur III's collapse and explore what powers sought to fill its place.

1 Albert Kirk Grayson, *Assyrian Royal Inscriptions*, Part 2, Records of the Ancient Near East 2, ed. Hans Goedicke (Wiesbaden, Germany: Otto Harrassowitz, 1976), 126.

Triumph and Collapse in the Second Millennium

As the god-kings of Egypt's Middle Kingdom restored stability in the Nile River valley, Mesopotamia reeled from the collapse of Ur III. The demise of Ur's hegemony, or political supremacy, around 2000 BC created a power vacuum in Mesopotamia, and newly freed city-states soon contended with one another to establish their own regional dominance. At first, the most prominent contenders were in Sumer, but the new powers emerging in northern and central Mesopotamia proved to be more successful.

Assyria began as a political backwater, whose cities were of little significance in northern Mesopotamia. First Sargon, then Ur III incorporated this area into their respective empires, but it was never a significant territory for either. Not until Ur III's rule ended did the region grow in importance, and the period known as "Old Assyria" (c. 2000–c. 1350 BC) begin.

In these early days, Assyrians were known for trade rather than terrorizing. Assyrian merchants established an extensive commercial network, with their city Ashur as its central hub. This city was named after the Assyrians' chief god, Ashur, and it occupied a promising site along the Tigris River. It soon served as a crossroads for trade caravans that entrepreneurial Assyrians organized. Tin from the east, textiles from the south, and gold and silver from the northwest passed through Ashur's gates and made it wealthy. Family businesses sought to expand their trade (and riches) by having members leave northern Mesopotamia to establish permanent trading depots in other regions. Men sometimes lived for years away from their families while the women at home oversaw the production or acquisition of goods. Investments were costly: traders needed to purchase donkeys as beasts of burden, hire personnel to protect their caravans, *and* prepare the actual products for sale. Nonetheless, commerce was lucrative; tin and textiles sold in Anatolia (modern-day Turkey) yielded profits as high as 100 percent.

Assyria was rapidly becoming an economic power, but it was not yet politically dominant. This situation began to change in 1807 BC. In that year, Shamshi-Adad I (r. 1807–1775 BC) seized control of Ashur. It is likely that he was the king of a nearby rival city, but we know little of his early life and reign. While he took the traditional Assyrian title ("governor of the god Ashur"), Shamshi-Adad's ambitions went far beyond those of Ashur's previous leaders. Over the next thirty years, he carved out a realm for himself to the north of ancient Sumer. This Kingdom of Upper Mesopotamia spread Assyrian practices—such as their method of dating documents—throughout the general region, but its influence came to an abrupt end shortly after Shamshi-Adad's death in 1775.

The next important ruler to govern in northern Mesopotamia was the most famous of them all. **Hammurabi** (r. 1792–1750 BC) ruled Babylon ("God's Gate"), a city in central Mesopotamia along the Euphrates River. His greatest asset was his patience. He understood that his small kingdom was not yet in a position to challenge the rule of Shamshi-Adad I to the north or the larger cities to the south. Instead, he waited. Even when Shamshi-Adad's death brought an opportunity to expand, Hammurabi continued to prepare. From 1780 to 1764, Hammurabi focused his efforts on Babylon's infrastructure and religious rituals.

His apparent passivity ultimately gave way to rapid conquests when Hammurabi decided to act. He began by using diplomacy to isolate rivals and pit them one against the other. By 1755—within ten years of his decision to send out his armies—Hammurabi had forged an empire as large as that of Ur III. His success redefined the political hierarchy of the entire Mesopotamian world: Babylon was now the mightiest city in the region, and its ruler confidently claimed that he was "the king who made the four quarters of the earth obedient."[2]

Hammurabi's Law Code. Made of basalt c. 1792–1750 BC. Currently in the Louvre Museum, Paris, France. This seven-foot stele is the most well-known version of the famous law code. At its top is a depiction of Hammurabi standing before Shamash, the god of justice. The empty part at its base originally had text, but a later king erased it.

2 Douglas R. Frayne, *Old Babylonian Period* (2003–1595 BC) (Toronto: University of Toronto, 1990), 341; quoted in Marc van de Mieroop, *A History of the Ancient Near East*, 3rd ed. (Oxford: Wiley Blackwell, 2016), 119.

Hammurabi took his responsibilities as king seriously. The best example of his desire to establish a legacy of justice and prosperity was his Law Code. This was not the first list of statutes in Mesopotamia, but it was the most influential—perhaps because it boasted at length of Hammurabi's achievements and encouraged later rulers to imitate him. The series of 282 pronouncements features "if, then" statements which describe a crime and then a corresponding punishment. Perhaps the most famous is Law 196: "If a man put out the eye of another man, his eye shall be put out." Most statements follow this "eye for an eye" reckoning of justice, though the social status of perpetrator and victim influenced punishment. Crimes committed against the socially important, for example, received harsher penalties than those inflicted upon the poor. Nonetheless, the document is not as straightforward as it first appears; there are a number of contradictions among its laws, and historians believe that it reflected the *ideal* situation that Hammurabi envisioned rather than the *actual* experience of Babylonian society.

Rebellions broke out in southern Mesopotamia after Hammurabi's death. It seems that the Babylonians suppressed these revolts so harshly that most people had to abandon the region. This would explain the mass emigration from the ancient cities of Sumer that occurred in the decades after Hammurabi's death. Among those leaving were students who abandoned clay tablets full of school exercises. Usually, these would have been reused by subsequent pupils, but the departing student body left them behind. The result was a treasure trove of students' work for future archeologists. Since students then, like those today, learned through repetition, scholars have found numerous examples of writing and mathematics. Sometimes our best versions of famous texts, such as *The Epic of Gilgamesh*, survive in these abandoned "workbooks" used by the students of this period. Other tablets reveal that Mesopotamians knew the square root of two and used principles from algebra and geometry.

As the population moved northward, fundamental changes in culture took place. The gods of northern and central Mesopotamia grew in importance, particularly the chief god of Babylon, Marduk. The southern deities, in contrast, declined. They were too associated with specific cities to survive in a new environment. Gradually, they either melded with other deities or faded altogether. The name Sumer itself was abandoned, and southern and central Mesopotamia became known as Babylonia. Nonetheless, this first period of Babylonian supremacy—known as "Old Babylon"—was relatively brief. In 1595 BC, a Hittite army from Anatolia invaded Babylon and sacked its capital.

The Hittites were a warrior people who began their rise to prominence around 1650 BC when Hattusilis (r. c. 1650–c. 1620 BC) took the city of Hattusa in central Anatolia and established it as his capital. The rugged terrain mirrored the hardy character of the people. They built massive walls and towers of defense and prized valor in battle. Their armies quickly humbled older powers—such as Babylon—through their use of chariots, military intelligence, and stratagem. Their society emphasized personal bonds of service and loyalty, but this did not prevent rival factions of warriors from supporting different claimants to the throne or assassinating unwanted kings. Despite its success against Babylon and others, the Hittite Kingdom itself soon devolved into internal chaos and temporary collapse.

What followed was a "Dark Age," a time when historians have few sources, and we must speculate about developments. In this particular situation, historians debate about the very length of the Dark Age. While some believe it lasted centuries, others argue it ended after several decades. Regardless of which chronology one follows, the ancient world that emerged from the Dark Age was very different from the previous era. Whereas previously Mesopotamian societies had focused on their own political and cultural development, after the Dark Age they increasingly interacted with lands further west.

This new focus brought Mesopotamia into consistent contact with the emerging New Kingdom of Egypt. The New Kingdom, as we have seen, was determined to avoid another foreign invasion and established a policy of expansion. Babylon and Hatti, having themselves recently experienced political upheaval, both entertained similar designs, and the stage was set for an epic clash of empires. Surprisingly, this did not happen. Instead, Babylon, the New Kingdom, the Hittites, and other powers formed a network of empires that corresponded with one another and sought to maintain a delicate balance of power through marriage alliances and the exchange of gifts. Historians sometimes call this era the **Club of Great Powers**. Eventually,

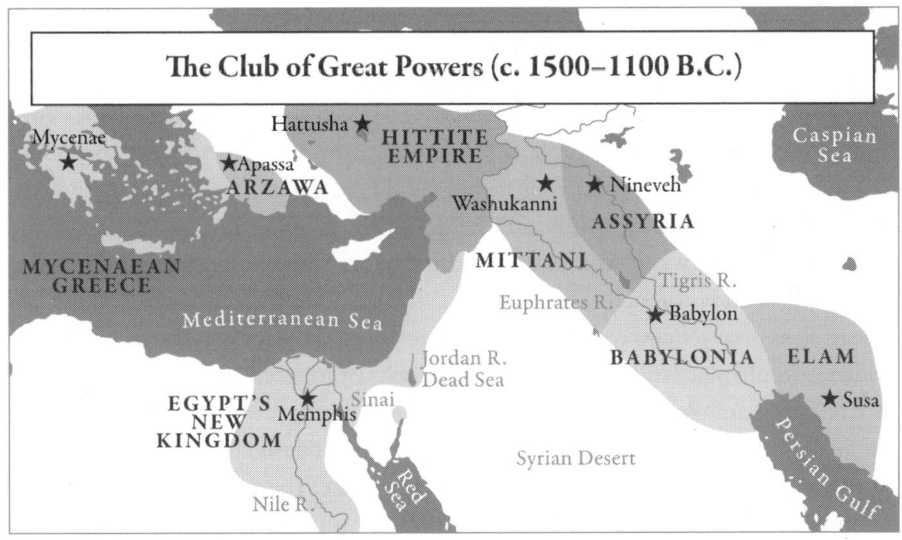

even Minoan Crete and Mycenaean Greece (see chapter 7) were interacting with this collection of rulers.

From around 1500 to 1200 BC, the Club of Great Powers generally succeeded in avoiding total war. There were exceptions, such as when Rameses II fought against the Hittites at Qadesh in 1274 BC, and some empires did fall. A beneficiary of the violence was Assyria. This region increasingly asserted its importance, but this time it had a more explicitly military—rather than economic—character. Rulers of Assyria now regularly summoned their subjects to serve in the army and awarded loyal service with land. It set an important precedent of power, but the glory of "Middle Assyria" (c. 1363–912 BC)—like that of the other members of the Club of Great Powers—soon passed into memory.

By 1100 BC, each of the major powers was either collapsing or experiencing great turmoil. We do not know precisely what brought about this situation at the end of the second millennium. What few records we have speak of foreign invaders, sometimes known as "sea peoples," but these accounts are confused and sometimes contradictory. Some historians have suggested that a sudden influx of new populations from the Russian steppe into Europe and West Asia undermined the stability of the region. What seems clear is that from around 1100 to 900 BC, the social order that had supported the commerce, communications, and infrastructures of the preceding era had disappeared. It was as though a heavy curtain set upon the stage of the ancient world. When this second Dark Age finally lifted, the land was a very different place. A fresh cast of peoples were carving out kingdoms for themselves and establishing new systems of relationships. Among these were the descendants of Abraham.

Israel: From Conquest to Division

When discussing the early history of the Israelites in Canaan, we are immediately confronted with problems in chronology. Evidence for the early history of the Hebrews in Canaan derives almost exclusively from the Old Testament, and many scholars dismiss the books of Exodus, Joshua, and Judges as unhistorical and also argue that the descriptions of glory and wealth during the days of Solomon are exaggerated. The archeological finds at Jericho are usually the first example that critics cite. While historians agree that Jericho was destroyed at one point, the dating of the archeological evidence would place this event centuries before the proposed arrival of the Hebrews in Canaan—assuming that the Exodus occurred during the reign of Rameses II. Archeologists, therefore, dismiss these accounts by saying that Joshua could not have destroyed a city that had already fallen centuries before. The same situation holds for a number of other sites described in the Book of Joshua. The Book of Judges adds

The **Merneptah Stele**. Made of black granite, c. 1208 BC. Currently in the Egyptian Museum, Cairo, Egypt. This presents the earliest extra-biblical reference to the ancient Israelites. In this monument, Merneptah (r. 1213–1203) declared that "Israel is wasted, its seed is not." While historians accept the stele as authentic, debates remain regarding which stage of development Israelite society had reached at the time of Merneptah's boast. Theories vary depending on which chronology of the ancient world one accepts.

its own thorny chronological issue. If we simply add the years that Judges provides sequentially, we have a period of approximately four hundred years between the death of Joshua and the rise of Samuel. However, Judges may not offer a straightforward chronology. It is possible, for example, that some judges were *contemporaries* rather than *sequential* (that is, they ruled alongside one another at the same time).

Understanding and then reconciling the biblical narrative with archeological evidence is a daunting task. That said, as noted in chapter 4's insert on the Exodus, a minority of archeologists and historians believe that a shift by several centuries in our chronological reckoning would align archeological evidence with the narrative offered in Exodus, Joshua, and Judges. The attraction of this theory is obvious, but regardless of whether it accurately synthesizes our current evidence or whether future findings will aid our understanding in some new way, we should remain confident that there exists a reasonable solution to these admittedly challenging historical questions regarding the biblical timeline.

According to the biblical narrative, the Israelites lacked a permanent central government or leadership when they first established their communities in Canaan. Moses had provided clear guidance during the Exodus and sojourn in the desert, while his lieutenant Joshua continued this legacy during his campaigns in Canaan. These initial conquests secured land for the Israelites that was subsequently divided among them. The organization of Hebrew society reflected its family history. Sections of land were designated for twelve tribes that roughly paralleled the twelve sons of Jacob. Unfortunately, these twelve tribes also manifested the jealousy and violence that had marked the relationships among Jacob's sons. Some tribes, for example, refused to fight on behalf of others and even warred amongst themselves. As a result, enemies could take advantage of these divisions to oppress various areas

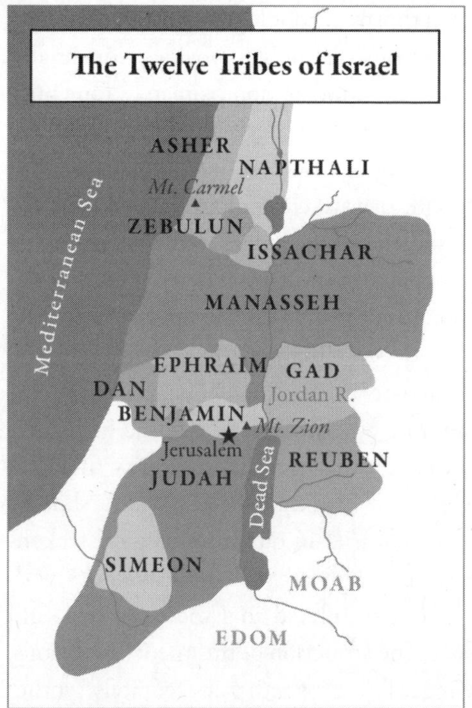

Technically, two of the twelve tribes of Jacob who occupied Canaan were the descendants of Joseph's two sons, Ephraim and Manasseh. There was no tribe of Joseph and the descendants of Levi did not receive their own exclusive division of land. Rather, the Levites lived among the other twelve groups as the priestly order within Israelite society.

in Israelite-held Canaan. Without leadership, the land promised to Abraham would soon slip from his descendants' control. This was the era recounted in Judges, when individual leaders from different tribes, known as judges, rose up to defend their people against external adversaries and internal corruption.

Worship of the Lord had been the unifying principle among the Israelites after their departure from Egypt. The Mosaic Law, that is, the body of religious and communal practices and prohibitions associated with God's revelations to Moses, gave the Hebrew community a focal point and common social foundation, but this cultural cohesion was gradually disintegrating as the fervor of the Israelites decreased over the generations. True, they had relics from the Exodus events enshrined in the Ark of the Covenant, as well as a priesthood, descended from Jacob's son Levi, that oversaw proper sacrifices to God. Furthermore, there was the Passover, the annual liturgical commemoration of their liberation from Egypt by God's hand. Nevertheless, the practices of the remaining Canaanites continually tempted the Hebrews to abandon their monotheism in favor of foreign gods. The most alluring of these deities was **Baal**. "Baal" ("owner" or "lord") was, at first, a general title of respect reserved for the gods, but it gradually became associated specifically with Hadad, the god of storms, rain, and fertility. Unlike Mesopotamia and Egypt, which had rivers to supply water regularly, Canaan had to rely upon rainfall. A weather god, therefore, held particular importance for the area's inhabitants. For lukewarm Israelites the worship of Baal promised social acceptance among their polytheistic neighbors as well as participation in their rites, which likely included licentious behavior. Some even went so far as to identify Abraham's God with Baal.

The Canaanites were not the only danger during the time of the judges. The Philistines, invaders from the Aegean, can likely be associated with the "sea peoples" that helped bring an end to the Club of Great Powers. Some historians believe that the Philistines were veterans or refugees from an earlier struggle in Anatolia known by legend as the Trojan War (see chapter 7). The Philistines eventually established a network of five cities along the Mediterranean coast and began to expand eastward towards the territory of the twelve tribes. The Old Testament has many famous episodes that highlight the animosity between the two peoples, such as those involving the judge Samson (see Jgs 13–16). Eventually, the Philistines' power went into decline as the first kings of Israel waged war against them. History today remembers them more as the enemies of Samson and David than for any achievement of their own. Nonetheless, their name outlived their historical influence: we still refer to the region as "Palestine," a term which derives from "Peleset," an alternative name for the Philistines.

What weakened Philistine power was the establishment of an Israelite kingdom. Indeed, the first decades of the so-called United Kingdom of Israel enjoyed many achievements. Under royal leadership, the Israelite people first pushed back their enemies and then inaugurated a golden era of prosperity and stability. Despite these successes, the biblical account emphasizes that the kingship was not originally a part of God's plan for the twelve tribes. When the Israelites demanded that their last judge, Samuel, anoint a king for them, they were rejecting God's leadership (in the form of divinely inspired judges) in favor of the political model of the societies around them. These cultures had kings that led armies and oversaw building projects. God gave the people their heart's desire, but not before Samuel had described all the obligations royalty would demand from them. This catalogue of future woes ended with a somber warning: "And in that day you will cry out because of your king, whom you have chosen for yourselves, but the LORD will not answer you in that day" (1 Sm [1 Kgs] 8:18).

It did not take long for the tribes to realize the truth of God's words. The first king, Saul (d. c. 1012 BC), initially drove back Israel's foes, but his fear that he would lose power saw him blend royal authority with that of the priesthood and attempt to offer sacrifice unlawfully. Furthermore, he jealously watched for any rivals and soon turned against his most skilled general, David. It was this David, the champion who had slain the Philistine Goliath, who became the next messiah ("anointed one") to rule Israel. He refused to slay Saul, despite the latter's increasing tyranny, and only assumed authority when Saul killed himself during a battle against the Philistines.

David (r. c. 1010–970 BC) inherited a tricky situation. Saul's son Eshbaal ("Fire of Baal") claimed the kingship, but David's own tribe of Judah promptly seceded and declared David king. The civil war lasted for two years until Eshbaal was betrayed by his own generals and assassinated. David now had no clear rival, but that did not mean he lacked enemies. He needed to unite the Israelite people and give them a new focus. He accomplished this through the daring campaign against the city of Jerusalem, a Canaanite stronghold in the territory allotted to the tribe of Benjamin. David made this fallen fortress his new capital and endowed it with religious significance by bringing the Ark of the Covenant to rest within its confines. David's son Solomon (r. c. 970–931 BC) added to Jerusalem's spiritual importance by building a massive temple for the Lord there. What is more, David's family became associated in Hebrew tradition with the coming of a Savior who would usher in a new era of glory for the Israelite people.

David had waged numerous wars—both foreign and civil—but his heir Solomon enjoyed a period of peace and prosperity that inspired an ambitious building agenda. This program severely strained the resources of his kingdom. The northern Israelites particularly resented that their labor and wealth went to benefit the southern capital. When Solomon died, they requested that his son Rehoboam (r. c. 931–913 BC) reduce these oppressive demands. Unfortunately for all involved, the new king's harsh response to their request caused the state to fracture in two: the northern Kingdom of Israel and the southern Kingdom of Judah. A religious schism accompanied the political break. The rulers of the North were not keen to have their people visit the Temple in Jerusalem, even though that was the official center of worship to the Lord. Instead, they built opposing shrines to the gods of their polytheistic neighbors.

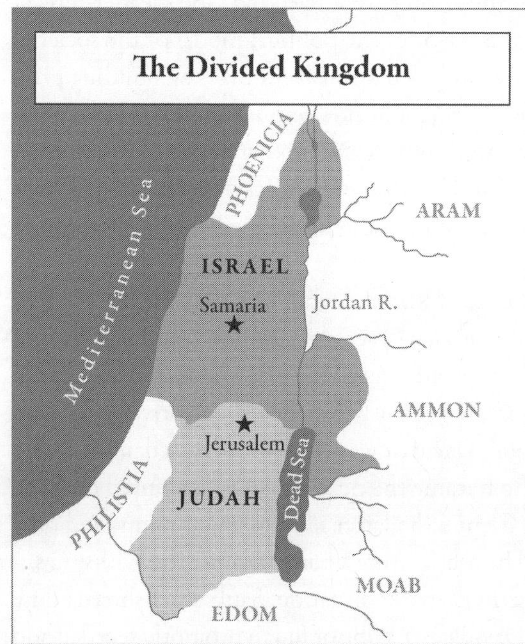

The North enjoyed much greater foreign contact and economic activity than did the less accessible, less fertile lands to the south. This was both a blessing and a curse. The blessing was that Israel was far more wealthy and powerful than its southern rival Judah. The curse was that this made the throne of Israel more attractive to would-be usurpers. Whereas the royal line of David had a

THE PROPHETS

Many people today associate prophecy with foretelling the future, but the Greek word *propheteia* originally meant interpreting the will of the gods. This is important to keep in mind when discussing the Old Testament prophets. While predicting events could be a part of their message, they were focused on teaching what God willed in the present. Furthermore, the prophets represented an important balance against royal overreach. Secular rulers have sought to co-opt or wield religious authority throughout history. As we have seen with Naram-Sin and others, the temptation to "become" a god was a real one. In contrast, the Hebrew prophets boldly condemned kings and others when their actions deserved it. Even generally pious kings were not exempt from censure, as we learn when the prophet Nathan condemned David for his adultery with Bathsheba and the murder of her husband. Nathan's rebuke—"You are the man!"—is perhaps one of the grandest moments in Hebrew history (2 Sm [2 Kgs] 12:7). It was a cry of defiance against human selfishness and a solemn declaration of the justice of the God who judges even kings.

The prophets, however, did more than criticize poor behavior or predict how it would be punished. They received the special task of unfolding God's inner life even as they responded to the social and political injustice of their own lifetimes. Thus, Amos (c. 760 BC) and Hosea (c. 740 BC) both warned Israel of the coming devastation of the Assyrian Captivity, but their messages stressed different attributes of the Lord. Amos spoke of God's righteousness and how the actions of all peoples received their just recompense from Him. Hosea emphasized God's love and spoke of Israel's faults with the metaphor of a faithless wife whose divine Husband nonetheless still cherishes her.

This pattern of revealing the depth of God's relationship with His people continued with the prophets of Judah. Isaiah's prophecies (c. 750–c. 680 BC) not only pointed to the future Messiah but also told of God's holiness. Jeremiah (c. 650–c. 570 BC) wept over the coming fate of Judah, but his messages emphasized the value of the individual soul before God. Ezekiel (c. 622–c. 570 BC) also guided his people to a better, richer understanding of God and His just love. As we will see in the next chapter, the people of Judah would require this deeper understanding if their faith were to survive the trials that were about to befall them.

religious aura that helped it avoid rebellions against its authority, the dynasties of Israel had no such deterrent. Assassinations and massacres brought chronic instability to the northern kingdom.

One of Israel's most notorious rulers was Ahab (r. c. 874–c. 853 BC). He was the north's seventh king and governed from his capital city of Samaria. His father had done much to increase Israel's prestige, including befriending the **Phoenicians** of Tyre. The Phoenician city-states occupied excellent harbors to the north of Israel.

This enabled them to develop their trade throughout the Mediterranean and to found colonies, including Carthage in northern Africa (see chapter 11). Ancient peoples highly valued Phoenician goods, particularly their textiles. (The Greek term *Phoenicia* references the purple dye used for their cloths.) However, historians agree that the Phoenicians' greatest contribution to history is the preservation of their writing throughout the Dark Age. Phoenician society had not collapsed at the end of the second millennium, and they were in a position to share the achievements of previous centuries with the emerging societies. Among these was their alphabet. Though the Phoenician script was inspired by Egyptian hieroglyphs, its characters were phonetic rather than pictographic. In other words, each symbol represented a sound rather than a specific item or concept. This meant that only a handful of characters were necessary to express a variety of ideas. Whereas cuneiform had hundreds of symbols, Phoenician writing had twenty-two. Its simplicity aided its spread, as did the presence of Phoenician merchants throughout the Mediterranean. Greek and Aramaic alphabets, for example, developed from the Phoenician script.

Ahab sought to promote friendship with the Phoenicians through his marriage to a princess from their important city of Tyre. His bride Jezebel ("Where is Baal?") was described by ancient historians as the great-aunt of Dido, the legendary founder of Carthage. While this relationship is unlikely, Ahab's marriage to Jezebel represented an important political and social triumph for Ahab. His political gain, however, brought spiritual devastation to the people of Israel. Jezebel insisted on worshipping Baal, and altars to her god proliferated throughout Israel. She also hunted down the prophets, individuals who spoke on the Lord's behalf and who frequently condemned the people for their worship of false gods. Eventually, only one of these messengers, Elijah, was left alive. This situation led to the memorable episode from the Book of Kings between Elijah and the priests of Baal during a time of prolonged drought. The latter called upon their sky god to show his might by raining down fire upon a sacrifice, but it was the God of the Hebrews who ultimately demonstrated His supremacy (1 [3] Kings 18). Despite this evidence of God's power, Ahab chose to tolerate Jezebel's gods until his violent death in battle.

Later kings of Israel continued to pursue foreign gods, alliances, and wars even though multiple prophets warned them of their errors and the coming consequences of their sins. In the end, the prophets' warnings proved true: Israel's habit of faithlessness led it to double-cross an empire that valued truth and was willing—and able—to punish those who violated their covenants. Retribution was thorough: the tribes of the northern kingdom would soon disappear from history.

The Neo-Assyrian Empire

The **Neo-Assyrian Empire** (911–609 BC) emerged from the Dark Age of the late second millennium with an energy and resolve that awed the ancient world. Whereas Old Assyria had sought economic influence and Middle Assyria desired to be a part of the Club of Great Powers, rulers of the Neo-Assyrian Empire embraced an ideology of strength through warfare. Kings now made a habit of leading military campaigns almost every year of their reign and brought multiple peoples under the "Yoke of Ashur," their administrative term for subjugated vassal states.

The first victims of this new aggressive spirit were the Aramaeans. This nomadic people never established a formal empire of their own, but they came to wield political power on a local level in the lands that had previously been incorporated into Middle Assyria. Their language, **Aramaic**, would eventually become the common language of the ancient world and would remain in use until the Muslim Arab conquests over one thousand years later. For the moment, Aramaean tribes felt the wrath of Assyria as it recovered the lands it had formerly controlled.

There were a number of factors that supported this initial expansion of the Neo-Assyrian Empire. One was its administration. It may be tempting to reduce Neo-Assyrian society to a war machine, but it possessed the most extensive bureaucracy that the ancient world had yet experienced. A hierarchy of administrators oversaw numerous cities, the collection of tribute and taxes, and maintained the network of roads that were crucial for staging military expeditions.

Royal ideology also aided Assyrian expansion. For Assyrians, warfare had become necessary to hold back the tide of chaos that continually threatened the world. Their polytheistic society worshipped Ashur above other gods and considered conquest as an opportunity to instill proper reverence for this deity. Thus, piety combined with a fierce resolve to punish those whom they felt dishonored their god. Breaking one's promises was particularly evil because it introduced disorder, and the kings felt obliged to punish oath-breakers—that is, those who resisted Ashur—in truly horrifying ways.

This brings us to the topic of Assyrian brutality. There is no underestimating the suffering that accompanied Assyrian conquests. We have abundant accounts of individuals being impaled, flayed alive, mutilated, forced to watch their children burn, and commanded to grind the bones of their ancestors so as to wipe out their very memory. For those who escaped these horrors, there remained the threat of forced removal. An estimated 4.5 million people suffered deportation at Assyrian hands. None of these cruelties, tragically, were new to humanity, but the Assyrians perfected them into instruments that both terrorized their opponents and supported their own goals.

The Assyrians realized that fear itself was an effective weapon in war. Their campaigns focused not on pitched battles but on the subjugation of small villages and cities. These could be taken quickly, and their sufferings turned to good advantage by weakening the resolve of others. In an episode recorded in the biblical Book of Isaiah (see chapter 6 for context), the Assyrians used their reputation for brutality to encourage despair. As the Assyrian commander proclaimed what awaited the people of Jerusalem, the defending leaders begged the Assyrians to speak in Aramaic rather than Hebrew, lest the common people understand the threats. The reply? "Has my master sent me to speak these words to your master and to you, and not to the men sitting on the wall, who are doomed with you to eat their own dung and drink their own urine?" (Is 36:12).

And yet the Assyrians were not mindlessly violent. They believed that such deeds gave glory to Ashur by punishing his enemies and furthering their interests. The practice of deportation, for example, typically involved an economic rather than punitive objective. Deported peoples even received Assyrian supplies and aid during their journey to their new home, which was typically a fertile but under-cultivated area of the empire. In this manner, Assyria utilized its agricultural lands efficiently even as it discouraged potential rebellion by isolating conquered people from their former homes.

By the middle of the ninth century, Assyrian kings had regained all the territory that Middle Assyria had held. The most famous of these "reclaiming" monarchs was Ashurnarsipal II (r. 883–859 BC). From 883 to 866 BC, he waged fourteen military operations. In addition to the vast amounts of treasure he imported from his conquests, he encouraged new forms of art inspired by the Phoenicians. Graphic depictions of hunts, battles, and the famous bulls with wings and giant human heads began to characterize Assyrian art. To climax his display of might, Ashurnarsipal built a new capital for his empire at Kalhu. Workers leveled decaying buildings of the original city and replaced them with a magnificent palace and ziggurat. Nearby, exotic animals populated fields overseen by a golden statue of Ashurnarsipal. The king hosted a ten-day party to celebrate his new capital and, according to his own reckoning, no less than 69,574 people attended.

Shalmaneser III (r. 858–824 BC) imitated his father and fought some thirty campaigns during his reign. One of the first was against a coalition that included Ahab of Israel. While Israel successfully warded off Assyrian domination for several years, it eventually paid tribute to avoid further war. Despite initial successes, Shalmaneser's reign experienced a massive rebellion in 827 BC that rocked the foundations of royal might. For the next eighty years, Assyrian kings struggled to regain their former authority and glory.

The **Lion Hunt of Ashurbanipal**. Made of gypsum alabaster c. 645-635 BC. Currently in the British Museum, London, England. This series of reliefs from the North Palace in Nineveh shows King Ashurbanipal performing a ritual hunt of lions in an arena.

Tiglath-pileser III (r. 744–727 BC) finally reestablished Assyrian stability and ushered in the last century of its domination. His armies marched west and south and added vast areas to his domain. The kingdom of Israel once again paid tribute and became a vassal state. However, the people of Israel, having long since violated their covenant with the Lord, found it easy to break trust with man. Their decision to ally with Assyria's enemies brought swift retribution. In 722 BC, the Assyrians seized Samaria, Israel's capital city, after a three-year siege. Orders soon arrived commanding the deportation of the population to the Zagros Mountains, some 750 miles distant. The former lands of Israel became the home to a people from Persia. The new inhabitants, soon known as the Samaritans, blended their own traditions with the beliefs and monotheism of neighboring Judah. Meanwhile, according to Assyrian records, 27,290 Israelites marched deep into the Assyrian Empire. There, the "lost tribes" of the **Assyrian Captivity** eventually assimilated into the surrounding population and became lost to history.

Conclusion

Assyria had come into its own after the collapse of the Club of Great Powers, and its conquests left a legacy of both piety and brutality on behalf of their god Ashur.

Lamassu from the Palace of Sargon II. Made of gypsum alabaster c. 713 BC. Currently in the Louvre Museum, Paris, France. These giant hybrid human-headed winged bulls were considered protective deities and placed near the entrances to the palace. They appear to stand when viewed from the front, to walk when viewed from the side, and to have five legs when viewed obliquely.

Caught in the midst of this vast empire's ambitions was the divided Hebrew world in Canaan. Its kingdom had enjoyed brief temporal success and unity, but this era of prosperity and peace soon gave way to intrigue, division, and religious turmoil. Israelite kings placed their security in wealth, power, and the gods of their neighbors, and long before they broke their word to Assyria, they had violated their covenant with God.

In the next chapter, we discuss the southern Kingdom of Judah. Once again, a mighty empire will shape the history of the Hebrew people, but it will not be Assyria. A new opponent was gathering strength within the heartland of Hammurabi's former realm even as Assyria sought to expand its borders ever further. It was the Babylonian Empire that initiated the last great flourishing of ancient Mesopotamian civilization. Unfortunately for the people of Judah, it was also the Babylonian Empire that brought an end to their independent Hebrew kingdom.

CHAPTER 6

Jewish Prophets and Gentile Kings

They read from the book, from the law of God, clearly; and they gave the sense, so that the people understood the reading . . . and the Levites who taught the people said to all the people, "This day is holy to the LORD your God; do not mourn or weep." For all the people wept when they heard the words of the law.

Nehemiah 8:8–9

The epigraph that begins this chapter refers to a climactic moment in Hebrew history, one that was centuries in the making. At first, it seemed likely, even providentially ordained, that the cruel fate suffered by the Kingdom of Israel would not befall its southern neighbor. Unfortunately, the same temptations that had led Israel away from the worship of God were present in Judah and yielded similar consequences. So far would Judah's people fall that their descendants, described in this eighth chapter of Nehemiah, would listen to the reading of God's law and weep in repentance for their sins. What internal and external factors contributed to this moral collapse and rebirth? To answer that question, we must intertwine the story of the Hebrew people with that of three great empires whose might and territory made the Kingdom of Judah seemingly insignificant.

Judah's Road to Captivity

The Kingdom of Judah had two advantages that enabled it to survive for over one hundred years after the Assyrian Captivity. That event had brought an end to the Kingdom of Israel in 722 BC, and the people to the south had reason to fear that such a scenario would soon befall them. Judah's terrain, however, offered its own benefits. Whereas Israel had fertile territory and access to the coastline of the

Mediterranean, Judah had neither. Its land was generally rocky, difficult to access, and not worth the effort of invading armies—unless they were intent upon punishment or the plunder of Jerusalem. More important to their endurance than geography was the people's attitude towards Judah's kings. Whereas multiple dynasties had ruled Israel, the Judeans remained loyal to the descendants of David and Solomon. Even though these heirs could be as foolish or wicked as the kings of the north, the people still believed that David's family had been anointed by God to rule. Furthermore, the Temple in Jerusalem provided the focal point for God's worship. These factors inspired stability, which both contributed to Judah's longer survival and enabled the restoration of proper worship whenever wayward rulers abandoned it.

This sense of God's presence in Judah's affairs undoubtedly provided support in the days following the split between the kingdoms of Israel and Judah. Rehoboam's foolishness (r. c. 931–913 BC) had brought about not only a political and religious schism but also encouraged Egypt to attack Judah and make it a vassal state. The worst consequence of this invasion was the Egyptian seizure of the Temple's treasures. Within a single generation much of the glory and influence associated with Solomon's legacy had been lost forever.

The next generations sought to restore their former united kingdom through force of arms, but these wars with the Kingdom of Israel accomplished little. Jehoshaphat (r. c. 870–849 BC) ultimately abandoned this effort to reconquer the North and instead offered peace and political alliance to Israel. The former rivals celebrated a marriage between the ruling families, and it seemed as though spiritual healing might take place. Jehoshaphat, for example, strove to reform Judean society through the removal of polytheistic shrines and the faithful observance of the Mosaic Law. Unfortunately, Athaliah, his new daughter-in-law, was of a different mindset. Her parents were Ahab and Jezebel, and she sought to introduce the worship of Baal to Judah. Athaliah eventually seized control of the kingdom, and her reign (c. 841–835 BC) began with a bloodbath as she eliminated all rivals to her power—including those in her own family. Only through desperate action was one of her grandsons hidden alive in the Temple. For six years, Athaliah ruled Judah and promoted the worship of Baal. Her young grandson eventually overthrew her, but the damage had been done. Polytheistic rituals remained so influential in Judean society that the new king later followed in his grandmother's footsteps and worshipped idols. He even ordered the execution of the prophet Zechariah.

The moral situation declined further with Ahaz (r. 732–716 BC). His reign coincided with the twilight of the Kingdom of Israel. He refused to join the North in its efforts against Assyria, but he also refused to follow the advice from the prophet Isaiah. Instead, he submitted to Assyria and even sent soldiers to aid its army in

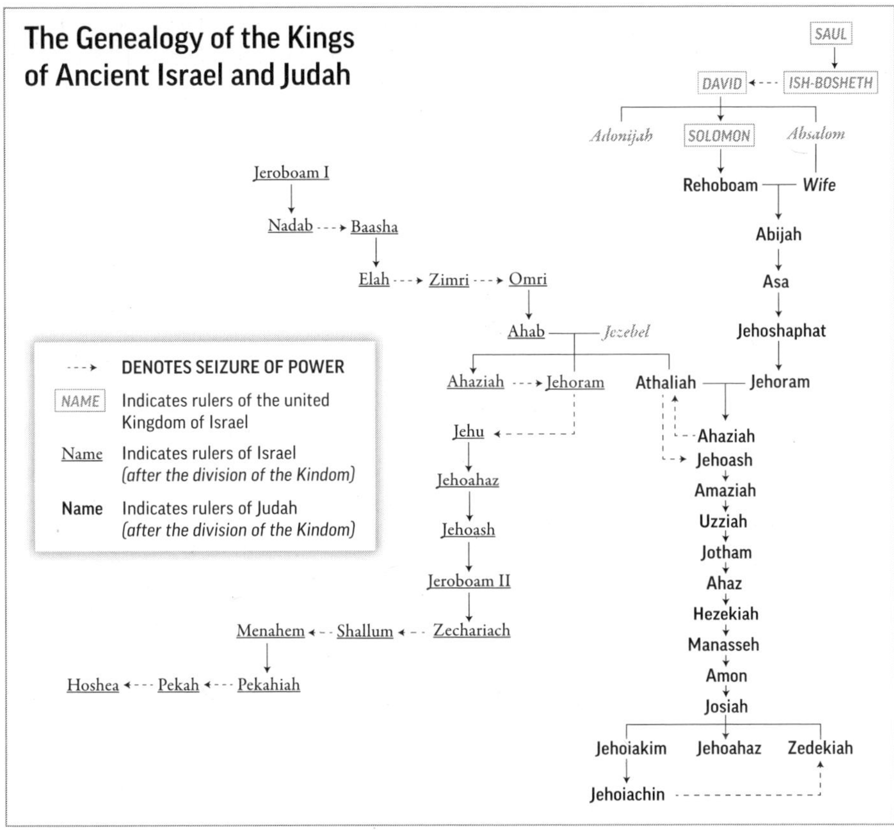

its campaign against the Kingdom of Israel and its allies. As the remnants of the ten tribes trudged into captivity, Ahaz incorporated Assyrian rituals and religious practices into the worship of the Temple. He went so far as to offer one of his sons as a burnt offering to the god Moloch.

Despite the frequent royal abandonment of monotheism, the prophets Micah (c. 760–c. 690 BC) and Isaiah (c. 750–c. 680 BC) continued to call for repentance and even foretold a future Messiah. Among Micah's messages, for example, we find his prophesy that Bethlehem would be the site of the Messiah's birth (see Mi 5:2). For his part, Isaiah promoted trust in God rather than submission to Assyria and even promised a sign to Ahaz to prove that God would be faithful. When Ahaz rejected this opportunity, Isaiah declared that God Himself would give the sign: "Behold the virgin will conceive and bear a son, and shall call his name Immanuel" (Is 7:14 ESV-CE).

While such prophecies regarding the coming Savior must have remained mysterious to Ahaz and his contemporaries, Isaiah's message also had two themes that were more immediately comprehended. First, Isaiah emphasized God's holiness and His presence in human history: the prophet's beautiful poetry revealed that God's perfect holiness did not prevent Him from confronting and resolving the messiness of humanity's affairs. Secondly, the prophet's message was often explicitly political and social. Earlier prophets had issued warnings about proper worship and personal immorality, but Isaiah included specific questions of royal policy. For example, the pressing issue at that time was how to avoid destruction at the hands of Assyria, particularly since Egypt began to challenge Assyrian dominance. While some at court favored remaining a subject of Assyria, others believed that Egypt represented Judah's best hope. Isaiah rejected both positions and called for conversion and confidence in God.

Ahaz's son Hezekiah (r. 716–686 BC) was a pious king who even destroyed the bronze serpent that Moses had fashioned in the desert (see Nm 21:6–9) in his zeal to remove all temptations to polytheistic worship. In 705 BC, he received news that Sargon II of Assyria had died in Anatolia in a defeat so disastrous that the army had failed to recover his body. It seemed to him and others that the shadow of Assyria had finally lifted. They were wrong. Assyria's new king, Sennacherib (r. 705–681 BC), quickly stabilized his rule and began to punish those who had sought independence after his father's death. Among the rebels was Hezekiah. The Assyrians besieged Jerusalem and, as we noted in the previous chapter, used terrifying threats to weaken the people's resolve. The city's destruction seemed imminent, but it was not to be. Sennacherib's army suddenly withdrew after suffering tremendous losses. Many scholars believe that a plague broke out among the Assyrian ranks, while the biblical account states simply that an angel brought overnight destruction to the invaders.

In the midst of the people's rejoicing at their deliverance, the idea became popular that Jerusalem would never face the same fate that had befallen Israel. After all, God's Temple was in their midst! Isaiah's sober warnings that Judah would enjoy God's protection only as long as it followed His covenant fell upon deaf ears.

Isaiah's warning proved all too accurate. Hezekiah's son Manasseh (r. 687–643 BC) mandated the worship of Baal in the Temple and persecuted the prophets who warned him of God's anger. So shocking were the abuses that took root during his reign that the prophet Jeremiah warned future generations that divine vengeance was required: "I will appoint over them four kinds of destroyers, says the LORD: the sword to slay, the dogs to tear, and the birds of the air and the beasts of the earth to devour and destroy. And I will make them a horror to all the kingdoms of the earth because of what Manasseh the son of Hezekiah, king of Judah, did in Jerusalem" (Jer 15:3–4).

Though Manasseh did eventually repent, it was not until the reign of his grandson **Josiah** (r. 640–609 BC) that the situation dramatically improved. Josiah destroyed polytheistic shrines throughout the kingdom and cleansed the Temple, which had been defiled by heathen rituals. During this purification, the Temple priests discovered a copy of the Mosaic Law and brought it to the king. When Josiah read it, he was astounded at how far the Hebrew people had fallen. This forgotten document, which was probably the biblical Book of Deuteronomy (Greek for "Second Law"), mandated many practices that had long been unobserved. The attention given to this text renewed the people's focus on the entire **Torah** (the first five books of the Bible) and the guidance that it contained. Future generations would continue this study and ensure that the Torah remained the center of their spirituality.

Nonetheless, Josiah's reforms fell under a cloud when he died in battle against an Egyptian army in 609 BC. That a pious king could still die in battle caused people to waver in their enthusiasm for his reforms. Some returned to the polytheistic cults Josiah had forbidden, while others recommended political alliances as the best way to safeguard Judah's well-being. Their solutions were in vain. In less than twenty years, the four destroyers foretold by Jeremiah would devastate their land.

The Rise of Babylon and the Babylonian Captivity

Despite its unstoppable appearance, Assyria's hold on power was fragile. Increasing resentment among subjugated peoples as well as the threat of external rivals brought a sudden end to Assyrian might. In its place rose antiquity's last great Mesopotamian empire, Babylon. For the people of Judah, the downfall of the god Ashur brought little reason to rejoice: Babylon's rise merely accelerated their own day of reckoning.

The Assyrian government relied on the exploitation of defeated lands. The heartland of Ashur could not sustain the demand for supplies and weapons required by its military. What Assyria could not produce it demanded as tribute from those lands who submitted to its armies. While this yielded short-term benefits, the animosity it aroused in conquered (and often deported) populations was a fundamental weakness in the Assyrian system. Many, like Hezekiah, merely awaited an opportunity to rebel—even under threat of brutal punishment.

This sense of resentment was especially intense among Assyria's subjects in Babylonia to the south. Assyria had a complex relationship with this region. Assyrian rulers acknowledged that their culture was intimately interwoven with the achievements of preceding Mesopotamian societies. For example, the city of Nineveh, which Sennacherib had expanded and turned into his massive capital, included numerous temples dedicated to Sumerian deities, and the last great Assyrian king Ashurbanipal (r. 668–631 BC) collected thousands of Mesopotamian manuscripts for his personal library there. These religious and historical connections made Assyrian kings hesitant to punish rebellion in Babylonia as harshly as they did elsewhere.

The region's diversity of peoples contributed to the discontent. Urban populations of the ancient city-states were surrounded by tribal nomads like the Chaldeans, who resisted Assyrian rule and easily avoided punishment by escaping to the marshlands at the far south of the Tigris and Euphrates Rivers. To make matters more challenging, Assyria—out of respect for their common past—still allowed Babylonia to have its own nominal king. Chaldean tribes frequently tried to seize the throne of Babylonia, and kings from Nineveh responded either by declaring *themselves* to be the kings of Babylon (and Assyria) or by installing puppet rulers to govern on their behalf. Neither solution brought success. In the face of continued resistance from the south, Sennacherib marched against Babylon and sacked the city in 689 BC. The king's wrath temporarily overcame any sense of respect for their shared cultural past, and he later boasted of its punishment: "So that in future days the site of [Babylon] and its temples would not be recognized, I totally dissolved it with water and made it like inundated land."[1] Though Sennacherib's successor, Esarhaddon (r. 680–669 BC), rebuilt the city, the region remained resentful and volatile.

Even as discontent built up within, Assyria overreached itself by attempting to expand into Egypt. The Nile's wealth and abundance proved irresistible to the kings of Nineveh, but they could not maintain direct control over a territory so far from their heartland. The height of their campaigning came in 663 BC when triumphant Assyrian soldiers sacked Thebes, the ancient capital of Egypt. It was all in vain. Egypt soon regained its independence, and Assyria had to deal with the consequences of its failed conquest.

Unfortunately, what precisely contributed to Assyria's final collapse remains uncertain. We know that in 626 BC, Nabopolassar, an Assyrian official in Uruk, declared a new Chaldean dynasty in Babylonia. He gradually gained control of the region and invaded Assyria's heartland in 616 BC. In desperation, the empire allied with Egypt, and Egyptian soldiers marched into Syria against Babylon. (It was to prevent the Egyptian pharaoh from joining the Assyrians that Josiah of Judah fought and died in battle in 609 BC.) In 605 BC, the Babylonians defeated a combined Assyrian-Egyptian army near Carchemish in northern Syria. Assyria, with all of its legacy of might and terror, disappeared forever with hardly a record to describe its last agony.

Nabopolassar had successfully overthrown the most powerful state of the era, but he died that very year. His son, **Nebuchadnezzar II** (r. 604–562 BC), received the formidable task of securing what historians call the "Neo-Babylonian Empire."

---

1 Daniel David Luckenbill, *Annals of Sennacherib* (Chicago: Chicago University, 1924), 834; quoted in van de Mieroop, *A History of the Ancient Near East*, 273.

The **Ishtar Gate** of Babylon. Constructed c. 575 BC by order of Nebuchadnezzar II. The portion shown in this photo is reconstructed in the Pergamon Museum, Berlin, Germany. This formidable gate was part of a walled thoroughfare leading into the city of Babylon. The walls were finished with blue glazed bricks and depictions of animals or deities. The prominent dragons, known as mushkhushshu, are associated with the god Marduk.

Its greatest threat lay to the west: Egypt may have suffered defeat at Carchemish, but this did not end its ambitions in Syria and Palestine. Over the course of the next twelve years, Nebuchadnezzar waged ten campaigns in these regions to establish undisputed Babylonian control.

It is in the context of these military operations that Judah's last, crucial years unfolded. Small states like Judah were caught between Egypt and Babylon, and the pressing question was which power would eventually triumph. In 605 BC, Judah pledged submission to Nebuchadnezzar, who deported a small segment of the population to Babylon to ensure its loyalty. Among this first group were the prophet Daniel and his companions. These hostages notwithstanding, Judah soon looked to Egypt for an alliance.

The prophet **Jeremiah** (c. 650–c. 570 BC) denounced this policy and urged leaders to remain faithful to Babylon. His message was a dark one: Judah had sinned grievously and had broken its covenant with the Lord; the punishments Moses had foretold centuries earlier would soon befall the people unless they repented. And yet, Jeremiah also looked forward to a time of renewal when a contrite, chastened people would return to God. Furthermore, his prophecies mark a significant development in the Hebrew tradition. Whereas previous prophets had emphasized the relationship of the community as a whole with the Lord, Jeremiah's message highlighted God's intimate concern for each individual—even before that person's conception (see Jer 1:5). On the eve of Judah's worst catastrophe, God was proclaiming His immense love for every individual soul.

Unfortunately, neither the beauty nor the warning of Jeremiah's message influenced Judean policy. Around 598 BC, Judah rebelled against Babylon. Egyptian assistance never came, and Nebuchadnezzar took Jerusalem after a brief siege. The second, and largest, deportation followed. Nebuchadnezzar forced the elites in Jerusalem and throughout Judah to journey to Babylon. Royalty, aristocrats, craftsmen, and priests left their homes forever.

King Zedekiah (r. 597–586 BC) was permitted to rule the predominately poor population left behind, but once again ambition blinded the leaders of Judah. Their appeal to Egypt brought swift punishment: In 587 BC, Nebuchadnezzar seized Jerusalem yet again. He executed Zedekiah's sons before his eyes and then blinded the king so that his last sight was his dead children. The city and the Temple he destroyed with fire. The trauma of the destruction of Jerusalem and its Temple cannot be overstated. The site of God's glory, the place pious Israelites assumed would never fall, was no more. (Scripture records that Jeremiah hid the Ark of the Covenant on Mount Nebo prior to the devastation [see 2 Mc 2:4–6].)

A third wave of exiles departed, but Jeremiah remained behind with the very poor who had been permitted to stay. He continued to offer guidance, but they ignored him, fled into Egypt, and forced him to accompany them. He apparently died in that land, stoned to death by his own people. For their part, the murderers found no refuge, for Nebuchadnezzar's armies soon invaded his imperial rival and placed a pharaoh sympathetic to Babylon on the throne.

Jehoiachin's ration tablets. Made of clay c. 580 BC. Currently in the Pergamon Museum, Berlin, Germany. These come from the archives of Nebuchadnezzar II and describe the oil rations given to prisoners in the city. The Akkadian cuneiform mentions a captive named "Jeconiah (Jehoiachin), King of Judah," and his five sons. Jehoiachin briefly ruled Judah before Nebuchadnezzar deported him in 597 and replaced him with Zedekiah.

The **Babylonian Captivity** (587–538 BC) was a turning point in Hebrew history. For the first time since their enslavement in Egypt, the descendants of Jacob found themselves cut off from their ancestral home and forced to live in captivity. True, the Babylonians did not enslave the Hebrews like the pharaohs had, but the danger that Hebrew society and religious beliefs would disappear was a real one. After all, the Israelites taken into Assyria failed to retain their Hebrew identity. Already, complaints were heard among the people that God had punished the innocent on account of the sins of previous generations. Such thinking could easily lead to the complete abandonment of God's worship. Many ancients, for example, assumed that defeat in battle demonstrated the relative weakness of one's deities versus those of the conquering armies. According to this logic, Judah's God was less powerful than Babylon's Marduk.

Here the prophets once again proved important. Their previous warnings about a coming punishment helped the captives preserve their conviction that their God was not weaker than the gods of the polytheists; rather, He had permitted this punishment because of their sins. Furthermore, these same prophets also spoke of a future time when the people would return to virtue and receive God's blessings once more.

Daniel and Ezekiel, for example, were prophets living in exile who nonetheless urged the people to remain true to the Mosaic Law. Ezekiel in particular criticized those who complained against God's justice and, complementing the insights of Jeremiah, taught that each individual soul received its own proper reward or punishment from God. Even as Ezekiel's teachings brought clarity and hope, the Hebrews revisited their own history and found within it further evidence of God's providence and mercy. It is likely that many historical books of the Old Testament were edited or written at this time using older sources. The ongoing narrative of sin, repentance, and restoration inspired those in captivity to look forward to the time when God would cease their punishment. A deeper understanding of God's transcendence also developed: His Temple may have been in Jerusalem, but His authority spanned all creation, and His praises could be sung even in lands far from Judah. As if to emphasize the exiles' renewed purpose and dedication to God, the ancient Hebrews came to be known by a new name. Babylonians still saw them as the people of Judah, and they became known as "Jews" and their religion as "**Judaism.**" Jews, meanwhile, referred to polytheists as *goyim* (Hebrew for "peoples"), a designation that was eventually associated with the Latin word *gentilis*, from which the term "Gentile" derives.

The Jews' ability to remain distinct was especially impressive in the context of Babylonian society. The conquests of Nebuchadnezzar created a cosmopolitan empire; foreign peoples interacted with one another as merchants, visitors from faraway states, or as exiles from fallen ones, and frequently blended together

The **Mul-Apin**. Carved on clay tablets c. 686 BC. Currently in the British Museum, London, England. One of the scientific achievements of Babylonian society was their astronomical precision. Treatises such as the Mul-Apin provided detailed observations of the stars alongside accurate calendars. The Babylonians frequently used this information for religious purposes.

through marriage as the years passed. The Babylonians themselves cherished their heritage and, though they held Babylon's god Marduk in highest esteem, they also emphasized the gods of Sumer. It was the last great flowering of Mesopotamian civilization.

After Nebuchadnezzar's death in 562 BC, the empire was rocked by two assassinations within six years. Power came to Nabonidus (r. 555–539 BC), one of the most mysterious rulers of the ancient world. He devoted himself to the god Sin and thus angered the traditional Babylonian priesthood with its devotion to Marduk. To make matters worse, he decided to move to a desert oasis in 552 BC and allowed his son Belshazzar to rule from Babylon. Scholars debate what motivated these decisions, but regardless of Nabonidus's plans for the future, the days of the Babylonian Empire were already numbered. In 539 BC, the Persians attacked. These enemies from the East defeated a Babylonian army at the Battle of Opis and soon entered the capital of Babylon itself without a fight. The last great empire of Mesopotamia perished with a whimper.

The Persian Empire and the Second Temple

Nabonidus's refusal to honor the god Marduk led to the collapse of his dynasty. At least, that is what the Persian king **Cyrus II** (r. 559–530 BC) proclaimed to the recently conquered people of Babylonia. According to the "Cyrus Cylinder," Marduk saw with dismay Nabonidus's wickedness and sought out a worthy man to replace him. His choice was Cyrus, and the new ruler restored the proper worship of Marduk and liberated the people from Nabonidus's oppressive rule. The cylinder's account was propaganda, but it also highlighted how the Persians consciously respected and incorporated the diversity of their subjects' cultures. This accommodation included the explicit respect Persian rulers showed to foreign deities like Marduk. We see this respect again when Cyrus listened to those Jews who showed him one of Isaiah's prophecies. This text foretold that he, Cyrus, would rebuild Jerusalem and its Temple (see Is 44:24–45:7). Modern secular historians dismiss the prophecy as a fabrication, but Cyrus did not. After decades of exile, the Jews of Babylon received permission to return to their homeland and rebuild. The Babylonian Captivity had come to an end.

The Persian Empire had humble origins. Its heartland was in modern-day southwest Iran, but almost nothing is known about its people until the rise of Cyrus II. A minor king in the region, he ultimately led his armies to create the largest empire yet seen. This journey from obscurity to glory began in 550 BC when he successfully defeated the Median ruler to the north and gained control over that land's resources. Three years later, he conquered Lydia in Anatolia. This kingdom was famous for its coinage, the first developed in Western history. Lydia also had control over the Greek colonies along the Ionian coastline; these now fell under Persian rule. This interaction set in motion the future contest between Persia and the Greek world (see chapter 8), but for the moment, the fall of Anatolia was but one of a string of victories celebrated by Cyrus. His greatest triumph came in 539 BC when he entered Babylon. Persia now dominated the Mesopotamian world and beyond, but Cyrus's ambition had not yet been satisfied. For nine more years, he worked to expand his rule until he died in battle in Central Asia.

As impressive as his conquests were, Cyrus's greatest legacy was to establish a new pattern of interaction with conquered peoples. Previously, invaders such as the Assyrians imposed their own form of government upon a vanquished people. The Persians, in contrast, allowed the existing bureaucracies of Babylon, Lydia, and other conquered territories to remain in place—as long as they paid tribute and acknowledged Persian overlordship. Cyrus and his successors realized that they could never effectively govern such a wide expanse of territory by themselves; while they required their subjects to acknowledge their sovereignty, they retained each region's traditional infrastructure. For example, Cyrus consciously chose to use the traditional Babylonian titles when he claimed lordship over that kingdom. His son did likewise when he extended Persian rule over Egypt in 525 BC. For most people of these regions, Persian hegemony did not bring about any significant change to their day-to-day life. The same royal titles, the same gods, the same culture, and the same body of local officials often remained in place. Official propaganda, like the Cyrus Cylinder, emphasized this aspect of Persian rule by praising the peace and order that they had bestowed upon all the people of their empire. This situation does not imply that Persians never massacred cities' inhabitants or deported populations. They did, but unlike the Assyrians, their official "messaging" did not emphasize those deeds.

The **Cyrus Cylinder**. Made of clay c. 539 BC. Currently in the British Museum, London, England. This inscription includes Cyrus's genealogy, a description of his restoration of and respect for Babylonian traditions, and a prayer to Marduk on his behalf.

Some changes, of course, were necessary. Persians occupied the very highest levels of administration and received special treatment to ensure their loyalty to the regime. The conquered lands were ultimately divided into various regions called *satrapies* (*satrapy* in the singular). The governors of these, known as *satraps*, were typically Persian and could enjoy near-royal authority depending on the favor (or the weakness) of the king. Furthermore, the Persian ruler, known as the "king of kings," required a worthy capital. Cyrus II founded one at Pasargadae, but the more famous capital city was Darius's Persepolis, a massive complex of stone palaces, gardens, and treasures. The audience hall of its largest building had columns almost sixty feet high. Here, too, Persia recognized the multiplicity of its peoples by blending a variety of regional designs into a single unified imperial style.

Unfortunately, our sources for Persia are woefully inadequate. We possess administrative documents but lack satisfying narratives of the wars and policies that saw the empire spread from the eastern Mediterranean to the Indus River in India. Our only detailed information derives from the far western areas of the empire, and these narratives can skew our understanding by giving those events undue importance (see chapter insert on historical perspectives and Persian history). Future chapters will present Persian interactions with the Greek world, but what was happening at the same time in India or Central Asia (modern-day Kazakhstan, Kyrgyzstan, Tajikistan, Turkmenistan, and Uzbekistan) remains unclear.

PERSIAN HISTORY: A CASE STUDY IN HISTORICAL PERSPECTIVE

Historians who study the ancient world face many challenges in addition to a simple lack of sources. Even an abundance of material may be misleading and difficult to interpret. This is the situation with ancient Persia. While we have administrative documents, we possess few narratives from the Persians themselves and are forced to rely upon external perspectives that may or may not be accurate. These outside sources tell us more about their own opinions of the Persian Empire rather than an objective assessment of its government, society, and other characteristics.

The majority of our information about early Persian history derives from either a Greek or Jewish perspective. As we will see in the chapters ahead, the Greeks and Persians were enemies. Greek historians, therefore, often depicted Persian culture as possessing values that were the opposite of Greek society's ideals. Considering that many Greeks cherished independence and a simple way of life, their descriptions of Persians emphasized their servitude and excessive opulence. In contrast, Jewish society had a generally positive attitude towards Persian rule. The biblical accounts of Daniel, Esther, Ezra, and Nehemiah typically portray Persian kings as imperfect but also well-disposed toward their Jewish subjects. This contrast is most evident when we consider how Herodotus's *Histories* and the Book of Esther differ in their attitude towards Xerxes (r. 485–465 BC). Herodotus's bias against the Persians frequently portrays this king as cruel and capricious. In contrast, the Book of Esther offers an overall sympathetic judgment of the king's character and blames his adviser Haman for his poor decisions. Neither work is simplistic in its attitude towards Xerxes, but the final impression is quite different depending on the perspective of the author recording the events.

Perspective and bias influence modern historians, too, though perhaps in more subtle ways. A modern interpretative bias that arises from our lack of Persian sources involves the Jewish faith. During the Second Temple period, Jewish texts increasingly emphasized the coming of the Messiah as well as the existence of demons who opposed God's plan. Because demonic activity is not highlighted in many books of the Old Testament, some historians conclude that these ideas derived from **Zoroastrianism**, the dualistic religion of the Persians. Its founder, Zarathustra (or Zoroaster in Greek), taught that the cosmos was engaged in a bitter struggle between the god of light, Ahura Mazda, and a god of darkness and lies. Different Zoroastrian ideas, such as this cosmic battle between good and evil, a bodily resurrection, and a last judgment, have obvious parallels to Jewish and Christian beliefs.

Historians seeking to disprove the uniqueness of Judaism use Zoroastrianism to demonstrate outside influence, while other scholars push back and claim that Judaism developed these beliefs in light of Jerusalem's destruction and the teachings of the prophets rather than through Zoroastrianism. To make the issue more complex, we do not know in what *millennium* Zarathustra lived! Estimates range from 1700 BC to 500 BC. In the end, how we interpret the relationship between these two religions is largely shaped by our preexisting worldview or bias. Historically speaking, our surviving evidence provides no clear answer.

The **Gate of All Nations** is located in the ruins of the ancient city of Persepolis, Iran. Made of clay c. 486–465 BC by Xerxes I. This area consisted of one large room with a door to the east guarded by a pair of giant lamassu, a door to the west guarded by two massive bulls, and a double-wide door opening to the south. Persepolis is a UNESCO World Heritage site.

The biblical narrative for this period also has frequent gaps in its record, and we remain uncertain about many details of this era in Jewish history. That said, we can retrace some of the most important moments.

Many, though not all, of the Jewish people took advantage of Cyrus' permission to return to Judah. Under the leadership of a descendant of David and the high priest, the Jews laid the foundations for another Temple. Their progress stalled when the Samaritans persuaded Persian officials to stop the reconstruction. The Samaritans, the people whom the Assyrians had settled in the former Kingdom of Israel, had initially offered to help but turned hostile when the Jews rejected their assistance. It was not until **Darius I** (r. 522–486 BC) came to power that the Jews finished rebuilding the Second Temple in 516 BC.

A reconstructed Temple did not automatically ensure a rebirth of piety. Fifty years after its refounding, two Jewish leaders from Persia, Ezra and Nehemiah, discovered that the Jewish community of Jerusalem was already intermarrying with those from the nearby polytheistic societies. Working together, these two reformers sought to reawaken in the hearts of their fellow Jews a desire to follow God's Law. Many of the Jews were unfamiliar with the demands of the Torah and wept at their negligence when Ezra read its contents publicly.

Under Ezra's guidance, the people returned to a more faithful observance of the Hebrew liturgical year. There were three important holy days. Each of these was tied to the agricultural cycle, but unlike their polytheistic neighbors, the Hebrews also associated these festivals with the remembrance of God's intervention in history. Passover, for example, marked the beginning of the yearly growing season, but, more importantly, it also called to mind the rescuing of the Hebrews from slavery in Egypt. Seven weeks later, they celebrated the Feast of Weeks, or Pentecost, in which they brought their first fruits to the Temple. They associated this ritual with the reception of the Law by Moses on Mount Sinai. The last major liturgical period came at the end of the growing season: The Festival of Tabernacles called to mind the forty-year sojourn their ancestors experienced in the desert. It also involved the beginning of the Hebrew New Year and a plea for purification on the Day of Atonement.

These feasts had been the liturgical holy days of their ancestors, and it was during the Festival of Tabernacles that Ezra read aloud the Law to the Jews of Jerusalem. From this reborn appreciation of their liturgical life and its annual reminders of God's providence came, slowly, a revitalized Judaism. Furthermore, the focus on the Mosaic Law in the Torah that Josiah had initiated centuries earlier continued. Never again would Jewish leaders openly promote polytheistic worship as had some kings of old. Never again would Judah as a nation turn away from their Law. The lesson had been learned. The Law and the Temple were the center of their identity, and many would prove willing to die rather than betray them.

Conclusion

The centuries after Israel's collapse in 722 BC brought tremendous upheaval to the Kingdom of Judah. This instability culminated in the destruction of the Temple and the Babylonian Captivity, but the Jewish people came to view these disasters as a part of God's plan for His people. Their very punishments inspired greater respect for their prophets and a deeper appreciation for the Torah. Furthermore, their exile had taught them that they could retain their Jewish identity even when absent from Jerusalem and Judah. Many in their community were thus poised to spread the knowledge of their beliefs throughout the larger world.

For their part, the Persians served as a catalyst in Western history. They had ended forever the great empires of Mesopotamia, and their relative tolerance towards those they subjugated enabled ideas and practices—such as those of the Jews—to spread throughout their vast domain. However, many still resisted Persian rule, as we will study in the next unit when we journey to Ancient Greece.

UNIT II

The Greek Odyssey

CHAPTER 7

The Origins of Greece

Let me not then die ingloriously and without a struggle,
but let me first do some great thing that shall be told
among men hereafter.

Hector, *The Iliad*.[1]

These words, taken from the Greek epic poem *The Iliad*, provide us with our first insight into Greek civilization. Despite facing mortal danger during the Trojan War, Hector is less concerned about defeating his Greek rival Achilles or even surviving; instead, his ambition is to fight with honor, even in the face of overwhelming odds, so that future generations will remember him as a valiant hero. This emphasis upon individual glory and one's place in history was a central value of early Greek culture. It reveals their confidence that their society would endure and remember the actions of past heroes.

One of the main reasons that Hector and the Trojan War have been so well remembered is the prominent role played by Greek society in the formation of Western Civilization. The Greeks ultimately spread their culture from Spain to India and made lasting contributions to a diverse array of fields that still influence the modern world, including philosophy, art, metallurgy, and science. Alongside their creativity, versatility, and resilience, however, there arose a pettiness and egocentrism that also became a (tragic) hallmark of ancient Greek culture.

---

1 Homer, *The Iliad*, trans. by A.T. Murray (Cambridge: Harvard University Press, 1924), 22.304–5.

Throughout this unit, we trace how Greek society came to focus on human individuality and rationality. Greek culture, like those we studied in the previous unit, certainly had religious rituals and promoted the worship of various deities. It also fostered the pursuit of nonreligious explanations for natural phenomena and celebrated individuals, such as Hector and Achilles, in a way that was foreign to the other cultures we have studied thus far.

Minoan Crete

While archaeologists date the earliest evidence for human settlements on Crete to around 3000 BC, it was closer to 2000 BC that its first island civilization, known today as **Minoan Crete**, flourished. This was, approximately, the same era that Ur III dominated in Mesopotamia and that the Middle Kingdom emerged in Egypt. Unfortunately, we do not know what these people called themselves. Our modern term "Minoan" was invented by scholars and derives from the mythological King Minos who was associated with the island.

The most notable structures from this civilization are its impressive palace complexes. Two of these, Knossos in the north and Phaistos in the south, extended about one hundred yards in length, the span of a modern football field. Their rooms were situated around a central plaza and included such luxuries as running water and flushing toilets. The palaces likely served as centers of administration as well as food storage and distribution. Although paved roads connected these complexes with their local communities, there is no surviving evidence that similar roads linked the different palaces with one another. This lack of infrastructure may indicate that each palace settlement was independent rather than ruled by a single dynasty. Yet, unlike the autonomous, or self-governing, city-states of Mesopotamia, Minoan settlements were unwalled; this suggests that Minoan society was stable and that its ruler(s) did not fear invasions or uprisings. Evidence for Minoan religious practices also seems to contrast with those of Mesopotamia. The Minoans did not build massive temples, and there is no evidence of a powerful class of Minoan priests. Instead, archeological discoveries indicate that Minoan religion consisted of ceremonies conducted at small shrines or caves in the countryside.

Minoans took advantage of their climate's abundant sunlight to cultivate a variety of crops, including olives for the production of olive oil. They also used their central location in the Mediterranean to establish themselves as merchants. From 2000 to 1400 BC, the Minoans enjoyed a virtual monopoly on trade across the Mediterranean. They also established a practice that later Greeks would adopt as their own: founding colonies across the Aegean Sea that supported and extended their commerce. Their trade thus grew to include interactions with Italy, the Greek

The **Palace of Minos** is located in the ruins of the Minoan city of Knossos, Crete. The archeological site was discovered in 1878 and underwent significant excavation and reconstruction during the early 1900s. The Palace North Entrance and the Dolphin Fresco from the Queen's Megaron are two examples of reconstruction which attempt to give modern visitors a glimpse of the palace's original grandeur.

mainland, the Balkans to the north, and Phoenicia, Egypt, and Assyria to the east. Furthermore, they developed their own goods for export, including stoneware, pottery, and jewelry. These items sometimes depicted Minoan leisure activities,

The **Octopus Vase**. Made of clay c. 1500 BC. Currently in the Herakleion Archaeological Museum in Crete, Greece. AND The **Dendra Cup**. Made of gold. Currently in the National Archeological Museum in Athens, Greece. The Octopus Vase is an excellent example of Minoan ceramics and has remarkable similarities to the octopuses and other sea creatures found on the Dendra Cup. This cup was found in an early Mycenaean tomb (c. 1400 BC) at the archaeological site of Dendra near Midea, Greece and indicates the Minoan influence on later Mycenaean art.

including boxing and bull-leaping. Bulls seem to have been important symbols of power to the Minoans, and bull-leaping was probably a test of bravery in their society. Facing a charging bull, the competitor would attempt to grasp the animal's horns and somersault over its back.

Later Greek stories painted a hostile picture of Cretan society. In these, Minoan rulers were typically bloodthirsty oppressors. Most famously, Greek myth claimed that King Minos kept a "Minotaur," a monster that was half man and half bull, in a labyrinth below his palace. Each year, Minos forced the Greeks to send unfortunate men and women to his palace, where he fed them to the beast. This yearly sacrifice continued until the hero Theseus killed the beast. It may be that Greek writers unfairly portrayed the Minoans as villains to emphasize the glories of their own later civilization. And yet, some archeological evidence suggests that the Minoans practiced ritual cannibalism as part of their religious ceremonies. Ancient Greek culture had deep misgivings about human sacrifices and condemned eating human flesh. While the evidence that the Minoans practiced cannibalism is far from conclusive, it is possible that the Greeks encountered customs on Crete that repulsed them and that these experiences contributed to the negative portrayal of the Minoans in Greek literature.

Our inability to read the Minoan language contributes to our uncertainties about its culture. Their script, known as Linear A, has never been deciphered, and the documents that survive until today remain unread by scholars. One reason that their writing system remains impenetrable to linguists is that the Minoan civilization collapsed around 1400 BC. From this point onward, Cretans stopped using Linear A, and so the surviving material available for scholars to study is limited.

Historians continue to debate various explanations for the collapse of the Minoans. A popular, longstanding explanation was that an undersea volcanic eruption caused a tsunami that destroyed the main Minoan cities. Other evidence suggests that this natural disaster took place almost two centuries earlier and did not seriously impact the Minoans. Currently, the most credible explanation is that invaders destroyed Minoan civilization. The main evidence to support this theory is that around 1400 BC, Linear A was replaced by a different writing system that archaeologists have cleverly designated Linear B. Scholars deciphered Linear B in 1953 and realized that it was a primitive form of Greek. Tablets that use Linear B and that date from around 1600 BC have been discovered on mainland Greece. Many historians have therefore concluded that people from the peninsula probably invaded and conquered the Minoans around 1400 BC.

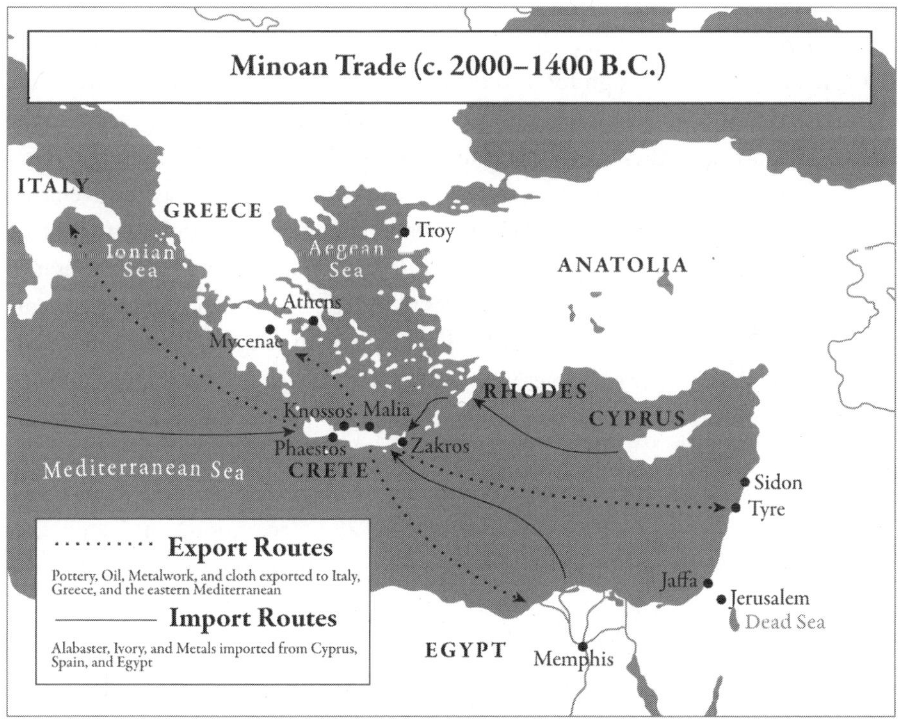

Mycenaean Greece

If Minoan Crete did collapse due to foreign conquest, the most likely culprits were the **Mycenaeans**. This people wrote using Linear B and established the earliest known civilization on mainland Greece around 1600 BC, approximately at the same time as Egypt's Second Intermediate Period. Archeological evidence suggests that they originally came from West Asia and settled in Greece, founding the city of Mycenae.

The geography of Greece differs significantly from the regions that we studied in the previous chapters. Whereas Mesopotamia, Egypt, and the societies occupying ancient Canaan were all connected by land, the Greek Peninsula is relatively isolated as it stretches southward into the eastern Mediterranean. The Adriatic Sea to its west separates it from Italy, while the Aegean Sea to the east divides it from Anatolia. The southernmost portion of the Greek Peninsula is itself another peninsula called the Peloponnesus, which is connected to the larger Greek Peninsula by the Isthmus of Corinth. In contrast to Mesopotamia and Egypt, Greece does not have a central river to provide a plentiful supply of water or to support extensive agriculture. In fact, the vast majority of its mainland, an estimated 80 percent, is mountainous. The Pindus range, for example, occupies the central region of Greece and divides the peninsula into small enclaves along the coast.

This rocky terrain limited the success of agriculture. The Greeks consistently struggled to produce enough food to feed their growing population. Furthermore, the uneven landscape discouraged the use of horses, except in the flatter region to the north. In contrast to these landbound limitations, Greece has over eight thousand miles of coastline, more than any other European country and surpassing even that of the state of Alaska. The peninsula is surrounded by a mass of islands, so many that the exact number remains disputed; some estimates reach as high as nine thousand! Most Greeks accordingly oriented their lives to the sea. They established settlements along the coast and became adept at fishing and maritime travel. Eventually, these voyages brought them into contact with other societies with whom they established trading relationships. So it was that ancient Greek sailors encountered the seafaring civilization of Crete.

The Mycenaeans initially traded with the Minoans and learned from them. They imitated Minoan pottery manufacturing and decoration, cultivated specialized crops like grapes and olives, and established their own colonies across the Mediterranean. They also apparently mirrored the Minoans' administrative practices: there was no unified state; rather, many independent cities formed loose and shifting alliances.

In other ways, the Mycenaeans were very different from the Minoans. They did not build undefended cities on the coast but instead established their population centers on defensible hills surrounded by large walls. Later Greeks believed that these so-called Cyclopean walls must have been built by Cyclopes, mythological one-eyed giants, because the stones used were so massive. Another example of Mycenaean building was the treasury of Atreus. This tomb of an unknown Mycenaean king was a tunnel hollowed out from the earth that culminated in a massive domed chamber. It remained the largest dome in the world for over a thousand years. Mycenaean society focused on its warrior-heroes, and each city had a king who led his champions in battle against others. Mycenaean art, while similar to the style of the Minoans, reflected this emphasis on warrior culture and celebrated violent human activities, such as boar hunting and chariot fighting.

The decline of Mycenaean society coincided with the collapse of the Club of Great Powers. As noted in chapter 5, the reasons for this breakdown remain unclear, and it may be that the success of the Trojan War (see chapter insert on

The **Lion Gate** of Mycenae, Greece. Made of limestone c. 1250 BC. This is the main entrance in the cyclopean walls to the ancient city, and it is named after the relief sculpture of two lionesses over the lintel. The heads of the animals are missing, and they rest their feet on an altar-like platform with a Minoan-type column between them. The gate is the only surviving example of Mycenaean monumental sculpture.

THE TROJAN WAR

Most modern historians prior to the twentieth century believed that the Trojan War and the city of Troy itself were purely mythological. Now, we are not so certain, and some argue that there was a war that inspired the later Greek legends surrounding Troy and its downfall. Archeologists, for example, have compared the descriptions of the landscapes and coastal features described in literary sources with the present geography and locate Troy at a site in modern-day Turkey where a wealthy Hittite city once stood. Evidence from these ruins as well as from Egyptian sources suggests to historians that the city fell in approximately 1184 BC. This date corresponds with the period of Mycenaean dominance and expansion in the Mediterranean. Egyptian records from this time refer to wandering "sea peoples," the Danuna and Akawasha, which titles are roughly equivalent to Homer's description of the Mycenaeans as the Danaans and Achaeans. Furthermore, these same Egyptian sources describe these sea peoples attacking settlements throughout the Mediterranean.

So was the Trojan war really fought to rescue the most beautiful woman in the world, as the literary account claims? Some suggest that this was, in fact, the case. Others have argued that this war was part of a wider conflict between rival trading federations and that the Mycenaeans destroyed Troy as part of their efforts to maintain their trading hegemony across the Mediterranean. The idea that warrior kings sailed to Anatolia to fight against their enemies and achieve lasting renown is thoroughly consistent with the ethos of Mycenaean culture, which glorified those who fought bravely for the honor of their cities and their families.

The period that followed the Trojan war was a dark one for ancient Greece. Many of the Mycenaeans' achievements were lost. Yet, centuries later, Greeks still gathered around the fires in the halls of their lords to sing the tales of Hector, Achilles, and other heroes whose examples of bravery and military prowess still inspired their descendants. These epic poems—known today as *The Iliad* and *The Odyssey*—were written centuries after the events they claim to describe. The former describes one episode from the war and assumes that its listeners/readers know how the war began and how it ended. The second epic recounts the journey home of the Greek hero Odysseus. They have 15,693 and 12,109 lines of poetry respectively and are written in a style known as dactylic hexameter. (A hexameter is a line of six "feet," each of which has either a dactyl, a long syllable followed by a pair of short syllables, or a spondee, a pair of long syllables.) A tradition developed that a single poet, a blind man named **Homer** (fl. 750 BC?), was the inspiration for their written form that we possess today. Regardless of whether the tradition of a single author is historically accurate, the themes of fate, fame, honor, pride, rage, homecoming, and hospitality established by these narratives captivated many, including future authors, and thus contributed to the foundation of the literature of Western Civilization.

the Trojan War) played a role in upsetting the delicate balance of power. Whatever the cause, the loss of stability in the region devastated the Mycenaean trading economy. As the different kingdoms in the peninsula competed against one another for the dwindling trade, a new people, called the Dorians, took advantage of their distraction and entered Greece from the north. Their arrival signaled the coming of a new era in Greek history, the Greek Dark Age.

The Dark Age

Since, by definition, few sources survive from a dark age, historians remain unsure what precisely precipitated the **Greek Dark Age** (c. 1050–c. 750 BC). Greek legends written many centuries later claim that the **Dorians** were warlike northern Greeks who invaded and conquered Mycenaean cities. The fact that the Dorian dialect became more prevalent in Greece at this time gives credence to this theory. We also know that the Dorians were formidable enemies since they used new, more powerful iron weapons and could produce the hotter kilns necessary for smelting this metal. Only the city of Athens and the Mycenaean colonies on the west coast of Anatolia, a region the Greeks called Ionia, maintained the Mycenaean dialect. This separation of Greece into Dorian and Mycenaean regions is consistent with the idea that the Dorians invaded the Greek mainland, while those Mycenaeans who could fled to Ionia. Nonetheless, some historians have expressed skepticism in recent years about whether there is enough evidence to support the idea of a full-scale military invasion by the Dorians. Instead, they have suggested that the Dorians migrating into Greece was only one part of the decline of Mycenaean civilization and was linked to the widespread chaos that shook all the powers of this era. Whatever the precise cause(s) for the Dark Age, the great urban settlements and impressive cultural achievements of the Mycenaeans largely disappeared during this period.

On the mainland, people no longer lived in cities or journeyed via distant trade routes. Instead, they lived in rural villages composed of mud-brick huts and thatched roofs. Most raised only enough food to feed their families with little or no surplus, a condition known as subsistence agriculture. Villages had a king, known as a *basileus*, who led warriors during wartime. When the king died, his nearest relative succeeded him, but this succession had to be accepted by the *ecclesia*, the council made up of all the freemen in the community. A freeman was someone who had received his own land from the king in return for a commitment to fight for the community in times of war. Their plots of land were worked by agricultural slaves, who were usually captives from successful raids and who possessed few, if any, rights in society. The *ecclesia* also had the power to ratify the laws and decisions made by the king, but they could not introduce any new laws of their own.

As the period of invasions and instability came to an end, the *ecclesia* developed into an aristocracy, or hereditary social elite, which owned most of the land and directed policy. In place of kings, they began to elect *archons* from among themselves to carry out important roles for a brief term of office. These positions included the formerly royal duties of acting as a priest or military leader. Eventually, population growth led to the formation of a larger community known as a ***polis***. (Our modern-day term "politics" derives from this Greek word.) Though these young *poleis* (the plural of *polis*), such as Corinth and Sparta, still had relatively small populations of a few thousand inhabitants, each *polis* had its own government and laws and competed with its rivals. Furthermore, an important ideological shift occurred. Whereas in a traditional monarchy a king ruled over *subjects*, a *polis* had *citizens*. That is, the eligible members of a *polis* participated, at least in a limited way, in the governing of their community. In these first aristocracies, the number of citizens was limited to members from the few elite families. These aristocrats might even preserve the formal title of king, as was the case in Sparta. Nonetheless, an important precedent had been set. The demand for citizenship and its accompanying right to participate in governing would ultimately expand the ranks of citizens in city-states throughout Greece.

The lack of writing during the Greek Dark Age does not mean that Greek society produced no lasting achievements. Wandering poets memorized and recited myths and legends about the origins of the Greek people. These stories created a common cultural foundation that encouraged listeners to achieve *arete* (Greek for "excellence"). This emphasis on greatness fostered a culture of competition and individualism among the Greeks.

This sense of rivalry is perhaps best seen in the Olympic Games. This series of contests in honor of the sky god Zeus began in 776 BC and was held every four years. There were no team sports. Individual participants competed in foot races, the most prestigious event, and chariot races, the most expensive and dangerous. In addition, they could participate in boxing, wrestling, the long jump, and discus and javelin throwing. Winning the pentathlon, a combination of all these events, was considered the supreme athletic achievement. The spirit of competition and excellence would inspire the Greeks to great achievements, but the balance between individual ambition and communal stability remained an unresolved tension in Greek culture. As we will see throughout this unit, this general spirit of competition for individual glory made it difficult for them to collaborate with each other.

One area in which the Greeks enjoyed unity was religion. Their religious practices and beliefs seem to have standardized during the Dark Age. Once society became more stable and literate, the Greeks began to write down records and stories.

An early example of this comes from the poet **Hesiod** (fl. 750 BC), who wrote *Theogony*, a text that offers a mythological genealogy of the Greek gods. Hesiod narrated that Uranus (the Sky) and Gaia (the Earth) gave birth to twelve gods, six males and six females, known as Titans. The Titans married each other and gave birth to different gods and heroes. According to Hesiod's account, Uranus hated his children, while their mother, Gaia, encouraged them to rise up against him. Only the youngest Titan, Cronus ("Time"), accepted the challenge. He successfully overthrew his father and became master of the cosmos. What was more, Cronus decided to avoid a similar rebellion by eating his own children. This gruesome policy failed, for Cronus's Titan-wife concealed her youngest child, Zeus, from her cannibalistic husband. Zeus later defeated Cronus and the Titans and cast them into Tartarus, an abyss of suffering and torment.

Theogony and other Greek myths reveal the priorities of early Greek society. Just as Baal, the god of rain, was among the most important deities in Canaan due to the necessity of rain for the region's well-being, so, too, the Greeks associated different powers with their deities to reflect their values and concerns. For example, the story of Cronus consuming his own children reflected their awareness of time and mortality as well as the inevitability of decay.

Meanwhile, each of the principal gods on Mount Olympus, the highest peak in Greece, had their own areas of expertise. Zeus, the lord of the gods, guided the heavens and guaranteed the good treatment of travelers and guests. The gods Poseidon and Hades ruled the sea and the underworld respectively. Zeus's sister (and wife), Hera, was the goddess of childbirth and marriage. She became the mother of Ares, the god of war, and Hephaestus, the god of metalwork. The myths also describe how Zeus had many adulterous affairs, sometimes with humans. Other gods were born from these relationships, such as Athena, goddess of wisdom; Apollo, the god of learning and medicine; Hermes, the messenger god; and Dionysus, the god of pleasure.

Despite their supernatural powers, none of Hesiod's deities were moral exemplars. In contrast to the Judeo-Christian belief that humans are made in the image and likeness of God, the mythical Greek gods were construed in humanity's image and likeness. They were human in shape and behavior and shared all the faults associated with humans. Even deities who personified reason and wisdom partook in sordid escapades. These unedifying episodes in their myths encouraged later Greek thinkers either to reject the gods entirely or to understand these accounts as incomplete, and misleading, portrayals of the divine nature. As we will see in coming chapters, these same individuals turned instead to a more rational, less mythological, explanation for the complexity of the world and its phenomena.

The Archaic Age

Greece emerged from its Dark Age around 750 BC and entered a period known as the **Archaic Age** (c. 750–c. 500 BC). By this point, Greek society had stabilized and increased in population. Merchants developed new trading partnerships across the Mediterranean to provide food for their growing city-states. These individuals brought back to Greece firsthand knowledge of the achievements of those societies we studied in chapters 5 and 6. Such interactions inspired further developments within Greek culture; for example, they adapted the Phoenician alphabet for their own use.

The **Peplos Kore** from the Acropolis of Athens. Made of white marble c. 530 BC. Currently in the National Archeological Museum in Athens, Greece. This is perhaps the most famous example among archaic Greek statues exhibiting the Archaic Smile.

The Greeks especially revered the antiquity and sophistication of Egypt. Early Greek sculptures from this period, such as the avenue of lion sculptures in Delos, demonstrate their conscious efforts to mimic Egyptian designs. Nonetheless, between 650 and 600 BC, the Greeks began to cultivate their own artistic style. These archaic Greek sculptures, though still based on Egyptian models, were less stiff and formal. They emphasized the individual humanity of their subjects and often portrayed them as smiling. This feature, known as the Archaic Smile, was intended to display a state of health and well-being. This can also be interpreted as a sign of the freedom of Greek citizens, who valued the liberty of displaying the full range of human emotions.

The Archaic Age witnessed a wave of Greek colonization. The growing mainland population outstripped the resources available to many individual city-states. The people of a given *polis* decided that the best way to relieve shortages and the social stress caused by overpopulation was to commission portions of their own people to establish a separate, but related, *polis* elsewhere. During this period, mainland city-states founded colonies around the Mediterranean and the Black Sea, as far west as Italy and as far south as Egypt. These colonies traded with their mother-city and typically adopted the political structures and laws of their original *polis*. The presence of these increasingly independent settlements spread Greek culture throughout the Mediterranean region and ensured that it would possess an influential role in the formation of Western Civilization.

In the meantime, society on mainland Greece did not remain static. Some merchants had become fantastically wealthy as a result of their far-flung trade. Yet they lacked political power at home because they were not part of the aristocracy. The social elites still enjoyed near-exclusive influence on account of their family claims to the land around the *polis* as well as their ancestral connection to the *polis's ecclesia*. Only members of the aristocracy could be citizens and thus participate in governing the community.

These privileged few could initially point to their role as the primary defenders of the *polis* in order to justify their elite status. According to the Homeric epic poem The *Iliad*, early Greek warfare primarily consisted of a series of honorable duels between the aristocrats of each side. A warrior would ride out in a chariot, declare his lineage, and challenge the aristocrats representing the opposing *polis* to fight him. Any challenger would also state his ancestry, and the two would typically fight by casting spears at one another from their chariots.

As the Archaic Age progressed, this older style of warfare evolved. Greek *poleis* had become wealthier and more jealous of their prestige. They were anxious to defeat their rivals and began to fund the development of larger armies to fight their wars. These new armies were primarily made up of infantry troops known as ***hoplites***. They wore armor made of bronze, carried eight-foot-long spears, and fought in a formation known as a *phalanx*. The *hoplites* would lock their shields together and the first ranks of soldiers would project their spears over the first line of shields, presenting a mass of spear points towards the enemy. As long as the formation did not break, casualties would be relatively low. Even a large-scale battle like the Battle of Plataea saw fewer than two thousand Greek casualties, while tens of thousands of Persians perished (see chapter 8). Battles between *phalanxes* were essentially pushing matches which depended on the valor of the men in the front ranks, while those to the rear maintained the army's forward pressure. By 650 BC, all major Greek city-states had adopted these powerful new armies. The Greeks gained a reputation as excellent warriors, and many were hired to fight as mercenaries in non-Greek conflicts across the Mediterranean. As the chariots of the aristocrats were replaced by the *phalanx*, merchants who had fought as *hoplites* successfully argued that their participation in the defense of the *polis* had gained them the right to govern the city alongside the aristocrats.

By the end of the Archaic Age, most Greek cities were no longer governed by the aristocracy; rather, they were governed by an oligarchy. This new governing class was composed of a combination of the wealthiest aristocrats and merchants. These oligarchies provided some of the most stable governments in Greek history and demonstrated a path for more inhabitants to become citizens and thus participate

The **Mykonos Vase**. Made of clay c. 675 BC. Currently in the Archaeological Museum of Mykonos, Greece. This is one of the earliest objects to depict the famous myth of the Trojan Horse, in which Greek warriors finally entered Troy by hiding in the hallow monument. The Greeks can be seen looking out windows of the wooden horse as they prepare to attack the city. Interestingly, no Trojan warriors are portrayed.

in the government of the *polis*. Nonetheless, the Greeks also kept alive the memories of their heroic age by reciting the deeds of the legendary warriors of their past. This was the context for the composition of *The Iliad* and *The Odyssey* (see chapter insert on the Trojan War). Greeks of all classes heard these accounts of the Trojan War and the travels of Odysseus across the Mediterranean and imbibed their lessons about heroism and *arete*. Although the aristocratic warfare described in these accounts was already fading, the Greeks of the Archaic Age, as well as the Golden Age yet to come, were still inspired by the deeds of Hector and his adversaries.

Conclusion

As we learned in chapter 4 when discussing Egypt and the Nile, geography can influence the development and even the beliefs of a given society. The mountains that so define the Greek Peninsula, as well as the waters that separate the nearby islands, encouraged a sense of political independence and individual freedom in Greek culture. Mycenaean warriors, as described in the Homeric epics, experienced fierce rivalry with one another and thirsted for personal glory. This heightened sense of self continued in the Archaic Age. By that time, the rise of city-states had expanded the role of warrior to a wider number of Greeks, who soon associated their ability to participate in their *polis's* wars with the right to participate in their *polis's* governance. At the same time, the sea served as a highway that connected them to other civilizations across the Mediterranean. The Greeks displayed a willingness to learn from these cultures and adopt their achievements and artistic styles, which contributed to their own efforts to depict the human figure and to capture the complexities of the human mind. These were but the first steps that would lead to later Greek glory.

In the next chapter, we compare in detail two of the most famous *poleis* in Greek history. We also return to the Persian Empire and discuss how it was that the small city-states of Greece came to clash with the largest empire the world had yet seen. That story, like Hector's at Troy, would be remembered and honored by future Greeks for millennia.

CHAPTER 8

Polis vs. Empire

Know thyself.

Thales of Miletus[1]

These words were inscribed in the forecourt of the Temple of Apollo at Delphi. Apollo was the Greek god of knowledge and harmony, and the ancient Greeks considered Delphi to be the center of the world. Those who traveled there to seek the god's guidance for their problems received often-cryptic messages from Apollo's priestess, known as the Pythia or Oracle. Though many held these messages to be of divine origin, the Greeks did not rely solely on their gods for wisdom. The inscription at Delphi was attributed, not to Apollo, but to Thales of Miletus. This philosopher, or "lover of wisdom," is traditionally seen as the first of the Greek sages who committed themselves to the pursuit of wisdom and who challenged others to use their reason to understand both themselves and their world. Their theories about the world and its composition were among the many impressive achievements of Archaic Greece.

In this chapter, we examine this Archaic Age in detail. The previous chapter has already outlined the broad contours of this era, so we focus here on this period's most famous Greek *poleis*: Sparta and Athens. The distinct values of these two city-states defined the everyday lives of their citizens and show us the range of priorities

1 Eliza G. Wilkins, "*ΕΓΓΥΑ, ΠΑΡΑ ΔΑΤΗ* in Literature," *Classical Philology* 22, no. 2 (1927), 121.

within Greek culture. In contrast to these small, independent *poleis* loomed the expanse of the Persian Empire. There, despite the limited liberties offered to its inhabitants, all people acknowledged the same king of kings and were subject to his whims. The Greeks could not imagine a starker contrast to their own emphasis on individual freedom, and the stage was set for a great struggle once the two cultures came into contact.

Sparta

Several characteristics distinguished **Sparta** from other Greek city-states. First, geographically, Sparta was located inland on the Peloponnesus, the peninsula in the south of Greece. Therefore, unlike most Greek communities, Spartans had little interaction with the sea and engaged in almost no trade. Instead, Sparta remained primarily agrarian and poorer than many other Greek cities. The main way to protect and increase its influence was through conquest of the surrounding lands. The Spartans consequently developed a culture that promoted excellence in warfare as the most noble act of citizenship. Its citizens' willingness to sacrifice their personal comfort and, to some extent, their own individuality for the greater glory of Sparta fascinated the other Greek *poleis*. It is one of the ironies of history that the generally individualistic Greek world was particularly fascinated by its most communal society. Indeed, much of what we know about Sparta comes from the writings of other Greeks, such as the Athenian Xenophon.

Sparta was founded by the Dorians during the Dark Age. According to Spartan tradition, the quasi-historical **Lycurgus** (see chapter insert on the legend of Lycurgus) established the laws and constitution of the city around 700 BC. During the Archaic Age, as we discussed in the previous chapter, many Greek city-states were transitioning away from rule by kings to oligarchies, but Sparta's government retained its two elected kings. Citizens of Sparta chose these from the *polis's* two leading aristocratic families, the Agaids and Eurypontids. These kings retained their status as military leaders and high priests who performed the community's most important rituals. Yet, their power was not absolute. Spartan kings were overseen by a group of five ***ephors*** who were elected for a one-year term and had the power to impeach, or condemn, the kings for misconduct. They also managed the daily activities of the *polis* and even governed foreign policy. War could not be declared without their vote. Thus, while the leadership of the kings kept Sparta in a state of readiness for war, the *ephors* served to check the power of the kings and make sure they did not become oppressive.

The chief law-making body in Sparta was the *Gerousia* ("gathering of elders"). It was a council of the two Spartan kings and twenty-eight other men who were at least sixty years old. These "elders" served in this position for life. The *Gerousia* was the only body that could approve laws, which were then proposed to the citizens of Sparta for a vote. It also served as the only law court with the power to condemn a citizen to death. The *Gerousia* was typically extremely conservative, so changes in Spartan society occurred only very gradually.

Sparta's citizens were a minority of its total population. For reasons explained below, there were seldom more than about six thousand Spartan warriors in the *polis*, an estimated 5 percent of Sparta's total population. (This number would, of course, decline during prolonged periods of war.) Another 15 percent were free noncitizens. These either were not accepted into the Spartan military when they turned twenty or had only one Spartan parent and were thus ineligible for military service and citizenship.

The majority of the population were ***helots***. They were the unfree descendants of nearby peoples whom the Spartans had conquered. They had no freedom of movement and could be bought and sold to work the land, but they were allowed to keep and sell anything they cultivated above the production quota set by the government. Some became quite prosperous and were able to purchase their freedom. Others could gain liberty by volunteering to fight in the Spartan armies as auxiliaries. Despite their dominant position, Spartans lived in constant fear of *helot* uprisings. Certain youth companies were assigned to spy on the slaves and to attack them if they appeared disloyal. This fear of *helot* rebellions played an important role in shaping the *polis's* foreign policy. Spartans generally kept their army close to home in case of a revolt and typically refused to join Greek expeditions beyond the Peloponnesus.

It was, in part, out of fear of *helot* uprisings that the Spartans maintained an austere system of education and training, designed to raise generations of elite warriors. Shortly after birth, all infants were inspected by members of the *Gerousia*. Sparta was a poor city and resources were scarce, so only the healthiest children were allowed to survive. Any that were considered unhealthy or malformed were cast into a chasm on one of the nearby mountains to die. Those children who did survive left home at the age of seven and were organized into packs. They were trained to write, sing, dance, and, above all, to fight in any condition. Sparta wanted hardened warriors, so their training encouraged endurance against all physical discomfort. Sometimes the boys were not given enough food and told to forage and steal. This hardship prepared them to survive in enemy territory. Failure to hide one's theft was severely punished. (There is a Spartan legend that a boy stole a fox and hid the animal inside his coat. Seeing his instructor approaching, he allowed the animal to wound him mortally rather than be discovered in the theft.) When Spartan boys turned twenty, they faced election into army squads of fifteen members. The candidates had to receive a unanimous vote

THE LEGEND OF LYCURGUS

The Spartans venerated Lycurgus (fl. eighth century BC?) as the founder of their constitution, but his biography remains shrouded in myth. Most of what we know about him is based on an account written by the Roman historian Plutarch (c. AD 46–119), who lived over seven hundred years after Lycurgus's proposed lifetime. Plutarch acknowledged that little could be known for certain about Lycurgus, but he also recognized that the legends about him revealed the values Spartans most admired.

According to the legend, Lycurgus was the younger brother of one of the Spartan kings. When his brother died, his sister-in-law offered to kill her infant son so that she and Lycurgus could assume the throne. Lycurgus pretended to agree to this plan but instead presented the child to the Spartans as heir to the throne and offered himself as guardian until the baby came of age.

Lycurgus as depicted in a marble relief over the gallery doors of the House Chamber of the United States Capital Building in Washington, D.C.

When rumors spread that he still sought to supplant the child, Lycurgus left Sparta and traveled throughout Greece. He learned effective ways to govern a *polis* as well as how to compose lyric poetry whose beauty helped to heal disagreements within a community. According to the tale, he also maintained that Homer's poems taught citizens valuable lessons about politics and discipline. (Lycurgus's proposed connection with Homer shows us that, although the Spartans distanced themselves from other *poleis* in many ways, they still wished to be associated with the general Greek values promoted by Homer's works.)

At the same time, instability at home led the Spartans to ask Lycurgus to return and govern them. Lycurgus reformed their laws and emphasized loyalty and discipline. He provided each citizen with an equal amount of land, large enough for him to be self-sufficient but not large enough to encourage excess. He also banned any currency based on precious metals to prevent corruption from trade and established rigorous systems of education for men and women.

After he had completed these reforms, Lycurgus left to consult the Pythia at Delphi. Those at Sparta promised to uphold his laws until his return. Once the Oracle assured him that his laws were excellent and would make his people famous, Lycurgus decided never to return to Sparta so that the Spartans' oath would bind them forever. In doing so, he sacrificed contact with his family and even his own identity since it was tied so closely with his *polis*. The legend's emphasis on the virtues of discipline, loyalty, and self-sacrifice reflected the communal values that the Spartans most prized. Whether or not Lycurgus was a historical figure, the story of his life shaped generations of Spartans and brought them their prophesied fame.

from the squad to gain a place. If they were not accepted into any of the squads, they could still live in Sparta, but they would not have the privileges of citizenship. If they were accepted, they would serve as full-time professional soldiers for ten years and develop unbreakable bonds of loyalty and friendship with their comrades.

Once they turned thirty, Spartan men gained the full rights of citizenship and received a plot of land from the *polis*. Such properties were large enough to allow individuals to be economically independent but not so large that someone could become corrupted by material desires and thus no longer be willing to make sacrifices for his city-state. These men were now encouraged to marry and raise up sons to be future warriors for Sparta. They were no longer considered active-duty soldiers, but they were expected to live with the other members of their squad rather than their families until they reached the age of forty-five. They also had to maintain their fitness and be available to campaign until they attained the age of sixty and could retire.

Spartan girls also received a vigorous physical education so that they could mother healthy children. They held a more equal status with male citizens than did women in other Greek cities. They married at about the age of eighteen and were the only Greek women who could inherit property in their own names. They also managed their households in times of war and supplied food for the army. Spartan women had a reputation for being fearless and encouraging their warriors to bravery. Mothers traditionally commanded their sons departing for war to come back either carrying their shields or borne upon them. The greatest honor was to die fighting for the *polis*, and survivors carried these heroes' bodies atop their shields back to Sparta. In contrast, it was the worst shame for a Spartan soldier to survive a battle by throwing away his weapon and shield as he escaped.

Statue of a helmed Spartan Hoplite. Made of marble c. 400 BC. Currently in the Archaeological Museum of Sparta, Greece.

While modern culture, especially in film, has frequently celebrated the Spartans' military prowess, an accurate historical understanding of Sparta acknowledges both the *polis's* great accomplishments and the abusive aspects of Spartan culture, which were substantial and ingrained. On the one hand, Sparta took unusual steps to promote equality among its inhabitants: women exercised greater public roles, and landholding was restricted to prevent individuals from increasing their wealth at the expense of others. Even *helots* had opportunities to gain their freedom. Furthermore, the Spartan system of education formed warriors who consistently displayed a willingness to disregard their individual safety and comfort for the greater glory of Sparta. Their loyalty and bravery won admiration and acclaim throughout Greece. On the other hand, the vast majority of the population were held as slaves with few legal rights and protections. Moreover, the natural bonds of family love were subjugated to the policies of the state, best displayed by the entrenched practice of infanticide. In a very real way, the value of the individual, which was so prized by most Greeks, became lost amidst Sparta's desire for security and military success.

Athens

Athens was the opposite of Sparta in many ways. The city was located near the coast and developed a thriving economy based on trade. Unlike the Spartans, who scorned work as the task of enslaved *helots*, Athenian culture promoted labor as a source of wealth and honor. Even their military contrasted with Sparta: whereas Spartans relied on infantry and famously decided not to build a wall around their *polis*, the Athenians developed their naval might and relied upon walls to defend the city of Athens. However, the most striking difference between the two was the emphasis that Athenian society came to place upon individual citizens and their role in the larger *polis*.

The Athenians were Ionian Greeks, descended from the Mycenaeans, and had retained control of their city during the Dark Age. Once the uncertainties of that era had receded around 800 BC, Athens followed the general pattern among Greek *poleis* of replacing their monarchy with a landed aristocracy. The aristocrats elected nine *archons* to serve as magistrates for ten years. After their term of office had ended, they became members of the *Areopagus*. This body proposed new legislation, which then received a vote from the *ecclesia*, the assembly of aristocrats which we introduced in the previous chapter.

By the seventh century BC, there was growing tension in Athens between aristocrats and the other members of society. The peasants were forced to rent land from the aristocrats every year at exorbitant rates and offer themselves and their families as security for any loan necessary to pay their rent. If a bad harvest followed and the farmer could not pay the loan, he and his family became slaves of the aristocrat landowner. Wealthy merchants were also dissatisfied. Aristocrats owned most of the city's land and held political power, but it was the merchants who fought the city's wars as *hoplites*. They insisted that aristocrats should at least write down the laws of the *polis* so that they could be known and applied equally to everyone rather than being subject to the interpretation of biased aristocratic *archons*.

In 621 BC, the *archons* finally attempted to quell this discontent by agreeing to appoint a man named Draco (fl. 621 BC) to write down the laws of Athens. Draco's law code established requirements for evidence and ensured that the laws were applied equally to all Athenians. Although Draco's laws were sophisticated in some areas—for example, he drew a distinction between murder and manslaughter—they were considered unbearably harsh by the Athenians. Many crimes were punishable by death, even stealing a cabbage! The severe nature of Draco's laws provoked such dissatisfaction that the aristocrats appointed **Solon** (c. 630–c. 560 BC) to revise them. On the one hand, Solon was from an aristocratic family, and many aristocrats assumed that his laws would benefit their party. On the other hand, Athenian merchants remembered that Solon's father had bankrupted his family due to his generosity to the poor and concluded that Solon, who had himself become a merchant to avoid poverty, would be sympathetic to their cause.

Overall, Solon's reforms benefited the non-elite. He abolished most of Draco's laws and made criminal penalties less severe. Thieves now paid ten times the amount they stole rather than face the death penalty. Furthermore, he released all Athenians who had been enslaved through debt and insisted that loans be paid with money or produce, not with one's freedom. He also established a standardized system of weights and measurements that helped merchants carry out trade. He even encouraged foreign merchants to settle in the *polis* by granting them citizenship. (Remember that citizenship was highly valued in Greek society.) Solon also laid the foundations for the future Athenian democracy by restructuring the government to permit wider involvement. Status in the *polis* was no longer determined by one's family lineage as it was in the aristocracy. Instead, he divided inhabitants into four classes based on their wealth. The office of *archon* was reserved for the two wealthiest classes and thus was still predominantly held by

Bust of Solon from the Farnese Collection. Made of marble c. AD 90. Currently in the National Archaeological Museum of Naples, Italy.

the aristocrats, but this change gave Athens's wealthiest merchants the opportunity to attain this office. Solon also established a new legislative body, the Council of Four Hundred, to advise and present the concerns of the wider *polis* to the *ecclesia*. Membership in this council was open to anyone from the three wealthiest classes. Although members of the poorest class were excluded, they were at least also exempted from any taxation.

Despite Solon's best efforts, unrest continued in the city. In 561 BC, **Peisistratus** (c. 600–527 BC), hero of a recent war, seized power as a tyrant. While today the word "tyrant" is associated with the abuse of power, for the Greeks at this time the term meant that a sole ruler held absolute power and was not limited by normal legal restraints. Typically, tyrants gained authority during emergencies or unrest; Peisistratus, for example, appealed to the unrepresented interests of the poor who resented the wealthy minority. Solon opposed Peisistratus, but by this point he was an old man. When he realized that no one was brave enough to challenge Peisistratus's coup, Solon displayed his *hoplite* equipment outside his door and declared that he had already done his part to maintain Athens's laws. It was up to others to defend them.

Although rebellions interrupted his rule several times, Peisistratus governed Athens successfully from 546–528 BC. During this period, he appointed the *archons* but otherwise allowed the system Solon had established to continue to function as before. He provided for the *polis's* merchants and farmers by funding loans and controlling the local silver mines. This latter policy had the additional benefit of supplying merchants with sufficient currency to trade effectively. He also improved the infrastructure of the city of Athens itself, especially its roads and water supply. Peisistratus had two sons, Hippias and Hipparchus, who succeeded him after his death. Resistance to their rule led to Hipparchus's assassination. In response, Hippias became paranoid and executed any Athenian he believed was plotting against him. Eventually, an alliance of Athenian opponents supported by Spartan troops drove him out of the city in 510 BC. His decision to flee to the Persian Empire was, as we will see, a fateful one.

An *archon* named **Cleisthenes** (c. 570–c. 508 BC) rose to prominence in the aftermath of the tyranny. With conflict continuing to plague the city, he again reformed Athens's government, this time from an oligarchy into a democracy. Solon had divided Athenians into four clans, which were then themselves divided into classes based on wealth. The few wealthiest Athenians had possessed access to the highest offices, which made its government an oligarchy in which "the few" held most authority. Cleisthenes, in contrast, divided the people according to the different regions where they lived in the *polis* without accounting for their wealth. These groups were known as "tribes."

Three institutions comprised the heart of his new government structure. He dramatically expanded membership in the *ecclesia* by opening it to all (male) citizens of Athens over eighteen years of age—about 40,000 out of an overall population estimated at 250,000. (About half of the population of Athens were slaves and ineligible for citizenship.) The *ecclesia*, now also known as the Assembly, met four times a year. On average, it seems about 5,000 citizens regularly attended these meetings. The Assembly could pass, reject, or amend measures proposed by the Council of Four Hundred. The Council of Four Hundred increased from its former four hundred members under Solon to five hundred. Fifty members from each of the tribes were chosen by lot to serve for a year. The Council met every day and carried out the administrative work of the government: supervising the military and government workers and drafting proposals for new laws to present to the Assembly. The third and final branch of Athenian democracy was the *Dikasteria*, the courts. Every day, five hundred men were chosen by lot from citizens older than thirty to serve on the jury. There was no police force in the city, so cases were prosecuted and defended by individual citizens.

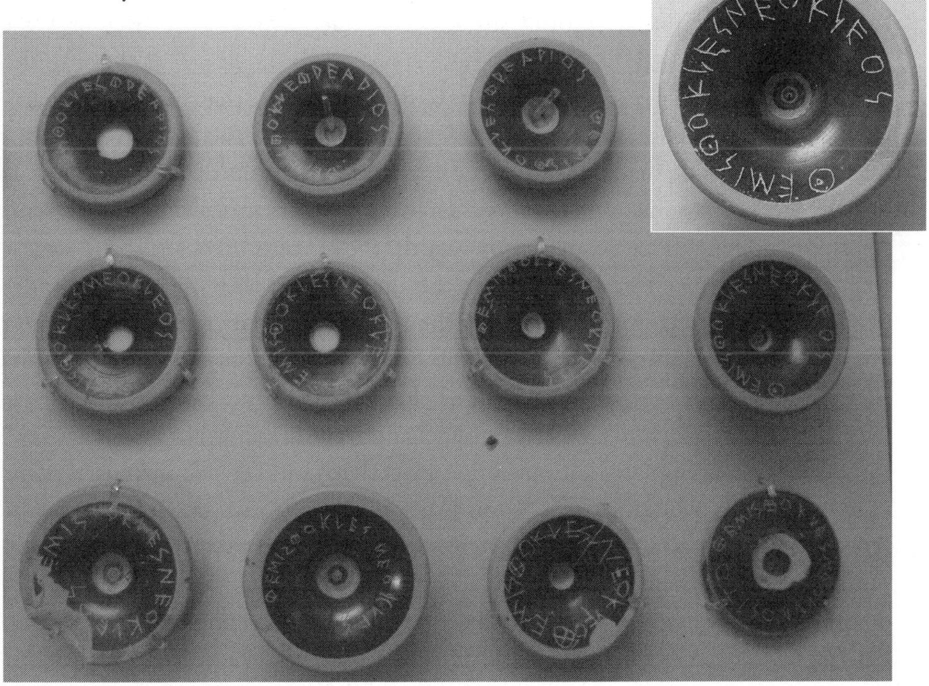

Ostraka. Made of clay c. 428 BC. Currently in the Museum of the Ancient Agora in Athens, Greece. Cleisthenes's reforms included ostracism. Athenians voted to exile a fellow citizen for 10 years. This was intended to protect the democracy from would-be tyrants while avoiding outright violence. According to Plutarch, it required 6,000 votes to be ostracized. The closeup shows an ostrakon reading ΘΕΜΙΣΘΟΚLΕΣ ΝΕΟΚLΕΟΣ ("Themistocles son of Neocles").

The structure of this democratic government emphasized the participation of all the *polis's* citizens and was one of the most striking political manifestations of Greek culture's individualism. Nonetheless, the other *poleis* of Greece were not impressed by this new form of government. They considered democracy chaotic and cumbersome. The official positions of the *polis* depended on those who gained the most votes and could change dramatically. Critics also pointed to the fact that voting in the Assembly was carried out by a show of hands. This left the process open to corruption through intimidation or through miscounting the votes. Sources tell us that some particularly contentious votes were even held in the dark to ensure the "correct" outcome. Such abuses convinced other Greek city-states, such as Sparta, to see this first experiment in democracy as consistent with their view of Athenian culture as superficial and decadently wealthy.

Ionia

Across the Aegean Sea from mainland Greece were the colonies that had been established on the western coast of Anatolia during the Mycenaean period. This region, known as **Ionia**, enjoyed sustained contact with the cultures of West Asia, especially the Persian Empire, whose conquests brought it ever closer to the different Greek Ionian *poleis*. The Ionian Greeks were more than just trading partners with the Persians; they were also highly impressed by the mathematical and scientific knowledge that came from the ancient civilizations of West Asia.

Whereas Spartans pursued heroism as loyal servants of the state, and Athenians sought to amass and enjoy wealth, the citizens of Miletus, the largest Ionian *polis*, embraced learning. Even in this undertaking, the Greek love for independence was not far from the surface. The Persians and Babylonians had desired knowledge of the natural world for religious and practical purposes. For example, they considered the best way to irrigate a field or the best time to worship a particular god. The Greeks broke with this model and went beyond the "best practices." Instead, they contemplated rational arguments that would enable them to *explain* (and not just describe) the natural world they inhabited. Such knowledge was not required for daily life. Yet, their conviction that the universe was orderly inspired some to dedicate their lives to discovering nature's patterns. These lovers of wisdom, or "philosophers," were convinced that humanity had an innate, or natural, longing to understand the world and further argued that human rationality can satisfy this urge and master the hidden riddles of the cosmos.

The earliest Greek philosophers flourished in Miletus from about 600 to 500 BC. These thinkers attempted to uncover a single principle that would explain the order they observed in the universe. The first was **Thales** (c. 625–c. 545 BC).

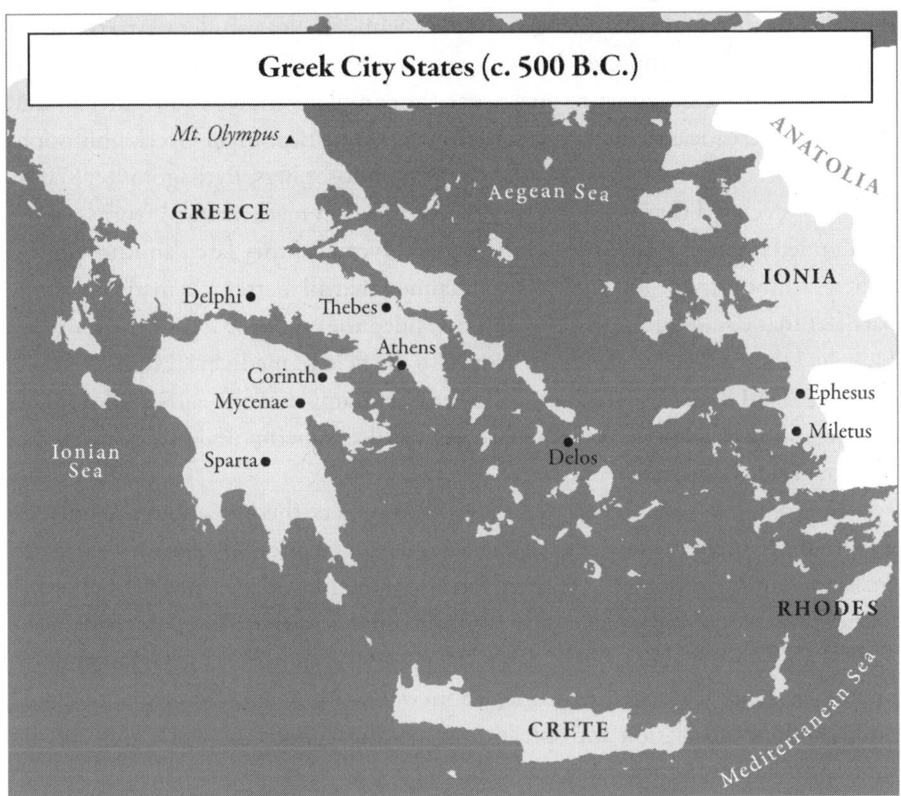

He was a great geometer and astronomer, who predicted eclipses, established that a circle could be divided by its diameter, and determined that the base angles of an isosceles triangle are equal. While he likely drew upon prior Babylonian and Egyptian achievements in his own observations, Thales wished to use this knowledge more broadly to explain the origins of the entire cosmos. Previously, the Greeks believed that cataclysmic events, like eclipses, were simply the result of the fickle wills of the gods, but Thales wanted a different explanation that was rooted in natural processes. He argued that water, which can nurture crops but also change landscapes, was the single substance that gave origin to all material things. Many mocked Thales as someone who was more interested in abstract theories about the universe than achieving the practical excellence that had made the Greeks famous. A popular contemporary story described him falling into a well because he was so busy trying to observe the stars. But Thales's efforts to explain the cosmos inspired a culture of philosophical inquiry at Miletus.

Inspired by Thales's example, others continued to develop theories about the composition of the universe. Anaximenes (c. 586–c. 526 BC), for example, argued that air was the single life-giving substance, while Thales's student Anaximander (c. 610–c. 546 BC) proposed that an indeterminate, unlimited, almost immaterial substance must be necessary to give rise to the complex variety of substances found in nature. These ideas demonstrate the growing sophistication of Greek philosophical thought. One of the most famous of these philosophers, Pythagoras (c. 570–c. 495 BC), declared that the universe was grounded in mathematical truths, which maintained harmony and order in the world. Over a century later, another philosopher, Democritus (c. 460–c. 370 BC), claimed that all matter was made up of tiny particles that could not be split up and that filled the empty spaces of the universe. He called these particles *atomoi*, or atoms. In the field of medicine, Hippocrates (c. 460–c. 370 BC) and his students followed the example of the early philosophers by attempting to demonstrate the natural as well as supernatural causes and remedies for various diseases.

The confidence that motivated these philosophers' theories about the universe was grounded in their knowledge of science and mathematics. All of them were mathematicians and astronomers. Yet there was also something more. They beheld beauty in the world's logic and order and firmly believed that such order could explain the natural phenomena about them. Later, the most well-known of the Greek philosophers—Socrates, Plato, and Aristotle, whom we discuss in the next chapter—would build on their foundation and spread concepts throughout the world that are still studied and debated to this day.

Persia

Their close proximity to the Persian Empire helped the Ionian Greeks increase their knowledge of prior civilizations, but it also led to conflict. While Persian and Greek interests were aligned in the area of education, the Persian model of a large and stable empire was opposed to the independence and individualism of the Greek *polis*. By the end of the sixth century BC, the Persians had defeated Croesus, the ruler of the Lydian Empire, and had even crossed into Europe, conquering territories as far north as the Danube River. Among their new territories were the Greek city-states of Ionia.

This subjugation brought the benefits of Persian rule—improved infrastructure, political stability, and relative autonomy, but the Greeks preferred their former independence. In 499 BC, the Ionian *poleis*, led by Miletus, revolted and appealed to mainland Greece for help. The Spartans—always aware of the danger of a *helot* uprising—rejected the idea of fighting such a remote campaign, but the Athenians recognized their kinship with the Ionian Greeks and sent twenty ships to support the rebels. The Athenians were also concerned by the presence of Hippias in the

Persian army and feared that he would use his powerful ally to restore his tyrannical rule over them.

The Greeks achieved some initial successes but were unable to overcome the might of the Persian Empire. Whenever they defeated a Persian army, another was mustered to replace it. After four years of fighting, the Persian king of kings Darius I finally captured and sacked Miletus. He deported any survivors to Mesopotamia. Darius's punishment of the rebels contrasted sharply with the Persian reputation for mild rule. (This Darius was the same Persian ruler who supported the Jews in the reconstruction of the Second Temple. See chapter 6.) The sack demonstrated the extent of Darius's frustration and his determination to make an example of the rebels to discourage further uprisings. It may also suggest that the Persians, who were renowned for understanding the different cultural predispositions of those they conquered, recognized that the Greeks would be far more reluctant to accept Persian rule than their other subjects. What is more, Darius did not forget the people from across the Aegean Sea who had dared to defy him by aiding Miletus and its allies. He ordered his slaves to proclaim "Lord, remember the Athenians" three times at every imperial meal.

The **Foundation Tablets of the Apadana Hoard**. Made of gold and silver, c. 510 BC. Currently in the National Museum of Iran. The Apadana Hoard was a collection of coins that were deposited under the foundation of the Apadana Palace in Persepolis, Iran. The coins were placed under stone boxes which contained gold and silver inscription tablets from Darius I. The trilingual inscription in Old Persian, Elamite and Akkadian is the same on each tablet and describes the geographical extent of Darius's empire.

Athens was in poor condition to resist the king of kings. Even within the city there was division between those who favored submission to the Persians and those who wished to fight for their independence. In 491 BC, Darius sent envoys to demand that the different Greek *poleis* submit to Persian rule. Approximately a third of the city-states, especially those to the north, accepted Persian overlordship. Their envoys returned to Darius bearing the traditional symbols of submission: earth and water.

The next year Darius arrived in Greece with an army of approximately twenty-five thousand soldiers and twenty ships to conquer Athens and force the Athenians to accept him as their ruler. The Athenians appealed to the Spartans for aid, but the Spartans insisted on observing a religious festival which prohibited them from marching before the next full moon. The Persian army landed on a plain called Marathon, and the Athenians occupied the high ground overlooking the bay. The armies faced one another for several days. The Persians hoped that the pro-Persian faction in Athens would seize control of the city itself and thus make a battle unnecessary, but the Athenians at Marathon knew that each day's delay gave their Spartan allies more time to join them. After a week, the Persians began to load their cavalry, their most powerful military force, onto ships to sail to Athens, while leaving the infantry behind to hold the Athenian army in place. One of the Athenian generals, Miltiades (550–489 BC), convinced the Athenians to attack the Persians during the confusion of this maneuver. He ordered his *phalanxes* to advance at a run, so as to minimize casualties from the numerous Persian archers.

The confines of the plain of **Marathon**—marshes to each side and the sea to their rear—prevented the Persians from making full use of their superior numbers to overwhelm the Athenian army. In contrast, their robust weapons and armor gave the Greeks a significant advantage while fighting at close quarters. The Athenians lost ground in the center of the battle, but they prevailed on the flanks and then began to surround the Persians. Panic spread, and the Persians retreated. Thousands died, but most escaped to Persian ships.

The Persian fleet now attempted to sail around the coast in the hopes of capturing Athens before its victorious army could return, but the Athenians sent a runner to encourage the city to stand firm. According to legend, this battle-weary *hoplite* ran about twenty-fives miles to the city and announced the news of the victory before collapsing dead. His mission was successful, for the city's inhabitants knew to resist until the army returned. (We honor this feat of distance running in our own modern-day practice of the "marathon." Though there were debates about the exact distance the runner was thought to have traversed, the official "marathon" was set at 26.2 miles in 1921.) The Persians did not have the strength to take the city as long as it resisted, so they sailed away.

The Athenians had won a remarkable victory. Despite being significantly outnumbered, they had repulsed the hitherto triumphant Persians. Over six thousand foes lay dead; only 192 Athenians fell in the battle. Athens had proved that the Greeks could resist the Persians, but even as they savored this victory, some of their shrewder citizens recognized that this was not the end. The Greeks' epic struggle against the might of the Persian Empire had only begun.

Conclusion

By 490 BC, the different city-states of Greece shared a common culture of excellence that led them to value the distinct characteristics of their individual *polis*. Sparta developed a society that raised elite warriors. Athens embraced the creation of wealth through trade and implicitly promoted the individual dignity of its citizens through its democracy. Further to the east, the philosophers of Miletus, building upon the achievements of previous civilizations, encouraged the pursuit of rational explanations for the world about them. The different political structures fostered by the Greeks supported their various ambitions, and many were determined to defend their *poleis* and their freedoms, even against the overwhelming odds that they would face in the years ahead.

CHAPTER 9

The Wisdom and Folly of Greece

Wonders are many, yet of all /
Things is Man the most wonderful.

Sophocles, *Antigone*[1]

The Parthenon stands above the modern city of Athens as a lasting tribute to the achievements of ancient Greek culture. Athenians built this temple to the goddess Athena, the patroness of their *polis*, in remembrance of her apparent aid during the Persian Wars. Its construction began in 447 BC, and they completed its final touches about fifteen years later. Historians estimate that its construction cost over one billion dollars in modern money.

The Parthenon's design is rightly famous. The ratios of the building's height and length, its front columns, and its façade all conformed to the ratio of four to nine. This pleasing proportion conveys a sense of order to the beholder. Furthermore, the architects compensated for the visual distortions caused by distance and angle so that its columns looked proportional and balanced regardless of the viewer's location. The temple itself was made of marble, and its different stones were carved in such a manner that they locked together without any need for cement.

The Athenians' architectural triumph symbolizes the many glories of the wider Greek civilization. Their military success against Persia, their great wealth through

1 Sophocles, *Antigone* in *Sophocles: Antigone, Oedipus the King, and Electra*, trans. by H.D.F. Kitto (Oxford: Oxford University, 2008), 13.

The **Parthenon** was the temple of Athena on the Acropolis in Athens, Greece. It was built during 447–432 BC as a public thanksgiving for the Greek victory in the Persian Wars. The name "Parthenon" derives from *parthenos*, the Greek word for "maiden," and immediately calls to mind the maiden goddess Athena.

trade, and their intellectual and artistic sophistication are, as it were, embodied in its very stone. Yet, despite this brilliance, the Greeks were unable to maintain the peace, stability, and order the Parthenon epitomized. Indeed, less than one hundred years after the Battle of Marathon, Greek society was in crisis and tearing itself apart.

The Persian Wars

Darius, the Persian king of kings, died in 486 BC. His son **Xerxes** (r. 486–465 BC) inherited not only the empire but also the desire to avenge the Persian defeat at Marathon. After securing obedience from the rest of the empire, Xerxes sent ambassadors to the Greek city-states ordering that they submit to his rule. Only thirty-one Greek *poleis*, about a third of their total number, rejected his demands. Athens and Sparta spearheaded this opposition to Persia.

Xerxes responded by assembling an enormous army of *at least* 150,000 soldiers. (Some estimate that it was closer to 500,000!) At its heart was an elite unit of 10,000 imperial bodyguards known as the Immortals. They received this name because as soon as one died or became ill, someone else was chosen to replace him. In theory, therefore, the warriors always numbered 10,000 and thus seemed "immortal." These Persian soldiers wore light armor with felt caps rather than helmets. They wielded shields made of wicker, short spears, and long daggers. They also carried composite bows made of horn and mulberry wood; these small but powerful weapons were among their most deadly.

The rest of Xerxes's army was levied from the territories of his empire. Persian nobles and *satraps* (provincial governors) were all expected to provide a certain number of soldiers who employed the traditional weapons, armor, and fighting style of their home region. Among these were Greek *hoplites* from those city-states that had submitted to the king of kings. The Persian navy followed a similar model and drew its strength primarily from Egyptian and Phoenician vessels. While the Persian military was impressive in its size, the diversity of languages and fighting styles within its ranks made it difficult to coordinate tactics across the army.

The Greeks, in contrast, had at most about 110,000 soldiers at their disposal. Of these, about 40,000 were *hoplites*; many of the rest were only lightly armored. While the Greeks had the advantage of speaking the same language and using the same fighting techniques, the rivalries that divided their *poleis* threatened to undermine their defense. Furthermore, when the Greeks consulted Apollo's Oracle at Delphi, they received little comfort. She predicted both the death of a Spartan king and the destruction of Athens.

The cause seemed desperate, but the Athenians did receive some hope from the Oracle: she encouraged them to trust their wooden walls. Many Athenians interpreted this vague statement as a reference to their navy. Indeed, the Athenians had significantly bolstered their fleet in the years following the Battle of Marathon by using a recently discovered seam of silver in their silver mines to fund new construction. This policy was championed by the *archon* Themistocles (523–469 BC).

The **Temple of Apollo** is part of a larger religious complex in Delphi, Greece. The ruins visible here are dated from c. 400 BC. This site was particularly famous for the Pythia, the temple's prophetess and high-priestess, who was also known as the Oracle at Delphi.

Whereas some Athenians had proposed to distribute the newfound wealth among the citizens to gain popularity, Themistocles convinced the Assembly that the best use of this wealth was to invest it in a state-of-the-art navy to resist future Persian invasions. The Athenians' commitment to defending their *polis*, even at the expense of political popularity, would be well rewarded.

Their fleet consisted of two hundred triremes, vessels with three banks of rowers that could make speeds of more than 10 miles an hour and turn 180 degrees in less than a minute. The prow of each ship was fitted with a 500-pound ram used to sink or disable enemy ships. Contrary to popular imagination, Athenians employed professional oarsmen—not slaves—to man these galleys.

The ***Olympias*** is a reconstruction built in the 1980s of an Athenian trireme, such as those used in the Battle of Salmis. Currently at the Hellenic Maritime Museum in Piraeus, Greece.

Xerxes's strategy was to travel by land and approach Greece from the north. His massive army relied on his fleet for many of its provisions, so the Greeks' counter-strategy was to defeat the Persian fleet and thereby limit the Persian army's supplies. Without sufficient food and other necessities, Xerxes's overland force would be compelled to withdraw.

The Persians reached the borders of Greece in the summer of 480 BC. The Spartan king Leonidas (540–480 BC) led a force of about 6,500 Greeks, including 300 Spartan *hoplites*, and occupied the crucial mountain pass of Thermopylae. Leonidas chose to defend this place since he and his allies knew that its narrow road would negate the Persians' numerical superiority. Xerxes assumed that the Greeks would retreat in the face of his huge army, but Persian scouts reported, to his shock, that the Spartans in the Greek camp were performing gymnastics and combing their

This bronze **monument of Leonidas** was erected at Thermopylae in 1955. The inscription below the statue reads ΜΟΛΩΝ ΛΑΒΕ ("Come and take them"), a reference to Leonidas's reply when Xerxes offered to spare Spartans who surrendered their weapons.

hair. This preparation for battle aroused Persian contempt, but that soon turned to begrudging respect as Leonidas's army repelled their tens of thousands. Finally, after two days of combat, a treacherous local showed the Immortals an alternative pass through the mountains that would enable them to surround the Greeks on the following day. Knowing the position was lost, Leonidas dismissed most of his force except for the Spartans, Thebans, and Thespians. (The Thespians refused to abandon the Spartans, but historians are unsure what motivated the Thebans to remain. According to the ancient Greek historian Herodotus, Leonidas forced them to stay against their will.[2]) The Spartans and Thespians fought to the bitter end: when their weapons broke, they used their fists and their teeth to attack their enemy. In contrast, many Thebans apparently surrendered as soon as they could. Two of Xerxes's brothers and many other noble Persians perished in Leonidas's final struggle. Xerxes finally ordered the surviving Greeks to be killed from a distance with arrows. Today, a pillar at the site of the battle bears testament to the valor of the Spartans. Its inscription reads: "Stranger, go tell the Lacedaemonians [another name for Spartans] that we lie here obedient to their word."

Later generations continue to marvel at the heroism of those who fought in the Battle of Thermopylae, but at the time, Leonidas's sacrifice seemed to have accomplished little. Xerxes's army was still an immense force, despite the losses it had suffered. Central Greece quickly capitulated, and the Persians advanced deeper into the peninsula. The Athenians evacuated their beloved city when they realized that no army stood between it and Xerxes. They watched from afar as the

Thermopylae pass.

2 Herodotus, *The Histories*, 493.

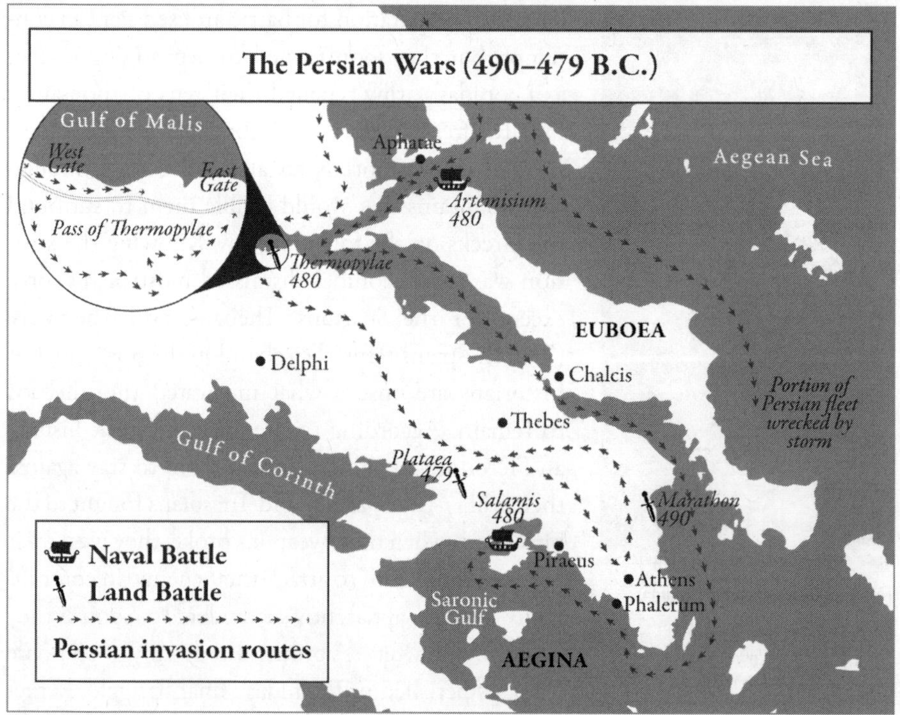

enemy burned Athens to the ground and destroyed the temples of their gods. Persian revenge against Athens seemed fulfilled.

One Greek force remained to challenge the Persians: the fleet led by the Athenians. It was situated in a bay that could only be entered through the straits between the Greek mainland and the island of Salamis. Xerxes initially avoided battle, but the wily Athenian leader Themistocles spread rumors that the Greeks were fighting among themselves. Xerxes therefore directed his ships to enter the straits—despite the advice of Artemisia, the queen of Halicarnassus, who personally led part of his fleet. In his confidence, Xerxes even set up his throne on the mountain overlooking this area so that he could observe the final capitulation of the Greeks and reward the commanders who performed well.

Xerxes gravely underestimated Greek resolve and cunning. The next day the Greek ships pretended to flee, drawing the Persians deeper into the straits before attacking their opponents who were confined by the tight quarters. The Persian losses were devastating. Of the estimated 800 vessels with which they entered the battle, almost half were lost, while the Greeks lost only about forty of their 375 vessels. Xerxes watched the destruction in helpless frustration from above. The wiser Artemisia avoided the slaughter by ramming and sinking another Persian ship to escape.

This **Battle of Salamis** (480 BC) marked a crucial turning point in the Persian War. With their navy now powerless, the Persians could no longer cross the Isthmus of Corinth into the Peloponnesus and complete the conquest of Greece. Instead, their army was now isolated on the mainland, giving the Greek *poleis* time to assemble their united forces to attack the invaders. By 479 BC, they had gathered the largest Greek army in history—about eighty thousand troops. Xerxes had departed Greece to attend to other areas of his empire, leaving behind the general Mardonius in command of an army of about one hundred thousand. Throughout the battles against Persia, the Greeks had shown that, if they could fight their enemy at close quarters, their superior weapons and armor enabled them to hold their own even when greatly outnumbered. Now with roughly equal numbers, the Greeks, led by the Spartans, soundly defeated the Persians at the Battle of Plataea (479 BC). At least half the Persian force perished.

After this battle, the Greeks took the offensive and drove the Persians out of the peninsula. Though the empire had suffered a surprising and costly defeat, this conclusion of the Persian Wars did not change its status as the most powerful realm in the Mediterranean and West Asia. For the Greeks, however, their astounding victory against overwhelming odds renewed their commitment to defending the freedom they possessed as citizens of their respective *poleis*. Their culture would achieve further triumphs in the Greek Golden Age that followed.

The Greek Golden Age

The **Greek Golden Age** (c. 500–c. 300 BC) produced many achievements in art, science, and mathematics. These accomplishments often stemmed from the Greeks' confidence that they lived in an ordered universe and that they could use human reason to explore and understand that order. This emphasis on rational explanation led a number of thinkers to question Greek polytheistic religion. As we mentioned in chapter 7, myths that indicated that gods could lie and quarrel undermined religious belief and encouraged this development of more rational, or reason-based, interpretations for natural phenomena. Early Greek astronomers and mathematicians laid the groundwork for this perspective by studying the consistency of mathematical principles as well as predicting the movements of planets and stars. This nonreligious outlook eventually encompassed other fields of endeavors such as history, philosophy, and theater. These pursuits contributed to a humanistic worldview, that is, an approach to life that focuses its attention on humanity, its deeds, its sufferings, and its quest for happiness. As our epigraph at the beginning of this chapter highlights, Greek culture celebrated these "wonders" and so promoted the importance of the individual.

History

Greek historians of the Golden Age reflected the emerging interest in establishing human explanations for the world. **Herodotus** (c. 484–c. 425 BC) was born four years before the invasion of Xerxes. In his account of the Persian Wars, he consciously emulated Homer's poetry by framing this conflict as an epic struggle between Greeks and a society from the east. Unlike Homer, who portrayed the Trojan War as orchestrated by the gods, Herodotus focused on recording the glorious deeds of men, both of Greeks and "barbarians" (that is, non-Greek peoples). While gods remained part of the world Herodotus sought to explain, they were no longer the sole agents or even leading actors.

Herodotus's younger contemporary Thucydides (c. 460–c. 400 BC) intensified this practice. Whereas Herodotus had included legends and anecdotes of divine intervention in his history, Thucydides completely removed divine activity from his account of the war between Athens and Sparta (see below). He concentrated on providing exclusively human explanations for the events of his era. This shift to explain events in terms of human activity rather than divine intervention helped lay the foundations for the modern discipline of history.

Philosophy

Even as these historians were crafting their narratives of the past, other thinkers explored the present by discussing what made for a fulfilling life. During the fourth century, the Athenian philosopher **Plato** (428–348 BC) wrote down his memories of the conversations and teachings of his mentor, **Socrates** (c. 470–399 BC). Previously, philosophers such as Thales had predominately practiced cosmology; they had sought to identify the underlying matter that composed the universe and had proposed theories suggesting that everything consisted of water, fire, air, or some other material. In contrast, Socrates shifted the discussion to questions about the intellectual and moral nature of humanity and about the relationship between the individual and the *polis*. Socrates did not write anything himself, but Plato's dialogues recounted Socrates's conversations with fellow Athenian citizens as he endeavored to define and practice virtues like justice and prudence.

Socrates realized that he did not understand what was necessary to live a fulfilled life, but he took comfort in the fact that he was aware of his lack of knowledge. While others disguised their ignorance with assumptions that were false to a greater or lesser degree, Socrates honestly admitted what he did not know—even when it was a seemingly basic idea such as "justice." His goal was to know truth itself, not to pretend to know it by teaching some half-truth or lie. Other philosophers, known as sophists, rejected Socrates's belief in objective truth. They argued that truth was

Diagram of the "Allegory of the Cave"

relative and merely an expression of individual desires. For the sophists, the highest aspiration was the mastery of rhetoric—the art of persuading others through the spoken word.

In *The Republic,* Plato laid out Socrates's theory of how humans come to truth in his famous "Allegory of the Cave." Socrates held that humans were fundamentally spiritual beings. He called this human spiritual core the soul and argued that all human souls were endowed with accurate knowledge of reality, but that they could be distracted from this knowledge by their senses. His allegory depicted the human soul as a prisoner who sits in a cave with his back to a fire. Out of view, puppeteers walk in front of the fire and their puppets cast shadows on the cave wall. The prisoner, seeing these shadows, mistakes the silhouettes for the actual objects they represent. This captive, Socrates explains, is each of us, and the shadows we see are the information we learn from our senses. The goal is to escape the cave with its limited light and puppet show and to emerge into the sunlight where we can encounter reality as it actually is. This knowledge involves not individual sense objects—such as a particular tree—but rather a universal, idealized form of "tree-ness" that embodies the perfection and qualities of all trees. For Socrates, a fulfilling life consisted in striving to contemplate these universal forms and to behold in them the Good, the

True, and the Beautiful. Sophists, meanwhile, were like prisoners who refused to leave the cave because they were too attached to their sense perceptions and desires.

Socrates's thought promoted the importance of the spiritual. He stressed that highest meaning and satisfaction were found in spiritual and intellectual pursuits rather than physical experiences. Unfortunately, his exclusive emphasis on intellectual knowledge and contemplation also implicitly denigrated the physical world. Humans were, according to his understanding, essentially spirits trapped in bodies. In fact, elsewhere Plato would write that we remember knowledge rather than learn it through life experiences. This perspective led many of Plato's disciples, known as Platonists, to have negative attitudes towards the material world, including the human body.

Socrates also challenged the traditional myths about the Greek deities, claiming that their selfish behavior was incompatible with the spiritual ideals of Goodness and Truth. In 399 BC, his enemies formally accused Socrates of impiety and of corrupting the youth. That same year, the Athenians condemned and executed him.

Socrates's death did not prevent Greek thinkers from engaging with his ideas. Plato's student **Aristotle** (384–322 BC), for example, pushed back against Socrates's hostile attitude towards the physical world. His philosophy was grounded in his scientific examination of nature. This study led him to conclude that the universe had been placed in motion by the Prime Mover. This spiritual being was uncaused in itself and yet the cause of all other movement. In other words, the Prime Mover was Aristotle's conception of a single, all-powerful God.

Aristotle integrated his study of the natural world into his theory of human nature. He accepted that human knowledge and satisfaction were primarily spiritual and intellectual but argued that this knowledge originated in human sense experience before being understood by the intellect. Aristotle, therefore, rejected the notion that humans were spirits imprisoned by their bodies and instead proposed that an individual was a material component (a body) moved or animated by a spiritual component (a soul).

This view of human nature shaped Aristotle's theory of ethics, where he argued that individual experiences shaped overall human behavior. For Aristotle, humans found happiness and fulfilment by practicing virtuous activity, and he defined a virtue as the habit of choosing the mean, or middle, behavior between two dangerous extremes. For example, by repeatedly navigating the balance between reckless spending and miserly thrift, an individual would eventually practice the virtue of generosity habitually.

Aristotle extended these ideas to his political philosophy. He proposed that the overall whole of a society was composed of individual families, who formed the most fundamental social unit; groups of families formed villages, and villages formed states. For Aristotle, the purpose of government was the promotion and encouragement of virtue among its citizens. He was therefore deeply skeptical of what he saw as the extreme liberty and chaos of Athenian democracy and instead was more supportive of structures like monarchy that were more stable and authoritative. The Aristotelian understanding of how an individual gained knowledge and lived virtuously exerted a powerful influence on future intellectual movements in the history of Western Civilization, most notably on medieval scholasticism, as future chapters will discuss.

Theater

Even as Socrates, Plato, and Aristotle developed their sophisticated theories regarding human nature and its flourishing, Greek interest in the human person found expression in theatrical performances. These productions, both comedies and tragedies, surveyed the emotional complexities and challenges of life. Greek theater had its origins in the performance of religious rituals. The Greeks believed that the gods deserved to be worshipped in public ceremonies that represented the participation of the whole community. Even those who questioned the traditional myths, such as Socrates, still participated. Among the foremost of these celebrations was the springtime festival in honor of Dionysus, the god of fertility and wine. Processions, songs, and sacrifices characterized the annual observances. A highlight of the procession came when one man stepped aside from the others to sing. His mournful song represented the goat who would soon be sacrificed to Dionysus, and his performance was known as the "song of the goat" (*tragoidia* in Greek). (This is the origin of our term "tragedy.") In answer, the other worshippers sang in chorus and responded to the "goat's" cries. Eventually, this grew into a dialogue between the "goat" and the chorus, which, in turn, evolved into a dramatic performance that became a part of Dionysus's worship.

By 508 BC, a theatrical festival in honor of Dionysus had been established in Athens. Tax revenues sponsored a competition among playwrights who composed a series of plays for the event. These productions were presented in an open-air theater built from stone. This could seat over ten thousand people, and its remarkable acoustics allowed the audience to hear the actors even when they were whispering. Men, women, children, and even prisoners attended the performances. The actors were assigned to perform in specific plays by lot and wore masks that both concealed the actors' identities and signified the role they were playing. These even helped project the actors' voices. In a circular area below the stage, known as the orchestra, the chorus danced and sang. An altar to Dionysus was placed in the middle of this area. Around 465 BC, a backdrop known as the *skene* was added to productions. Our modern term "scene" has its origins in these first "scenic" backgrounds.

Other *poleis* participated in the growing tradition of dramatic performances, and theaters proliferated throughout the Greek world. Playwrights drew inspiration for their tragedies primarily from their traditional mythology. Though audiences already knew these stories, skillful authors emphasized certain themes or characters so that those attending the performance were thrilled to experience familiar stories made new, as it were, through the drama's interpretation. Tragedies engaged with questions about whether individuals shaped their own destiny or whether their fate was controlled by the gods. The sufferings of the human protagonists demonstrated the apparent limitations of their freedom while simultaneously revealing the great dignity of human nature as understood by the Greeks. On the lighter side, Greek comedies typically satirized current politicians and political debates and were full of raucous humor.

The Athenian theater of the Golden Age produced three renowned playwrights: Aeschylus, Sophocles, and Euripides. Aeschylus (525–456 BC) was a veteran who fought at Marathon, Salamis, and Plataea. He wrote ninety plays, only seven of which survive today. Drama had its origins in the exchange between the "goat" and a chorus, and the first plays imitated this structure. Aeschylus, however, introduced a second speaking role in Greek plays, initiating the practice of dialogue between two characters on stage, accompanied by the chorus. In his tragedies, Aeschylus defended the justice of the gods. In the *Oresteia*, for example, he dramatized the sordid tale of how Clytemnestra and her lover Aegisthus murdered her husband Agamemnon when he returned from Troy. According to the myth, Clytemnestra herself soon faced death when her son Orestes avenged his father by striking her down. However, this act of matricide deserved its own punishment, and Orestes was tormented by the Furies. The costumes for these goddesses, who were described as having hate drip from their very eyes, were apparently so terrifying that pregnant women in the audience went into labor. Aeschylus used this myth to suggest to his audience that the gods were guiding human beings away from the vicious cycle of violent revenge and promoting a more just system of jury trials in Athens.

The **Mask of Agamemnon**. Made of gold c. 1500 BC. Currently in the National Archaeological Museum of Athens, Greece. This funeral mask was found at the archaeological site of Mycenae, Greece. Despite its name, we do not know to whom it belonged.

Sophocles (497–405 BC) was an aristocrat who had led the boys' chorus in the celebration of the victory at Salamis. Between 465 and 405 BC, he won twenty-four of the thirty competitions he entered. His innovative contribution to Greek theater was the introduction of a third speaking role, which made multiple stage conversations possible. Sophocles was a pious Greek, but he did not share Aeschylus's confidence that he could explain how the gods' will always benefited humanity. Instead, Sophocles's plots introduced situations where there was no clear solution. His so-called *Theban Plays*, for example, highlighted the suffering that resulted when

SLAVERY IN GREEK SOCIETY

Slavery had existed in Greece at least since the Mycenaean period. By the end of the eighth century BC, it was such an integral part of everyday life that only the very poor did not own slaves. This practice continued in the Archaic and Golden Ages of Greek history. Each *polis* had its own significant slave population. About a quarter of the Athenian population was in servitude, and Sparta's *helots* made up as much as 80 percent of its inhabitants.

Individuals did not become slaves because they were from a particular race or background, as in some other societies. Rather, force of circumstance typically ended their freedom. Usually, they were war captives or had become so indebted they were compelled to sell themselves into slavery. Though there were variations in practice among the different *poleis*, slaves generally possessed few, if any, social, legal, or political rights. For example, it was common for them not to be able to testify in court or to own property. Their families were typically not recognized by the *polis*, and children born to slaves inherited their parents' servile status. In theory, they could purchase their freedom, but this was rare and normally required a kind master who was willing to let them save money or grant them a loan.

Most slaves engaged in agricultural labor, though others worked in the households of their masters. While domestic work presumably offered a more comfortable environment, it also brought its own dangers of personal abuse, particularly to female slaves. Other slaves were the property of the *polis* and served to construct and maintain public infrastructure. The most degrading and deadly occupation was work in mines and quarries. There, shifts lasted as long as ten hours and the toil continued around the clock.

As far as we know, there were no abolitionists in Greek society. Even the most brilliant minds of ancient Greece took slavery for granted. Aristotle, for example, considered slaves as living property. He acknowledged that some had become slaves through misfortune but argued that there were many humans who lacked the ability to live rationally. These, he concluded, benefitted from serving their masters, who could direct their lives towards rational ends. Though Greek culture celebrated the individual, many were blind to the common human dignity they shared with those enslaved about them.

the protagonist, Oedipus, unwittingly fulfilled a prophecy that he would murder his father and marry his mother. These dramas featured impossible choices, which made for great drama, but which also pointed to a weakening of traditional piety. For example, the epigraph from *Antigone* that opened this chapter was an affirmation of the classic Greek optimism and esteem for human achievement, but the play itself was a tragedy that involved the destruction of Antigone, a young woman forced to choose between loyalty to her brother and to her *polis*. Another example comes from *Oedipus the King*, considered by Aristotle to be the model tragedy. This tells of Oedipus's genuine efforts to punish a great wrong only to realize at the end that *he* was the (unsuspecting) villain he sought to punish. Audiences probably writhed in their seats as they heard Oedipus's dialogue, which they realized foreshadowed future suffering but which the doomed king did not.

Sophocles's contemporary Euripides (480–406 BC) reflected the growing loss of confidence in the traditional order of Greek culture. His plots emphasized the arbitrary pettiness and destructiveness of the gods while his protagonists openly doubted divine wisdom. He rejected Aeschylus's and Sophocles's portrayal of suffering as ennobling and instead showed how it could debase an individual. His ability to explore complex human emotions gave his plays great depth, but he was never as popular as the more optimistic Sophocles. Nonetheless, Euripides's unsympathetic attitude toward traditional relationships and piety underscored how that older worldview was rapidly crumbling in the midst of the Peloponnesian War.

The Peloponnesian War

Euripides's skepticism reflected Greece's growing political turmoil as destructive competition replaced the spirit of cooperation among those city-states who had resisted Persia. The seeds for this rivalry began when some city-states turned to the rebuilt Athens for leadership and protection. In 476 BC, these *poleis* formed the **Delian League**, an alliance of city-states intended to protect one another against any future Persian aggression. The League met once a year at Delos, the mythological birthplace of Apollo, and they maintained a common treasury there. (This connection to Delos gave the alliance its name.) Each *polis* held one vote. The larger city-states contributed ships to the League, while the smaller ones contributed taxes to pay for the construction of additional vessels in Athenian shipyards.

Athens soon dominated the Delian League. It was the most powerful of the allies and came to see its fellow members as subordinates rather than equals. In 468 BC, when the *polis* of Naxos attempted to withdraw from the League, Athens led a fleet against its own ally and conquered it. Naxos lost its membership privileges and was reduced to the status of a conquered territory. Soon the Delian League

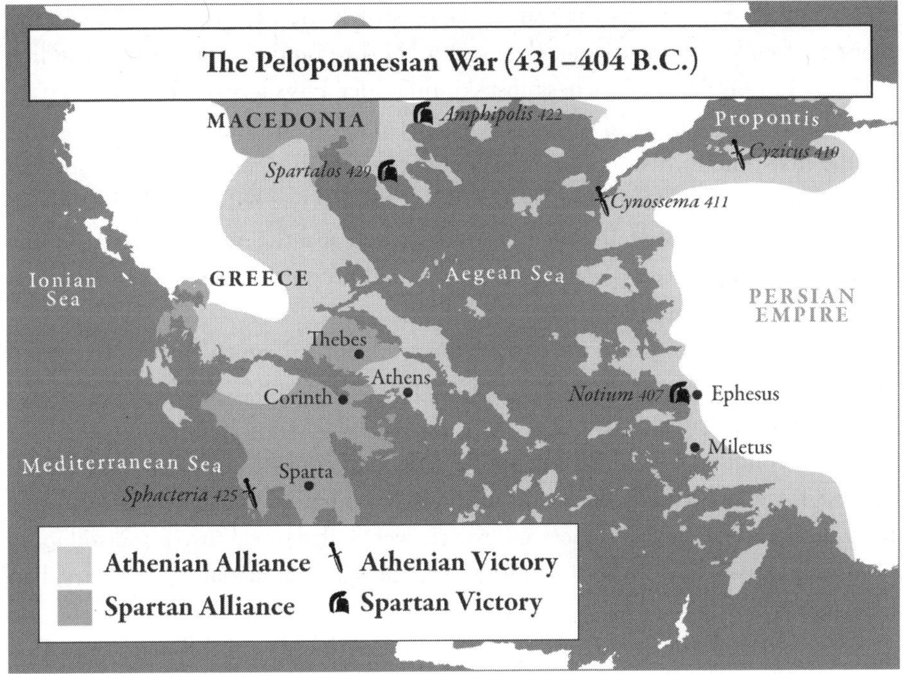

controlled most of the Greek cities in the Aegean and the Black Seas, giving Athens commercial dominance of the eastern Mediterranean. In 454 BC, Athens relocated the League's treasury from Delos to Athens; from this point onwards, the Athenian Assembly effectively ruled the League. The democracy of Athens was rapidly becoming a tyrant over its allies.

Other *poleis* realized that unchecked Athenian power could threaten their own independence and turned to Sparta for protection. These cities formed the Peloponnesian League. As Athens increasingly interfered with these city-states, attacking them and imposing crippling trade restrictions, the Spartans faced a choice of either going to war or seeing their influence collapse. They chose war.

The resulting **Peloponnesian War** (431–404 BC) was ancient Greece's most destructive war. Ironically, it occurred at the same time as much of the cultural flourishing described above. (Socrates, for example, fought in one of its early battles.) Neither Greek superpower had the capacity or desire to expend the resources necessary to defeat the other conclusively. Nonetheless, aggressive politicians on both sides continued to encourage the conflict. The first phase of the war followed a predictable pattern. Sparta would invade Athenian territory each year and destroy Athenian crops, forcing the populace to retreat behind the fortifications of the city itself. Athens would then use its navy to attack Spartan allies from the sea.

In the second year of the war, a plague struck the overcrowded Athens and raged for four years. Approximately one third of the population perished, including Pericles (495–429 BC), Athens's most skillful leader. His successor's aggressive policies seemed to be successful at first. They even led to the surrender of a Spartan army for the first time in history, but Sparta countered with a campaign that captured Athens's important silver mines. By 421 BC, both sides wanted peace. The Athenian farmers were weary of seeing their crops destroyed and the Spartans were running out of troops. Peace terms were agreed upon and prewar boundaries restored. Ten years of war had resolved nothing.

Direct conflict between the two *poleis* ceased, but Athens still sought to expand the power of the Delian League at Sparta's expense. In 414 BC, the Athenians sent a large force west against Syracuse in Sicily. This island was rich in resources, and they hoped its conquest would further secure Athenian control of the Mediterranean. Although the expedition began promisingly, it ended in disaster. Approximately forty thousand Athenian soldiers and rowers were killed or captured, and still more significantly, two hundred ships were lost. Athens's great advantage, its navy, had been destroyed.

Sparta seized this opportunity to recommence the war the following year. This time, an old enemy of Athens aided them. The Spartans formed an alliance with the Persians, granting them uncontested control over the Greek *poleis* in Anatolia in exchange for Persian funds to build a Spartan navy. Amazingly, the Athenians rallied to build a new navy and even defeated the Spartan fleet! Sparta hurriedly proposed peace on the same terms as before. Athens refused. Its pro-war politicians exploited the instability of Athenian democracy to create a paranoid mob that was willing to vote for the death or exile of anyone who favored bringing the war to an end. Finally, backed by Persian funds, the Spartans were able to destroy the second Athenian fleet and blockade Athens by land and sea. In 404 BC, the Athenians were forced to surrender and give up their empire. The Spartans destroyed the walls that protected the city and forced Athens to make peace with them.

Although Sparta had won the war, it was too exhausted to lead Greece effectively. In reality, the Persians were the great victors of the Peloponnesian War. They both had their revenge on Athens and realized that their great wealth allowed them to influence the policies of the Greek city-states. They began to use their resources to propel different *poleis* into prominence; once their current favorite became too successful, the Persians redirected their riches and promoted a competing *polis*. The result was chronic warfare as Persian wealth encouraged various city-states to attempt to dominate their neighbors in exchange for acknowledging Persian rule in Ionia.

Nothing symbolized the self-inflicted decline of Greece better than the destruction of the Athenian democracy at the end of the Peloponnesian War. Sparta, previously the defender of Greek independence, now forced Athens to accept the rule of the Thirty Tyrants. These Spartan-backed rulers promptly executed over a thousand political opponents and exiled five thousand more. The ambition and blindness of Athenian politicians had led democracy to disaster, and now the general populace suffered the consequences of their officials' policies. Democracy—with its self-serving politicians and inflammatory rhetoric—had enabled, rather than prevented, the Athenians' tragedy.

Conclusion

The fifth century BC was a pivotal period for Greek civilization. The Greeks collectively achieved *arete*, or excellence, by successfully uniting to defeat the Persians and thus preserving the independence of the Greek *poleis*. Their victories against overwhelming odds inspired and supported the immense achievements of the Greek Golden Age in the fields of history, philosophy, and drama. These accomplishments deepened their understanding of human nature, its most profound goals, its most dramatic emotions, and its role in history. The value of the individual was at the forefront of their culture. Yet this emphasis on the individual came with a risk. The different city-states were unable to create a stable political environment as different governments sought to gain dominance. Sophists encouraged individual ambition and justified the use of rhetoric to sway the masses for selfish ends. Unbridled competition and rivalry pitted Sparta and Athens against one another in a destructive war. In its aftermath, the desire for power and wealth spread and led Greeks to sacrifice the freedom their fathers and grandfathers had died to secure. Persia, once their most feared and hated enemy, had become their most useful ally in defeating their fellow Greeks. What the Athenians, Spartans, and others failed to realize was that the Greek peninsula had been conquered in all but name.

CHAPTER 10

Alexander the Great and the Hellenistic World

Who is he, and what has he achieved, to assume the right to vilify [Alexander,] a man of that stature who reached the height of human success and made himself unambiguously king of two continents, with his name spread throughout the whole world? By comparison the critic is an insignificant creature, toiling away at some insignificant work, and not even master of that.

Arrian, *The Anabasis*[1]

Under the shadow of the mountains in northeast Afghanistan, in one of the remotest areas in the world, lie the ruins of Ai Khanoum. In AD 1961, the Afghan king discovered this site during a hunting expedition. While ancient sites can be found throughout central and western Asia, a team of French archaeologists discovered that Ai Khanoum had more in common with Athens than Afghanistan. Among their finds were one of the largest gymnasia of the ancient world, a six-thousand-seat theater, and temples to Greek gods, all built using Greek techniques. Even its statues that represented local deities had been crafted in a Greek style. How had the Greeks, whom we left in the last chapter fighting with one another and manipulated by Persian wealth, spread their culture so far afield?

The answer is the young Macedonian king known to history as Alexander the Great. While he reigned for only thirteen years, Alexander transformed the legacy of ancient Greece and the trajectory of Western Civilization by exporting Greek culture from the eastern Mediterranean to Egypt, West and Central Asia, and even to India. Ai Khanoum, which some archaeologists believe was originally named

1 Arrian, *Alexander the Great: The Anabasis and the Indica*, trans. by Martin Hammond (Oxford: Oxford University Press, 2013), 224–225.

"Alexandria," demonstrates the amazing influence of this man who gave his name and culture to locations over three thousand miles from his homeland.

In this chapter, we examine the historical context of Alexander's rise to power and explore how Greek society developed after his conquests. As we will see, Greek culture did not remain static but evolved significantly during this era of expansion. While some peoples embraced this new "Hellenistic" culture, others, most notably the Jews, resented the expectation that they conform their traditions and beliefs to Greek standards. The ensuing war between partisans of Judaism and Greek culture demonstrated both the prominence and the limitations of Alexander's legacy.

Philip II and the Rise of Macedon

To the north of Greece lay **Macedon**. This kingdom was more fertile and less mountainous than the Greek peninsula to the south, and it could sustain the domestication of horses. Cavalry therefore became an integral part of its military. Furthermore, the frequent dangers posed by nomadic raiders from the north meant that Macedon, in contrast to the Greek *poleis*, never lost the need for kings who could unify and command the whole kingdom. These rulers governed in collaboration with an assembly of the army, which included the Macedonian nobility. These aristocrats formed the elite cavalry force known as the king's "companions."

The Greeks and the Macedonians were unsure what to make of one another. Macedonians thought the Greeks were effeminate and unruly. Greeks, in turn, saw Macedonian culture as barbaric and dangerous. While sources indicate that Macedonian life did emphasize hunting, drinking, and blood feuds, they also maintained a consistent interest in the intellectual achievements of their neighbors to the south. They invited Socrates to come to Macedon and teach philosophy, but he refused. The playwright Euripides was said to have accepted a similar invitation after he was driven out of Athens, but he was reportedly killed by a pack of wild dogs. Perhaps Greek impressions of Macedon were not far from the mark.

Greeks and Macedonians came into closer contact during the reign of **Philip II** (r. 359–336 BC). During the period after the Peloponnesian War, the city of Thebes briefly became the most powerful Greek *polis*. Despite being outnumbered, they had defeated a Spartan army at the Battle of Leuctra in 373 BC by deploying an innovative military tactic known as an oblique formation. Traditionally, Greek leaders placed their best soldiers on their right flank, that is the right-most position of the army. In contrast, the Thebans at Leuctra arranged their soldiers so that their *left* flank was the most powerful by quadrupling the number of men in this leftmost column. This weakened their own center and right flank, but, as the two armies marched towards each other, the Thebans held back at an angle these depleted portions of their force.

This oblique formation allowed their massive left to attack and crush the Spartan right before the other sections of the army were fully engaged. Soon the oversized Theban left threatened to surround the utterly bewildered Spartan army, and they fled the battlefield. Five years later, the Thebans likewise defeated the Macedonians and took the teenage Philip as a political hostage. He spent three years in Thebes and received Greek intellectual formation and Theban military training.

Philip put both to good use when he became king in 359 BC. He improved the Macedonian military, making the infantry more mobile and equipping them with longer pikes than the spears used by Greek *phalanxes*. Philip also developed a corps of engineers who constructed siege equipment and kept the army supplied. This made longer, more effective campaigns possible. These reforms, combined with the traditional Macedonian cavalry charge, made his army the most effective military force in the Mediterranean world.

Philip displayed a keen sense of strategy in his efforts to expand Macedonian influence. He seized Greek colonies on the Aegean coast that had access to gold and silver mines and used these resources to fund his future campaigns. He next exploited the division among the Greek *poleis* to isolate and then force individual city-states

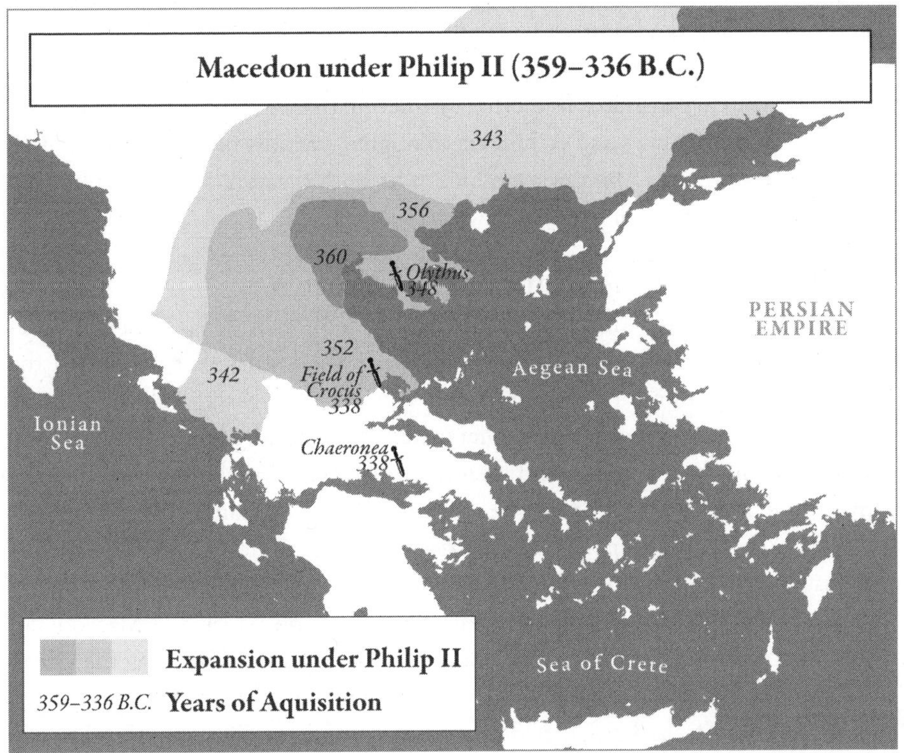

to "ally" with him. Their constant bickering and competition blinded them to the threat, even though the Athenian orator Demosthenes warned that Philip intended to conquer all Greece.

Indeed, Philip effectively controlled the peninsula after defeating a combined Athenian-Theban army at the Battle of Chaeronea in 338 BC. While he promised to defend Greece from Persian interference, he also established the League of Corinth and compelled all *poleis* to join it. This confederation was, of course, led by Macedon. At a banquet held to celebrate both his own wedding and this peace agreement among the Greeks, a standard-bearer carried Philip's image in procession alongside depictions of the twelve principal gods of Mount Olympus. The message was clear: a "thirteenth god" now exercised power throughout Greece.

This wedding celebration proved to be Philip's undoing. His new marriage alliance involved the rejection of his former wife Olympias. She was ruthless in the pursuit of her own ambitions and those of her son. Philip's repudiation threatened them both, and she probably orchestrated Philip's assassination two years later. Her twenty-year-old son, **Alexander** (r. 336–323 BC), seized control and killed anyone in his family who posed a threat to his position. He had received an elite intellectual education under the tutorship of the philosopher Aristotle and a rigorous physical training in the Spartan tradition from one of his uncles. He had already shown his bravery and ability to lead during the Battle of Chaeronea when he commanded Philip's cavalry. Furthermore, his mother taught him that he was the son of Zeus and descended from Hercules and Achilles, two mighty warriors of Greek legend. This formation and presumed lineage gave Alexander both the ability and the ambition to attempt the conquest of the known world.

The Conquests of Alexander the Great

Many Greeks expected that Macedonian control of their *poleis* would disintegrate when Philip died. They did not understand the loyalty that permeated the Macedonian army, nor did they appreciate his son Alexander's unparalleled military ability. When Thebes rebelled, Alexander marched five hundred miles in two weeks, defeated the shocked Thebans, and then razed their city. Six thousand died in the carnage, and thirty thousand more were sold into slavery. Alexander had dramatically displayed two predominant characteristics: his daring military leadership and his ruthless punishment of those who resisted him. Other *poleis* quickly fell into line.

In 334 BC, Alexander led an army of forty thousand Greek and Macedonian troops into Anatolia, vowing to carry out his father's plan of liberating the Greek cities in Ionia from Persian rule. While invading the mighty Persian Empire might appear reckless, Alexander had two important advantages. First, the Greeks were confident in their training and in Alexander's leadership. They had learned during the fifth century that they could overcome Persia's superior numbers if they could fight in close quarters.

Second, Persian authority was unstable. King of Kings Darius III (r. 336–330 BC) had only come to power after a murderous palace coup. He was inexperienced and lacked the necessary respect of his *satraps* to respond effectively to Alexander's invasion. At the same time, some, especially in Egypt, were eager to welcome Alexander as their liberator. Darius also failed to use Persian money to encourage Greek resistance to Macedonian rule at home, which might have proved an effective strategy. In short, the Macedonian army—experienced, disciplined, and loyal—was primed for success in Asia due to its own strengths and Persia's current weakness.

The Persians foolishly allowed Alexander to enter West Asia unopposed in 334 BC. The Macedonian king first made a point of visiting Troy, the site of Greece's famous victory and the location where his "ancestor" Achilles had won immortal glory. Soon thereafter, he defeated a Persian army at the Battle of the Granicus. Alexander was almost killed leading the decisive cavalry charge, but his personal bravery inspired the admiration of his troops. He celebrated this battle not as a victory of the Macedonian Empire but as the triumph of all Greeks over the Persians. This act of propaganda swayed the Ionian

The ***Alexander Mosaic***. Made of over a million tiny painted tiles c. 120–100 BC. It is currently in the National Archaeological Museum in Naples, Italy. This floor mosaic originally came from the House of the Faun in Pompeii, Italy. It likely depicts the Battle of Issus between Alexander the Great (far left) and Darius III of Persia (center).

The ***Hermes Azara***. Made of marble c. 1st century AD. Currently in the Louvre Museum, Paris, France. This a Roman copy of a bronze sculpture of Alexander the Great which has been lost. Lysippos, the personal sculptor of Alexander, made the bronze original c. 4th century BC.

Greeks to join the League of Corinth and accept Macedonian rule.

Alexander defeated a second army at the Battle of Issus and marched south to secure the Mediterranean coast. Most cities surrendered immediately, but Tyre and Gaza resisted. Tyre seemed secure from foreign conquest; it was half a mile from the seashore, and the sea, at its deepest, was hundreds of feet. Alexander spent eight months building a pier—a platform on pillars reaching out from the mainland to the citadel—from which his troops could bombard the city. Using vessels from his new allies along the Mediterranean, he finally took the city after a seven-month siege. He crucified two thousand inhabitants and sold the rest into slavery. When he captured Gaza, the young king dragged its ruler's body behind his chariot in grim imitation of the *Iliad*'s account of Achilles's desecration of Hector's body. The Egyptians, by contrast, welcomed Alexander and treated him as the son of a god.

The final battle against Darius took place in 331 BC at Gaugamela in Mesopotamia. Darius had assembled yet another large army—estimates range from 100,000 to 250,000—and had even flattened the ground to make the terrain more suitable for his chariots. Alexander could have forced the Persians to fight him on another battlefield, but he recognized that, if he defeated Darius here, he could capture the whole Persian Empire. Apparently, Alexander was so confident of victory that he overslept on the morning of the battle. He defeated the Persians by using the oblique formation first introduced by the Thebans. When the Greeks charged, the weight of their attack applied more concentrated pressure to a specific point in the Persian line than if they had attacked all at once across a wide front. Although the Persian right flank achieved some success against the Macedonian left, Darius lost his nerve and fled from the battlefield. Disenchanted Persians murdered him shortly thereafter. The Persian army, as well as the empire it defended, collapsed. Alexander claimed the title of "king of kings" and captured Babylon, Susa, and Persepolis, the Persian capital. This last city he burned to the ground in revenge for Xerxes's destruction of Athens.

He then campaigned to the north into Afghanistan and Central Asia. Here his army encountered mountain strongholds covered with ice and snow, yet they were still victorious. The young king inspired his soldiers with his willingness to endure their hardships and to help stragglers. These campaigns were perhaps Alexander's greatest triumphs; few armies in the two thousand years that followed have achieved such military success in Afghanistan. Alexander's final campaign took place in northwestern India. Here the Macedonians encountered new dangers: huge rivers, terrifying snakes, war elephants, and inhabitants that fought fiercely from village to village. Even though Alexander was still victorious in battle, by now his troops had had enough of campaigning. They had marched over three thousand miles and had been away from their homes for eight years. They refused to comply with his ambition to conquer the entire Indian subcontinent.

Deeply disappointed, Alexander eventually agreed to turn back. He decided to return to Babylon by marching through the outer reaches of his empire, the southernmost deserts of Iran. Here, the desert heat and the hit-and-run tactics of local tribes inflicted the greatest losses Alexander ever experienced. More soldiers died on this march than during all the previous battles combined. Alexander himself was wounded in the lung by an arrow and never walked without pain again.

Once back in Babylon, Alexander suffered another loss—the death of his closest friend, Hephaestion. Again, in imitation of the *Iliad*, he ordered his horses' manes and tails to be shorn as part of elaborate mourning and funeral rituals. From this point

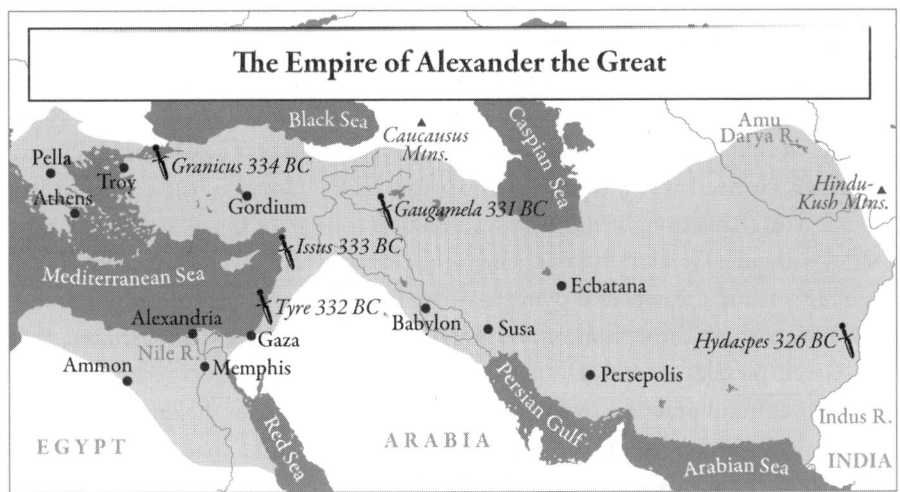

onwards, Alexander appears to have sunk into a state of depression. He drank heavily, further damaging his already weakened health. He developed a severe fever, which some suggest was brought on by poison, and died in 323 BC at the age of thirty-two.

The **Theater of Pergamon**. Constructed in the 3rd century BC. Pergamon, located in modern Turkey, was a rich and powerful ancient Greek city that became a center of Hellenistic culture. Its theater is still largely intact and seats 10,000 people. Pergamon is a UNESCO World Heritage site.

Hellenization

Alexander's empire quickly broke apart, but the effects of his conquests endured. He and his army had introduced Greek culture throughout West Asia and beyond. This was partly because Alexander founded seventeen new colonies, such as the one discovered at Ai Khanoum. (These he humbly named "Alexandria" after himself.) As Greek emigrants settled in these places, their values and their language became a foundation that united these hitherto disparate regions. Language was particularly important for developing this shared culture. Most spoke *Koine* (literally, "common") Greek. This simplified dialect was relatively easy to learn and enabled non-Greek peoples to have access to Greek literature and philosophy more easily. The ideas contained in these texts became part of the collective cultural identity. Historians call this shared culture "**Hellenistic**" and the process by which this culture developed "Hellenization." These terms derive from the Greek term "*Hellenes*," the name that Greeks used to identify themselves.

Though he did not live long enough to see it flourish, Alexander desired this adoption of Greek culture throughout his realm. He was well aware that he could not rule the inhabitants of his new lands as conquered slaves if he wished his empire to survive. He needed to integrate them as citizens. For example, he recruited thirty thousand Afghans to fight in his army. Practical aspects of Greek culture became part of daily life. Greek military science and tactics spread throughout Alexander's conquests, while theaters and gymnasia—built using Greek architectural styles—were constructed throughout these regions. These projects demonstrated that non-Greek peoples were not only adopting Greek construction techniques but also their cultural practices by building the same buildings for the same uses. Even as far away as India, sculptors created statues of the Buddha that reflected Greek influence in their artistic realism and proportionality.

Buddha Shakyamuni Meditating in the Indrashala Cave [top] **and Buddha Dipankara** [bottom]. Made of schist, c. AD 101-300 in Gandhara (modern Pakistan). Currently in the Art Institute of Chicago in Chicago, Illinois. This relief is notable for the striking contrast between the traditional Eastern depiction of the meditating Buddha in the upper portion and the Hellenized Buddha in the lower portion who is standing, receiving visitors, and even has a classical Greek Hercules as a body guard.

These changes did not flow in one direction only. The cultures of these lands began to exercise a similar influence in Greek society, especially in the areas of education and politics. Just as exposure to Mesopotamian knowledge had encouraged Ionian learning in the Archaic Age, so now even easier access to Persian and Babylonian insights inspired further Greek achievements. During this period, Euclid (fl. 300 BC) developed his famous textbook, the *Elements*, which demonstrated proofs for geometric theories. Meanwhile, Archimedes (287–212 BC) discovered how to calculate the areas of circles and parabolas and laid the foundations for modern calculus.

It was in government, however, that Persia most influenced Greek culture. Alexander adopted Persian court customs. Previous Macedonian kings were leaders of the assembly of warriors; Alexander now walked in the footsteps of the Persian king of kings and required his subjects to prostrate themselves in his presence. Greeks and Macedonians alike found such behavior demeaning to their sense of freedom, but Alexander's successors adopted similar practices.

Hellenistic Society

The dying Alexander was said to have left his empire "to the strongest." This clearly did not include his infant son or his mentally impaired half-brother Philip. Each of these attempted to seize power (or, rather, others sought to seize it on their behalf) and were ultimately executed. In the end, Alexander's generals divided his conquests into four separate empires. His cousin Cassander (r. 305–297 BC) claimed the throne of Macedon; Antigonus (r. 306–301 BC) seized most of Anatolia; Seleucus (r. 305–281 BC) took control of Babylon and the eastern territories; and to the south, Ptolemy (r. 305–282 BC) secured Egypt. All of these rulers, with the

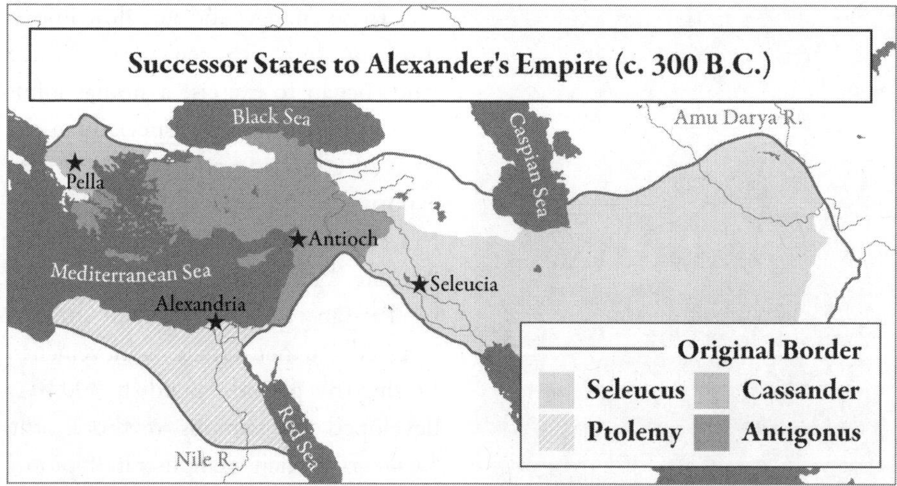

exception of Cassander, founded dynasties named after them, and "Antigonids," "Seleucids," and "Ptolemies" competed against one another for dominance.

These rulers faced the challenge of governing a complex diversity of different ethnicities, languages, and religious practices. The process of Hellenization certainly helped in this regard, but its influence was uneven. Empires faced different local challenges and traditions while some specific regions within a given empire were, as we will see, unsympathetic to the ideals of Hellenistic culture. Furthermore, the generals-turned-emperors realized that not *everything* Greek was desirable for their new realms. In the traditional Greek *polis*, citizens performed all the roles of government and military as their duty. While this encouraged a sense of freedom and self-determination, it also led to the chaos and infighting that had dominated the *poleis* during the Peloponnesian War. Something needed to change if the new empires were to enjoy peace and stability.

The Hellenistic *cosmopolis* (literally, "world city") thus replaced the Greek *polis*. Whereas *poleis* were relatively small and included one major city and its surrounding territory, the *cosmopoleis* engulfed vast areas and populations. The government of these states was very different. Monarchs now wielded absolute authority, and a divide emerged between the ruling elite and everyone else, which contrasted starkly with the *polis's* sense of equality among its citizens. In Ptolemaic Egypt, for example, Greeks and upper-class Egyptians spoke Greek and benefitted from a Greek legal system, while the rest of the population lived as they had before. (Manetho, who wrote the history of Egypt that we discussed in chapter 4, was a part of this Greek-speaking elite.)

Contributing to the divide between elite and everyone else was the professionalization of warfare and government. Motivation from a sense of duty or desire for personal glory all but disappeared among soldiers and statesmen. This transformation had begun in the period immediately following the Peloponnesian War, but it reached its climax in the Hellenistic empires. Soldiers fought for money and switched sides based on the amount offered. Government officials, meanwhile, carried out administrative tasks not out of civic duty but for income. These new values reduced the importance of individuals who were not wealthy. They were no longer crucial *citizens* of a small community who debated about causes close to heart and home; they were now insignificant *subjects* of absolute monarchs. Such persons were easily replaced by someone similarly expendable.

As individuals became politically superfluous, they paradoxically became the focus of Hellenistic culture. Without an opportunity to play a significant role in the decisions and actions of the community, individuals increasingly focused on their own interests and comforts (see chapter insert on Hellenistic philosophies). Ironically, as men found themselves excluded from public decision making, women became more prominent in society. Previously, Greek women had been generally restricted in their public appearances and had few interactions outside of the home. When they realized that Greek males in foreign lands desired Greek wives, many Greek women seized the opportunity to demand more freedoms. Potential brides in Egypt, for example, now set the terms for their marriages and even stipulated monetary recompense if their husbands failed to live up to their expectations.

The **Grave *Naiskos* of an Enthroned Woman with an Attendant**. Made of marble, c. 100 BC. Currently in the Getty Villa Museum, Los Angeles, California. A *naiskos* is a small temple or shine frequently found at graves. In this *naiskos*, a woman wears bracelets on her wrists and upper arm and sits upon an elegant chair carved with an eagle and lion paws. Her obvious wealth and dignity reflect the increased prominence of women in late Hellenistic culture.

The art of this period reflected this shift to domestic life and featured numerous personal portraits and busts. Even the depictions of the gods changed. Praxiteles's Apollo did not display the austerity of divinity but instead a human beauty that was even slightly effeminate. The portrayal of the gods as the human figures of the past encouraged the deification of contemporary rulers, who were increasingly promoted as living gods for their subjects.

Rulers might claim divine honors, but that was not the only religious change during this period. When the

HELLENISTIC PHILOSOPHIES

Individuals in the Hellenistic *cosmopoleis* lacked the ability to influence their communities as had their Greek ancestors of old. They turned away from the traditional ideal of individual heroism or participation in their cities' governments and instead resigned themselves to political insignificance and focused on their own personal lives and pleasures. Such attitudes were reflected in the major philosophies that developed during this era.

Cynicism, whose name derived from the Greek word for "dog," was associated with Diogenes of Sinope (412–323 BC). This controversial figure taught that individuals have little control over their lives. Chance determined one's fate, so rather than struggle against it we should break free from social conventions and the things of the world, including the obligations and rights of marriage, property, and citizenship. Diogenes was notorious for flaunting social norms and offending others' sensibilities in his effort to live "naturally." This was probably why, in part, he and his followers were called "dog-like" or cynics. Our modern term "cynical" derives from Diogenes's mistrust of society.

Epicurus of Samos (341–270 BC), like Diogenes, rejected much of contemporary Hellenistic society. His philosophy, known as Epicureanism, was hedonistic, or pleasure-focused. For him, pleasure and happiness were the same, but his definition of pleasure was the absence of pain and fear. He encouraged his followers to choose contentment with simple pleasures in moderation rather than worry about achieving some greater success. Furthermore, in his desire to liberate people from fear of death, he rejected belief in the gods as well as life after death.

Finally, Zeno of Citium (334–262 BC) founded the philosophical school of Stoicism. He accepted that the universe was divinely ordered to a particular end and that humans had free will, but he denied that individuals could use this will to alter the natural progress of the universe. To attempt to do so only resulted in suffering. Instead, he taught that individuals should embrace the duties that were associated with their position in society and not struggle for change. Stoicism encouraged many natural virtues, such as patience and fortitude, which later Christian writers would also emphasize.

Greeks migrated eastwards, they found it difficult to take their traditional local cults with them. Devotions to different Greek gods had always been associated with a specific place like Athens or Delphi. Cut off from its geographical roots, public piety towards the classical gods of ancient Greece weakened. Some Greeks adopted the foreign gods of the places they now ruled, though they sometimes associated those deities with the names and powers of the Greek gods back home. More importantly, a new, individualist form of spirituality took shape with the so-called **Mystery Religions** that arose from the myths and rituals of Mesopotamia, Egypt, and elsewhere. These different sects each had their own deities and rituals, but they shared a common emphasis on secrecy and the necessity of initiation in order to participate in their ceremonies and promised blessings in the afterlife.

The Mystery Religions affected Hellenistic society in two ways. First, they provided a sense of belonging. Previous generations had been able to identify with their *polis* and its culture; now that the Greek world was much larger, people needed a new anchor for their values and their identity. The Mystery Religions provided this by appealing to certain segments of the population, such as mothers or soldiers, and offering them a community.

In addition to providing a social network, the Mystery Religions also tapped into the evolving individualism of the Hellenistic era and directed it towards spirituality. In particular, these cults fostered a hope in individual salvation. Many of them promised special blessings and rewards in the afterlife that were only available to those who had formally participated in the cult. This emphasis on the spiritual worth of the individual was an important leap that helped prepare the Mediterranean peoples for the future message of Christianity.

There were many Mystery Religions, and people began to adopt a syncretistic approach to religion. They joined any number of cults while still observing public state rituals. This syncretism, or blending, of religious practices seemed to offer a solution to the challenge of incorporating the diverse beliefs that existed within the Hellenistic empires. However, the more straightforward this solution appeared to the Hellenistic monarchs, the more severe their wrath became towards those who rejected it.

Judaism in the Hellenistic World

Hellenism had profound ramifications for Jewish society. While unique in their worship of one God, Jews were not entirely dissimilar from their neighbors. Semitic people generally practiced circumcision and observed religious holy days based on the agricultural cycle. What made the Jews different was the theological-historical significance that these practices held for them. As noted in chapter 6, Passover was not simply a celebration of the earth's returning fertility as it was for the Jews' neighbors; it was the annual commemoration of God's dramatic intervention to liberate the Hebrews from Egyptian slavery.

This broader Semitic cultural context changed in 331 BC when Alexander conquered the Persian Empire. As Greek values and philosophy spread, Jewish society became increasingly isolated. The Greeks, for example, considered circumcision a barbaric practice that denigrated the perfection of the male figure. As a result, the practice ceased among most Semitic peoples in the former territories of the Persian

Empire; it was more important to integrate with Hellenistic society than it was to retain a ritual that their new rulers found objectionable. In contrast, the Jewish world refused to abandon this visible sign of Abraham's covenant with God. They also rejected attempts to identify their God with Zeus or some other deity. This resolute resistance to Greek influence aroused animosity and mistrust.

Although pious Jews remained steadfast regarding circumcision, they had to adapt other aspects of their spirituality in light of the Hellenistic *cosmopolis*, especially since the Jewish population had become scattered. While many returned to Judah (or, as the Greeks said, "Judea") after the end of their captivity, others stayed in Babylonia. This began the **Diaspora** (Greek for "scattering") of Jewish life. Soon, Jewish communities, attracted by trade or other opportunities, were growing in Syria, Egypt, and the Mediterranean. These groups obeyed local laws, spoke local languages, and lived lives akin to their nearest neighbors—insofar as the Torah's precepts allowed. Furthermore, they retained connections with Jerusalem and contributed annually to the Temple's material upkeep.

Because these Diaspora communities could not participate in the Temple's sacrifices, they developed an alternative for this worship. The synagogue probably has its roots in the Babylonian Captivity when formal sacrifices to God, as described in the Mosaic Law, could not be observed. This new institution emphasized the reading and understanding of the Torah and did not require the participation of a priest. In theory, any Jewish man could lead the community in its prayers as its *rabbi* or teacher. Local synagogues thus became the communal site for worship among those who lived outside of Judea.

Judea itself fell under the authority of the Ptolemies of Egypt after Alexander's death. This new dynasty of Greek pharaohs ruled from Alexandria in the Nile delta. Alexander had founded this city, but it was Ptolemy and his successors who turned it into a wonder of the world through its famed lighthouse and its massive library. The Jewish community there thrived and became one of the largest in the world, but it also lost connection with its Palestinian roots. The majority did not speak Hebrew and could not understand the Scriptures when they were recited at the synagogue. A translation was necessary, but this was itself a problematic situation. Many held that the inspiration that Moses and the prophets had received was rooted in the Hebrew words themselves. How could they be translated into Greek without losing that divine meaning?

According to tradition, God's providence intervened. Ptolemy II (r. 284–246 BC), a great patron of learning, commissioned seventy-two Palestinian scholars to translate the Hebrew Scriptures into Greek. Each was said to have worked independently for seventy-two days; when the scholars later compared their translations, they discovered that each copy coincided perfectly with the others. The Greek text became known as the Septuagint (Greek for "seventy") after the seventy-two scholars. Our source for this account comes from a single letter, purportedly written by one of Ptolemy's courtiers. Though most modern scholars consider this letter to be a later invention, many ancient Jews thought otherwise. Belief in a miraculous intervention calmed their fears that a Greek translation would not be accurate. Indeed, the Septuagint enjoyed much prestige among the Diaspora communities, and New Testament authors later quoted its text in their own writings.

Affairs changed dramatically for the Jews in Palestine when the Seleucid Empire seized control of the region from Ptolemaic Egypt. Their new king, Antiochus IV (r. 175–164 BC), wanted to covert Jerusalem into a Hellenistic city, complete with a theater, gymnasium, and other Greek institutions. Social pressure mounted to accept these changes, and many Jews, especially among the social elite, chose to "Hellenize." They gave Greek names like Jason or Philip to their children. They also attended the theater that portrayed the Greek gods and exercised in the Greek gymnasium. This last activity was particularly scandalous since the cultural expectation was that men exercised nude. This practice discouraged Jews from circumcising their sons, lest this physical "blemish" be noticed in later years when the boys exercised.

To make matters worse, Antiochus interfered with the high priesthood and removed the current high priest, whose family had held that office since Solomon's reign. Instead, he appointed "Hellenizers" as high priests. These Jews desired power and only nominally exercised their office. Ambitious candidates competed with one another for Antiochus's favor, and one high priest even sent financial support to the Greek games.

Even as some Jews "Hellenized," others resisted. These generally came from among the poor and called themselves the *Hasidim* ("devout"). Their loyalty to Judaism was put to the test in 169 BC when Antiochus's program of Hellenization became more aggressive. He outlawed the observance of the Torah with its practice of circumcision and rededicated the Jewish Temple to Zeus. A pig was sacrificed in the Temple, a particularly horrific act to the *Hasidim* since pigs were considered ritually unclean. Antiochus's ferocity against practicing Jews led to numerous martyrdoms, such as that of Eleazar (see 2 Mc 6:18–31) and the seven brothers with their mother (see 2 Mc 7).

Such bloodshed might have convinced many to Hellenize, but others rallied around Judas "Maccabee" and participated in the **Maccabean Revolt** (167–138 BC) in defense of their faith. Historians debate whether Judas's epithet "Maccabee" meant "hammer" and referred to his vigorous fighting or whether it was an acronym for the Torah verse that was his battle cry ("Who is like thee, O LORD, among the gods?" Ex 15:11). Regardless, Seleucid armies learned to fear this brilliant general. In 165 BC, he won the Battle of Emmaus. He retook Jerusalem one year later and cleansed the Temple from its profanation, an event remembered annually by the feast of Hannukah.

After decades of fighting and skillful diplomatic maneuvering, the Maccabees won. The Seleucid Empire withdrew its armies, and Jerusalem once more became the capital of an independent Jewish realm. Judas's surviving brother established the Hasmonean dynasty and held both royal and priestly authority. In claiming the high priesthood, the Hasmoneans effectively ensured that the descendants of Zadok, the high priest during the days of Solomon, would never again hold that position. This change, combined with the disappearance of King David's descendants early in the Second Temple era, brought about a new attitude among the Jewish population. Both family lines associated with traditional leadership were gone, and many felt that they now lived in an unprecedented and uncertain time. It is not a coincidence that Jewish leaders considered the era of biblical books to have ended shortly after the revolt and did not consider any new writings to be scriptural.

Conclusion

Alexander's conquests had fundamentally transformed the world. The resulting Hellenistic society laid the groundwork for a common culture that spanned three continents. Disparate regions now spoke the same language and had access to the achievements of Greek culture. To the Jews of the time, however, Hellenism was a danger to their faith. Though the Maccabees were successful in defeating Seleucid armies, the challenge represented by Greek culture still remained.

The Maccabean Revolt pointed to the next stage in Western history. In the midst of winning battles, Judas had carefully cultivated friendship with the enemies of the Seleucid Empire. Among these were the Spartans, with whom he formed an alliance. But even more important than these famed soldiers of the Greek past was a new power rising in the western Mediterranean. When the Maccabees celebrated their final victory over the Seleucids, they did so knowing that it was Roman pressure that ultimately convinced their enemies to negotiate peace. In the next unit, we introduce the Roman world, its origins and institutions, and its journey to become the ruler of the known world.

UNIT III

The Glory of Rome and the Humility of Christ

CHAPTER 11

Rome Becomes a Ruler

Lucius, consul of the Romans, to King Ptolemy, greeting.
The envoys of the Jews have come to us as our friends and allies....
We therefore have decided to write to the kings and countries that
they should not seek their harm or make war against [the Jews]
and their cities and their country, or make alliance with
those who war against them.

1 Maccabees 15:16–19

The Maccabean warriors were valiant, but they could not overcome the Seleucid Empire alone. This realization motivated their friendship with Rome. By the era of the Maccabean Revolt, the Italian city-state dominated the western Mediterranean and was extending its authority to the Hellenistic kingdoms of the East. In fact, shortly before hostilities broke out in Judea, Antiochus IV had a dramatic encounter with Roman influence in Egypt. A single Roman ambassador stood before Antiochus's invading army and demanded that they withdraw, or else Rome would declare war. When Antiochus requested time to consider the matter with his advisers, the Roman drew a circle around the king and ordered him to deliberate there. It may be that this humiliation drove Antiochus to lash out against the Jews shortly thereafter when they, too, thwarted his plans. Regardless of what motivated the persecution, the Maccabean leaders correctly realized that friendship with Rome could shift the war in their favor.

What were the origins of these Romans, and why did established powers, such as the Seleucid Empire, fear their opposition? What role did alliances, such as that between Rome and the Jews, play in the development of Roman might? In this chapter, we explore the rise of the Roman Republic and the challenges that confronted it as it grew to become the ruler of the Mediterranean.

From Kingdom to Republic

It is worthwhile to explore the myths Romans told about their origins before we discuss the historical evidence for their early history. These stories help us understand what Romans valued and how they understood their own past. One striking characteristic is how frequently acts of violence and warfare saturate their early legends. Not only did Romans claim that they were descendants of the mythical Aeneas and his Trojan warriors, but they also believed that Mars, the god of war himself, was the father of their first king. According to this story, Mars violated a princess of the Latin people in central Italy and fathered twin sons, **Romulus and Remus**. Years later, these brothers decided to establish their own city but soon argued about who would rule it. When Remus contemptuously jumped over the wall that his twin was building, Romulus responded in rage and killed him. The murderer claimed undisputed authority as king and gave his name to the city.

The **Capitoline She-wolf**. The dating of this bronze sculpture is widely debated, with estimates ranging from 400 BC to AD 1100. Currently in the Capitoline Museum in Rome, Italy. This depicts the she-wolf who, according to myth, rescued Romulus and Remus from death and nursed them as infants. It is commonly agreed that the statues of the twins are later additions to the piece.

Other legends tell of Rome's earliest inhabitants. Many were outcasts from nearby cities, whose citizens refused to allow their daughters to marry these rough-and-tumble vagabonds. This presented a significant problem, for most Romans were male, and Romulus's little kingdom faced an impending population crisis unless something changed soon. His solution was characteristically aggressive. The Romans invited the nearby Sabine community to attend a religious festival, but that was only a ruse to distract the men while the Romans abducted their daughters. The ensuing warfare between the Sabines and the Romans ended only when the women surprisingly intervened and made peace between their fathers and their new husbands. Force had brought about Romulus's birth, and fratricide had secured his rule. Now the first generation of Roman children were, according to their own stories, born from relationships that had pitted father against grandfather.

The myths surrounding Rome's second king emphasize very different qualities, and Romans considered his rule a new beginning. Numa Pompilius agreed to become king, but only after receiving favorable omens from Jupiter, king of the gods.

Coin from the reign of Nero (r. AD 54-68). The obverse depicts the Temple of Janus. The gates were the primary focus of the temple, and this coin shows the double doors closed and draped with a garland, a symbol of peaceful times. The interior of the temple was just large enough to house a statue of the god Janus.

He desired wisdom rather than aggression, justice rather than force. He dismissed Romulus's private army of bodyguards and ordered the construction of a temple to Janus. This deity was the god of entrances, and the doors of his new temple symbolically represented when the entrances into Rome—that is, its bridges—were lowered for access or raised to prevent enemies from entering the city. Open doors at Janus's temple were associated with the bridges being raised and therefore indicated that Rome was at war. Numa shut these doors and avoided war throughout his reign. He also reformed the Roman calendar and emphasized sacred days and festivals. Roman tradition further attributed to Numa the foundation of the Romans' civic priesthood and the Vestal Virgins. These last tended the sacred fire in the temple of Vesta, goddess of the home and family; this became one of the most important devotions of the Roman religion. Nonetheless, Numa's emphasis on piety and peace could not entirely undo the example of Romulus. Rome's third king promptly reopened the doors of the Temple of Janus, and they remained open for the next four centuries.

According to tradition, Rome's seventh and last king was Tarquin the Proud. He became notorious for his injustice against prominent Romans, but it was his son who brought about the end of the monarchy. This prince assaulted Lucretia, the honorable wife of a nobleman who was away fighting Rome's wars. She summoned her husband and demanded vengeance for the crime. As he debated what course of action to take, Lucretia drew a dagger and committed suicide, lest she live in shame since her purity had been dishonored. The tragedy precipitated an uprising against the monarchy and the formation of a republic. This was not a revolution that rejected social hierarchy or the authority of a ruler. Rather, it was a defense of the domestic virtues that the Romans held most dear and that they saw as endangered by a tyrannical king.

Romans believed all these myths transpired between 753 BC, the year Romulus founded the city's walls, and 509 BC, the year Tarquin's rule came to its inglorious end. But what are we as historians to make of these legends? What can we learn from archeology about the origins of the Roman state?

We begin with the second question. Around 1000 BC, about the same time that King David ruled Israel, warrior peoples entered the Italian peninsula from the north and established communities along the Apennine Mountain range that runs down the territory like a spine. About two hundred years later, some of their descendants left the mountains and established control over the fertile lands of western Italy, including the region that became the site of Rome. These ancestors of the future Romans were not the only people in the peninsula. Greek colonists had begun establishing trading centers along the northern coasts of the Mediterranean in the eighth century. By 600 BC, their settlements included a number of colonies in the Italian peninsula. The Greeks settled predominately in the "toe" and "instep" of the Italian "boot" as well as in the bountiful island of Sicily. (As we learned in chapter 9, Sicily's resources later inspired Athens's disastrous Sicilian Expedition in the fifth century.)

There were also the **Etruscans** to the north. Historians debate about the origins of this people, whether they migrated to Italy or were indigenous. Regardless of how they arrived, their league of city-states ruled northern Italy and by the sixth century had extended their network southward to include Rome itself. Roman legends admit as much by featuring Etruscans among their last kings, including Tarquin the Proud. The Roman revolt against Etruscan dominance did not immediately bring an end to their influence in Roman culture or their power in northern Italy. They remained a political rival and intellectual influence for some centuries until Rome conquered Tuscany around 300 BC.

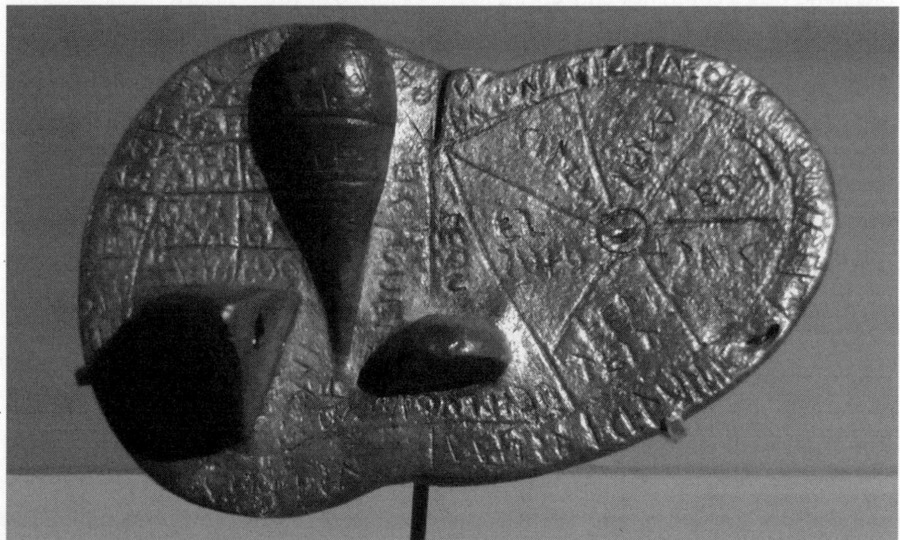

The **Liver of Piacenza**. Made of bronze, c. 2nd century BC. Currently in the Municipal Museum of Piacenza, Italy. This model of a sheep's liver was used by an Etruscan priest know as a haruspex. Such priests were devoted to the interpretation of entrails from sacrificed animals as a way to know the will of the gods. The names of the gods associated with each part of the liver is engraved on the piece.

Etruscan culture influenced the development of Rome's religious attitude. Rome, for example, adopted the Etruscan ritual of divination, the art of trying to determine the future through various methods. Etruscan priests, for example, studied the flight pattern of birds (making note of kind, number, and direction) or the path of lightning. They also sacrificed animals and cut open their livers in an attempt to understand current affairs or future ones. Romans incorporated such practices into the very fabric of their emerging state by endowing certain civil offices with religious duties.

Etruscan architecture also inspired Roman temples. Greek examples, like the Parthenon, were often centrally located in a sacred location and could be approached or viewed from all angles. In contrast, Italian sacred sites focused one's attention on an elevated temple structure placed at the far end of the holy grounds. This elevated zone reminded Etruscan (and Roman) worshippers of the hierarchy that separated the gods from humanity.

Roman traditions, such as those about Romulus, Numa, and Lucretia, tell us much about what Romans celebrated in their own culture. They glorified warfare and the skills that enabled them to succeed in that craft. Yet for all their violence, the Romans saw themselves as a pious people. As an example of piety, a roofless area (known as the *auguraculum*) was set aside for the proper observance of omens in the sky on the Capitoline Hill in Rome. It was so important to trace the paths of birds or lightning that a nobleman's house was torn down when officials discovered that it impeded their view. This devout attitude extended from the temple into the home, and the Romans reverenced many gods who, like Vesta, were believed to oversee the homestead.

The central figure in the Roman family was the ***paterfamilias***, the senior male member of the extended family. The *paterfamilias* acted as priest when honoring the household gods, made decisions for junior family members, and worked to ensure that family honor and prestige continued into the future. A Roman wife, meanwhile, ran the household and sometimes also had a role in her husband's business. Children studied the brave deeds of their ancestors so that they could imitate them. They learned the importance of tradition and their own role in continuing the family name and prestige.

Unfortunately, this education could lead to a disproportionate concern for family honor. Lucretia's example of death rather than shame highlights how this unbalanced concern for reputation could lead to deeper suffering. Marriage itself often became a union sought, not for the mutual love of future spouses, but for the mutual glory that would result for the two *patresfamilias*. Moreover, a *paterfamilias* held literal life-and-death authority over others. While social pressure could moderate his decisions, no one questioned his right to execute a wayward son or daughter if he thought that individual dishonored the family. Despite these excesses, Romans still valued and emphasized the dignity of the family more than many other contemporary cultures whose gods were not so tied to the daily life of the home.

Early Roman stories help us understand the virtues and the weaknesses of their society. On the one hand, much like Mycenaean Greece, there was violence and an unhealthy regard for honor. On the other hand, there was respect for the family and a sense of duty directed toward the fulfillment of their gods' will. Regardless of whether the details of a given story accurately portrayed an event or historical person, the Romans believed that their society and political independence derived from both the legacy of martial virtues and their emphasis on piety and family. Warriors may have driven out Tarquin, but it was the attack on Lucretia's marriage that inspired their courage.

The **Togatus Barberini**. Made of marble, c. 1st century AD. Currently in the Capitoline Museum in Rome, Italy. This full-sized figure holds the heads of his ancestors in his hands. It is notable because multi-generational sculptures are rare, and the figures here are realistic rather than idealized. The composition and realism indicate the individuality of each family member and the responsibility of descendants to honor their ancestors.

Rome, the Italian City-State

Our term "republic" derives from the Latin *res publica*, literally "the public thing." This concept of a public government contrasted with the *res privata* ("private thing") of the kings who had ruled Rome as their personal possession. According to tradition, the uprising inspired by Lucretia's anguish established the *res publica*, or Republic, of Rome in 509 BC. So hated was the legacy of Tarquin's family that no Roman, even the most tyrannical, ever again claimed the title of "king." While governance was now a public affair, the monarchy's overthrow did not immediately transform Roman society into something else. The Romans valued tradition and were conservative in matters of change.

There were two principal classes in Roman society: patricians, who were elites, and plebeians, who were commoners. The former had been wealthy advisers to the kings during the days of the monarchy, and they retained their influence during the early Republic. The most important of these patrician families belonged to the **Senate**, an advisory body that effectively governed the Republic. Plebeians, in contrast, lacked formal authority or influence. These farmers, tradesmen, and laborers were connected to the patrician elite through a system known as clientage. In exchange for physical labor and political support (that is, voting in elections for a given patrician), the plebeians gained economic, legal, and physical protection from their patrician patron. This patron/client arrangement remained an integral part of the Republic throughout its history.

The early Roman Republic limited political positions to the patrician class. The highest of these elected officials, the consuls, exercised much of the former royal authority. This was known as *imperium*, and it included the prosecution of war, overseeing religious rites, and punishment (by execution, if necessary). Unlike the king who ruled for life, a consul held authority for only a year. His *imperium* had geographical limits as well. Consuls possessed the authority over life and death while waging war abroad, but they could not exercise that judicial authority within the city's boundaries. Furthermore, two consuls held *imperium* simultaneously and could negate one another's decisions. The consuls tended to work closely with the Senate. It was in their best interests to do so since former consuls automatically joined the ranks of senators; from the Senate's perspective, influence in the consuls' decisions added to their overall control of the Republic and its policies.

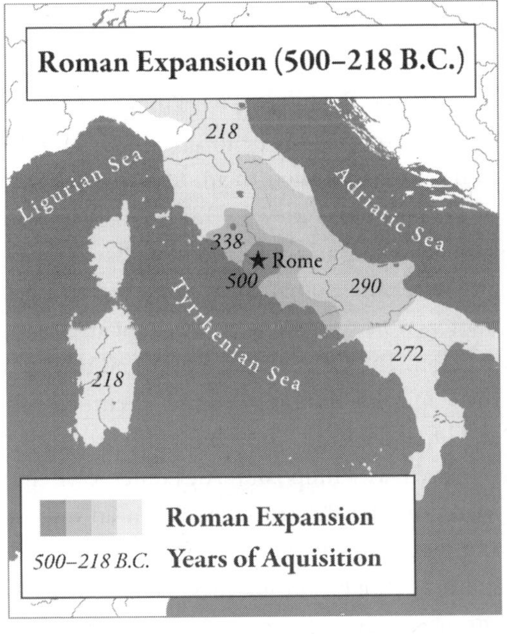

As the Republic expanded its domain, military campaigns took place farther from the city of Rome and sometimes lasted more than a year. The Romans therefore developed the position of proconsul. This permitted former consuls to continue to act as generals in specific regions for longer than their appointed year as consul. Furthermore, for times of emergency, Romans harkened back to Rome's royal past and instituted the unelected role of *dictator* (derived from *dicto*, "I order"). These leaders received absolute authority during times of upheaval. Neither geographical limitations nor a colleague restricted their *imperium*. Nonetheless, Romans sought ways to avoid potential abuse by limiting a dictator's authority to an established duration, such as a six-month term.

Roman expansion brought to the fore the plebeian desire to participate in government. While patricians appeared to hold most advantages, the plebeians possessed substantial leverage since they did most of the fighting, dying, and conquering for the Roman state. By refusing to partake in Rome's wars, they could effectively bring the patricians to the bargaining table. This era of social transformation, known as the **Struggle of the Orders** (494–287 BC), began with a plebeian victory: the creation of the office of tribune in 494 BC. Tribunes came from the plebeian order and had the authority to veto (literally, "I forbid") any action by a magistrate or bill proposed in assembly. This success inspired further advances for the plebeians over the next two hundred years. In addition to a written law code, known as the Twelve Tablets, they secured the right to marry patricians (445 BC), to hold office as consul (367 BC), and, most importantly, to enact laws in a plebeian assembly that were binding on all Romans (287 BC). These reforms shifted the elite ranks within the Republic. One's birth became less important than one's private resources, and wealthy plebeians grew in influence. Their ultimate goal was a seat in the Senate, which retained its overall authority and significance throughout this period.

Roman armies advanced even as patricians and plebeians wrestled with one another over the internal workings of the Republic. By 400 BC, the city-state was a growing power in the peninsula, but it soon faced a new rival. The Celts, or "Gauls" as the Romans called them, had crossed the Alps and undermined Etruscan rule in the Po River Valley. In 387 BC, a Roman diplomatic mission to stop the Celts from besieging an ally ended in warfare. The conflict initially did not go well for the city-state. The Roman army panicked and fled the battlefield in disgrace. To make matters worse, the soldiers left Rome itself vulnerable as they retreated to a different location. The Celts sacked Rome and then besieged those civilians who had fled to the Capitoline Hill for defense. Eventually, the Roman army recovered its courage and lifted the siege. The rebuilt city promptly resumed its territorial expansion.

Even as Philip and Alexander contemplated the conquest of Persia from Macedon, the Romans engaged in an important struggle against rivals in central and southern Italy. The Samnites occupied the highlands controlling the land to the south of Rome, and for two generations (343–290 BC), they fought against one another to shape the future of Italy. In 295 BC, the Romans won a decisive battle against a coalition of Samnites, Etruscans, and Gauls. According to tradition, the Romans secured their victory through desperate means. The consul Decius decided to offer himself as a human sacrifice for the Republic and cursed himself and his enemies to the gods of the underworld in exchange for victory. He charged into the place where the battle was most fierce and quickly met death. The Romans believed that it was at that moment that the battle's tide shifted, and they conquered.

Rome had become the dominant power in the peninsula, but the Greek colonies in the south still sought to maintain their independence by summoning a mercenary captain from the East. **Pyrrhus of Epirus** (319/8–272 BC) technically fought for the interests of the Greek colony Tarentum, but his ambitions went beyond this. He believed that he was a descendant of Achilles and that the Romans were descendants of Trojans and thus his sworn enemies. Not content with this, he also claimed that he would conquer the West just as Alexander the Great had triumphed in the East five decades earlier. He landed in Italy in 280 BC and quickly gained a victory in that year and the year following. The war elephants that accompanied his army initially terrified the Romans, but they fought with such valor that Pyrrhus realized that the significant losses he suffered in his victories actually undermined his hope of winning the war. He reportedly said that one more victory against the Romans would ruin him. (This is the origin of the term "Pyrrhic Victory," a win that comes with such cost that it jeopardizes one's overall success.) Pyrrhus withdrew in 275 BC, and the road was open for undisputed Roman control over the Italian Peninsula.

Rome had grown significantly from its earliest years as a small city-state. While it may be tempting to see its initial growth as the legacy of Romulus's aggression, the Romans themselves attributed their success to their piety. Rome was a desirable friend; its armies were resilient and (usually) courageous. Therefore, beleaguered communities often appealed to Rome for an alliance. These connections soon entangled Rome in their friends' struggles. From the Roman perspective, their growing hegemony was a blessing from the gods for their faithfulness in friendship. Even in the war against Pyrrhus, Rome had first been approached by some Greeks who sought to be Roman allies. Technically, Roman soldiers were piously fighting for the benefit of others and thus combined their inheritance from both Romulus *and* Numa.

Furthermore, Rome treated those within its political network well. Those nearest Rome received citizenship, an enviable position since Roman success brought ever greater wealth and prestige. Other allies retained their self-government, though Rome required them to send soldiers in time of war (which, of course, was frequent). The possibility of Roman citizenship in the future encouraged loyalty, and there was a sense that everyone had a vested interest in aiding Rome's expansion.

Pyrrhus was one of the most esteemed generals of the Hellenistic era, and his defeat signaled a new stage in Roman history. The city-state was now the head of a coalition of territories that spanned the peninsula. Its roads connected its friends and facilitated the movement of its armies. Its veterans received land in various areas to help minimize any rebellion against its authority. Even as Hellenistic kingdoms competed with one another in the East, Rome was uniting the West. One great challenge in the western Mediterranean remained: The city of Carthage in northern Africa.

Rome, Ruler of the Mediterranean

The geography of the western Mediterranean created narrow, fertile strips of land along the Italian, French, Spanish, and African coasts that ended in mountains or plateaus as one progressed inland. These interior obstacles encouraged those dwelling along the coasts to look toward the sea for expansion and trade. Large rivers facilitated water travel, while islands, such as Sicily and Sardinia, offered convenient places of shelter and rest for those seeking to journey from one area to another via the sea. Once Rome had secured its control over Italy, it was inevitable that its alliances, ambitions, and central location would draw it further into this Mediterranean network. However, its growing influence soon brought it into conflict with another power that sought dominance.

The Phoenicians had founded a series of colonies that brought their culture from the Near East into the western Mediterranean. These settlements spread predominantly along the African and Spanish coastlines. Of particular interest to Phoenician merchants were the valuable mineral resources, such as copper and tin, found in the Iberian Peninsula (modern-day Spain). The resulting trade brought great wealth to the Phoenicians, and it was in the context of the city-state Tyre's

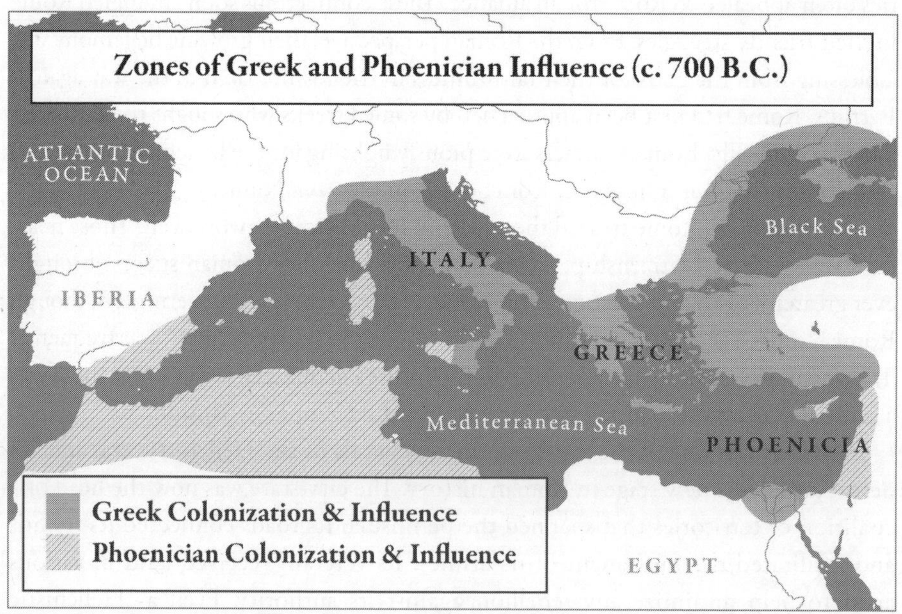

In Italy, the Apennine Mountains run like a spine down the heart of the peninsula while the Alps separate the entire peninsula from the interior of Europe. In southeast France, the Alpine and Cévenol mountain ranges create a distinct coastal region. Meanwhile, the Spanish central plateau and the Atlas Mountains of Africa delineate the beginning of more arid and less fertile regions, such as the Sahara Desert to the south of the Atlas range.

commercial power that King Ahab of Israel sought to marry the infamous Jezebel. Several decades later, according to tradition, Jezebel's great-niece Dido founded the greatest of all Phoenician colonies, Carthage.

Carthage (literally, "New Town") came to dominate the trade of the western Mediterranean. Its location in North Africa was ideal, for it possessed both a natural harbor and a fertile hinterland that supplied the city and provided many agricultural exports. By the third century BC, Carthage had grown from a trading port to an empire in its own right. Libya to the east, southern Spain to the west, and the islands to the north, including parts of Sicily, were firmly within its zone of influence.

Its political institutions were praised by the Greek philosopher Aristotle and paralleled those of the Roman Republic. The two highest offices, like Roman consuls, were annually elected and shared power with the members of a senate. Measures proposed by senators required a vote from an assembly of citizens. Nevertheless, the two societies had more differences than similarities. First of all, Carthaginians focused on commercial expansion and the increase of their riches. Theirs was a maritime power, whose tariffs and trade generated fantastic wealth. The city's harbor, for example, had over two hundred docks to service the vessels laden with goods that

THE ROMAN ARMY

The Greek *phalanx* was the model for the earliest armies of the Roman Republic. Historians are uncertain whether the Romans learned *hoplite* warfare directly from the Greeks in southern Italy or from the Etruscans, who themselves had adopted the Greek style of fighting. Regardless of how they learned this type of warfare, the Romans modified the *phalanx* and perfected it.

The principal unit of the Roman army was the **legion**. Originally, "*legio*" had referred to the annual levy of citizen soldiers able to fight for the Republic. By the fourth century BC, it described a specific unit that, at least ideally, consisted of 4,200 soldiers and 300 cavalry. This legion was further divided into 1,200 *velites*, or light infantry, and thirty *maniples*. In battle formation, the *maniples* formed three rows of ten. Each *maniple* in the first two rows included two *centuries* of sixty men. The *maniples* in the third row only had one *century* each, but these soldiers were the most experienced. By the time of the Punic Wars, these legionaries no longer fought with the long spears of the Greeks. Instead, they wielded the javelin (*pilum*) and the short sword (*gladius*). The former had an effective range of about fifty feet and was designed to puncture shields and wound the warrior behind. The latter came from Spain and may have been incorporated into Roman warfare as a result of fighting against Hannibal's Iberian soldiers.

One of the most remarkable features of Roman military life was the army's daily camp. At the end of a day's march, the Roman soldiers established a camp—complete with streets and a defensive ditch and walls. Each *maniple* had an assigned place within these daily camps, and soldiers knew their specific duties whenever they set up a camp. These structures were not intended to withstand a siege or assault; instead, they delayed enemy attacks and enabled the legionaries within to organize and prepare for immediate battle.

Though the specific structure of the Roman army would evolve significantly over the centuries, the underlying discipline and organization would remain a key component of Roman success for centuries.

frequently visited the city. Its leading citizens valued their economic opportunities, and there was a sense that their wealth could buy whatever was required for success. Many of their soldiers were foreign mercenaries. Rome, in contrast, was a land power whose wealth lay in the agricultural yields produced by its farmers. Romans, at least in their ideals, valued simplicity more than wealth and celebrated the military prowess of their farming citizenry. Rome's network of alliances was the keystone to its strength. Naval trade and warfare were virtually unknown to them.

The greatest contrast between the two societies was their religious beliefs. Carthage had retained its cultural connections to Phoenicia. This close relationship included the worship of their ancestral gods such as Baal. This god and his consort, Tanit, goddess of love and fertility, demanded child sacrifice, and ancient reports tell of a Carthaginian statue of Baal whose stomach was a furnace designed to consume doomed children. Carthaginians sometimes sought various ways to avoid killing their own children, usually by purchasing others to die in their stead. This economic solution, however, met with resistance when Carthage suffered a military defeat in 310 BC. Baal, they feared, had abandoned them because they no longer gave him the children of nobles. According to the Greek historian Diodorus, the Carthaginians promptly sacrificed more than two hundred children from wealthy families to regain Baal's favor. The Carthaginians won that war.

The practice of child sacrifice divided Roman and Carthaginian societies. While Romans did expose unwanted children and leave them to die, they have no record of killing children as an act of worship. Roman gods upheld marriage, family, and the home. For them, the Carthaginian deities who demanded one's own children for continued economic blessings were dangerous. While it can be tempting to emphasize hostility between these two religious worldviews, Rome could and did sign treaties with its southern neighbor; no less than four agreements, spanning the years from 509 BC—the year of the Republic's foundation—to 279 BC, linked the two powers. Yet once the Romans defeated Pyrrhus, it became increasingly clear that the competing ambitions of Rome and Carthage could no longer be resolved through diplomacy.

The immediate cause for conflict between the two arose in Sicily, where Roman and Carthaginian spheres of influence collided. A dispute in the city of Messana caused two factions to appeal for outside help, one to Carthage and the other to Rome. Carthage swiftly established a garrison in the city. To the Romans, this Carthaginian presence so close to the Italian coast was a serious threat, and they responded by sending troops to support the opposing faction.

Thus began the series of three wars known collectively as the **Punic Wars** (264–146 BC). ("Punic" is the Latin term for "Phoenician.") These wars were the

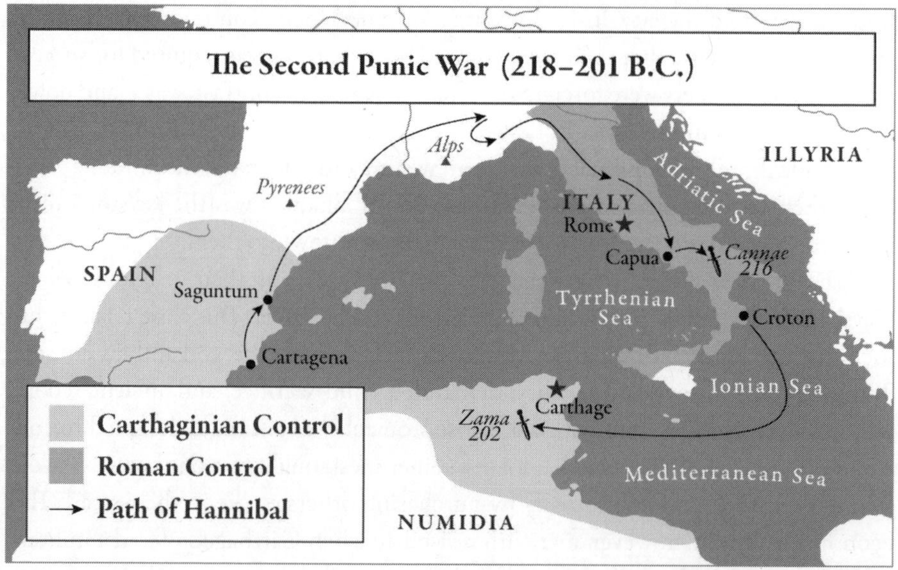

crucible in which Roman dominance of the Mediterranean was forged. As the First Punic War opened in 264 BC, Carthage seemed to hold the upper hand because it possessed a powerful navy. The Romans, for their part, had never even built ships before. According to tradition, they reverse-engineered a shipwreck they found on the coast to construct their first ship and practiced rowing as a team by sitting on two benches on the beach. Despite these shaky beginnings, they nevertheless developed a navy that went toe-to-toe with the might of Carthage. Three separate times their entire fleet was almost destroyed, but they rebuilt again and again. In the end, the Carthaginians were not willing to sustain this price in men and resources and sought peace terms. They gave up some territories, but, more importantly, Rome gained control of the sea. Carthage's greatest asset had been neutralized.

The Second Punic War (218–202 BC) was the most famous. The Carthaginian commander **Hannibal** (247–181 BC), whose name literally means "the grace of Baal," had sworn undying hatred for Rome after the first Carthaginian defeat. He surprised the Romans by invading from the Alps in the north and defeated numerous Roman armies in displays of breathtaking tactical mastery. At the Battle of Cannae, for example, he succeeded in surrounding the entire Roman force before annihilating it. Both consuls and numerous senators lost their lives in the disaster.

Rome faced the greatest threat it had ever known. There were no armies left to send, and Hannibal's forces still occupied Italy. Nonetheless, many of Rome's Italian allies refused to join the Carthaginians and remained loyal to Roman rule. The Roman system of alliances and benefits was too generous to abandon, even in the face of great danger. Slowly, the Romans rebuilt their forces, while the Carthaginians, who had grown jealous of Hannibal, refused to send him sufficient reinforcements to enable the decisive, final attack. Instead, the Romans launched their own invasion and took the war to the gates of Carthage. Hannibal hurriedly returned to lead the defense. There he faced a young general named Scipio who had studied Hannibal's tactics; Scipio defeated the great general at the Battle of Zama in 202 BC. Carthage surrendered, and Hannibal ultimately went into voluntary exile and advised other enemies of Rome until he died almost two decades later. Some historians suggest that he committed suicide to escape Roman capture.

The Second Punic War was a catalyst for the expansion of Roman power. Carthaginian territories became a part of the Roman network, and the city itself was reduced to a dependent ally of Rome. The Republic now controlled the western Mediterranean, but its appetite for expansion proved insatiable. New alliances with kingdoms to the East soon encouraged Roman activity in the eastern Mediterranean. Already in 200 BC—just two years after defeating Carthage—Roman armies were fighting in Greece. Shortly after that victory, Rome fought against Antiochus III of the Seleucid Empire. The Republic forced him to sign the humiliating Treaty of Apamea (188 BC), which severely limited his army and navy. As we discussed at the beginning of this chapter, Antiochus IV learned a similar lesson in submission when he attempted to invade Egypt. Though the Republic did not yet rule the lands of the eastern Mediterranean directly, there was no doubt whose armies were supreme.

Conclusion

This rise of Roman power was the context for the alliance between the Maccabees and the Roman Republic. The Jewish leaders knew that all powers feared Rome's military might; for its part, the Republic was eager for any opportunity to showcase its leadership and to humble any would-be rivals. As if to accentuate that a new era of Roman power was dawning, the Romans demanded that the Carthaginians surrender all their weapons and leave their city in 149 BC. When Carthage refused, Rome declared war and easily defeated their much-weakened rival three years later. This Third Punic War ended with the city of Carthage burned to the ground. That same year, the Romans sacked Corinth as a message to Greece and others that true military power in the Mediterranean world lay in Roman hands and no other.

CHAPTER 12

The Death and Rebirth of Rome

Then followed long years when earth was stained with blood
and men released their souls to hell, justice/
A word forgotten; brothers dipped their fingers into brother's blood . . . /
Thus right and wrong became confused; mankind in darkness,
bewildered now ignored the gods. /
Never again do gods return to earth or walk with men
in the bright sun of noon.

Catullus, *Poem 64*[1]

The Roman poet Catullus (c. 84–c. 54 BC) was infamous for his hedonistic poetry, but in this particular instance he revealed the intense emptiness of his decadent life and his disgust at the corruption he witnessed in Roman society. Both he and Rome seemed to possess access to whatever they desired, but neither was content, neither was happy. Indeed, Rome was tearing itself apart. Generals strove one against the other for ultimate power, and it appeared that the values of home and family that characterized the myths of the early Republic were now replaced by greed and ambition. This was an era of violence and lawlessness that brought about the collapse of the Roman Republic. Nonetheless, Rome survived even if the Republic did not: a final civil war brought to power a self-styled savior who promised to restore Rome to its old glory, virtue, and friendship with the gods. Who was this political savior? What reforms did he enact, and were they successful? To answer these questions, we must first ask what events brought about the death of the Roman Republic and its rebirth as an empire.

1 Catullus, *Poem 64;* quoted in Stringfellow Barr, *The Mask of Jove* (New York: J.B. Lippincott, 1966), 119.

The Hazards of Success

Rome had begun as a city-state. The Republic's early officials and institutions presupposed a small society that was geographically based around the city itself. The story of Cincinnatus perfectly captures this early context. Tradition reports that Cincinnatus served as dictator during a crisis in the fifth century BC. He famously left his farm while plowing his fields to assume control of the Roman army, only to return two weeks later to that same farm once the threat had been removed. As this story shows, the early wars saw Roman soldiers campaign relatively close to their homes. Their reward was gratitude and respect rather than riches. Furthermore, the Roman strategy of granting either citizenship or limited autonomy (self-government) to its neighbors made new territorial acquisitions a natural extension of Rome's current borders. This wise practice convinced many allies to remain loyal during the trials of the Second Punic War. Yet Carthage's defeat heralded a new era in Roman policy, and the old order steadily broke down.

This collapse occurred in part because Roman success outpaced its original city-state institutions and mindset. Men in positions that had originally been responsible for local affairs were now called upon to make decisions regarding territories far away from Rome. A more developed infrastructure with a more elaborate bureaucracy was desperately needed, but it was difficult for this conservative society to change. Instead, leaders applied stopgap measures, often inadequate in the long run, to Rome's new situation as ruler of the Mediterranean. These "solutions" lacked the nuance and balance that characterized the earlier positions within the Republic. For example, territories far from Rome became provinces ruled by governors who did not have checks on their authority. Provincial governors possessed full *imperium* and could enjoy their position for multiple years in a row. (In contrast, consuls were expected to wait as long as ten years before seeking that office again.) Also, the peoples under the governors' authority did not become Roman citizens or even enjoy limited self-governance as Rome's allies in Italy did. As if to underscore their subordinate status, they provided tribute money instead of military service. Such policies indirectly discouraged loyalty to Rome, for the provinces possessed little vested interest in Rome's continued success.

This failure to integrate new territories is perhaps best reflected by Rome's conflicting attitudes towards Hellenistic culture. Romans had no equivalent to Greek philosophy and literature. They had celebrated hierarchy, order, and martial valor rather than intellectual achievement. Confronted by Greek art and thought, some Romans responded by denigrating or dismissing Greek culture as effeminate and cowardly. From this perspective, the political divisions within the Hellenistic world as well as its love for subtle philosophical distinctions highlighted Greek

The **Roman Forum** was the center of life in the city of Rome for centuries. Today, the archeological site houses the ruins of some of the oldest buildings in the ancient city, including temples, the senate house, monuments, and other important public structures. Along the south edge of the Forum stretches the ruins of the Regia, the historic residence of the Roman kings and later the *pontifex maximus*, the highest religious official of Rome. This residence dates from the 8th century BC.

shortcomings. For others, the opposite was true. Roman arms might be supreme, but Greek culture offered an escape from Rome's traditional rustic ways. These individuals often hired (or bought) Greek tutors to accompany them for conversation and to instruct their sons. Many Romans soon believed that knowledge of Greek language, literature, and philosophy was an integral part of their education, and a blended "Greco-Roman" culture began to take root. The divided Roman response to Greek civilization pointed to the numerous cracks that were forming in society at large.

Even in religion, the Roman world was splintering. Though Roman gods were typically identified with Greeks ones—for example, the Roman Jupiter was the Greek Zeus—some deities from the eastern Mediterranean, such as Dionysus, promoted worship that involved rites and behavior that undermined classic Roman values. Though the Senate outlawed the worship of these suspect deities, its official condemnation could not stop all Romans from engaging in the new rituals.

Foreign conquests brought their own problems. While plunder and slaves flooded Roman markets, many Romans found themselves in increasingly difficult economic situations. Roman alliances spanned the Mediterranean, and wars were no longer local or even regional affairs. Roman soldiers, therefore, were usually absent from their homes for years. When they returned, their small farms were often unprofitable or approaching ruin. (Some never recovered from the devastation of Hannibal's Italian campaign.) Many veterans sold their lands and sought work as farmhands or as laborers in a city.

This situation increased the divide between the wealthy and the poor within Roman society. Roman elites bought the farms of returning soldiers and formed vast estates, later known as *latifundia*. These plantations focused on profitable cash crops, that is, those foods that brought the most wealth rather than fed the most people. This practice further increased the wealth of their owners. At the same time, landless veterans found themselves struggling amidst a glut of laborers who all sought the same types of jobs. Not only did they have competition among themselves; the influx of slaves from foreign conquests gave employers another source of inexpensive labor.

Roman slavery included all the negatives one rightly associates with the loss of freedom. Owners could and did abuse, overwork, and even kill their "property." Slaves had no legal recourse, though in 135 BC slaves in Sicily did rise up to fight against oppression. This First Servile War (135–132 BC) ended in defeat for the slaves but not before they had terrorized and killed some of their Roman masters.

Despite the cruelty that frequently accompanied Roman slavery, Romans could be surprisingly tolerant towards former slaves who had received freedom. They often blended in with society at large and could avoid the stigma of previously belonging to the slave class. Once freed, or manumitted, the "freedmen" became Roman citizens and were incorporated into the families of their former owners. There are even rare cases in which former slaves became the eldest surviving male in a family and thus its *paterfamilias*! Nonetheless, the chasm between "property" and "fellow human" was a real one, and to the tens of thousands taken captive by Roman armies the possibility of future freedom was only a distant dream.

Roman veterans searching for work did not have much sympathy for slaves. To a potential employer, buying slaves was often more cost-effective than hiring someone else. To make matters worse for the veteran, once he sold his family farm, he (and his sons) could no longer serve in the Roman military, since normally one had to be a property owner to be a soldier. Several problems were thus all interconnected: as more Romans sold their lands, recruitment in the army declined, which threatened the Republic's influence in the Mediterranean; furthermore, the inability to join the army limited the options of the poor and contributed to the growing gap between wealthy landowners and their impoverished, landless fellow Romans. Many of these destitute poor flocked to Rome to receive government support.

Roman society stood at a crossroads without any easy answer to the shifting cultural and political landscape. In 133 BC, a young tribune, **Tiberius Gracchus** (168–133 BC), proposed a solution to the situation. Tiberius was no newcomer to public life. He had gained fame as a soldier in the Third Punic War by being the first to scale Carthage's wall. Moreover, his deceased father had served as a consul while his maternal grandfather was the general who ended the Second Punic War. Everything seemed in place for Tiberius to enjoy a fruitful political career. Yet Tiberius chose to champion what he saw as necessary measures to reform society, regardless of how unpopular such policies might be to the social elite. To his admirers, Tiberius was sacrificing a comfortable life of political success in order to benefit the downtrodden among the Romans; to his enemies, he was a rabble-rouser intent on using the ignorant masses to gain unlawful power over the Republic. At stake were state-owned lands that the wealthy had effectively absorbed into their *latifundia*. Tiberius proposed to break up these plots and give them to the landless veterans. He believed that this would lessen the wide disparity between the abject poor and the fantastically wealthy, while simultaneously solving the army's recruitment problem.

Tiberius realized that resistance from the elites would be severe, but things escalated once he illegally removed a fellow tribune from office in order to pass his law. Senators became convinced that Tiberius would use his popular support to overturn the legal structures of the Republic. When Tiberius broke the law again by seeking reelection as tribune, riots followed, and he and about three hundred of his followers were killed.

Roman politics were quickly unraveling due to Tiberius's willingness to ignore the law and the Senate's introduction of violence. Two factions developed: the *populares* (literally, "supporters of the people"), who saw the masses as the key to winning political victories, and the *optimates* (literally, "best men"), who upheld the traditional authority of the Senate. Neither party necessarily had the greater good of society in mind, and it became convenient to see the opposition as responsible for all of society's ills.

The situation became even more tense in 123 BC when Tiberius's younger brother Gaius (c. 159–121 BC) became tribune. Gaius sought to win the support of the equestrian order. This sector of Roman society was wealthy—their title reflected their ability to serve as cavalry in the Roman army—but was not as wellborn or as influential as the *optimates* in the Senate. Gaius hoped to appeal to equestrian self-interest by showing how Tiberius's reforms could enhance the army and thus the equestrians' ability to plunder other lands. However, Gaius moved too quickly and lost support from many Romans when he argued that Roman citizenship should extend to all Italians. Once again, violence was unleashed as *optimates* and *populares* fought in the streets regarding Gaius's proposals. Again the Gracchus lost, and his foes threw Gaius's decapitated body into the Tiber. This time, some three thousand Romans also lost their lives. Both sides had accepted violence as a realistic and almost inevitable method of settling Rome's political debates.

Last Years of the Republic

The murder of the Gracchi brothers only temporarily reestablished the Senate's authority. More than anything, the recourse to bloodshed highlighted how the old network of patron-client relationships was falling apart. That system assumed that the different parts of society were working together, but it became increasingly apparent that the interests of the *optimates* did not include the concerns of the *populares*. The vast divide between wealthy and poor, the needs of the landless, and the recruitment problem for the army all remained pressing issues for the majority of Romans, but senators refused to support measures that altered the status quo. The shortsighted among them believed that Gaius Gracchus's death had ended the crisis. Little did they realize that within one hundred years the Republic they knew would be overturned by civil war.

Such complacency revealed the corruption at the highest levels of Roman government. Bribes bought senators, and inept military leaders among the *optimates* focused more on their own ambitions than on defeating their enemies. One such opponent, the North African king Jugurtha, once declared that Rome was a city for sale and would perish when it found a buyer.

It was Jugurtha's success against Roman legions that led to the election of the *populares* candidate **Gaius Marius** (c. 157–86 BC) as consul in 107 BC. *Optimates* looked down on him as an equestrian "new man" who lacked the proper connections to the ancient families of the Roman elite, but Marius ignored their scorn and promptly reformed the military. To solve the recruitment problem, he removed the land requirement for Roman soldiers. Volunteers desperate to improve their indigent state filled his ranks, and he won their confidence as he restructured the legion to make it more effective on the battlefield. He replaced the legion's *maniples* with cohorts—smaller, more maneuverable units—and gave each legion its own standard, an eagle that came to embody that particular legion's history and pride. This new, predominately landless soldiery offered its loyalty not to the Republic or the Senate but to their commander, who

Aquila. Made of bronze c. 1st-3rd century AD. Property of the British Museum, London, England. The *aquila* was a figure of an eagle, typically situated atop of a Roman legion's military standard. The standard would be carried by an *aquilifer*, or "eagle-bearer," and held special importance to the men in that legion. If seized by enemy forces, it was considered a disgrace and an omen of misfortune.

The **Arch of Constantine**. Constructed in AD 315, but nearly all its ornamentation was taken from other, older monuments. Located between the Colosseum and the Palatine Hill in Rome. Perhaps no two symbols are more commonly associated with Rome than the eagles of its legions and the phrase *Senatus Populusque Romanus* ("The Roman Senate and People," often abbreviated as SPQR). Both symbols can be seen on the Arch of Constantine: "SPQR" is visible in the inscription above the center arch, and the eagles can be seen atop the military standards in the carved relief panels flanking the inscription.

promised them plunder now and land once they retired. The Republic's civilian army was evolving into a professional, full-time military devoted to its generals.

Marius became the darling of the Roman people by defeating Jugurtha and securing land grants for his veterans among the territories conquered by Rome. The people elected him consul for five successive years, despite such reelections being illegal. The *optimates* resented Marius's power and popularity and turned to his rival, **Lucius Cornelius Sulla** (138–78 BC), a member of an ancient but impoverished family.

Sulla defeated Marius's partisans in the civil war that followed, but the *optimates* soon regretted what sort of champion they had supported. He engineered his appointment as dictator and emphasized his authority by ordering the execution of six thousand prisoners of war as he met with the Senate. Their screams accompanied his speech, and every senator realized that Sulla supported the old order on *his* terms. Political purges soon followed. He composed lists of his enemies that included how much he would pay to those who killed them. These "proscription lists" were posted publicly and enabled Sulla to amass vast wealth by auctioning off the estates of the recently murdered.

Despite this butchery, Sulla saw himself as a protector of the Republic. He limited the power of the regional governors and tribunes, whom he believed had become too influential, and sought to return authority to the Senate. Ironically, Sulla's bloodthirstiness weakened senatorial leadership even as he believed he was restoring it. His proscription lists had eliminated many senators, and he added four hundred new members, largely drawn from the equestrian class. This reform expanded the Senate to an unprecedented size and weakened the *optimates*' ability to pursue a single strategy. Sulla relinquished his dictatorship in 79 BC and died one year later, confident that he had restored the former constitution of the Republic. His lieutenants, however, came to a very different conclusion regarding his legacy.

Both **Marcus Licinius Crassus** (115–53 BC) and **Cnaeus Pompey** (106–48 BC) had fought under Sulla's command but neither shared his desire to restore authority to the Senate. Instead, they immediately began to maneuver themselves into position to take control of Rome. Crassus initially focused on wealth. During Sulla's proscriptions, he took advantage of opportunities to buy property inexpensively. Some believed that he even added names to the list so that he could purchase lands once their owners had been killed. In addition, Crassus formed Rome's first fire brigade. These five hundred men would rush to the site of a fire—which was nearly a daily event due to the city's many wooden residences—and then wait while Crassus offered to buy the burning building at a fraction of its worth. If the desperate owner refused, Crassus's "firefighters" simply watched the home burn. If the victim agreed to sell, Crassus ordered his men to put out the fire. Using unscrupulous methods such as these, Crassus amassed an estimated 7,100 talents of gold, the equivalent of 229 tons.

Crassus soon realized that he needed military prestige, too. He received his opportunity in 73 BC. That year the gladiator Spartacus led a slave revolt that terrified Rome. Crassus offered to equip and fund private legions to bring down the rebel, but his army lacked morale and dedication. After a part of his army fled a battle, Crassus resorted to the practice of decimation: he ordered his own soldiers to kill one out of every ten Romans who had fled. He wanted them to fear him more than the enemy. Such cruelty worked, and Crassus crushed Spartacus's army in 71 BC and crucified the six thousand survivors.

His rival, Pompey, was also busy expanding his authority. In 67 BC, the Senate bestowed on him unlimited authority (*imperium infinitum*) to eradicate pirates that were active in the Mediterranean. He completed his mission in three months. One year later, he was commanding legions in the eastern Mediterranean against a rival of Roman authority. From 66 to 62 BC, his armies marched throughout Anatolia, Syria, and Palestine and brought those regions more firmly under Roman control. Pompey founded cities, oversaw treaties, and increased the tribute to Rome by an estimated 70 percent. (We will discuss his role in Judean history in the next chapter.)

The Senate was wary of Pompey's growing prestige. In 63 BC, there had been an attempted revolution in Rome itself. The plot to arm the slaves was discovered by the consul Cicero, a famous orator and Roman philosopher, and the Senate remained on guard against any perceived threat to its authority. It feared Pompey's

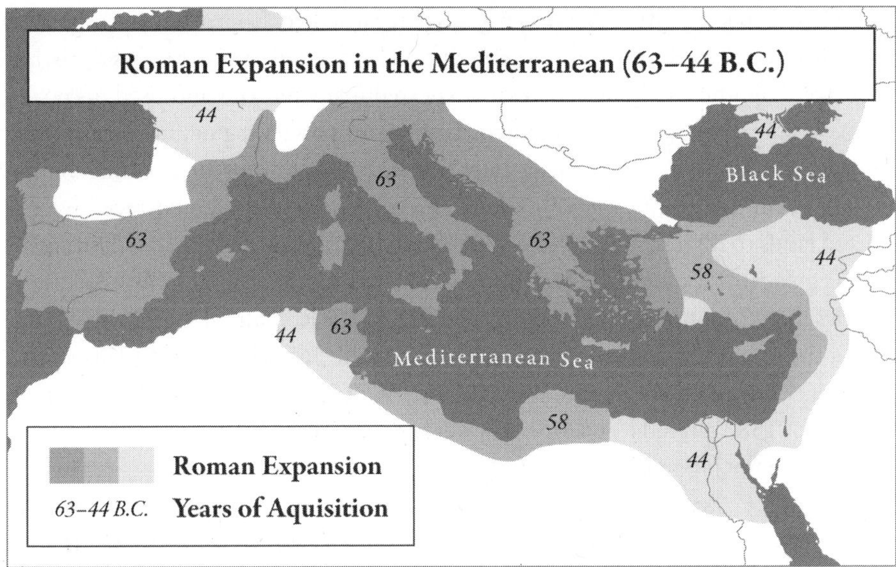

power and deliberately refused to accept the decisions he made in the East. This drove the furious Pompey into an unlikely alliance with both Crassus and **Julius Caesar** (100–44 BC).

This alliance is often referred to as the **First Triumvirate** ("rule by three men"), though it is important to note that the three men were rivals even in the midst of their collaboration. Julius Caesar, a member of the *populares* who had survived Sulla's proscriptions, was the weakest of the three, but he moved quickly to increase his influence. He received appointment as provincial governor of transalpine Gaul (modern-day southern France) and gradually subdued the Gauls and even invaded Britain. He was careful to record (and exaggerate) his victories against barbarians in simple prose so that he could gain popular support in Rome. (Latin students today still read his *Commentary on the Gallic War*.) By 50 BC, he had spent almost a decade in Gaul, had amassed private wealth, and gained both important military experience and a dedicated, battle-hardened army. He was ready to make the next move.

The triumvirate ultimately collapsed. Crassus died in 53 BC while on campaign against the Parthians to the east (see below and the insert on the Parthian Empire in chapter 15). Pompey, meanwhile, reconciled with senatorial leadership. In 49 BC, the Senate, fearful of Caesar's ambition, revoked his command. Rather than lay down arms, he illegally led his soldiers across the Rubicon River, the geographical border of his provincial governorship, and began civil war. Caesar defeated Pompey one year later, though the war dragged on until 45 BC.

Many expected the worst when Caesar returned to Rome, but he began his rule with clemency. There were no proscription lists and no murder of his rivals, but there were significant changes. Caesar advocated many reforms and used his power to make sure they were implemented. Laws were passed regulating wealth, promoting large families, and reducing debt. He increased the Senate to nine hundred members, limited the power of regional governors, and distributed recently conquered lands to his veterans. His longest-lasting reform was the calendar. During his campaign against Pompey, he had journeyed to Egypt and become embroiled in the politics there. Upon returning to Rome, he altered the Roman calendar so that it followed the solar calendar of Egypt and instituted the 365.25-day year. (This "Julian Calendar" remained the standard calendar of Western Europe until the Gregorian Reform of 1582 altered how leap years were spaced. Some branches of Christianity still observe the Julian Calendar.)

Though Caesar attempted to rule with moderation, he was not interested in sharing power. He became dictator for life in February 44 BC and declared that he would appoint future consuls and tribunes. Positions that had once been elected now became the gift of a dictator who would undoubtedly give them to those who would do his will.

The Republic had effectively ended, but its demise was long in the making. Many had played a role in undermining its traditions and stability. Decades of disintegration had culminated in Caesar's triumph, but he would not enjoy his success for long. The *optimates* hoped to recover their authority by a desperate move. On March 15, they assassinated Julius Caesar as he entered the Senate building. Some sixty men gathered around him and stabbed him over twenty times. But one man's death could not revive the Republic.

Birth of the Empire

Julius Caesar's assassins proclaimed that they had restored the Republic, but popular opinion was against them. Many Romans loved Caesar, and their affection for the dead dictator only increased when they learned that his will divided his fortune among the people of Rome. Those closest to Caesar, encouraged by this goodwill, formed a Second Triumvirate. This alliance included two of Caesar's former officers, **Mark Antony** (83–30 BC) and Marcus Aemilius Lepidus, and Caesar's great-nephew and adopted heir **Octavian** (63 BC–AD 14). The three men sealed their alliance by writing a list of several hundred individuals they wanted dead once they seized power. This included not only the orator Cicero (despite his initial support for Octavian) but also Mark Antony's uncle and even Lepidus's brother—this last at the request of Lepidus himself. The three men ruthlessly eliminated their enemies, including, of course, those responsible for Caesar's assassination. For its part, the Senate promptly recognized Julius Caesar as a god, thus beginning the practice of deifying emperors after their deaths.

As with the First Triumvirate, ambition soon brought the members into conflict. The teenage Octavian was in a particularly weak position. He had poor health and less military experience than either Antony or Lepidus. Nonetheless, when they partitioned the Republic's territory among themselves, Octavian outmaneuvered Lepidus. The latter received the title of *pontifex maximus*, or high priest of Rome, and theoretical control of the city of Rome itself. Nevertheless, true power resided in the army, and Mark Antony and Octavian claimed for themselves the territories, east and west respectively, that had the greatest number of Roman legions. As Lepidus faded into insignificance, his two colleagues prepared for war.

Augustus of Prima Porta. Made of marble, c. 1st century AD. Currently in the Vatican Museums, Vatican City. This sculpture depicts Octavian Augustus and is believed to be a marble copy of a lost bronze original. The decoration on the breastplate shows a Parthian returning a military standard (including an eagle) to a Roman in a gesture of peace.

Mark Antony appeared to be the best situated. He controlled the vast resources of the eastern Mediterranean and had more military experience. However, two factors undermined his position. The first was military in nature. The Seleucid Empire had gradually been replaced by the Parthians, a people from northwestern Iran. By 100 BC, the Parthians ruled a vast territory that included parts of modern-day Turkey and India. They represented a continual threat to Rome's eastern border, and Crassus's attempt to push them back in 53 BC ended in his death and the ruin of his army. Now, thirteen years later, the Parthians overran the border and defeated the Roman forces there. This setback was a significant blow to Antony's military prestige, but his failure was compounded in the eyes of his fellow Romans by his relationship with the Egyptian queen Cleopatra VII (69–30 BC).

Cleopatra was among the last of the Ptolemaic line that had ruled Egypt since Alexander the Great's death. Though the land of the Nile had long been under the influence of Rome, it now had an able, determined leader in Cleopatra. Earlier, she had seduced Julius Caesar when he came to Egypt pursuing Pompey's army and convinced him to support her right to the throne. Now she devoted her attention to controlling Mark Antony. Their relationship played into Octavian's hands. He could already criticize Antony for neglecting the defense of Rome's borders. Now he condemned his rival for abandoning his Roman wife and family. Octavian also asserted that Antony intended to make himself king and to divide Roman territory into petty realms for his children by Cleopatra.

War broke out between the rivals, but Octavian was careful to depict this struggle as a foreign, rather than a civil, conflict. He wanted people to see him as Rome's defender, not just another would-be dictator. In 31 BC, his navy won a decisive victory against the fleet of Cleopatra and Antony near Actium. Antony committed suicide in the aftermath of this defeat. Cleopatra may have attempted to seduce Octavian (third time's the charm!), but she killed herself once she realized that he intended to parade her in triumph through the streets of Rome. Egypt and its vast wealth were now under Octavian's personal control.

When Octavian returned to Rome in 29 BC, he was the undisputed master of its armies and its resources. All the same, Octavian was conscious of the mistakes that his great-uncle had made. Caesar's willingness to disregard tradition, to insult the Senate, and to publicize his authority through titles such as Perpetual Dictator had resulted in his death. His heir was determined not to make the same mistakes. Instead, he cast himself as the protector of Roman tradition and values.

An image of Octavian as the political savior of the Roman Republic began to form. He avoided executions and emphasized how he had brought about peace by closing the doors of the temple to Janus. His most brilliant move came in 27 BC. In that year, he publicly relinquished his authority to the Senate and declared a new beginning to the Republic. The result was precisely what he desired; the senators begged him to retain his authority lest the age of civil wars return. They gave Octavian everything that an emperor needed: control of the armies; a private bodyguard, known as the Praetorian Guard; and a new title of "Augustus" (literally, "venerable") that bestowed on him a religious aura. All that was lacking was the candid acknowledgement that he was indeed the real ruler of Rome. Eventually, Augustus (as Octavian was now known) took the title *princeps* ("first citizen"). This enabled him to claim that the Senate and the Republic still held their traditional authority even as he used this informal role of *princeps* to guide Roman policy.

Augustus had no less ambition than Caesar to remake Rome, but he carefully crafted his reforms in terms of tradition and piety. For example, he promised a religious renewal for the Roman people. The shameless, despairing poetry of Catullus

VIOLENCE AS ENTERTAINMENT

Perhaps nothing shows the dissolution of Roman morals more dramatically than the widespread enjoyment of gladiatorial combat. This "entertainment" originated as a means of honoring those who had died. Private individuals offered *munera* (Latin for "gifts") to the deceased in the form of combat that honored the memory and courage of the one who had died. The earliest *munera* occurred in 264 BC during the First Punic War. Prisoners, criminals, and slaves were forced to fight one another as gladiators using names and armor that reflected the enemies of Rome.

By the first century, *munera* had assumed a political dimension. In theory, they still honored a specific deceased Roman, but in practice, they were used by ambitious individuals to curry popular favor. The one who funded the most extravagant gladiatorial combat could win votes when he ran for office. This is why, for example, Julius Caesar had over six hundred gladiators fight in honor of his father. It did not matter that his father had died twenty years earlier; he needed the votes now.

Shin guards. Made of bronze, c. 1st century AD. Currently part of the touring exhibit, "One Day in Pompeii." Gladiatorial armor could be very expensive and ornate. These shin guards, found in the gladiatorial barracks of Pompeii, have elaborate decorations showing the god Bacchus at the top, the god Silenus in the center, and a stork fighting a snake at the bottom.

Wild beast hunts also emphasized the widespread power and influence of Rome. Each exotic animal brought before the people to be killed showcased how Rome could plunder far-off lands with impunity. Those who offered the most outlandish animals received the greatest praise. Thus, Pompey displayed hundreds of lions and leopards for the slaughter and even managed to bring the first rhinoceros to Rome. Caesar countered with the killing of hundreds of other animals, including Rome's first giraffe.

Augustus realized the importance of keeping people entertained and content, so he institutionalized the *munera*. He had the resources to fund the most lavish combats ever seen, and he combined these with wild beast hunts and the execution of prisoners so that poor Romans, in particular, would remember his munificence and not make trouble. It was no coincidence that the first permanent amphitheater, or arena, dated from his reign. Almost three hundred other permanent amphitheaters would follow.

showed how far astray Rome had gone from its earlier, virtuous myths. The atheistic poetry of Lucretius (99–55 BC) abandoned that tradition even further by declaring that the gods themselves were fictitious. Roman society was in critical need of spiritual rebirth, and Augustus set about to provide it. He promoted laws that advocated fidelity in marriage and the procreation of children. He restored many traditional religious observances and renovated numerous temples. When Lepidus died in 12

The **Ara Pacis**. Made of marble, 13-9 BC. Currently in the Museum of the Ara Pacis, Rome. This altar celebrated Augustus's triumphant return and the establishment of the *Pax Romana*. It is covered with intricate relief panels depicting various scenes of mythological or historic significance to Rome. The so-called "Tellus panel" shows a central female figure nursing two infants, reminiscent of the Capitoline She-wolf. The goddess is commonly identified as Tellus (mother earth), Italia (Italy), or Pax (peace).

BC, Augustus assumed the title *pontifex maximus* and thus formally united both religious and political supremacy in his person.

Influential writers during Augustus's time collaborated with this image of a restoration of Roman values. The historian Livy (59 BC–AD 17) wrote a massive history of Rome titled *Ab Urbe Condita* (*From the Founding of the City*) that spanned the seven centuries from Romulus to Augustus. Much of his work is now lost, but the Romans of his day reveled in his stories of past glory and virtue. The poet Virgil did even more to link the era of Augustus with the glory days of Rome. His epic poem *The Aeneid* borrowed liberally from Homer's *Iliad* and *Odyssey*, but the hero, Aeneas, embodied the values of Rome rather than Greece. Aeneas was dutiful, pious to the gods, and destined to be the ancestor of the Romans. To promote Augustus as explicitly as possible, Virgil's narrative included a vision of him as the one "who shall bring once again an Age of Gold".[2]

In addition to restabilizing Roman society, Augustus sought to reform Rome's government. The era of the city-state had long since passed, and he centralized and streamlined the old structures into an imperial system that integrated the different provinces. He promoted men based on their ability rather than their birth and worked hard to curb corruption by rewarding those governors who oversaw provinces well. His policies promoted trade and wealth, and he funded the construction of beautiful marble monuments, such as the Altar of Peace. Rome even gained a real fire department that actually helped people! It was a decisive success when his stepson, Tiberius, received formal recognition as Augustus's heir and the future leader of Rome. A new era of empire had dawned.

Conclusion

Many considered Augustus the savior of Rome. His rule effectively ended decades of proscriptions and civil wars and ushered in a new era of peace, stability, and prosperity know to historians as the *Pax Romana* ("the Roman peace"). And yet his authority was bolstered by lies and propaganda. He himself may have admitted as much when, on his deathbed, he asked those around him whether he had played his part well. When they agreed that he had, he asked for applause as he died. Nevertheless, the yearning for a savior was real. Catullus had voiced this desire for reconciliation with heaven when he lamented that the gods would never again walk on earth. Little did he know that the Son of God was soon to be born in a humble stable in Bethlehem.

2 Virgil, *The Aeneid*, trans. by Robert Fitzgerald (New York: Vintage Classics, 1990), 187.

CHAPTER 13

The Fullness of Time

But when the time had fully come, God sent forth his Son, born of woman, born under the law, to redeem those who were under the law, so that we might receive adoption as sons.

Paul of Tarsus, *Epistle to the Galatians* 4:4

Perhaps no verse in the entire New Testament so perfectly conveyed the significance of history for Christians. If God became man and entered physically into time, then everything before and after God's coming possessed a deep purpose, a meaning that transcended—or went beyond—this world into eternity. The choices made by ancient Mesopotamians, Hebrews, Egyptians, Greeks, Romans, and all other cultures were not meaningless. Instead, each mysteriously contributed to the "fullness of time" that was the era of the Incarnation.

Such an attitude encouraged the first Christians to look back upon the preceding centuries and see in their events the unfolding of God's Providence. The best of Greek philosophy, for example, taught the importance of truth and virtue. Alexander's ambitions spread these ideas and the Greek language, resulting in a widespread Hellenistic culture that facilitated communication. Hellenism's individualism also included an emphasis on individual salvation and spirituality. Finally, Roman rule under Augustus brought political unity and social order to the Mediterranean during the so-called Roman Peace, or "*Pax Romana*."

In this chapter, we resume our narrative of Jewish history in the decades immediately before and after the life of Jesus of Nazareth. As we explore the Hasmonean dynasty, the rise of the Pharisees and Sadducees, and the coming of the Romans, we can better understand details in the Gospel accounts and come to a deeper understanding of why God chose *this moment* to dwell among us and to send forth His apostles to spread the message of His coming, death, and resurrection.

On the Eve of the Incarnation

In 142 BC, the last surviving brother of Judas Maccabeus, Simon, claimed leadership of the Jewish resistance. The Seleucid Empire, tired by two decades of warfare and wary of Simon's alliance with Rome, granted Judea limited autonomy shortly thereafter. The Roman Senate also acknowledged Simon and his **Hasmonean dynasty** (141–c. 37 BC) in 139 BC. For their part, the Jewish people embraced Simon and his descendants as their leaders and high priests "until a trustworthy prophet should arise" (1 Mc 14:41).

Judea had gained partial independence, but the Seleucids could not resist interfering with Jewish life. They were concerned about the growing power of the Parthians to the east, and an independent Judea was a potential threat to their crumbling stability. In 135 BC, the Seleucid governor of Syria murdered Simon, and an army soon approached Jerusalem itself. The new high priest and Jewish leader, Simon's son **John Hyrcanus** (r. 135–105 BC), looted the treasures in King David's tomb in desperation and gave them to the Seleucid king as tribute. The army withdrew, but the Seleucids forced John to participate in a war against the Parthians. Fortunately for John, the Seleucid king died in battle in 128 BC, and John seized this opportunity to turn Judea's dream of full independence into a reality. He hired a mercenary army with more riches plundered from David's tomb and began his own expansion. His soldiers conquered Idumea in the south and forced its inhabitants to convert to Judaism. John then turned his attention to Samaria in the north.

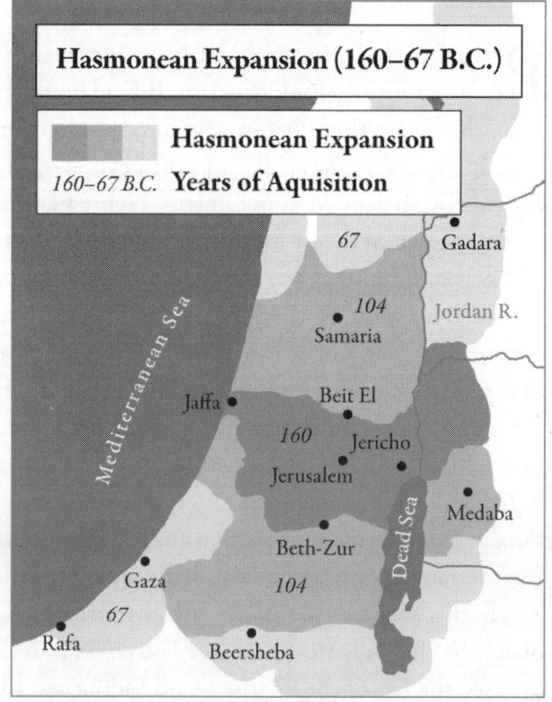

The Samaritans and Jews had become increasingly antagonistic toward one another in the years following the Jewish return to Judea. This enmity began when the Jews refused the Samaritan offer to help build the Second Temple, but the division became even more pronounced when the Samaritans constructed a rival temple near Sichem on Mount Gerizim. The mutual hostility boiled over during the time of the Maccabean Revolt. The Samaritans distanced themselves from the efforts of Judas Maccabeus and renounced any association with the Jewish people. They also embraced Hellenism and rededicated their temple on Mount Gerizim to Jupiter. John struck hard against these despised northern neighbors. By 110 BC, his army had destroyed their temple, leveled their capital city of Samaria, and ordered the population to observe Jewish customs.

John's authority brought political and military success, but lingering tensions between Jewish and Hellenistic cultures resulted in two factions within Jewish society. The **Pharisees** (literally, "those set apart") championed Jewish traditions and were the spiritual successors to the *Hasidim*, those earlier Jews who had rejected all compromise with Hellenism. The Pharisees emphasized the strict observance of the Mosaic Law and also taught that there was an "Oral Torah," a body of tradition that held parallel authority to the written Scriptures. Their ideological opponents were the **Sadducees**. The designation "Sadducee" probably derived from the name of Zadok, the high priest during the days of Solomon, and this party consisted of many Jewish priests and social elite. These welcomed Hellenistic culture and philosophy and upheld the literal interpretation of Sacred Scripture, which for them consisted of the Torah. Their literal reading of the Torah and their love of Greek philosophy led them to scorn the Pharisees' concept of an Oral Torah, their emphasis on rituals and ceremonies, and their belief in such teachings as bodily resurrection.

Most Jews looked to the Pharisees for spiritual leadership. Their strict observance of the Mosaic Law and their willingness to suffer on account of this observance won the esteem of many. John initially favored the Pharisees since his family had fought and died to preserve Jewish traditions. But this friendship soured when a Pharisee publicly cast doubt on the legitimacy of John's birth and, therefore, his eligibility to be high priest. This suspicion outraged John so much that he embraced the Sadducee faction and promoted its interests.

Hasmonean corruption worsened this ideological conflict. John attempted to separate religious and political authority in the Jewish world upon his death in 105 BC. He entrusted civil power to his wife and made his eldest son, Aristobulus I, high priest. The ambitious Aristobulus imprisoned three brothers, murdered a fourth, and ordered that his mother be starved to death. Now firmly in control, he embraced Hellenism and declared himself to be *basileus* (Greek for "king")—the first of the Hasmonean line to claim that title. He died one year later. His younger brother, Alexander Jannaeus (r. 103–78 BC), claimed both the throne and the high priesthood. He continued promoting Hellenism and openly ignored Pharisaic rituals when acting as high priest. When some criticized his behavior, he sent soldiers against them. Six thousand Pharisees died in this initial clash, and soon a full civil war was tearing Jewish society apart. Perhaps Alexander's most brutal act was the crucifixion of eight hundred Pharisees who were forced to witness the execution of their wives and children as they hung dying. Alexander himself looked on as he dined with his concubines.

Alexander's death brought a brief respite to the Pharisees, but the power struggle between Alexander's sons created another civil war. The two would-be kings foolishly appealed to a third party to decide their fate: the Roman general Pompey. In 63 BC, Pompey was at the height of his power and was in the process of bringing the eastern Mediterranean firmly under direct Roman authority. He brought an end to the civil war, captured Jerusalem, and even entered the Holy of Holies in the Temple.

The Hasmonean Kingdom was now under the authority of the Roman governor of Syria. Roman officials divided the territory into regions: Judea, Galilee, and Samaria. Technically, a king still ruled. There were also local religious councils known as the *Sanhedrin*, the most important of which was in Jerusalem. Unfortunately, we know little about the origin of these councils or how they worked. The term itself is Greek and means "sitting together" or "council."

Meanwhile, an ambitious Hasmonean official, Antipater the Idumean (c. 113–43 BC), worked behind the scenes to gain Rome's good graces and replace the Hasmoneans. The antagonism between Pompey and Julius Caesar gave him his chance. Antipater was initially an ally of Pompey, but he switched sides and sent soldiers to Caesar and Cleopatra in Egypt. For this support, Caesar declared Antipater a Roman citizen, a personal friend, and the procurator of Judea.

This close connection with those in power at Rome continued with Antipater's son, **Herod the Great** (c. 72–c. 4 BC). He cultivated friendship with Caesar's successor, Octavian, and ultimately received from the Roman Senate the title of king. Accompanied by Octavian, Herod gave public thanks at Rome's Temple of Jupiter before returning to Jerusalem and his new kingdom. Once there, he began an ambitious building regimen that included the construction of cities, theaters, hippodromes, and gymnasia. The most important of these cities was Caesarea in Palestine, which was named in honor of Octavian.

Though he also built a number of temples to Roman gods, Herod was most famous for his reconstruction of the Second Temple at Jerusalem. Herod's Idumean ancestors had been forced to convert by John Hyrcanus, and Herod wore his Judaism lightly. Still, he needed at least some support from those he ruled. Thus, around 22 BC, he began gathering the materials necessary to enlarge and beautify the Temple. Though the new Temple itself was built in a year and a half, construction on its courts and other buildings continued for the next eight decades, and even the Pharisees admitted that Herod had made the Temple far more glorious than it had been. Nonetheless, the common people detested this non-Jewish king who had been imposed by a foreign power and who only superficially followed their religion.

Herod's building projects highlighted the splendor and wealth of his court, but there was a darker side to his kingship. As king, he murdered suspected rivals, including his children by a Hasmonean wife. Indeed, Herod's execution of two sons made Augustus remark that it was better to be Herod's pig than his child. Herod became so universally unpopular that, as he lay dying in Jericho, he asked his family to gather together important men and kill them upon his death so that people would mourn at the time of his passing. Fortunately, his family prevented this last act of brutality.

The **Western Wall**, also known as the "Wailing Wall," is a limestone retaining wall for the Temple Mount in the Old City of Jerusalem. The lower half of the wall with larger stones is believed to have been begun by Herod the Great in 19 BC, while the upper half is believed to have been added later. Due to restricted access to the Temple Mount, it is considered the closest location to the Holy of Holies where Jews can pray.

Such was the king who ruled Jerusalem when the divine King of Kings drew His first breath in Bethlehem.

The Son of Man and the Kingdom of Heaven

Jesus of Nazareth (c. 4 BC–c. AD 30) was born in Bethlehem during Herod's last years. Only Matthew's Gospel records Herod's decision to slaughter the male children of Bethlehem lest there arise a rival king, but what we know of his ruthlessness makes this scenario plausible even for those who reject the Gospels as historical sources. Herod had requested that his kingdom be split among three sons, a wish that Augustus honored. Herod's son Archelaus (23 BC–c. AD 18) became the "ethnarch" of Judea, and Herod Antipas (c. 20 BC–after AD 39) became "tetrarch" of Galilee. Unfortunately, Archelaus's cruelty mirrored his father's; he killed thousands, and Augustus finally exiled him to Gaul in AD 6. In contrast, Herod Antipas carefully maintained good relations with Rome and generally avoided acts of violence. However, he did violate Jewish marriage law by marrying his sister-in-law while his brother Herod Philip (c. 27 BC–AD 34) still lived. (This Herod Philip should not to be confused with Philip the Tetrarch.) This relationship later led to his decision to execute John the Baptist.

Jesus lived as a poor Jewish carpenter in the backwater town of Nazareth until, around the age of thirty, He entered public view as a traveling preacher. Reports of miracles drew crowds to Him, but His criticisms of the Pharisees and the scribes, a class of legal scholars of the Torah, made Him enemies. Both groups were highly regarded by pious Jews, but Jesus's rebukes of their excessively complex legal interpretations threatened to undermine their social and religious prestige. Jesus's own teachings were controversial. Crowds might admire His parables and moral instructions, but His statement that His followers must eat and drink His body and blood caused many disciples to leave. His interactions with the Samaritans certainly raised eyebrows, especially when he used a

Samaritan as the model of good behavior in one of His parables and spoke with the Samaritan woman at the well (see Lk 10:25–37; Jn 4:4–30). Even His closest friends did not understand Him and frequently saw Him as a political figure who would bring about the establishment of an independent Judea.

The desire for Jewish independence came to the forefront in the decades immediately before Jesus's public career. When Augustus exiled Archelaus, he made Jerusalem and its surrounding areas into the Roman province of Judea and placed a Roman prefect in charge with troops stationed at Caesarea. Whereas taxes had previously been gathered by Jews, who then gave part of this income as a "gift" to the emperor, tax collectors now worked directly on behalf of the polytheistic Roman state. A deep division in Jewish society resulted, and some held that paying taxes directly to Caesar violated their beliefs. Some Jews, known collectively as "Zealots," even went so far as to encourage violent opposition to the Roman occupation.

Denarius of Emperor Tiberius. Made of silver c. AD 18-35. The tribute penny shown to Jesus would have been like the one shown here. The front of the coin shows Tiberius with the words TI[berivs] CAESAR DIVI AVG[vsti] F[ilivs] AVGVSTVS ("Caesar Augustus Tiberius, son of the Divine Augustus"). The back shows Tiberius's wife, Livia, with the words PONTIF[ex] MAXIM[us] ("the greatest bridge-builder").

Jesus thus faced a tricky situation when asked whether it was lawful to give tax money to Caesar. His command to give to God and to Caesar what was due to each solved the dilemma. It also undermined the system of divine rulers that had characterized human politics since ancient Mesopotamia. Whereas previous societies took for granted the blending of political and religious authority, Jesus boldly claimed that one's obligations to God were distinct from anything owed to a temporal ruler. Perhaps He had privately given this lesson to reconcile His own disciples. After all, He numbered among His closest followers both Matthew the tax collector and Simon the Zealot.

Jesus's wisdom did not placate His enemies. The Pharisee and Sadducee leaders who formed the *Sanhedrin* of Jerusalem conspired to have Jesus condemned before the Roman prefect. Historians debate whether the *Sanhedrin* merely advised the high priest or whether it was a deliberating body under his presidency. Regardless, we know that by this point the office of high priest had effectively become political. The Romans threatened to depose uncooperative priests and stored their vestments in Herod's royal palace. Every morning, the high priest symbolically acknowledged

Roman authority by receiving his ceremonial clothing from them. To make matters worse, Roman officials auctioned the high priesthood every two years to the leading (Sadducee) families, who competed with one another for the privilege. The high priest at this time was the Sadducee Caiaphas (c. 14 BC–c. AD 46). He retained his priesthood for almost twenty years, a notable achievement and a testimony to his ability to work well with Roman officials. Caiaphas saw Jesus as a threat to the fragile status quo in Judea, and he convinced "the chief priests and the Pharisees" of the *Sanhedrin* that Jesus must die so that the people could live (Jn 11:47). Yet what was His crime?

Jesus frequently described Himself as the "Son of Man" and declared the arrival of the "Kingdom of Heaven."[1] Both phrases drew from the prophecies of Daniel, a sixth-century Jew associated with the Babylonian Captivity and the beginning of Persian rule. Daniel's prophecies linked the Messiah, whom he called the Son of Man, with the coming of the Kingdom of Heaven. He described this kingdom as small in its beginning but ultimately growing to fill the world. In addition, Daniel foretold the specific timeframe of this Messiah's coming.

Jesus's contemporaries therefore expected the Messiah to appear, and His use of Daniel's terms indicated His claim to that role. But He did more. Jesus subtly indicated His equality with God throughout His public ministry. His encounter with the rich young man (see Lk 18:18–27) is a good example. When the man called Jesus "good," He did not deny His goodness but rather indicated His divinity by declaring that "only God is good." Jesus also made following *Him* equal in importance to obeying the commandments given to Moses—a truly shocking claim. The Gospels are full of these subtle exchanges where Jesus revealed, without explicitly declaring, His identity as the Son of God. He reserved those open assertions of divinity, as seen, for example, in John 8 and 10, for key moments in His ministry. Each time He did so many among His audience sought His life.

His final entry into Jerusalem shortly before Passover heralded a change. Each action consciously contributed to the clearer revelation of who the Son of Man was and was not. He both insinuated His royalty and definitively rejected the political liberation anticipated by Zealots and others by entering Jerusalem on an ass rather than at the head of an army. (For the precedent of a Jewish king entering Jerusalem on a mule, see 1 [3] Kgs 1:38.) He did not storm the Roman garrison but cleansed the Temple of its money changers. Furthermore, after years of debates, He conclusively silenced His enemies with His question about the "Son of David," a riddle that set the stage for His final, formal declaration of His identity before the highest

---

1 Many of the following observations are adapted from Brant Pitre's *The Case for Jesus* (New York: Image, 2016). We encourage interested students to read his excellent book in its entirety.

authority in Judaism. Everything came to a head when Jesus was brought before the *Sanhedrin* on the night of Holy Thursday. The high priest Caiaphas solemnly ordered Jesus to answer a direct question regarding His claims as the Son of Man. Jesus's reply was the history-shaking avowal that He was equal to God.

No Roman prefect would be troubled by debates over the Jewish God, which is why the *Sanhedrin* had to frame Jesus's offense as a threat to Rome's rule. They emphasized Jesus's claims of kingship and thus made Jesus a rival to Caesar. Pontius Pilate (r. AD 26–36) was no friend to Judaism. His refusal to respect their traditions, such as when he used Temple funds to pay for a new aqueduct into Jerusalem, had led to violent clashes between Romans and Jews. Many of those who protested his misappropriation of funds died. Such behavior earned the rebuke of the emperor himself. Pilate realized that he must avoid further turmoil if he wanted to retain his position and perhaps even his life. (Pilate ultimately disappeared from history in AD 36 after the emperor summoned him to Rome on account of his massacre of some Samaritans.) This explains the politically charged accusations against Jesus as well as the significance of His own declaration that His kingdom was not of this world. In the end, the threat of turmoil overwhelmed the voice of justice, and Pilate ordered the crucifixion of Jesus of Nazareth.

Ecce Homo ("Behold the Man") by Antonio Ciseri. Oil on canvas, c. 1860–1880. Currently in the Cantonal Art Museum of Lugano, Switzerland.

Such a death was the most shameful end to Jesus's career that could be imagined. If we consider how frequently movements collapse after the death of their leaders, we can begin to understand what the life of Jesus *should* have been in the eyes of history. His small following was in an obscure corner of the Roman Empire, and it apparently ended in catastrophe. We could rightly expect that His legacy would be merely a footnote in larger studies about more important topics. And yet in every subsequent generation, His followers have spread the message of His teachings and His death. Indeed, no king, no emperor, no warlord ever changed history as much as He did.

The Era of the Apostles

Jesus of Nazareth was dead. The movement that had followed its leader in triumph into Jerusalem a week before was now on the verge of disintegration, but no collapse happened. About eighty years after Jesus's execution, the Roman historian Tacitus recorded that Pilate had executed a certain Christ, but that this had proved to be only "a temporary setback" for Jesus's disciples, who were soon spreading their "deadly superstition" into Rome itself.[2]

"A temporary setback"?

How could this be?

The answer, of course, is Jesus's resurrection on Easter Sunday. This ushered in a new era, and the realization that He had triumphed over death ultimately transformed His followers' discouragement and despair into fearless zeal. The seeming defeat of His crucifixion became but a "temporary setback" as His disciples boldly announced the message of His victory over the grave. We see this clearly throughout the Gospel accounts. What should have been catastrophe became the disciples' source of hope and confidence in Jesus's message and divinity. Interestingly, we have no historical account of the Resurrection itself. The evangelists passed over this moment of divine glory in silence and resumed their narrative with encounters that took place afterwards. The Resurrection—that brilliant burst of eternity into time—was beyond history's descriptive capabilities.

Fifty days after Passover was the Jewish feast of **Pentecost**, and numerous Jews from communities throughout the Roman Empire and beyond had gathered in Jerusalem. Despite their different languages, all received the same message in their own tongue when, as recorded in The Acts of the Apostles, the disciples received the Holy Spirit and began to preach openly the message of Jesus's resurrection (see Acts 2:1–11). They invited everyone to join them as members of the new community of

2 Tacitus, *The Annals of Imperial Rome*, trans. by Michael Grant (New York: Penguin, 1996), 365.

THE GOSPELS AS HISTORICAL SOURCES

Secular scholars reject out of hand Jesus's various miracles, especially the Resurrection, and typically seek to discredit the historical reliability of the Gospels by questioning their authorship, their dating, and their accuracy.[3] For example, New Testament scholars such as Bart Ehrman suggest that the Gospels were not written by Matthew, Mark, Luke, and John; rather, they claim that the original texts were anonymous and only gradually came to be associated with those names to give them greater authority and trustworthiness. Furthermore, such scholars hold that these Gospels were written after AD 70 and contain later traditions that "corrupted" Jesus's original message with miracle accounts and claims of Jesus's divinity. (The analogy of the "Telephone Game" is commonly used to describe this process by which an original idea becomes garbled as it is transmitted from one person to another over time.) Still another approach argues that the Gospels were never intended to be historical at all. They were just folk tales that the simple accepted as fact.

How should the Catholic reply to these academic claims?

First of all, while damaged or incomplete manuscripts may be missing the author's name, those copies that are complete or that include the beginning of a Gospel all reference their authors. What is more, these all assign a given Gospel to the same author that we acknowledge today. If these were truly anonymous, we could expect to see a given Gospel attributed to different people in different copies. We do not. Every existing copy of Luke's Gospel, for instance, is identified as his. Therefore, the witness of our earliest primary sources indicates that the four Gospels were indeed attributed to the four people we know today. (Incidentally, it makes sense that Matthew would write a Gospel since he, as a tax collector, was the most likely to be literate from among Jesus's apostles.)

Regarding the dating, there are many arguments back and forth among academics about which Gospel came first and when each was written. Nearly everyone agrees that John's Gospel was written last. Secular historians have assumed that, because Jesus prophesied the destruction of the Temple in the Gospels of Matthew, Mark, and Luke, they also were written after the event in AD 70. But there is no scholarly proof that indicates this. In fact, Jesus's prophecy has many details that would be unnecessary if one were writing *after* the fact. Why include, for example, Jesus's command to pray that the event not take place in winter if it was known that the siege historically took place during the summer? More importantly, why not include that the prophecy was fulfilled? Luke emphasized the fulfilment of a prophecy regarding a famine during the Acts of the Apostles (see 11:28)—why would he not do the same for the much more important prophecy of Jesus? It seems possible, if not probable, that the three synoptic Gospels (Matthew, Mark, and

3 Again, the authors encourage students to read Pitre's *The Case for Jesus* for in-depth discussions on each of these points.

Luke) were composed in the decades prior to the Temple's fall. In fact, if Luke wrote before 70 and drew upon earlier Gospels that were already circulating (see Luke 1:1–4), then an early date of composition for Matthew and Mark is likely. This, in turn, undermines the suggestion that corruption gradually distorted an "original" (and presumably nonmiraculous) account of Jesus's life.

Finally, the claim that the Gospels are not historical documents flies in the face of the statements of the Gospels themselves. Matthew's and John's Gospels claim to be written by eyewitnesses of the events described, while Luke's explicitly addresses his use of witnesses in order to construct his narrative. Furthermore, the Gospels follow many conventions of ancient biography, which told their readers to view the recorded events as history. Regardless of whether we choose to accept them as fact, there is no doubt that the authors intended the Gospels to be read as such. What is more, eyewitnesses to the events would still be alive even if we accept the later dates for the composition of the Gospels. Surely, those who saw with their own eyes the events of Jesus's life would protest against a fictitious rendering of His biography.

Those who desire not to believe will find reasons to discredit the witness of the Gospels. We should confront their arguments and theories by confidently exploring the evidence more deeply.

God's adopted sons and daughters, which they called "the Way (of Life)" and which we know today as the Catholic Church.

These apostles (literally "messengers") were convinced that God had prepared the world to receive the "Good News" (*euaggelion* in Greek) of Jesus's coming. For example, among the Jews there was both a renewed loyalty to the teachings of Moses and a conscious need for reform. On the one hand, the generations after the Babylonian Captivity had faithfully preserved the exclusive worship of God and had even suffered martyrdom for their belief. On the other hand, corruption had weakened the Jewish priesthood and leadership. Even many who tried to follow the Law scrupulously were focusing on their own prestige and traditions rather than on true piety. Many Jews were hungry for genuine spiritual renewal and were open to the apostles' message that Jesus had come to save humanity.

The first Christians found a similar, favorable situation in the polytheistic Roman world. As we noted earlier, not only was there political unity and relative peace throughout the Mediterranean (the *Pax Romana*) but there was also the shared Hellenistic culture and language. Christians could easily travel and communicate, and their audiences had already encountered ideas regarding virtue and truth from Greek philosophy as well as that of individual salvation from the Mystery Religions. Furthermore, the Diaspora, the scattering of Jewish communities throughout the Mediterranean, had exposed non-Jews of good will to the beauties of the Jewish

Scriptures and worship. These sincere non-Jews, or Gentiles, were known as "God-fearers" and attended or supported their local synagogue. They became fellow recipients of the apostles' earliest preaching. It seemed as though everything was coming together to benefit the earliest followers of "the Way."

Nonetheless, even the most optimistic realized that the new community faced significant challenges from both within and without. Corruption and pettiness were the enemies within. As the ranks of early believers expanded, the temptation to claim membership while retaining one's old life was strong. We see this in the story of Ananias and Sapphira, who kept a portion of their wealth for themselves despite claiming otherwise (see Acts 5:1–11). Others, such as Simon Magus, desired to imitate and even purchase the spiritual powers of the apostles and to use them for their own ambitions (see Acts 8:9–24). Another source of contention was the natural desire to help one's family or friends rather than strangers. Acts 6:1–6 describes how those converts who came from outside of Judea did not receive the same attention and care as those from Jerusalem. The apostles temporarily solved the matter by appointing deacons (from the Greek *diakonos* meaning "servant") to oversee the equal distribution of goods, but as we will see in the chapters ahead, internal corruption caused by false conversion, ambition, or selfishness remained a constant peril for the Church.

The dangers posed by external powers were simultaneously worse and more helpful for the community of believers. Worse because faithfulness to Jesus led to persecution. Jewish authorities resisted the apostles' teachings and resented the growth of what they perceived as a heresy within the Jewish community. Some, such as Stephen the Deacon, lost their lives for boldly declaring their allegiance to Jesus. And yet such acts of witness in the face of death also confirmed many believers' faith and won new converts. For example, as disciples fled persecution in Jerusalem, they brought the Gospel to new regions. Furthermore, God used the conversion of the most fervent persecutor of the Early Church, **Saul (or Paul) of Tarsus** (c. AD 5–c. 64), to expand the ministry of the Church from Jews and God-fearers to the Gentile world itself. Already the Apostle Peter (d. c. AD 64), who had assumed a prominent leadership role on Pentecost Sunday, announced a vision that indicated that the Gentiles were to be welcomed as fellow members of "the Way." When Peter received the Roman centurion Cornelius into the Church (see Acts 10), it raised a number of questions about how such Gentile converts should behave. Were they obliged to follow the Law of Moses through circumcision, dietary restrictions, and other rituals? To put the question more directly: did belief in Jesus make the "Way of Life" something different from Judaism?

This was the question that the apostles and others debated at what is often called the **Council of Jerusalem** (c. AD 50). Paul of Tarsus championed the belief that the

Mosaic Law did not apply to the followers of Jesus, particularly its commandment that all males be circumcised. He had already seen the desire for conversion among the Gentiles, particularly in Antioch, the place where followers of "the Way" were first called "Christians." (*Christos*, the Greek word for "anointed," is a translation of the Hebrew "messiah" and is commonly used to identify Jesus of Nazareth.) The leaders of the Church of Jerusalem, including its bishop, the Apostle James the Just, believed that Paul's claim that the Gentiles did not need to be circumcised jeopardized their efforts to convert their fellow Jews to belief in Jesus. Nonetheless, they also acknowledged that the miracles experienced by Paul and Peter had indicated divine favor for their ministry among the Gentiles. Unfortunately, our understanding of the events at the council is incomplete, but we know that ultimately the leaders agreed with Paul that circumcision was unnecessary for Gentiles to become followers of Jesus.

This apparent success soon unraveled as more divisions and disputes broke out—this time over the dietary restrictions imposed by the Mosaic Law. Paul remained firm and even rebuked Peter for not remaining consistent in his position that certain parts of the Mosaic Law were no longer binding. The division ran deep, and Paul's fiercest critics were fellow Christians.

Even as Christians debated among themselves, the Jews of Judea had become increasingly hostile to Roman rule. In AD 66, a revolt broke out that soon required the presence of no less than three Roman legions. After four years of devastating warfare, the legions besieged Jerusalem itself. Josephus, a contemporary witness, wrote *The Jewish War* and provided details of this horrific time. Pharisees, Zealots, and others fought amongst themselves even as the Romans came ever closer to seizing control of the Temple. Famine raged within the besieged Temple and the Romans crucified those whom they caught foraging for food outside its walls. According to Josephus, they eventually ran out of wood because they had executed so many. Within the Temple walls, opponents accused the high priest of conspiring with the Romans. In anger they killed him, his sons, and other members of the *Sanhedrin*. The hunger was reportedly so overwhelming that there were acts of cannibalism. Finally, in AD 70, on the same day that Nebuchadnezzar's army had destroyed Solomon's Temple centuries earlier, Jesus's prophecy of the Temple's destruction became reality as Roman soldiers set fire to the Temple complex in their efforts to seize control of Jerusalem.

For the Jews, it was a pivotal turning point in their history. According to contemporary sources, hundreds of thousands perished during the siege, and many survivors were brought as slaves to Rome and soon put to work building the famous Colosseum. Among the Jews still left in Judea, there was a crisis of leadership. People blamed the tragedy on the leadership of both Sadducees and Zealots and turned toward the Pharisees for leadership. The *Sanhedrin* became a formal governing body, and the title "rabbi"—once merely a title of respect—now became a recognized office invested with teaching authority by the Pharisees of the *Sanhedrin*. This was the beginning of Judaism as we experience it today.

The Christians interpreted the Temple's destruction as God's sign that Christianity was distinct from Judaism. Most abandoned the idea that Gentile converts needed to follow the Mosaic Law, and Christians developed their own particular rituals and worship inspired by Jesus's example that were independent of those of the Jewish Temple. The split between Christian and Jew expanded to the point that Christians of the following century no longer centered their devotional life in Jerusalem. Indeed, other cities that had larger Christian communities, such as Caesarea, Antioch, and Alexandria, became more important. The most prominent of these new focal points was Rome. There, as we will see in the

The **Arch of Titus**. Constructed c. AD 81. Located on the Via Sacra in Rome, Italy. This celebrated the victory of Titus and Vespasian over the Jewish rebellion in Judea. The inner panel on the south side shows the items taken from the Temple, including the Menorah, the Gold Trumpets, and the Table of Showbread.

next chapter, Christians endured their first imperial persecution, and it was then, in the years immediately preceding the Temple's devastation, that both Peter and Paul accepted martyrdom for Christ.

Stories abound of the different missions the apostles undertook to spread the "Good News" of Jesus. Most of these belong to the realm of tradition rather than history because, without further evidence, we cannot responsibly claim to know what actually happened historically and what may have arisen from well-meaning, but unverifiable, devotion.[4] A notable exception is the belief that the Apostle Thomas went to India and established Christian communities there. Our meager historical records at least partially corroborate this tradition.

Conclusion

The "temporary setback" of Jesus's crucifixion had given way to Christianity's rapid expansion across the Mediterranean. Through the preaching of Paul and others, both Jews and Gentiles embraced the "Way of Life" and shared the "Good News" of Jesus throughout the Roman Empire. Even setbacks, such as the persecution in Jerusalem, promoted conversions as the disciples settled in new areas and gave witness to their love for Jesus.

Nonetheless, Christians were yet but a small minority in a much larger, hostile Roman world. The internal and external dangers that they had faced in the decades immediately following Jesus's resurrection amplified as the movement spread and grew in numbers. In the next chapter, we trace how the small, growing mustard seed of Faith survived in the midst of persecutions, heresies, and the political turmoil of the Roman Empire.

---

4 Students interested in reading more about the apostles, with a brief mention of the later traditions that arose, should consult Pope Benedict XVI, *Jesus, The Apostles, and the Early Church* (San Francisco: Ignatius, 2007).

CHAPTER 14

Wheat Among Weeds

I asked at their own lips whether they were Christians, and if they confessed, I asked them a second and third time with threats of punishment. If they kept to it, I ordered them for execution; for I held no question that whatever it was that they admitted, in any case obstinacy and unbending perversity deserve to be punished.

Pliny, Letter to Trajan

You have followed, my dear Secundus, the process you should have done in examining the cases of those who were accused to you as Christians. . . . They are not to be sought out; but if they are accused and convicted, they must be punished.

Trajan, *Reply to Pliny*[1]

Romans gradually realized that Christianity was distinct from Judaism in the years following the destruction of the Jewish Temple. This recognition did not lead to respect, for conservative Romans interpreted this new religion as a dangerous "superstition" and considered their Christian neighbors a threat to traditional Roman morals. We see this attitude expressed in our epigraphs for this chapter. Pliny the Younger ("Secundus"), a governor in Anatolia, suspected that the region's Christians were causing social unrest and wrote to the Emperor Trajan for advice. On the one hand, these letters highlight Rome's hostility: those accused of practicing Christianity faced imminent death. On the other hand, Trajan's command to avoid seeking Christians revealed a more complex attitude than simple hatred. He was suspicious enough of their beliefs to execute them but fair enough to maintain that Rome should not ignore its own laws in order to eradicate them. As the years advanced and Christians became more numerous, Roman suspicion gradually evolved into intellectual debate which, in turn, led to eventual acceptance. Still, Rome's conversion was far in the future; for the moment, many

1 John W. Coakley and Andrea Sterk, eds., *Readings in World Christian History Volume I: Earliest Christianity to 1453* (New York: Orbis, 2018), 23–4.

assumed that public adherence to Christianity destabilized the Empire. For their part, Christians frequently withdrew from Roman society, lest they be corrupted by its vices. They evangelized in the midst of suspicion and persecution, but their greatest challenge came from within as rival interpretations of Christianity developed into formidable heresies.

In this chapter, we trace the parallel stories of Christianity and the Roman Empire in the period immediately following the life of Jesus of Nazareth. We highlight early imperial dynasties and their interactions with Christianity, concluding in the midst of a Roman golden age. We also explore the early Church's institutions and core teachings and their heretical alternatives. In contrast to the empire's prosperity, the Christian Church of this era seemed fragmented and already overwhelmed with setbacks. To contemporary Christians, persecutions and heresies must have seemed like weeds planted by the enemy to destroy God's harvest (see Mt 13:24–30). They could only trust that God would ensure the survival of the "wheat" He had planted.

Imperial Rome's First Dynasties

Augustus had initiated a period of peace, promoted Rome's traditional moral values, and avoided further civil disorder. Nonetheless, he had no son to succeed him and reluctantly adopted his stepson Tiberius (r. 14–37) as his heir.[2] The Senate acknowledged Tiberius as the new *princeps* ("first citizen") and thus established the **Julio-Claudian dynasty** (27 BC–AD 68). This first imperial dynasty derived its name from the two families (Julius and Claudius) that became intertwined through Augustus's adoption of Tiberius. Each subsequent member was related to both families even though none of them was the biological son of his predecessor. Unfortunately, some were also among the most infamous rulers in Roman history.

The shift from Augustus's diligence to his successors' decadence happened swiftly. Tiberius was already in his fifties when he became *princeps* and, after about a decade, he decided to withdraw from Rome to the island of Capri. Stories of his cruelty and debauchery there made him despised in the capital, but he still wielded enough authority to torture and kill those in the Senate who resented his absence and depravity. When he died in 37, the populace of Rome openly celebrated and desired to dishonor his body by throwing it into the Tiber River. Such was the emperor whom the *Sanhedrin* had declared to be their king on the day Pilate ordered Jesus's crucifixion (see John 19:15).

2 Now that our journey through history has taken us beyond the traditional BC/AD split, all dates are "AD" unless otherwise noted.

Tiberius's death brought little respite. Gaius, his successor, was better known to history by his nickname "Little Boot," or, in Latin, Caligula (r. 37–41). Years earlier, soldiers serving under Caligula's father had affectionately bestowed this name on the little toddler who visited their camp. Now, as Tiberius's adopted heir, he received the titles of *princeps*, *Pontifex Maximus*, and emperor. He was twenty-four. Sources conflict about whether Caligula was already a degenerate when he rose to power or whether absolute power corrupted him. It is possible that the horrors he experienced as a teenager under Tiberius's tutelage on the island of Capri had warped any sense of right and wrong years before he became emperor.

Regardless of when insanity took hold, Caligula's brief reign witnessed numerous murders and acts of irrationality. Reports circulated that he sent soldiers to the English Channel in order to collect seashells along the beach and that he intended to make his horse a consul. In 40, he proclaimed that he was a god and ordered all the empire to worship him. This was a shocking development. Previous rulers, such as Julius Caesar and Augustus, had been declared divine after their deaths, but Caligula, like Naram-Sin of old, desired such honors while still alive. Less than a decade earlier, Jesus had taught His followers to give what belongs to God to God alone, and now the emperor planned to erect a statue of himself in the Jewish Temple. Caligula's divinity was short-lived. Many in Rome wanted his death, and members of the emperor's private army, the Praetorian Guard, murdered the twenty-eight-year-old "god."

The next Julio-Claudian ruler made sure to pay the Praetorian Guard well to secure his rule. This was Caligula's uncle, Claudius (r. 41–54). Many considered him too physically weak to be effective since he suffered from a limp and partial deafness. Nonetheless, his reign was a partial lull from the lawlessness of Tiberius and Caligula. He even established Roman control over much of Britain before his wife decided to murder him.

The **Palentine Nero**. Made of marble, c. mid-1st century AD. Currently in the Antiquarium of the Palatine, Rome, Italy.

Nero (r. 54–68), the most notorious of the Julio-Claudians, became *princeps* at the age of sixteen after his mother killed his stepfather, Claudius. He showed restraint during his first years of rule, but lure of unbridled power proved too overwhelming. He became increasingly unstable, ordered the deaths of his tutor and mother, and devoted himself to music, literature, and his passions. Nero's reputation for shamelessness was so prevalent that when a fire broke out in Rome in 64, many believed that he had started the inferno. The fire continued for days, killing thousands and destroying two-thirds of the city. Whether Nero actually started the fire is still debated. He did organize efforts to put out the conflagration and provided food and shelter for the survivors at his own expense. However, he also set aside recently devastated areas for his newest palace. Resentment grew, and it did not help when people learned that he—ever the aspiring musician—had sung about the fall of Troy as he watched flames consume his capital. Whether responsible or not, Nero needed a distraction.

Thus it was that the first formal Roman persecution of Christians began. Romans already viewed them with suspicion, making them the perfect scapegoat for the disaster. The tortures inflicted upon these early martyrs showcased Nero's depravity: some were fed to beasts, others he burned as human candles to light his nighttime parties. According to tradition, this persecution claimed the lives of the apostles Peter and Paul. As we will see, their martyrdoms at Rome gave that city and its Christian community special significance to many in the wider Christian world.

By this point, the Julio-Claudians had largely disregarded the empire's general well-being for decades. The empire's ability to survive such misrule suggested its underlying strength, but developments in its provinces indicated that it could not sustain this neglect indefinitely. For example, a significant revolt arose in Judea in 66 when Romans seized treasures from the Temple as tax money. Fighting continued for seven years, and Rome needed approximately sixty thousand soldiers to subdue the region. The destruction of the Jewish Temple in 70 was its most dramatic moment, but Nero never learned that the legions reestablished control. He had committed suicide in 68 when he realized that a rebellion had arisen against him.

Nero's death led to civil war, and the ultimate victor was Vespasian (r. 69–79), who established the Flavian dynasty (69–96). Unlike the Julio-Claudians, Vespasian did not come from society's aristocratic elite. His was a rural family, and his father had been a tax collector. He had served ably during Claudius's campaign in Britain and was the commander charged with subduing Judea during the Jewish Revolt. He was practical, financially prudent, valued simplicity, and brought a much-needed dose of sensible government to Rome. His most famous architectural achievement was the Flavian Amphitheater, better known as the Colosseum. Treasures seized from the Jewish Temple funded its construction, while Jewish captives labored in its building for eight years.

Vespasian left the empire more stable and financially secure than it had been in decades, but affairs began to unravel once again after his death. His son Titus

The **Flavian Amphitheater** (or **Colosseum**). Built of limestone, tuff, wood, bricks, and concrete. Construction began under Vespasian in 72 and was completed under Titus in 80. The amphitheater seated about 60,000 people. The name "Colosseum" probably first referred to a colossal statue of Nero that stood nearby. It was used for public spectacles such as gladiatorial combat, reenactment of battles, and dramatic performances. There was a retractable awning which covered two-thirds of the arena to keep the audience comfortable.

(r. 79–81) had overseen the fall of Jerusalem when Vespasian left to secure the throne, but Titus's reign was brief and overshadowed by the eruption of Mount Vesuvius in 79 and another massive fire in Rome. Rule passed to his brother, Domitian (r. 81–96), who declared himself "lord and god" (*dominus et deus*) and did away with Augustus's fiction that the Senate still mattered. He oversaw every aspect of government and strictly enforced its laws. This attention to the public order was theoretically good, but Domitian's severity created an oppressive atmosphere. People feared the savage punishments he inflicted. (According to tradition, Domitian exiled John the Evangelist to Patmos Island, where the apostle wrote the Book of Revelation. Later Christians assumed that this was part of a general persecution, but there is little evidence of widespread anti-Christian violence.) Domitian's unpopularity did not extend to the army. He realized that loyal legions were his best defense and paid them very well. Nonetheless, the military could not protect him from everyone. A group of conspirators—which may have included his own wife—assassinated him in 96.

Rome stood at an important crossroads. Though the Flavian dynasty had ended, the Senate realized that a century of emperors had made it difficult to abandon the monarchy. They chose Nerva (r. 96–98), a fellow-senator who was already sixty-six, to succeed Domitian. Perhaps some senators genuinely hoped to restore authority to the Senate and intended Nerva's reign to be a step in that direction. If so, they were disappointed. The Praetorian Guard and the army remained loyal to Domitian's memory and coerced Nerva to appoint an heir who was acceptable to the army. He chose the general Trajan, who took control when Nerva died several months later. Ancient Rome's golden age had dawned.

Roman Renewal and the Question of Christianity

Trajan was part of a group of rulers that historians call the **Five Good Emperors** (96–180). These men differed from each other in many ways, but they shared a common desire to promote Rome's stability and avoid the destructive, selfish pursuits that had characterized earlier reigns. These "Good Emperors" oversaw the pinnacle of polytheistic Rome's achievements: its borders expanded, culture flourished, and its laws—at least some of them—became more humane and just. Yet despite Rome's outward success, rampant poverty and moral rot still endured. Cruel practices like gladiatorial combat were now commonplace, and many elites focused solely on amassing more treasures. Those who felt spiritual hunger often sought fulfillment in traditional piety or in the "Mystery Religions" from the eastern provinces and looked upon Christianity's teachings as dangerous and subversive.

Historians generally identify Nerva as the first "Good Emperor," but his brief reign was important primarily because he appointed Trajan as his successor. While Nerva represented the Roman senatorial elite, Trajan (r. 98–117) was a warrior through and through. He came from Rome's provinces rather than its heartland. His focus was the military, and he remained with his army along the empire's borders for eighteen months before making his first journey as emperor to the city of Rome. He was soon with his soldiers again, and he expanded Roman might north of the Danube, conquered the Sinai Peninsula, and even occupied the heartland of Mesopotamia. In the midst of these conquests, Trajan did not neglect affairs closer to home. He supported building projects that improved infrastructure and dutifully showed respect to the Senate. By the time of his death, Trajan apparently enjoyed near-universal popularity among the people. Later generations continued to look upon his reign favorably: a medieval legend suggested that the sixth-century Pope Gregory I was so moved by Trajan's sense of justice that he successfully prayed for Trajan's entry into Heaven; Dante likewise described the emperor as enjoying Paradise in his *Divine Comedy*. Nonetheless, as we saw above in our epigraph for this chapter, Trajan viewed Christians as subversive and tolerated their execution. He also staged massive gladiatorial games to celebrate his achievements and to keep the Roman people entertained through bloody spectacle.

If Trajan was a daring military commander who personally led his soldiers on multiple fronts, his successor, Hadrian (r. 117–138), was a man of letters and culture. This is not to say that Hadrian neglected his armies. He spent years touring the empire's frontier and living among the soldiers, but his heart was not in campaigning. Instead of Trajan's dynamic expansion, Hadrian withdrew from Mesopotamia and established a defensive wall in England to create what he thought were more defensible borders. Hadrian reveled in the glories of Greek philosophy and culture and was more at home in Athens than in Rome. His love of philosophy inspired beneficial reforms, such as the outlawing of human sacrifice and the castration of slaves. However, his eagerness for Greco-Roman culture also unleashed the worst war of his reign.

The **Mausoleum of Hadrian**. Built on the west bank of the Tiber River in Rome between 134-139. According to popular tradition, the archangel Michael appeared there in 590 to signal the end of a plague. This led to the mausoleum being known as Castel Sant'Angelo ("Castle of the Holy Angel"). A large marble statue of St. Michael was added to the top in 1536, and the current bronze statue was placed in 1753. The popes converted the mausoleum into a castle during the 14th century and connected it to St. Peter's using a fortified corridor. It has served as a papal fortress, residence and even prison.

The Bar Kochba Revolt (132–136) took its name from the mysterious "Bar Kochba" ("Son of the Star"), an otherwise unknown figure who identified as the Jewish messiah. Hadrian's intention to reestablish Jerusalem as a Hellenistic city complete with polytheistic temples started a rebellion led by Bar Kochba. The consequences of this uprising were catastrophic: hundreds of thousands of Jews perished, countless villages were destroyed, and the survivors were sold into slavery. Romans forbade Jews to enter *Aelia Capitolina* (as the rebuilt Jerusalem was now known) except on the anniversary of the Temple's destruction. The former Temple area became the site of a temple to Jupiter, while Mount Calvary became a temple to Venus. For their part, surviving Jewish leaders became more cautious and began to interpret the prophecy of a messiah as a purely spiritual message rather than a prediction of someone to come.

The next emperor was Antoninus Pius (r. 138–161). He spent the majority of his reign in or near Rome and enjoyed one of the most peaceful and uneventful periods of Roman history. He was an able administrator and enacted laws that promoted more humane treatment of slaves. For example, one law mandated that consistently mistreated slaves had to be sold to a different, more benevolent owner. As we will see in the next chapter, his choice of successor was his most important decision.

It was during this era of the Five Good Emperors that Christianity increasingly came to public attention. Some Romans were willing to interpret Christianity within the framework of their own myths and practices. It was not difficult for them to accept Jesus's claim to be the Son of God since many Roman myths told of the gods having children. Christians resisted this syncretism, or blending of religions, and Romans intent on preserving social order came to view their unwillingness to blend in with the rest of society as subversive.

Roman religion permeated the day-to-day life of the empire's inhabitants. Numerous statues of the gods were in public places, and Roman games, theaters, or other pastimes included a public sacrifice or acknowledgement of Rome's gods. Romans, like peoples of other ancient societies, believed these public demonstrations secured divine protection for the empire and its people. They saw those who refused to participate in such devotions as antisocial and irreligious. (A parallel can be made with modern society's reverence for the nation state, embodied in the practice of participating in the national anthem before sporting events. Just as many today would consider it unpatriotic to refuse to stand for the national anthem before a ballgame, so, too, many saw the refusal to participate in a sacrifice or ritual as a rejection of their society and its values.)

Furthermore, Romans argued that the gods had blessed the empire. Did not Rome's rise to power demonstrate their providence? They concluded that those who condemned their public rituals were irrational and considered their gods unnecessary. Romans supposed that such impiety must derive from a superstitious belief in unchanging fate, which, they argued, ultimately led to disbelief in the gods and atheism. This explains why Roman judges often denounced Christianity as a "superstition" and executed Christians on the charge of atheism. Their refusal to partake in public rituals convinced Romans that they rejected the concept of providence and were ultimately undermining respect for the divine. For pious Romans, like Trajan and Pliny, the good of society demanded that Christians be chastised.

Speculation also arose regarding Christian activities, and rumors spread that Christians engaged in cannibalism and other revolting practices. Pliny alluded to this gossip when he wrote to Trajan that Christians claimed to eat only "normal" food. Such allegations persisted, and some Christians decided to correct the misunderstanding by explaining their practices to a polytheistic audience. These writers, known collectively as the apologists (*apologia* is Greek for "defense"), hoped their explanations would convince the broader Roman community that Christians were pious, had goodwill towards everyone, and did not deserve punishment.

The most famous of these apologists was **Justin Martyr** (c. 100–c. 165). He had converted to Christianity after seeking wisdom in different philosophical schools. Justin concluded that all truth led to Christ and that everyone who sought it sincerely, such as Socrates, discovered "seeds of truth" that God scattered throughout creation. Therefore, Justin argued, all that was best in society was actually Christian, for Jesus was the Truth and unified everything good in Himself.

The apologists dispelled misconceptions about Christian practices and encouraged their polytheistic opponents to take its moral claims seriously. Celsus (fl. 170),

The **ichthys** (ΙΧΘΥΣ in Greek characters) is an acronym for the Greek Ἰησοῦς Χρῖστός Θεοῦ Υἱός Σωτήρ ("Jesus Christ, God's Son, Savior"). The circular depiction to the far right is made by combining all the Greek letters together. This particular ichthys was carved into marble in the ruins of ancient Ephesus in modern day Turkey.

the earliest known Roman author to write specifically against Christianity, may have written his *True Doctrine* in response to Justin, but, unfortunately, only fragments of this text survive. He apparently did not mention cannibalism or other horrors but rather advanced intellectual arguments against Christianity's beliefs. Among his criticisms were that Christians worshiped two gods and were not true monotheists and that they borrowed their ideas from Greek philosophy. Celsus and many others remained hostile, but thanks to the apologists, they now viewed Christianity as a parallel spiritual and intellectual position that both possessed its own moral code and required a sophisticated response.

The apologists also played an important role in Christianity's development. Previously, Christian texts had predominately targeted fellow believers; now, Christians began to engage with the educated Greco-Roman world and its philosophies. Justin, for example, encouraged deeper reflection on Christianity's beliefs through his confidence that all truth belonged to Christ. This perspective inspired later Christians to see philosophy, despite its association with polytheism, as a tool to understand and express their beliefs more clearly. Furthermore, Roman rebuttals to the apologists, like that of Celsus, helped Christianity to mature. These intellectual challenges to their convictions forced Christians to reevaluate why they held a given belief, why it was important, and how they could defend it. As we will see in the next section, such intellectual development was desperately required, for early Christians also had to identify false teachings within their own communities.

The Apostolic Tradition and Its Challengers

Christianity continued to spread despite Roman suspicion. Much like the small mustard seed that became the greatest tree in the garden (see Mt 13:32), belief in Jesus slowly took root and blossomed. Much of this early growth, again like the sprouting mustard seed, occurred quietly and without fanfare. For a number of reasons, including the threat of persecution, Christians did not produce many texts that described their ideas and practices in the generations immediately following the Apostles. Surviving documents hint at traditions and institutions that later became prominent, and historians still debate about when a given practice or role arose within Christian history. To complicate matters, there were competing interpretations of Christianity. Each of these claimed to offer the original teachings of the apostles, and early Christians, already harried by Roman opposition, had to develop means of distinguishing truth from error. It was in this context that many embraced apostolic succession as the criterion of orthodoxy, or right belief. This position upheld the authority of bishops because they were the successors of the apostles and therefore shared in the apostles' leadership role within the Christian community.

MITHRAISM AND CHRISTIANITY

We introduced the Mystery Religions in chapter 10, but it is worthwhile returning to the topic in the context of Roman society. While many Romans mistrusted Christianity, they generally, like the Hellenistic Greeks before them, found Mystery Religions very attractive. Roman soldiers, for example, adopted the Persian god Mithras as their especial deity and underwent a series of initiations into his worship. This involved a subterranean sacrifice of a bull and a sacred banquet that honored Mithras and the Unconquered Sun (*Sol Invictus*).

Unfortunately, we do not know much about **Mithraism** because adherents consciously shrouded their beliefs and rituals in secrecy. This has not stopped some historians from stressing superficial parallels between it and Christianity. To these scholars, Christianity is simply another Mystery Religion since Christians did not discuss their beliefs openly and often met secretly to avoid unwanted attention. They argue that Baptism, the Holy Eucharist, and other aspects of Christian life derived from practices in Mithraism. Initiates into Mithraism, for example, underwent a type of baptism ceremony which concluded with a mark on the initiates' foreheads, which some identify as a parallel to the sacrament of Confirmation. However, the evidence is not conclusive, and other scholars suggest that it was Mithraism and other Mystery Religions that were borrowing from Christianity. Contemporary Christians, for their part, held that Mystery Religions were diabolical counterfeits intended to lead people away from Jesus's salvific sacraments. They were unlikely to imitate something they considered demonic.

Mithras Killing a Bull. Made of marble, c. 100–200. Currently in the Louvre Museum, Paris, France.

Furthermore, unlike Christianity, Mystery Religions were a supplement to Roman piety—not a replacement. Soldiers could easily worship Mithras *and* Jupiter by attending a secret ritual *and* participating in the public cult of Rome. This is why Romans accepted and tolerated these religions while simultaneously rejecting Christianity as superstitious. Christians refused to blend their beliefs with other religions and to partake in official acts of worship, and that made all the difference.

The earliest, and perhaps most striking, example of this apostolic tradition was the ***Epistle to the Corinthians*** by Clement, the fourth bishop of Rome (r. c. 92–c. 100). Later Christians taught that Clement was either a freed slave or the son of one; moreover, they thought that he died in exile during the reign of Trajan. (The fact that there is no known grave for him in Rome may be evidence of this tradition's accuracy.) He possibly wrote his letter shortly after Domitian's death in 96 to heal a schism that existed in Corinth. For reasons unknown, some Corinthians had rebelled against their *presbyters* (Greek for "elders") and installed a group of younger, would-be leaders for the community.

Clement's defense of the displaced *presbyters* is notable for several reasons. First, the letter clearly claimed the Roman Church's authority to intervene in the affairs of the Corinthian Church.[3] Clement believed that both Peter and Paul had suffered martyrdom in Rome, and he argued this unique double-apostolic foundation gave the Roman Church special authority. (It is worth noting that John the Evangelist was probably still alive at this time, but both Clement and the Corinthians accepted Rome's role as arbitrator.) Secondly, he emphasized obedience as the foundation for proper Christian life. Just as most soldiers in an army are not generals, so not all in a given Christian community are *presbyters*. (Again, it is worth noting that his argument assumed as established fact that there existed the formal distinction between the laity [that is, nonordained members of the Church] and an ordained leadership or hierarchy.) So influential was Clement's *Epistle* that many early Christians considered it a part of Sacred Scripture.

The letters of **Ignatius of Antioch** (c. 35–c. 108 / c. 60–c. 140) reveal even more about the hierarchy within early Christian communities. This bishop of Antioch was sent to Rome for execution, probably during the time of Pliny's persecution. He

---

3 Those who wish to argue that this letter is *not* an early example of papal authority usually point to the fact that Clement is writing on behalf of the Roman Church rather than explicitly invoking his own role as bishop. Indeed, this aspect of the epistle has been used to suggest that the Church of Rome did not develop the office of the monarchical bishop (that is, one bishop for the diocese) until after Clement. These observations are intimately tied to the dating of the epistle. Most historians believe that it was written c. 96 because 1) the fourth-century historian Eusebius of Caesarea recorded that Clement became bishop of Rome toward the end of Domitian's reign, and 2) Clement mentions recent misfortunes, which historians have long associated with a persecution during the reign of Domitian. However, as it becomes clearer that there was no systematic persecution during Domitian's reign, the dating for the epistle has begun to be reevaluated. Most notably, Thomas Herron claims that internal evidence (that is, evidence within the document) suggests that the epistle's misfortunes actually reference the period prior to the Temple's destruction in 70. He proposes that Clement wrote as a secretary, which is why he does not claim his own authority but rather stresses that of the Church of Rome. It was not until decades later that he himself became Rome's bishop. If this reading is accurate, it helps explain why there is no clear reference to a bishop in Rome since it was possibly written in the early aftermath of Peter and Paul's martyrdoms when the Roman Church was transitioning from the apostolic era to that of their successors. For further details, please see Thomas J. Herron, *Clement and the Early Church of Rome: On the Dating of Clement's First Epistle to the Corinthians* (Steubenville, OH: Emmaus Road Publishing, 2010). The authors would like to thank Otto Feil for pointing us toward Herron's thesis.

wrote a series of epistles to different communities during this journey. In them he clearly differentiated a structure of authority, beginning with the bishop and extending to presbyters and deacons. Furthermore, he described a bishop as "the vicar of God" and "the vicar of Jesus," and stressed that everyone ought to obey his local bishop—even to the point of not marrying unless he gave consent. Ignatius was also the first we know to have used the term "Catholic Church." "Catholic" is Greek for "universal" or "general," and his use of this term expressed the conviction that Jesus's Church transcended local identities and was meant for all.

"Catholic" would become the standard designation for Christian by the fourth century, but in Ignatius's day many communities still emphasized their regional characters and customs, which included alternative terminology and arrangements of authority. Some churches, for example, did not have "bishops" but instead used "apostle" and "prophet" as titles. Others, such as that in Jerusalem, emphasized the authority of a committee of *presbyters* which was probably modeled on the Jewish *Sanhedrin*. The term "presbyter" only gradually came to have the restricted meaning of ordained minister. For decades, the term could reference any number of (non-ordained) roles, thus making it difficult for later historians to piece together the practices of a given community. Another office that existed in some places was that of deaconess. These virgins or widows helped instruct women or aided them when, for example, they were being baptized. Unlike deacons, there is no evidence that they had liturgical roles. As the second century progressed, these regional differences disappeared as bishops, *presbyter*-priests, and deacons increasingly became the standard organization for Christian Churches.

Ignatius's early witness to the authority of bishops has been controversial. John Calvin, the sixteenth-century Protestant, dismissed his letters as forgeries because Calvin considered episcopal authority a later invention. Modern historians, in contrast, view the letters as authentic but debate when precisely Ignatius died. It does not help that even his contemporaries were uncertain about his fate: Polycarp, a disciple of John the Evangelist and the recipient of one of Ignatius's letters, wrote that he did not know whether Ignatius had died a martyr.

In contrast to Ignatius's vision of a universal Church united under the authority of bishops, there were alternative interpretations of Christianity that were later condemned as heretical and are known collectively to historians as **Christian Gnosticism**. *Gnosis* is the Greek word for "knowledge," and a common thread that united the different Gnostic beliefs was their emphasis on special teachings that were clandestinely passed down to select disciples. Gnosticism—that is, this emphasis on hidden, spiritual knowledge—predated Christianity and could be found in multiple religions, including Judaism. According to tradition, the first

Christian Gnostic was Simon Magus, the man who attempted to purchase spiritual power from the Apostle Peter (see Acts 8:9–24). Simon apparently turned to secret (and diabolical) knowledge when Peter refused to sell the gifts of the Holy Spirit. There is also evidence that the Apostle Jude was responding to early Gnostic tendencies in his epistle. Nonetheless, just like the Mystery Religions (see chapter insert on Mithraism), the Gnostic emphasis on secrecy deprives us of a clear understanding of what precisely their beliefs were and how they arose.

Despite this incomplete information, we can identify certain common traits among the various Christian Gnostic sects. Their emphasis on knowledge and the spirit frequently led to the condemnation of the body and the material world. In its most radical expressions, the created world was seen as sinful and under the authority of an evil god (usually associated with Yahweh of the Old Testament). Some even taught that the serpent in the book of Genesis was a hero because he showed Adam and Eve the hidden knowledge that freed them from Eden. Some Gnostic texts survived and have gained much attention in modern society. The *Gospel of Thomas* and the *Gospel of Mary* are perhaps the most famous of these. Even the casual reader quickly discerns how different these are from the Gospels of the New Testament. Their emphasis on hidden truth and secret rites stands in stark contrast to the relatively straightforward narrative of the four canonical Gospels.

Though not technically Gnostic, the teachings of **Marcion of Sinope** (c. 85–c. 165) paralleled Gnostic hostility to the material world and the God of the Old Testament. Our biographical information for Marcion is sketchy, but we know that the Roman Church excommunicated him in 144. He denied any allegorical interpretation of Sacred Scripture; only a literal reading was true, and he concluded that the Hebrew Scriptures referenced a deity other than Jesus's Father. After all, these texts described God as, for example, ignorant (He asked Adam questions) and spiteful (He hardened pharaoh's heart). He concluded that the Yahweh of the Jews had created the material world, which Marcion viewed as a place of corruption and sin. Marcion contrasted Yahweh with a "god of the spirit," that is, Jesus's Father. This deity, Marcion explained, sent Jesus to save us, though he also clarified that Jesus only *appeared* to be a man since the material world is evil.

He further taught that Christians should avoid anything that implied continuity between the God of Judaism and that of Christianity. The only Scriptures, therefore, that he accepted were some of the epistles of Paul and the Gospel of Luke. (Even here, Marcion had to edit out verses that suggested continuity with Judaism and claimed that later Judaizers had inserted them to corrupt Paul's teaching.) Ironically, his collection of Scriptures was the first attempt to create a "table of contents" for the New Testament. (At this time, different local Churches recognized different texts as scriptural. Many books were the same from community to community, but some recognized certain titles—such as Clement's *Epistle to the Corinthians*—that would later be excluded from the New Testament canon.)

Marcion's community gained many adherents. In fact, Justin Martyr described his teachings as spreading "even to the ends of the earth," and for over a century the Marcionite Church was a significant rival to Catholicism. It was not until the fifth century that it at last faded from history.

Conclusion

Rome had weathered the chaos of the Julio-Claudians to enjoy an unrivaled period of prosperity and stability during the period of the Five Good Emperors. However, these model rulers could not address the underlying moral corruption that infected Roman society. The fascination with bloodshed, represented by gladiatorial combat, and the precedent of military takeover pointed to the coming era of violence and social breakdown. By contrast, the first centuries of Christianity witnessed intense trials. Not only did Christians endure the suspicions and persecutions of the Roman Empire, but they also encountered rival interpretations of Christianity. Many beliefs still needed to be clarified and explained, and yet there was an underlying strength. The "weeds" of persecution and heresy did not choke out the slow spread of Catholic belief. As we will see in the next chapter, one of the darkest periods in early Christian history would ultimately give way to an unanticipated triumph.

UNIT IV

Seeds of Christian Europe

CHAPTER 15

Crisis and Refoundation

And while [Constantine] was thus praying with fervent entreaty, a most marvelous sign appeared to him from heaven . . . he saw with his own eyes the trophy of a cross of light in the heavens, above the sun, and an inscription, CONQUER BY THIS, attached to it.

Eusebius of Caesarea, *Life of Constantine*[1]

According to Constantine, he received this famous vision shortly before he battled his rival Maxentius at the Battle of the Milvian Bridge in 312. Constantine, like many soldiers of the Roman Empire, participated in the Mystery Religion of Mithras and worshipped *Sol Invictus*, the "Unconquered Sun" (see insert on Mithraism in chapter 14). This apparition signified to the soldier-emperor that there was a greater Power than Mithraism's "Unconquered Sun" since the sun itself was overshadowed. How precisely Constantine described his vision remains debated. While the Christian historian Eusebius wrote that the heavenly apparition was a cross, Constantine actually ordered his soldiers to paint not a cross but the "Chi-Rho" on their shields. These were the first two Greek characters for the word *Christos*. Constantine's victory against his anti-Christian enemy secured his authority in the western half of the Roman Empire and initiated a new era of cooperation between the empire and the Church.

This development was unexpected. The preceding century had witnessed an increase in anti-Christian sentiment as the Roman Empire struggled to regain

1 Eusebius of Caesarea, *Vita Constantini* quoted in J. Stevenson, *A New Eusebius: Documents Illustrating the History of the Church to AD 337*, 2nd ed. revised by W.H.C. Frend (London: SPCK, 1987), 283–4.

The **Triumph of Constantius II**. Made of silver, c. 4th century. Currently in the State Hermitage Museum, St. Petersburg, Russia. This dish shows emperor Constantius II on horseback, being crowned by Victory (right) and accompanied by a soldier holding a shield with the chi-rho (left).

The **Chi-Rho** as depicted on a sarcophagus plaque. Made of marble, c. 4th century. Property of the Vatican Museums, Vatican City.

its footing after the prosperous era of the Five Good Emperors collapsed. Church leaders, meanwhile, continued to confront opposing interpretations of Christianity even as they debated what they should do with those who abandoned their Faith to avoid persecution. Nonetheless, events were soon set in motion that would end Roman intimidation and elevate Christianity to an influential place within Roman society.

Furthermore, as we will discuss in this unit's subsequent chapters, Constantine's conversion convinced many that Christianity and Rome were now intertwined and even unified. Emperors assumed the right to interfere with theological debates, and rival Church leaders increasingly used imperial might to silence each other. Church unity fragmented, and the vision of a combined Empire-Church quickly proved fragile. Rome's political stability was deteriorating, and wiser Church leaders warned that it was dangerous to assume that the Gospel was somehow permanently interconnected with the fate of the Roman Empire. When the Western Roman Empire became a historical memory, Christianity arose from its ashes to be much more than merely an aid for imperial unity. It laid the foundation for a new society and took what it could from Rome as it forged the new culture of Christian Europe. These were centuries of tremendous debate and change, and we resume our study in this chapter with the last flourishing of polytheistic Rome's golden age.

From Prosperity to Crisis

The era of the Five Good Emperors culminated in the reign of **Marcus Aurelius** (r. 161–180). It was a particularly good moment to be alive in the Roman Empire, for there appeared to be no limit to its influence and wealth. Indeed, the first Roman embassy reached China around this time and heralded even more opportunities for trade. Best of all, Marcus Aurelius seemed to embody all the virtues of the preceding "Good Emperors."

Centuries earlier, Plato had written in his *Republic* about the ideal "philosopher-king" who ruled from a sense of duty and for the greater good rather than for selfish gain. It appeared to many that Rome had achieved this ideal in Marcus Aurelius. Their new emperor was a Stoic who believed that the highest virtue was fulfilling one's duties (see insert on Hellenistic philosophies in chapter 10). He personally preferred a life of thought and meditation over that of action and conquest, but he embraced his responsibilities as emperor. Nonetheless, as if to make it clear that he did not desire lordship over others, he convinced the Senate to recognize a second emperor with whom he shared authority.

The **Equestrian Statue of Marcus Aurelius**. Made of bronze, c. 175. Currently in the Capitoline Museum, Rome, Italy. This is one of the few imperial equestrian statues which was not melted down to recycle its bronze in later centuries. It owes its preservation to the popular, but mistaken, identification of the figure as a statue of Constantine.

Unfortunately for Marcus, his reign was a tumultuous one. His troubles began when the Parthians invaded Rome's eastern border. Though Roman soldiers repulsed the attack, they became infected with a plague which soon spread throughout the empire. This epidemic was either smallpox or measles, and historians estimate that approximately 10 percent of the empire's population perished from the disease within a handful of years. Marcus's own coruler succumbed to the plague in 169. This sudden population loss reduced economic productivity and the tax revenues available to the empire. It also became more difficult to maintain a strong military. To make matters worse, barbarian incursions along the Danube intensified.

In general, the Germanic peoples north of the Danube were nomadic herdsmen whose cultures celebrated raiding and intertribal warfare rather than trade or urban life. Their societies emphasized kinship and loyalty to a tribal chief, who was likely elected by a body of warriors. The most powerful of these chiefs were essentially kings, whose primary responsibilities were to defend their followers and to provide sufficient plunder for their warriors. These kings did not rule formal territories or maintain borders; rather, their "realms" were based on the connections among families within the clan. (Some historians see this emphasis upon shared culture and family heritage as the seed for the later concept of a nation.) Legal disputes were resolved by appealing to the gods, who were then trusted to protect the virtuous and punish the guilty. For example, an accused individual might have to walk through fire unharmed to demonstrate innocence. Others might have to combat their accusers, with the assumption that the gods would grant victory to the just side. So ingrained were these practices that trial by ordeal remained a part of Germanic life centuries after the various tribes had converted to Christianity.

The Romans had a complex relationship with those barbarians who lived closest to their borders. Some Romans, like the second-century historian Tacitus, praised the Germans' simplicity of life and contrasted their virtues with the decadence of Rome. Others were less sympathetic and saw the barbarians as hopelessly uncivilized. Some barbarians in later centuries would develop a strong desire to be a part of the Roman world and eagerly traded for imperial goods. These items gave them prestige among their own kin group and encouraged further exchanges between Romans and barbarians. By the time we come to the fourth and fifth centuries, we will see that the Germanic tribes closest to the empire wanted nothing more than to become incorporated into Roman society. Such an attitude lay in the future; in the late second century, the interactions between these Germanic peoples and the Romans was primarily hostile and violent.

Hence, for the remainder of Marcus's life the would-be philosopher-king became a warrior, leading his armies to the north in an attempt to protect the frontier from Germanic attacks. Some in Rome grumbled at the emperor's absence, but Marcus Aurelius won their favor by doing his best to pay for the expensive wars in the north without raising taxes. He instead sold the treasures of the imperial palace—including his wife's royal robes!—to help fund the war effort. He satisfied his longing for an intellectual life by writing philosophical reflections after the long days on campaign. This work, commonly known as *The Meditations*, offers us a fascinating insight into the challenges faced by Marcus and how he responded to them.

On the one hand, the philosopher-king's reign was a success. Roman borders did not crumble under his watch, and though plague afflicted the population, the

THE PARTHIAN EMPIRE (C. 247 BC–C. AD 224)

The Parthians were a nomadic people from the steppes of Central Asia who settled in the north-eastern area of the Iranian Plateau. This region became part of the Hellenistic Seleucid Empire after the death of Alexander the Great, but the Seleucids did not retain power over the Parthians for long. By approximately 247 BC, they had gained their independence, and by 129 BC, Parthian warriors had pushed their Seleucid enemies west of the Euphrates. Under the leadership of its king, Mithridates II (r. 124–91 BC), the Parthian realm covered a vast expanse that stretched from the Indian subcontinent to Anatolia. This central location led to contact with China; by 100 BC, trade between the two empires had developed into the famous Silk Road.

Internal disputes over the Parthian throne attracted Roman interference. As we mentioned in chapter 12, Crassus invaded the Parthian Empire in 53 BC in his effort to outmaneuver Julius Caesar and Pompey. The result was a catastrophic defeat at Carrhae; mounted Parthian archers used their mobility to unleash a devastating rain of arrows before the Roman infantry could respond. (Their tactic of firing arrows as they rode away came to be known in proverb as the "Parthian Shot." Today, the phrase is still used to indicate a last insult or argument before the speaker leaves the room.) Augustus stabilized the border several decades later, but the possibility of aggression from one or the other empire continued. Trajan, for example, occupied Parthian territory during his reign, while the Parthians launched their own attack during the time of Marcus Aurelius.

Parthian society retained elements of its nomadic roots, but it was also deeply influenced by Hellenism and traditional Persian society. Hellenistic culture was particularly influential in the first centuries of the Parthian Empire. This situation changed in the first century AD when classical Persian themes in art and traditional Persian names became popular once again. At the same time, Zoroastrianism received encouragement from later Parthian rulers, though they themselves tended to be polytheistic. They were generally tolerant of new faiths such as Christianity.

Ongoing conflict with Rome as well as domestic intrigue brought down the Parthian Empire. The Sassanid dynasty (224–651) replaced it and used propaganda to portray the Parthians as foreign invaders and themselves as the rightful heirs to Cyrus, Darius, and Xerxes. Nonetheless, the Sassanids preserved the legacy of the Parthian Empire in two ways: they remained an important trading hub for Asia, and they continued the ongoing struggle with the Roman Empire for dominance in West Asia.

stability and prosperity that Augustus had set in motion two hundred years earlier remained intact. On the other hand, Marcus Aurelius dealt Rome's golden age a fatal blow. Rather than follow in the footsteps of the other Good Emperors and appoint a successor from outside his family, Marcus Aurelius chose Commodus, his self-absorbed son, to be his heir.

Commodus (r. 180–192) was the first Roman emperor "to be born in the purple" (that is, to be born while his father was emperor), but he used this privileged position to pursue a debauched and shameless lifestyle. He rejected his father's intellectual pursuits and instead declared that he was the reincarnation of Hercules, a demigod of enormous strength in Greek myth. To showcase his physical prowess, Commodus publicly competed in gladiatorial combat as well as in staged hunts against wild animals. His vanity morphed into paranoia after one of his sisters attempted to assassinate him in 182, and for the next decade he ordered the execution of anyone he suspected of foul play. Finally, in 192, his physical trainer strangled him at the behest of one of his concubines.

Commodus's reign marks the beginning of the empire's descent towards anarchy. The emperor's private army, the Praetorian Guard, murdered his successor, and rival generals quickly realized that they could seize power for themselves. A civil war ended in victory for Septimius Severus. His **Severan dynasty** (193–235) was effectively a military dictatorship. He replaced the Praetorian Guard with soldiers loyal to him personally and spent much of his time fighting wars along Rome's borders. On his deathbed, he reportedly advised his two sons to be at peace with one another, to pay their armies, and to despise everyone else. Unfortunately for Rome, the two brothers soon fell to fighting, and different family members plotted against one another in an attempt to control the empire.

In addition to a crisis of leadership, Roman society struggled to overcome two interrelated problems. The first involved the army. Military life had become increasingly unattractive to many Romans, and the empire's frontiers were simply too extensive for the border legions to defend adequately in their reduced state. Severus, therefore, left the frontiers relatively weak and instead established a mobile army that responded to threats wherever they arose along Rome's borders. To make enlistment as attractive as possible, he increased soldiers' pay and reduced military discipline. He also recruited primarily from among the poor in the empire's least civilized provinces to create this army. This established a dangerous precedent: future generations would continue to recruit soldiers who did not necessarily have a strong association with the empire and its history. As we will see in chapter 17, this eventually resulted in an army composed of "barbarians" rather than Romans.

The second predicament involved the economy. Commodus's irresponsible spending had depleted the imperial treasury. Emperors had to incorporate new territory, gain access to more gold or silver mines, or increase the taxes of their own citizens if they desired to rebuild the state's wealth. Each of these options had significant disadvantages or difficulties, so the Severan emperors decided that the best short-term solution was to debase the coinage.

The Roman economy depended on precious metals such as gold and silver. These metals formed the bulk of a given coin's substance and gave it its inherent value. Debasing coins involved melting them down and then adding a non-precious, or base, metal into the mix to increase its volume. This resulted in the production of more physical coins, but it also meant that these same coins had reduced value since their precious metal content was now diminished. The result was a downward spiral: emperors needed to increase the pay of soldiers to attract them, so they debased their currency in order to give them more physical coins. These possessed less worth, of course, because they had been debased, so soldiers demanded even more pay and thus initiated the cycle anew. As emperors debased their currency again and again, inflation set in: prices increased dramatically, and people's purchasing power declined as their money decreased in value.

With the struggling economy, social order broke down. Brigandage and piracy increased, roads and infrastructure deteriorated from neglect, and laborers abandoned low-paying agricultural work. Food shortages swiftly followed. In response, the state forced wealthy members of society to fill administrative roles in local government and then seized their wealth if expected tax revenues were not met. This arrangement could mean financial ruin for those forced to participate, and the wealthy attempted to avoid local administrative roles as much as possible. Their reduced social involvement further harmed the economy.

This deteriorating situation led Severus's son Caracalla to grant universal citizenship to all the inhabitants of the empire in 212. For centuries, Rome had maintained different levels of involvement in its political life so that most people within the empire technically did not possess full citizenship. Now, all non-Romans, or "barbarians" as Romans called them, living in the empire could claim to be full members of Roman society. These new citizens still retained their loyalty to their ancestral culture and to their own leaders, creating a situation that weakened the cohesion of imperial society. Meanwhile, universal citizenship was no act of generosity from

The **Severan Tondo**. Made of tempura painted on a panel, c. 200. Currently in the Staatliche Museen zu Berlin, Germany. A tondo is a circular piece of art, and this particular work is a painting of Septimius Severus, his wife Julia Domna, and their sons Caracalla (lower right) and Geta (obliterated).

Caracalla. Since citizens paid certain taxes that others did not, the emperor intended universal citizenship to increase tax revenue. It was still not enough.

In 235, the army killed the last Severan emperor and initiated the period known as the **Third-Century Crisis** (235–284). For the next forty-nine years, Rome had twenty-two official emperors and numerous would-be usurpers. The stability enjoyed by previous generations disappeared as civil wars, economic turmoil, and social unrest ripped apart the achievements of the Five Good Emperors. In the midst of the chaos and violence that gripped the empire, some rulers concluded that the best way to return to the peace and prosperity of the preceding era was to eliminate from society everything that threatened traditional Roman piety. The era of the empire-wide persecutions against Christianity had begun.

The Church in the Third Century

Violence against Christians was largely a local phenomenon in the period before the third century. Nero's executions after the Great Fire of 64 focused on those Christians in the city of Rome itself. The Five Good Emperors discouraged attempts to seek out Christians, but as we saw with Pliny, local governors could punish Christians who refused to participate in public rituals. By the end of the second century, Rome's growing troubles focused hostile attention on Christian communities.

Despite the efforts of Celsus and other Roman traditionalists, Christianity had gained converts as more people sought spiritual comfort in the midst of social uncertainty. While motives for conversion were, of course, personal, the Christian practice of caring for others during natural disasters such as plagues won the respect of many non-Christians. Furthermore, the Christian emphasis on the dignity of all people made their Faith attractive among the poor, slaves, and others who were frequently overlooked or neglected. This appeal to those disregarded by Roman society fueled conservative fears about the potential revolutionary consequences of Christian influence.

Persecution intensified in the early third century. Historians are uncertain whether the Severan dynasty promoted this bloodshed; while some sources state that Severus employed Christians and even intervened to save them from mob violence, others describe him as a persecutor who forbade any conversions to Christianity or Judaism. It may be that Severus began his reign favorably disposed towards Christians only to become hostile later in life. Regardless, regional persecutions did occur during Severus's reign, and the most famous martyrs of this time were the North African noblewoman Perpetua and her slave Felicity.

The dangers confronting Christians only increased with the onset of the Third-Century Crisis. Not only did they have to navigate social disintegration alongside everyone else, the Emperor **Decius** (r. 249–251) also initiated the first empire-wide persecution of Christians. Decius had successfully rebelled against his predecessor, and he realized that he would likely face a similar revolt against his rule unless something changed. At the same time, the plague that had afflicted the empire during Marcus Aurelius's reign reappeared and devastated the population once more. Decius concluded that Rome needed to honor the gods more fervently, leading him to issue an edict in 250 mandating everyone in the empire (with the exception of Jews) to offer sacrifice. This was a formal, public act—complete with witnesses and written documentation that a given person had complied with the edict. Punishment awaited those who refused. Decius died in battle one year later, but Church leaders understood that his actions set a precedent for future empire-wide persecutions.

Papyrus Oxyrhynchus 3929. Made of papyrus c. 250. Currently in the Art, Archaeology and Ancient World Library of Oxford, England. This is an example of a libellus, or brief document, certifying that the owner had offered sacrifice to the gods.

Christian communities needed strong leadership to face such difficult situations, and during this period the Church continued to refine its teachings about its own sources of authority. In the previous chapter, we had discussed Gnosticism and Marcionism. The former emphasized the authority of secret knowledge and presented different scriptures. The latter taught that Marcion's (edited) collection of Paul's writings represented the true Christian revelation. Confusion spread, and many wondered what authentic Christian teaching really was. This was the situation when **Irenaeus of Lyons** (c. 130–c. 202) began to write on behalf of the apostolic tradition. He was born in Anatolia and received instruction as a young man from the elderly Polycarp, who, in turn, had been a disciple of John the Evangelist. Irenaeus eventually journeyed to Rome before becoming the bishop of Lyons in Gaul (modern-day France). Tradition holds that he died a martyr during the reign of Septimius Severus.

For Irenaeus, contemporary disputes about Christianity revolved around the authority of the apostles and their successors. He disregarded the Gnostic claim that there were secret teachings and insisted that, because the apostles had taught openly, they must have ensured that their instruction would continue in a visible manner by appointing public successors. Furthermore, he upheld the bishop of

Rome as a preeminent guide for true Christianity since that bishop was the successor of two apostles, Peter and Paul. He applied a similar "apostolic" approach to Marcion's claims. He condemned Marcion's hostility to the Hebrew Scriptures and argued that *all* apostolic writings (not just Paul's) should be included in the emerging collection we know today as the New Testament. This apostolic standard also meant that some texts considered scriptural by local churches, such as *The Shepherd of Hermas* and Clement's *Epistle to the Corinthians*, ultimately fell outside of the biblical canon.

Irenaeus helped establish apostolic succession as the visible standard for Christian unity and doctrine, but could God supersede, or overwrite, episcopal authority with a new revelation? **Montanus** (2nd century), a former polytheistic priest from Anatolia, argued that God guided His Church through continual public prophetic revelation. He claimed to receive new teachings from the Holy Spirit and encouraged his followers to practice extreme self-denial and to embrace martyrdom. This claim required measured consideration. After all, a new public revelation from God was possible, and groups of bishops, perhaps gathering for the first time since the apostles, met to discuss whether Montanus's call to austere discipline and zeal for martyrdom was God's newest message. Montanus's disciples championed their "pure" form of Christianity even after some of his predictions failed to come true. Some even went so far as to suggest that Montanus *was* the Holy Spirit. By this point, the bishop of Rome and others had condemned the movement and declared that God's public revelation had ended with the death of John the Evangelist. Nonetheless, Montanism persisted for several more centuries, in part because their fervor during persecution convinced many that Montanism had to be the true expression of Christian belief.

Thousands, including Montanists, had chosen death rather than sacrifice during the Decian persecution, but many abandoned their Faith or pretended to comply with Decius's edict by purchasing false documentation. Was any pardon possible for these apostates and dissumulators? This question highlighted the tension between "rigorists," who, like Montanists, saw austerity and eagerness for martyrdom as the core identity of a Christian, and others who were less demanding or more forgiving in their assessment of Christian behavior. This was a different challenge from that of Gnosticism or Marcionism: all sides embraced the principle of apostolic succession and firmly believed that their particular branch represented the apostles' public teachings.

The division was particularly pronounced in Carthage and Rome. The respective bishops of these two cities, Cyprian and Cornelius, argued that, while apostasy was a grievous sin, it, too, could be forgiven. Rigorist opponents, in contrast, often believed that this sin was unpardonable. They began to establish separate, parallel churches for those Christians who had remained steadfast in the face of persecution. They chose rival bishops to lead their communities, and the alternative bishop of Rome, Novatian, established a parallel "Novatian" Church that lasted for several centuries.

Caught in the midst of such developments were two of the greatest early theologians of Christian history. Tertullian (c. 160–c. 230) was a North African Christian who wrote numerous works about Christian life and belief. His Trinitarian theology, in particular, influenced Western Christian thought. He was the first to make the important distinction between the concepts of "one substance" and "three Persons" when describing God's nature. Also, unlike some earlier Christian authors, he clearly identified the Holy Spirit as divine. Tertullian became a fervent adherent to Montanism later in life and championed its severe lifestyle. This led him to discredit some of his earlier writings, particularly on the topics of marriage and repentance. We know very little about his last years.

Origen (c. 185–c. 254) was another African who had a significant impact on future Christian thought. His father had been martyred in Alexandria during Severus's reign, and this proved to be the defining moment in Origen's youth. He committed himself to Christianity and devoted his life to exploring its doctrines. This led him to learn Hebrew so that he could understand the Jewish Scriptures in their original language. His most famous work, the *Hexapla*, was a side-by-side comparison of Hebrew Scriptures with four different Greek translations, including the Septuagint. He eventually settled in Caesarea in Palestine, and his massive library turned that city into a center for Christian intellectual life.

Origen was eager to discover truth, but his speculations sometimes contradicted themselves, and he left it to his readers to come to their own conclusions regarding different theories. Furthermore, Origen often explored positions that later Christians found troubling or even heretical. For example, he apparently suggested that God had created all souls before He fashioned the material world. At first, these souls were equal in love for their Creator, but as their love lessened, most drifted away from Him. Those whose love weakened the most became demons, while others, whose love still remained somewhat intact, eventually become incarnate as humans. The Word united with the only soul to preserve absolute loyalty to God and became incarnate as Jesus Christ. Later Christians also rejected as problematic his specific theories regarding the universal salvation, or *apokatastasis* ("restoration"), of all, including Satan. Centuries later, in 553, the Second Council of Constantinople condemned these teachings and added Origen's name to the list of anathematized heretics. (We should note that this condemnation did not imply that Origen died a formal heretic but rather signified the spiritual danger to those who hold the now-formally condemned positions.)

Origen readily admitted that much of his thought was speculation, and there is no reason to believe that he wanted to introduce erroneous ideas. Later Church Fathers, such as Athanasius and Basil of Caesarea, held Origen in great esteem and incorporated his thought into their own theological writings, and many of his contemporaries considered him a faithful Christian, especially when he died from tortures he had endured during the Decian persecution.

From Persecution to Conversion: Diocletian and Constantine

The Third-Century Crisis brought the Roman Empire dangerously close to collapse. Rebellions were breaking the empire apart, and barbarian raids reached Italy itself. Furthermore, the new Sassanid dynasty in Persia demonstrated its strength when it captured and enslaved an emperor in 260. Finally, after six emperors came and went in less than a decade, the army proclaimed **Diocletian** (r. 284–305), the captain of the imperial bodyguard, to be the next emperor. He was a capable soldier who came from a humble background in the Balkans; more pointedly, he was willing to make revolutionary changes to steady the empire.

The ongoing chaos convinced Diocletian that the empire had become too unwieldy for one man to rule effectively. Opposing generals frequently challenged a given emperor's reign, and the resulting civil wars merely weakened Rome further. To break this cycle, Diocletian divided the empire into two halves, East and West, and allowed a potential adversary to become his co-emperor in 285. Furthermore, he adopted a practice of the Five Good Emperors and clearly designated as his successor not a family member but another ambitious general. This new system is known as the Tetrarchy, "rule of four," because each half of the empire eventually had two emperors: a senior emperor and a junior emperor who was next in line for succession. Diocletian theoretically retained overall authority over the entire empire, but

The **Portrait of the Four Tetrarchs**. Made of porphyry, c. 300. The sculpture's original location is unknown, but it was displayed in Constantinople from the days of Constantine until the Fourth Crusade in 1204. It was taken as spoils and placed at St. Mark's Basilica in Venice, Italy. This group of statues depicts Diocletian, Maximian, Galerius, and Constantius I.

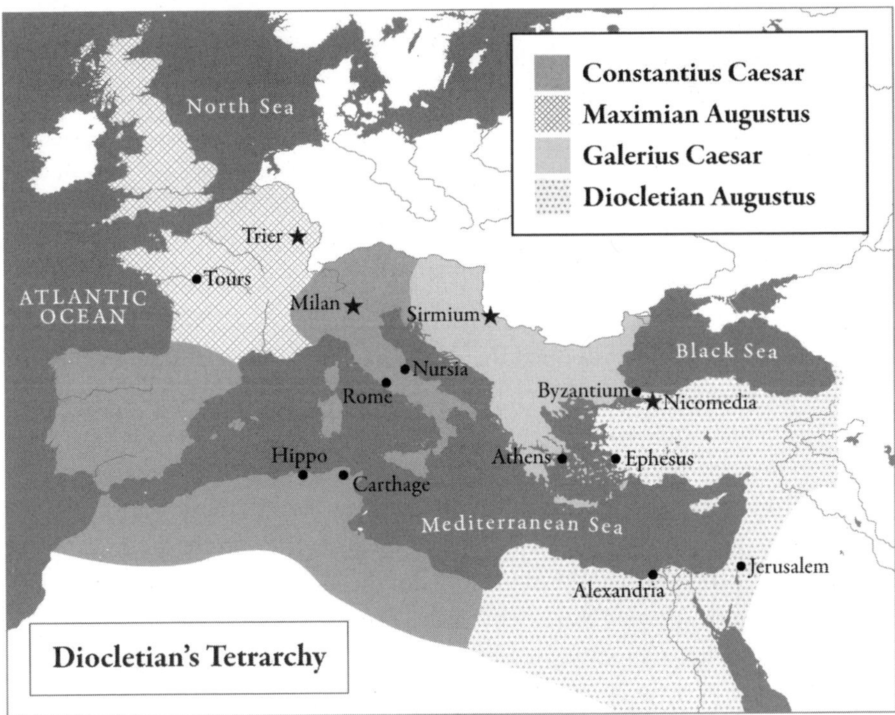

he hoped that he could avoid conflict by incorporating three other powerful military leaders into his government.

Diocletian chose to allow his co-emperor to rule the western half of the Roman Empire (essentially Italy and everything to its west) while he ruled the eastern half directly. The Western Roman Empire might have the historical city of Rome, but most of the empire's wealth and population were located in the eastern Mediterranean. Egypt, for example, possessed the empire's richest farmland, while many soldiers, like Diocletian himself, came from the Balkan peninsula. Diocletian's eastern location also enabled him to respond in a timely manner to any threats along Rome's border with the Sassanid Persian Empire.

Reforms were not limited to the imperial throne. Diocletian realized that ambitious governors could instigate rebellions in the provinces, and he sought to restructure the empire to minimize that threat. Previously, provincial leaders had possessed both martial and civil authority, but Diocletian divided this power into two offices. The one position, *dux*, retained military command while the other, *comes*, held civil authority. (The medieval titles "duke" and "count" have their origins in these two Roman offices.) This separation of powers reduced the threat of rebellion since governors no longer had control over both the region's army *and* its treasury. Furthermore,

Diocletian linked provinces together in new administrative units known as "dioceses." These increased the number of civil servants, or bureaucrats, which further reduced the authority of any one individual. The increased bureaucracy also enabled Diocletian to enact tax reform. Rather than merely collecting near-worthless debased coinage, he mandated that some taxes be paid "in kind." This meant that some taxes were now in the form of items, such as crops, which were then redistributed to the army and civil service. This policy was a first step towards economic recovery.

Diocletian's reorganization fundamentally changed the relationship between the people of the provinces and the Roman state. Previously, although Rome ruled, it had not profoundly transformed the day-to-day life of most people; Hellenistic culture had remained the primary unifying force in the eastern Mediterranean. Now, Diocletian's restructured, enlarged bureaucracy tied Roman subjects more closely to imperial policies. For example, not only did farmers pay their taxes "in kind" but they were also forbidden to leave their farms and move elsewhere. This restriction of mobility was intended to ensure adequate harvests for the government tax collectors. (This also laid the foundation for the medieval institution of serfdom in which peasants were tied to a given locality. See chapter 24.)

In 295, Diocletian promulgated an edict promoting marriage and declared that morality and respect for law ensured the favor of the gods. This effort to reinvigorate Roman piety included an attempt to restore respect for the office of emperor. Imperial dignity had suffered much during the chaos of the Third-Century Crisis. It was hard to feel awe and respect for emperors when it was likely that their reign would last, at most, a handful of years. Diocletian tried to counteract this by creating a divine "lineage" for each of the senior emperors that connected their ancestors to the gods. Furthermore, he ordered that everyone who approached his throne first prostrate themselves and address him as "lord and god."

This agenda to restore reverence for authority reawakened the empire's hostility towards Christians. By this time, the threat of another empire-wide persecution had seemingly receded, and Christians met openly in worship. There was even a church close to Diocletian's palace in the city of Nicomedia. Then, during a sacrifice in Diocletian's presence in 299, the presiding priests declared that Christians among Diocletian's attendants had thwarted the ceremony by crossing themselves. The pious emperor responded by ordering everyone in the bureaucracy and army to offer sacrifice; if they did not, they lost their post.

Imperial antagonism flared again in 303 when Diocletian and Galerius, his co-emperor of the East and chosen heir, promulgated an empire-wide edict calling for the destruction of Christian churches and their Scriptures. From Diocletian's perspective, his reforms of the past two decades had been largely successful, and he could now turn his attention to less-pressing challenges such as the Christians' refusal to worship the gods. Galerius was particularly hostile and convinced Diocletian to publish another edict one year later that demanded that all subjects (with the exception of Jews) offer sacrifice to the gods.

The Great Persecution (303–313) occupies a prominent place in Christian memory. Thousands of Christians suffered execution, mutilation, or other punishments for their Faith. The implementation of the persecution, however, was far from even. The emperors of the Western Roman Empire were not particularly enthusiastic in executing the decrees, and there were fewer Christians in the West anyway. Even Diocletian had no real heart in the matter. It was Galerius who prosecuted the persecution with vigor, and he received his opportunity to crush Christianity permanently when Diocletian announced in 305 that he was stepping down from the imperial throne to pursue a quiet life of growing cabbages on his estates in modern-day Croatia.

Diocletian's abdication revealed his confidence in his reforms. After two decades of rule, he had successfully reestablished imperial authority and social stability without any serious uprisings against him. The tetrarchy and its program of succession would

Wall painting of Martyred Saints from Wadi Sarga, Egypt. Made of stucco, c. 6th–7th century. Property of the British Museum, London, England. This honors martyrs from the Great Persecution. The painting's center is likely an older portion which depicted the three young men cast into the fiery furnace in the biblical book of Daniel (see Dan. 3). Beneath this is a Coptic inscription referencing "sixty martyrs of Samalut" which are otherwise unknown. The larger figures flanking the central portion are SS. Cosmas (left) and Damian (right) and the smaller figures below are their brothers Leontios, Eupredios, and Anthinmos. All five brothers and their mother Theodote were martyred during the Great Persecution.

preserve his achievements for future generations, or so he hoped. Unfortunately for Diocletian, unhappy reports soon troubled his peaceful retirement.

The problems began when the senior emperor of the Western Roman Empire, Constantius, died prematurely in 306. Constantius's army immediately declared his son **Constantine** (r. 306–337) to be the next emperor, but this action violated Diocletian's plan for the tetrarchy in two ways. First, the surviving emperor in the West had not chosen Constantine; second, Diocletian had consciously avoided appointing family members as heirs. Constantine's irregular claim to power inspired others, and soon no less than six different emperors asserted their right to rule. Diocletian apparently took his own life in despair as Rome prepared to fight against itself yet again.

The civil war ultimately gained a religious dimension. Constantius had not shared Galerius's anti-Christian sentiment and had been unwilling to enforce anti-Christian edicts. Constantine likewise showed no inclination to punish Christians for their Faith, and it was no secret that they hoped he would be victorious and end the persecution. Constantine's rival emperors, particularly Maxentius in Italy, increased their anti-Christian violence as Constantine's armies gradually gained dominance. The civil war's most dramatic moment came in 312 when Constantine declared that he had received a vision from the Christian God and won a climactic battle against Maxentius.

One year later, the two surviving claimants to imperial power agreed to divide the empire between them. Constantine received the Western Roman Empire, while his ally Licinius commanded the Eastern. They also promulgated the **Edict of Milan** (313), which officially legalized Christianity in the Roman Empire. Nonetheless, peace between the two did not last long. Fighting broke out once again, and once more religion played a role. Licinius restricted public activities of Christians and mandated traditional sacrifices among his soldiers. In contrast, Constantine, though still not baptized, publicly honored Sunday as the day of Jesus's resurrection and promoted Christians to positions of influence. The war between the last two competing emperors finally came to an end in 324. Constantine's forces were triumphant. Once again, a single emperor ruled the entire Roman world, but now for the first time that emperor openly promoted Christianity.

Conclusion

The century and a half after Marcus Aurelius brought many changes to the Roman Empire. The former days of the Five Good Emperors were gone beyond recall, but so, too, was the chaos of the Third-Century Crisis. Though Diocletian died convinced that his reforms had ended in failure, he had single-handedly rescued Roman society from anarchy. His expanded bureaucracy created more bonds of connection between the empire and the average Roman and stabilized, indeed refounded, the Roman government. This more effective administration enabled Diocletian's imperial successors to endure in the eastern Mediterranean for over a thousand years after his death.

Ironically, Rome's battle against Christianity actually promoted that Faith. The fortitude that Christian martyrs displayed inspired respect and convinced many to abandon their suspicion that Christians were subversive. Furthermore, more people became interested in joining Christianity themselves if a less hostile environment ever arose. Constantine's reign gave them their opportunity. Christians, meanwhile, had weathered the first debates about the nature of their religion and now consistently looked for leadership to their bishops, who were the successors of those who had first followed the call of Jesus of Nazareth. Nonetheless, the authority of bishops did not guarantee tranquility. Even as Constantine marched against Licinius, a theological storm was brewing that would rend Christian communities and reveal the dangers presented by the new *Christian* Roman Empire.

CHAPTER 16

The Challenges of a Christian Roman Empire

Experience had taught [Julian] that no wild beasts are as dangerous enemies to man as Christians are to one another.

Ammianus Marcellinus, *Rerum Gestarum*[1]

Christians rightly rejoiced at Constantine's rise to authority; he openly promoted their Faith and worked to bring the imperial government into alignment with Christian values. And yet Constantine and his successors envisioned a role for Christianity that paralleled the ancient religion of Rome: just as previous emperors had enforced public acts of worship, so now the first Christian emperors sought to mandate a particular theology for Christian belief. This made theological disputes harsher since winners could use imperial force to punish their opponents. At the same time, adversaries of Christianity, such as the historian Ammianus Marcellinus, pointed out the personal flaws of opportunistic Church leaders as well as those of the emperors they sought to manipulate.

Furthermore, Christianity, like Rome's traditional religion before it, did not guarantee the preservation of the empire from wars or instability. If anything, opponents of Christianity argued, it added to Rome's problems by adding theological divisions to society. A backlash against the Christianization of the Roman Empire formed amidst threats from Persians and barbarians, and Christians discovered that their new, positive

1 Ammianus Marcellinus, *The Later Roman Empire (AD 354–378)*, trans. by Walter Hamilton (New York: Penguin, 2004), 239.

status within the Empire did not mean the end of their troubles. Instead, Christians had to work out all the more clearly how to express their beliefs and how to navigate the relationship between the Roman world and their eternal goal.

Constantine's Christian Empire

Constantine (r. 306–337) was a little over fifty when he defeated his last rival in 324. His journey to the imperial throne had included surprising victories against more powerful adversaries, and many Christians, grateful for the Edict of Milan, attributed his ultimate success to God. While Constantine distanced himself from his anti-Christian predecessors, he also realized the wisdom of Diocletian's reforms. He continued the trend of expanding the bureaucracy as well as that of separating military and civil authority. He even retained Diocletian's division of the empire into four administrative regions despite the fact that he ruled alone. Furthermore, Constantine shared Diocletian's awareness that the eastern Mediterranean, with its wealth and resources, was more vital to the empire than the Italian Peninsula and regions further west.

The **Colossus of Constantine**. Marble, 4th century. Displayed in the Capitoline Museum in Rome, Italy. These fragments belonged to a giant statue depicting the emperor Constantine, most of which has been lost. The head and parts of the hands, feet, knees and elbows survived, probably because they were made of marble while the rest the statue was made of brick, wood, and plaster.

Diocletian had used Nicomedia as his *de facto* capital. This city in Anatolia was situated near crossroads that enabled Diocletian to remain informed about events throughout the Eastern Empire. Constantine wanted this same advantage for his own new capital, but he also wanted to avoid direct association with Diocletian or his legacy of persecution. He found the perfect site for both goals in the town of Byzantium. This former Greek colony was alongside the Bosporus Strait, a waterway that granted access from the Black Sea to the Mediterranean. This made its port an important hub of maritime travel and trade. Additionally, its strategic location at the place were Europe and West Asia practically touch made it a logical focal point for communication with both the empire's northern border along the Danube and its eastern border with Persia. As if to complete this perfect scenario, Byzantium was on a peninsula, which made the construction of a defensive wall much easier.

Constantine began building his capital of "New Rome" in 324. People soon called the city **Constantinople** ("Constantine's city"), and Constantine gave it all the trappings of grandeur that he could imagine. It possessed a Senate and received grain supplies from Egypt; he even ransacked ancient temples so that he could use their most precious items as ornaments. Nonetheless, these polytheistic items did not compromise Constantine's pro-Christian stance. It was no coincidence that, when he dedicated the city in 330, he did so on May 11, the anniversary of the death of the martyr Mocius who had been executed at Byzantium during Diocletian's reign.

Many treasures seized from the temples were melted down into coins to pay for the construction of Constantinople. This action had two important effects. First, the circulation of non-debased currency stabilized the Roman economy. Constantine's gold *nomisma* (or *solidus* in Latin) maintained a consistent percentage of gold and weight ($^{1}/_{72}$ of a pound). Public trust in its value remained the anchor point for the Roman economy for the next several centuries. Second, the confiscation of temple wealth impoverished these sites and weakened their cultural influence.

Traditional religion suffered another blow when Constantine officially forbade sacrifices to the gods or divination. He also sought to bring social behavior more in line with Christian morals by outlawing gladiatorial combat and "sacred prostitution," a ritual that encouraged promiscuity. He even attempted to prevent infanticide by providing money for poor parents. Of course, his reforms did not immediately transform Rome into a Christian society. Polytheistic devotions and festivals continued, and many temples remained open. Christians were, after all, only a minority within the empire, and most Romans still valued their ancestral beliefs.

The **Solidus of Constantine**. Made of gold, c. 324-325. Property of the Art Institute of Chicago in Chicago, Illinois. The front of the coin shows Constantine with the words CONSTANT-INVS P[ius] F[elix] AVG[ustus] ("Constantine the Dutiful and Happy Augustus"). The back shows Constantine on horseback with a spear with the words AOVENTVS [sic] AVGVSTI N ("The Coming of Our Augustus"). The lower text is the Antioch mint mark SMAN ("Sacra Moneta Antioch").

Nonetheless, Constantine's support mattered. A good example of this was his refashioning of Jerusalem into a Christian city. Christians certainly associated Jerusalem with Jesus's life, but early Christians had emphasized the heavenly Jerusalem rather than the earthly one. The latter had, after all, rejected Jesus. At the time Constantine began his reign, Jerusalem was still Hadrian's *Aelia Capitolina*. A temple to Jupiter occupied the site of the Jewish Temple, while another dedicated to Venus was located at the site of Jesus's crucifixion. Constantine and his mother, Helena, changed this situation by building the massive Church of the Holy Sepulcher, which replaced the temple to Venus. A desire to visit the places where Jesus had actually stood grew among Christians throughout the empire, and pilgrims made their way to the church that many now considered the holiest place on Earth.

Though Constantine promoted Christianity and its values, he retained Rome's traditional perspective towards religious belief, which explicitly linked political well-being with public piety. Worship of the gods had previously united Roman society, and now Constantine intended Christianity to be Rome's new foundation. In exchange for his pro-Christian policies, Constantine expected God to bless his reign just as He had apparently assisted Constantine's battles against non-Christian rivals. This does not mean that Constantine was insincere or conniving in his beliefs. Centuries of tradition had ingrained this attitude in the Roman mind, and it is understandable that his religious perspective reflected ancient assumptions.

Constantine was, therefore, particularly disturbed to learn that Christian communities were arguing among themselves regarding various theological questions. Such a disturbance was unlikely in polytheism. The multitude of myths and gods,

The **Church of the Holy Sepulcher**. Built by Constantine in the Old City of Jerusalem over the sites of Jesus's crucifixion on Calvary and His nearby tomb (see Jn 19:42). The rotunda has the larger dome and covers the burial site. The basilica has the smaller dome and includes the crucifixion site with the Rock of Calvary encased in protective glass. The church has been damaged and rebuilt numerous times throughout its history.

as well as the tendency to identify different deities with one another, made polytheism more open to alternative, even seemingly contradictory, beliefs. In contrast, Christianity, like Judaism before it, possessed a stricter understanding of truth and an inability to compromise with falsehood. This inflexibility meant that theological divisions presented greater implications for the Christian than they did for the polytheist, and disputes became all the more bitter because error jeopardized the eternal salvation of those involved.

Ironically, the legalization of Christianity contributed to its division. During the era of persecutions, local Churches had only infrequent or imperfect communication with one another, and it was easy to overlook diverging practices and beliefs by focusing on their common, embattled Christian identity. After the Edict of Milan, some bishops began to communicate more closely and recognized the need for a uniform articulation of their Faith. One such bishop was Alexander of Alexandria (d. 326). He requested that his presbyters comment on certain theological issues and was shocked to learn that **Arius** (c. 256–336), one of the most popular presbyters in the city, taught that God the Son had been created by God the Father.

While nearly all denominations of Christianity today condemn Arius's position as heresy, his teachings underscored hitherto unresolved tensions in early Christian theology. The Gospels clearly referred to "the Father" and "the Son," and some Christians were confused whether this terminology implied that the Father was superior to the Son. In other words, did the divine relationship mirror human ones in which fathers are older and have authority that sons do not? Certain verses, including Jesus's statement that "the Father is greater than I" (Jn 14:28), seemingly supported this position. Arius took this logic and joined it with other scriptural passages, particularly one from the Book of Proverbs (see 8:22–31). These verses stated that the Lord created wisdom before anything else. Since Christians used the title "Wisdom" to refer to the Son (see 1 Cor 1:24), Arius concluded that the Son must have been created. The very names "Father" and "Son," Arius argued, implied that the former must have preexisted the latter, just as human fathers preexist their sons.

In contrast to Arius, Bishop Alexander and his supporters held that "Father" and "Son" demonstrated the equality between the two. These intimate terms showed a common nature; therefore, the Son must be fully divine and thus coeternal with the Father. Passages such as Jesus's declaration that "no one knows the Son except the Father, and no one knows the Father except the Son" (Mt 11:27) lent support to their position.

The debate soon spread as both Alexander and Arius sought support outside Alexandria. Bishops were divided over the question, and there appeared to be no easy way to solve the issue. For Constantine, all of these subtle theological arguments were both bewildering and frustrating. The unbaptized emperor decided that a gathering of the bishops would solve this issue. He therefore summoned as many bishops as could come to Nicaea, a location not far from his future capital of Constantinople.

The **Council of Nicaea** met in 325 and addressed a number of issues that Constantine realized were causing dissent in the Christian world. The most pressing was Arius's teachings. Constantine himself sat in attendance, and his advisor, Ossius, the bishop of Cordova, served as the effective leader of the gathering. (The papal legates from Rome were shown especial deference, and, though they were only priests, they signed the acts before all the other bishops present except Ossius.) Most bishops were against Arius's position and decided that the best way to condemn it was to compose a statement of Faith, or creed, that expressed their beliefs. This was easier said than done: every time they incorporated scriptural texts to show Arius's errors, they realized that Arius could interpret them in a way that still supported his position. To break the impasse, Constantine recommended that they insert the word "consubstantial" (*homoousios* in Greek) into the creed to describe the relationship between Father and Son. This term from Greek philosophy expressed unity of being or substance. Arius vehemently rejected the term, so the bishops promptly included it and denounced Arius's teachings as heretical. The emperor confirmed their decision by exiling Arius.

PERSPECTIVES ON ECUMENICAL COUNCILS

The history of ecumenical councils can be challenging for Christians. Unedifying debates, the personal failings of those involved, and the reality of human ambition can easily lead us to view Church gatherings with suspicion or disgust. (See, for example, the epigraph from St. Gregory of Nazianzus at the start of chapter 18.) In such cases, it is important to remember that a lack of charity does not necessarily negate the theological position held by a given individual. A person can, for example, express the truth forcefully, even harshly; this approach may not convince anyone and may not be advisable for any number of reasons, but it does not compromise the basic truthfulness of the position.

These important points have not stopped some modern historians, such as the atheist Ramsay MacMullen, who have used ecumenical councils as a stick with which to beat the Church. MacMullen's book *Voting about God in Early Church Councils* highlights the moral and intellectual failings of those bishops who attended the early ecumenical councils. For him, these gatherings were unruly affairs in which the attending bishops' pride and ignorance were influential factors that helped determine which theological positions were either accepted or condemned. If read without care, his research can undermine our confidence in the Church's teachings since it can seem that dogmas of the Faith were decided by mere human leaders whose selfishness guided their decisions.

Yet, when we look to Sacred Scripture, we see that similar human failings have continually been present in sacred history. There are many examples we could cite, but perhaps one of the most obvious comes from the Book of Jonah. God called Jonah to warn the people of Nineveh of their impending punishment unless they repented, but this prophet *wanted* the city to be destroyed. He even became angry when they returned to God and thus avoided punishment. Fortunately, Jonah's message and its capability to inspire conversion were not restricted by the prophet's own desires. Jonah's spite could not overcome the grace of God.

When viewed with the eyes of faith, ecumenical councils can likewise reveal the work of the Holy Spirit in the Church. Despite the fallen human nature of theologians, bishops, and popes, the ecumenical councils, taken together, present us with a body of Christian teaching that is internally coherent, or consistent, and that does not formally contradict the general body of tradition and morals held by previous generations of Christians. This is *not* because all those who attended an ecumenical council were necessarily pious or even good willed. Nor is it because a council's teachings were universally accepted or clearly defined. Many times, it took an additional council to clarify or confirm what was taught at an earlier gathering. Rather, in a mysterious way, it is the very weaknesses of those attending a council which best demonstrates the Holy Spirit's guidance. The Church is both divine and human. God does not negate the bishops' free will or ensure that everything is taught as lucidly as possible, but He does make certain that the truth is proclaimed, even if many bishops involved were, like Jonah, neither moral exemplars nor effective teachers. As Catholics, therefore, we should not ignore the moral ugliness and confusion that frequently accompanied ecumenical councils; rather, we should understand these gatherings as reflecting both humanity's fallen nature *and* the grace of God which acts through our fallen nature to bring about His purposes.

Constantine rejoiced. From his straightforward soldier's perspective, the issue had been solved. The debate, however, intensified rather than ended. The term "consubstantial" was not found in the Scriptures, and many bishops had serious reservations about its use. After all, some interpreted it to mean that the Father and Son not only shared the same divine substance but were actually *identical*. In other words, one could understand "consubstantial" to mean that the Father and the Son were simply two names for the same person. This reminded many of a third-century heresy known as Modalism that had taught the Trinity was really one person with three modes (that is, three personas or masks). In 268, a local council of Antioch had even condemned the use of the term "consubstantial" as heretical. Many bishops, therefore, soon distanced themselves from Nicaea and its controversial creed and instead sought other ways to express the Son's relationship to the Father. The "Arian" Crisis was just beginning.

The "Arian" Crisis

Arius initiated a long-lasting theological dispute within Constantine's new Christian Roman Empire, but it is important to note that not all people identified by opponents or later generations as "Arians" agreed with Arius. In fact, many "Arians" condemned him as a heretic. For this reason, historians often use "Arian" in quotation marks in order to emphasize that most "Arians" actually rejected Arius's teachings and frequently disagreed among themselves. What united them as "Arians" in the eyes of their opponents was their common hostility to the Nicene Creed and its term "consubstantial."

The lack of precise theological terminology made things very confusing. The challenge was to develop a vocabulary whose meanings could be understood clearly by everyone. The council fathers of Nicaea, for example, did not offer a precise definition for their use of "consubstantial", and so its meaning could still be interpreted in multiple (and heretical) ways. To make everything even more difficult, there was no theology of ecumenical councils in the fourth century, and Christians only gradually came to uphold Nicaea as more authoritative than its many rival "Arian" councils in the fourth century. Indeed, the Nicene Creed was essentially overlooked for nearly two decades after the council due to its universally controversial, and to some heretical, "consubstantial" terminology.

Another factor that prolonged the conflict was the interference of the emperors. Constantine and his immediate successors considered theological nuances less important than imperial unity. Furthermore, the belief that the Son was a creature subordinate to the Father was attractive to some fourth-century emperors. If both emperor and the Son were creatures, the two could be seen as parallel, even approximately equal, subordinates to the Father. If the Son were a creature under the Father and yet—as the Scriptures clearly taught—held spiritual authority, then emperors likewise could piously see themselves as creatures under the Father holding all *temporal* authority. "Arians," such as the historian Eusebius of Caesarea, encouraged this interpretation in their writings. Some "Arian" bishops also attended Constantine's court and acted as advisors. They realized that Constantine's desire to unify Christianity could be manipulated to punish their theological opponents, who soon suffered exile thanks to Constantine's "Arian" counselors.

One powerful court bishop, who was a stalwart ally of Arius, convinced Constantine to recall the exiled presbyter and to order the anti-"Arian" bishop of Constantinople to receive him with honor. Though Arius died in 336 before he could publicly be readmitted to communion, Constantine's decision to end Arius's exile demonstrated the influence of the anti-Nicene position. As if to emphasize this fact, it was an "Arian" bishop who baptized the dying Constantine in 337.

Constantine was a crucial transitional figure in Roman history. On the one hand, he embodied traditional Roman piety. He, as emperor, remained the *Pontifex Maximus*, the "bridge maker" between heaven and earth, and he considered it his right to exile bishops and to summon a council for theological debate. On the other hand, Constantine integrated Christian morality into imperial laws, enabling Christian principles to begin to transform Roman culture at its core. Though Constantine likely did not realize the profound ramifications of his reign, he nonetheless deserves credit for contributing to the foundation of Christian Europe.

Constantine's three sons divided the empire among themselves after his death, but warfare and murder ultimately reduce their number to one. This surviving heir, Constantius II (r. 337–361), chose to remain unbaptized until his deathbed, but this decision did not prevent him from promoting "Arian" Christianity even more directly than his father had. He supported the work of the "Arian" missionary Ulfilas, who had great success in converting people north of the Danube. He also ordered the execution of those who worshipped idols or attended polytheistic sacrifices.

In addition, Constantius continued his father's support for Christians within Sassanid Persia. Initially, Christianity had enjoyed relative toleration under the polytheistic Parthians, but the Sassanids overthrew the Parthians in 224. The new dynasty sought to revitalize everything connected with the ancient glories of Persia, including its dualistic Zoroastrian religion. They viewed Christianity suspiciously and became even more mistrustful when Constantine portrayed himself as the protector of Christians throughout the world. Sassanid rulers now saw Persian Christians as potential traitors. Brutal persecutions followed. Constantine died before he could oversee a campaign against the Sassanid oppressors, but Constantius continued his father's plans. The fighting lasted over a decade, but Constantius had little to show for his effort. To make matters worse, a usurper claimed imperial power in 350, and Constantius had to fight a civil war, too.

In the midst of these battlefield struggles, the emperor labored to unite Christians under a single theological banner. He remained hostile to the teachings of Nicaea and summoned numerous councils to win bishops to his position. Like Constantine, he exiled and replaced those who opposed him. This coercion was an effective tool for enforcing "Arian" belief, and ultimately most bishops either publicly supported an "Arian" position or, as in the case of Pope Liberius, had signed a document that could be interpreted as compromising or outright rejecting Nicaea's position that the Son was "consubstantial" with the Father. Imperial pressure even targeted the nearly one-hundred-year-old Ossius and finally compelled him to sign an "Arian" creed shortly before his death.

Only a handful of bishops continued to resist. The most famous of these was **Athanasius** (c. 293–373). He had succeeded Alexander as bishop of Alexandria and opposed "Arianism" in all its forms. His stalwart defiance led to five separate exiles by several emperors, but he still remained dedicated to fighting for the Son's equality with the Father. For Athanasius, the heart of the issue was our understanding of salvation. If the Son were not fully divine, Athanasius argued, then He could not have redeemed us from our sins. Only God could offer infinite reparation for Adam's offense against His infinite Goodness. Therefore, the Son had to be equal to the Father and also become incarnate if He were truly to redeem humanity. This insight convinced Athanasius that the Nicene Creed—with its term "consubstantial"—was the surest way of clearly rejecting every type of "Arianism." In 343, he successfully persuaded other anti-"Arian" bishops to forego drafting another creed and, instead, to support the creed of Nicaea as the touchstone of orthodoxy.

Athanasius also realized that many "Arians" were Christians of good will who had genuine fears that "consubstantial" was heretical. As we noted above, that term could be interpretated as teaching that the Father and Son were the same person. To alleviate these fears, Athanasius clearly rejected any heretical interpretation of "consubstantial" and stressed how this term alone, properly understood, could adequately defend the Son's divinity and equality with the Father.

Constantius II died without children in 361, and his cousin Julian (r. 361–363) became his heir. Though he had been baptized, this young man had secretly denounced Christianity and embraced polytheism. He worked to undo Christian influence and attempted to destabilize it in different ways. For example, he permitted all exiled bishops to return to their cities. He knew, as his admirer Ammianus Marcellinus scathingly noted in our beginning quotation, that infighting would reach a fevered pitch once multiple bishops attempted to lead the same congregations. His policies also included the restriction of employment opportunities for Christian teachers and the refusal to punish those who killed Christians. Perhaps his most dramatic decision was his attempt to discredit Christianity by rebuilding the Jewish Temple and thus restoring the ancient Jewish sacrifices. Such a program had obvious support from the Jewish population, which had been effectively exiled from their holy city since the days of Hadrian. Historians, including Ammianus Marcellinus, record striking events—such as fireballs emerging from the earth—which soon ended the effort. The undaunted Julian continued his program to reinvigorate polytheism and, ironically, encouraged its priests to live according to the same moral standards as Christian priests. When devotion to the gods still floundered, Julian decided to show their power by successfully invading Persia. Unfortunately for him, the invasion ended with defeat and his death in 363.

The threat of renewed persecution vanished, and there was further good news for Athanasius and his pro-Nicene camp. Different schools of "Arian" thought had developed throughout the decades, each seeking to express better the Son's relationship with the Father.[2] Some taught that the Son was "similar-in-substance" with the Father, while others declared that the most we could say was that the Son was "similar" to the Father. A branch of "Arian" theology gained prominence during Julian's reign that argued that the Son was "unlike" the Father. These "Arians" went so far as to replace the terms "Son" and "Father" with "Begotten" and "Unbegotten" in order to emphasize the Begotten's status as a creature. This position was shocking to other "Arians," and some began to listen to Athanasius's claims regarding the Nicene Creed.

Constantine's dynasty ended when Julian died without an heir. The army decided to choose the next emperor from among their officers and eventually selected Valentinian, who decided to share rule with his younger brother Valens. Valentinian was mildly pro-Nicene and ruled in the West, while Valens (r. 364–378) took an aggressive pro-"Arian" position and governed in the East. Julian's defeat had left the Eastern Roman Empire in a weakened state, and Valens was desperate to restore its military might when a seemingly fortuitous opportunity arose. The Goths across the Danube requested permission to enter and settle within the empire. Though Roman prejudice still considered them to be "barbarians," they had been interacting with Roman society for years and had incorporated many elements of Roman culture. There were even "Arian" Goths thanks to the missionary endeavors during Constantius's reign. Valens concluded that he could settle the Goths in regions that were not as productive agriculturally *and* recruit them into the army. They would

2 For the sake of clarity, we will not explore the intricacies of the various "Arian" schools in our narrative, but we did want to include more details for the interested student. Three predominate "Arian" theologies developed during the fourth century. The first was the *Homoiousian* ("similar-in-substance") position. Sometimes described as "semi-Arians", these bishops and others sought to condemn Modalism and therefore rejected the term "consubstantial" with its potential Modalist interpretation. In its place, they advocated "similar-in-substance"; this, they felt, correctly distinguished the Son from the Father. The problem, of course, with this wording is that if the Son is merely "similar" in substance, than He must also be "dissimilar" in some regard. Otherwise, you could use the term "same." They were the "Arians" most likely to join cause with Athanasius after the rise of Heterousian theology. The second position was the *Homian* ("similar"). Its adherents rejected the use of substance terminology and instead emphasized a generic "similar-ness" between the Father and Son. This was the "Arian" theology that many barbarian converts in the fourth, fifth, and sixth centuries held. The last, and most radical, "Arian" position was that of *Heterousian* ("different-in-substance"). This faction is also known as *Anomoian* ("unlike"), Eunomian (after one of its most prominent leaders), or Neo-Arian. It applied the principles of Aristotelian logic to Christian teaching. This emphasis on logic led them to believe that they understood God in His essence. Their emphasis on the terms "unbegotten" and "begotten" demonstrated their confidence that the human intellect could comprehend God.

increase his tax income, solve his military dilemma, and presumably support his theology. It seemed like the perfect solution—until it fell apart.

The Goths crossed the Danube with their families only to find themselves without the resources they needed to survive. What was more, the Romans in charge of their migration were neither provisioned enough to supply all the immigrants' needs nor numerous enough to govern the new inhabitants. They consequently used harsh measures to attempt to maintain control. The Goths felt betrayed and mistreated. They rose up in rebellion, and Valens found himself marching against the very people he had hoped would strengthen his own army. They met in battle at Adrianople in 378. The defeat was one of the worst in Roman history. Tens of thousands of Roman soldiers died, including Valens. To make matters worse, his older brother Valentinian had died several years earlier when he became so angry that a blood vessel burst in his head. With Valens's violent end, the entire empire was now in the hands of Valentinian's nineteen-year-old son Gratian.

Obelisk of Theodosius. Made of red granite and first erected by Pharaoh Thutmose III c. 15th century BC in Egypt and then moved in AD 390 to the center of the Hippodrome of Constantinople by Theodosius I. Each of its four sides bears an inscription in hieroglyphics praising Thutmose III. The pedestal under the obelisk is made of marble and has Greek and Latin inscriptions praising Theodosius, including the phrase *omnia Theodosio cedunt subolique perenni* ("all things yield to Theodosius and his eternal offspring"). Today, the obelisk remains in its same location in what is now Sultanahmet Square, Istanbul, Turkey.

Gratian realized that he could not save the empire single-handedly, so he turned to **Theodosius** (r. 379–395), a military officer from Spain, and appointed him co-emperor. After three years, Theodosius subdued the Goths' rebellion, but the losses at Adrianople now made it necessary to recruit soldiers from those he had just fought. Defeated Goths became Roman allies, or "federates." These soldiers ostensibly fought for Rome, but they also retained a strong allegiance to their own leaders, who served as their military officers. The empire's military became increasingly "barbarian" in its composition.

In 380, while still pursuing victory against the Goths, Theodosius fell dangerously ill and asked for Baptism. He, like Constantine and others, had assumed that ruling required decisions that were sometimes morally compromising. They postponed Baptism, therefore, until their death so that they received its absolution without any need to perform penance for subsequent sins. Yet Theodosius's plan fell apart when he recovered from his illness *after* receiving Baptism. He was now formally integrated into the Church and under the authority of its leaders and its discipline. This unexpected situation brought the theological questions of the preceding decades to the forefront of his agenda.

Theodosius decided to summon a council at Constantinople to deal conclusively with "Arianism." Due in part to Athanasius's efforts before his death in 373, the pro-Nicene position had become increasingly stronger and united, while the "Arian" position had fragmented further and now included an explicit denial of the Holy Spirit's divinity. In 381, the Council of Constantinople affirmed the Council of Nicaea's teaching that the Son was consubstantial with the Father and expanded its creed to include statements regarding the divinity of the Holy Spirit.[3] (This expanded Nicene-Constantinopolitan Creed is still recited today at every Divine Liturgy and Sunday Mass.) While "Arianism" would remain alive for centuries among those barbarians whom Ulfilas had evangelized, orthodox Christian practice within the empire now clearly emphasized the divinity and equality of the Father, Son, and Holy Spirit.

New Trials and New Solutions

Theodosius's support for Catholic Christianity (as opposed to "Arianism") enhanced its spiritual, social, and political influence in the empire. Of course, adherents to Rome's traditional religion remained, particularly among those living in the conservative countryside. These became known as "pagans" (from the Latin *pagus*, "rural"), but their numbers steadily dwindled over the next centuries. Many celebrated the growing prevalence of Christianity and the decline of paganism, but some feared that this success compromised the fervent spirit that had characterized earlier Christians. Previous generations had shown their commitment to Jesus despite persecution and death. In contrast, imperial support seemed to encourage laxity and merely superficial devotion. A desire arose to imitate the martyrs of previous generations by dedicating one's life entirely to Christianity.

Thus began the ascetic movement. The term "**asceticism**" comes from the Greek verb for training and exercise (*askein*), and ascetics strove for "spiritual training" by

3 It is worthwhile to remember St. John Henry Newman's teachings on the development of doctrine and how later insight can deepen our understanding of, but never contradict, a previous doctrine of the Church. Thus, Constantinople I clarified and completed the teachings of Nicaea regarding the three Persons of the Holy Trinity without contradicting that prior gathering. We will encounter this phenonmenon again when we discuss the councils of Ephesus and Chalcedon.

voluntarily embracing harsh living conditions and penances. They could no longer die for Jesus's name, but they could renounce temporal pleasures for His sake. The most famous of the early ascetics was Antony of the Desert (251–356). His decision to live in Egypt's wilderness and to practice severe mortifications inspired others to follow in his path. They became known as "monks" since they technically lived alone. (*Monos* is "alone" or "solitary" in Greek.) These early monks, often called the "Desert Fathers," practiced continual fasting and other physical deprivations. Later, monks outside of Egypt decided to increase their "spiritual training" by living alone atop pillars. These "stylites" dedicated their lives to prayer while exposed to the elements.

There were also groups of monks who formed communities, and the practice of **monasticism** eventually included societies in which ascetics lived together and helped provide for the well-being of their fellow members. **Basil of Cappadocia** (330–379), often known as "Basil the Great," was a bishop in Cappadocia in northern Anatolia who contributed to the development of communal life within monasticism. He composed a rule of life for monks that de-emphasized extreme environments and penances and focused instead on moderate practices of self-denial in community. His *Rule* was very influential and has shaped the practice of monasticism throughout Eastern Christianity even until today. Furthermore, Basil founded a monastery called the *Basileias* that served as the ancient inspiration for modern hospitals. This community blended monastic ideals of prayer and self-denial with free medical treatment for the poor. In Basil's vision, monks were both desirous of personal sanctity and benefactors of the general population.

As Christianity slowly transformed Roman society, the underlying tensions between the old Roman order and the new Christian ethos became more pronounced. One clear example was the question of classical pagan education. Christians wondered whether their children should study non-Christian texts such as the Homeric poems or the Platonic dialogues. In response, Basil defended the study of pagan literature and emphasized that many such texts taught important truths and helped guide young Christians to virtue. After all, he argued, Moses had learned from the polytheistic Egyptians before God called him to lead the Israelites. Basil himself quoted or referenced Homer, Hesiod, and many other pagan authors in his writings. He did warn against those works that taught vice and said that such teachings should be avoided, and he praised Odysseus and his flight from the deadly sirens in *The Odyssey* as an example of how Christians should respond to any moral baseness in pagan literature. The explicit support Basil (and other Church Fathers) gave to the study of the intellectual achievements of pagan Greece and Rome ensured that future generations of Christians continued to learn from these important sources.

Another dramatic moment exemplifying the tension between old Roman power and new Christian authority occurred when a bishop publicly rebuked Emperor Theodosius for his involvement in the slaughter of thousands of innocent people after a riot around the year 390. (Historians debate whether Theodosius had directly ordered the slaughter or whether his soldiers exceeded the emperor's command in their aggression. Regardless, many held Theodosius responsible.) Former emperors had also engaged in unjust acts of violence, but Theodosius was a baptized member of the Christian community and lived under the spiritual authority of his bishop, Ambrose of Milan (c. 339–c. 397). The drama of this moment is hard to exaggerate. Ambrose's bold move to demand repentance from the most powerful man in the Roman Empire was matched by Theodosius's equally surprising decision to humble himself and repent. To put this in context, less than one hundred years earlier, Theodosius's predecessors had been hailed as "lord and god" before someone approached them. A demand for public penance from a "god" would have been unthinkable.

Theodosius's actions touched upon important questions that, for many contemporaries, had no clear answers: Was there an inherent "sympathy" or connection between the Christian Roman Empire and the Catholic Church? Was working for Rome's glory equal to working for the glory of Jesus's kingdom? This question of the proper relationship between political and spiritual life within the empire came to a head in the decades following Theodosius's death in 395. He had divided his empire between two sons, but, unfortunately for the empire, neither was talented or even competent. Advisors were soon controlling their decisions behind the scenes. Even worse, these powerful counsellors soon plotted against one another. Armies marched east and west as the brothers' advisors tried to outmaneuver their rivals in the other half of the empire. In the midst of this turmoil, one Roman general—the Goth Alaric—became tired of being a mere pawn in the power plays of ambitious officials and decided to lead his army on his own behalf. Their target was the city of Rome itself. In 410, an imperial army—composed primarily of Goths and led by a Goth—sacked the city of Rome.

The psychological impact of Rome's fate was tremendous. True, the city by this point was a cultural and historical site rather than one that had administrative importance, but as a symbol it represented the health and glory of the empire. The event shocked those Christians who believed that Christianity's success depended upon the survival of the Roman Empire. For pagans, the catastrophe was a sign from the gods to return to the old religion, and it intensified their condemnation of Christianity.

This situation inspired the bishop **Augustine of Hippo** (354–430) to write a lengthy treatise refuting pagan claims that Christianity had weakened the Roman Empire, as well as challenging Christian attitudes that Rome's survival was necessary

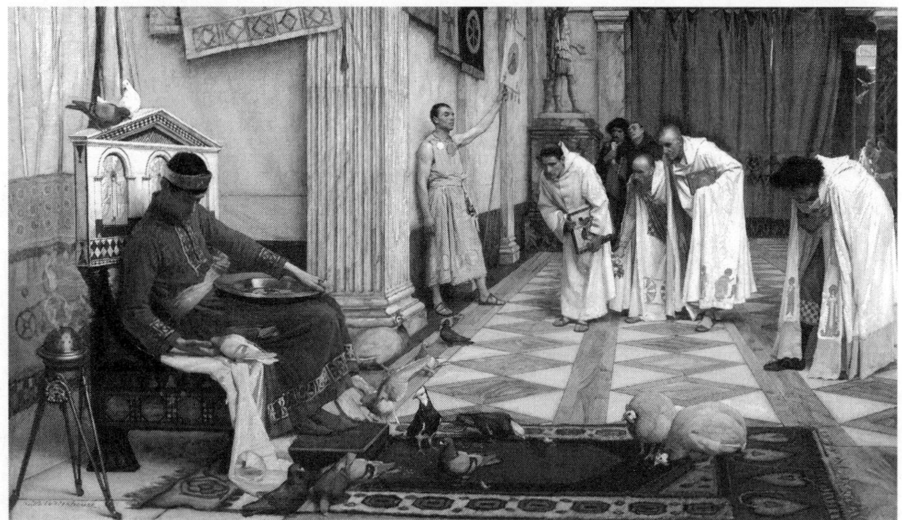

The Favorites of Emperor Honorius by John William Waterhouse. Oil on canvas, c. 1883. Currently in the Art Gallery of South Australia, Adelaide, Australia. This painting alludes to an infamous episode in Rome's history, one that provides a striking example of Rome's decline. Honorius, Theodosius's younger son and the incompetent ruler of the Western Roman Empire, broke down crying when he learned of the sack of Rome. However, this was because he mistakenly believed that the message that "Rome had perished" referenced his pet chicken named "Rome" rather than the city. He cared more for his bird than he did for the ancient capital of his empire.

for the spread of Christianity. Augustine's *The City of God* proposed the model of two cities: one heavenly and of God, the other earthly and of Man. Christians, he wrote, are temporary residents of the secular world. They should not allow the distractions of the earthly City of Man—money, fame, and power—to distract them from pursuing their heavenly goal of eternal fellowship in the City of God. Furthermore, the authority possessed by temporal rulers was limited and should not interfere with the religious sphere.

Augustine viewed even Christian emperors with mistrust. All too frequently in history, temporal rulers had attempted to use and control religion to support their political agendas, and Augustine sought to protect the Church from that danger by arguing that political and spiritual authority—even in Christian realms—should be separate rather than intertwined. (This is different from modern arguments regarding the separation of Church and State; these typically are not concerned about safeguarding the Church from political interference but instead seek to prevent any religious influence from limiting the state's power.)

The revolutionary nature of Augustine's ideas may not be immediately obvious to us of the modern era. That spiritual and political authority should be distinct has become so commonplace in the modern worldview that we can forget that the ancient world took it for granted that "State and Church" formed one single entity, what we might call a "**State-Church**." In this "State-Church" political allegiance and religious belief were coterminous, or overlapping. When ancient rulers, such as Naram-Sin, the pharaohs, or the early Roman emperors, claimed spiritual power or even divine honors, their subjects saw this as a natural development. This perspective also explains why Christianity was so mistrusted by early Romans; they saw traditional polytheistic practices as part of the duties of those living in the Roman Empire. Augustine's *The City of God* rejected this on two levels. First, it disputed the idea that the "State," or temporal order, should be the more important. In ancient societies, it was typically his political power that enabled a ruler to dictate religious belief; spirituality was subordinate to temporal interests. Secondly, it denied the very notion that religion and politics needed to be intimately intertwined.

Nonetheless, it is one thing to propose that the Church should be independent from political interference. It is another to work out what that means in practice. Even Augustine himself blurred the lines between religious and political authority when he encouraged the use of coercion to help suppress a rigorist branch of Christianity known as Donatism. Donatists argued that the personal failings of the clergy invalidated their sacraments. The movement had begun during Diocletian's persecution and eventually became an outright schism in the African Church. Augustine sought to heal the breach, but when they became violent, he enlisted imperial power to end the schism. Was this a violation of the principles he articulated in *The City of God*? Or were there justifiable reasons for either the spiritual or political authority to intervene in the other's sphere? As we will see in later chapters, questions such as these would become increasingly important in the medieval era.

Augustine's vision of history and political life has influenced Christian thought ever since, but his significance is not limited to *The City of God*. Even before that work, he had composed his *Confessions*. This spiritual autobiography retraced his early childhood, his belief in Manichaeanism—a dualistic religion which enabled him to blame an evil god for his moral failings—and his conversion to Christianity under the spiritual guidance of Ambrose of Milan. The work became a classic and has continued to influence theological and philosophical discussion even until today. Augustine ultimately became bishop of Hippo in his native North Africa. Here he wrote about key concepts such as Original Sin, grace, and free will, and successfully integrated Greek philosophical language and concepts with Christian theology in a way that influenced Western Christian theology for centuries. As we will see in volume II, contradictory interpretations of Augustine's theology would become an important part of the debates surrounding the rise of Protestantism over a thousand years later.

Conclusion

Constantine could not have foreseen the fundamental changes that would take place within the century after his victory in 324. His decision to support Christianity transformed that Faith from an embattled, persecuted minority into a dominant influence in imperial life. The decisions of Constantius II, Theodosius, and others showed how emperors saw Christianity as an integral part of their rule. Ordinary Christians came to consider the empire as a coworker with the Church itself, and the lines between secular and eternal began to blur. The Sack of Rome in 410 provided an important challenge to that assessment, and Augustine's *The City of God* laid the foundations for a more detached interpretation of the Church-Empire relationship that sought to defend the Church's ability to proclaim the truth without political compromise or interference. His understanding that Christ's Church could continue even without Rome may have seemed shocking to some, but already monastic foundations in the Egyptian desert and elsewhere demonstrated that Christian society was beginning to forge an independent path. The ideas of Augustine and the work of monks would become crucial in the next decades as the Western Roman Empire crumbled apart.

THE FORMATION OF THE BIBLE

The designation "Bible" comes from the Greek *biblia*, which is the plural form of the word for "book." We do not know when the term first became commonplace, but, at the latest, people of the ninth century were using it in the same way that we do today.

When discussing the Bible, it is important to note two distinct, but related, concepts. The first is "Sacred Scripture," which consists of the texts that are divinely inspired. The second concept is that of a canon. "Canon" can refer to either a set of rules (as in Canon Law) or a list. The biblical canon indicates the list of Scriptures that Christians accept as divinely inspired. Technically speaking, Scripture does not require a canon. There was no canon for the Hebrew Bible for centuries; in fact, the Jews developed their biblical canon *after* Christians did. Even if not required, Christians by the fourth century had become convinced of the advantages of having a standard "table of contents" for the Bible.

In 367, Athanasius drafted the first list that included the same twenty-seven books of the New Testament that most Christians accept today. Some argue that Pope Damasus first defined the canon of Scripture, both Old and New Testaments, in a Council of Rome in 382. However, the evidence for this claim is debated among historians since the surviving texts seem to suggest that the work was written in the late fifth century under Pope Gelasius I. The fact that the prolific, scholarly Jerome (see below) never mentions any such council of 382—despite being in Rome—has also been seen as evidence that it did not take place.[4] It is not until 393, at a synod in Hippo, that we have the first undisputed historical promulgation of the list of Scriptures that coincides with the biblical books that Catholics accept today. This African synod's decision was confirmed by two separate local councils held in Carthage in 397 and 416. Augustine, who became bishop of Hippo in 396, supported these declarations and declared that Christians should accept as Scripture those books recognized by "all the Catholic Churches," which is why he accepted the Epistle to the Hebrews even though he personally doubted that the Apostle Paul wrote it.

Another significant development in biblical history was Jerome's Latin translation. Jerome (c. 347-420) was an educated ascetic who lived both in Rome and Palestine and who devoted much of his time to the study of Scripture. He realized that current Latin translations of the Greek texts were inadequate and, at the request of Pope Damasus, set about creating a new translation of the Old Testament that would be based, not on the Greek Septuagint, but on the original Hebrew. His work, known as the Vulgate, became an authoritative translation for Latin-speaking Christians and was later declared to be the official translation for the Catholic Church at the Council of Trent in the sixteenth century.[5]

---

4 The argument that this council did not take place because it is not mentioned in Jerome's writings is what is known as an "argument from silence." These can be fraught with danger. The fact that Jerome never mentioned a council that defined the Biblical canon, for example, could be attributed to any number of factors that do not undermine the existence of that council. It may even be that he *did* write about a council in 382, but that particular letter or document has been lost to history. Historians must use prudence when assessing a given argument based on someone's (literary) silence. Such evidence can have merit, but it can also be misleading if one does not understand its potential weaknesses. In this particular situation, Jerome's numerous writings, which include those of a historical nature, make it surprising that he never mentioned such a meeting if it took place and supports the position (but does not by itself prove) that the council did not happen.

5 Pope Pius XII later emphasized that Trent's pronouncement that all should use the Vulgate as the authentic Latin translation applied only to the Latin Church (as opposed to the Eastern Catholic Churches) and in no way "diminish[ed] the authority and value of the original [Hebrew and Greek] texts." (See *Divino Afflante Spiritu*, § 21-2.)

CHAPTER 17

Monks and Barbarians

"If you will give me victory over my enemies, and if I may have evidence of that miraculous power which the people dedicated to your name say that they have experienced, then I will believe in you and I will be baptized in your name."

Clovis in Gregory of Tours, *History of the Franks*[1]

Clovis, king of the Franks, uttered these words during a particularly desperate battle. He had begun to weep as he watched his soldiers cut down around him and in desperation called upon the God of his wife for aid. Shortly thereafter, the tide of battle turned as his enemies' leader perished and the remaining foes fled the battlefield. Such is the tradition surrounding Clovis's decision to accept baptism, but we have little evidence to confirm it. Few historical records survive from this period, and we must instead rely on texts of doubtful accuracy that were written long after the events they describe.

Our lack of sources for the fifth century is intimately tied to the contemporary challenges confronting the Roman Empire. Even as Romans struggled to recover from their defeat at Adrianople in the east, other barbarian tribes were poised to enter the western provinces. Many of their leaders desired to maintain the wealth, art, and education of the empire, but they were unable to do so in the growing instability of the fifth century. Instead, the strength of their warriors, who followed them out of tribal loyalty and a desire for plunder, contributed to the breakdown of order and the growth of violence. Those caught between Roman and barbarian armies

1 Gregory of Tours, *The History of the Franks*, trans. by Lewis Thorpe (New York: Penguin, 1974), 143.

focused on mere survival, and the knowledge of reading and writing declined. The relative religious unity Christianity promised Rome was also broken. The new arrivals were either pagan or "Arian," and they reintroduced the division and conflict of earlier religious debates. Yet even in this time of transition from the world of Rome to that of the barbarian kingdoms of **Early Medieval Europe** (c. 500–c. 1000), pious Catholics worked to preserve the Christian Faith and ancient civilization.

England after Rome

Britain had been the northernmost part of the Roman Empire for centuries. Roman involvement had begun with Julius Caesar, and Emperor Claudius had completed the subjugation of the Britons by the year 50. In 122, the third "Good Emperor," Hadrian, commissioned the construction of "Hadrian's Wall" across Britain to fortify the empire's northern boundary against the barbarian tribes of Scots and Picts. For over three hundred years, Roman rule provided Britain with the same peace, wealth, and education as its other provinces, and it was during this period that Christianity was first introduced to the island.

Nonetheless, once imperial frontiers on the continent had been breached, Britain was the first region to lose the protection of the Roman legions. In 406, barbarian tribes crossed the Rhine River into Gaul. Despite the Britons begging them to stay, Roman troops were withdrawn from the island to defend the empire's beleaguered continental border.

The Britons had to defend themselves after centuries of relying on Roman military power. Celtic peoples from Ireland and Scotland raided and devastated their towns and farmlands. In one of these raids, pirates captured a teenager named **Patrick** (385–461), whom they sold as a slave in Ireland. The young man was put to work as a shepherd, and he found comfort by turning to his Christian faith as he tended the flocks in contemplative solitude.

Escaping Ireland, Patrick eventually traveled to Gaul where he was ordained a priest and then a bishop. He dedicated the rest of his life to preaching the Gospel to the Irish. Powerful religious leaders called druids opposed him. They practiced human sacrifice and held much influence throughout the land. Ireland's first missionary-bishop, Palladius (fl. 431), had already worked to convince the Irish to abandon their paganism, but it was under Patrick that the druids' sway decisively collapsed. By the time of Patrick's death, many had embraced the Christian Faith and sought to learn as much as they could about its teachings. Soon Irish monasteries multiplied and became centers of learning and literacy.

Back in England, the situation was grim. The Britons still faced Scottish attacks as well as raids from the continent by the Germanic Angle and Saxon

The **Sutton Hoo Helmet**. Made of silver, gold, iron, bronze and garnets, c. 620–625. Property of the British Museum, London, England. The image here shows the replica produced by the British Royal Armouries in 1973. This Anglo-Saxon helmet was included with other treasures in a ship burial. Its elaborate decorations has encouraged speculation that the helmet may have doubled as a crown.

tribes. According to legend, the famous King Arthur rallied the Britons to fight against the Saxons, but after his death, they were defeated, and the land was overrun. As the Angles and Saxons increased in number, much of Britain became known as "England," the land of the Angles. Four main Anglo-Saxon kingdoms divided most of the land among them: East Anglia and Northumberland were to the east and north, respectively; Mercia in the center; and Wessex in the southwest.

The Anglo-Saxon era shaped English culture. Their dialects formed the basis of Old English and established the Germanic foundation of the English language. Germanic customs, tales, and practices spread throughout the island. Their society emphasized kinship. They lived in large family halls built of wood and reeds, and the kings led the warriors of the tribe in battle. The Saxon burial sites that have survived show that they equipped the dead with the most precious items they could produce for the journey to the underworld: swords, helmets, pottery, and intricate metalwork. The Saxons worshipped their traditional pagan gods and goddesses such as Thunor, god of thunder, Tiw, god of war, Frigg, goddess of love and motherhood, and Eostre, goddess of spring. Though Britain had earlier adopted Roman practices enthusiastically, many now reverted to paganism, and Christianity almost completely disappeared from the land.

The Vandals

The **Vandals** were originally from southern Poland. In 406, they crossed the Rhine River and made their way across Gaul, sacking and plundering the towns and villages they encountered. This destructive behavior forever associated their name with acts of wanton violence, and "vandal" and "vandalism" remain part of our vocabulary even until today. After initially settling in Spain, they move southward and invaded North Africa. In fact, the Vandals besieged the city of Hippo even as its famous bishop Augustine lay dying in 430. By 435, they had completed their conquest.

The fall of North Africa was disastrous for the Romans. First, a wealthy province close to the city of Rome was now lost to the empire. Second, and more remarkably, the Vandals, who had previously been an entirely inland people, learned the navigational and shipbuilding skills of this region. Within a generation, they had followed in the footsteps of ancient Carthage and had created the most powerful naval force in the Mediterranean.

The Vandals were devastatingly effective pirates, looting coastal towns, seizing goods, and destroying vessels. The Roman Mediterranean trading network, a vital source of wealth for the empire, collapsed, and with it much of what remained of the imperial economy. The Romans attempted to make peace with the Vandals by arranging a marriage between the emperor's daughter and the son of the Vandal king, but the Romans' own infighting betrayed them. A coup brought a new emperor to the throne, and the Vandals seized on this pretext to attack. In 455, their forces landed in Italy and sacked Rome itself. Vandal dominance and Roman weakness were evident to all.

Despite this violence, the Vandals actually desired to preserve and to participate in Rome's traditional system of stability and wealth. In 476, for example, the African Vandal Kingdom established peace with the Eastern Roman Empire. Nonetheless, the disruptive nature of their arrival had damaged the cohesion of western Roman society in ways that were not easily healed. One area of tension associated with the Vandals was their aggressive promotion of "Arian" Christianity. They beheaded Catholic bishops and seized their property; they also attempted to establish a rival "Arian" hierarchy. This religious persecution contributed to the instability and ultimate collapse of the Vandal Kingdom, which we will discuss in chapter 19.

The Visigoths

The group of tribes known as the Visigoths (or sometimes simply as the "Goths") had long lived on the borders of the empire along the Danube and had established trading partnerships with the Romans. Missionaries sent north during the reign of Constantius II had evangelized them and, like the Vandals, the Visigoths were committed "Arian" Christians. As we saw in the last chapter, the Visigoths initially entered the empire as allies, but abuse from Roman soldiers and lack of resources drove them to rebel. Emperor Theodosius eventually subdued and even incorporated the Visigoths into his army as *foederati*, or allies. Yet mistrust remained on both sides, and the Goths did not develop a sense of exclusive loyalty to the empire. Instead, from 395 onwards, many became increasingly-independent agents, dismissing Theodosius's incompetent sons and instead following the leadership of **Alaric** (370–411).

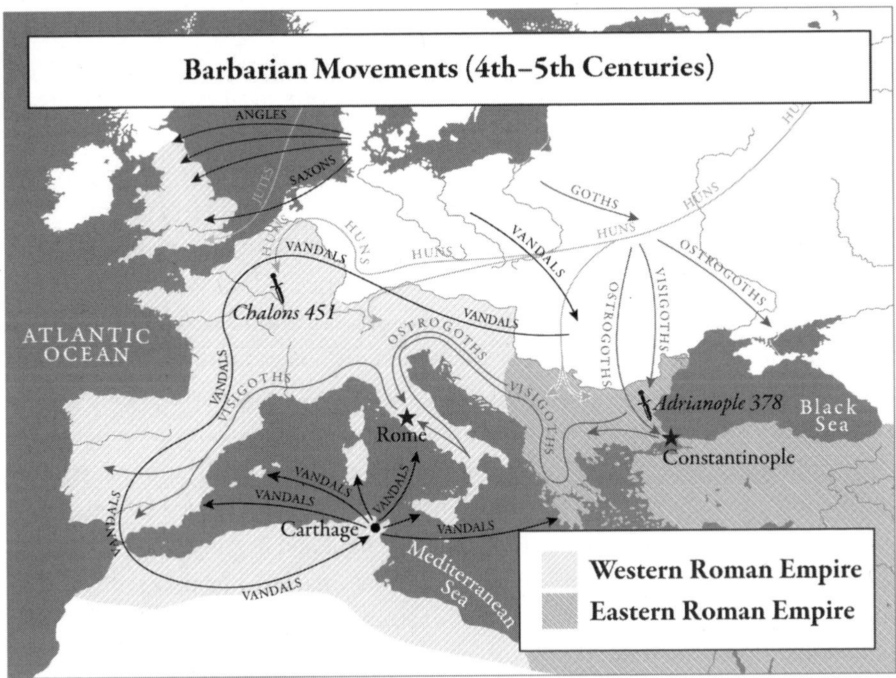

Historians debate when and even whether Alaric claimed the title "king of the Visigoths." If he did assert this authority, he did not intend to carve out a separate Gothic realm. Instead, for the first decade of the fifth century, he negotiated with Roman officials in an attempt to gain an imperial position such as "consul." His efforts were repeatedly rebuffed, and violence ensued. So determined was the Goth to receive Roman recognition that he temporarily proclaimed a rival emperor who promptly bestowed upon Alaric the title he craved. When this situation fell apart, the frustrated Goths ultimately vented their wrath on the city of Rome. On August 24, 410, Visigothic soldiers entered the ancient capital and began a three-day sack.

Alaric's quest for imperial recognition is particularly fascinating because it took place within the context of Rome's decline. The empire's growing weakness was all-too-discernible, yet Alaric did not immediately seek to overthrow the Roman government with some barbarian kingdom. Instead, he wished to gain the prestige still associated with a high position in the Roman regime. Alaric's immediate successors shared his aim of being affiliated with the empire even though they also openly used the title "king of the Visigoths." Indeed, in 414, the Visigoth king married the western emperor's sister, and the two sides eventually formed an alliance against the Vandals in Spain. In return for this military support, the Romans granted their allies land in southern Gaul. This effectively acknowledged

Visigoth independence, though their king still theoretically accepted the overlordship of the emperor.

The Romans had unwittingly taken a step that pointed toward the final breakup of their government in the west. Imperial officials had collected a land tax, which was used to pay for roads, aqueducts, other infrastructure, and, most importantly, the military. By granting the Visigoths land, the Romans had permitted the creation of an independent Visigothic kingdom in the heart of the empire that no longer paid taxes. The loss of this revenue further crippled the Romans' ability to maintain the military protection, unity, and sophistication that had been typical of life in the empire for so long. For their part, the Visigoths did not have a centralized government that could ensure its soldiers' loyalty by paying them in cash. Instead, they subdivided the land and granted it to their warriors in exchange for their military service. The exchange of land for service made the warriors more independent of their rulers. The transition from Rome's centralized model of governance to the decentralized medieval feudal system had begun.

The Visigoths were becoming an independent nation, but they still contributed one last significant effort on behalf of Rome. The Huns, a warlike, nomadic people, had established their own realm in Central Asia during the fourth century. Their steady advance towards the Danube had been the occasion for the Visigoths' request to Valens for permission to cross that river and so enjoy imperial protection. A century later, the Huns were conducting raids against both halves of the Roman Empire under their most famous king, Attila (r. 434–453). So powerful had Attila become that he demanded the western emperor's sister for a bride as well as half of the Western Roman Empire. When this was refused, the Huns crossed the Rhine River intent upon conquest. Attila's massive force attacked cities throughout northern Gaul and threatened many others, including Paris. (This city's preservation is often attributed to the spiritual leadership of a consecrated virgin named Geneviève.) The outnumbered Roman general received desperate aid from the Visigoths, and their combined forces inflicted a decisive defeat against the Hun invaders at the Battle of Châlons in 451. It was one of the final victories ever won by a Roman army in the West.

Attila's surviving army could still terrorized the Roman world. In 452, he invaded Italy, but, to the surprise of many, Pope Leo I convinced Attila not to attack Rome. Later tradition ascribed Leo's accomplishment to a supernatural vision.[2] Attila died the following year during a marriage feast when he suffocated while in a drunken state. His empire swiftly fell apart.

2 Unfortunately, Leo was not able to stop the Vandal sack of Rome three years later.

In contrast, the Visigoths were slowly developing their independent domain. Frankish pressure during the sixth century convinced them to move further southward and settle in the Iberian Peninsula. Here they maintained a Visigothic kingdom which still preserved a version of Roman law combined with their own Gothic customs. They established a court in the city of Toledo, and a council of nobles and bishops elected each new king. Although they did not persecute Catholic Christians as actively as did the Vandals, their promotion of "Arian" Christianity meant that divisions remained between themselves and the native Hispanic and Roman populations whom they ruled.

Ostrogoths

The Ostrogoths entered the Eastern Roman Empire in the fifth century after living in close proximity to the empire for years. The emperors struggled to control them, and the Ostrogoths frequently made war against one another and plundered the provinces of the empire. Meanwhile, in Italy, the second half of the fifth century saw the ever-weaker Roman emperors become puppets controlled by powerful barbarian warlords. The most successful of these kingmakers was Odoacer (c. 433–493). In 476, he deposed the eleven-year-old Romulus Augustulus (r. 475–476) and sent the imperial regalia to the Emperor Zeno in Constantinople. Though this moment is traditionally seen as the decisive "fall" of the Roman Empire in the West, it is important to note that Odoacer claimed to restore Italy to Zeno's authority. He even appealed to the emperor to recognize him as a patrician, or a member of elite Roman society. This request again reveals that the barbarians of this era desired to preserve the Roman world on their own terms rather than overthrow it completely. Only when Zeno rejected Odoacer's appeal did the general declare himself king of Italy.

Mosaic of Theodoric. Made c. 6th century. Currently in the Basilica of Sant'Apollinare Nuovo in Ravenna, Italy. It is believed that the name "Justinian" was added later during a restoration. It is unclear whether the addition was a mistake or was a deliberate attempt to erase Ostrogothic history.

Zeno ultimately encouraged a leading Ostrogoth warrior named **Theodoric** (r. 493–526) to take his army west to Italy. (We discuss Zeno and the situation in Constantinople in the next chapter.) In 489,

Theodoric arrived in Italy and proceeded to establish his own authority at Odoacer's expense. He won several battles, took the important city of Ravenna, and ultimately murdered his rival in 493 by cutting him in two with his sword during a feast that was supposed to celebrate peace between them. (Odoacer's last words were "Where is God?" At which point, Theodoric replied "This is what you did to my friends.")

Theodoric was now the undisputed king of Italy, but like Odoacer before him, he did not desire to overthrow Roman society. Indeed, Theodoric had spent his youth as a hostage in Constantinople, where he had received a comprehensive Roman education. Now in power, he attempted to restore Roman peace and culture while preserving his own independent rule of Italy.

Theodoric, for example, rebuilt the city of Ravenna, restoring the aqueduct, constructing a palace modelled on the great palace in Constantinople, and building new churches, including a cathedral that is famous for its beautiful mosaics. He also repaired other nearby cities in northern Italy, building walls, aqueducts, churches, and baths. Theodoric was an "Arian," but he tolerated the Catholics who lived in his kingdom, and he claimed to respect the office of the papacy. He appointed as his chief minister the Catholic philosopher Boethius (480–524), whose Latin translations of Plato's dialogues and Aristotle's works on logic provided many early medieval students in the West with their sole access to Greek philosophy.

In addition to his efforts to rebuild Roman culture and infrastructure, Theodoric also attempted to restore the political unity of the former Western Roman Empire. He pursued this goal using a system of marriage alliances that was more typical of Germanic culture than imperial Rome. He married the sister of the Frankish ruler to the north and gave his own sister in marriage to the Vandal king in North Africa. In 511, he gained control of the Visigothic Kingdom in Spain when he became regent for his grandson, forming an "empire" of influence that stretched across the Mediterranean from the Atlantic to the Danube.

During his long reign, it must have seemed as though Theodoric would restore the Roman Empire in the West, reenergized by an infusion of Germanic culture. He dressed as a Roman, oversaw a period of peace and prosperity, and successfully promoted important aspects of Roman culture. Toward the end of his life, however, these ambitions failed. Fighting broke out among the different barbarian kingdoms and, frustrated by the fickleness of his allies, Theodoric became increasingly paranoid in his old age and began persecuting Catholics. He even executed Boethius, who wrote his famous *The Consolation of Philosophy* while in prison. Pope John I likewise faced his wrath and died in prison after failing to secure benefits for the "Arians" of the East during the first papal visit to Constantinople. Theodoric's death from dysentery in 526 possibly saved the Catholic Church in Italy from a severe persecution.

The **Arian Baptistry** and the **Basilica of Sant'Apollinare Nuovo**. Both built by Theodoric in Ravenna, Italy, in the early 6th century. These two sites are significant because of their numerous well-preserved mosaics which give insight into the artistic style of period that has largely been lost elsewhere. Both the basilica and the baptistry are UNESCO World Heritage Sites.

The Franks

The **Franks** were different from the other barbarian groups who entered the Roman Empire during the fifth century in two important ways. First, they did not migrate into the Roman Empire but instead expanded from their lands in modern-day northwest Germany into the Roman province of Gaul. Second, the Franks were not "Arian" Christians but pagans, and they were therefore less invested in the Christian debates and persecutions that occurred in other kingdoms.

Binding Plate of St. Remi. Made of carved ivory c. 870. Currently in the Musée de Picardie, Amiens, France. This plaque depicts three different miracles associated with the life of St. Remigius. In the top register, he restores a young girl to life, while in the middle scene, the Hand of God (far left) fills the two vials with the Oil of Catechumens and the Holy Chrism so that the bishop can baptize a dying pagan. In the bottom scene, the Holy Spirit fills a single vial for the baptism of Clovis. These last two miracles, both associated with Christian initiation, became the foundation for legends surrounding the origin of the Holy Ampulla, a glass vial which held the chrism oil for anointing the French kings from the twelfth century until the French Revolution.

According to legend, the Franks fought alongside the Visigoths and the Romans to defeat the Huns at Châlons. Later, they demanded their own land in Gaul, but the Romans rejected their request and mocked **Clovis** (r. c. 481–511), the Frankish king, because of his youth and long hair. If this encounter actually happened, Clovis had the last laugh, for his warriors seized control of northern Gaul after defeating the Roman army at the Battle of Soissons in 486. From the Romans' perspective, this must have felt like the utter collapse of civilization: the last independent Western Roman province was now overrun by barbarians who were not even Christians.

Clovis's name means "pillaging warrior," which succinctly highlights Frankish goals and culture at this time. It would take many decades to convince the Franks to abandon their warlike and pagan values, but Clovis's marriage to the Burgundian princess Clotilde (474–545) set in motion the ultimate Christianization of his people. The Burgundians were another barbarian people who had established an independent kingdom within the declining Roman Empire. Many Burgundians had embraced "Arianism," but Clotilde was Catholic. Once married to Clovis, she allied with Bishop Remigius, who had been elected bishop of Reims at the age of twenty-one on account of his piety. Clotilde and he worked together to preserve Catholicism in the Frankish realm and to exhort Clovis to convert.

Clovis scoffed at the idea of abandoning the Franks' traditional gods in favor of the God of the defeated Romans, and, at first, he must have thought that his mistrust was well placed. Their first son received baptism at Clotilde's insistence but died in infancy. Clovis attributed the death to the weakness of Christianity and became still more resistant to conversion. His wife, nonetheless, remained confident in her own Faith and later sought to baptize their newborn second son. Clovis begrudgingly permitted his heir to receive the sacrament, perhaps an indication of his own love and respect for his bride as much as a new openness towards her religion.

It was shortly thereafter that the king found himself losing on a battlefield. As we described above, his prayer to Clotilde's God was followed by a sudden change in fortune. Clovis was convinced that God had intervened to give him the victory, and he honored his promise to become a Christian. In fact, not only Clovis but also many of his warriors received baptism from Remigius at the cathedral of Reims.

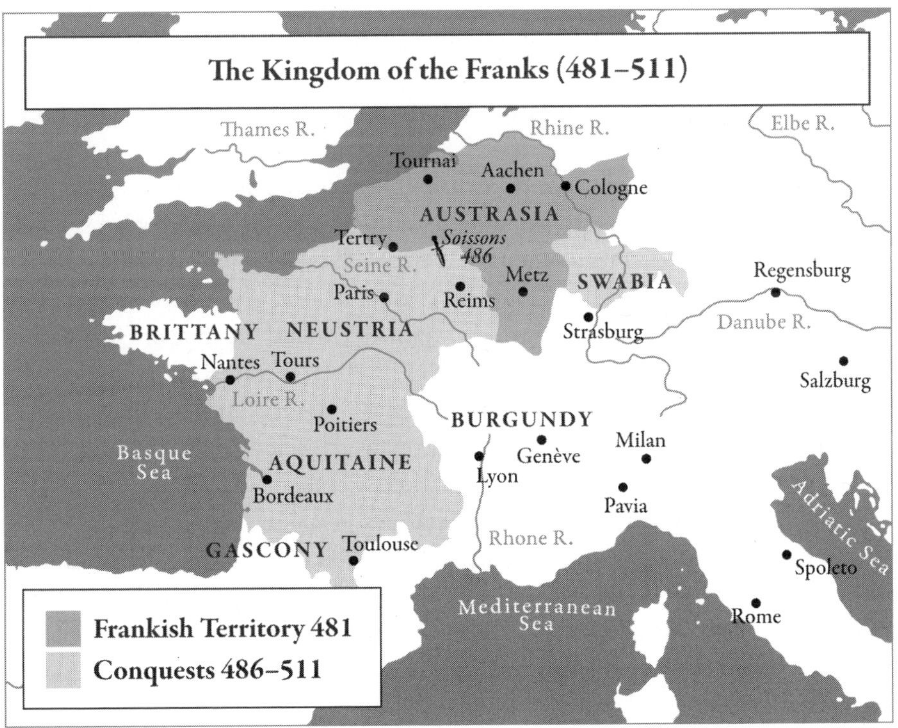

Clovis's conversion provided Catholics with a much-needed protector among the Germanic rulers who had replaced the Roman Empire. It also strengthened his own position. Whereas the authority of Vandal, Visigothic, and Ostrogothic rulers was undermined by religious divisions, Clovis had the support of his Roman subjects, who, encouraged by their bishops, were willing to fight alongside his Frankish warriors.

Furthermore, Clovis remained a successful warrior. His victories, such as when he drove the Visigoths out of Gaul and into Spain in 507, enabled him to establish a large Frankish kingdom, which ruled over both Franks and the region's remaining Roman citizens, known as Gallo-Romans. By the time of his death in 511, this land of Frankia (which gave modern-day France its name) was poised to be the most powerful of all the barbarian kingdoms.

Nonetheless, the king's adoption of Catholicism did not immediately transform the often selfish and violent behavior of the Frankish nobles. Brutal customs and practices persisted and were considered necessary to survive. Clovis is said to have immediately executed a warrior who challenged his authority. Even Clovis's and Clotilde's sons fought with one another and murdered their own nephews.

In this turbulent time, devout Christians did not look to Frankish kings and elite for piety but rather turned to those who had withdrawn from society as monks and nuns. These ascetics took inspiration from the example of Martin of Tours (316–397), the first famous monk in Western Europe. He was a former soldier who renounced his military career to live as a hermit. Later he became bishop of Tours and used his position to promote asceticism in Gaul on the eve of Roman decline.

A generation later, a monk from Palestine named John Cassian (360–435) traveled to Western Europe to promote monasticism in the region. He especially encouraged monks to live in community. Cassian's disciples founded a monastery on the rocky island of Lerins, off the southern coast of France, which became an oasis of peace and stability as the Roman world crumbled. Around the time of Clovis's conquest of Gaul, a young man named Caesarius (468–542) joined the community at Lerins. He received his formation at the monastery but ultimately became bishop of Arles in southwest France. As bishop, he encouraged his flock to practice self-denial and to strive for spiritual progress through monasticism.

Among those who responded to Caesarius's preaching was Radegund (520–587), a Germanic princess who had been seized by a Frankish prince. She was forced to live as one of his concubines, but she refused to become absorbed by her own sufferings. Instead, she devoted her life to prayer and the service of others. She also founded convents that enabled nuns to give alms to the poor and care for the sick in the midst of their lives of prayer.

FALL OR TRANSFORMATION

How Should We Interpret the Last Years of the Western Roman Empire?

The last years of the Western Roman Empire has been a topic of constant fascination for historians. Their discussions often concentrate on the probable cause(s) behind the empire's decline, and many theories have been advanced and debated. Was it external invasions, interior weakness and corruption, or some combination of the two that brought the empire to the point of no return?

In the eighteenth and nineteenth centuries, historians like Edward Gibbon advanced the popular thesis that Rome was weakened by Christianity and invaded by uncivilized Germanic barbarian armies. They argued that this combination destroyed the intellectual and artistic achievements of pagan Roman civilization and replaced them with a dark age of economic and intellectual poverty.

This interpretation has since fallen out of favor, thanks in large part to a new generation of historians in the second half of the twentieth century. These scholars, led by Peter Brown, proposed that the transition from Roman to medieval society was a process of gradual transformation rather than one of sudden and traumatic collapse. Historians like Walter Goffart further claimed that Rome was not overrun by hostile waves of Germanic invasions. Instead, they argued that these peoples were slowly integrated into imperial territories as mercenaries and that their rise to power was so gradual that the inhabitants barely noticed until later that the empire had effectively ended.

Nonetheless, other recent scholars, such as Bryan Ward-Perkins, have pushed back against this "transformation" interpretation. This second school of thought emphasizes the violence and trauma of this period and uses archeological findings to demonstrate the breakdown in supplies and quality of tools. Such evidence indicates to these historians that the fall of Rome *was* noticeable and very painful to those who lived at the time.

This historiographical debate (that is, a debate about historical *interpretations* rather than the events themselves) will doubtless continue, and both sides have made good points and clarifications. While it may seem surprising that historians cannot agree about something as "big picture" as the fall of Rome, their conversation highlights for us how various scholars can interpret the same evidence in different ways.

One of Radegund's allies was Venantius Fortunatus (530–610), a poet from Italy. He had come to the kingdom of the Franks on pilgrimage to the shrine of Martin of Tours. He remained at the Frankish court and encouraged Radegund's literary endeavors. He himself composed hymns such as *Vexilla Regis* that remain part of the liturgical life of the Church.

Clovis's baptism had not immediately remade the Franks into a Christian people, but it did enable Christian culture to continue amidst one of the most difficult and uncertain times in the Church's history. Individuals such as Radegund and Venantius enriched the tradition of the Church with their artistic talents and pointed forward to an era when the Franks themselves would understand their new faith better and contribute to its flourishing.

Benedict of Nursia

The rise of western monasticism played a significant role in the history of Western Civilization, and no one influenced monasticism in the West more than **Benedict of Nursia** (480–547). As a young man he came to Rome around 500 to study. This was an era of relative peace in Theodoric's Ostrogothic Kingdom, but Benedict rejected the prosperous culture that he found in the city. Benedict's fellow students lived corrupt, dissolute lives, and even his instructors mixed their teachings of past wisdom with private ambition. Other inhabitants were desperately poor, having fled to the city after their homes were destroyed by the barbarian armies of previous decades. Vice and illiteracy were common, and many were returning to pagan religious practices.

Benedict despaired of finding a path to the contemplation of God in the city, and he left Rome for the hills of the Italian countryside. Here he dedicated his life to prayer and asceticism. His reputation for holiness attracted followers, later known as Benedictines, and they began to live as a community with Benedict as their teacher. As the number of Benedict's followers grew, he founded his first monastery south of Rome on a mountain that overlooked the town of Cassino. A large pagan temple dedicated to Apollo had stood on this site, but Benedict destroyed the shrine and replaced it with the new abbey of Monte Cassino. This foundation came to symbolize an emerging medieval culture rooted in Christianity.

At Monte Cassino, Benedict wrote his famous *Rule* to provide practical principles for organizing monastic life. Benedict intended their way of life to be more balanced and less austere than that of the hermits in Egypt. He established a schedule for the monks to gather as a community eight times throughout the day to pray the psalms. It also included a daily routine of manual and intellectual labor. Benedict's sister, Scholastica (480–543), established a similar foundation for women nearby.

Among the changes and turmoil of the sixth century, the Benedictine Rule provided a flexible and balanced system of communal prayer and labor that has helped men and women pursue sanctity for over 1,500 years. His contemporaries of Early Medieval Europe embraced his teachings, and the desire to follow Benedict's way

Monte Cassino is the site of the first Benedictine abbey, established by St. Benedict of Nursia c. 529. It is located approximately 93 miles southeast of Rome, Italy. The current abbey building dates from 1964 due to destruction of the prior buildings during World War II. Though these buildings are technically modern, those responsible for the reconstruction attempted to recreate the older structures that had been lost in the war.

of life encouraged many to read and reproduce the *Rule*. This work helped preserve literacy in these ascetic communities even as such knowledge declined across Western Europe. In this area, as in many others, Benedictine monasticism laid the foundation for medieval civilization.

Conclusion

The Ostrogothic mosaics in Ravenna, the Visigothic art in Spain, and even the Saxon helmets in England revealed both these peoples' remarkable artistic skills and also their deep appreciation for the achievements of Roman culture. All the same, such esteem was not enough to keep the Western Roman Empire alive. The efforts of the Ostrogoths, Visigoths, and Vandals to preserve or resurrect Rome all failed, for the very presence of barbarian kingdoms unraveled the delicate balance of society within Western Europe. The court of Theodoric did preserve art, learning, and culture within its limited sphere, but the rest of the lands descended into cultural uncertainty. The collapse of the security and prosperity provided by Roman trade and Roman armies meant that most people had to focus on feeding and defending themselves rather than devoting time to intellectual activities. Nonetheless, Frankish rulers played a key role in preserving Western Civilization by collaborating with their Roman subjects to forge a new society during this distressing period. Yet even more important than Clovis and his successors were the efforts of Benedictine monks and nuns who blended lives of prayer, labor, and intellectual activity and thereby helped lay the groundwork for medieval society.

CHAPTER 18

The First Great Schism

For my part, if I am to write the truth, my inclination is to avoid all assemblies of bishops, because I have never seen any council come to a good end, nor turn out to be a solution of evils. On the contrary, it usually increases them. You always find there love of contention and love of power.

Gregory of Nazianzus, *Letter* 130[1]

The previous chapter explored the rise of barbarian kingdoms in Western Europe and how each interacted with the legacy of Rome. As the last Western Roman emperors faded from memory, Frankish warriors and Benedictine monks established new sources of political, intellectual, and spiritual authority that laid the foundations for medieval European society. This chapter returns to the fifth century and investigates what took place in the *Eastern* Roman Empire as the West gradually collapsed. Historians often designate the Eastern Roman Empire as the "Byzantine Empire" or "Byzantium" because its capital, Constantinople, was built atop the Greek colony of Byzantium. We will use this terminology, but we should remember that "Byzantines" called themselves "Romans" and rightly understood their empire to be a continuation of the Roman world—even though Greek replaced Latin as the imperial language.

Religious division and political intrigue dominated fifth-century Byzantium. New theological debates led to unrest, and emperors followed Constantine's example by summoning new councils to find an acceptable consensus. Even as these

1 Gregory of Nazianzus, *Epistle CXXX* quoted in J. Stevenson, *Creeds, Councils, and Controversies: Documents illustrating the History of the Church, AD 337–461*, 2nd ed revised by W.H.C. Frend (London: SPCK, 2003) 118–119.

assemblies met, barbarian leaders were seizing lands of the Western Roman Empire, and the court at Constantinople found itself in a complex duel with its own powerful barbarian generals. Unlike the West, eastern emperors overcame their rivals, and Byzantium survived. Tragically for the Church, no one successfully reconciled the theological factions tearing Christianity apart. Instead of healing the discord, each council seemed to add to it until there were three opposing branches of Christianity.

Such an unfortunate situation would not have surprised Gregory of Nazianzus. He was a close friend of Basil of Caesarea and temporarily presided over the Council of Constantinople in 381 until church infighting forced him to step down. Though he did not live to see the disputes covered in this chapter, Gregory would likely have believed that his assessment above was as valid for them as it was for those of his own lifetime.

Seeds of Rivalry

The "love of power" decried in Gregory's letter became more apparent as bishops grew in prosperity and social prestige during the fourth and fifth centuries. Imperial gifts as well as the practice of bequeathing part of one's inheritance to the Church enriched many churchmen. Soon men more interested in their status than in spiritual service sought to become bishops. At the same time, episcopal authority was extending into the countryside. Previously, Christian communities had been predominately urban, but in the fourth and fifth centuries, more converts came from rural areas. These newly baptized required spiritual guidance, and bishops decided to adapt the existing imperial administration to serve the needs of the Church. They created "dioceses" which, though smaller than Diocletian's administrative unit of the same name, formally extended a bishop's authority into a city's hinterland, or surrounding countryside.

This reorganization was not the first time that the Church had followed imperial models. The Roman designation "metropolis" indicated the capital city of a regional province. Since the third century, Christians considered the bishop of a metropolis to have authority over the other bishops in a province. A metropolitan bishop, for example, could veto a local episcopal consecration or settle a dispute among bishops in his region. The metropolitan cities of Rome, Antioch, and Alexandria were particularly important in the Church's hierarchy, and the decrees, or canons, of the Council of Nicaea explicitly acknowledged their preeminence and authority.

This accepted arrangement suffered a shock at the Council of Constantinople in 381. As we discussed in chapter 16, this gathering expanded the Nicene Creed to include statements explicitly defending the Holy Spirit's divinity. In addition to this teaching, however, the council fathers also declared that the bishop of

Constantinople was next in dignity to the bishop of Rome. This decision assumed that Constantinople, as the new imperial capital, should share a similar ecclesiastical standing as that enjoyed by Rome, Alexandria, and Antioch. Yet these cities possessed more than just imperial significance. Their Christian communities traced their origins to either the apostle Peter or his close associate, the evangelist Mark. Constantinople, in contrast, lacked an obvious historical connection to Peter. (A later tradition sought to address this issue and claimed that Peter's brother Andrew founded Byzantium's Christian community.) Though Rome accepted the council's revision to the Nicene Creed, it was not until 1215, at the Fourth Lateran Council, that the Roman Church accepted Constantinople as next in rank after itself.

In the East, however, the canons were held to be valid, and Antioch and Alexandria resented this usurpation of their status. Soon, Constantinople's bishopric became a "battleground" between these two cities' metropolitan bishops. Each strove to install their respective candidate as bishop in the capital in order to defend their own diocese's prestige and influence.

Adding to this competition was the fact that Antioch and Alexandria championed two opposing approaches to theology. (Historians refer to their methodologies as "schools," but neither was an established institution; rather, "school" refers to their shared perspectives in theology and biblical exegesis.) Alexandria's "school" defended Origen's use of allegorical interpretation for Sacred Scripture; this interpretation emphasized the typological character of the Old Testament; in other words, the historical significance of Moses, King David, or the prophets was generally considered not as important as how their actions and messages could be understood as prefiguring Christ. Furthermore, this "school" focused upon Jesus's divinity before turning to His humanity. As the historian Leo David describes it, Alexandrian theologians began with the eternal Word in John's Prologue and then tried to understand how God could become man.[2] In contrast, Antiochene theologians began with the historical Jesus of Nazareth in the synoptic Gospels of Matthew, Mark, and Luke and then explored how this man could also be God. The Antiochene "school" generally emphasized a literal, historical interpretation of biblical texts, though some adherents did admit that, on rare occasion, an allegorical reading was beneficial. To complicate matters, there was no standard theological vocabulary for either "school" to use, and their imprecise terminology could be misunderstood by those outside of their own tradition.

2 Leo Donald Davis, *The First Seven Ecumenical Councils* (Collegeville, Minnesota: The Liturgical Press, 1990), 142.

The rivalry between Antioch and Alexandria took a deadly turn when Theodosius's son Arcadius (r. 395–408) chose **John Chrysostom** (c. 349–407), or John the Golden-mouthed, to be the next bishop of Constantinople in 397. John, an ascetic from Antioch, was famous for his eloquent preaching, and later generations honored him alongside Basil of Caesarea and Gregory of Nazianzus as one of the three great Church Fathers of the East. Unfortunately, John's contemporaries were not so enamored of him. Theophilus, the bishop of Alexandria, was particularly outraged that John, a representative of the Antiochene "school," could now use his position to influence Arcadius. The fact that John boldly deposed a corrupt bishop in one diocese and intervened in another convinced Theophilus that John was power hungry.

Furthermore, John, as bishop of the Eastern Empire's capital, soon became entangled in political intrigues. The most important of these involved an "Arian" barbarian general. This general had murdered Arcadius's adviser and was positioning himself as the dominant power behind the throne. The people of Constantinople were on edge, and John's stalwart refusal to allow an "Arian" church inside the capital helped inspire a popular uprising against the barbarians in 400. The general and his soldiers fled the city, and the danger passed.

The emperor's gratitude to John for his role in averting the threat cooled when the bishop began to preach against the excesses of the imperial court. To make matters worse for John, a theological dispute about Origen's teachings had arisen, and Theophilus of Alexandria used the controversy (and his vast wealth) to convince Arcadius to exile John—twice! He died in 407 from the ill treatment he received from imperial soldiers.

The contrast between Arcadius and his father, Theodosius, could not have been clearer. Whereas Theodosius had repented at Ambrose's rebuke, Arcadius rejected John's admonitions and indirectly contributed to the bishop's death. Arcadius's attitude proved to be prevalent in Byzantine history, as eastern emperors commonly considered themselves above the bishops of Constantinople and replaced them at will. Many also believed that they had the right to intervene in Church issues and frequently did so. Nonetheless, Arcadius's son Theodosius II (r. 408–450) repented of his father's actions and returned John's body to the city with great honor in 438.

Centuries of development in Christian piety inspired Theodosius II's respect for John's bones, or relics. It began with the admiration for martyrs. As early as the second century, we have reports of Christians honoring martyrs' bodies. Burial sites became focal points for devotion and prayers, and soon church buildings housed the remains of those who died for Christ. Such enthusiasm was particularly revolting to Roman piety. According to pagan tradition, proximity to corpses brought ritual uncleanness. From the Christian perspective, Jesus's resurrection had ended

Relic of St. John Chrysostom. Currently on display at the Residenz Munich in Germany. Devotion to relics was a common form of Christian piety, but there were differing opinions on how it should be accomplished. Many in the West thought that the bodies of saints should be honored whole and not divided. In the East, SS. Basil of Caesarea and Gregory of Nazianzus promoted the division of the bones among various sites in order to spread devotion to a given saint throughout the land.

death's dominion. By bringing bodies of saints into the buildings of the living—particularly churches—Christians proclaimed the connection between heaven and earth. The dead were not gone but rather remained an integral part of the Church community and even interceded on behalf of those who sought their prayers. The churches that held these remains possessed special importance, and Christians soon came from great distances to honor the relics that they housed.

Pilgrimage thus became a popular expression of Christian piety. Journeys to the places associated with martyrs became religious acts, though the motives for these arduous and potentially hazardous trips varied. Penance for sins committed or a desire for some blessing were the most common goals among pious pilgrims. While sites associated with the life of Jesus had special value, Rome and other places that had witnessed the martyrs' courage or that now housed their bones also attracted Christian pilgrims. Furthermore, the respect Christians held for martyrs extended into the fourth and fifth centuries to include ascetics, and soon their relics—like those of John Chrysostom—were highly valued.

The developing devotion to the saints included veneration of Jesus's mother, Mary of Nazareth. The earliest evidence for Marian devotion comes from the second and third centuries as figures introduced in previous chapters—Ignatius of Antioch, Justin Martyr, and Irenaeus of Lyons—wrote in defense of Mary's perpetual virginity and spoke of her with great honor. Irenaeus even identified her as the "New Eve," whose obedience enabled Jesus's incarnation and our redemption. A fourth- or fifth-century text known as the *Six Books Dormition Apocryphon* described Mary's assumption into Heaven and her status as queen. This work also served as a liturgical guide for public devotions in honor of Mary. Moreover, our earliest evidence of Marian devotion comes from a third-century papyrus of the *Sub Tuum Praesidium* ("We fly to your protection") prayer. This invoked Mary's help under the title ***Theotokos***, a Greek term that translates as "God-bearer," or "Mother of God." This title and its wider theological significance became the initial focal point of the great theological debates of the fifth century.

EARLY MARIAN DEVOTION

Perhaps the most controversial devotion of early Christians—at least from a modern Protestant perspective—is their esteem for the Virgin Mary. As noted previously, Irenaeus and others promoted respect for Jesus's mother, while the work known as the *Six Books Dormition Apocryphon* explicitly endorsed prayers to Mary and recounted various miracles attributed to the Mother of God. What is more, Gregory of Nyssa, one of the three Cappadocian Church Fathers of the fourth century, mentioned in 380 the earliest known account of a Marian apparition. According to Gregory of Nyssa, another Gregory, the third-century saint Gregory the Wonderworker, had a vision of the Virgin Mary and John the Evangelist. These two comforted the saint as he prayed about the heresies then dividing the Church.

The **Sub Tuum Praesidium Papyrus**. Greek Papyrus 470 in the Catalogue of the Greek and Latin Papyri in the John Rylands Library, University of Manchester, England. This fragment of papyrus records a Marian prayer written in brown ink c. 3-4th century. The Greek text of lines 4-9 translates to, "Mother of God [hear] my supplications: suffer us not [to be] in adversity, but deliver us from danger. Thou alone..."

Despite this early evidence, Protestants sometimes point to the relative silence that many Church Fathers practiced regarding the Virgin Mary and claim that Marian devotion did not really arise until after the Council of Ephesus. While it is true that Marian devotion became more prominent after the council, we should also note that it evidently had popular support in the period leading up to the events of 431. The best example of this is the *Sub Tuum Praesidium* papyrus, a third- or fourth-century fragment of a prayer to the Virgin Mary; Marian devotion, in at least some form, preceded the council by over a century.

Nonetheless, Catholics may be surprised that various Church Fathers wrote only infrequently about the Virgin Mary or, in the case of the fourth-century Epiphanius of Salamis, were even suspicious of devotion to her. The reason for this hesitation may reside in the heresy of Gnosticism. Christian Gnostics claimed to have secret knowledge about Jesus's mysteries, and there is evidence that some Gnostics used devotion to the Virgin Mary as an opportunity to circulate their beliefs. The fourth-century *Book of Mary's Repose*, which described Mary's Assumption, included many Gnostic elements and claimed that she gave birth to the "Cherub of Great Light" who was also the Angel of Death in Exodus. It may be that the Gnostic emphasis on Mary's "secret knowledge" convinced certain Church Fathers to avoid explicit Marian topics. Nonetheless, popular devotion remained strong and, as the dangers of Gnosticism faded, Marian devotion enjoyed more explicit support from Church leaders and theologians until it blossomed in the years after the Council of Ephesus.

A Tragedy of Terminology

The ecclesiastical tragedy that unfolded in the fifth century began with three dominant personalities, each of whom sought to win support for their position from the pious, but weak-willed, Theodosius II. The first protagonist was Theodosius's sister **Pulcheria** (399–453). Unlike her brother, she had a strong sense of purpose for her life. In 413, at the age of fourteen, she publicly dedicated her virginity to God and transformed the court into a quasi-convent. She also used her unique status as an empress-turned-consecrated-virgin to steer her brother's policies. Pulcheria herself drew inspiration from Atticus, bishop of Constantinople, and his associate Proclus. Both priests encouraged Marian feasts in the capital and upheld the *Theotokos* as the ideal for consecrated virgins like Pulcheria.

The second important personality entered the stage in 428. When the bishop of Constantinople died, a debate arose about whom the emperor should choose to replace him. Though Pulcheria favored Proclus, Theodosius chose **Nestorius** (c. 381–c. 451), a monk from Antioch known for his opposition to heresy. Nestorius reportedly told Theodosius, "With me, Sire, overthrow the heretics; with you, I will overthrow the Persians."[3]

This explicit association between the health of the empire and that of the Church came less than two decades after the Sack of Rome and embodied a very different sentiment from that expressed by Augustine. As we saw in chapter 16, Augustine's *City of God* emphasized that Christians should not place their hope in temporary political structures. After all, by 428, the Vandals were about to conquer northern Africa and the Western Roman Empire had already begun its dissolution. The fate of the Church, Augustine argued, was distinct from whatever befell the Roman Empire.

3 Davis, *Seven Ecumenical Councils*, 139.

This sentiment was not widespread in the East. It was far more common here to agree with Nestorius's assumption that the success of empire and Church were interwoven. This was all the easier to do since Byzantium's neighbor, the Sassanid Empire, had waged a vicious persecution against Christians earlier that decade. The most prominent external political and religious threats were therefore one and the same for most Byzantines. Under such circumstances, we might expect that Nestorius's desire to link piety and policy would win the support of Pulcheria, but another issue made them bitter foes.

Conflict erupted when, in 428, an Antiochene priest who had accompanied Nestorius to Constantinople denounced the title *Theotokos* in a sermon. It was impossible, he claimed, for a woman to give birth to God. Many were outraged. Pulcheria felt particularly attacked because she interpreted her consecrated virginity as a special act of imitation of the Virgin Mary. Furthermore, Origen, Athanasius, and Gregory of Nazianzus had all used the term *Theotokos*. Nestorius, in contrast, supported his priest and condemned the Marian title.

There were two different, but connected, theological issues at stake. The more obvious—and easier to understand—was the role of Marian devotion in the Church. The reaction against Nestorius revealed the depth of popular piety toward the Virgin Mary, and most people understood the principal issue at stake to be the justification of Mary's title as Mother of God. More difficult to explain was the related mystery of Jesus's identity as both God and Man. Later Catholic teaching explicitly taught that Jesus was one divine Person (God the Son) with two natures (divine and human). At this stage in her history, however, the Church was still struggling to find the proper terminology to express her beliefs. Earlier attempts to explain this relationship had led to heresies that claimed the Son had either *appeared* to become a man (Docetism) or was a man who had been *adopted* as the Son of God at His baptism (Adoptionism). Nestorius wanted to avoid these errors by explaining that Jesus was truly both God and man, but, unfortunately, his solution had its own problems.

Nestorius's terminology was inspired by the Antiochene "school," which believed it was crucial to uphold the reality of Jesus's human nature. Nestorius concluded that it was necessary to emphasize a complete distinction between the two natures. Jesus's human nature performed the human actions recorded in the Gospels, such as feeling tired or hungry. His divine nature performed divine actions, such as raising someone from the dead. Using this logic, it was improper to say that God died or to describe Mary as the Mother of God, since she could only give birth to a human nature. Instead, Nestorius used the term "Christ" as a meeting ground for both human and divine activity. For example, we could not say that God suffered and died, but we *could* say that "Christ" did because the term "Christ" acted as an

Our Lady of the Sign, also known as the Great Panagia. Icon panel painted c. 1130. Currently in the Tretyakov Gallery, Moscow, Russia. This icon depicts Mary as *Theotokos* ("God-bearer") holding Christ within her womb at the moment of the Annunciation.

umbrella and included both divine and human actions; in a similar way, Nestorius argued that we could use the title *Christotokos* ("Mother of Christ") but not *Theotokos*. This "solution" was, at best, confusing, and seemed to introduce a third entity into Nestorius's already-puzzling division between Jesus's humanity and divinity.

While he genuinely attempted to defend Jesus's two natures, Nestorius failed to preserve the unity of personhood between the historical man Jesus of Nazareth and the eternal Son of God. His efforts to emphasize how both natures remained distinct ultimately suggested to others that he was dividing the Savior into two persons—a divine person and a human one. To muddy matters further, there was no agreed theological terminology to discuss this topic, so Nestorius's teachings could easily be misconstrued. In fact, if you are still scratching your head about what Nestorius taught, take comfort in the fact that historians remain uncertain even to this day what precisely Nestorius believed. It seems likely that his intent was orthodox, but he lacked the ability to express his thought clearly and found himself promoting heresy through his teachings. He later denied that he taught the errors associated with him and which came to be known as "Nestorianism", but, unfortunately for the Church, his theological expressions had a life of their own.

The competition between Alexandria and Antioch added to the unfolding upheaval by encouraging a third important figure to join in the debate. **Cyril of Alexandria** (c. 376–444) was the successor to and nephew of Theophilus, and he shared his uncle's hostility to Antioch. He once declared that praying to John Chrysostom was like returning Judas to the number of the apostles. (To his credit and as an example of his willingness to admit error, he later repented of this and publicly honored John.) As a zealous bishop, Cyril was distraught at the implications of Nestorius' teachings regarding the Virgin Mary's dignity and the Person of the Incarnate Word. However, as the leader of the Alexandrian community, he also saw the dispute as a perfect opportunity for him to promote Alexandrian theology over and above that of its Antiochene rival.

Cyril's own theological position emphasized the unity between the Savior's divinity and humanity. Whereas Nestorius denied that Mary of Nazareth could give birth to a divine nature, the Alexandrian "school" correctly taught that mothers give birth to persons—not natures. Therefore, Mary gave birth to the divine person, God the Son, and truly was the *Theotokos*. Cyril lacked the precise theological vocabulary that would later be developed, and he expressed his belief in Jesus's divinity and humanity using terminology that could be interpreted as though He possessed one nature that was both divine *and* human. Nestorius assumed Cyril's position denied Jesus's full humanity, and both he and Cyril exchanged passionate letters

PELAGIANISM

In addition to the dispute over Nestorius's teachings, the Council of Ephesus also addressed the teachings of Pelagius (d. after 418) and his disciples. This monk from Britain had arrived in Rome sometime in the 380s and sought to reform the moral laxity that he found there among the people. He and his followers held that Jesus's exhortation to be perfect as God the Father is perfect (see Mt. 5:48) implied that humanity could achieve moral perfection since Christ would not command the impossible. After all, Pelagius reasoned, Jesus had shown us how to live an exemplary life, and we, through our free will, could choose to imitate that life and avoid sin. Furthermore, Adam's fall in Eden was a personal sin rather than something shared by all his descendants, and there was no need for infant Baptism since children were already in the primordial state of innocence that Adam had enjoyed prior to disobeying God.

Augustine of Hippo vigorously challenged this position. He based his arguments on both St. Paul's epistles and his personal experience, citing, for example, his observations of how even an infant can become jealous of others. With Rome's support, a series of condemnations successfully undermined the spread of Pelagian thought and culminated in its rejection as a heresy at Ephesus in 431. Though Pelagianism did not spread any further in the East, pockets remained active in the West for a number of years. What was more, interpretations of Augustine's critiques of free will and its limitations, as well as his teachings on the nature of grace and Original Sin, would have profound ramifications later in Church history during the early years of the Protestant era.

that condemned the other's position. Cyril wrote to Pope Celestine I (r. 422–432), who agreed with Cyril regarding the errors in Nestorius' theology, but who was also unaware of how Cyril's language could be interpreted problematically. For his part, though he favored Nestorius, Theodosius II decided that the best way to solve the crisis was to summon an ecumenical council. Many assumed that Cyril was about to be placed on trial for arguing with the emperor's bishop, but the pope delegated Cyril to represent him at the upcoming council, and Cyril arrived prepared to battle for the honor of the Virgin Mary.

The **Council of Ephesus** (431) was a mess. Cyril did not wait for bishops sympathetic to Nestorius to arrive. Instead, he convinced the leading imperial official to convene the council officially by reading Theodosius' authorization for the bishops' gathering. Once the session had begun, Cyril showed a letter from Celestine that supported his defense of the title *Theotokos* and swiftly condemned Nestorius as a heretic. When Nestorius's allies came shortly thereafter, they proceeded to hold their own council, which promptly accused Cyril of heresy! Lastly, the papal legates arrived and, acting under orders from the pope, sided with Cyril's condemnation of Nestorius' theology; they also stressed, in a rather dramatic display of early papal authority, how Celestine expected the council to accept the papal position against Nestorianism without debate. The imperial officers in charge of the proceedings were utterly befuddled by two conflicting councils and promptly placed both Nestorius *and* Cyril under house arrest. This situation did not last long. Cyril, taking a page from his uncle's playbook, soon used the wealth of his diocese to bribe officials in the capital. These men released Cyril and convinced the emperor to depose and exile Nestorius.

What the Church desperately needed at this moment was another Athanasius. If you recall, Athanasius had realized that some "Arians" possessed a genuine desire to preserve belief in God the Son's divinity; they rejected Nicaea because they feared it compromised the Son's distinct personhood. Athanasius, therefore, had looked past the formal heresy of their position and sought to win them to the pro-Nicene position by appealing to their honorable intentions. In contrast, neither Cyril nor Nestorius examined their assumptions to see if the other side possessed goodwill. Had they done so, they would likely have realized that they both desired to defend the same truth even though their respective statements both failed to express that truth clearly and unambiguously. (For example, since there was no agreed upon theological vocabulary, it was possible to read Cyril's document known as the Twelve Anathemas as saying that Christ did not have a full human nature even if this was not what he meant.) The long-lasting competition between Antioch and Alexandria merely exacerbated, or intensified, the tragedy. Pope Celestine I probably recognized as much when he wrote to Cyril some months before the council reminding him that God did not desire the death of the sinner (in this case, Nestorius) and warned the bishop of Alexandria not to be among those condemned for being swift to shed blood. Indeed, one of Cyril's own allies wrote to him to condemn his behavior at the council: "Favor obscures the view, but hatred blinds completely. . . . A number of those who have been at Ephesus represent you as a man burning to avenge an injury of his own, not to seek in orthodoxy the glory of Jesus Christ. He is, they say, a nephew of Theophilus. . . . The fury of the uncle was unleashed against John [Chrysostom], the friend of God; [Cyril] too, though the cases are very different, has sought for a success about which he can boast."[4] Perhaps taking such a rebuke to heart, Cyril ultimately made peace with one of the leaders of the Antiochene "school". This John of Antioch agreed to condemn Nestorius's errors while Cyril no

DOCTRINE AND THE CHURCH FATHERS

The tragic schism that ultimately fragmented Christianity into three branches highlights for us the difficulties of this era in Church history. Church Fathers are rightly celebrated for laying the foundations for later theological insight, but they often struggled with their lack of a precise theological vocabulary. In attempting to develop ways of expressing his Catholic belief, a given Church Father—for example, Origen, some of whose ideas were condemned but whom Pope Benedict XVI called a "great master of faith"—could easily introduce phrases and ideas that later generations would reject as problematic.[5] Furthermore, in attempting to combat error, their own occasional imprecision in language, like that of St. Cyril of Alexandria, contributed to the confusion which led to additional challenges. Therefore, the writings of the Church Fathers should be approached with both respect and care. Not everything they wrote proved to be as clear or as orthodox as they intended. Nonetheless, they successfully identified serious errors and laid down principles that reaped much fruit in future centuries. Perhaps St. Augustine's words in his treatise *The Trinity* best express the theological endeavors that marked the Patristic Era:

"Dear reader, whenever you are as certain about something as I am go forward with me; whenever you hesitate, seek with me; whenever you discover that you have gone wrong come back to me; or if I have gone wrong, call me back to you. In this way we will travel along the street of love together as we make our way toward him of whom it is said, 'Seek his face always.'"[6]

5 Pope Benedict XVI, *Church Fathers: From Clement of Rome to Augustine* (San Francisco, Ignatius Press, 2008), 37.

6 Augustine, *The Trinity*, 1.3.5; quoted in Robert Wilken, *The Spirit of Early Christian Thought*, 107.

4 Isidore of Pelusium quoted in Davis, *Seven Ecumenical Councils*, 160.

longer insisted on certain terminology that was especially troubling to his theological opponents and prone to heretical interpretation. Nonetheless, many supporters of both bishops disliked this attempt to find common ground, and the general theological breach between Alexandria and Antioch remained. The breakdown of Church unity had begun.

Ecclesiastical Fragmentation

The first act of the drama had ended in triumph for defenders of the *Theotokos*. People celebrated in the streets when Cyril announced Nestorius's condemnation, and the pope in Rome honored the Council of Ephesus (that is, the one presided over by Cyril) by dedicating the church of St. Mary Major several years later. Theodosius II, meanwhile, decided to champion a theology entirely opposed to that of Nestorius. His new favorite cleric was Eutyches, a monk who lived near Constantinople. Eutyches proposed that God the Son had two natures *before* the Incarnation but only one divine nature *after* He became flesh. This perplexing position was a muddled mixture of Cyril's theology and the teachings in a manuscript which many at the time thought had been written by Athanasius. Unfortunately, the work was heretical and undermined belief in Jesus's human nature by suggesting that He lacked a human mind. Eutyches concluded that Jesus's divinity had effectively absorbed whatever humanity He possessed.

Many disagreed with Eutyches's theology, but Cyril died in 444 and could not clarify his position in light of the confusion caused by this abbot's teaching. Instead, Alexandria's new bishop, Dioscorus, suspected that resistance to Eutyches's theology was actually a clandestine effort to restore Nestorius's errors. Once again disagreement erupted, and Theodosius II decided that another ecumenical council was necessary. He invited Pope **Leo I** (r. 440–461) to join, but Leo refused since no previous pope had attended a council. Instead, he sent delegates who brought with them a text known as the *Tome of Leo*, which presented the pope's harmonization of the best insights from both Alexandria's and Antioch's theological traditions.

The bishops gathered at Ephesus in 449. Dioscorus led the gathering. He refused to read Leo's *Tome* and forced a vote in which many bishops were not allowed to participate. This approach secured the condemnation of those who disagreed with Eutyches. The papal legate, who could not speak Greek, finally realized that Dioscorus had no intention of permitting discussion and shouted "*veto*" (Latin for "I forbid [this]"). At the same time, several bishops approached Dioscorus to request that he stop the proceedings, but the bishop of Alexandria yelled that he was being attacked. In burst soldiers and pro-Alexandrian monks who began physically beating bishops into submission. The papal legate later considered himself fortunate to have escaped the scene alive. Dioscorus forced those who had not escaped to sign blank sheets of paper that would be filled in later with his own theological position.

Pope Leo was outraged when he heard of the proceedings. He declared that it was no council but rather a gathering of robbers, and Catholics still refer to the event as the *Latrocinium*, or "Robber Council." In contrast, Theodosius praised the gathering, and Eutyches's theology seemed poised to spread across the Byzantine Empire. Such was the situation when the childless Theodosius II died unexpectedly in 450.

Pulcheria was next in line for the throne, but Roman society was not yet ready to accept a woman ruler. She needed a husband to act as emperor, but finding a husband was complicated for the consecrated virgin. Fortunately for Pulcheria, the general Marcian (r. 450–457) agreed to respect her vows in exchange for receiving imperial status through marriage. Now married and officially empress, Pulcheria could address the theological chaos caused by the *Latrocinium*.

At Leo's urging, she summoned yet another council, this time closer to Constantinople so she could maintain control over the proceedings. Leo's *Tome* became the focal point for the **Council of Chalcedon** (451). This taught that the Incarnate Word was one divine person with two natures. The pope's formula brought together Cyril's emphasis on the unity of personhood with the Antiochene "school's" clear insistence that Jesus was both fully divine *and* fully human. The bishops proclaimed that the Apostle Peter had spoken through Leo and embraced the *Tome*'s teachings. They deposed Dioscorus, and it seemed that the drama begun in 428 was finally ending in peace.

In reality, the tragedy had only begun. Many followers of Cyril's theology held firm to his ambiguous terminology and believed that Jesus possessed one nature that was both human and divine, or, as Cyril had expressed it, "one incarnate nature of God the Logos." These "**Miaphysites**" (Greek for "one nature") rejected Eutyches's position since he denied Jesus's full humanity.[7] They also believed that Chalcedon taught heresy since they interpreted the teaching that Jesus had two natures as Nestorian. Reports that Nestorius agreed with Chalcedon when he learned of its teaching only further convinced Miaphysites that the "Chalcedonians" were heretical.

Miaphysite riots broke out in Egypt and Palestine when the council's decisions became known. Violence in Alexandria was particularly intense and took the form

7 Both "Miaphysite" and "Monophysite" reference "one nature." While scholars used the term "Monophysite" for many generations to describe the Cyrillian theology of the Oriental Orthodox Churches, modern scholarship generally uses the term "Miaphysite" and reserves the term "Monophysite" to reference Eutyches's theology. While we will use "Miaphysite" in this text when mentioning the Oriental Orthodox Churches, note that other histories use "Monophysite" and "Miaphysite" interchangeably.

of a popular uprising. Miaphysites attacked imperial soldiers and trapped them in a pagan temple, which they then burned down. The empire responded with more troops, but the unrest continued. Amidst the fires and tumult, the Miaphysite community severed itself from Chalcedonian theology and took an important step towards the formation of a distinct Church, known today as the Oriental Orthodox Church. Christianity was rapidly splintering into three factions: the Nestorians of the East (see insert on the Church of the East in chapter 21), the Miaphysites of Egypt and Palestine, and the Chalcedonians, who remained loyal to Leo's *Tome*.

This rupture was not the only setback to Church unity that arose at this time. Despite the bishops' proclamation that Peter had spoken through Leo, the Council of Chalcedon was a turning point in papal relations with Eastern Christianity. Leo and other popes believed their authority was rooted in Peter's leadership of the apostles. In contrast, the council fathers at Chalcedon affirmed an ecclesiastical structure that incorporated *imperial* priorities. Canon 28 explicitly decreed that Rome had ecclesiastical precedence because it was "the imperial city," while New Rome (Constantinople) would enjoy "equal privileges" as the new imperial city. Eastern bishops did not see this as an attack on papal authority but rather as a part of the restructuring of the Eastern Church's governance, which now focused on the five "patriarchs," or bishops, of Rome, Constantinople, Alexandria, Antioch, and

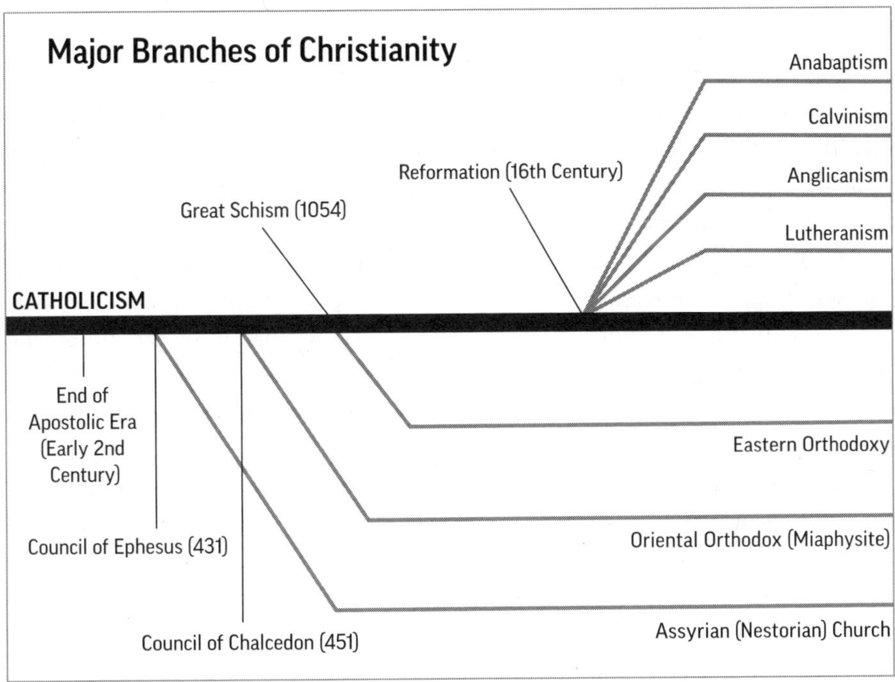

Jerusalem. Leo and subsequent popes, however, perceived this as a usurpation of authority and rejected canon 28. Already, the seeds for the "second" Great Schism, which separated Catholicism and Orthodoxy centuries later, had been planted.

Imperial Revival

Even as the Church experienced these wounds, the Eastern Roman Empire slowly recovered its strength. What contributed to Byzantium's success even as the Western Roman Empire gradually fell apart? Constantinople itself played a role in the empire's survival. Whereas the West lacked a centralized capital that could easily be protected, Constantinople was ideally situated for defense. Its location on a peninsula made it difficult to besiege from all sides, while the impressive series of defensive walls that had been built during Theodosius II's reign made it secure from sudden land attack. Secondly, the relative security of Constantinople enabled the Eastern Empire's infrastructure, that is its bureaucratic administration, to remain secure, even as western lands succumbed to barbarian conquests.

Nonetheless, it takes more than walls to preserve an empire. The people themselves need to be invested in the state's survival. We already saw the people's commitment during the time of John Chrysostom. It was not the emperor who saved his capital but rather the people, who used their bishop's opposition to a barbarian heretic as an inspiration for popular resistance. This resolve revealed itself again when an earthquake damaged Constantinople's new walls in 447. Attila the Hun was terrorizing parts of the Roman world when he learned that the capital's defense had been weakened. The people, however, rebuilt the walls swiftly and preserved their city from Attila's attack. This success stands in stark contrast to the fate of the West. Unlike Constantinople, with its walls and its dedicated population, many cities of the West—including Rome itself—were at the mercy of barbarian armies.

A final strength that the East possessed that the West did not was its leadership. This advantage was not apparent in 457 when one of the barbarian generals selected the next emperor. His choice was Leo I (r. 457–474), a man in his late fifties who had no son and was not known for leadership. It seemed like the East was embarking on the same pattern of weak emperors that was currently happening in the West, but Leo slowly began rebuilding imperial strength. He began by asking the patriarch of Constantinople to crown him emperor. This gesture—which became standard for future generations—gave his authority spiritual significance. Furthermore, he decided to recruit an independent military force from southern Anatolia. This army was not under the leadership of barbarian generals, and Leo married his daughter to their captain, Zeno. By 471, Leo felt strong enough to assassinate several barbarians who were trying to control his throne.

Rule eventually passed to Leo's son-in-law **Zeno** (r. 474–491). Zeno balanced the ambitions of the remaining barbarian generals by favoring the two most powerful rivals at the same time. These men, both named Theodoric, held one another in check as they jealously worked for their own dominance. The emperor took advantage of their competition to play one against the other. If either Theodoric became too influential, Zeno simply supported the other.

Zeno's problems included more than barbarian threats. His mother-in-law plotted against him, the Western Roman Empire faced imminent collapse, and the different theological factions continued to pull the empire apart. The intrigues within the imperial family forced Zeno to flee Constantinople in 475. Thankfully for him, the conspiracy fell apart, and Zeno returned in 476. He resumed control of Constantinople just in time to receive word that Odoacer, whom we met in the previous chapter, had overthrown the western emperor in Italy. Zeno refused to accept this situation and ordered Odoacer to acknowledge Zeno's candidate as emperor. Odoacer refused and declared himself king.

To add to Zeno's headaches, the theological debate over Chalcedon remained divisive. He needed unity if he was to avoid the fate that had just befallen the West. Therefore, in 482, he promoted the *Henoticon* ("Act of Union"). This statement neither confirmed nor rejected the Council of Chalcedon, but simply tried to restate the issue using terminology that everyone would accept. The compromise failed, and Zeno's support for it led to another revolt against his reign—this time from pro-Chalcedonians.

Things looked bleak for Zeno, especially since one Theodoric had died and the surviving Theodoric demanded greater influence. But Zeno was a survivor. By 488, he had outlasted the pro-Chalcedonian rebellion and had even solved his barbarian problem. In that year, as we discussed in the previous chapter, he commissioned Theodoric and his Ostrogoths to reclaim Italy for the empire. Both men realized that, in truth, Theodoric would be establishing his own kingdom there. It was the classic "win-win" scenario: Theodoric gained a kingdom, and Zeno preserved his empire. The consequences for Byzantium were tremendous. For the first time in generations, the emperor held power without a threatening barbarian figure attempting to control decisions in the background.

Conclusion

When Zeno died in 491, he left behind an empire free from barbarian control. Not only had it survived when the West collapsed, but it was poised to enter into a glorious period of economic prosperity and military expansion. Nonetheless, the religious divisions remained deep. The opposing theologies of Nestorianism, Miaphysitism, and Chalcedonianism became intertwined with regional identities so that attempts, like Zeno's *Henoticon*, to appease various sides met with failure and increasing hostility. Tragically for the Church, the "first" Great Schism split her community into three rival camps which remain alienated from each other even today.

UNIT V

Gain and Loss

CHAPTER 19

The Ambition of Justinian

For when you reach the point of supreme danger nothing else seems best other than to settle the matter at hand in the best possible way.

Empress Theodora in Procopius, *History of the Persian Wars*[1]

Empress Theodora's advice is probably sound counsel for anyone confronted by difficult circumstances, but it was especially valuable for her husband, Justinian. This emperor faced a desperate moment early in his reign as riots raged throughout Constantinople. He was tempted to flee the city, but Theodora urged him to stand firm. Her pragmatic response and willingness to take on the challenge at hand reflected her own difficult background. She had come from humiliating circumstances, and she would not return to them.

Her dauntless attitude also perfectly captured the energy and ambition that motivated both her and Justinian as they sought to take the Byzantine Empire to ever greater triumphs. Whereas in the fifth century new barbarian rulers of the West had tried to preserve the achievements of the Roman Empire and had largely failed, now, in the sixth century, Justinian and Theodora strove to restore the glories of Roman law, Roman expansion, and even Christian unity. As they pursued these goals, they and their successors encountered invasions, disease, and continued religious discord. Faced with these difficulties, they did not achieve all their goals, but both their successes and failures shaped the subsequent course of European history.

1 Prokopius, *The Wars of Justinian*, trans. by H.B. Dewing, revised edition by Anthony Kaldellis (Indianapolis; Hackett, 2014), 64.

Justinian's Ascendancy

Zeno died in 491. For all his success in warding off the threat of barbarian dominance, he did not establish a dynasty to succeed him. Instead, his widow married again and chose as her second husband and new emperor the administrator **Anastasius I** (r. 491–518). Her choice of a sixty-one-year-old official probably raised eyebrows, but her decision benefited the empire in ways few could have imagined.

Thanks to the efforts of Leo and Zeno, Anastasius did not have to worry about powerful rivals undermining his rule, and he focused his attention on reforming the Byzantine economy and military. For generations, many taxes had been paid in kind, that is, paid with goods such as grain. This system was inherently inefficient; consumable food was expensive to transport and could spoil before the government brought it to where it was needed. Anastasius reinstituted taxes paid in cash. This change increased the government's overall income and reduced waste. Furthermore, the emperor introduced a pure copper coin, known as the *follis*. The *follis* made ordinary transactions much easier by providing smaller denominations

Mosaic of Empress Theodora and attendants. Made c. 547 for the Basilica San Vitale in Ravenna, Italy. The basilica is important as one of the best preserved examples of early Byzantine art and architecture. It is a UNESCO World Heritage Site.

Barberini Ivory. Made of ivory c. 6th century. Currently in the Louvre Museum, Paris, France. This is a carved diptych showing a victorious emperor identified as either Zeno, Anastasius I, or Justinian. The figure holding the emperor's foot is likely an allegory for the conquered territory, while an angel holding the palm of victory crowns the emperor.

that could be used in day-to-day activities. (It was worth approximately 1/180 of Constantine's gold *nomisma*, which remained the foundation for the imperial economy.) Its ease of use encouraged more economic activity, which in turn increased tax revenue.

Anastasius also improved the pay for the Byzantine military. Previously, the government had allotted soldiers their weapons, uniforms, and supplies. Now, Anastasius gave soldiers a generous allowance of money, which they used to purchase their equipment. The wage more than paid for their gear, and soldiers thus received a nice monetary "bonus" that they could keep. This income made serving in the army more attractive than it had been for generations. More Byzantines saw military service as a viable career, and the empire no longer had to rely predominately on barbarian recruits to defend its borders or wage its wars.

As Anastasius's reign continued, the empire became wealthier and stronger. His reforms eliminated much of the corruption in the bureaucracy so that the imperial treasury actually increased even though the total rate of taxes decreased. Nonetheless, his successes did not include reconciling the different theological factions.

Anastasius was a Miaphysite and had initially embraced Zeno's *Henoticon* as a way of reconciling Chalcedonians and Miaphysites. This compromise—which deliberately refrained from either accepting or condemning the decisions of Chalcedon—failed to bring together the different parties during Zeno's reign. The pope had condemned it and even excommunicated Acacius, Zeno's patriarch of Constantinople, for promulgating its vague terminology. This resulted in the Acacian Schism, which temporarily severed relations between Rome and Constantinople. Zeno had not troubled to resolve the issue. For his part, Anastasius was confident that his many accomplishments would convince people to support Miaphysitism; he decided to move beyond the vague terminology of the *Henoticon* to promote Miaphysite theology outright. This led to a pro-Chalcedonian rebellion, but it failed to dislodge the elderly emperor.

Mosaic of Court of Emperor Justinian. Made c. 547 for the Basilica San Vitale in Ravenna, Italy. This shows Justinian (center) flanked by his generals Belisarius (left of Justinian) and Narses (right of Justinian), and the archbishop of Ravenna, Maximian, with deacons and other court members.

Anastasius left no obvious successor when he died in 518, so the imperial bodyguard chose one of its own officers named Justin to occupy the throne. Justin (r. 518–527) was a poor farmer from the province of Illyricum in Eastern Europe. He was already sixty-eight and had no experience in government. He did not even know how to write his name and had to use a stencil to "sign" imperial decrees. Throughout his reign, therefore, he relied heavily on his better-educated and loyal nephew to help govern the empire. This was Peter, better known to history by the name **Justinian** (r. 527–565), which he took to honor his uncle.

While Justin and Justinian both spoke Greek, the language of their home province (one of the westernmost in the Byzantine Empire) was Latin. They felt a strong loyalty to Latin Christianity and the papacy and desired to end Miaphysitism. In 519, Justin sent a delegation to Rome that condemned the *Henoticon* and brought an end to the Acacian Schism by approving the Council of Chalcedon for the entire empire.

Using the resources carefully collected by Anastasius, Justin and Justinian also attempted to strengthen and expand imperial influence. Their generals secured the empire's northern border by defeating the Slav armies that raided from the northeast. Furthermore, they encouraged the western Persian provinces to rebel against their rulers even as they undermined Theodoric's Ostrogothic influence in the Mediterranean by developing diplomatic relations with the Vandal Kingdom in North Africa. The Byzantines also encouraged the East African Christian kingdom of Aksum to defend the Christian population in the southern Arabian Peninsula. This alliance, which we discuss more in the next chapter, secured Byzantine access to lucrative trade with India through the Red Sea. Such efforts displayed the renewed wealth and military power of the Byzantine Empire. Moreover, they served as a preparation for Justin's and Justinian's ultimate ambition to recover those former imperial territories in the West that were currently under barbarian rule.

Justinian also worked to improve his position within the empire. He increased his popularity by funding chariot races in Constantinople. Anastasius had suppressed these because he personally disapproved of them and because they cost the empire money. Justinian, in contrast, was an enthusiastic fan. The different chariot racing teams in Constantinople had passionate groups of supporters, who were known by the colors worn by their teams: Blue, Green, Red, and White. Among these, the Blues and the Greens were the largest and most powerful. Justinian supported the Blues, and it was through this association that he first met his future empress, Theodora (500–548).

Theodora was an actress whose beauty was famous and whose immodest performances were notorious among the Blues faction. She and her sisters had tragically been forced to enter this degrading lifestyle at a very young age when their father died and their mother could not provide for them. Although imperial law prevented a member of the court like Justinian from marrying an actress, he would not be deterred and convinced his uncle to make an exception that enabled him to marry Theodora if she repented. Justinian's commitment to his new bride was typical of his ability to recognize talented collaborators even among the poorest and most despised in society. For her part, Theodora energetically helped other actresses reform their lives and leave the corruption of the Byzantine theater. She also became a bulwark of strength for Justinian when he became emperor in 527 after the death of Justin.

The Law and the Cathedral

Emperor Justinian dreamed of achieving three great goals: reconquering the western provinces of the empire, reorganizing Roman law, and suppressing Miaphysitism in imperial territories. Just as in his marriage, Justinian avoided appointing ministers from the self-serving elite of society and instead chose loyal and efficient lieutenants from more humble backgrounds to help him pursue these goals.

These subordinates delivered Justinian an early success in 529 when, after a year of intense research, a body of selected jurists presented him with the completed ***Justinian Code***. This text was an enormous undertaking and a remarkable accomplishment. For more than five hundred years, the Roman Empire had developed and enforced a variety of laws. During that time contradictions had arisen as well as confusion regarding what laws were still in force and where. Justinian's comprehensive codification clearly listed those laws that were standard throughout his empire.

He immediately commissioned further legal projects that were also successful. In 533, the commission produced the *Digest* and the *Institutes.* These textbooks for students provided commentaries and explanations for the different laws contained in the *Code*. Even after Justinian's death, his commission published the *Novellae,* a collection of all the new laws enacted by Justin and Justinian.

These works preserved the achievements of Roman law by making the decrees and their explanations readily accessible. This enabled later peoples to learn about Roman law and to incorporate it into their own societies. Indeed, the *Justinian Code* influenced legal developments long after the empire's final collapse, and most European countries still base their own law codes on Justinian's codification.

Despite this early success, the emperor almost lost his throne in 532 when riots broke out in the capital. While modern sports fans can occasionally become violent, the Blues and the Greens were notorious for celebrating their team's victories or mourning its losses by attacking their rivals. Justinian had some of these ruffians executed for murder after one such bout of violence, but a mob comprised of both factions demanded the release of the surviving prisoners. When Justinian refused, the mob became unmanageable. The rioters took up the popular sports cheer "*Nika*!" ("Win!") and burned much of the center of the city. They took control of the Hippodrome and even proclaimed a rival emperor.

Many leading senators supported the so-called **Nika Revolt**. They resented Justinian's peasant background and the efficient steps he had taken to stamp out the corrupt practices they used to enrich themselves. Justinian prepared to flee the city, but Theodora urged him to stand firm and act decisively. Using the language quoted at the start of this chapter, she exhorted him not to give up the throne and boldly declared that imperial purple made a fine color for a burial shroud. Justinian took courage and sent his general Belisarius into the Hippodrome with loyal soldiers. These troops bloodily suppressed the riots and executed the hapless rival emperor.

With the coup quashed, Justinian continued to pursue his agenda, but now with the additional project of rebuilding the heart of Constantinople. He decided to construct a series of splendid buildings that would showcase his empire's might. The most famous of these was the ***Hagia Sophia*** (Greek for "Holy Wisdom"), a massive cathedral dedicated to Christ. This church, the largest in the world at that time, had an imposing exterior that focused attention on its principal dome. Domes had long been a feature of Roman architecture, but the *Hagia Sophia* adjusted the model by

The **Hagia Sophia** ("Holy Wisdom"). Built by Justinian between 532–537 in Constantinople (modern Istanbul, Turkey). This cathedral, dedicated to the Son of God, was the largest cathedral in the world for almost one thousand years. After the fall of Constantinople to Ottoman Muslims in 1453, the structure was converted to a mosque, the minarets were added, and many of its mosaics were covered with plaster. Several mosaics with Christian imagery managed to survive. The *Deësis* ("Entreaty") mosaic probably dates from the 13th century and shows the Virgin Mary and St. John the Baptist interceding with Christ at the Final Judgement. The refinement of the facial features make this mosaic one of the finest remaining in the structure. The Hagia Sophia is a UNESCO World Heritage Site.

setting one very large dome atop smaller half domes. Furthermore, the main dome had windows at its base. As light streamed into the church from high above, those within described the main dome as floating between heaven and earth. The building itself was clad in white marble which, combined with the gilded domes, gave it a shimmering effect. Its interior was decorated in green and white marble with purple porphyry and gold mosaics.

The *Hagia Sophia* was consecrated on December 27, 537, less than six years after construction began. The great size and beauty of the cathedral symbolized both that Justinian had secured his hold on the throne after the Nika Revolt and also that Roman power was again on the rise. Less than fifty years earlier, Theodoric the Ostrogoth had initiated an impressive building program in Ravenna. While this included many beautiful churches, Justinian's rebuilding of Constantinople, crowned by the construction of Hagia Sophia, emphasized that even the most sophisticated western kingdoms could still not compete with the engineering resources and artistic brilliance of the empire.

Reconquest and Plague

Justinian soon embarked on the goal that was especially close to his heart, the restoration of the western provinces of the Roman Empire. Justinian had been preparing for this task for years. Beginning in 530, imperial armies won a series of victories against the Bulgars and the Slavs, two recently arrived barbarian peoples who had been raiding along the imperial border in Eastern Europe. In 532, after a series of minor conflicts with the Persians, Justinian purchased a peace treaty with that empire for 5.5 tons of gold. These efforts had secured both his northern and eastern borders and provided his army and its generals with experience. Now that his position at home had stabilized after the Nika Revolt, the emperor could shift his gaze westward.

Justinian's program of conquest began in North Africa. The Vandals' determination to convert their subjects to "Arianism" had turned their Roman subjects against them. Furthermore, because they were more concerned about rebellions than invasions, the Vandal kings had torn down most of the walled fortifications of their cities. Such policies had severely weakened the Vandal Kingdom.

When the imperial force under Belisarius landed in 533, the Vandal army was away on the island of Sardinia suppressing a rebellion. The Byzantines quickly defeated their forces while the Vandals were still confused and disorganized. Belisarius conquered the barbarian kingdom in less than a year. Even better for Justinian, the entire Vandal treasury, once plundered from the Romans, was recaptured. These spoils enabled the Byzantines to pay for the invasion and still have resources to fund future campaigns.

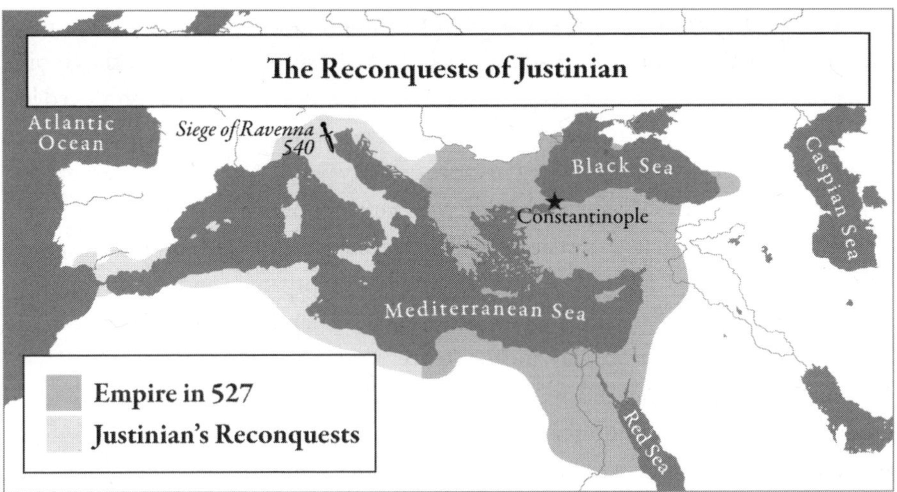

Justinian now turned his attention to Italy. Theodoric had died in 526 and was succeeded by his daughter Amalasuntha (r. 526–535). She ruled as regent for her ten-year-old child and formed an alliance with Justinian to protect her against her rebellious Gothic nobles. She ended Theodoric's persecution of Catholics and even defended the papacy. These positions only made the other Goths more suspicious of her, and when her son died in 534, they rose up in rebellion and eventually executed her.

Justinian used the death of his ally as a pretext to launch his long-intended invasion of Italy. Belisarius quickly captured Sicily, while another Byzantine army attacked the Ostrogoths from the north. Despite having only a small army, Belisarius continued to win victories for the empire, recapturing Naples and then Rome in 537. By 540, it seemed as though Belisarius was poised to defeat all the Ostrogoths. Justinian would have recovered two of the most important provinces of the western half of the empire and could begin planning further campaigns of reconquest. Then, at the height of his success, disaster struck.

Ironically, the source of this disaster was one of the greatest strengths of the Byzantine economy: the alliance with Aksum and the trade it enabled with Asia. In October 541, the **bubonic plague** made its first appearance in the Mediterranean, arriving in Egypt either from India or East Africa. The disease was transmitted by the bites of infected fleas which lived among rats, and the outbreaks were most severe where the rat and human populations were most densely concentrated. The plague's spread was swift and devastating. Within six months it raged throughout the Mediterranean. Of those who contracted the disease, as many as 75 percent died. Over 200,000 died in Constantinople alone.

This epidemic dramatically weakened the empire just when it appeared most powerful. The Byzantines now had fewer troops to defend the borders of the empire, fewer recruits to replace their casualties, and a smaller population that produced less tax revenue with which to pay for these campaigns. While the Goths and Slavs also suffered from the disease, they lived in more sparsely populated village communities. They were therefore less affected than their Byzantine enemies. The Byzantines were further weakened when Justinian himself contracted the plague and fell gravely ill. The Ostrogoths took advantage of this reprieve to reorganize and recover most of Italy. In the east, the Persians also invaded the empire and forced the Byzantines to pay a large sum of money to buy another truce.

Amazingly, not only did Justinian recover his health but he also, to his great credit, restabilized the empire. After making peace with the Persians in 545, he raised more troops to defeat the Slavs, who had once again invaded the empire from the north. He even completed the conquest of Italy in 554. These victories were impressive achievements, and Justinian added to them by conquering part of Spain for the empire. However, the dream of reestablishing the rest of the western provinces of the empire was over. Throughout the last decade of Justinian's reign, his armies struggled to defend the imperial frontiers, and there were clear signs that the empire had grown weaker and was less well-equipped to repel challenges from both within and outside its borders.

A Fragmented Empire

Part of the empire's weakness came from its ongoing religious division. One of Justinian's chief goals was to eliminate the Miaphysite heresy from the empire. Initially, he was successful and oversaw the replacement of the Miaphysite bishops of Alexandria and Constantinople with bishops who supported the Council of Chalcedon. In 536, he hosted a synod at Constantinople at which some leading Miaphysites accepted Chalcedon's decisions. Genuine Christian unity in the empire seemed more likely than at any time since the controversy had begun over a century earlier.

The plague played an important role in the failure of this project, but Justinian's efforts were also sabotaged by one of his closest companions. Justinian had taken the pragmatic step of confining the Miaphysite bishops in Constantinople. He left them undisturbed on the understanding that they would consecrate no new bishops. Even if the Miaphysites did not compromise with the emperor, they would eventually have no priests to serve them and would be forced to accept the leadership of clergy who accepted the theology of Chalcedon.

The Miaphysites, however, had a powerful ally in Empress Theodora. When Justinian was incapacitated by the plague, she allowed the Miaphysites to consecrate two new bishops. These bishops were supposed to limit their ministry to missionary territories outside the empire, but one of them, **Jacob Baradaeus** (500–578), revived Miaphysitism throughout the empire. He dressed as a monk to evade government officials and ordained priests and consecrated bishops throughout Mesopotamia, Palestine, Syria, and Egypt. The new clergy established a separate Church hierarchy, transforming Miaphysitism from a theological position into a schismatic Church.

When Justinian recovered from the plague, he realized that his goal of suppressing Miaphysitism had failed. Now he was the party who would be forced to compromise if he wished to achieve full religious union during his lifetime. Another factor that perhaps weighed on Justinian at this time was the death of Theodora. The empress died in 548, probably of cancer. Justinian had loved her to the end and did not wish to accept that she had died in heresy and that her soul could be lost. This reason helps explain why, despite his committed support of Chalcedon during the first half of his reign, he attempted a series of compromises with Miaphysitism during his later years.

First, the emperor issued the *Edict of the Three Chapters*. This anathematized Nestorius's teacher Theodore of Mopsuestia, who had died before the Council of Ephesus. It also condemned the pro-Nestorian writings of two theologians who later attended Chalcedon and affirmed that council's teachings. Justinian hoped that the Miaphysites would accept the council if they realized that Chalcedonian Christians fully rejected Nestorius and his partisans. Justinian's edict did not win much Miaphysite support, and it aroused severe opposition in the West. Many there saw his attack on dead theologians as a judgment against the Council of Chalcedon and a harsh condemnation of men who had died at peace with the Church.

Eventually, Justinian summoned an ecumenical council at Constantinople in 553. Almost all the bishops who attended were from the East, and they agreed to the *Edict of the Three Chapters* while also reaffirming Chalcedon. This fifth ecumenical council nevertheless did not achieve Justinian's goal of Church unity. Its condemnation of Nestorianism was not sufficient to convince the Miaphysites to abandon their schismatic Church, and Justinian's strongarm tactics to force bishops, including the pope, to agree to its decisions left even the emperor's theological allies unhappy.

In a desperation that bordered on obsession, an elderly—and perhaps senile—Justinian attempted one final compromise in 565, arguing that Christ had a fully human nature, but that His body was incapable of suffering. This compromise convinced no one. Even most Miaphysites rejected this theory as an excessive limitation of Christ's humanity, and the schism remained unresolved when Justinian died a few months later.

The ongoing division between the Miaphysites and the Chalcedonians was the chief failure of Justinian's reign. His efforts to restore Roman law and the city of Constantinople were overwhelming successes, and his wars of reconquest added more territory to the empire than any previous campaign aside from those of Trajan and Augustus. No emperor could have foreseen the outbreak of bubonic plague, which contributed heavily to Justinian's failure to reconcile the Miaphysites and left a weakened empire more vulnerable to attack.

Justinian's successors needed similar wisdom and energy if they were to navigate this difficult situation, but his nephew and heir, Justin II (r. 565–578), lacked both. Although Justin achieved some initial success reconciling the Chalcedonian and Miaphysite bishops, the Miaphysite laity convinced their leaders to reject any endorsement of Chalcedon. Frustrated, Justin unleashed a savage persecution against the Miaphysites, but this only hardened the religious division.

Justin's second great mistake was to reduce support for the Byzantine armies in order to save money. Byzantine forces were soon defeated in Italy by the **Lombards**, a new barbarian group that had just arrived in the peninsula from the northeast, in Spain by the Visigoths, and in North Africa by the indigenous Berber tribes. As the emperor refused to spend the money necessary to reinforce these armies, most of Justinian's gains in the West disappeared.

JUSTINIAN AND THE SILK ROAD

The Silk Road is well known as the famous set of trade routes that developed in the second century BC and that connected the Mediterranean with China. The name of this network comes from the highly lucrative trade in silk textiles that were produced almost exclusively in China and that were wildly popular in Egypt, Greece, and Rome.

The Romans inherited the western portions of the Silk Road from the Greek kingdoms of Alexander the Great's successors. This trade remained an important source of wealth for the empire, even after its western provinces had fallen. The Turkish peoples, who had recently migrated to Central Asia, established themselves as merchants, trading and transporting horses from the west and silk from the east. Their rulers and the Byzantine emperors provided protection along a route that stretched from the Caspian Sea westward into their imperial provinces. Tombs found in the high passes along this route contain traces of silk fabric and Chinese documents. We know little else about these merchants, and we are left to wonder at the amazing lives they lived, traversing the remote lands of the Asian steppe over fifteen hundred years ago and knowing the glory and achievements of both Rome and China.

Justinian attempted to establish an imperial monopoly over the silk trade so that the merchants would buy and sell through government officials only. This would grant him tighter control over the prices they charged and the revenue they generated. Unfortunately for him, the consistent high demand for silk within the empire encouraged Persian merchants to form a black-market network where they sold silk to private buyers at high prices and avoided imperial taxes.

The historian Procopius records that, in his frustration, Justinian turned to monks who had knowledge of China and the East to learn from them how to bypass the Persian merchants. The monks explained that silk was woven by silkworms and that, while it was impossible to transport the worms, their eggs could be moved more easily. With Justinian's support, the monks smuggled eggs from China into Byzantium, covering them with dung heated by a lamp until the worms hatched. They then sustained the silkworms by feeding them mulberry leaves. The Byzantine Empire thus began its own silk production and established a highly profitable monopoly for centuries by selling its silk in Europe. Once again, Justinian had revealed his understanding of the world beyond the borders of the Byzantine Empire as well as his determination to find the solutions necessary to achieve his goals.

Justin's frugality also affected the eastern border. He had hoped to save money by refusing to pay tribute to the Persians, but the result was a Persian invasion in 573. When they captured Dara, an important border city, Justin was so devastated and consumed with guilt that his mind appears to have given way to madness. His attendants were reduced to pulling him around in a little wagon and restraining him from jumping out of windows. His wife Sophia and his friend Tiberius II (r. 578–582) took control of the empire.

Imperial Crisis

Subsequent Byzantine emperors encountered two intertwined crises that threatened to destroy the empire. On one hand, following the depopulation of the plague, the empire could no longer raise the revenues necessary to defend its borders. On the other hand, they faced attacks from powerful enemies: the Persians to the east and the Avars and Slavs to the north. If the emperors did not strengthen their armies, they faced defeat and invasion. If they enlarged their forces, they plunged the empire further into debt.

Unlike Justin, Tiberius was successful on the battlefield. His victories against the Persians secured temporary peace along the eastern frontier, but this effort also depleted the empire's financial reserves and made it impossible to deploy sufficient troops along the empire's northern border. As a result, both the Slavs and the Avars, a coalition of Huns and other ethnicities, now raided the empire's European territories with increasing impunity.

Conditions briefly improved under the leadership of Tiberius's former general and imperial successor, Maurice (r. 582–602). An insurrection against the Persian shah, or king, led both the embattled ruler and his would-be usurper to appeal to Byzantium for help. Maurice sided with Shah Khusrau II (r. 590–628) and provided crucial support that defeated the rebellion. This victory meant that the Byzantines now had a Persian ally who granted new territories to the Byzantine Empire in gratitude for their fight to secure his throne.

Maurice also enjoyed success against the Avars, but his efforts to save money by reducing the soldiers' pay made him dangerously unpopular. In 602, his cost-cutting policies led to an uprising of imperial troops. They seized Constantinople, executed Maurice and his family, and installed as emperor one of their junior officers, the fifty-five-year-old **Phocas** (r. 602–610).

Phocas lacked any semblance of legitimate claim to the crown and became suspicious of all potential rivals. Still more problematic, Khusrau took advantage of this turmoil to invade the empire. He claimed that Maurice's eldest son had escaped from Constantinople and that the Persians were fighting to restore the rightful Byzantine ruler to power. As Persian armies won victories across West Asia, plots against Phocas increased. The emperor responded by torturing and even burning alive those whom he thought were plotting against him.

The **Jeweled Cross of Heraclius**. This photograph was taken c. 1920 and is part of the G. Eric and Edith Matson Photograph Collection in the Library of Congress, Washington, D.C. Heraclius gave this cross to the Church of the Holy Sepulcher in Jerusalem in 628.

Eventually, the Byzantine governor of North Africa rebelled. He secured control of Egypt and cut off the capital's supply of grain before sending his son **Heraclius** (r. 610–641) to remove Phocas. In 610, Heraclius seized control and had Phocas beheaded. According to one source, Heraclius and Phocas had a brief exchange before the latter's death.

"Is this the way you rule, wretch?" Heraclius asked.

"Will you do any better?" Phocas replied.

It was a fair question.

Heraclius's rise to power did not resolve the empire's problems. By the time he had seized the throne, the Persians had conquered Mesopotamia, Armenia, Syria, and parts of Anatolia, and were even closing in on Constantinople. Byzantine fortunes continued to deteriorate even after Heraclius took personal command of the army. The Persians promptly defeated him and then marched into Palestine. There they captured Jerusalem, deported the Christian population, and seized the relic of the Cross.

Still the plight of the empire worsened. The Slavs captured most of the cities of Greece, and in 620 the Persians completed the conquest of Egypt. Heraclius no longer had the supplies to feed the people of Constantinople. The empire was so short of funds that he was able to halve the soldiers' pay without rebellion. The clergy of Constantinople even agreed to melt down the precious metal that decorated churches to forge new coins. These coins were minted with the inscription, "God help the Romans," a desperate prayer for divine aid in distress. Heraclius sent ambassadors to Khusrau to try to broker peace, but the shah was now confident of total victory. He allowed the Byzantine ambassadors to starve to death in captivity. After ten years on the throne, Heraclius held perhaps the worst military record of any emperor in Roman history.

Byzantine Hexagram. The front shows Heraclius with a short beard (left) and his son Heraclius Constantine (right). The back of the coin has the inscription DEUS ADIUTA (sic) ROMANIS ("God Help the Romans"). Herakleios, Silver, Hexagram, Constantinople, circa 615-625 (BZC.2015.015), Image courtesy of Dumbarton Oaks, Coins and Seals Collection, Washington, D.C.

Facing the complete destruction of the empire, Heraclius recognized the need to respond with a fresh offensive against the Persians. In 624, he combined all his armies under his leadership and made a truce with the Avars. Then, in a desperate final effort, he led his combined forces past the Persian army and marched directly for the Persian capital of Ctesiphon, hoping to coerce Khusrau to negotiate a peace treaty.

Heraclius won several victories, but the shah then imitated Byzantine strategy and sent an army to attack Constantinople itself. The Persians allied with the Avars and the Slavs, and the three allies placed the city under siege. This attack was perhaps the empire's greatest moment of peril, but it also proved to be the turning point. Khusrau had become nervous that his own general would rebel and had sent a letter ordering the execution of this officer. The Byzantines intercepted this letter and promptly showed it to the doomed general. He prudently withdrew with his army to Egypt and took no further part in the fighting. For their part, the Avars and the Slavs began fighting one another, and the siege fell apart.

Heraclius continued his assault on the heartland of the Persian Empire. Now he won victory after victory. Khusrau was bewildered by how quickly total conquest had slipped from his grasp. He refused Heraclius's offers of peace until, in 628, Khusrau's own son executed the shah and accepted peace. All prisoners were exchanged and the frontier between Persia and Byzantium was restored to where it had been in 602. Heraclius returned the Cross to Jerusalem with great joy and was widely revered as the savior of the empire. Nonetheless, Heraclius's extraordinary achievement of perseverance and skill did not automatically restore the former strength of the empire.

Conclusion

Over the hundred years covered in this chapter, the Byzantine Empire had experienced a dizzying sequence of success, failure, and stabilization. After Justinian became emperor in 527, he achieved a series of remarkable accomplishments in the areas of the law, infrastructure, and military conquest. For a moment, it seemed as though he would even achieve his ambition of restoring the entire Roman Empire in the West, but this dream was destroyed by the devastation of the bubonic plague.

From this point onwards, the empire was dragged into a destructive spiral of financial crises, military weakness, and political unrest. Some of the Byzantine accomplishments from this era, such as the Justinian Code and the *Hagia Sophia,* stand today, but the empire had sustained grievous wounds that festered in the shadows of Heraclius's triumph. Byzantium was still financially and militarily exhausted by the plague and divided by the conflict between the Chalcedonians and Miaphysites, which neither Justinian nor Heraclius were able to resolve. Furthermore, the thirty-year war with Persia had required every ounce of its strength and resources. Byzantium was ill-prepared to face the religious and political whirlwind that was stirring in Arabia.

CHAPTER 20

Muhammad and the Submission to God

O believers! Bow down, prostrate yourselves, worship your Lord, and do what is good so that you may be successful. Strive for the cause of Allah in the way He deserves, for it is He Who has chosen you, and laid upon you no hardship in the religion—the way of your forefather Abraham. Who named you "the ones who submit" in the earlier scriptures and in this Qur'an. . . . So establish prayer, pay alms-tax, and hold fast to Allah.

Qur'an 22:77–78

Even as Heraclius's Byzantium fought for survival against Persia, a new religious and political power was arising in Arabia. Around the year 613, Muhammad, an Arab merchant, announced to his fellow tribesmen that he was receiving revelations from God. These collected messages comprise the *Qur'an* ("Recitation"), the sacred text of Muhammad's new religion of Islam. The *Qur'an*'s call to conversion and its warning of the coming Day of Judgment transformed Arab society and enabled this assortment of separate tribes to become one of the great powers of the eastern Mediterranean and beyond.

The above excerpt from the *Qur'an* introduces several important characteristics of Islam. The first involves the relationship between God and those who serve Him. "Islam" means "submission," and those who practice this religion are known as "Muslims," or "the ones who submit."[1] This emphasis on God's dominion and

1 There can be confusion over the proper use of the terms "Islam," "Islamic," and "Muslim." "Islam" refers to the religion itself and the adjective "Islamic" is used when discussing attributes of the religion of Islam, its ideals and ideas, or its influence in culture (for example, "Islamic law," "Islamic art," or "Islamic architecture"). "Muslim," in contrast, refers to people rather than ideas or practices. It can be used both to indicate the people themselves, that is as a noun, and as an adjective (for example, "Muslim worshippers" or "a Muslim architect"). That said, there can be fine lines of overlap in the use of "Islamic" and "Muslim," so it may be that the author of a given piece is intending to suggest some subtle nuance by a deliberate choice of one or the other.

power governs the overall tone of the *Qur'an* and presents a very different perspective from the Christian emphasis on God's fatherhood and the individual's ability to participate in His own divine life through Baptism. Secondly, Muslims consider their religion to have begun with the Lord's revelation to the Hebrew patriarchs and to have continued with the Gospel of Jesus. This perspective explains why the selection above references Abraham and the "earlier Scriptures," that is, the sacred texts of Judaism and Christianity. Finally, we see here a simple outline of Muslim piety and worship. One must bow down before the one true God and hold fast to Him in prayer while also engaging in almsgiving. These simple, straightforward concepts were easily grasped and, as we will see, facilitated conversion.

In this chapter, we explore the world of early Islam and discuss the life of Muhammad, his teachings, and Muslim theology. We begin our story many decades before Muhammad's public preaching and in locations far from his birth city of Mecca. To explain the rise of Islam, we must first understand the history of the Arabian Peninsula and its neighbor, the African kingdom of Aksum.

Aksum and Arabia

Geography brought both challenges and blessings to the people of Arabia. Its northern landscape, for example, presented a rugged, severe terrain in which only the infrequent oasis provided dependable water and food. This harsh environment encouraged the development of two interdependent lifestyles. There were agricultural communities that settled near oases and produced crops of dates and wheat, and there were pastoralists, or **Bedouins**, who reared camels and goats and who migrated as the needs of their herds dictated. These nomads sometimes plundered agricultural settlements or attacked one another, and the resulting hostility between opposing Arab tribes could be very violent. Still, it was generally in one's best interests to cultivate mutually beneficial relationships, and many Bedouins traded—rather than raided—when they visited oasis communities. The camel's ability to traverse long distances in arid environments enabled the Bedouin merchants to form caravans that brought trade goods from one region to another. These included luxury items from outside of the peninsula, and the resulting commerce brought great wealth to the region.

In contrast to the north, the southwestern corner of Arabia (modern-day Yemen) experienced relatively high amounts of rainfall and yielded bountiful agricultural harvests with proper irrigation. This more hospitable geography enabled the rise of densely populated regional kingdoms in the centuries before Muhammad. The region's most famous early kingdom was Saba', which is frequently associated with the biblical realm of Sheba (see 1 [3] Kings 10:1–13). While

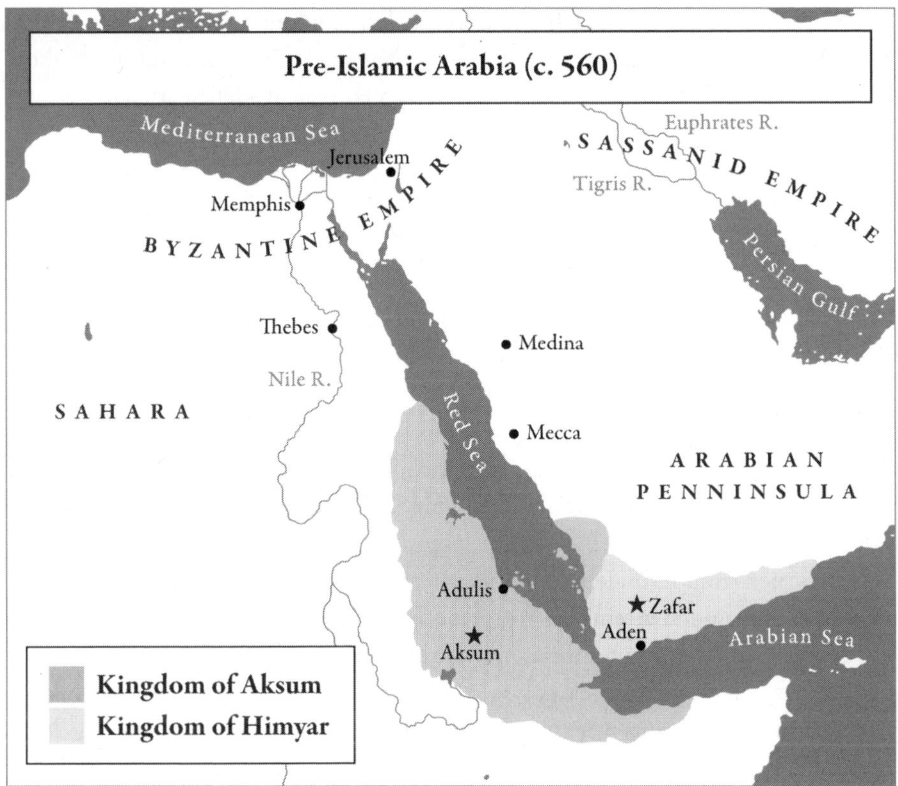

scholars debate when precisely this kingdom began, most agree that its wealth and its sophisticated irrigation system were justly famous in the ancient world.

Arabia's central location between Africa and Asia, as well as its proximity to the Mediterranean, made it an important commercial hub. The Bedouin caravans mentioned above were only part of the flow of trade from one region to another. Also lucrative—particularly for southern Arabia—were the maritime routes that enabled luxury items to be shared among communities in India, Africa, and ultimately the Mediterranean. Those Arab cities along the coast, as well as those further inland along major caravan routes, enjoyed the fruits of this commerce and became prosperous.

A nearby area that likewise profited from intercontinental trade was the **Kingdom of Aksum** (c. 100–c. 940) in eastern Africa (modern-day Ethiopia and Eritrea). Aksum, its capital city, was situated in fertile highlands, while its most famous port, Adulis, lay along the arid Red Sea coast. This city exported slaves, ivory, frankincense, and gold from Africa's interior to nearby southern Arabia and elsewhere.

Aksum's trade brought riches and made the kingdom a cultural melting pot. Most Aksumites, for example, spoke a Semitic language akin to those of the Arabian Peninsula. At the same time, the kingdom also embraced Hellenistic culture and even minted coins with Greek phrases. What is more, Buddhists from India established communities in Aksum's cities. So cosmopolitan was the African realm that one prominent third-century Persian declared that Aksum was one of the four great empires of the world (the other three being Persia, Rome, and China).

Unfortunately, we know little about the rise of Aksum as a territorial power. It emerges in our sources around the year 100 and was by that time already a developed kingdom that interacted with both Arabian and Mediterranean societies. Aksum's relationship with imperial Rome was relatively strong despite the fact that they did not share a common border, and historians believe this friendship facilitated the Aksumites' conversion to Christianity in the fourth century.

The first reference to African Christianity comes from the Acts of the Apostles (see 8:26–40). In a famous episode, the deacon Philip baptized an Ethiopian eunuch as he returned from Jerusalem to Nubia, a realm south of Egypt. While we can surmise that the eunuch attempted to spread his new Faith, there are no records of indigenous Christian communities in the area of Aksum until the fourth century. A personal tragedy served as the catalyst to change this situation. A Christian philosopher and his two students were traveling to India, a route that involved sailing down the Red Sea. When their vessel landed at Adulis, some of the city's inhabitants killed the philosopher and seized his two young pupils for Aksum's king.

Frumentius, one of the enslaved boys, eventually rose to great influence with the king and even became an adviser to the next ruler, Ezana (r. c. 320–356). This king permitted Frumentius to organize Christian merchants at Adulis and even allowed him to journey to Alexandria, where Athanasius consecrated him as bishop of Aksum. Interestingly, this connection with the great opponent to "Arianism" resulted in a letter from Constantius II to Ezana warning him about Athanasius's theology and encouraging the Aksumites to return Frumentius to the Roman Empire so that Constantius could evaluate his teachings. Ezana apparently turned down the request, and he became the first African king to receive Baptism. Furthermore, Aksumite Christianity remained closely tied to Alexandrian thought and spirituality and supported Miaphysite theology after the Council of Chalcedon.

Shortly after Ezana embraced Christianity, the world of southern Arabia had its own religious conversion. The **kingdom of Himyar** (c. 275–c. 570) had conquered Saba' and established its authority over the region. Within one hundred years, the Himyarite kings had reformed the area's language, calendar, and religion. The last was the most significant, as the rulers broke with their polytheistic past and embraced Judaism. By 380, Jewish traditions had officially replaced polytheistic practices in Himyar. Furthermore, the kingdom began expanding its influence and by the mid-fifth century had become the predominate power not only in the south but also in central Arabia.

Meanwhile, Arabs to the north found themselves caught between Byzantium and Persia. Each power supported a different northern Arab kingdom and used its warriors to attack the other empire. The Persians, in part due to their proximity to the peninsula, were more successful in maintaining consistent influence in Arabia. In contrast, the Byzantines generally failed to dedicate enough attention and resources to maintain advantage in the region. However, in 519, a new development rekindled Byzantine enthusiasm: for reasons not entirely known, Himyar had gradually become more dependent upon Aksumite influence until, in that year, the Africans placed one of their own as a puppet-king over southern Arabia. This new Christian ruler of Himyar was willing to attack pro-Persian tribes, and the Byzantines envisioned a Byzantine-Aksumite-Himyarite operation against Persia.

Affairs suddenly changed in 522 when a coup returned a Jewish king to the Himyarite throne. Dhu Nuwas, also known as King Joseph (r. 522–525), assumed that Arab Christians supported Aksum and lashed out against them. His most notorious action occurred at the oasis of Najran. He deceived and then massacred over four thousand Christians. As news of the atrocity spread, the Aksumite king responded by launching an invasion force of over sixty vessels. These soldiers not only retook the throne but also initiated their own bloody persecution of Jews in retaliation.

Aksum once again placed a Christian puppet-king in Himyar, and Emperor Justinian in Constantinople proposed joint military action against Persia. He also encouraged Aksum to seek new routes for the silk trade that would bypass Persia. He hoped in this way to bring economic hardship to his imperial rival. (Only later did Justinian successfully break Persia's stranglehold on the silk trade. See insert on Justinian and the Silk Road in chapter 19.) Unfortunately for Justinian, Byzantine ambitions again met with delay. This time, an Aksumite general seized the throne of Himyar for himself. This military leader, Abraha (r. c. 535–c. 565), sought to reestablish Himyarite independence, with himself at its head.

Abraha oversaw one last flourishing of the Himyarite Kingdom. In 547, he hosted a diplomatic meeting for Byzantine, Aksumite, and Persian representatives. Unfortunately, we do not know precisely what they discussed, but the fact that Abraha organized such a meeting indicates that his desire to restore Himyar as an independent regional power had been successful. Abraha also initiated an ambitious church-building program in southern Arabia. The most famous church was the cathedral in San'a, his capital city. This structure was reportedly one of the grandest churches of its era—which is impressive considering that the Hagia Sophia had only recently been built. Abraha hoped to turn San'a into a major pilgrimage site, but such ambition aroused the envy of those who lived in Mecca.

Mecca was situated on a trade route north of Himyar and established its prominence in Arab life through its numerous polytheistic shrines. Abraha's new church threatened Mecca's religious importance, and pagan Bedouins retaliated by desecrating its altar and cross with dung. Abraha responded to the outrage by sending an army to Mecca. He himself rode on a white elephant at the head of the Himyarite soldiers, and the sight of such a beast in Arabia made such an impression that later generations still spoke of the "Year of the Elephant." Unfortunately for Abraha, his attempt to punish the city failed, and he was defeated around the year 565. What is more, this defeat likely contributed to the collapse of the Himyarite Kingdom in the years immediately following.

These **rock carvings** from Najran, Saudi Arabia, likely depict the Year of the Elephant. Exact dating is not possible due to weathering, but scholars agree that Abraha and his "Companions of the Elephant" are the subject matter. The carvings were discovered in November 2014 by the Franco-Saudi Archaeological Mission of Najrān about 6 miles from the Wells of Ḥimà, a UNESCO World Heritage Site.

In fact, Arabia as a whole entered into a difficult period of its history. Islamic tradition recounts famines, poverty, and social turmoil in the Arabian Peninsula in the decades following the Year of the Elephant. Historians debate what precisely caused these crises. Some believe that the bubonic plague was the culprit, as it appears that Abraha's campaign collapsed in part due to disease. Regardless of what factors contributed to Arabia's plight, Mecca developed into an important city. Its leading tribe, the Quraysh, were regarded as "the people of God" after their victory against Abraha's army. Furthermore, they capitalized on their fame by organizing trade fairs and promoting acts of piety to the numerous gods "resident" in their city. The inhabitants of Mecca were poised to become a dominant power in Arabia for years to come. The stage had been set for Muhammad's religious revolution.

The Life of Muhammad

Most of what we know of Muhammad's life comes from Islamic tradition. This is based on three different types of sources. The earliest, but also the least useful, is the

Qur'an. We will discuss this text more below, but for now, we simply note that while the *Qur'an* offers insights into Islamic belief, it does not provide much biographical data about Muhammad himself. The second type of source we can use to reconstruct Muhammad's life is the *hadith* ("talk" or "discourse"). These numerous accounts claim to record Muhammad's conversations with his closest companions. The *hadith* have become very important for Islamic religious law, but they are potentially misleading if one seeks biographical information. Even early Muslim scholars admitted that there were many forgeries among the *hadith*, and scholars do not agree upon which details may actually reflect historical reality.

The final group of sources for Muhammad's life is the *sira* ("life" or "journey"). These narratives would seem to be the best option for historians to use, for they present a chronological story of the Muslim prophet's accomplishments. However, the earliest *sira* account was written over one hundred years after Muhammad's death. What is more, this text survives only in fragments quoted by later authors. The earliest complete *sira* narratives that survive date from the ninth and tenth centuries, over two hundred years after Muhammad's death. These likely include later Islamic traditions and interpretations and should not always be accepted at face value.

Nonetheless, most historians accept the traditional Islamic account of Muhammad's life and base their biographies upon that information. We follow this general practice here, but it is worthwhile pointing out that, in comparison to the biographical sources for Muhammad, the accounts describing the life of Jesus have a much stronger historical foundation. Even the most skeptical academics believe that the Gospels were written within one hundred years of Jesus's life. Furthermore, as we discussed in the insert "The Gospels as Historical Sources" in chapter 13, there is reason to believe that at least one of the Gospels was written within a handful of years of the events it records.

Muhammad (c. 570–632) was born into a minor clan of the Quraysh tribe of Mecca shortly after its victory against Abraha's army. He had been orphaned by age seven, and his uncle Abu Talib raised him and provided a family network. Familial relationships were crucial in Arab society since they gave an individual protection, hospitality, and support. Without his uncle's kindness, Muhammad would likely have come to an unfortunate and early end. Instead, he became a successful merchant and accompanied caravans north into Syria. He eventually married his employer, the rich widow Khadija, around 595. The two had six children together, four daughters and two sons. Both boys died in infancy.

According to Islamic tradition, Muhammad began to show dissatisfaction with the polytheistic shrines of Mecca around the year 610. His earlier travels had led to interactions with Jews as well as Chalcedonian, Miaphysite, and

Nestorian Christians. The confusing array of theological positions in Christianity and the resulting bitter hostility among Christians reduced the likelihood of his conversion, but Muhammad did become convinced that the Jewish and Christian central belief in one God was true. He avoided Mecca's religious devotions to its numerous gods and instead meditated in a cave. Muhammad claimed that it was there that God sent him his first revelation through the angel Gabriel: "Recite in the name of your Lord who created: Created man from a blood clot." (*Qur'an* 96:1) Though this verse occurs towards the end of the *Qur'an* as we know it, Muslims believe this was the calling that began Muhammad's career as God's last prophet.

The **Hira Cave**. Located on Mount Jabal al-Nour, near Mecca. According to traditional Muslim belief, this site is where Muhammad received the first revelation of the *Qur'an*.

After about three years of self-doubt, Muhammad finally began publicly preaching in Mecca. His early message emphasized the need to repent and the coming Day of Judgment. The heart of his theology was easy to grasp: there was only one God, and Muhammad was His prophet.

His initial efforts met with disappointment. Only a few "submitted to God"—thus becoming the first "Muslims"—and many of these came from his own family. Abu Talib, Muhammad's uncle, joined the movement and used his influence to shelter his nephew from those who disliked his message. The majority of Mecca's population resented Muhammad's claim to be a prophet, particularly since he challenged the status quo of Meccan society. After all, the city made its wealth through its polytheistic shrines, and the call to end such worship presented, at the very least, a financial danger for the Meccan elite.

Resentment grew to enmity, and by 615, some of the earliest Muslims fled to Aksum to escape Meccan hostility. The Aksumite king likely interpreted Muhammad's monotheism as a step towards Christianity, and he welcomed Muslims and treated them with respect. This kindness ultimately benefited Aksum and Ethiopia in general. In the centuries to come, Muslim conquests in Africa would surround but not include Aksum.

The **Great Mosque** in Mecca, Saudi Arabia. This photo was taken during the *hajj*.

By 619, the situation in Mecca had become untenable for Muhammad and his followers. Both Khadija and Abu Talib died that year, and Muhammad was in an increasingly dangerous position without his uncle's support. Fortunately for him, some pilgrims to Mecca's shrines heard his preaching and wanted to learn more. They invited his community to Yathrib, a city about two hundred miles north. Muslims began leaving Mecca in small numbers so as not to attract attention. Muhammad, his close friend Abu Bakr, and his cousin and son-in-law 'Ali were the last three to remain. According to tradition, Muhammad hid in a cave while 'Ali slept in Muhammad's bed so that their enemies did not realize that the Muslim prophet was escaping. Muhammad and Abu Bakr arrived in Yathrib on September 24, 622. Later Muslims would commemorate this event, known as the ***hijra*** ("migration"), by beginning the Islamic calendar with this year.[2]

Muhammad's years in Yathrib were transformative for the Muslim community. At first, they were a minority among the resident polytheistic and Jewish clans. Possessing little authority and faced with potential hostility, Muhammad attempted to make his new faith as attractive as possible. In particular, he hoped to win converts among the city's Jewish population. After all, Muhammad considered Islam to be the continuation of Judaism, so he incorporated Jewish ideas into Muslim practice in order to make Islam a viable alternative for Jews. For example, initially, Muslims were expected to pray five times a day in the direction of Jerusalem. This changed to prayer facing toward Mecca after Yathrib's Jewish communities rejected Muhammad's status as prophet. Muhammad's setback with Jews was offset by his progress with Yathrib's pagan population. So many converted that

2 Just as Christians mark time by estimating when Jesus's birth took place, so Muslims calculate the year in terms of the *hijra*. Since the Islamic calendar is lunar, its years do not have the same number of days as a solar calendar and its months gradually migrate across the solar year. This is why, for example, the month of Ramadan can occur in different seasons from year to year. To have an approximate reckoning of the Islamic year, or *anno hegirae* (AH), you can subtract 622 from the related year in our Gregorian calendar. This method, however, becomes less accurate the farther away you are from the historical *hijra* since the discrepancies between lunar and solar calendars lead to greater divergences between the two.

the city was later known as Medina, a shortened form of *Madinat al-nabi* ("the city of the Prophet").

His success alarmed Mecca. Muhammad's authority in Medina could challenge Mecca's regional preeminence, and in 624, Meccan soldiers marched northward. A series of battles followed over the course of several years. Though the Meccans did defeat the Muslims once, the overall victory belonged to Muhammad's followers. Furthermore, each victorious battle strengthened the prophet's control over Medina, and he no longer felt the need to compromise with the city's non-Muslim inhabitants. He expelled certain Jewish communities and seized their property for the Muslim faithful. When the Meccans enlisted Jewish aid in their war against Muhammad, those remaining Jews in Medina faced further reprisals. Ultimately, these last remnants were either executed or enslaved.

This harshness contrasted with Muhammad's treatment of those who lived at Khaybar, an oasis that was the home of many Jews, including some whom he had expelled from Medina. Khaybar was only one hundred miles from Medina, and the Islamic prophet decided that its inhabitants needed to be subdued. In 628, he captured the oasis, the first conquest by a Muslim army. Muhammad's authority was now secure enough that he could be lenient towards its inhabitants. He did not execute them but, instead, recognized the Jews as "**People of the Book**." He applied this identification to all Jews and Christians to indicate their Scriptures' connection to Islam. Muhammad even permitted the Khaybar Jews to practice their religion, though they had to pay a tax for the privilege. This approach set an important precedent for future generations of Muslims who, at least officially, continued to permit Jews and Christians to observe their respective beliefs, provided that they paid a tax. Later Muslim generations expanded the "People of the Book" to include Samaritans, Persian Zoroastrians, Buddhists, and Hindus.

Muhammad's greatest triumph was his reentry into Mecca. He had laid the groundwork for this in 628 by using his skills as a merchant to bargain with Meccans for permission to enter their city. However, the truce that the parties accepted was violated by disgruntled Meccans, and Muhammad responded with the threat of violence. As his army approached the city, the Meccan leaders met Islam's prophet and made their peace. In January 630, Muhammad purged Mecca of its polytheistic shrines. Pagan idols were destroyed, and Mecca was from henceforth to be a Islamic city.

Muhammad's last two years saw him campaign in eastern and northern Arabia and bring those areas under his authority. He then returned to Mecca for what became known as the Farewell Pilgrimage. This was the first *hajj* (discussed more below), and Muhammad's actions during this time set the precedent for all Muslims to follow. He died in 632, a mere ten years after the *hijra* to Yathrib. Yet those ten years were crucial, for in them he had cemented the foundations for one of the world's most influential religions.

The Religion of Islam

Muhammad's success lay in his claim to have received messages from God. These sayings were collected and codified in the decades following his death into the text we know as the ***Qur'an*** ("Recitation"). Muslims believe that the *Qur'an* itself is a miracle, and contemporary orthodox belief holds that it is an *uncreated* book which the angel Gabriel dictated to Muhammad. Whereas Christians hold that God, the ultimate author of the books of the Bible, employed different human authors who received inspiration from the Holy Spirit, Muslims maintain that God is the direct author of the *Qur'an*. Furthermore, due to the early codification of the text and the destruction of alternative versions, there are no variations in the manuscripts that have survived from Islam's earliest centuries.

The *Qur'an* consists of 114 chapters or *suras*. These are organized in order of descending length: earlier *suras* generally have more verses than those which come later. An exception is the very first *sura*, which is a brief prayer. Each chapter has its own title (for example, *The Cow*, *Jonah*, and *The Pilgrimage*), which reflects some portion of its content. However, scholars do not know why a given title came to be associated with a given *sura* or even why the *Qur'an* is organized the way that it is.

The *suras* themselves can present narratives or a series of connected verses, but often the verses will seem to jump from one theme or topic to another. Part of the reason for this is that the messages are not recorded in chronological order. Most scholars, as noted above, believe that Muhammad's first message is in *sura* 96—almost the very end of the *Qur'an*—while his last (chronologically) message apparently is in the fifth *sura*.

The teachings and themes of the *Qur'an* are straightforward. There is one God and Muhammad is His prophet. God created the angels, humanity, and jinn (invisible creatures on earth who, like us, can choose good or evil and will be judged). The *Qur'an* emphasized that God is solitary and clearly rejected the belief that Jesus was the Son of God. Nonetheless, at the end of the world there will be a Day of Judgment in which Jesus, a mere prophet according to Islamic theology, will return as judge. Those who have accepted God's message and submitted to Him will enter into bliss, while those who rejected it will be damned to torments. Unlike Christianity, there is no concept of redemption from sin or sharing in God's own divine life.

Interestingly, the *Qur'an* includes many hints of Jewish and Christian Scriptures and traditions. Often these retell familiar stories (such as the Annunciation) but with additional details or a different emphasis. (In the annunciation account, for example, the Virgin Mary does not consent but is simply told she will conceive a son.) It is likely that Muhammad blended together various apocryphal texts from other traditions into his own. This gives the *Qur'an* a unique feel of being both recognizable and unfamiliar to first-time Jewish and Christian readers.

Muhammad's message as recorded in the *Qur'an* had obvious success in converting many of his fellow Arabs. What precisely appealed to his audiences? Of course, an individual's decision to convert is just that—individual—but several factors likely played a key role. First of all, the *Qur'an* (and Muhammad) were Arab. Other scriptures were in different languages and had not been adequately translated or spread throughout the peninsula. In contrast, Muhammad's message emphasized the importance of the Arab people, referenced their tales and history, and made their language the very language of God. Whereas previously they had been shaped by Persian, Byzantine, and Aksumite interests, Arabs now had a heightened sense of their own value and purpose.

Secondly, its message was simple and expressed in a graphic manner. Many non-Christian Arab merchants (and probably some Christian ones too!) were undoubtedly confused by the subtle theological distinctions in Christianity. Disagreements among Chalcedonians, Miaphysites, and Nestorians were not edifying and discouraged a unified missionary endeavor. In contrast, one could easily understand Muhammad's teachings about Jesus and other topics. For example, in contrast to Christianity's ethereal report of Heaven (see 1 Cor 2:9), Muhammad described its bliss in easy-to-grasp images of rivers and abundant food, while the torments of Hell likewise received memorable (and disturbing) details.

What was more, the central practices of Islam, known as the Five Pillars, were also straightforward. The first is the profession of faith, a simple acknowledgement that there is no God but God and that Muhammad is His prophet. The second is the practice of prayer five times a day. Originally, as noted above, this was directed towards Jerusalem, but Muhammad later changed it so that one faced Mecca. Specifically, one turned towards the ***Ka'ba***, a cube-shaped building that housed a black meteorite. This had previously been associated with polytheism, but Muhammad stressed its importance as a religious site where the patriarchs Noah and Abraham had worshipped. It is the most sacred location in Islam and the destination for those who complete the *hajj*. This pilgrimage to Mecca is the third "pillar" of Islam. Pious Muslims seek to perform this devotion at least once during their lifetimes, and the event takes place over several days once a year. There, multitudes of Muslims replicate the devotions and animal sacrifice performed by Muhammad during his Farewell Pilgrimage. The last two "pillars of Islam" involve

The **Ka'ba** ("the Cube") stands at the center of the Great Mosque in Mecca, Saudi Arabia, and contains the Black Stone. During the *hajj*, Muslim pilgrims circle the Ka'ba seven times counterclockwise and many kiss the Black Stone in imitation of Muhammad.

giving alms to the poor and observing the fast from food and drink during the daylight hours of the sacred month of Ramadan.

Finally, Islam called upon the Arab tribes to abandon their petty rivalries and to embrace a cosmic mission of spreading God's message throughout the world. Even during Muhammad's life, Islam had involved the subjugation and conversion of polytheistic Arabs. Just as Christian and Jewish kingdoms in the region had waged bloody wars against others, so now the Muslim world embarked on its own conquests. Eventually, this precedent would develop into what we know today as the Islamic practice of ***jihad*** ("striving"). According to later Islamic tradition, there are two kinds of *jihad*—the greater (which involves a spiritual struggle for self-control) and the lesser (which involves physical struggle against those polytheists who reject Islam). Pious Muslims should practice both forms of *jihad*, and, as we will see, this perspective will lead to a rapid expansion of Arab rule across three continents—especially because the *Qur'an* taught that those who died in battle on behalf of God entered Heaven.

Conclusion

Muhammad's role as prophet and ruler of Medina and Mecca blended together spiritual and political leadership for the Islamic community. This brought a certain simplicity to the power structure of the early Muslim world, but it also led to tension after Muhammad's death in 632. Muhammad's sons had died young, and there was no clear heir to succeed him as leader. Ultimately, authority passed to his close friend and early convert, Abu Bakr (r. 632–634). He became the first caliph ("successor"), and during his two-year rule, he secured Islam's place in Arabian society. He did this through the sword.

Muhammad had died while planning an expedition against Roman Syria, but before Abu Bakr could accomplish this Syrian invasion, he had to confront growing discontent at home. Even during the prophet's lifetime there were complaints among various Arab tribes, and rebellions broke out shortly after Muhammad's death. For Abu Bakr and others, there was no distinction between political unrest and religious apostasy. Those who disagreed with Abu Bakr's rule, therefore, had rejected Islam itself and needed to return to the community or be punished. The caliph led the so-called Ridda Wars ("Apostasy Wars") against the rebels and regained control of the entire Arabian Peninsula. When he died shortly thereafter, he left the Muslim world better unified and, perhaps even more importantly, better trained for its future wars of expansion.

JUDAISM AFTER THE TEMPLE

Jewish belief and practice influenced early Islam, but it had evolved in many ways since the days of Jesus. The Great *Sanhedrin*, a governing body of Pharisaic rabbis, guided the Jewish world through the difficult period following the destruction of the Jewish Temple and the defeat of the second-century Bar Kochba Rebellion (see chapter 14). Among its notable achievements was the creation of the *Mishnah* ("repetition" or "study"). This text recorded the oral traditions of the Pharisees so that future generations would have access to their interpretations of the Scriptures, particularly the Torah. The *Mishnah* helped the dispersed Jewish communities, such as those in Arabia, to maintain a common Jewish tradition despite the fact that Byzantine authorities abolished the Great *Sanhedrin* in 425.

There was no longer any central Jewish authority in Palestine, and for the next several centuries effective leadership passed to the ancient Jewish community in Babylon. The ancestors of these Jews had decided to remain in Mesopotamia while others had returned to Judea. Babylonian Jews enjoyed relative peace and prosperity during the era of the Parthian and

Sassanid dynasties. Their political leader was the Exilarch or "Prince of the Exiles." This office was hereditary, and those who held it claimed to be descended from King David. Many Jews also recognized two spiritual leaders from two different schools of interpretation. These two scholars were known as the *Geonim*, or "Excellencies," and they received questions regarding the interpretation of Rabbinical tradition. Their decisions influenced Jewish practices for over four hundred years.

The *Geonim* focused on the proper interpretation of the *Talmud* ("teaching"). This massive text included both the *Mishnah* and the *Gemara* ("supplement"), an unsystematic assortment of interpretations and discussions regarding the *Mishnah*. As the *Mishnah* was a written collection of rabbis' oral commentaries on Scripture, so the *Gemara* was a written collection of commentaries on the *Mishnah*! Together these formed the *Talmud*. Despite its confusing organization, the *Talmud's* contents shaped many aspects of Jewish law, piety, and life. Modern rabbis, for example, frequently study the *Talmud* more than the Torah itself.

Though leadership had passed to Babylon, Palestinian Jews were by no means inactive. They had already created their own (Palestinian) *Talmud*, but this was both shorter and less influential than the Babylonian *Talmud*. Of greater significance to the majority of Jews was the Palestinian scholars' effort to produce an accurate, standard biblical text. As books were copied by hand, the possibility that a scribe might make an error was high. Attempts to correct a mistake by writing "in the margins" usually only made matters worse since future readers did not know what was commentary and what was supposed to be a correction. Jewish scholars, known as the *Masoretes* ("masters of tradition"), took it upon themselves to create a standard text for the Hebrew Bible. This process lasted centuries (c. fifth–tenth centuries) and was made more complex by the fact that written Hebrew only contained consonants. The vowels were typically left to the reader to supply. Of course, a change in vowels could dramatically alter the meaning of a word. (To invent an example in English, "pst" could be interpreted as "past," "pest," "post," or "paste"!) The *Masoretes* established systems of standardizing the vowel choice of a given word by adding dots or flourishes. Furthermore, they destroyed copies of the Scriptures that did not coincide with their now-standard interpretation. This is partly why there can be such dramatic differences between the Septuagint, the ancient Greek translation of the Hebrew Bible, and the current text of the Hebrew Bible.

CHAPTER 21

The Achievement of the Umayyads

We shall not manifest our religion publicly nor convert anyone to it. We shall not prevent any of our kin from entering Islam if they wish it. We shall show respect towards the Muslims, and we shall rise from our seats when they wish it.

The Pact of 'Umar[1]

In the decades that followed the death of Muhammad, the warriors of Islam won a series of spectacular victories and defeated both the Persian and Byzantine Empires. They established an empire of eleven million square miles that stretched from the western coasts of Europe and North Africa, across West Asia and into India. They achieved and maintained these conquests despite their own civil war and the emergence of a lasting schism between different Islamic factions. What was more, their first dynasty successfully ruled over their empire for generations, even though most of their new subjects did not share their Islamic faith.

This chapter's epigraph from *The Pact of 'Umar* highlights the pragmatic approach that Arab rulers adopted when confronted with different religions. Christians and others could keep their traditional beliefs without threat of death or official pressure to convert to Islam. Nonetheless, they could not practice their faith openly. Furthermore, only conversions to Islam were permitted; no Christian was allowed to proselytize a Muslim. While this suppression of public practice was harsh, many Christians and Jews at the time accepted these circumstances and even collaborated

1 "Pact of Umar," available on Paul Halsall, *Internet Medieval Sourcebook*, December 7, 2022. https://sourcebooks.fordham.edu/source/pact-umar.asp.

with their new Muslim rulers in governing. The result was one of the great accomplishments of the Umayyad dynasty—a period of relative peace and coexistence among different religious groups. And yet, like the barbarian kings of the West and the Byzantine emperors, the Umayyad caliphs did not replace the Roman Empire or reunite Europe and the Mediterranean under their rule. Instead, as we will see in this chapter, their trail of conquest was halted and they themselves were overthrown.

Conquest

When Abu Bakr died in 634, he designated his close associate **'Umar** (r. 634–644) as his successor. 'Umar, a member of the Quraysh tribe from Mecca, had initially opposed Muhammad, but once he converted, he was a committed disciple. According to tradition, he was the first Muslim to pray openly at the Ka'ba. He was also a brilliant general.

Abu Bakr had already devised plans for raids against the Persian and Byzantine Empires, partly to keep the Arabs focused on expansion rather than fighting one another. His soldiers soon discovered that the recent long war between Heraclius and Khusrau II had left both empires exhausted. The Persians were particularly poorly organized. In the decade following Heraclius's surprising victory, they had experienced a series of coups that led to ten different claimants to the throne in as many years.

The new caliph 'Umar sensed an opportunity and transformed raids into invasions. Nonetheless, their first major engagement against the Persians, the Battle of Qadisyyah in 636, began poorly. The Persians had brought war elephants, which terrified the Arab warriors for several days. Finally, the Muslims realized that they could wound the elephants by attacking their trunks. This caused the animals to stampede and contributed to a great victory. 'Umar's forces quickly seized Ctesiphon, Babylon, and most of Mesopotamia. The Persians retreated across the Zagros Mountains to the east in complete disarray and in utter amazement that they had lost their capital to a scruffy group of Arab tribesmen, whom they had previously considered little more than an annoyance.

'Umar allowed his enemies to retreat. However, when the Persians began to launch raids into Mesopotamia, the caliph realized that the Muslims would never have peace until the Persians were completely defeated. He launched an invasion across the mountains into the Persian heartland and defeated the last Persian army at the Battle of Nahavand in 642. The ancient Persian Empire collapsed. The Muslim realm now extended into modern-day Afghanistan and Turkistan, even reaching the northern limits of Alexander the Great's historic conquests.

Arab incursions into the Byzantine Empire enjoyed similar successes in 634 and 635. Heraclius sent an army to push them back, but the great Muslim general Khalib

Ibn al-Walid (592–642) brought reinforcements on a two-day march across the desert, just in time to defeat the Byzantines. This victory enabled the Muslims to seize the cities of Damascus, Gaza, Acre, and Tyre.

Heraclius, though now in his sixties, was still an astute general. He recognized both that this Arab army was far more dangerous than the raiding parties of the past and that they were still inexperienced at siege warfare. He withdrew Byzantine forces into the walled cities of the region and waited for the Muslim armies to exhaust themselves attacking the fortifications. Khalid also understood his army's strengths and weaknesses and refused to be drawn into a conflict that would favor the Byzantines.

Eventually, Heraclius's generals became impatient and attacked the Muslims at Yarmuk in 636. The Yarmuk River, a tributary of the Jordan River, was to the southeast of the Sea of Galilee, and the battle took place near ravines, some over six hundred feet deep, that channeled its water. Once again, the Muslims fought on the defensive for the first several days of the battle. More than once their battle line was almost broken, but each time they reformed and held firm. Finally, on the sixth day of the battle, they defeated the Byzantine cavalry and cut off the escape route for the rest of the army. 'Umar's soldiers took no prisoners, and many Byzantines fell to their death trying to escape down the ravines. Almost half of the imperial army perished.

The **Valley of Yarmuk** in modern-day Jordan.

The **Battle of Yarmuk River** was a catastrophic defeat for the Byzantine Empire. Heraclius recognized, as the Persians did not, that he could not continue to fight against the Muslim armies when his own forces were so exhausted. Instead, he made the sound but personally heartbreaking decision to withdraw across the Taurus Mountains into Anatolia. This decision meant that he gave up the provinces of Syria, Mesopotamia, and Palestine, which he had fought heroically to recover from the Persians just six years before. The ancient holy cities of Antioch and Jerusalem now fell into Muslim hands.

Heraclius had hoped that he would still be able to save the province of Egypt with its rich grain-producing regions and formidable natural defenses, but the Muslim army was unstoppable. In 641, they invaded Egypt and conquered Byzantium's most valuable province. Heraclius's tactical retreat enabled the Byzantine Empire to survive, but only as a much smaller empire with its territories heavily concentrated in Europe and modern-day Turkey. The Islamic caliphate was the new, dominant empire.

How had this happened? How was an army of Arab tribesmen able to defeat both the Persian and Byzantine Empires in less than ten years? Several reasons provide an explanation. First, and perhaps most important, was the combined exhaustion of Persia and Byzantium. After expending all their energies in a thirty-year war with one another, neither had the military or economic strength and energy to take on a new enemy.

By contrast, the Muslim armies were brilliantly led and highly maneuverable, making excellent use of their familiarity with the desert to escape from difficult situations and exploit their enemies' weaknesses. They were also totally committed to their cause and saw each campaign as an act of devotion to God and each victory as a further sign of divine approval.

Finally, religious divisions among Christians within the Byzantine Empire contributed significantly to the Muslims' success. Justin II's persecutions of the Miaphysites had so embittered this schism that the Miaphysites were willing to support the Muslims against their fellow Christians, confident that they would be treated more leniently by the new rulers. Miaphysite support was especially important in Egypt, where these inhabitants critically weakened resistance to the Muslim invasion.

Civil War

Despite their many impressive successes, the Muslims soon developed their own destructive divisions. 'Umar did not live long enough to enjoy the victories his armies had won. In 644, he was assassinated in his bath by a Persian slave who had been captured at the Battle of Qadisyyah.

Medallions with the names of 'Umar, 'Uthman and 'Ali. Painted by calligrapher Kazasker Mustafa Izzet Efendi c. 1847. Currently in the Hagia Sophia, Istanbul, Turkey. There are five additional medallions displaying the names of Allah, Muhammad, Abu Bakr, Hasan and Husayn. Because many Muslims believe that God forbids any depiction of animate beings, these ornate calligraphic names are the only acceptable way to represent famous individuals from Muslim history.

The new caliph was 'Uthman (r. 644–656). Another of Muhammad's early followers, he was a member of the wealthy and influential Umayyad clan, and his conversion to Islam had angered his relatives. Under 'Uthman, the territory governed by the caliphate continued to grow, but 'Uthman was a merchant and an administrator, not a popular general. He governed the Muslim community from the safety of Medina, rather than from the front lines of the battlefield. In 656, he was assassinated by a group of rebels, who accused him of loving his own safety and luxury more than the advancement of Islam.

With the death of 'Uthman, conflict broke out as the Muslims attempted to determine his successor. One obvious candidate was 'Uthman's cousin **Mu'awiyah** (r. 661–680), who was the governor of Syria and controlled the largest Muslim army. Though Mu'awiyah had made himself an important part of the Muslim hierarchy through his skills as a general and an administrator, his past weighed heavily against him. It was well known that he had not been among Muhammad's initial disciples and had not converted to Islam until Muhammad returned and gained control of Mecca. Some even whispered that he had been among those who initially drove the prophet out of the city and pursued him across the desert. They found it hard to accept that someone who had persecuted Muhammad might become his successor and the leader of Islam.

The party that was most opposed to Mu'awiyah supported the candidacy of Muhammad's son-in-law, **'Ali** (r. 656–661). This faction had always argued that Islamic religious leadership should be passed to those with the strongest biological connection to the prophet. They had conceded to Abu Bakr's and 'Umar's candidacies because they were fathers of Muhammad's wives and in that way related to him. They also assented, more grudgingly, to 'Uthman's caliphate, confident that once the men of Muhammad's generation had passed away the field would be clear for 'Ali to assume his rightful role. But they were not willing to see their candidate passed over again, especially for a former enemy of Muhammad like Mu'awiyah.

Mu'awiyah's checkered past doomed his candidacy and 'Ali assumed the caliphate. However, some of Mu'awiyah's faction refused to accept this resolution and civil war, or *fitna*, soon broke out. For the first time, Muslim fought against Muslim in battle. 'Ali was desperate to avoid the fratricidal violence and sought to negotiate a peace with his enemies. Some of 'Ali's more extreme supporters, a group later called the Kharijites ("those who go out"), left his army and rejected 'Ali's attempt at diplomacy. The Kharijites were some of the first proponents of a radical Islamic school of thought which held that any tolerance of error was an act of apostasy from Islam and deserved the death penalty. In their eyes, 'Ali had committed apostasy by negotiating to end the *fitna* with Mu'awiyah, and in 661, a Kharijite assassinated Muhammad's own son-in-law.

'Ali's followers argued that he should be succeeded by his son, but Mu'awiyah was now too powerful. He secured control, was acknowledged as caliph in Jerusalem,

The **Mosque of 'Ali** in Najaf, Iraq. The current structure was built 1621–1631, but there have been various shrines at the location since 786. Many Shi'ite Muslims believe it contains the tomb of 'Ali as well as the remains of Adam and Noah.

and took up residence at Damascus. The Syrian location of this capital signified that Islam had expanded its influence beyond Arabia and now aimed to extend its rule westward across the Mediterranean. Mu'awiyah successfully founded the **Umayyad dynasty** (661–750). His descendants would lead the Muslim community for the next hundred years. 'Ali's followers did not accept Mu'awiyah and his descendants as legitimate caliphs and even attempted to seize the caliphate for 'Ali's grandson. This coup met with defeat, and a permanent split developed within Islam. The majority of Muslims accepted Mu'awiyah's caliphate and embraced the idea that an individual received the authority to lead Islam by the approval of the community of believers. These became known as **Sunni Muslims**. ("*Sunna*" means "custom" and refers to the traditions surrounding Muhammad's ideal conduct.)

THE CHURCH OF THE EAST

When the Umayyads conquered Persia, they encountered a branch of Christianity that had largely developed in isolation from the broader Catholic tradition which took root in the Roman Empire. Christians under Persian rule never had a Constantine who embraced and promoted their religion and instead suffered one of the worst persecutions in all Christian history. Historians estimate that nearly 200,000 martyrs died in Persia during the fourth century. Despite the suffering, few abandoned their Faith, and the Persians ultimately issued an edict of toleration in 410.

That same year, the bishops of the region took advantage of the opportunity to meet in synod and to address issues of theology. They entrusted the leadership of their communities to the bishop of Seleucia-Ctesiphon. He received the title "*catholicos*," which was roughly equivalent to the authority of a patriarch. Furthermore, a bishop from the Roman Empire attended the gathering. He told them about the decisions of the Council of Nicaea from nearly a century earlier and asked the eastern bishops to accept its teachings. This request was met with agreement, and, for the moment, the Church of the East, while effectively independent, was in union with the wider Christian world.

Persecution resumed in the 420s. The *catholicos's* authority grew as he guided his beleaguered community through this renewed hardship, and many Christians in the Persian Empire considered his authority to be the equal of any other leader in Christianity. The situation also severely limited contact between Roman and Persian Christians. Most interactions took place in Syria at the so-called School of the Persians in Edessa. This school educated future bishops of the Church of the East according to the principles of the "Antiochene School" of theology. When these leaders learned about the controversy between Nestorius and Cyril, they sided with Nestorius and his Antiochene-based theology.

This support became even more pronounced when the Miaphysite Emperor Zeno closed the School of the Persians in an effort to limit the growth of Nestorius's position. His decision backfired. Persian Christians were now effectively isolated and doubled down on the teachings that they had received from trusted Antiochene theologians. In 486, the *catholicos* summoned another synod and enacted a series of reforms that shaped the future of an independent Church of the East. Some decisions involved discipline; for example, the synod permitted bishops to marry. More important was its rejection of both Miaphysite theology and the Council of Chalcedon.

The ramifications of this schism cannot be properly weighed. To the bishops within the Roman Empire, the Church of the East was now officially "Nestorian" and therefore heretical. This included not only Christians in Persia but also those in India and even the first Christian missions to China—all of which were under the authority of the *catholicos*. These communities continued to develop their own traditions, including a different biblical canon that omitted several books from both the Old and New Testaments. Once the Umayyads had effectively pushed the Byzantines out of Syria, contact between Chalcedonians and the Church of the East—and any hope of healing—was effectively eliminated for centuries. Only in the 1990s has significant progress been made in reconciling this ancient branch of Christianity, known today as the Assyrian Church of the East, with Catholicism. Its half-million faithful are predominately located in the Middle East and India.

Those who rejected Mu'awiyah insisted that only those with the closest biological connection to Muhammad had the authority to lead the Muslim community. These were the **Shi'ite Muslims**. ("*Shi'a*" is an abbreviated form of "partisans of 'Ali.") They considered 'Ali to be the prophet's chosen guardian for their community, second only to Muhammad in holiness. Shi'ite Muslims also held that Muhammad's authority passed down to their leaders, known as *imams*. They believed that these men received divine inspiration to interpret religious law and to reveal the hidden meanings of the *Qur'an* to their followers. Sunni Muslims rejected this Shi'ite theology of additional revelation, and tension between Sunnis and Shi'ites continues to divide Islam even to the present day.

Limits of Umayyad Expansion

Despite this ongoing internal division, the Umayyads continued to expand their rule. Their armies marched east into India and west along the northern coast of Africa and into Europe. Although the Umayyads were still victorious on many occasions, they were defeated in three battles in the early eighth century that helped determine the boundaries of their empire and limited the initial spread of Islam.

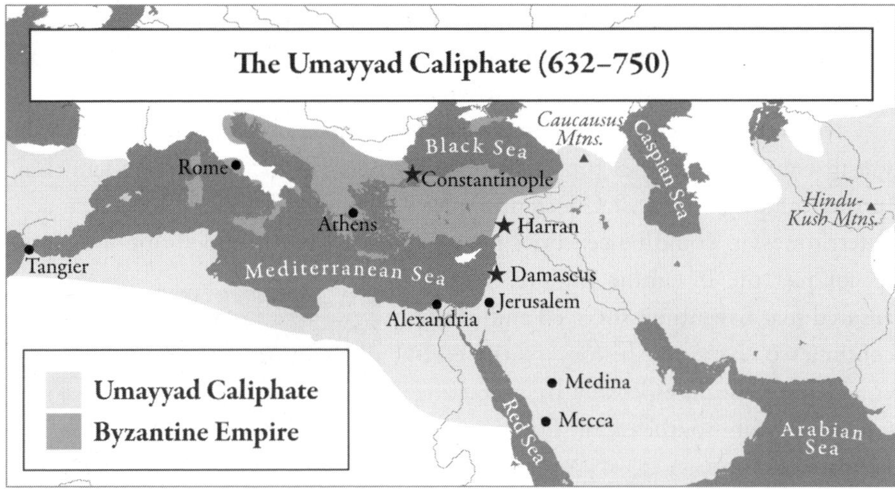

Heraclius had withdrawn from Syria, but the victorious Muslim armies had no intention of halting their attacks against the Byzantine Empire. By 717, they were aiming for the greatest prize of all, the city of Constantinople. Building upon the foundations laid by ʻUthman and Muʻawiyah, they had constructed the first Muslim navy. Like the Vandals, the Umayyads had little or no experience of naval warfare, but this first fleet was largely built and staffed by Miaphysite Christians who preferred the relative tolerance and financial penalties they endured under Muslim rule to the religious persecution the Byzantines had inflicted.

In 717, the expedition set sail and laid siege to Constantinople. Due to the city's unique location, the besieging army had to control both the Bosporus strait to the east and the land approaches to the city from the west to prevent the inhabitants from receiving food during the siege. The Muslim forces were initially successful. The navy gained control of the Bosporus and then transported troops to the western side, where they cut off the city from outside assistance.

The Byzantines, however, had a new secret weapon known as Greek fire that they used to resist this attack. This weapon was a highly effective incendiary that burned on water and was almost impossible to extinguish. The Byzantine ships used Greek fire to defeat the Umayyad navy and regain control of the Bosporus.

Now the tide turned. The Byzantines were able to use the navy to resupply the city from Anatolia. For their part, the Muslim army was trapped on the western side of the city amid a hostile population. Throughout the winter their damaged fleet struggled to provide them with the necessary supplies, and soldiers were reduced to eating their horses and even their dead comrades. Effective Byzantine raids further increased their casualties, and their generals decided to abandon the siege and return home the following spring. On the way, an undersea volcano erupted, showering the fleet with rocks and molten lava and sinking many of the ships. Byzantine historians claim that only five vessels returned to Syria.

This setback was an astounding defeat for the previously unstoppable Muslim war machine. The scale of the catastrophe discouraged the Arabs from launching further campaigns against Constantinople. While they continued to raid imperial territories, it would be centuries before another Muslim expedition attempted to conquer the Byzantine Empire. Victory ensured that Byzantium survived and would continue to shape the history of the eastern Mediterranean, especially by protecting Christianity in southeastern Europe from Islamic expansion.

Further south, Muslim forces continued to enjoy success. From Egypt, they spread west across Africa, and by 708, they had captured Carthage and Tangiers, gaining control of the entire Roman province of North Africa. They then began to expand inland and conquered the indigenous Berber and Moorish tribes.

Votive crown of the Visigoth King Recceswinth. Made of gold, blue sapphires, and other precious stones c. 650. Currently in the National Archaeological Museum in Madrid, Spain. The crown was part of the Treasure of Guarrazar, a set of 26 votive crowns and crosses offered to the Catholic Church by several Visigoth kings in the seventh century as a gesture of submission to ecclesiastical authority. The "crowns" were not intended to be worn but were rather designed to be suspended over an altar. The Treasure was discovered in an orchard near Toledo in 1858–1861. The hanging letters spell [R]ECCESVINTHVS REX OFFERET meaning "King Recceswinth offers [this]."

The increasing Muslim strength in northwest Africa posed a growing challenge to the Visigothic Kingdom in Spain. We will discuss the Visigoths more in chapter 22; for the moment, we merely note that by 700, Visigothic kings had succeeded in unifying Spain. Their one great failing was that they never succeeded in establishing a dynastic kingship with a clear line of succession from father to son. Each new king was elected by the nobles after the death of his predecessor. This system lacked the stability of a dynastic monarchy in which a prince could grow up well-known and recognized as the heir to the throne and ready to assume power after the death of his father. Instead, when a king died, there was frequently an unstable transition period. Powerful nobles squabbled and postured to try to win the election, and a new king might even face military challenges from those who had supported other candidates.

In 711, the election for the kingship was so bitter that the losing party rebelled and turned to the Muslim governor of North Africa for support. A Muslim army arrived in Spain and won a series of conclusive victories, seizing control of most of the peninsula for themselves. Once again, conflict among Christians had played a key role in the expansion of Islam.

A few Visigoths refused to accept this defeat. They retreated to the mountains in northern Spain and there lived in relative independence, occasionally launching raids against the new rulers. At first, the Umayyads were unconcerned about this small band of outlaws, but eventually the raids became costly enough that they sent out an army to stamp out this resistance permanently.

Around 722, Muslim soldiers cornered the Visigoth rebels on a mountain. According to later accounts of the campaign, the Umayyad general dismissed the Visigoths as "thirty barbarians perched on a rock" and predicted that they would soon die. Even a bishop who had accepted Muslim rule attempted to convince the Christians that their cause was hopeless and encouraged them to give up their resistance. Still, the Visigoths refused to surrender. During the ensuing Battle of Covadonga (718 or 722), the Christians made use of their local knowledge and the steep slopes of the mountains to win an unexpected victory. They attributed this triumph to the Virgin Mary's intercession and saw it as a sign that God would eventually restore all of Spain to Christian hands. About a hundred years later, a local bishop announced he had discovered the bones of the Apostle James the Greater in a Roman cemetery at Compostela in northwestern Spain. This site now became the focus of pilgrimages from across Western Europe, and Spanish Christians adopted the apostle as another heavenly patron in their struggle to reclaim their lands.

While the memory of Covadonga remained a rallying cry for later generations of Spanish Christians, this victory did little at the time to challenge Muslim control of the Spanish Peninsula. The Umayyads were surprised and disappointed, but they were content to leave the Visigoths to their small kingdom in the northern mountains of Spain and continued to push further north, launching raids across the Pyrenees and into France.

In the years since Clovis, the Frankish kingdom of the Merovingians had been weakened by the Frankish custom of dividing their inheritance among their children. This practice meant that kings became weaker with each generation while nobles with a single heir could make their families more powerful. By the early eighth century, one of these nobles, **Charles Martel** (688–741), had become Mayor of the Palace. This office gave him tremendous authority, including command of the royal armies.

Charles had seen Muslim raids from Spain increasing and knew that eventually they would come north in strength. Although the Franks had no cavalry at the time, Charles prepared for the clash he knew was coming by training a disciplined army. In 732, the long-expected raid occurred. A large Muslim army crossed the mountains intending to plunder the city of Tours, which had become enriched by pilgrims visiting the city to honor the tomb of St. Martin.

The Muslim forces were not expecting resistance, and Charles was able to position his army on ground of his choosing at the top of a hill that blocked the invaders' advance. Wave after wave of Arab cavalry charges hurled themselves up the hill. Attacks like these had shattered the power of the Persian and Byzantine Empires, but here the thin line of motley Frankish soldiers held firm. The following day, in the midst of another attack, Charles sent a raiding party to attack the Muslims' supply wagons. Confused by the disruption to their rear, the Muslims halted in the midst of their latest advance, and the Franks seized their moment and charged, routing their enemies and driving them back into their camp. The Franks were ready to resume the battle the following day, but the Muslims slipped away back to Spain under the cover of darkness.

Charles Martel's victory at the **Battle of Tours** (732) proved to be decisive for the future of Christian Europe. Had Charles failed to defeat the Umayyads, there was no remaining significant force that might conceivably have protected Western Europe from additional Muslim raids and conquest. Indeed, Arab raids into France still occurred for some years after the battle, though by 740 Charles had secured the Frankish kingdom's southern border and put an end to most of these attacks. The victory at Tours set a northern limit to the spread of Islam and allowed Christianity to continue to grow in influence throughout Western Europe. This success also strengthened Charles's prestige among the Franks. Even though he remained Mayor of the Palace, most Franks realized that Charles, and not their king, was the effective ruler and protector of the kingdom.

Umayyad Society

Despite these defeats, the Umayyads still ruled over a vast empire where many of their subjects were not Muslim. How did they govern this realm? What was society like under Islamic rule for the large Christian and Jewish populations living in former Persian and Byzantine territories?

Like the barbarian kings of Europe, the Arabs had next to no experience raising taxes and maintaining the infrastructure of large empires. Unlike the barbarians, they were far more successful in preserving established practices by convincing their non-Muslim subjects to assist them in governing the caliphate. With the exception of the army, which was still almost entirely composed of Arab soldiers, Christians and Jews held the same government positions they had held before, just now under the direction of their new Muslim rulers. Provincial governors were exclusively Arab and appointed by the caliph. These regional leaders raised taxes and oversaw the administration of the army, government, and religious officials. Any surplus tax was sent to the caliphs in Damascus.

Most of the conquered people were content to serve the new rulers, in large part because the Umayyads did not pressure them to convert to Islam. The Muslims did not see these conflicts as wars of conversion, nor did they immediately feel a strong sense of obligation to encourage their new subjects to become Muslims. For them, these were campaigns of conquest. By triumphing on the battlefield and governing their lands according to Islamic teachings, they had satisfactorily proved that they were the true followers of God, whose actions enjoyed divine approval.

As noted in the previous chapter, Muslims considered Christians People of the Book, meaning that they were guided by some aspects of divine revelation. They had accepted the teachings of Abraham and Jesus, but not Muhammad. The Umayyads gave those who adhered to Christianity (or another tolerated religion) a protected status and they were known as ***dhimmis***. (This word derives from the Arabic word *damma*—"to blame"—since these protected people had the right to accuse their Muslim rulers if they failed to protect them.) Each Christian was required to pay a poll tax known as the *jizya*, they were required to wear certain clothes to distinguish them from Muslims who were subject to Islamic teaching, and they were forbidden from openly practicing or promoting their religion. For example, they were not allowed to build new churches, display the cross in public, or ring church bells. Such policies did not attack Christianity directly as much as suffocate it slowly.

Non-Muslims were the majority of the caliphate's population, and so *dhimmi* status was a pragmatic solution for the Umayyads. It meant they did not have to attempt some kind of forceful program of mass conversion, and the *jizya* payments made the caliphate wealthy and funded further wars of conquest.

Eventually, a distinct Islamic culture began to develop within the caliphate. Whereas most early government records were still written in the Greek and Persian languages, Arabic soon became the empire's common, unifying language. Byzantine and Persian currency underwent a similar unification under Umayyad rule. An Islamic architectural style also developed, which fused together the large interior spaces characteristic of Roman buildings with the curves common in Persian constructions.

The **Umayyad Mosque**. Built by Caliph al-Walid I c. 706–715 in Damascus, Syria. It was the former site of a Roman temple and then the Christian cathedral dedicated to St. John the Baptist. Although the building has been altered and repaired numerous times, it retains the original Umayyad architectural style with its innovative blend of the Roman basilica layout with Persian domes and extensive mosaic decoration. It is considered the basis for most subsequent Islamic architecture.

Over time, members of the conquered populations also began to convert to Islam. This process posed new challenges for the Umayyads. After a while, they could no longer afford to release their subjects from the *jizya,* even if they converted to Islam, because the tax was an important source of revenue. Instead, they began to require this tax on their subjects on the basis of their biological background rather than their religion. Non-Arab Muslims, known as *mawalis,* were treated as second-class citizens who were required to pay higher taxes. Such a situation naturally led to resentment.

In 750, this bitterness brought about a revolution. The Umayyads were overthrown by a new 'Abbasid dynasty (750–1258). The 'Abbasids claimed descent from Muhammad's uncle, 'Abbas, and promised to reform the luxuries and excesses of the Umayyad Caliphate and to rule with a purer Islamic zeal. This position won them support from both Shi'ite Muslims and *mawalis.* They raised an army in Persia, defeated the Umayyads in Mesopotamia, and captured Damascus, killing all the Umayyads they could find. One surviving member of the dynasty fled to

THE "NEW MARTYRS" UNDER ISLAM

There is a common misperception that conversion to Islam was spread by the sword. Muslim military conquests—which were, of course, spread through violence—established political Muslim rule, but that is a different phenomenon than the spread of the religion of Islam. Various verses within the *Qur'an* indicated Islam's intended universal character. However, the earliest generations of Muslims considered Islam to be an *Arab* religion. This attitude, coupled with the reality that the Muslim state relied on the tax money gained from the "People of the Book," helps explain why there were no widespread violent persecutions of Christians during the first centuries of the caliphate. Muslims had little to gain spiritually or materially by compelling Christians (or Jews or Zoroastrians) to accept their religion. Meanwhile, some Christians chose to convert to Islam to avoid the *jizya* tax and to increase their social standing. Those Christians who had been enslaved after the conquest had particular motive for conversion since this increased the possibility of their manumission. In the late eighth century, the number of conversions had apparently grown so great that the monk John the Stylite recorded in dismay that Christians "turn to Islam faster than sheep rushing to water... This was done not only by the young, but also by adults, the elderly... even by senior priests and so many deacons they cannot be counted."[2]

The lack of formal violent persecution and the "rush" towards Islam recounted by John did not mean that there were no Christians killed for their Faith during these early centuries. We know of approximately 270 martyrs during the period from, roughly, 660-860. Most of these died in large groups or within a handful of years from one another. Muslims condemned them as apostates and blasphemers, but Christians hailed them as the "new martyrs," a term that was meant to evoke a continuation of the ancient Roman martyrs' legacy. Certainly, their individual acts of courage and witness harkened back to that earlier age. They often endured great tortures and died by crucifixion or some other horrifying death. What is more, Muslim judges sometimes mandated that their bodies be burned so as to destroy any possible relics.

Despite the obvious parallels between the Roman martyrs and the "new martyrs", the immediate contexts for each were dramatically different. First, the Christians of ancient Rome had been a mistrusted minority, whereas they comprised the majority population under the Umayyad dynasty and during the early years of the 'Abbasid dynasty. Secondly, Roman judges typically executed Christians for not participating in the state religion or from suspicions about the supposedly evil nature of their beliefs. In contrast, most martyrs under early Muslim rule died because they abandoned Islam. Most were originally Christian, had decided to convert to Islam, and then renounced their new allegiance to return to Christianity. Therefore, a Muslim judge did not execute a given Christian *for being Christian* but rather because that person had

2 John the Stylite, *Chronicle of Zuqnin* quoted in Christian C. Sahner, *Christian Martyrs under Islam: Religious Violence and the Making of the Muslim World* (Princeton: Princeton University Press, 2018), 29.

dared to renounce Islam. Other martyrs were condemned for blasphemy, that is the public disparagement of Muhammad or some Islamic practice. The most famous of these were forty-eight Christians of Córdoba who actively sought martyrdom by publicly denouncing Islam between the years 850 and 859. Again, these suffered death not because of their Christian beliefs as such but because of what they had said publicly against Islam.

Interestingly, the *Qur'an* did not explicitly call for the execution of either apostates or blasphemers. Rather, this ultimate penalty became a part of the teachings of the various Islamic legal schools only after the death of Muhammad. Regarding apostacy, the watershed moment was the Ridda Wars during the caliphate of Abu Bakr. This attempt by various Arab tribes to break free from Muslim rule encouraged the conviction that the punishment for abandoning Islam was death. Legal theories about blasphemy developed more gradually, though, by the 850s, there was enough consensus that Christians knew it likely meant death to disparage Muhammad or Islam publicly.

Why inflict torment and death in certain cases when the wider caliphate did not generally execute Christians? Quite simply, these martyrdoms served as public examples. Many took place during the early years of the 'Abbasid dynasty, when the 'Abbasids needed to justify their revolution by emphasizing their devotion to Islam. Various caliphs promoted an explicitly Islamic character for their rule by destroying churches and synagogues and replacing them with mosques. Furthermore, the ongoing wars with Byzantium heightened fears that Christians might be collaborating with the enemy. Muslims who returned to Christianity must have only confirmed those fears. The occasional execution by a local judge could be an effective preventative measure.

For their part, Christians must have feared their eventual assimilation in the growing Muslim population, and so some sought opportunities to emphasize the distinction between the two religions through their dramatic witness. And yet, by the end of the ninth century, martyrdom had become rare once more. Christians turned to argumentation and theological refutation as tools for resisting the spread of Islam within their ranks, and the now established 'Abbasids had their own internal concerns that were more pressing than the activities of a small percentage of the Christian population. It was not until centuries later, with the rise of the Mamluks in Egypt and the Ottoman Empire, that the Church witnessed more "new martyrs" in Muslim lands.

Spain, known to Muslims as al-Andalus. Here he established an independent government which was ruled by descendants of the Umayyad dynasty for the next three centuries. The 'Abbasids established their own capital in the Mesopotamian city of Baghdad, which quickly became one of the largest and most important cities in the world. The 'Abbasids would lead the disciples of Muhammad to new and still more impressive achievements, but they were never able to expand the borders of Muslim rule that had been established after the Umayyads' defeats in Europe.

Conclusion

The Umayyad dynasty could boast of many achievements. After the dramatic success of the early Muslim victories over the Persian and Byzantine Empires, they cemented these conquests and successfully ruled over a huge empire that included large non-Muslim populations in the Mediterranean region and beyond. Islam became a prominent rival to Christianity, ironically due, in part, to the support it received from disaffected Christian populations. It also emerged as a tremendous political, military, and cultural influence. The spread of Arabic as the new common language throughout the vast Umayyad realm was but one example of its growing significance.

Despite these successes, the Umayyads also experienced several important failures. They were unable to reunify the Islamic community after the death of ʿAli. Muʿawiyah's contentious rise to power and the resulting split between Sunni and Shiʿite Muslims remained a point of discord at the heart of Islam. They also suffered important defeats at either end of Europe that discouraged their further expansion into that region. Their most significant failure was their inability to satisfy their own Muslim subjects, who ultimately rebelled and overthrew them in 750.

In the next chapter, we return to Western Europe and resume our narrative in the aftermath of Justinian's reconquests. As we will see, the papacy became increasingly important not only in the Italian Peninsula but also throughout Western Europe as it promoted Christian missionary activity in the barbarian kingdoms. At the same time, friction between the popes and the Byzantine emperors contributed to tensions that threatened once again to divide Christians into hostile theological camps.

CHAPTER 22

Papal Authority, West and East

"[A bishop] must, therefore, be the model for everyone. He must be devoted entirely to the example of good living. He must be dead to the passions of the flesh and live a spiritual life. He must have no regard for worldly prosperity and never cower in the face of adversity. He must desire the internal life only."

Pope Gregory I, *The Book of Pastoral Care*[1]

During the sixth and seventh centuries, Christian Europe was in dire need of brave and selfless spiritual leaders. The infrastructure provided by the Roman Empire had collapsed across western Europe. In its stead were the Germanic kingdoms we introduced in chapter 17. The ensuing political turmoil frequently contributed to the deterioration of the people's spiritual condition: persecution from "Arian" rulers or a resurgence of pagan belief could undermine generations of missionary activity.

To the east, the Byzantine Empire remained vulnerable to foreign attack, and several emperors attempted to reinforce their position by increasing their influence within the Church. For them, the pursuit of political stability intertwined with the quest for religious truth, and they frequently supported whatever theological positions exalted their own imperial authority. They exerted formidable pressure on Church leaders, threatening them with imprisonment or even death if they dared to question the emperor's spiritual role.

Meanwhile, a few lonely voices sought to re-establish spiritual order in the midst of the tumult. As seen in this chapter's epigraph, Pope Gregory I worked to clarify

1 Gregory the Great, *The Book of Pastoral Rule,* trans. George Demacopoulos (Crestwood, NY: St. Vladimir's Seminary Press, 2007), 49.

and promote the characteristics of a good bishop. His pastoral insight and concern stood in stark contrast to the self-serving ambitions of many others during this era.

In this chapter, we will examine the expansion of papal influence in the West, as well as the challenge to its authority that it faced in the East. Both established important precedents that would shape medieval civilization and the role of the papacy.

Successes in the West

Gregory I (r. 590–604) began the papacy's shift towards the Germanic West and away from the Byzantine East. He came from a wealthy Roman family whose piety was well known. (Both his parents and two of his aunts were eventually canonized.) Whereas Benedict of Nursia had fled Rome and its moral depravity about a century earlier, Gregory's family saw themselves as responsible for guiding and protecting the Roman community. They used their wealth to minister to the poor and served as public officials in the city. Gregory received the best education his family could provide and took up the family's mantle of public responsibility when he became prefect, or mayor, of the city in his early thirties. Nonetheless, Gregory felt called to renounce the world and sold his family's possessions before entering a monastery. Gregory's monastic years quietly prepared him to serve not only the physical but also the spiritual needs of his beloved fellow Romans. He later described these years as the happiest of his life.

As we saw in chapter 19, Justinian's reconquests had made the city of Rome part of the Byzantine Empire once again. However, plague and other setbacks seriously compromised the imperial army's ability to retain control over its new territories. This weakness encouraged the Germanic Lombard tribes to enter northern Italy.

The **Caelian Hill** in Rome was the site of Pope Gregory I's family home. The family lived in a villa across the street from the ruins of the emperors' palaces on the Palatine Hill, with the Colosseum at the north end of their street and the Circus Maximus at the south end. Today, the street is known as Via di San Gregorio in honor of Gregory.

Soon Lombard armies were camped almost at the gates of Rome, and refugees from their raids flooded the city in search of safety and food.

In 578, Gregory became senior deacon of Rome, a role which he received on account of his education and administrative experience. His duties soon sent him to Constantinople to plead with the emperor for more troops to defend Italy. Gregory was unsuccessful in his petition, and his experiences in Constantinople showed him that imperial strength was declining throughout the Mediterranean. He returned to Italy convinced that more effective leadership was desperately needed for those in the West. To his surprise and regret, that new leadership would come from him: in 590, despite his protestations, he was chosen to be the bishop of Rome.

As pope, Gregory resumed his family's traditional role as the benefactor of Rome. He negotiated with the Lombards and persuaded them to refrain from attacking the city. When a plague broke out among Rome's overcrowded and undernourished population, he organized a series of processions throughout the city praying for the Virgin Mary's protection. (According to tradition, the Archangel Michael appeared atop Emperor Hadrian's tomb to signify that the prayers had been heard. The mausoleum was later renamed Castle of the Holy Angel.) Gregory also sold Church land to provide food and clothing for the poor, a deed that inspired wealthy families to do the same. Gregory wept when even these actions failed to stop his people from starving but continued to do all in his power to care for the poor.

Pope Gregory I dictating chant. Illuminated miniature made c. 1000. Currently "Cod. Sang. 390 page 13" in the Stiftsbibliothek Monastic Library, St. Gallen, Switzerland. This image is from the *Antiphonary of Hartker*. An antiphonary is a book of music used to assist a community or choir in chanting the Liturgy of the Hours. The *Antiphonary of Hartker* from the Abbey of St. Gall is one of the earliest complete chant manuscripts containing both text and music.

Gregory also ministered to the people's spiritual needs. He reformed the liturgy of the Roman Church by establishing standard practices throughout the diocese, such as when certain prayers like the *Pater Noster* ("Our Father") were recited during Mass. Furthermore, he loved music and codified different traditions of liturgical chant, contributing to the development of what we know today as "Gregorian chant." Gregory also completed several important spiritual works, including his *Book of Pastoral Care*. This was the first book written specifically to teach bishops the responsibilities of their office. The composition of such a work emphasized the papacy's moral example and authority to the other bishops of the Church. It and other writings also encouraged bishops to take on civic responsibilities within their communities since the Roman Empire was no longer able to provide effective protection and guidance. This in turn contributed to the Church's future influence in medieval society.

Others, too, were working to improve the situation for Catholics in the former lands of the Western Roman Empire. Several of the most influential of these were Frankish princesses. These pious women lived during a challenging period. Clovis may have converted to Christianity, but his Merovingian dynasty was best known for its brutality and corruption. His descendants frequently fought with each other and did not hesitate to kill even children who might grow up to be their rivals. Nor did they observe basic Christian teachings like monogamy; one of Clovis's sons, Chlothar (r. 511–558), had multiple wives simultaneously.

These semi-Christian rulers often exercised ruinous control over the local Church and its resources. It became the custom after Clovis that all bishops required royal approval before their consecration. As bishops frequently possessed large amounts of land—typically as the result of pious Christians bequeathing their possessions to the Church—Frankish rulers regularly appointed their friends and warriors to episcopal positions. Many of these "churchmen" had little or no understanding of Church teaching or of their own liturgical duties, but they did provide the wealth and troops their rulers required. (Chlothar, for example, taxed Frankish bishops a third of their land's revenue.) Consequently, there were few efforts made to promote genuine Christianity within France, and many people mixed Christian devotions, such as the veneration of local saints like Martin of Tours, with pagan rites that came from their own Roman, Gallic, or Frankish traditions.

Despite this daunting environment, a number of heroic Frankish princesses not only remained committed to the practice of Christianity in its fullness but even saw their marriages as opportunities to introduce Catholic Christianity into the hostile "Arian" courts of the Visigoths in Spain and the Lombards in Italy. Pagan England likewise owed its conversion to Christianity, at least in part, to a Frankish princess who promoted Gregory's mission to the island.

The Visigoths had defeated Byzantine efforts to reconquer the Spanish Peninsula and enjoyed unity under King Leovigild (r. 568–586). He was one of the greatest of the Visigothic kings and promulgated a law code that granted equal rights to both Visigoths and the peninsula's original population, known as Hispano-Romans. This political and legal reform notwithstanding, the kingdom was religiously divided between the predominately "Arian" Visigoths and the overwhelmingly Catholic Hispano-Roman population. Leovigild attempted to persuade the Catholics to adopt "Arian" rituals as a sign of harmony, but the Catholics refused to comply for fear that altering their liturgical practices would ultimately undermine their pro-Nicene beliefs.

Meanwhile, Leovigild's son and heir, Hermenegild, married the Catholic Frankish princess Ingund (567–584). Bishop Leander, a close correspondent of the future Pope Gregory, encouraged and supported Ingund, and it was perhaps through her influence that Hermenegild announced his conversion to Catholicism. He rebelled against his "Arian" father, but Leovigild captured and executed him. Later generations venerated him as a martyr. Hermenegild's example may have convinced his younger brother **Reccared I** (r. 586–601) to convert to Catholicism after he became king in 587. Most "Arian" Visigothic bishops and nobles followed his example and entered the Church.

In 589, Reccared organized a council in the Visigothic capital of Toledo. There he solemnly recited the Nicene Creed and promised to defend the Church's teachings. Catholic Christians in Spain had won a decisive victory over "Arianism," which never again enjoyed widespread support in Europe. To emphasize this triumph, Spanish clergy began reciting the Nicene Creed at every Mass. Furthermore, the council introduced a clause to the creed, known as the ***Filioque* clause**. This emphasized Jesus's divinity by proclaiming that the Holy Spirit proceeded from the Father "and the Son" ("*Filioque*" in Latin). This addition to the Nicene Creed eventually became common across Western Europe, though, as we will see in chapter 25, it tragically contributed to the division between Catholic and Orthodox Christianity. Even so, for the moment, it was a jubilant sign of the new unity that existed among Spanish Christians.

The influence of Frankish princesses was even more pronounced in Lombard Italy and Anglo-Saxon England. In 588, the Lombard king Authari married a Frankish princess named Theodelinda (570–627). Authari died two years later, but Theodelinda was so popular that she remained queen and married his successor, Agilulf (r. 590–616). Pope Gregory corresponded with Theodelinda regularly and encouraged her to exhort her husband and his subjects to convert to Catholicism. Although Agilulf remained an "Arian," he allowed Theodelinda to baptize their son as a Catholic and tolerated Catholics at his court. Her influence was widespread, and her efforts ultimately contributed to the conversion of the Lombards to Catholic Christianity later in the seventh century.

Bertha (539–612), yet another Frankish princess, also participated in the expansion of Catholicism during Gregory's pontificate. She had married Aethelbert (r. 589–616), ruler of the Anglo-Saxon kingdom of Kent in southeast England. By this point, England had been effectively cut off from the rest of the Roman world and had all but reverted to pagan beliefs. Aethelbert, nonetheless, allowed his wife, a granddaughter of Clovis, to practice her Christian faith freely.

In addition, Pope Gregory vowed to send missionaries to England after he saw Angle prisoners in Rome. Tradition holds that he declared that these pagans were "Angels, not Angles." In 597, one of Gregory's subordinates, a monk known to history as **Augustine of Canterbury** (d. 604), arrived in the kingdom of Kent with forty other monks. Aethelbert, likely acting under the influence of Bertha, agreed to hear Augustine preach, but only outside and surrounded by warriors. He feared that Augustine would use sorcery to control him, but in the end, he and thousands of other Anglo-Saxons accepted baptism that same year. With funds provided by the king, Augustine and the monks built a monastery in the old Roman town of Canterbury where Augustine, at Gregory's instruction, assumed the duties of archbishop.

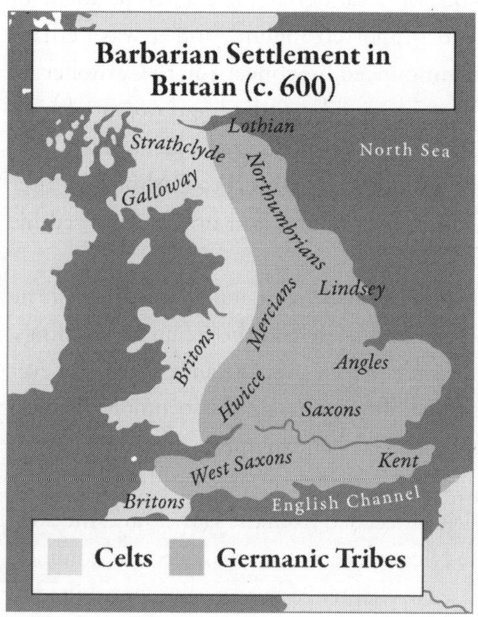

Augustine continued the work of evangelizing England and established bishops in the ancient Roman cities. Acting on Gregory's instructions, Augustine did not destroy the Anglo-Saxons' pagan temples and shrines but rather converted these places into churches. This pastoral policy did not break the spiritual instincts of the people who were used to worshipping at these sites but rather directed these religious impulses toward Christianity. Augustine died less than three months after Gregory in 604, but his inspiring preaching, combined with the pope's prudent care for this new Christian community, inspired a deep loyalty to the papacy in England and, as we will see, ultimately contributed to the revival of Christian practice across Europe.

Advances in the North

In the years before Augustine of Canterbury and other Roman missionaries reestablished the Church in southeast Britain, Celtic missionaries from Ireland were evangelizing the island from the north. The first of these Celtic missionaries was

Columba (521–597). He was a large man with a powerful voice and a quick temper. Though a monk and a priest, he apparently instigated a battle when he refused to part with a copy of the Book of Psalms which another monk claimed was his. Since books were rare and very valuable, Columba's refusal to compromise led to a fight in which, according to report, over three thousand men died. Columba was horrified by the slaughter and vowed to do penance by converting a soul to God for every life lost as a result of his anger.

He traveled with twelve monk-companions to Scotland and established a monastery on the island of Iona in 563. This site became a center of learning in an otherwise illiterate society. Columba himself was said to have copied over three hundred books. He then took up the challenge of converting the pagan Celtic peoples of northern Scotland. According to legend, he even fought with a prehistoric monster living in Loch Ness, the largest and deepest lake in Scotland! By the time of his death in early June 597, almost the exact time that Augustine arrived in Canterbury, Columba had established a stable Christian community in Scotland.

Iona Abbey as seen today. The buildings had been in ruins since the late 16th century, but they were restored and reopened in the 20th century.

As Columba's Celtic mission spread southwards, Augustine's Roman mission stretched northward. In between their two zones of influence was the powerful Saxon kingdom of Northumberland. In 627, the king of that land accepted baptism at the encouragement of his wife, Aethelburg, who was a daughter of Aethelbert and Bertha of Kent. Roman missionaries from Kent attempted to capitalize on

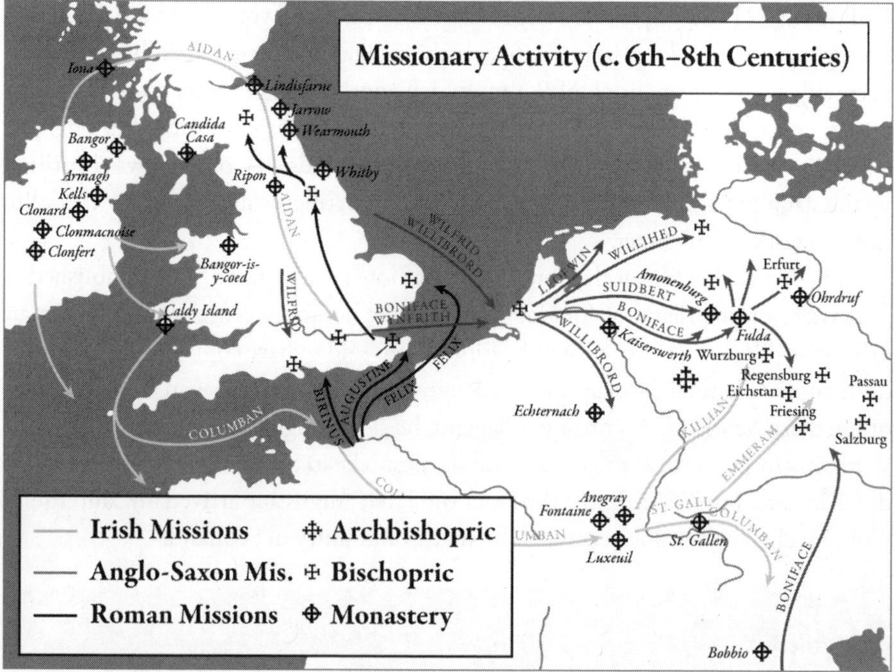

this opportunity to spread Christianity, but Northumberland experienced a pagan uprising which overthrew its Christian king. For one year paganism had the upper hand until a second war brought another Christian to the throne. King Oswald (r. 633–642) had been converted to Christianity not by the Roman mission but by the Celtic monks associated with Columba. In fact, the evening before his battle against his pagan rival, Oswald reported a vision of Columba promising that God would give him victory the next day. He planted a wooden cross in the ground and convinced even the pagans in his army and council to join him in prayer and to convert to Christianity after the battle.

After his victory, Oswald petitioned Celtic missionaries to help complete the Christianization of his people. In response came Aidan (590–651), a monk known for his gentleness and persuasive preaching. In 635, Oswald granted him the island of Lindisfarne to establish a monastery. Lindisfarne became another center of literacy and evangelization as Celtic Christianity continued to spread among the Anglo-Saxons under Oswald and his successor Oswui (r. 642–670).

In 648, a teenager named **Wilfrid** (633–709) arrived to study at Lindisfarne. From his earliest days at the monastery, Wilfrid displayed exceptional intellectual ability, and he was chosen in 652 to travel to Kent. There he worked with the missionaries from Rome and eventually traveled to Rome itself on pilgrimage. This

THE LINDISFARNE GOSPELS

Celtic missionaries both revived Christianity in Britain and encouraged literacy and learning. Indeed, beginning around 650, Britain became one of the most important centers of learning in Europe. Anglo-Saxon monks played a significant role in the formation of British and medieval culture through their preservation and composition of texts. One of the most famous examples of their work is the Lindisfarne Gospels, which was produced in the Northumbrian monastery of Lindisfarne.

The process of producing the materials required for the manuscript was both time-consuming and labor-intensive. Its pages were *vellum*, a form of parchment made of calfskins. This particular manuscript required an estimated one hundred and fifty calfskins, all of which had to be processed for this use. Meanwhile, the many different inks used in the manuscript were collected from a wide variety of animal, vegetable, and mineral sources.

Once the materials had been collected, the monks spent hours copying the texts of the Gospels into the manuscript. Yet this labor was not the simple copying of words; it was a spiritual task that inspired great beauty. The monks illustrated the margins of the pages and the initials of the chapters with beautiful and intricate decorations that included geometric designs, animals, and even human characters. For the monks of Lindisfarne, copying the Gospels was not only an act of literary service, nor merely a necessary task for the rituals of the abbey; it was itself an act of worship of the God Who had revealed His all-conquering love for mankind in the narratives they were faithfully duplicating.

A page from the Lindisfarne Gospels. Illuminated manuscript made c. 700. Currently "Cotton MS Nero D IV" in the British Library, London, England. This image shows the Greek letters "chi" and "rho" at the top to indicate the word "Christi" with characters for the rest of the verse from Mt. 1:18 following immediately below: "Christi autem generatio sic erat cum esset desponsata mater eius Maria Ioseph..." ("The birth of Christ took place in this way; when His mother Mary had been betrothed to Joseph...")

experience was profoundly moving. While there, he venerated the relics of martyrs, encountered Benedictine monasticism, and embraced Roman liturgical practices even though they differed from those he had been taught at Lindisfarne. Wilfrid returned to England determined to convince others to adopt the practices he had witnessed on the continent so that they might be fully united with other Christians.

The most notable difference between Celtic and Roman traditions involved the celebration of Easter. The Celtic reckoning was earlier than the Roman, and this created tension between the missionaries from Rome and those from Ireland. After all, the Irish monks and those who followed their tradition were feasting to celebrate Easter while those who obeyed the Roman tradition were still observing the fast in Lent.

In 664, representatives of both the Celts and the Romans met at the **Synod of Whitby** to determine one dating system that the kingdom would follow. The Celts claimed that their calculations for dating Easter were drawn from the teachings of John the Evangelist, but Wilfrid argued that the Roman practices could be traced back to Peter, the head of the apostles. Eventually King Oswui decided in favor of Wilfrid and the Romans, saying that he ought to conform to the apostle who held the keys to the gates of Heaven lest they be shut against him. Although the chief issue at stake in the synod was not one of Faith or morals, the result had profound ramifications. It ensured that English Christianity was not practiced in isolation but would be united with the Church on the continent under the leadership of the papacy.

In the aftermath of this triumph, Wilfrid continued his efforts to integrate Anglo-Saxon Christianity with the Roman leadership of the Church. He became bishop of York and instructed the monasteries under his jurisdiction to adopt the Benedictine Rule. He built new churches according to the styles he had seen in Rome and even used stones from Hadrian's Wall in their construction. Inside these churches, he placed relics of Roman martyrs that he had brought back from the continent. This explicitly Roman architecture and the relics further united the Anglo-Saxon Christians with their Roman brethren.

Wilfrid's reforms were not always well received. Many devout Celtic clergy saw him as uprooting their traditions, while some Saxon kings felt that he was undermining their authority by encouraging Christians to observe a stronger loyalty to the papacy. A number of times he was exiled, but each time he traveled to Rome to gain papal support and then returned to continue his work. His reliance on the papacy established another important principle. Although kings exercised a powerful influence within the English Church, as demonstrated by Oswui's decisive contribution at Whitby, the Roman pontiffs claimed the right to choose the island's bishops.

On one of these voyages, the ship carrying Wilfrid was blown off course and landed in modern-day Belgium and the Netherlands. Wilfrid discovered that it was not only the Anglo-Saxons who required evangelization and preached to the local pagans. When Wilfrid died in 709, his disciple Willibrord (658–739) continued his missionary vision. Willibrord had studied in an English monastery and in Ireland and had a reputation for great learning. At the age of thirty-three, he traveled to the Frisians in the Netherlands to preach the Gospel. He was initially successful, converting the local ruler and many of his subjects to Christianity as well as building a new church. Once this king died, however, his successor reverted to the pagan practices that were entrenched in Frisian culture. The new king drove out the missionaries and burned down the churches. This experience taught Willibrord that, although the populations of these regions might be ready to accept Christianity, he and his companions would struggle to sustain these converts in the practice of the Faith without the support of their rulers. Future missionaries would take this lesson to heart.

Tensions in the East

While the influence of the papacy was growing in northwest Europe, it was increasingly under threat in the Byzantine Empire. The Miaphysites and those who supported the Council of Chalcedon remained unreconciled. During the reign of Heraclius, the Patriarch of Constantinople Sergius (r. 610–638), proposed a compromise between these parties by teaching that Christ had both divine and human natures, but only one *energy*. This position was known as "Monoenergism." Heraclius's dramatic victory over the Persians enabled the emperor to convince the patriarchs of Alexandria and Antioch to adopt this teaching, too. Even the current pope, **Honorius I** (r. 625–638), wrote a letter seemingly supporting Sergius's teaching regarding Christ's single will, though he also called for discussions about Christ's "energy" to end for the sake of Church unity.

Many Miaphysites and Chalcedonians disliked the compromise, and the religious unity that Monoenergism had seemingly fostered soon disintegrated. This collapse mirrored the decline of the emperor himself. The defeat at the Battle of Yarmuk in 636 broke Heraclius's spirit. He was convinced that God was punishing him, both for failing to achieve Christian unity and for marrying his niece—a relationship most Byzantines viewed as sinful. The emperor who had boldly attacked the Persians in the empire's greatest hour of need had become a quivering old man, afraid even to cross the narrow Bosporus to Constantinople for fear that God would sink the boat and send him to Hell.

Three years later, Heraclius supported a new doctrine in a document called the *Ecthesis* ("exposition" in Greek). This document forbade discussion about whether

The **Church of St. Agnes Outside the Walls**. Built by Pope Honorius I c. 625 in Rome over the Catacombs of St. Agnes. The mosaic in the apse is original and shows St. Agnes in the center with Honorius on her right holding a model of the church building.

Christ had one or two energies and instead asserted that Christ had two natures but only one will. The eastern patriarchs of Antioch and Alexandria accepted this new doctrine of Monothelitism (Greek for "one will") and once again it appeared as though Patriarch Sergius and Heraclius had achieved Christian unity in the empire.

Honorius's papal successor, Severinus (r. 638–640), refused to sign the *Ecthesis*, and the desperate emperor turned to coercion. At this time, papal elections were conducted by the clergy of Rome, though the emperor still had to approve of their choice. Heraclius initially refused to acknowledge Severinus till he accepted the *Ecthesis*. To add even more pressure, the imperial representative in Italy, known as an exarch, incited a mob to plunder the papal treasury and to threaten the pope into accepting Monothelitism. These tactics did not work, and the pope died without offering support for Monothelitism. The next pope, John IV (r. 640–642), denounced the *Ecthesis* outright. Heraclius's health was already in decline, and the condemnation of his final attempt to heal the religious divisions in the empire led him to renounce Monothelitism before he died in 641. Nonetheless, it still remained the official theological position for many eastern bishops.

In 645, **Maximus the Confessor** (c. 580–662) arrived in Rome from Carthage. This monk was an astute theologian and had convinced many North African bishops that Monothelitism was erroneous. He stressed that Jesus could not be fully human unless He could suffer and be tempted, and he used as evidence both Jesus's temptations in the desert and His agony in Gethsemane. This last example was particularly compelling since Jesus clearly distinguished His human will from the divine will of the Father when He prayed "not my will, but thine, be done" (Lk 22:42). Jesus, therefore, had to have *two* wills—one divine and one human. Maximus's theology found support in Rome, and the pope ultimately excommunicated the patriarch of Constantinople as a heretic for teaching that Christ had only one will.

The papacy's continued opposition did not sit well with the new emperor, Heraclius's grandson **Constans II** (r. 641–668). Constans had become emperor at the age of eleven, and the young boy soon demonstrated a remarkable ability to govern the empire. He defeated the Slavs and restored imperial control over much of southeastern Europe. He also negotiated peace with the Muslims and used the civil war between ʿAli and Muʿawiyah as an opportunity to restructure the Byzantine military. Rather than pay his soldiers money that the embattled empire did not have, he gave them land which they could use for their own benefit. In exchange, these soldier-farmers were expected to come to the defense of their territory if an enemy approached. Soldiers were thus scattered throughout the empire in military regions known as *themes*. The *theme* system proved remarkably successful: soldiers responded quickly to local threats and had a vested interest in protecting areas close to their own homes. Constans's reform enabled the Byzantine army to recover from its defeats by Arab armies and even set the stage for later victories.

Focused on these endeavors, Constans was frustrated by the seemingly never-ending religious debates. He issued the *Type* (Greek for "edict"), in which he forbade further debate on the topic of Christ's will(s) and declared that either position could be held because the discussion was unimportant. For Constans, theological unity was a tool for strengthening political stability, and he could not understand why Maximus the Confessor and his allies had a very different perspective.

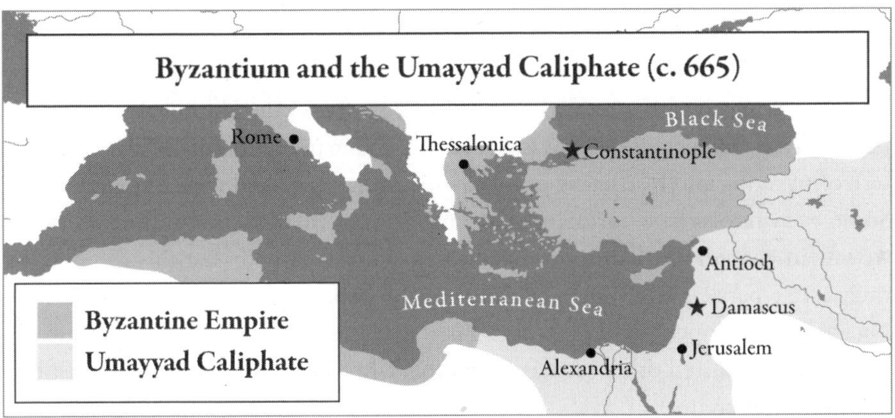

The divergence in attitude became all too apparent when Pope Martin I (r. 649–655) explicitly condemned both the *Ecthesis* and Constans's *Type* at the Lateran Council of 649. This gathering formally taught that Christ had both divine and human wills, and Martin's defiance of the emperor's claim to spiritual authority resulted in a swift response from Constans. The exarch of Italy led troops into the Lateran Basilica and seized both Martin and Maximus. Maximus was exiled; later, his tongue and his right hand were cut off so that he could no longer defy the emperor through his preaching or his writing. Martin was dragged through the streets of Constantinople in chains, declared a heretic, and also sent into exile.

Constans insisted that the Romans elect a new pope, and Martin agreed to resign to avoid the confusion of two men simultaneously claiming to hold the papacy. When Martin died in 655 many honored him as a martyr, the last pope to be venerated with that title. His sufferings inspired the Romans to continue their resistance to Monothelitism, and his papal successor refused to support Constans's theology. This uneasy state of affairs continued until 668, when an assassin struck down Constans II while he bathed.

The next emperor, Constantine IV (r. 668–685), decided to summon an ecumenical council to resolve the theological tension. The Third Council of Constantinople lasted from 680 until 681 and had its own drama. One Monothelite priest claimed he would prove the supremacy of this teaching by raising the dead to life and even had a corpse brought into the chamber. Despite the priest's whispering into the body's ears, the cadaver remained dead. Though the patriarch of Antioch remained adamant in his support for Monothelitism, the rest of the council fathers enthusiastically supported the teaching of Pope Agatho (r. 678–681) and condemned Monothelitism. Martin and Maximus, though both deceased, were vindicated, and the Monothelite controversy ended.

The debates about Monothelitism had revealed significant practical limitations to papal authority. First, it showed that the Byzantine Empire, while weakened by Muslim conquests, still intended to exercise control over the Church, including the papacy. Despite exceptions like Constantine IV, many emperors followed a pattern of rejecting and restricting papal teaching if it conflicted with imperial policy. Some even resorted to torturing and imprisoning their theological enemies. As we saw in chapter 16, Constantine and Constantius II had set this precedent by their active participation (or meddling) in the debates about "Arianism" and the Nicene Creed. Popes gradually realized that a defense of their independent spiritual authority required other secular protectors who could protect them against this imperial interference.

Second, it revealed that popes could contribute to crises within the Church, especially if they ignored the nuances of theological debates. As noted above, Pope Honorius had written to Sergius apparently supporting the idea that Christ had only one will. A careful reading of the letter showed that Honorius merely agreed with Sergius that Christ could not have two *opposing* wills; he never asserted that Christ had only one will. Nonetheless, the council fathers at Constantinople condemned Honorius as a heretic, though they indicated that he had subverted the Faith through association with heretics rather than active promotion of heresy.[2]

This distinction was crucial when, centuries later, the attendees of the First Vatican Council (1869–70) discussed papal infallibility and how to reconcile that belief with the popes' fallen human nature. Ultimately, Vatican I taught that popes are infallible under very limited circumstances when they formally instruct the entire Church on a matter of faith or morals. Even this restricted understanding met with opposition, and those who argued against papal infallibility used Honorius's status as a heretic as evidence against infallibility. Those in favor of papal infallibility successfully counterargued that Honorius had never formally promulgated error in matters of faith and morals. Instead, he had failed to combat heresy as rigorously as he should have. (We already encountered a similar situation in chapter 16 when Pope Liberius signed a creed that *could* be interpreted as "Arian." Nonetheless, he never formally taught "Arianism.") The personal failings of Honorius also pointed forward to a coming era, which we will study in chapter 24, when many popes' scandalous lives added to the moral crisis of the Church rather than worked to heal its divisions.

Conclusion

The seventh century was a critical period in the history of the papacy and the Early Medieval Church. Gregory the Great recognized the need for spiritual and civil leadership in the developing barbarian kingdoms, and he inspired bishops by his exhortations and example to serve the people both spiritually and in temporal matters. Whereas Byzantine emperors sought their own agendas and sometimes attacked those popes who resisted them, local political rulers in the West supported papal aspirations. Again and again, Gregory and other popes received assistance from royal women of France who travelled to foreign lands and worked to convert

---

2 Philip Schaff and Rev. Henry Wallace, ed. *Nicene and Post-Nicene Fathers*, 2nd Series Vol. 14 (New York: Cosimo Classics, 2007), 342–3: "And with these we define that there shall be expelled from the holy Church of God and anathematized Honorius who was some time Pope of Old Rome, because of what we found written by him to Sergius, that in all respects he followed his view and confirmed his impious doctrines.... To Honorius, the heretic, anathema!"

their new husbands and kingdoms. Their influence was crucial to the adoption of Christianity in Italy, Spain, and England. English Christianity, in particular, thrived and ultimately contributed its own missionaries to support Europe's evangelization. Slowly but surely, a new civilization was rising, one in which Christianity would exercise greater influence than ever before. Its next step—as we will see in chapter 23—was an alliance between the Roman pontiffs and the Frankish kings.

UNIT VI

The Rise of Christendom

CHAPTER 23

Charlemagne's City of God

Without the patronage of the Frankish prince I can neither govern the faithful of the Church nor protect the priests, clerics, monks and nuns of God, nor can I forbid the practice of heathen rites and the worship of idols in Germany without his orders and the fear he inspires.

Boniface, *Letter to Bishop Daniel of Winchester*[1]

Boniface (675–754) could speak with authority about preaching the Gospel in Germany and among the Franks. A missionary from England, he had joined Willibrord's mission to Frisia (the modern-day Netherlands) but was driven out when a new king attacked the Christians in 716. The undaunted Boniface returned to the region one year later, this time as a papally appointed bishop. In a dramatic gesture, he boldly cut down a tree sacred to the pagans while a surrounding crowd waited expectantly for the gods to strike down this impudent stranger. Boniface's biographer records that the witnesses converted to Christianity when nothing happened. Boniface even used the wood of the tree to construct a new church on that site. Yet, as the above epigraph highlights, this courageous cleric recognized that, for all his resolve, he still required the backing of temporal rulers.

In the mid-eighth century, a new Frankish dynasty emerged which both supported missionaries' efforts to evangelize northwestern Europe and protected the papacy from Lombard and Byzantine threats. In return, the popes endowed these rulers with the authority to govern the Christian people in Western Europe.

1 Boniface, "Letter to Bishop Daniel of Winchester," quoted in George Washington Robinson, "Letters of Saint Boniface to the Popes and Others," in *Papers of the American Society of Church History* (1923), second series, vii, 157–86.

Establishing the limits of these Frankish rulers' influence in the Church would prove challenging, but their alliance with the See of Rome nevertheless played a crucial role in the development of Early Medieval Europe.

Origins of the Papal-Frankish Alliance

The eighth-century popes faced two significant challenges: Lombards and iconoclasts. The Lombards had become the dominant barbarian power in the Italian peninsula. Though many had converted from "Arianism" to Catholic Christianity by the end of the seventh century, Lombard rulers still saw the bishops of Rome as rivals and attacked those who dared to oppose them. Popes had initially looked to the Byzantine Empire for protection, but their hope for support soon disappeared. A theological controversy over images had erupted in Byzantium, and the emperors were not eager to help those whom they viewed as threats to their spiritual authority.

The latest breakdown in papal-imperial relations had its roots in the failed Umayyad assault on Constantinople in 717. The hero of the Byzantine resistance was Emperor **Leo III** (r. 717–741). He believed that God was displeased with Byzantine society and had allowed the Muslims to win so many victories as a punishment for the empire. To win divine favor, Leo promulgated the *Ecloga* ("Selection"), a law code that emphasized biblical morality. It mandated harsh punishments for abortion and homosexuality and restricted the use of the death penalty. (Many Christians in the East, following the teaching of Basil of Caesarea, believed that any killing—not just murder—was immoral.) Leo also believed that converting the Jews would win God's favor, and he attempted to compel Jews living within imperial territories to accept baptism.

Such reforms failed to secure immediate military success, and Leo concluded that the cause of God's wrath was the practice of venerating icons, or images, of Jesus, the Virgin Mary, and the saints. Islam strictly forbade any artistic depiction of a person, and the emperor decided that this must be the key to Muslim victories. His theory that icons violated God's commandments was seemingly confirmed when a submarine volcano erupted in the Mediterranean in 726. This produced a tsunami that destroyed several towns and killed many people, a sure sign to Leo that God was angry with the empire.

That year, Leo ordered a prominent icon of Jesus removed from the palace gate. This decision is commonly seen as the beginning of Christian **Iconoclasm** ("image breaking"). Most Byzantines rejected Leo's iconoclast policy, and some rioted when soldiers arrived to take down the icon. Leo persisted in his policy: iconoclasts substituted simple crosses for crucifixes in churches while representations of flowers and animals replaced images of Jesus and the saints. In 731, Pope Gregory III held a synod at Rome that condemned Iconoclasm as a heresy and declared that anyone

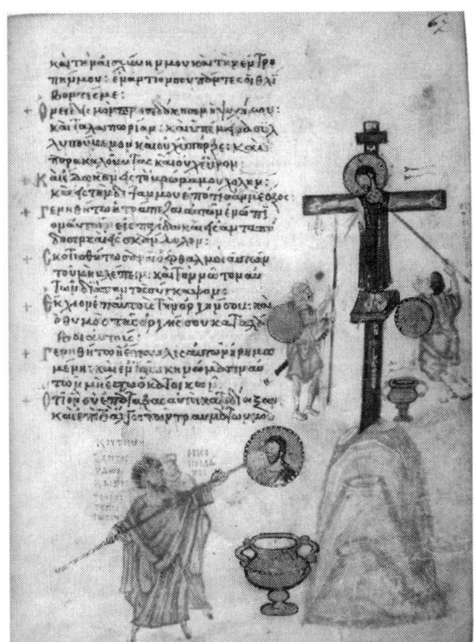

An Iconophile Depiction of Iconoclasm. Illuminated Miniatures made c. 850–875. Currently "MS. D.129, folio 67r" in the State Historical Museum, Moscow, Russia. This image is from the *Chludov Psalter*, a book of psalms with illustrations explicitly referencing iconoclasm. This page illustrates Ps. 69:21 "They gave me poison for food, and for my thirst they gave me vinegar to drink." The image of the soldier offering the crucified Christ a sponge of vinegar attached to a pole is paired with the bottom image of the iconoclast Patriarch of Constantinople, John the Grammarian, destroying a painting of Christ with a sponge attached to a pole. For iconophiles, those who destroyed images effectively crucified Jesus once again.

who willingly damaged a religious image was excommunicated. Despite papal hostility and popular outrage, Leo noted that the more he removed icons from public view, the more his armies won battles against the Arabs. God, he believed, had restored His blessing upon the empire.

Leo's son and heir, Constantine V (r. 741–775), was likewise convinced that Iconoclasm was righteous. He promoted his father's policies aggressively, especially since Byzantine armies were now on the offensive against the Muslims and had even regained territory in southeast Europe that had been lost to the Slavs and the Bulgars. Such successes contrasted starkly with the disasters that the empire had experienced before Iconoclasm, and many Christians, especially those in the army, now agreed with Constantine that God was showing His approval for the imperial position.

Others, particularly monks, still opposed Iconoclasm, and an "iconophile" (icon-lover) rebellion broke out against the emperor. Constantine defeated it and concluded that monasticism was the seedbed of this resistance and needed to be abolished. Monks were tortured, exiled, or forced to violate their vows. Their monasteries became soldiers' barracks. Extreme iconoclasts even rejected the veneration of relics and began destroying shrines and burning the bones of saints.

In 754, Constantine summoned a council to proclaim Iconoclasm as a formal teaching of the Church. 340 bishops attended the Council of Hieria, which was named after the imperial palace where it was held. None of the five patriarchal sees were present or represented. Nonetheless, the council rejected all images of Christ as heretical and praised the emperor as a standard-bearer of orthodoxy.

The pope explicitly condemned the gathering, further heightening tensions with Constantine. The Lombards supported this disagreement because it undermined

The **Hagia Irene**. Built by Justinian c. 532 in modern-day Istanbul, Turkey. The church was damaged during an earthquake in 740, and Constantine V oversaw its repair and redecoration in a stark iconoclast style, as exemplified by the simple black cross mosaic in the apse. The Iconoclast Council of Hieria declared that icons of Christ were heretical because they either depicted Jesus' human nature apart from His divine nature (Nestorianism) or attempted to mix His two natures in one image (Miaphysitism). This conclusion arose from their belief that an image, by definition, shared the same substance as the original. They reasoned that no painting could possibly be consubstantial with God so they must be idols.

both imperial and papal authority in central Italy and provided an opportunity for them to become the dominant power in the peninsula. Worried about Lombard encroachments and aware of Byzantine hostility, popes turned to the Franks for protection.

By the early eighth century, the Merovingians had ceased to be the most powerful figures in Frankia. As noted in chapter 21, they practiced partible inheritance. According to this custom, a father divided his inheritance more or less equally among his children. This led to different Frankish kingdoms in which each individual king consequently controlled less land and wielded less power with every generation.

As Merovingian power declined, a new family grew in influence among the Franks. Its rise to power began in 613 when Pepin of Landen (c. 580–640) became Mayor of the Palace for one of the Frankish kings. This role included authority over the king's army, and Pepin's grandson Pepin II (c. 635–714) used his own appointment as Mayor of the Palace to wage war against other Frankish leaders. While Pepin's king technically ruled the newly reunited realm, everyone knew that the "Pippinid" family possessed more effective authority than the Merovingian rulers they served.

When Boniface came to the Frankish court, the Mayor of the Palace was Pepin II's son Charles Martel (c. 688–741). Charles had fought a number of battles to secure and expand his authority, one of which was the Battle of Tours in 732, which we discussed in chapter 21. Though he never claimed the title of king, it was Charles who ruled Frankia until his death in 741.

During these decades, the Frankish church remained in a semi-pagan state. Charles had gained new lands through his battles and granted many of these possessions to churches and monasteries. However, like the Merovingians before him, he chose abbots and bishops based on their military capability and loyalty to him rather than for any spiritual disposition. The recently arrived Boniface reported with horror that some whom Charles appointed as priests were unrepentant murderers and adulterers. Boniface knew if he openly rejected the company of such men, he would lose Charles's support and would be unable to continue his missionary activity. The bishop decided to refrain from any public approval of corrupt clerics and their actions, but he did not publicly condemn them either. This policy of discretion caused Boniface much concern, and he wondered whether his desire to promote the Church's missions justified his silence in the face of liturgical abuse and worse. Nonetheless, his tact was rewarded in 737 when Charles created four new dioceses in Bavaria (modern-day southern Germany) and granted him full authority over the Church in these lands as archbishop. Boniface finally had the opportunity to establish a Church hierarchy that was free from the frequently corrupt candidates favored by political leaders.

Though missionaries complained of Charles's abuses and the semi-Christian state of the Franks in general, there were some examples of genuine piety among the elite of Frankish society. We saw this among the Frankish princesses of the previous chapter, and we encounter it again in Charles Martel's son, Carloman. Carloman and his brother Pepin had assumed power upon Charles Martel's death in 741; Carloman, however, renounced his land one decade later and entered the Benedictine monastery at Monte Cassino. This decision reunited the Pippinid lands under his brother Pepin III, commonly known as **Pepin the Short** (r. 741–768). Pepin, like his father Charles, had become both Mayor of the Palace and the most powerful man in Frankia.

Pepin III supported Boniface's regional councils, which reformed the Church by enforcing ecclesiastical law. Pepin nonetheless remained reluctant to surrender his authority to appoint bishops. He feared that without this ability, he would not be able to rely on his bishops to provide him with troops in times of need.

Pepin also resented his lack of royal title. He wrote to Pope Zachary (r. 741–752) asking whether it was just that the man who actually wielded power in the kingdom did not receive formal recognition as king. Zachary wrote back affirming that it was fitting for the most powerful figure in the kingdom to hold the royal title. Pepin used this letter as justification to depose the final Merovingian monarch. The following year, the same year as the Council of Hieria, Pope Stephen II (r. 752–757) crossed the Alps and anointed Pepin as king in Paris.

The practice of anointing a king derived from biblical precedent (see 1 Sm [1 Kgs] 10:1) and was important for two reasons. First, the pope was effectively claiming that the reigning pope, not the Byzantine emperor, had the authority to determine who ruled in the former lands of the Western Roman Empire. Second, the anointing became a sign to many Franks that their kings possessed both political and spiritual authority. Some later medieval theologians even concluded that this anointing was a sacrament that marked the king's soul. Such ideas contributed to the future conflict over the precise nature of a king's, or an emperor's, (spiritual) authority.

Pope Stephen had more immediate concerns. Pepin was now king of the Franks, and the pope turned to him for support against the Lombard threat. Pepin entered Italy with his army and temporarily subdued the Lombards in 756. Stephen received a document, often known as the ***Donation of Pepin***, which listed all the cities and territories in central Italy whose inhabitants had been compelled by Pepin to accept the pope as their political ruler. The papal office now possessed explicit regional authority and oversaw the accompanying resources and wealth. Popes hoped that these territories would provide political strength and independence so that they could govern the Church free from coercion by earthly rulers, but this situation distracted many from their spiritual obligations and, even worse, attracted men who cared more for temporal gain than for the salvation of souls. The papacy had gained physical safety from the Lombards, but it was entering a time of grave spiritual peril.

Charlemagne and the Carolingian Renaissance

In 768, Pepin died and bequeathed his kingdom to two sons, Charles and Carloman. Three years later, Carloman died, and power was once again consolidated in the hands of a single successor. Charles, better known as Charles the Great or **Charlemagne** (r. 768–814), dramatically expanded the authority of the Frankish kingdom and played a crucial role in the formation of medieval European society. Indeed, Pepin III's dynasty would be named "the Carolingians" after Charles, its most famous member.

Charlemagne was first and foremost a mighty warrior. His biographer Einhard described him as exceptionally tall, and excavations of his tomb revealed a skeleton measuring between six feet and six feet, six inches tall at a time when the average male was only five feet, seven inches tall. Einhard also described him as sturdily built with a short, fat neck, a large nose, and large, lively eyes. He was an intimidating figure. On the battlefield, his armies were only rarely defeated.

Charlemagne expanded Frankish authority by first definitively defeating the Lombards in Italy and claiming the iron crown of the Lombard kings for himself. His armies ultimately pushed northward into Bavaria, westward into the eastern

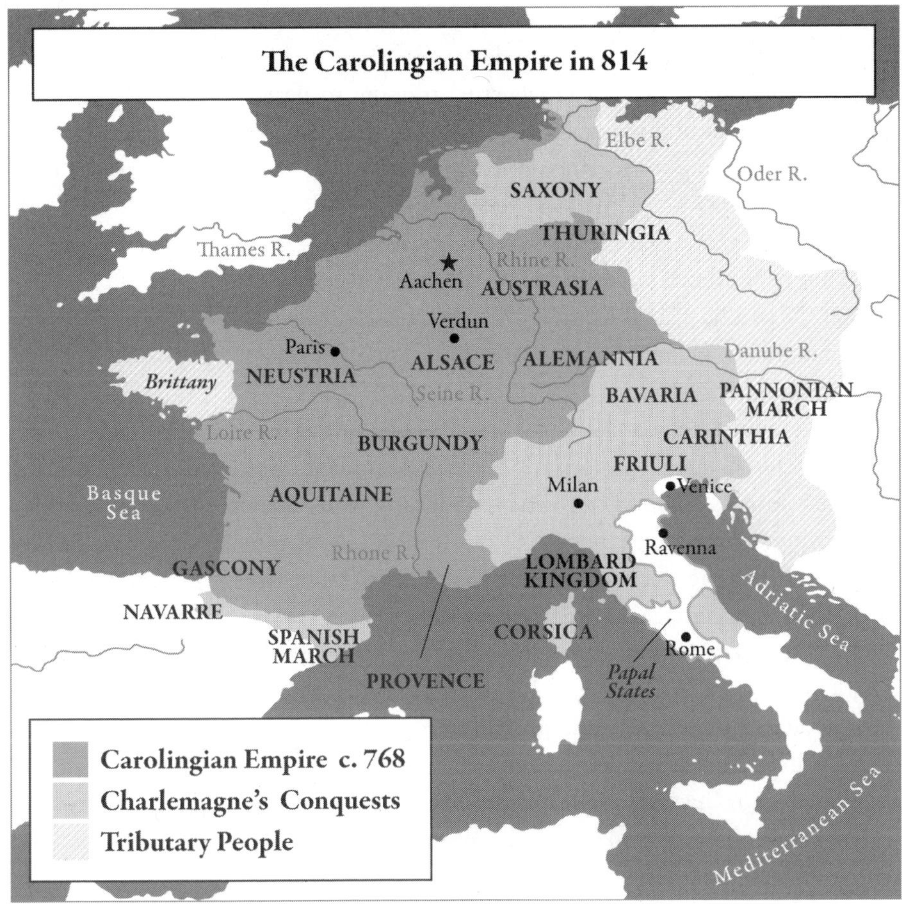

corridor of Spain, and as far east as modern-day Hungary. Most of his campaigns were fought against the Saxons, a Germanic people on the northeastern borders of his Frankish kingdom.

The struggle between the Saxons and Franks lasted for thirty-two years. The fighting had a distressing cycle. Charlemagne would first conquer territories and establish monasteries to convert the inhabitants to Christianity, promote literacy, and cultivate the lands effectively. Then the Saxons would rebel and destroy these monasteries, killing any Frankish settlers. Charlemagne would defeat the Saxons again, sometimes violating truces and resorting to brutal reprisals to punish them. On one occasion, he ordered the mass execution of four thousand Saxon prisoners. Others were forcibly baptized into Christianity despite the objections of the bishops and monks who advised the Frankish king. By the year 800, he had united much of Western Europe under his rule.

Though Charlemagne saw Christianity as an integral part of his growing realm, he had inherited a society whose understanding of Christianity was fragile at best. Clerics frequently lacked the intellectual training to perform their duties. Many had no access to a Bible or missal and could not read even if they did. Such priests mumbled the wrong words when offering Mass and improvised rubrics for the liturgy. Charlemagne was convinced that this situation displeased God and that only a uniform practice of Christianity would peacefully unite the various peoples he ruled. He realized that widespread education was necessary to improve the Frankish Church. When he visited Rome in 774, he received from the pope several texts to guide his efforts, including some writings of Pope Gregory I, a copy of canon law, and the Benedictine Rule.

These works helped shape the royal decree issued by Charlemagne in 789, known as the "General Admonition." In this document, the king described himself as a "new Josiah," a reference to the Jewish king who restored correct observance of the Mosaic Law after a period of corruption (see chapter 6). The parallel was clear: Charlemagne intended to purify lax Frankish practices by enforcing proper ones. The king decried abuses among the clergy, such as not preaching or instructing their congregations or even demanding money in exchange for the sacraments. Charlemagne now ordered Frankish priests to give sermons on Sundays and holydays, to administer the sacraments, and to teach their congregations basic prayers, such as the "Our Father" and psalms. He also insisted that Frankish liturgies be celebrated according to the rubrics of the Roman Rite. For their part, the laity were instructed to observe Sundays as a day of rest, to fast on the appropriate days, and to give alms to the poor.

Charlemagne disseminated such decrees through the *missi dominici* ("messengers of the lord"). These officials travelled in pairs—one knight and one cleric—and ensured that local administrators implemented the laws and reforms of the king. Any assault on them was punished with the same severity as an attack on the king himself. Their work as representatives of the king helped unify royal and local administrations into a more centralized form of government.

Although Charlemagne was eager to reform the Frankish Church at large, he was unwilling to address several compromising aspects of his personal life. He had public relationships with five different concubines and had several illegitimate children. Furthermore, he allowed his daughters to engage in extramarital relationships while refusing to permit them to marry lest a rival dynasty arise. Many clergy, including bishops, lacked the courage to confront him or condemn his behavior.

The clergy were also slow to implement Charlemagne's proposed liturgical reform. It was only in 813, shortly before Charlemagne's death, that Church

Bust of Charlemagne. Made of silver, gold, and precious stones c. 1350. Currently in the Aachen Cathedral Treasury, Aachen, Germany. The reliquary contains parts of Charlemagne's skull. It is considered a masterpiece of silver-gilt, or silver painted over with gold, Gothic metalwork and realistic sculpture.

leaders began holding local synods to implement his decrees. Bishops gradually enforced standard practices for training priests according to the norms found in the Roman liturgical books and emphasized codes of conduct for the clergy. Dioceses were subdivided into parishes, and the people began to observe fast days and holy days of obligation. Such changes laid the groundwork for unified liturgical practice throughout Western Europe.

Charlemagne also recruited international scholars to establish schools and to lead an intellectual renewal. The most prominent of these educators was the English monk Alcuin (735–804). Although he composed some original works, Alcuin displayed greater talents as a teacher and administrator. Together with other intellectuals from Spain and Italy, he constructed a liberal arts curriculum inspired by Roman tradition for Charlemagne's new schools. These reforms contributed to a renaissance (French for "rebirth") of learning in Western Europe.

Charlemagne envisioned his schools not as training centers for careers but as opportunities to deepen the students' faith. Rich and poor, boys and girls, were all encouraged to attend. Of course, in addition to any spiritual benefit, better access to education resulted in better administrators and other officials for his kingdom. Charlemagne himself was an enthusiastic student and learned to speak Latin fluently. He even kept instructional materials under his pillow so that he could practice writing in his rare moments of leisure, but his biographer concluded that he began too late in life to master the skill.

Monasticism also flourished during this time. Reformers like Benedict of Aniane (747–821) spread knowledge of the Benedictine Rule and standardized its practice. The growing number of monasteries served many functions in society: the monks prayed for society's well-being, prepared missionaries to go among pagan Germans, and produced the books necessary to promote both Charlemagne's

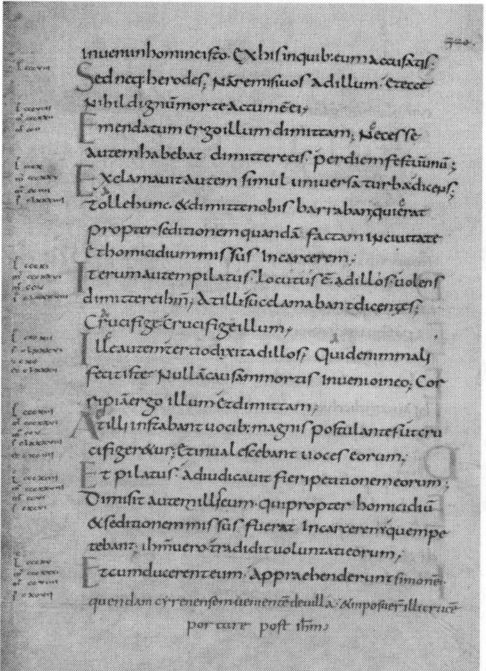

Carolingian Minuscule. Illuminated manuscript made c. 820. Currently "MS Add. 11848 Folio 160v" in the British Library, London, England. This image is from the *Carolingian Gospel Book*. The Latin Vulgate is Luke 23:14–26 during the trial of Jesus with Pilate. The top line reads "[non] inveni in homine isto ex his in quibus eum accusatis" ("I did not find this man guilty of any of your charges against him.")

educational program and his desire for standard liturgical practices in the empire.

We know the names of only a few of these Carolingian monks, but they played a crucial role in the formation of Western Civilization. They developed a standardized script known as Carolingian miniscule. This introduced "miniscule" (non-capitalized or lower-case) lettering, spaces between words, and punctuation symbols. Such innovations were lacking in the earlier Merovingian script and made Carolingian-era books easier to read and to produce.

When preserving manuscripts, the monks' first priority was to reproduce liturgical books and theological treatises, such as the writings of the Church Fathers. Yet, such was their respect for the ancient world that eventually monastic communities copied any ancient text that was available. Mistakes in the Latin grammar suggest that many scribes did not understand the ancient Roman texts they were duplicating, but their efforts preserved these works for later generations.

The **Carolingian Renaissance** was not a movement of great intellectual creativity and invention. Copying texts from earlier ages may seem like an underwhelming leading achievement, but it played a crucial role in preserving the wisdom of the Roman world: an estimated 90 percent of the texts we possess from Roman society can be traced back to a manuscript copied in a Carolingian monastery. To give but one example of their industry, the library at the monastery of Reichenau swelled from fifty books in the year 800 to over a thousand volumes by the year 850. What was more, the monks' tireless efforts to promote learning helped establish a medieval intellectual culture that valued human thought and considered the pursuit of knowledge as an opportunity to glorify God.

The Carolingian "Roman" Empire

Charlemagne had successfully ended the Lombard threat and initiated the Carolingian Renaissance, but the Byzantine iconoclast controversy remained unresolved. The worst of the iconoclast persecution ended with Constantine V's death in 775. His heir, Leo IV (r. 775–780), was not as zealous in punishing iconophiles, but he was furious when he discovered that his wife Irene (750–803) was venerating religious images in the palace. He sentenced her to exile but died shortly thereafter from a sudden fever. While there is no conclusive evidence that Irene was responsible for her husband's death, her later actions made peoples' suspicions of foul play not unreasonable. As her son Constantine VI would later learn, she was ruthless in her efforts at self-preservation. Irene used her husband's death as an opportunity to undo his iconoclast policies. She outwitted her iconoclast enemies in the army by ordering them to campaign against Muslims. Once the army was safely away, she removed its iconoclast officers from power and summoned a council in 787.

Solidus with Irene and Constantine VI. Made of gold c. 792-797 and currently in the Dumbarton Oakes Research Library and Collection, Washington, D.C. This solidus was issued during the period when Irene and Constantine VI were co-rulers of the empire.

The **Second Council of Nicaea** embraced the teachings of John Damascene (c. 675–749), a Christian bureaucrat in the Umayyad government who later retired to become a monk and had written three treatises against Iconoclasm. John had argued that reverence given to an icon—for example, bowing or praying before it—was actually given to the person that the image represented, much like an embrace given to an absent loved one's garment is directed towards the person, not the cloth itself. (A more modern example would be blowing a kiss to a photo of your mother. Your kiss is directed towards your mother, not the pigments and paper of the photo itself.) John thought that Iconoclasm was a return to Docetism and Manichaeanism since it seemingly denied the reality and goodness of Jesus's Incarnation by denying our ability to honor the Incarnate God the Son through physical means.[2] John taught that icons were an affirmation that God had really dwelt among us and had been seen by human

2. Docetism was the belief that God the Son had not become incarnate but only appeared (*dokein* in Greek) to have a human body. We briefly mentioned Manichaeanism in chapter 16 when discussing Augustine of Hippo. It was a dualist religion that held that the material world was created by an evil god. John interpreted Iconoclasm's prohibition of material images to be an echo of Manichaeanism's hostility to physical objects.

eyes and heard by human ears, and this reality is what justified and even necessitated our images of His humanity. Such images were not mere decorations; they taught us through our sense of sight that God the Son had truly become man. Using John's logic, the council fathers concluded that iconoclasts erred when they associated icons with idolatry; rather, the veneration of images was a holy and proper method of worshipping God and showing homage to Him by honoring His saints.

Though the Church would have more ecumenical councils, Nicaea II was the last to address central Christological issues. The Church had for centuries slowly been clarifying her beliefs about Jesus's identity and His divine and human natures, and now she had affirmed these decisions by asserting that the Incarnation could indeed be depicted and reverenced in icons.

Unfortunately, like the preceding councils, the immediate result of Nicaea II was confusion. The Latin translation of the council's teachings appeared to promote idolatry because it blurred the crucial distinction between worship given to Jesus and the respect given to His icons. As Charlemagne and his advisers did not know Greek, they read the Latin translation and were horrified. Charlemagne ordered his theologians to write a refutation of the council's decrees which explained why the worship of images was sinful. The pope attempted to clarify the situation, but the Franks were convinced that the council was heretical. They were also disgruntled that Frankish bishops had not been invited to attend.

Throne of Charlemagne. Made of marble and erected by Charlemagne c. 790. Currently in the Aachen Cathedral, Aachen, Germany.

The Byzantines saw the Frankish response as embarrassingly ignorant. It confirmed their long-held suspicions that the Germanic tribes were unlettered barbarians incapable of understanding complex theological discussions. Byzantines increasingly disassociated themselves from western "barbarian" Christian communities and emphasized the superiority of their own theological formulas and liturgical practices. As the decades progressed, the divide between Eastern and Western Christians grew until they came to see each other's devotions not only as different but also as wrong.

The growing gulf between Eastern and Western Christians was exacerbated by the deepening alliance between the Franks and the popes. Enemies of Pope Leo III (r. 795–816) had accused him of holding office invalidly. (This Leo III is different from the iconoclast Emperor Leo III who had died in 741.) In 800, Charlemagne came to Rome to chair an assembly of bishops and nobility to decide the issue. The gathering announced that they did not have the intention to judge Leo, since they believed that no earthly power could pass sentence on Peter's successor. Instead, the pope took an oath denying the charges. Though Charlemagne did not technically decide the question of Leo's innocence, the entire situation had the appearance that he had authority to determine a pope's legitimacy. This interpretation fit well with an earlier letter Charlemagne had sent to the pope in which the Frank declared that it was his responsibility to both defend and spread Christianity; the pope's role, meanwhile, was merely to pray for the king's military

THE FIRST CENTURIES OF PAPAL LEADERSHIP

The close relationship between Frankish kings and popes ushered in a new era of development in papal authority. The Donation of Pepin laid the practical groundwork for papal political rule in central Italy, even as Charlemagne's coronation at the hands of Pope Leo III intimately associated the papacy with the restored Roman Empire. While this emphasis on an explicitly political role for the papacy was new, the popes of the preceding centuries had not been hesitant to claim their spiritual authority over the Church.

It was apparently in the third century, during a heated debate between Cyprian of Carthage and Pope Stephen I (r. 254-7), that a pope first explicitly invoked Matthew 16:17-19 to justify the papacy's intervention in other dioceses. Cyprian had maintained that those who had been baptized by the schismatic Novatian clergy had not received a valid sacrament and needed to be rebaptized before joining the Catholic Church. Stephen dismissed this position and claimed the authority to recognize such baptisms as valid. It seemed as though a schism would develop between the communities of North Africa and Rome. The outbreak of persecution averted this misfortune, and both Cyprian and Stephen's successor, Pope Sixtus II, died as martyrs.

The fourth and fifth centuries witnessed a further maturing of papal prerogatives. For example, the Council of Serdica in 343–the same council where Athanasius advocated reemphasizing the Nicene Creed as the best defense against "Arianism"–invoked the memory of the Apostle Peter and urged those bishops who believed that they had been wronged to petition the bishop of Rome as the court of last appeal. Several decades later, Pope Damasus wrote to other bishops as "sons" rather than the hitherto traditional "brothers", thereby signifying a not-too-subtle evolution in papal attitude towards other bishops. Innocent I (r. 401-417) considered the papacy to be the supreme law-giver in the Church and understood it as his right and duty to help

John Chrysostom when the latter had been unjustly condemned, despite the fact that the case involved the pope of Alexandria and the see of Constantinople.[3] (Unfortunately, his efforts were not able to rescue John from mistreatment.)

Among the Roman bishops of these first centuries, it was Pope Leo I who possessed the most elevated understanding of papal authority, for he described an almost mystical connection between the Apostle Peter and his successors. For example, Leo held that the Council of Chalcedon ought to accept his *Tome* without debate, for he firmly believed that Peter *always* taught through the popes. That said, Leo was also careful to note that this spiritual connection between the apostle and the bishop of Rome indicated an obligation to serve rather than a right to domination. The popes were, in Leo's thought, custodians of the Apostolic teaching—not innovators or rulers.

Overt clashes between the emperors in Constantinople and the bishops of Rome became more intense in the aftermath of the fall of the Western Roman Empire. The pro-Miaphysite policies of Emperor Anastasius I, for instance, led Pope Gelasius I (r. 492–496) to write a stern rebuke. In this, he reminded the emperor that there were two authorities in the world, the spiritual and the royal. The former, he continued, was the superior, for even an emperor was required to obey priestly authority, particularly that of the bishop of Rome, if he wished to be saved. Though Gelasius's reproach failed to convince Anastasius to change, Pope Hormisdas I (r. 514–523) witnessed the triumph of Gelasius's position when the new emperor, the pro-Chalcedonian Justin I, mandated that the eastern bishops accept a formula of union with the papacy that acknowledged papal primacy and the necessity for Catholics to have communion with the bishop of Rome.

These achievements notwithstanding, respect for papal authority also suffered from self-inflicted wounds. Pope Vigilius (r. 537–555) was an unscrupulous character who engineered the deposition of his predecessor and his own election as pope soon thereafter. When the displaced pope appealed to Emperor Justinian for support, Vigilius promptly exiled his predecessor to an island where he died of malnutrition several months later. Vigilius's pontificate was off to a bad start, and his reputation did not improve. He had accepted money from Empress Theodora in return for his promise to support the Miaphysites. He broke that promise by reaffirming the teachings of Chalcedon, but he did not escape imperial pressure for long. Justinian was eager to placate Miaphysite sensibilities and hoped that a fifth ecumenical council would heal the division. In particular, he intended to secure support for his condemnation of the writings of three theologians who were associated with Nestorius but yet had died in union with the Church. Vigilius initially refused to support the council, despite being arrested and brought to Constantinople. In the end, however, he buckled under imperial pressure and recognized the decisions of the Second Council of Constantinople. Vigilius's recognition of the council, which

3 It was not until the sixth century that the title "pope" became reserved by custom to the bishop of Rome. Previously, some other bishops, most notably that of Alexandria, were also designated by the title "pope." This, however, did not necessarily imply to contemporaries the same level of authority that the title "pope" does for Catholics today.

many in the West (inaccurately) believed had repudiated the Council of Chalcedon, led to several schisms, including one in Italy that lasted for about one hundred and fifty years.

Many regarded the legacy of Vigilius's pontificate as a unsightly stain on the tapestry of papal activity, but Gregory I, one of the greatest popes—perhaps *the* greatest—helped restore the papacy's prestige and moral standing. He asserted that the papal charism was one of both authority and humble service. This is why Gregory criticized the designation "Ecumenical Patriarch" when the Patriarch of Constantinople assumed that title. To Gregory, this claim detracted from other bishops and their authority; in response, he chose to describe himself as *servus servorum Dei* ("servant of the servants of God"). He also permitted a wide range of liturgical practices in order to foster devotion among different populations like the new converts from paganism in England. Furthermore, Gregory's emphasis on the keys promised to Peter in Matthew 16:19 captured the imaginations of recent converts like the Anglo-Saxons. Peter's keys would remained a potent symbol for papal primacy and the necessity of being in communion with Peter even until today.

Since the Church had become the largest single landowner in the West, Gregory mobilized its resources on behalf of those suffering from the Lombard conquests in Italy. This created ties with local communities and established connections of patronage that paralleled those of the old Roman order. In other words, the first foundations for the medieval papacy's political power and influence were being laid. And yet, despite this growing temporal role during Gregory's pontificate, he remained convinced that the pope's authority was spiritual in nature and that he was under the authority of the Byzantine emperor in secular matters. This is why, even though he wrote a scathing letter to Emperor Maurice condemning Maurice's decision to prohibit active soldiers from becoming monks, Gregory still obediently distributed the related imperial edict.

Ironically, it was during an era when many popes were from the East that the split between Roman popes and Byzantine emperors became wider. The condemnation of Pope Honorius, which we discussed in chapter 22, had emphasized the problems that could arise when popes failed to weigh the nuances of a theological argument. Since that time, however, many clergy, monks, and theologians from the East had come to Rome. As these clerics rose to positions of prominence during the seventh and eighth centuries, a number of them became pope. The eastern popes brought a more refined awareness of the convoluted intricacies of theological arguments regarding Miaphysitism, Monoenergism, and Monotheletism. They also introduced eastern devotions and saints, for example Cosmas and Damian, to the Roman liturgy. Nonetheless, they offered staunch resistance when Byzantine emperors attempted to impose Byzantine customs on the Roman Church. For example, when Emperor Justinian II (r. 685–695; 705–711) forbade the pictural representation of Jesus as a lamb, Pope Sergius I (r. 687–701) responded by introducing the invocation *Agnus Dei* ("Lamb of God") into the Roman liturgy. Such acts of resistance to imperial interference contributed to the eventual re-alignment of the papacy away from the Byzantine Empire and toward the Franks of the West.

victories and to obey Church law. It appeared that the bishop of Rome had merely exchanged Byzantine interference for Frankish meddling.

To make the matter more complex, on Christmas Day of that same year, Leo crowned Charlemagne "Emperor of the Romans." The motives surrounding this coronation are unclear. Had Charlemagne demanded this from Leo in exchange for supporting the pope against his enemies? Or was Leo attempting to reclaim his independence by asserting his ability to grant the title "emperor" to Charlemagne? While we cannot be sure if either of these motives is accurate, subsequent generations understood that the popes had claimed the authority to bestow the title of Roman emperor in the West. Future candidates could not claim the title of emperor, regardless of how much land they controlled, until a pope had crowned them as such.

For his part, Charlemagne saw himself as a Christian King David attempting to create a Christian empire that would bring about Augustine's vision of a City of God. Ironically, even though Augustine had emphasized that the City of God was distinct from any earthly realm, Charlemagne (and his successors) embraced the notion of sacred kingship and saw the restored Roman Empire as having a spiritual character in addition to a temporal one. To the new emperor, the Carolingian state and the Church worked together, just like the knight and the cleric worked side-by-side as *missi dominici*. What was more, Charlemagne firmly believed that the spiritual realm was greater than the worldly. We might even say that the medieval society that subsequently arose after his empire was a *spiritual* society due to the prominence and centrality of its religious belief.

The result of Charlemagne's vision was a profound shift from the ancient world. Whereas many ancient rulers had focused on the temporal world and used religion to help their political aims, Charlemagne and his successors recognized that religious faith is not simply a political tool or an individual choice. Rather, one's beliefs have profound ramifications for society as a whole, and Charlemagne and those who ruled after him saw it as part of their duties to preserve the well-being of society by actively promoting Christian morals. In the process, they were effectively replacing what we called in chapter 16 the ancient "State-Church" with a medieval "Church-State" in which the spiritual was recognized as having primacy but was also affected by the temporal order. This developing "Church-State" vision had advantages, but it also brought challenges. In particular, monarchs (including Charlemagne) believed that their political authority participated in this spiritual realm (as when Charlemagne forced the Saxons to convert to Christianity). As we will see in future chapters, this would lead to a bitter contest between the popes and emperors.

Meanwhile, papal coronation did not improve the Byzantine opinion of Charlemagne. They rejected him as an imposter, but they had their own problems.

Irene had blinded her son Constantine VI when he attempted to govern without her influence. She now claimed authority as empress, but Charlemagne and others argued that the imperial office could only be held by a man and was therefore vacant. When reports circulated that Charlemagne and Irene might marry to reunite the Roman Empire, the Byzantines took matters into their own hands and forced Irene to abdicate in 802.

Irene's overthrow set in motion a period of Byzantine decline in the early ninth century. As imperial armies began to lose battles and territory, Iconoclasm revived among the soldiers. Several more iconoclast emperors came to power, but this second stage of Iconoclasm soon passed. Theodora, another icon-loving empress, came to power after the death of her husband and restored the veneration of images in 843. This final victory over Iconoclasm is still celebrated every year among Eastern Catholics and Orthodox on the First Sunday of Lent, which is known as the Feast of Orthodoxy.

In the West, Charlemagne's empire faced its own challenges in the decades after 800. Even though he was now Roman emperor, Charlemagne remained a Frank in his mentality: his roles as Roman emperor, king of the Franks, and king of the Lombards were all distinct. He apparently never considered merging his authority into a single, imperial power. That explains why he continued to divide newly gained territories among his warriors in return for their faithful service and bestowed upon them the titles of margrave or count. As long as Charlemagne continued to conquer new lands, the Frankish nobles remained united and loyal to him. Even so, by the time Charlemagne died in 814 at the age of seventy-two, fragmentation was setting in: Frankish nobles were claiming territories as their own possessions rather than holding them as rewards from their king. Without Charlemagne's force of personality and military leadership, the empire started to fall apart.

Charlemagne's heir was his one surviving legitimate son, **Louis the Pious** (r. 814–840). Louis earned his epithet by quickly dismissing concubines and others of dubious character from his court and surrounding himself with priests and monks. These advisers encouraged him to promote monasticism and the Carolingian Renaissance. They also supported his decision to have Carolingian succession follow the Roman system of having one primary heir instead of the Frankish system of partible inheritance among multiple heirs. Thus, even though he had three sons, Louis named his eldest son as his imperial successor in 817. The other two received much smaller territories.

Everyone involved seems to have accepted this situation until Louis himself changed his will in 829. Louis had married again after his first wife's death, and he doted on the son of this second marriage. He decided to revert to the Frankish system of partible inheritance so that this youngest child would also receive lands.

Louis's older sons were outraged at their father's change of heart and soon took up arms to fight against their father and each other. The next ten years were dominated by civil war and ever-shifting alliances. Louis watched in anguish as the mighty Carolingian military tore itself and the empire apart. Even after Louis's death in 840, his sons continued to war among themselves. The worst of their encounters was in central France at Fontenoy; according to one source, that single battle claimed the lives of forty thousand soldiers.

Charles the Bald receiving the Vivian Bible. Illuminated miniature made c. 845 and commissioned by Count Vivian of Tours. Currently "Ms. Latin 1 folio 423r" in the National Library of France, Paris, France. This image is from the *Vivian Bible* and shows Count Vivian (left) presenting the Bible as a gift to Charles the Bald (seated in center) when Charles visited the church of Saint Martin de Tours in 846.

Finally, in 843, the surviving rivals sought peace and agreed to the terms of the **Treaty of Verdun**. Charlemagne's former empire was divided into three parts. The oldest son, Lothar (r. 840–855), received Middle Frankia consisting of Italy, the Rhine Valley, and modern-day Belgium and the Netherlands. His brother Louis the German (r. 843–876), received East Frankia, which included much of modern-day Germany. Their half-brother, Charles the Bald (r. 840–877), received West Frankia. This treaty shaped the future history of Europe. West Frankia became the kingdom of France, and East Frankia formed the basis of the German-speaking regions of Europe. Middle Frankia, divided and weakened by its own mountains and rivers, experienced repeated attacks from its two larger neighbors and ultimately fragmented into smaller sections within a century of its creation.

Conclusion

Charlemagne's reign was remembered in the medieval imagination as a "golden age" of security and prosperity, and subsequent rulers wished to link their authority with his example. Even when, as we will see, emperors disputed with popes, they still desired to receive the imperial crown from papal hands because that was what

THE CAROLINGIAN ARMY

The Carolingian army typically waged a campaign every year during the summer months. Rulers like Charlemagne summoned Frankish freemen to muster shortly after Easter and punished with death those who failed to respond. The frequency of their military operations, combined with the necessity to participate in them, created a core of highly experienced veterans who were crucial to the expansion and defense of the Carolingian lands.

The bulk of the army was made up of levies of peasant infantry. Each local noble was expected to supply their levies with spears and shields. Though the Franks did not generally use Byzantine coin, the cost of this equipment was approximately two Byzantine *solidi*. (For point of reference, a cow was typically valued at three *solidi*.)

Nobles formed the elite units of the Carolingian army. Charlemagne typically fought alongside a group of young nobles whom he provided with arms, armor, food, and lodging at the court. These advantages encouraged the nobles to demonstrate their loyalty and military prowess in the hope that the king would make them counts and grant them their own lands.

Reconstruction of Carolingian solider from Aachen City Hall, Aachen, Germany.

Counts who held land were expected to invest the wealth they gained from their holdings in their own weapons and armor. Therefore, they arrived at the muster armed with a sword, which would cost approximately three *solidi*, as well as a spear and shield, a horse, and a suit of chain mail armor. The armor was by far the most expensive military item, costing as much as forty-four *solidi*. A count who arrived at the muster without armor could be deprived of his lands. Charlemagne underlined the high value the Carolingians placed on chain mail by forbidding merchants to export the steel that was used to make armor. He both wanted it for his own soldiers and sought to restrict opposing armies' access to it.

Another important ingredient for the Carolingians' victories seems to have been their mobility. Contrary to popular imagination, they had not yet developed the stirrup. (This technology would enable later generations of knights to hold themselves in place during the shock of a charge.) Nonetheless, Carolingians still used horses to move swiftly and catch their opponents by surprise.

Carts carrying food for three months also joined the muster at the beginning of the campaign. These, too, enhanced the speed of Carolingian armies as soldiers did not have to delay as they foraged for provisions. Bringing their own supplies had the added benefit of not alienating local populations by seizing their resources. Though we do not typically associate armor, mobility, and compulsory military service with education and spiritual ideals, without the strength of his army, Charlemagne's great reforms would never have been able to take root within his realm.

Charlemagne had done. And yet, that very act had its own uncertain meaning. Did the pope confer the crown because the papacy was above the empire? Or did the emperor undergo the ceremony to demonstrate how he was the head of both the temporal and religious spheres?

We must emphasize here that neither Charlemagne nor the popes thought in our modern terms of "Church" and (a secular) "State." Rather, as noted above, Charlemagne saw the spiritual and political as firmly intertwined. Such had been the common perspective in ancient societies stretching back to Mesopotamia and the god-kings of Egypt. Even Christian rulers like Constantine retained this perspective; that is why Roman emperors in Byzantium so frequently intervened (or interfered) in ecumenical councils and in other religious affairs. Their understanding of Christianity's relationship with the political realm was rooted in the ancient assumption that religious belief and political well-being were intimately associated. (This is why, as we discussed in chapter 16, Augustine's proposed separation of the temporal and spiritual spheres in *The City of God* was such a revolutionary idea.) Charlemagne retained this attitude but shifted the emphasis. The political and religious still formed one unity, but it was a "Church-State" rather than the reverse; in other words, though Charlemagne saw his own role as touching upon both spiritual and political spheres, he also maintained that spiritual concerns were more important than the temporal order.

The assumption that spiritual and political authority were interconnected laid the groundwork for ever more challenging questions concerning the relationship between popes and monarchs in Western Europe. Each new situation forced them to consider more deeply just what their relationship implied. Could political authority legislate Christian belief? Could it force unbelievers to accept baptism? Did the king have the right to appoint bishops, especially when they were motivated or corrupted by political ambitions? Was the ruler still subject to all the disciplines of the Church, or was he above its moral laws? Could the Church truly be catholic, that is "universal," when its policies reflected the ambitions of a given ruler? These questions and the various answers offered to them would shape medieval history.

CHAPTER 24

Fiefs and Vassals

By the Lord before whom this sanctuary is holy, I will to N. be faithful and true, and love all which he loves and shun all that he shuns, according to the laws of God and the order of the world. Nor will I ever with will or action, through word or deed, do anything which is unpleasing to him, on condition that he will hold to me as I shall deserve it, and that he will perform everything as it was in our agreement when I submitted myself to him and chose his will.

Anglo-Saxon Oath of Fealty[1]

During the tenth and eleventh centuries, many European warriors swore oaths of fealty to powerful lords or even to their king himself. In return for these pledges of loyalty and service, they became vassals and received the authority to govern a specific land, or fief. This exchange of land for service was at the core of **feudalism**, a type of society that emphasized the duties of personal relationships and that became prominent in parts of Europe during the centuries after Charlemagne.

Trust that members of society would fulfill their promises was crucial for feudalism. To ensure that people kept their word, oaths, like the epigraph above, acquired explicitly sacred qualities. Individuals promised God that they would uphold their commitments to their lord or vassal, and the saints were invoked as witnesses—often by swearing one's fealty while in the presence of a saint's relic. The consequences for violating one's pledge also gained spiritual significance; oath-breakers would answer for their infidelity to God Himself. This conscious effort to integrate God into the feudal order became one of the most striking characteristics of medieval culture.

1 E. P. Cheyney, trans., *Translations and Reprints from the Original Sources of European History*, vol. 4 (Philadelphia: University of Pennsylvania, 1898), 3–5.

In this chapter we explore how the breakdown of social order in the ninth and tenth centuries encouraged the rise of such feudal relationships. The civil war among Charlemagne's grandsons, which we discussed in chapter 23, encouraged the collapse of Carolingian society, as did the arrival of powerful new adversaries who raided Britain, France, and Germany. Local nobles took advantage of the chaos to pursue their own interests. Violence became endemic. To make matters worse, the Church entered its own period of turmoil as corruption infected the highest offices in the ecclesiastical hierarchy. Both politically and spiritually, these centuries stand alongside the darkest Europe had ever faced.

The Coming of the Vikings

Among those who attacked Carolingian lands were the pagan raiders from Scandinavia known as **Vikings** or Norsemen. Unfortunately, we know little about early Scandinavian history. Scholars even debate the origin of the English term "Viking." Nonetheless, historians believe that we can reconstruct certain characteristics of their culture.

Nordic society was predominately agrarian. Most were farmers who also engaged, part-time as it were, in piracy. They valued bravery and honor and sought to be known as a *drengr*. This term originally meant a solitary rock standing in the sea, but it came to designate someone who possessed great, even reckless, courage. Such courage was necessary to confront whatever fate had in store for a person. According to Norse belief, you could do nothing to change when you were destined to die, but you could choose to face death bravely.

The concept of fate also permeates the surviving myths of Nordic culture. Even Viking gods must face their destiny, and many will meet their deaths at *Ragnorak*, a future cataclysmic struggle between the gods and their enemies. The king of these Norse deities was the one-eyed Odin, who hung himself on the mystical tree Yggdrasil at the center of the universe for nine days in order to learn wisdom. Other well-known gods included Thor, whose name means thunder; Loki, a trickster who often allied with the gods' enemies; and Freya, a goddess often associated with love, fertility, and war. Some Norse deities even remain in our common day-to-day vocabulary: "Wednesday" derives from "Odin's day," while "Thursday" and "Friday" honor Thor and Freya, respectively.

Norse concepts of the afterlife reflected their belief in fate and their desire to be a *drengr*. Whereas most dead entered Hel, a land without joy, others—those who fell fearlessly in battle—went to Valhalla. There they feasted with the gods, fought each other, and awaited *Ragnorak*. This understanding of the afterlife encouraged Viking men to fight when possible; if they were fated to die that day, it was better to die violently than to go to Hel.

An important feature of Viking society was the public gathering known as a *thing*. These meetings served many functions, including the collective acceptance of a new king, the promulgation of laws, and even the sale of land. Local chieftains and their *thingmen*, or retainers, attended these gatherings and voted to decide important matters.

While men were prominent at *things*, Norse women were not without their own authority. Unlike the women of ancient Rome, Scandinavian wives and daughters could own land in their own name, and the wealthiest tombs excavated by archeologists have belonged to women. Furthermore, Norse belief associated women with magic and prophecy. They thus had an important role in religious rituals, though it does not appear that the Vikings ever developed a priesthood.

In the summer months, many Scandinavian men left their homes seeking glory and wealth before returning to harvest their crops at the end of the growing season. Their navigational and shipbuilding skills enabled them to be among history's most successful explorers. They traveled east to modern-day Russia, south to Constantinople, and westward to Iceland and even to North America. Those in Russia established extensive trading networks with the Slavs and Byzantines, but Vikings are best remembered for their raids into Western Europe.

Tjängvide Image Stone. Made of limestone c. 700–900. Currently in the Swedish Museum of National Antiquities in Stockholm, Sweden. An image stone is an ornately carved slab of stone raised as a memorial to a deceased person but generally not placed beside graves. This particular stone is from Viking-era Scandinavia and shows a Viking longship on the bottom half.

Several factors likely contributed to the rise of the Viking attacks that began at the end of the eighth century. During this period, Norse kings were consolidating their power and frequently banished potential rivals. Many of these exiles sought their fortunes in ever-further voyages. Scandinavian lands could yield only so much food due to the harsh climate and rocky terrain, so the growing Norse population meant that these adventurers had a steady supply of men eager to join their expeditions in the hopes of improving their fortunes. Meanwhile, Charlemagne's successes against the Frisians to the north of his empire brought the Franks into contact with the Vikings. Although their initial interactions likely focused on trade, the line between trading and raiding for the Norse was thin, and their presence in Frankish lands became increasingly aggressive as Carolingian power waned.

Monasteries were a frequent objective. These institutions were isolated, vulnerable, and contained altar vessels and other precious objects. Furthermore, the Vikings realized that most men who lived there were woefully incompetent warriors. Bands of thirty to sixty marauders struck these sites quickly and without warning.

The first target of the Vikings' European raids was the eastern coast of England. The great monastery of Lindisfarne was destroyed in 793; others soon followed. The monks were either killed or taken as slaves. Viking raids along the English coast increased in frequency until they became a struggle for outright conquest in 850. Fifteen years later, the Vikings assembled the so-called "Great Army" and inflicted one defeat after another against the Anglo-Saxon defenders. Finally, in 878, the last remaining Saxon king, Alfred of Wessex (r. 871–899), rallied his remaining soldiers and withdrew into marshland to regroup. Later that year, he led the Saxons to a great victory over their Viking enemy at the Battle of Edington. The Viking king agreed to accept baptism and to rule the north and east of England while Alfred governed the rest as king of the Anglo-Saxons.

"Alfred the Great" is considered the first king of England because his predecessors had ruled only portions of the Anglo-Saxon world. (Alfred himself was originally just the king of Wessex, that is, the land of the "West Saxons.") Alfred established the tradition of a powerful English navy that could protect the island from foreign attacks. Perhaps more importantly, he also supported the recovery of learning. Many monastic centers of education had been destroyed, and Alfred set about to restore a culture of literacy in his kingdom. Furthermore, he was a pious Christian and kept a book of the Psalms with him throughout his reign to meditate on in times of both failure and success. His reform of Anglo-Saxon laws reflected his piety and knowledge of Scripture. For over a century, Alfred's descendants continued to rule much of England, fostering a revival of Benedictine monasticism and keeping in check the threat of Viking conquest.

The Travails of West and East Frankia

England emerged from the Viking invasions in a relatively stable condition, but the same could not be said for the nearby kingdom of West Frankia. Its long, exposed coastline and rivers presented a wide array of potential destinations. The fact that Viking long ships, with their shallow draft, could navigate rivers far upstream made their raids impossible to anticipate and added to their terror. As Carolingian kings could not predict where they would attack, the Vikings could often withdraw before any adequate response was mustered. The results could be disastrous even when Frankish soldiers confronted the raiders. In 845, on Easter Sunday, the Vikings sacked West Frankia's capital city of Paris. To add to the horror, they hanged over one hundred defending Franks as a sacrifice to Odin.

The inability of Carolingian rulers to defend their people accelerated the breakdown of their authority and the rise of feudal relationships. Rural populations now looked to local leaders, often known as dukes or counts, for protection rather than to the king and his soldiers. These regional nobles promised to provide a more immediate response to any threat. Many began to build strongholds for protection. These constructions were technically a violation of royal authority, but the same kings who could not stop Viking raids were also powerless to prevent their warriors from establishing independent areas within their realm.

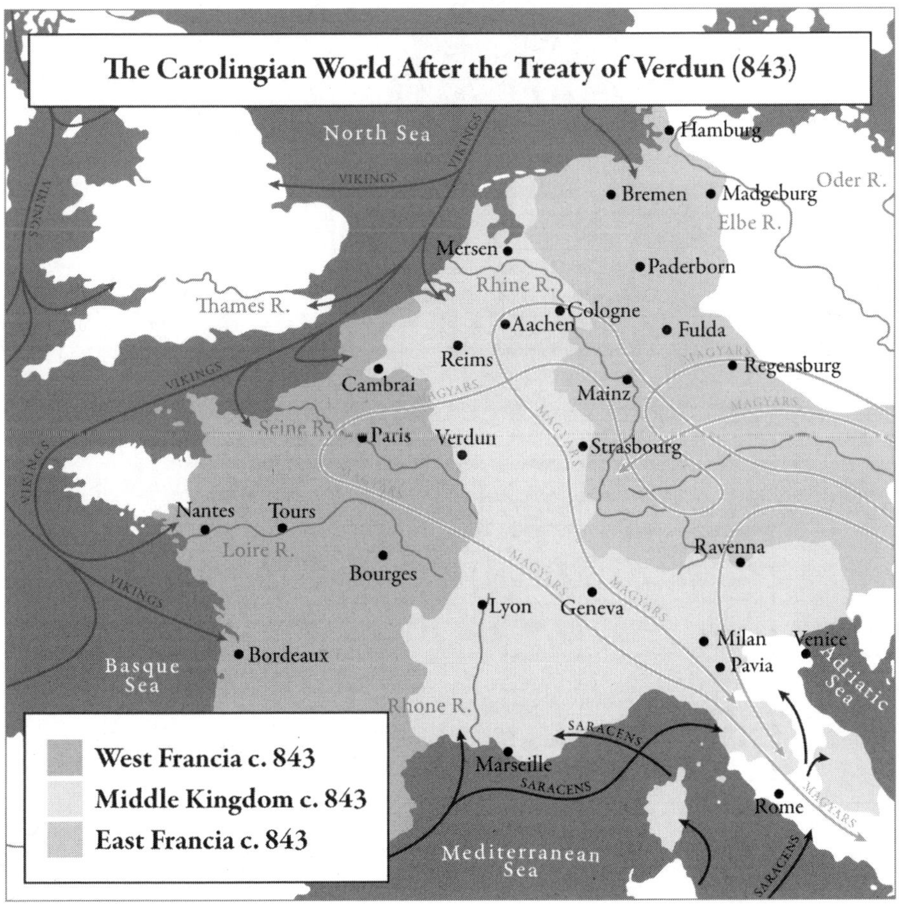

These early castles were built from earth and timber. Though not as strong as later stone fortifications, these structures, known as a **motte and bailey**, still provided protection. What was more, the required materials were inexpensive, readily available, and did not require skilled labor. Fifty people could complete one motte and bailey in about six weeks. The motte, or keep, was the castle stronghold, while the bailey provided a protected space for villagers to shelter with their animals. From these places of security, defenders could defy their attackers until help arrived or their enemy lifted the siege.

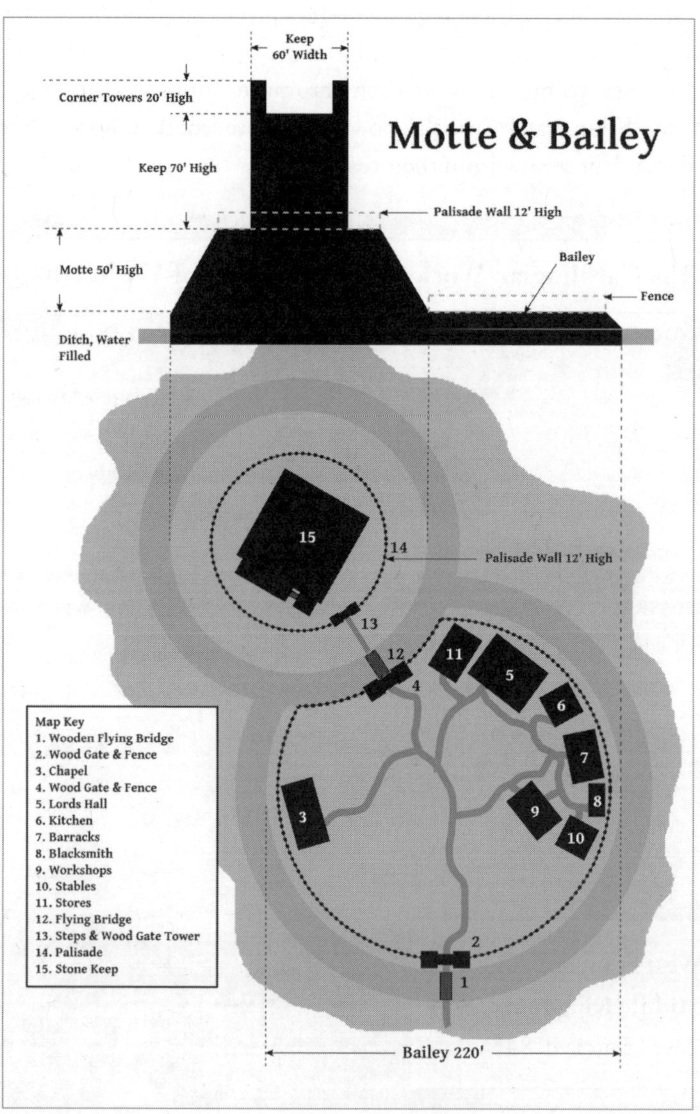

Secure in their new fortifications, nobles were soon tempted to raid the lands of those who were less powerful. Franks marched against each other, attacking and then withdrawing into their own fortifications if anything threatened them in return. These warlords recognized no overlord or law, and West Frankia became increasingly violent even when there were no Viking raids to repel.

The feudal system was an attempt to restore order to this desperate situation. Kings in Paris agreed to acknowledge the nobles' effective control of the land in exchange for recognition of their (often-theoretical) royal supremacy and a commitment to provide military service when summoned. A ritual developed to confirm this relationship: The one pledging service, the vassal, came to the residence of the lord, the one granting authority over the land. The vassal approached bareheaded and weaponless and swore to be faithful to the lord as "his man," sometimes while holding a saint's relic. In return, the lord gave his new vassal some earth as a symbol of his fief, that is, the land granted in exchange for service.

This lord-vassal relationship became the model for different tiers of society in the developing feudal system. Nobles subdivided the fief they received from the king among their own warriors. These men, known as knights, swore to serve faithfully in exchange for the land and those who worked it. The knights, in turn, established a similar relationship with their serfs. These peasants farmed the land that surrounded the villages where they were born. Their status was typically hereditary and passed to their children, who were also expected to farm in the same area. Serfs provided their knight and his household, or manor, with food. In return, they were leased strips of land which they could cultivate for their own use. They also pastured any animals on village common land. Historians refer to this arrangement as **manorialism**.

The feudal world was far from perfect. Lords could mistreat their vassals; knights could abuse their serfs. Furthermore, violence remained commonplace. Nonetheless, feudalism established bonds of trust and honor that clearly identified those who violated their oaths. This broadly acknowledged standard of behavior eventually fostered effective methods to curb the worst abuses.

The Vikings provide a good example of this gradual stabilization. After years of terrorizing West Frankia, one of their leaders, Rollo, converted to Christianity in 911 and became the vassal of the king in return for a section of northwestern France. He even agreed to defend his new fief against other Norse raiders. Rollo's "northmen" came to be known as Normans, and his land received the name of Normandy. They were certainly still violent, but the worst chaos of the preceding decades was over. As we will see in the next chapter, the Normans also played an important role in the formation of multiple regions of medieval Europe.

East Frankia did not have a long, exposed coastline and thus did not suffer from prolonged Viking incursions as did Britain and West Frankia. Instead, it was menaced by a threat from the Asian steppes. In 862, the **Magyars**, ancestors of today's Hungarians, first appeared along the borders of East Frankia. Once again, we know very little about this people's early history. Early Magyars left behind no surviving written records, and those who did write about the Magyars often misleadingly associated the nomadic horse riders with previous peoples in history.

Magyar paganism apparently involved the veneration of ancestors and horses, as well as belief in a "world tree" that connected the sky, the earth, and the land under the earth. In ritual, it was shamanistic, a shaman (known as a *taltos* in Hungarian) being a person who served as a medium from this world to another. The shaman usually entered a trance in which he claimed to receive knowledge and messages from a spiritual realm.

Their society consisted of a coalition of tribes, each of which had its own duke. (Although the Magyars spoke a Finno-Ugric language, our term "Hungarian" derives from the Turkic word *Onogur* or "ten tribes.") By the time they appeared in East Frankia, the Magyars also had two kings who technically ruled over all the tribes, but it appears that this authority was largely nominal. The raids that the Magyars inflicted upon the East Franks, for example, indicated a decentralized society where warbands followed individual leaders rather than a king's grand strategy.

These attacks were nonetheless devastating. While Vikings certainly destroyed communities and set monasteries afire, the Magyars seemed to have delighted in being thorough in their destruction. Contemporary accounts indicate that the Magyars burned every village they encountered and spared only young women and children, whom they enslaved. The rest they left as mounds of corpses.

As we saw with West Frankia, the arrival of pagan marauders upset the fragile Carolingian world. By the early tenth century, the Magyars had inflicted a number of defeats and had even raided into West Frankia and Italy! Local nobles, rather than the kings themselves, were once again more effective at defending the land against raids. Their exploits helped them establish greater independence from the Carolingian ruler, and power in the realm coalesced in the hands of the five most influential dukes. These nobles ruled the lands of Franconia, Bavaria, Swabia, Saxony, and Lotharingia.

East Frankia entered a new stage in its history when its last Carolingian ruler died in 911. The five dukes promptly claimed the authority to elect future rulers of East Frankia and chose a new king from among their own number. At first, they chose the *weakest* candidate among themselves because they desired to retain as much independence as possible. This shortsighted policy did nothing to alleviate

The **Imperial Crown of the Holy Roman Empire**. Made of gold and precious stones c. 962. Currently in the Imperial Treasury at the Hofburg in Vienna, Austria. Beginning in the eleventh century, rulers of the reconstituted Roman Empire claimed the title "king of the Romans" until their imperial coronation. This was the crown that was used in those coronations from the time of Otto I until 1806, when Emperor Francis II (r. 1792-1806) effectively dissolved the Holy Roman Empire in response to the victories of Napoleon Bonaparte.

Magyar raids, so the nobles decided that their next king should be the most powerful among them. Their choice was Henry of Saxony (r. 918–936). He enjoyed dominance largely because of a recently discovered silver mine in Saxony that enabled him to fund an army that could resist the Magyars. When Henry died in 936, the other nobles, still desiring a powerful protector, elected his son **Otto I** (r. 936–973) as his successor.

Otto was already an experienced general by the time he ascended the throne, and he defeated the Magyars at the Battle of Lechfeld in 955 despite being badly outnumbered. This victory effectively ended the Magyar threat. The defeated raiders ultimately settled in the region of modern-day Hungary and within a century had converted to Christianity and established their own kingdom.

The victory at Lechfeld dramatically increased Otto's prestige, and he desired to associate himself with the imperial legacy of Charlemagne. The problem, of course, was that Otto was "king of the Franks" and no emperor. The popes had initially continued to bestow the title of "Roman emperor" on one of Charlemagne's descendants, but no one had received the imperial crown since 924. Such was the situation when the pope entreated Otto to come to Italy and defend him from his rivals. Otto jumped at the chance. This was an opportunity to imitate Charlemagne as a defender of the papacy and, in turn, to receive the crown as Roman emperor. The pious Otto, however, was about to discover just how low the papacy had fallen.

Papal Controversy and Corruption

Rome had been suffering its own turmoil. In 827, Muslim soldiers from Algeria began their conquest of Sicily, a strategic center for transportation in the region. Though it would be decades before they controlled the entire island, those ports in Muslim hands became staging points for raids along the nearby coasts of Italy, France, and Spain. They even sacked St. Peter's Basilica in 846. Three years later, an Italian coalition summoned by the pope defeated a Muslim fleet at the Battle of Ostia. The immediate threat of Muslim invasion receded, but the popes soon had other concerns to occupy their attention.

Nicholas I (r. 858–867) sought to assert the pope's position of leadership as the Carolingian order broke apart. He emphasized his authority to adjudicate disputes

among bishops in the West. He also upheld the Church's teachings on the indissolubility of marriage and refused to allow Frankish rulers to divorce their wives as many had previously done.

Unfortunately, during his reign a brief, but historically significant, division arose between the Roman and Byzantine Churches. There were several factors involved in this relatively short-lived schism. The immediate issue was a dispute about the current patriarch of Constantinople. In 863, the Emperor Michael III (r. 842–867) deposed the current patriarch, Ignatius (c. 798–877), and replaced him with the lay scholar **Photius** (810–891). Ignatius had condemned the scandalous behavior at court, and Michael desired a new patriarch who would be less forthright in upholding the Church's teachings on marriage. Photius promptly received ordination and was consecrated as bishop, but Pope Nicholas was outraged at Ignatius's removal and refused to acknowledge Photius as a valid priest.

Wrapped up with this issue was the conversion of the pagans in Eastern Europe. As the Slavs and Bulgars began to seek instruction in Christianity, Roman, Byzantine, and Frankish missionaries competed with one another to be the dominant influence. Photius, for example, had sent the missionaries Cyril and Methodius to the Slavic kingdom of Moravia in 863. These two brothers developed a way to write Slavic and even translated the Greek liturgy into that language. Unfortunately, the conversion of Slavs and Bulgars soon took on a political dimension as the pope, Franks and Byzantines competed to establish cultural and ecclesiastical authority over the different regions. Photius's disputed status became an opportunity to criticize the other side's missionaries.

In 867, the embattled Photius held a council that claimed that the pope was deposed. Among the reasons for this decision were two liturgical "abuses": the Roman Church used unleavened bread in the celebration of the Holy Eucharist, and she permitted the addition of the *Filioque* clause to the Nicene Creed. (For the *Filioque* clause, see chapter 22.) These differences in custom had generally been overlooked by previous generations, but they now became prominent points of contention. (Some historians, like Christopher Dawson, have suggested that the Churches first drifted apart culturally and only later emphasized theological reasons, such as Photius's denunciation of the *Filioque* clause, to justify their distanced relationship.)

Eventually a council met in Constantinople in 869 and restored Ignatius as the patriarch. This Fourth Council of Constantinople was the first ecumenical council that did not address any pressing question of Christology. It thus set a precedent for an ecumenical council to focus primarily on issues of discipline and practice rather than doctrine. Though Photius died in union with Rome, his earlier attacks on Western liturgical practice set an important, and tragic, precedent for future controversies.

The decades after this council saw the popes face increased pressure both from Muslim raids and from local nobles who desired to control Rome and the papacy. Perhaps the most shocking example of political interference was the Cadaver Synod of 897. Pope Formosus (r. 891–896) had opposed a certain political faction, but his enemies had their revenge after his death when one of their own became pope. The new successor to St. Peter exhumed Formosus's body and placed the skeleton on trial. The synod found Formosus unworthy of the pontificate, and any priestly ordinations he had conferred were proclaimed invalid. They ceremonially stripped his skeleton of its papal vestments, cut off the three fingers of his right hand used to bless, and threw his body into the Tiber. Some subsequent popes condemned the ghastly synod, but Pope Sergius III (r. 904–911) reaffirmed the trial for political reasons. The result was that the validity of Formosus's priestly and episcopal ordinations remained an open question for years as a result of the contradictory papal rulings.

Violence and irreverence became the norm as the rivalry continued among nobles and the popes they controlled. Of the next eighteen popes after Formosus, two were deposed and three were murdered. One had been previously stripped of his orders, and others were reputed to be murderers and adulterers.

When Otto arrived in Rome in 962, the pope was the infamous John XII (r. 955–964). He had become pope in his late teens or early twenties when his noble father

The Cadaver Synod by Jean-Paul Laurens. Oil on canvas c. 1870. Currently in the Nantes Museum of Arts in Nantes, France.

forced the Romans to accept him as their bishop. Sources claim he performed ordinations while in the stables preparing for hunting trips, arranged the assassinations of those who reproved him, and frequently committed acts of fornication and adultery.

John crowned Otto as Roman emperor in exchange for his assistance in waging war against John's enemies. Otto was horrified by the pope's lifestyle and, before leaving on campaign, exhorted him to reform his ways. This disapproval worried John, and he began planning an alliance with the Magyars to attack the new emperor. Otto moved more swiftly than John and summoned a council that declared John deposed and elected a new pope in his place. Once the emperor left, John returned to Rome with an army and executed or mutilated those of his enemies he could capture. He declared his deposition invalid and reclaimed his position as the bishop of Rome.[2] According to one tradition, he met his death when a nobleman threw him out of a window after finding the pope committing adultery with his wife.

This legacy of papal corruption can be a difficult one for modern Catholics to face. For those expecting the pope to be a moral exemplar, it can be shocking to learn that popes like John XII have lived so scandalously. Such behavior, of course, is distressing, but apostolic succession does not guarantee that a given bishop or pope will be a worthy successor to the apostles. Nor does the Church's teaching on infallibility claim that the Holy Spirit protects the bishop of Rome from all error or temptation. As we learned during our discussion on Pope Honorius I, infallibility only applies to formal papal teachings on matters of faith and morals. Popes can be in error both in their personal lives and in their informal teaching as private theologians.

Political decentralization and papal corruption not only weakened the authority of the kings of West Frankia but also contributed to the corruption of the Christian clergy. This decline was especially obvious in monasteries. Frequently, local nobles appointed abbots because of their loyalty as warriors rather than for any spiritual considerations. Many of these abbots did not reside with their communities and were not even monks. Instead, they simply used the revenue from their monastery's lands to enrich themselves.

In 910, Duke William of Aquitaine (875–918), fearing his violent life deserved God's judgment, established a monastery to offer continual prayers for his soul. He chose the monk Berno (850–927) to serve as abbot on account of his reputation as someone who actually lived his monastic vocation. William entrusted the new

2 Otto's replacement, Leo VIII (r. 963/4–965), is sometimes described as an antipope, but the *Annuario Pontifico*, an official Vatican directory that was first published in 1912, includes a list of popes that recognizes Leo VIII's reign as beginning after John XII had died and after John's immediate successor, Benedict V (r. 964), had resigned at Otto's insistence. Leo VIII does not appear to have been formally re-elected or reinstalled as pontiff.

abbey at **Cluny** to the protection of the apostles Peter and Paul and gave it the right to elect its abbot without the potentially corrupting influence of temporal rulers.

The monks of Cluny faithfully lived the Benedictine Rule, and their community grew rapidly under the leadership of pious and capable abbots. People became convinced that the prayers of these Cluniac monks were especially pleasing to God, and in time nobles throughout Western Europe requested monks from Cluny to come and reform the monasteries in their lands. In this way, a Cluniac reform of monasticism steadily spread. Eventually, the monks constructed an enormous abbey church, which remained the largest church in Western Europe until the seventeenth century when the current St. Peter's Basilica was finished in Rome. Tragically, today there are few remains from Cluny's massive church.

Cluny and its daughter-houses became oases of peace and shelter for the sick and homeless in the violent landscape of Early Medieval Europe. Moreover, their unapologetically rigorous lifestyle attracted many from warrior backgrounds. These nobles and soldiers were attracted to the emphasis on the liturgical life and saw the chanting of the psalms for approximately eight hours a day as a heroic conflict waged against Satan on behalf of God and His Church. Hands that once held swords and lips that cursed were learning to sing praises and wield quills to preserve literacy and civilization throughout Western Europe.

Cluny Abbey. Established by Duke William of Aquitaine c. 910. It is located in the city of Cluny in central France. It was the largest church in Europe until St. Peter's Basilica was completed in 1626. Nearly the entire abbey and library were destroyed during the French Revolution, and the stones from its walls were used for other buildings. Only the southern transept with its bell tower and the lower parts of the two west front towers remained intact. These date from c. 1120.

During the tenth century, however, the Cluniac movement was still relatively small. At this time, Christians began to look to Otto and his descendants for leadership. After all, had not Charlemagne effectively spearheaded the reform of Carolingian society? For Otto's part, the temptation to use the spiritual to aid his temporal ambitions was great—especially when the opportunity to emphasize his leadership role in Church affairs coincided with his own dynastic agenda. Otto was now

DAILY LIFE AT CLUNY

The monastic community at Cluny placed a special emphasis on liturgical prayer. Their day began at two thirty in the morning with the night office, known as Matins. This office of psalms and readings was concluded by five o'clock and was followed by time for individual spiritual reading. As the first rays of dawn began to filter through the windows of their church, they consecrated the new day to God by praying Lauds, which honored the Resurrection. Next came Prime and Terce around eight o'clock and then the private Masses of those monks who were priests. At the Chapter, there was a spiritual reading as well as the confession of any faults monks had committed against the Rule the previous day, for which the abbot assigned penance. After three hours of manual labor, they gathered again at noon to pray Sext in honor of the crucifixion. The community Mass and the office of None followed. Mass was celebrated after Terce on Sundays and feast days to shorten the fast.

At this point in the day, around two o'clock in the afternoon, the monks broke their fast and ate their main meal, usually a combination of bread and vegetables, occasionally supplemented by dairy or fish. They ate in silence while a monk read a text from Scripture or the lives of the saints. After the meal there was another period of work–usually reading and copying books–until the evening prayer of Vespers. This office evoked the ancient rites of the Jewish Temple. The monks listened to another spiritual reading as they ate a small meal, perhaps with a cup of ale, around five o'clock. They prayed the final office of Compline before retiring for the night as early as six thirty in the evening.

emperor, but he did not have a secure dynasty. Instead, his potential heir would first need to be elected king by the other great dukes of East Frankia. The Ottonian family needed trustworthy subordinates who would support their efforts to become *the* imperial dynasty of East Frankia.

Since Otto shared Charlemagne's vision that Church and empire should work together, the new emperor began appointing bishops as administrators within his government. This choice was logical, considering that these men were usually among the best educated in society. Bishops became Otto's vassals and received their dioceses as fiefs. This arrangement supported Otto's agenda. Not only did bishops still have a vassal's obligation to supply soldiers in times of war but also their fiefs automatically returned to him after a given bishop died, as bishops did not have any recognized heirs. Otto, therefore, had a constant supply of lands he could use as an incentive to encourage loyalty and service among his followers. This arrangement, called the **imperial Church system** by historians, wedded feudal relationships with the "Church-State's" assumption that spiritual and temporal orders were intimately

Crowning of Emperor Otto II and Empress Theophano. Made of ivory c. 982. Currently in the Musée de Cluny, Paris, France. Theophano was a Byzantine princess who married Otto II. Some historians credit her with introducing the fork as a dining utensil to Western Europe, though others believe that this honor should go to her cousin who married a Venetian doge.

intertwined. It was also susceptible to corruption, though for the moment the emperors were more likely to appoint pious and conscientious bishops than the popes.

Otto's plans bore their fruit; both his son and grandson became emperor after him. Otto II (r. 973–983) even married a Byzantine princess, which intimately associated his rule with that of the ancient Eastern Roman Empire. Their son, Otto III (r. 983–1002), saw himself as the heir of Constantine and described his reign as the renovation of the Roman Empire. He made Rome his formal capital and worked closely with the friend he chose to be Pope Sylvester II (r. 999–1002). (The pope had selected the name "Sylvester" to echo the name of the pope during Constantine's reign.)

The childless Otto III died unexpectedly in 1002, and his vision for a restored Constantinian empire collapsed. His successor was Henry II (r. 1002–1024), the only medieval Germanic ruler to be canonized. Henry championed clerical reform, particularly in regard to the vow of celibacy. He also shifted the focus of East Frankia so that its kings now used the title "king of the Romans" before they received the imperial crown from the pope. Perhaps his most important legacy for the eleventh century was to increase, to its greatest extent, the number of bishops who oversaw imperial land as imperial vassals.

While the emperors' influence within the Church grew, the papacy's, for the most part, continued to shrink. With the exception of those chosen by the emperors, most of the popes of this period were dominated by the Roman nobles. Among the most notorious was Benedict IX (r. 1032–1045; 1047–1048). He became pope around the age of nineteen when his father bribed the electors to choose him as the next pontiff. Reports soon spread that Benedict had engaged in murder and assaults against women. By 1044, Benedict's lifestyle had become so scandalous that the Romans drove him out of the city and elected a rival pope, Sylvester III, to replace him. Benedict raised an army with the help of powerful patrons, retook the city, and reclaimed his papal authority. Soon afterwards, still a young man and now desiring to marry, he offered the bishopric of Rome to his pious godfather in exchange for money equal to the amount that Benedict's family had spent securing his election. (The new pope, Gregory VI, was hailed as a reformer despite the fact that some had misgivings since he had, in essence, paid money to become pontiff.) Perhaps unsurprisingly, Benedict and the lady in question lost interest in marriage, and Benedict yet again demanded the papal office, even though Sylvester and Gregory both still claimed to occupy the papal see.

Where could the Church turn to resolve this contemptible state of affairs? Who had the authority to determine the true pope in this disastrous scenario? The one viable option appeared to be Henry III (r. 1039–1056), an emperor known for his commitment to reforming the Church. Both clergy and laity besought him to come to Rome and restore order. Henry arrived in Italy in 1046 and summoned a meeting known as the Synod of Sutri. After an investigation into the state of the papacy and hearing the crimes imputed to Benedict, he declared that both he and Sylvester were deposed and successfully encouraged the more virtuous Gregory to resign. Benedict IX apparently retired to a monastery and ended his days as a penitent.

Conclusion

Could an emperor depose a pope when that pope was as corrupt as John XII or Benedict IX? Did the emperor have the right to choose the next pope? Furthermore, what was the proper boundary of authority when bishops became the vassals of an emperor or king? Did they receive their *ecclesiastical* position from their *political* lord?

Such were the questions prompted by the feudal order and the "Church-State" perspective that were arising in Western Europe. The political chaos of the Viking and Magyar raids had receded, but the spiritual confusion caused by the declining moral authority of the popes remained an open wound. So far, German emperors had chosen pious men to be popes, but surely this situation would eventually be compromised. For the moment, Henry III's choices proved beneficial. In 1049, he selected his close friend to be pope. Leo IX shared Henry's desire to reform the Church, but he also indicated that, in order to do so, the popes needed independence: he refused to accept his new status until the clergy and people of Rome had accepted him as their bishop. He therefore made the long journey to Rome on foot to beg for their approval. Each step brought the papacy closer to reform . . . and the beginning of its catastrophic struggle with the German emperors.

CHAPTER 25

Reform and Crusade

I. The Roman Church was founded by God alone.
II. Only the Roman Pontiff may by right be called universal.
III. He alone can depose or restore bishops.

Gregory VII, *Dictatus Papae*[1]

These formidable assertions were written by Pope Gregory VII, a central figure in the drama that rocked both empire and Church during the eleventh century. He penned a total of twenty-seven statements, all of which described the nature of papal authority. According to Gregory, this included the exclusive right to establish Church laws, to use the imperial insignia, and the power to depose emperors. Though Gregory never promulgated this document and historians still debate what motivated him to write it, his ideas perfectly communicated the aspirations of the papal reform movement.

By 1050, two parties—one papal, the other imperial—had emerged in reaction to the corruption within the clergy, and within the papacy in particular. Both genuinely desired to purify the Church, and both took for granted Charlemagne's model of a combined "Church-State." This vision of society, as we discussed in chapter 23, saw political and spiritual authority as part of a unified whole. This is why imperial reformers believed that Christian emperors were an indispensable authority for purifying the Church. They pointed to pious emperors, such as Charlemagne and

1 Gregory VII, "Dictatus Papae," in *Power and the Holy in the Age of the Investiture Conflict: A Brief History with Documents,* ed. Maureen Miller (Bedford: St Martin's, 2005), 81–82.

Otto I, who had intervened to root out corruption and immorality at the highest levels of the Church hierarchy. Clearly, they argued, imperial authority included the right to intervene in ecclesiastical affairs.

In contrast, Gregory VII and other papal reformers contended that the political order was subservient to the spiritual and should not attempt to control the appointment and reform of the clergy. These papal reformers considered Cluny's independence from worldly oversight to be the model for reform and sought to remove any temporal influence from Church governance. During the second half of the eleventh century, these two factions engaged in a titanic conflict that shaped the relationship between Church and State throughout the High Middle Ages (c. 1000–c. 1300) and beyond.

The Norman Expansion

The eleventh-century controversy between the popes and emperors was complex and involved many different people. One group that became increasingly important during this period was the **Normans** of northwestern France. In the last chapter, we discussed how the Viking Rollo had agreed to convert to Christianity and to become a vassal to the king of West Frankia. His fief of Normandy witnessed the

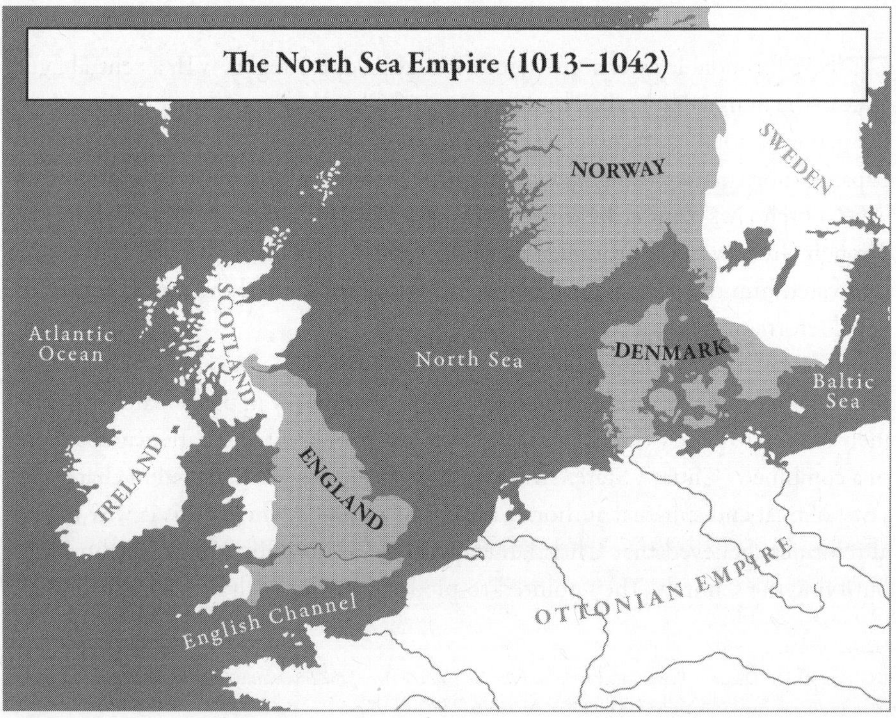

blending of Carolingian culture and Viking traditions. Rollo's Norman followers, for example, retained their esteem for courage and remained eager to explore and travel, but they also converted to Christianity and now journeyed as pilgrims seeking spiritual experiences rather than plunder.

In 999, some Normans were returning from pilgrimage to Jerusalem and put into port at Salerno in southern Italy. They witnessed Muslim pirates from North Africa demanding tribute from Salerno's prince and drove off the raiders. Word spread among adventurous Normans that opportunities for military service abounded in southern Italy, and newly-arrived Norman mercenaries helped deter the threat of invasion from the south. Some captains, however, began to fight for their own interests and carved out Norman domains in the region. This expansion aroused bitter hostility between the Normans and Byzantium because southern Italy had remained culturally connected to the empire. Some areas, such as Bari, were still ruled by Byzantine officials.

King Cnut and Queen Emma. Illuminated miniature made c. 1031. Currently "Stowe MS 944 Folio 6" in the British Library, London, England. This image is from the *New Minster Liber Vitae*, a confraternity book register of the names of pilgrims to the New Minster Abbey in Winchester, England. It is one of only two surviving Anglo-Saxon confraternity books. This scene shows King Cnut and Queen Emma presenting a cross at the altar of the abbey.

Byzantium had enjoyed a military revival during the tenth century and once again harbored dreams of restoring its rule in the former lands of the Western Roman Empire. The greatest of these recent warrior-emperors was Basil II the Bulgar Slayer (r. 976–1025). As his epithet indicates, he was a relentless foe to the Bulgars along his northern border, but he was also famous for his alliance with the Vikings of Russia. Vladimir I (r. 980–1015) ruled Kievan Rus and agreed to convert to Christianity and send six thousand soldiers, known as the Varangian Guard, in exchange for Basil's sister in marriage. This alliance intimately connected Russia with Byzantium, particularly in regard to the practice of Christianity. (We will discuss the origins of Russia at greater length in volume II.) It seemed that the Byzantine Empire was once again on the ascendancy, but a series of foolish rulers followed Basil's reign and brought about a catastrophic, rapid decline in the eleventh century. To add insult to injury, the struggling Byzantines watched as the Normans took advantage of the situation to secure Norman control over southern Italy and Sicily and even to attack Byzantine territories along the Adriatic Sea.

During this period, events in England provided other Normans with opportunities for exploits closer to Normandy itself. Alfred the Great's successors had ruled England for over a century after his death, but in 1013 the Anglo-Saxon king and his family fled to Normandy when a Viking invasion threatened. Most Nordic leaders were Christian by this time, but this did not prevent their desire for conquests. The Danish prince Cnut (r. 1016–1035) had secured his rule over England by 1016. Two years later, he was king of Denmark. In 1028, Norway also came under his authority, and historians speak of his realms as a so-called North Sea Empire. It seemed likely that England, despite its proximity to France, would now be integrated into Scandinavian culture and politics.

After Cnut's death in 1035, English nobles rebelled against Nordic rule and welcomed the return of an Anglo-Saxon king. Edward the Confessor (r. 1042–1066) had spent most of his life in exile in Normandy and was famous for his piety. He attended Mass every day and gave generously to the poor. (He was canonized in 1161 and venerated as the patron saint of England for many years.) Despite his personal virtue, Edward's reign precipitated a crisis in England, for he had no children to succeed him.

Three contenders for the English throne emerged. Harold Godwinson was a powerful Saxon and the choice of the English nobles. Harald Hardrada was the ruler of Norway and claimed the crown as Cnut's descendant. Finally, William, the duke of Normandy, declared that Edward had promised him the crown during

The **Bayeux Tapestry**. Embroidered linen made c. 1067-1079. Currently in the William the Conqueror Center of Bayeux in Normandy, France. The tapestry is 224 ft long and shows 58 scenes depicting the Norman Conquest and the Battle of Hastings in 1066. The left image shows William the Conqueror. The right image shows the death of the Anglo-Saxon King Harold Godwinson at the Battle of Hastings.

Edward's period of exile. He enjoyed the pope's support and received a papal banner to accompany his army. Though Harold seemed likely to win the contest among the three, it was **William the Conqueror** (r. 1066–1087) who won the Battle of Hastings and gained the English crown.

This development permanently altered the trajectory of English history. Whereas Cnut had oriented the island toward Scandinavia, under William it was now increasingly tied to the affairs in France. In fact, William, though king of England, was still Duke of Normandy and therefore a vassal to the king of West Frankia. This connection between the two realms meant that England would now be more influenced by political changes and religious movements on the continent than in previous centuries.

Another consequence was that England became more unified. William conducted a comprehensive survey of the lands and possessions within his recently conquered kingdom. His so-called *Domesday*, or *Doomsday*, *Book* recorded this survey and made note of the taxes owed to him. He also seized all lands held by Saxon lords and redistributed them among his faithful Norman warriors. These loyal servants received their fiefs with the understanding that William could take them back if the noble were found to be disloyal. Elsewhere in Europe, the feudal relationship, at least for the most powerful lords, had evolved differently. In East Frankia, for

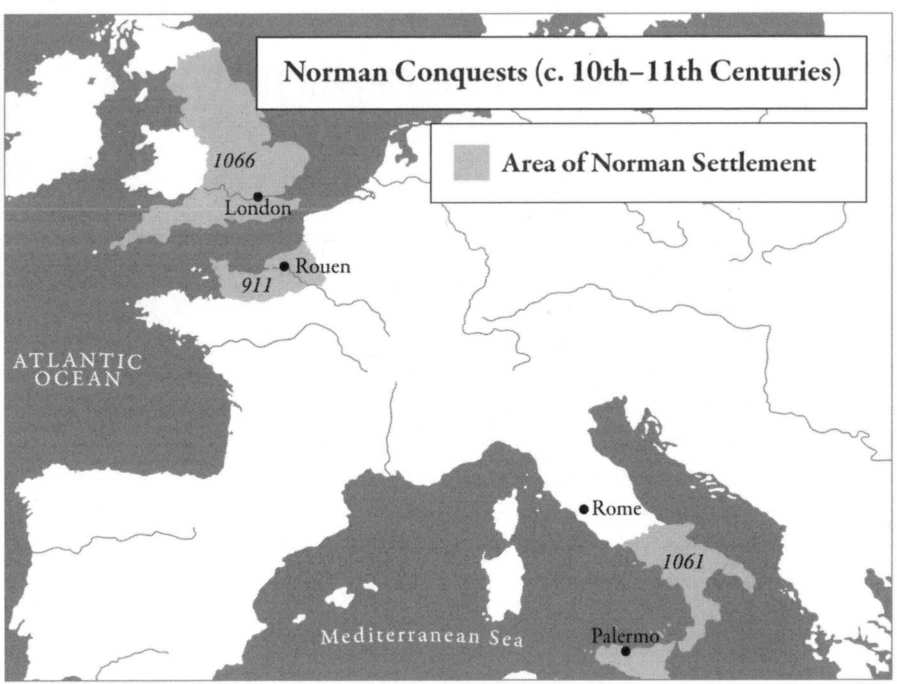

example, the five most powerful dukes held their land from generation to generation without worrying that the king might seize it and give it to another. In contrast, English lords, or barons, were more susceptible to royal oversight and confiscation. Such centralization made the Norman kings of England stronger than their neighboring counterparts and a more powerful force in European politics than the size of their kingdom might suggest.

Leo IX, Reform, and the Great Schism of 1054

When we introduced Pope **Leo IX** (r. 1049–1054) in the previous chapter, he was walking to Rome to seek confirmation of his appointment as bishop of Rome. Both he and Henry III, the Roman emperor who selected him, ardently desired to purify the Church, and Leo was the first of a series of reforming popes.

For Leo, the two main forms of corruption among the clergy were clerical concubinage and simony. Abuses concerning celibacy were prevalent in part because local nobles often appointed friends and loyal warriors to serve as priests and abbots regardless of any spiritual vocation. Such appointees frequently took concubines and lived with their families. Monasteries became akin to social clubs where men lived comfortable lives in complete disregard of their religious vows. Even more problematic to Leo was the practice of simony, that is, the selling of religious offices.

THE DONATION OF CONSTANTINE

Leo IX and later reforming popes based their understanding of papal authority's expansiveness in part on a forged document known as the *Donation of Constantine*. The *Donation* accepted as fact a legend that Pope Sylvester I baptized Constantine and even cured him of leprosy. It claimed that this miraculous event inspired Constantine both to establish the bishop of Rome as supreme above every other bishop and to give the pope Constantine's own imperial power. It went so far as to claim that the pope received sovereignty over the provinces of Italy and other western regions of the empire. This explains in part why Gregory VII made such sweeping claims in his *Dictatus Papae*. Historians debate when and why precisely this text was written, but it seems likely that someone associated with the papacy penned it in the decades following the alliance between the popes and Pepin the Short in the eighth century. It was not until the fifteenth century that most churchmen realized that the document was forged. The evidence that its vocabulary and style could not have originated in the fourth century was too convincing for subsequent popes to use the *Donation* as a support for their authority. Nonetheless, Leo IX, Gregory VII, and many other pontiffs we will discuss in the following chapters firmly believed that the *Donation* was both true and binding.

(This vice received its name from Simon, who tried to buy spiritual power from the apostles; see Acts 8:9–24.) Those bishops who bought their religious office usually perpetuated the abuse by selling priestly ordinations in an effort to recoup the money they had spent. Pious Christians became concerned that this behavior invalidated episcopal consecrations. This undermined confidence that priestly ordinations were valid, which, in turn, jeopardized the laity's access to the celebration of Mass and the sacraments.

Leo travelled throughout Europe holding synods in each region to investigate those religious who were suspected of taking wives or participating in simony. The guilty were either forced to repent or resign. He also transformed the college of cardinals. This was originally a body of Roman clerics who aided liturgical functions, but now cardinals became trusted papal representatives enrolled from across Europe who supervised reform in other dioceses.

Leo's desire to reform the Church led to ever-bolder claims of papal authority. Whereas previous generations had seen the emperor as the temporal leader and the pope as the spiritual leader of Christians, Leo and likeminded churchmen now emphasized the pope as the *sole* head of the entire Christian world. This position was not exactly new. Leo I, Gregory I, Nicholas I, and other popes had all contributed to the growing understanding of papal leadership, but Leo IX and his immediate successors also employed blunt terminology that minimized the traditional roles of emperors and other bishops in the "Church-State."

While it may be tempting to view Leo as simply desiring power, he and his successors became increasingly convinced that a pope's authority had to be as extensive as possible within the Church to bring about the proposed reform of the clergy. This placed the papal reform movement on a collision course with the program of imperial reformers. The latter were often no less devout or desirous for reform, but they were convinced that the emperor was the rightful leader of the "Church-State." A bitter conflict was brewing for the decades ahead.

Leo's rhetoric also contributed to the **Great Schism of 1054** between Catholicism and Orthodoxy. At this time, many Eastern Christians had recognized Rome as the greatest of the patriarchal sees, but to them, this meant that the pope was the first among equals. The patriarch of Constantinople saw Leo's claim to universal authority as a usurpation that threatened his dignity as a fellow patriarch of the Church. Furthermore, the papal attempt to eliminate clerical concubinage in Sicily and southern Italy aroused the anger of many Byzantine clergy who lived there. The custom of married priests had long been upheld in the Byzantine Church, and they resented papal assumptions that all clerical marriage was an abuse.

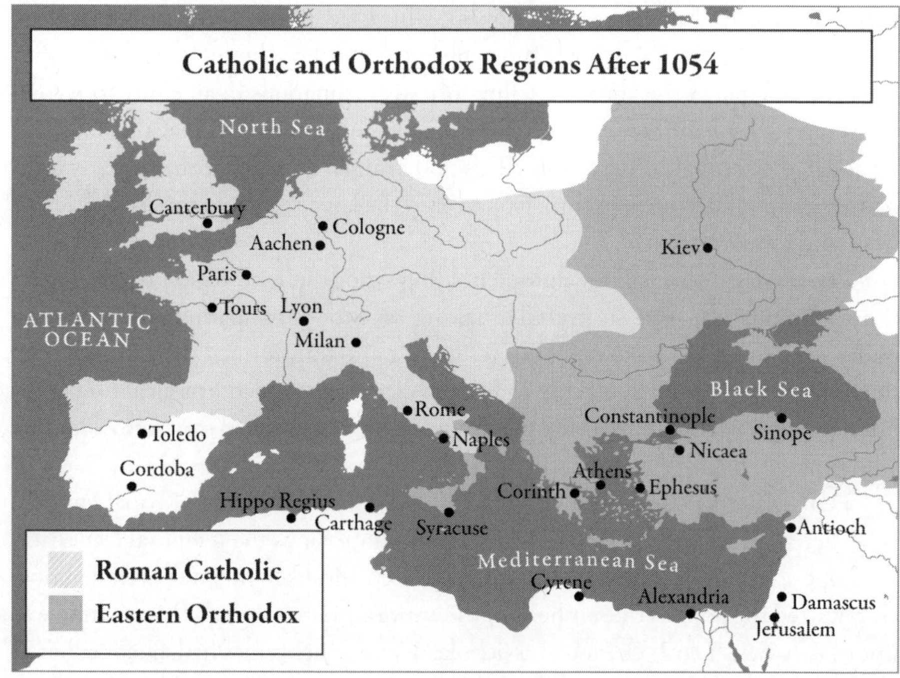

Personal ambition also played a role in the growing divide. The patriarch of Constantinople, Michael Cerularius (1043–1058), was known for his intrigues and desire to influence imperial policy. He encouraged hostility between Latin and Byzantine Christians by forbidding the use of the Latin rite in Byzantine territories and condemning Western liturgical practices that differed from those of the Byzantines, such as the suppression of the "Alleluia" during Lenten liturgies, the recitation of the *Filioque* clause during the Creed, and the use of unleavened bread for the Holy Eucharist. There were even reports that he had consecrated hosts from Latin churches trampled because he assumed that they were invalid.

Ironically, popes had only recently permitted the use of the *Filioque* clause in Roman liturgies. Pope Leo III, for example, had refused to add the phrase to the recitation of the Nicene Creed despite Charlemagne's insistence that he do so. Leo was not rejecting the theology of the clause itself so much as emphasizing the papacy's role to preserve what it had received—in this case from an ecumenical council—rather than to innovate. To make this point rather dramatically, Leo had the Nicene Creed (without the *Filioque*) engraved in silver plaques in both Latin and Greek and then placed on the tombs of the Apostles Peter and Paul. Leo's request that Charlemagne suppress the clause went unheeded, and it was only at the beginning of the eleventh century that the popes, encouraged by Emperor

Henry II, finally decided to insert the *Filioque* into the creed when it was recited at Mass.

Cerularius's actions prompted Leo to send a delegation to Constantinople in 1053. He was hopeful that a reconciliation could be achieved; that same year, he personally led an army against the Normans of southern Italy in a dramatic display of papal support for Byzantine interests in southern Italy. The Normans did not want to fight the pope, but they defended themselves successfully and even captured Leo. To make matters worse for the imprisoned pontiff, his legate to Constantinople, Cardinal Humbert (1015–1061), had an abrasive personality and was not inclined to seek common ground with Cerularius. He chose to conduct negotiations solely with the emperor and ignored the patriarch. The legate achieved union with the emperor, who was eager to promote an alliance with the See of Rome against the Normans, but Humbert also declared that Cerularius was excommunicated. He placed the bull, or decree, of this sentence upon the high altar in the Hagia Sophia.

Technically, only Cerularius was excommunicated. (Even this action was questionable. Unbeknownst to Humbert, Leo had died before the excommunication, and the delegation's authority to act on his behalf had ended.) Nonetheless, the document was interpreted as an attack against all Byzantine Christians. They rallied behind their patriarch, who issued a letter condemning the Latin Church for separating itself from traditional Christianity through its liturgical "abuses." Other Eastern Churches, such as that of Russia, were concerned by papal claims to universal authority and sided with Constantinople. The Great Schism between Catholicism and Eastern Orthodoxy had begun.

The effects of 1054 are still with us today. This is, in part, because the debate about the *Filioque* clause had no obvious path to resolution. Both sides could and did appeal to Scripture and interpreted key passages in different ways. The fact that most medieval churchmen from either side could not read the language of the other only added to the impasse.

Eastern theologians saw the Father as the Trinity's unifying principle and looked upon the insertion of the Holy Spirit's procession from the Father and the Son into the Nicene Creed as an illicit innovation. They argued that the *Filioque* took away from the dignity of the Holy Spirit and that it implied two principles of unity (Father and Son) and thus came dangerously close to polytheism. In contrast, theologians in the West—building particularly upon Augustine—argued that it was the Holy Spirit's procession from the Father and the Son that united the three Persons of the Trinity. Western theologians stressed that the *Filioque* preserved the Son's equality with the Father, and some even argued that it was impossible to distinguish the Son and Holy Spirit if they both proceeded in the same manner from the Father.

This important dispute about the nature of the Trinity was relatively abstract, but it became intertwined with the more visible divisions arising from the different liturgical traditions. The result was that one's theological position became closely aligned with one's culture so that it was often impossible to pursue genuine theological discourse without the threat of significant cultural upheaval. As historian Christopher Dawson emphasizes, schisms have a cultural component that can be at least as problematic as the actual theological issue when attempting to heal the conflict.

The papacy's developing struggle with the empire in the West added to the crisis. The more popes expressed their independence from temporal interference by asserting their own authority, the more they used terminology that indirectly reinforced the divide between East and West. It was a perfect storm of tragedy.

The Investiture Controversy

Pope Leo IX had died in early 1054, several weeks after the Normans released him from captivity. The emperor Henry III followed his friend Leo to the grave in 1056. The pious Henry had been influential in deposing two popes and selecting three more, and he had achieved the difficult feat of both increasing imperial oversight of the Church and contributing to its reform. Peter Damian (1007–1072), a Benedictine monk who championed Leo's efforts, described Henry as the model Christian ruler.

Henry's six-year-old son Henry IV (r. 1056–1106), succeeded him. Nobles within the empire used the long years of young Henry's minority to increase their power and independence. They even took control of lands that were traditionally held by the emperors. Papal reformers also seized this opportunity to try to limit imperial influence in the Church. In 1059, Pope Nicholas II (r. 1059–1061) issued a decree reforming the election process for popes. Previously, temporal influence—either from Roman nobility or the emperors—had often played a decisive role in the selection of the next pope, with public acclamation from the people of Rome confirming the appointment. Nicholas's decree stated that the pope could be elected only by the cardinals in assembly.

Furthermore, Nicholas condemned lay investiture. Emperors often chose the bishops for imperial territories, but even more troubling to papal reformers was that emperors also gave the episcopal candidates a crozier and ring, symbols of the bishop's *spiritual* jurisdiction. This implied that the emperor—though a layman—had the ability to invest, or endow, a bishop with spiritual authority. The investiture ceremony also included the candidate's feudal act of homage, which took place shortly before the consecration itself. For the emperors, as for any feudal lord, this act of homage was a vital component of ensuring the loyalty of their subordinates before entrusting them with the lands and resources of the empire. For reformers like Nicholas, this practice was a variation of simony, for bishops seemingly received their office in exchange for promising their loyalty, men, and resources to the emperor. Nicholas's decree of 1059 banned any cleric from receiving an abbey or diocese from a lay lord.

Papal reformers saw these changes as part of the necessary purification of the Church from worldly influences. Yet many devout Christians believed these efforts undermined the established traditions of the Church and threatened the tenuous stability achieved by the feudal system. Emperors had ratified papal elections for centuries, and the integration of Church and State had brought order, peace, and the Faith to much of Europe. Many, therefore, saw the emperors rather than the popes as fighting to maintain the traditions of their Church and of their culture.

The **Investiture Controversy** between papal and imperial reformers broke out in earnest during the pontificate of **Gregory VII** (r. 1073–1085). His passionate desire to end lay investiture came to characterize the entire papal reform movement, which is now known as the "Gregorian Reform." And yet, Gregory's own election to the papacy was technically illicit. The fact that he was chosen as pope by popular acclaim violated Nicholas's new procedure of election by the cardinals. Gregory, ironically, appealed to Henry IV to approve his election.

Hugh of Cluny, Henry IV, and Matilda of Tuscany. Illuminated miniature made c. 1115. Currently "Vat.lat.4922 folio 49r" in the Vatican Library. This image is from the *Life of the Countess Matilda of Canossa.* The scene shows Henry IV at Canossa Castle begging the owner Matilda of Tuscany (right) and abbot Hugh of Cluny (left) for an audience with Pope Gregory VII to obtain the pope's forgiveness. Matilda and Hugh were instrumental in securing this meeting.

Henry had come of age in 1065. Though he ruled Germany as king, he had not yet been crowned emperor and desired to recover the authority that had been lost to the German nobility during his minority. He needed a papal ally and so confirmed Gregory's appointment. Once Henry realized the new pope's desire to reduce imperial influence within the Church, he increasingly saw papal reform as yet another effort to strip him of his rightful authority. Meanwhile, Gregory was convinced that he was called to reform the Church and liberate her from any threat of outside corruption.

His confidence in his own calling and holiness of purpose made him unwilling to back down from a confrontation, though he could and did compromise when he was convinced that the good of souls required it.

THE PEACE AND TRUCE OF GOD MOVEMENTS

Reformers of the tenth and eleventh centuries not only addressed abuses among the clergy but also developed two initiatives that targeted knightly culture and sought to establish a more Christian ethos among warriors. The first was the Peace of God. This initiative began in 989 when the bishops of southeast France established a code of conduct that threatened excommunication for anyone who attacked women, children, or clergy or who stole from peasants. Bishops held devotional assemblies during which local knights were expected to swear on saints' relics to uphold these ideals. Several decades later, in the early eleventh century, another endeavor took root. This was the Truce of God, and it focused on establishing greater peace among Christian warriors by attempting to restrict when knights could fight. In theory, warriors were now forbidden from acts of violence on all Sundays as well as during the seasons of Advent, Christmas, Lent, and Easter.

The Peace and Truce of God movements contributed to later concepts of chivalry. "Chivalry" has its roots in the Old French word for "horsemanship," and the term came to encompass the expected behavior of a Christian knight. Unlike, for example, the Viking raider of the ninth century, the Christian warrior not only needed to be brave and valiant in battle but he also had to live a life of service and devotion to God. Thus, the rituals surrounding knighthood took on an explicitly religious character. In the period leading up to their knighting ceremony, warriors fasted, confessed their sins, and kept vigil in the church with their weapons upon the altar as a sign of their dedication to God. Recent advances in metallurgy allowed them to engrave sacred images and inscriptions on their helmets and swords, and some carried relics with them into battle to call down divine assistance. These relics also served to remind knights of the ideals they had sworn to uphold and to limit their fighting to actions approved by the Church.

The transformation of warriors' behavior was neither easy nor swift. In one account, when local monks told a knight that he must forgive an enemy who had wronged him, the knight angrily fell to the ground and even gnawed at the dirt in rage. The monks responded by throwing the relics of a local saint on the ground and telling the outraged warrior that he was hurting the saint. This sight convinced the knight to make peace and embrace his adversary. Even when knights disregarded the Church's attempt to limit violence, they realized that there was a growing expectation that they should conform to these ideals. In this way, the very existence of the Peace and Truce of God movements helped establish a society that looked to laws for standards of right and wrong behavior rather than to mere physical might.

Conflict between the two began in the Italian city of Milan and escalated quickly. Gregory rejected Henry's episcopal candidate on the grounds of simony. Henry, for his part, wanted a bishop that he could trust to uphold imperial authority. When no compromise could be reached, Henry summoned a diet, or meeting, at Worms in which he declared Gregory deposed because of his interference. Gregory responded by excommunicating the ruler in 1076 and releasing his vassals from their feudal oaths.

Gregory's declaration was unprecedented and threatened the very foundation of Henry's government and the stability of feudal society. Several dukes quickly rebelled and sought to secure full independence from Henry's reign. Their battlefield victories convinced Henry to seek the pope's pardon and so have Gregory restore the feudal bonds. The king journeyed to the papal residence outside Canossa and requested an audience. Gregory suspected that Henry was motivated by worldly interests rather than contrition and forced him to stand outside in the snow dressed as a beggar for three days before receiving him and, at least temporarily, reconciling with him. Though Gregory reinstated all feudal oaths to Henry, the iconic image of the king begging outside for forgiveness strengthened the papal claims that popes could judge, excommunicate, and depose monarchs.

For the moment, the German king was triumphant. He consolidated his authority over the nobility, who felt betrayed by a pope who had encouraged them to rebel only to reverse his position and abandon them. They would be far less willing to support the papal cause with arms in the future. Furthermore, Henry soon attacked Gregory again. In 1080, he declared Gregory deposed and supervised the election of an antipope who took the name Clement III. To imperial reformers, Henry, like his father and others before him, had removed a corrupting, even revolutionary, influence from the Church's highest office.

Gregory excommunicated Henry, but without military support from the Germans, he could only flee as Henry's army approached. The victorious king entered Rome and received the imperial crown of his father at the hands of Clement III in 1084. The desperate Gregory appealed to the Normans of southern Italy for support, and the Normans responded by forcing Henry out of Rome. Unfortunately, they also sacked the city. The people of Rome were enraged that Gregory had exposed his flock to death and suffering while pursuing his reform agenda. They drove the pope out of the city, and Gregory died in exile the following year.

Henry IV, Clement III, and the imperial party seemed to have won. Though Gregory's papal successors considered Clement to be an antipope—an illicit claimant to the papacy—Clement and his supporters held the city of Rome for much of the decade that followed Gregory's death.

The First Crusade and Aftermath

Urban II (r. 1088–1099) was a successor to Gregory VII but pursued the papal agenda with greater diplomatic finesse. Barred from Rome, he followed Leo IX's example and conducted a preaching tour, promoting reform and demonstrating his authority by his deeds. Urban also received help from an unexpected quarter: the Byzantine Empire.

We will discuss events in the 'Abbasid Caliphate in the next chapter. What we need to know here is that by 1055, a new power, the Seljuk Turks, had arisen in the Muslim world. These warriors, under their capable leader Alp Arslan (1029–1072), inflicted a devastating defeat on the Byzantine Empire during the Battle of Manzikert in 1071. Arslan captured the Byzantine emperor and most of Anatolia, Byzantium's former heartland. Arslan hoped to consolidate his authority within the Muslim world before continuing his advance against Constantinople, but his death in 1072 precipitated a civil war among his sons. Syria and Palestine became the battlefields for a confusing series of shifting rivalries and conflicts among Arabs, Turks, Shi'ites, and Sunnis.

The Byzantine Empire underwent a succession of violent coups in response to the disaster at Manzikert. In 1081, these conflicts catapulted a young and energetic leader, Alexius I (r. 1081–1118), to the throne. Alexius realized that his empire was too weak to face the Turks alone and so he took the bold step of appealing to the pope for support. He begged Gregory VII to send troops to assist their fellow Christians and even suggested that such goodwill could help reconcile the schism of 1054. Gregory was locked in the desperate struggle with Henry IV and unable to respond, but Urban II saw Alexius's continued pleas for help as an opportunity to promote Church reform as well as the defense of Byzantium.

The critical moment came in November 1095 during a local council at the town of Clermont. This site was near Cluny, the center for the papal reform movement and the place where Urban had been a monk. After addressing issues such as simony and clerical concubinage, Urban held a public gathering in the fields outside the city. This gathering mirrored the Peace of God meetings where knights swore on relics to refrain from unrestrained violence (see chapter insert on the Peace and Truce of God movements). Now, however, Urban exhorted the warriors present to make a different commitment. He explained the Turkish threat to Byzantium, but his most effective appeal was his account of Jerusalem. He declared that this holy city where Jesus Himself had walked and died for humanity's salvation was profaned by Islamic rites, the desecration of holy places, and the persecution of Christians. Urban urged those in attendance to put aside local feuds and instead vow to travel on pilgrimage to the Holy Sepulcher. This band of pilgrims would fight to deliver the Holy Land and the Christians of the region from the oppression of unbelievers. He offered an indulgence to all who made this vow, promising Heaven to those who died and remission of temporal punishment for sins previously committed to those who lived. According to accounts of this council, the knights present cried out "God wills it!" Many vowed their service to the campaign and wore crosses as a sign of their vow. Contemporaries called these oath-takers "pilgrims" or "crossbearers"; later generations called them crusaders. Soon knights across Europe were vowing to join the effort.

Crusader Graffiti. It is typically thought these crosses etched into the stones of the Church of the Holy Sepulcher in Jerusalem were left by crusaders and other medieval pilgrims. However, some recent scholars argue that these were the work of professional masons who carved the crosses on behalf of pilgrims who came after the medieval period. Regardless of their specific origin, it is likely that the fragments of the stones became pious "souvenirs" to commemorate the pilgrims' journey to Jerusalem.

Though medieval sources did not use the term "crusade," historians are justified in using this later designation to signify a new development in Christianity. The idea of fighting to defend others was not new, but what the crusades did differently was to associate this act of defense with penance and an indulgence. Those who vowed to go on crusade were undertaking an act of propitiation for their own sins. They were expected to pray, fast, and live a quasi-monastic life until they had fulfilled their vow to visit the Holy Sepulcher. Closely connected to this was the promised indulgence, a guarantee that participation was a spiritually meritorious act which gained grace for their souls.[2]

---

2 An indulgence is the remittance of the temporal punishment due to sins that have already been forgiven (see *CCC* §1471). However, at the time of the First Crusade, the theology of indulgences was in its infancy and had not been fully articulated or defined. Phrases such as "remittance of sins" were employed side-by-side with "remission of penances" when describing the crusade indulgence. This seemingly contradictory terminology has its roots in changing practices for the sacrament of Confession. Earlier in the Church's history, penitents confessed their sins, performed the required penance (e.g., fasting, pilgrimage, etc.) and only received absolution after the priest decided the penance had been sufficiently completed. By the eleventh century, the custom of granting absolution *prior* to the performance of penance had begun to spread. This, in turn, led to a more explicit emphasis on the infinite merits of Christ—as opposed to the merit of a given individual's penitential act—as the motivation for God's forgiveness of our sins. This focus on God's mercy and the spiritual "treasury of the Church" helped develop the budding theology of indulgences until it reached a more consistently recognizable form during the pontificate of Innocent III in the early thirteenth century.

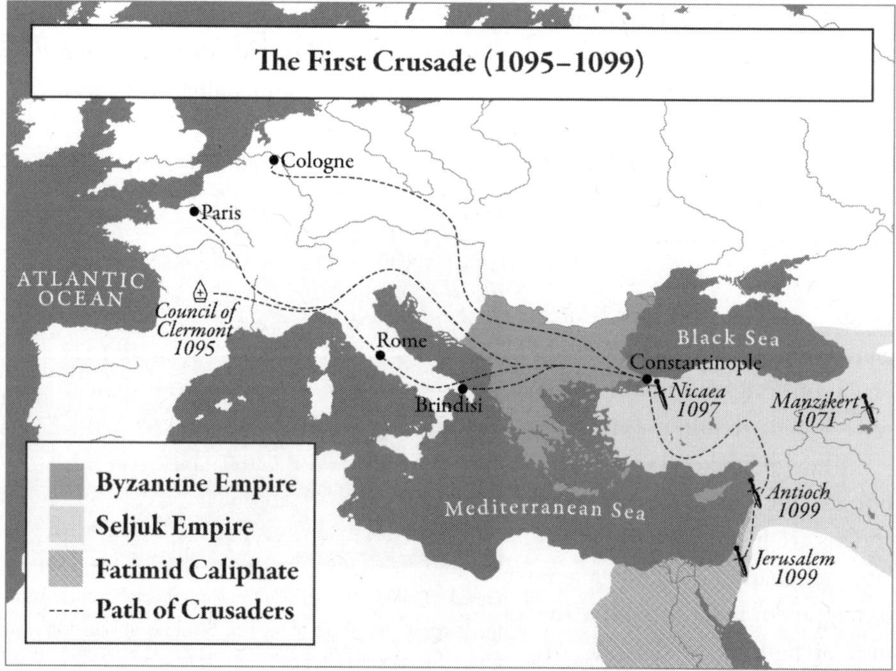

The organization of what became known as the **First Crusade** (1095–99) was shaped by feudal society. The pope appointed a legate as nominal head, but the participants in the crusade followed their local lords. The principal crusading armies agreed to begin the march eastward on the date set by Urban II, August 15, 1096.

Unfortunately, the enthusiasm for crusade made some see any delay for preparation as a lack of trust in God. A charismatic preacher, Peter the Hermit, rallied thousands who began the journey to Constantinople, confident that God would grant them victory. This so-called "Peasant's Crusade" was disorganized and poorly armed. Alexius had envisioned the pope contributing money or a small group of highly trained mercenaries. When this first wave of crusaders arrived, he was beyond disappointed. He promptly ferried them across the Bosporus; shortly thereafter, they encountered a Seljuk army and were butchered. Peter the Hermit, with a few fellow survivors, returned to Constantinople.

Some German crusaders never even made it to Constantinople. They, too, had fallen under the influence of Peter the Hermit but set out after his "Peasant's Crusade" had left. These groups encountered wealthy Jewish communities in the Rhine country and decided to attack them since they blamed all Jews for the death of Christ. They seized the Jews' possessions and forced them to convert. Many Jews turned to the local bishops for help, but not even episcopal protection prevented crusaders, such as the notorious Count Emicho of Leiningen, from committing atrocities against them. The Jews were so terrified of being brutalized that many killed their own families and themselves to avoid falling into the hands of their Christian attackers.

The main crusading armies began to arrive in Constantinople in late 1096 and early 1097. Alexius was even more perturbed by these soldiers than he had been by the misguided peasants. These were not the mercenaries he expected but rather independent armies with their own goals and ambitions other than serving the Byzantine Empire. What was more, among them were Normans from southern Italy who had attacked Byzantine territory just a few years before. The emperor persuaded almost all the leaders to swear oaths that they would return any territory they captured to the Byzantine Empire and then transported them to Anatolia.

The crusade began its campaign by defeating a Seljuk army and regaining Nicaea for the empire. After a difficult siege, the crusaders were able to gain control of some parts of the ancient Christian city of Antioch, but they themselves were soon besieged by a larger Turkish army. The fate of the crusade stood on a knife-edge. Alexius had been on his way to join the crusaders, but when he learned of their situation, he decided it was his responsibility to save his army and withdrew. Trapped in the city and without food, the crusaders boldly attacked their surprised enemy, and seemingly against all odds, won a spectacular victory.

Squabbling now distracted the crusaders. Many felt betrayed by Alexius and considered their vows to him void. Bohemond, a Norman, claimed the city of Antioch for himself, and the precedent was set for individual leaders to claim different territories along the Levant for themselves. The leaders bickered amongst themselves, but ultimately the rank and file of the armies shamed them into resuming the crusade and fulfilling their vow.

Divisions among different Muslim factions in the region aided the crusaders' advance. Local rulers were often happy to grant the crusade a peaceful passage if they were left unmolested. For their part, Sunni Muslims openly rejoiced that crusaders would attack their Shi'ite rivals in Jerusalem.

The siege of Jerusalem saw the crusaders benefit from seemingly miraculous events, such as when Genoese and English ships arrived with materials that they used to build siege engines to attack the walls. Nonetheless, the siege was brutal, and on July 8, the army began a period of fasting and barefoot processions before making the final effort. One week later, the city fell. Unfortunately, the slaughter of the city's inhabitants followed. Later accounts, echoing imagery in the Book of Revelation, described the streets as so overflowing with blood that it reached the knees of their horses. While this was an exaggeration, there is no denying that medieval warfare was often brutal and pitiless. The First Crusade was no exception.

Many today point to the fall of Jerusalem and other massacres and conclude that the crusades represent the worst attributes of medieval Christianity. They mistakenly present Urban's call to arms as an *offensive* campaign against Islam rather than a *defensive* measure to protect Christians and the holy sites in Palestine. Some historians of the twentieth century went so far as to suggest that crusaders were attempting to colonize Palestine and Syria in order to enrich themselves. More recent research has discredited this theory. These studies have highlighted how the majority of nobles who joined the crusades sold lands and mortgaged others to pay for the travel and weapons for themselves and their vassals. Far from having nothing to lose, they were willing to sacrifice everything to fight for the Holy Land's liberation. The same holds for many of the knights and peasants who joined. Of course, not everyone had lofty intentions or necessarily preserved those they had at the start of the crusade, but many saw participation in the coming battles as an act of love for their Christian neighbor. Furthermore, crusading contributed to the development of the ideals of chivalry by showing knights that their lives of warfare could be directed towards selfless, and even spiritual, goals. Rather than a mere "might makes right" perspective, Christian knights increasingly identified their role as defenders of the weak. (See chapter 28 for more on chivalry.)

Henry V, Holy Roman Emperor. Fresco painted c. 1130 in the Prüfening Abbey Church of St. George near Regensburg, Germany.

Unfortunately, the First Crusade also exacerbated the divide between Constantinople and Rome. The Byzantines felt betrayed as crusade leaders began establishing their own territories, or crusader states, in Palestine and elsewhere. The soldiers who were supposed to help the empire regain territory had simply taken former Byzantine lands for themselves. The crusaders also felt betrayed by Alexius and reports of his withdrawal from Antioch suggested to many that Byzantines were liars and untrustworthy. The schism deepened.

In contrast, many in Western Europe saw the success of the First Crusade as a sign of divine approval for papal claims to leadership in the "Church-State." Popes had both encouraged moral renewal through the reform movement and now successfully fused military might with devotion. Warfare, prayerful penitence, and even the forgiveness of sins had been connected

St. Peter's Cathedral in Worms, Germany. This church was the site of the Concordat of Worms in 1122, as well as other historic events such as the Diet of Worms in 1521. The current structure was built c. 1160–1181 and is considered an excellent example of Late Romanesque architecture.

in a campaign that had been launched, not by the emperor, but by the pope. The papacy's prominent role laid the groundwork for what became known as **Christendom**, a culture whose political and social vision reflected the beliefs and morals of Christianity under papal leadership.

Urban II's successor and fellow Cluniac monk, Paschal II (r. 1099–1118), attempted to capitalize on the crusade's success and insisted that the emperors renounce the right of investiture. He supported the rebellion of Henry IV's son, Henry V (r. 1105–1125). This act of filial treachery broke the aging Henry IV's will, and he died one year after losing his throne without ever receiving absolution from his excommunication. For his part, Henry V proved to be a fickle ally and imprisoned Paschal in an attempt to preserve the royal right of investiture.

Ten more years of conflict convinced many that neither the popes nor the emperors would achieve all their goals. Representatives of the emperor and the new pope, Calixtus II (r. 1119–1124), finally agreed to a compromise known as the **Concordat of Worms** in 1122. This agreement stated that bishops must be canonically elected by the priests of the cathedral, but before their consecration, the candidates would do homage to the emperor for their lands. The emperors gave up the right of investing the bishop with his ring and staff but retained the ability to veto any candidate they considered unacceptable.

On the one hand, the concordat, or agreement, seemed to favor the emperors; they retained a veto power over the appointment of bishops and, as we will see, still harbored ambitions of controlling the Church. On the other hand, the papacy won an important ideological battle. The papal reform had withstood imperial might and had even inspired what many thought was the miraculous liberation of the Holy Land. The pope's status as the supreme leader of all Christians was now more enthusiastically acknowledged in Western Europe. Though many battles remained ahead, the gains were celebrated in 1123 at the First Lateran Council, the first ecumenical council located in Western Europe and the first convoked by a pope rather than an emperor. Several hundred bishops attended and approved canons that confirmed the Church's independence from temporal control and established rules governing clerical celibacy and the consecration of bishops.

Conclusion

The Investiture Controversy seemingly answered the pressing issue between empire and Church. Church leaders had rejected the imperial program of reform and established boundaries that limited, at least in theory, rulers' religious powers. Nonetheless, future conflict remained inevitable. Charlemagne's vision of society as a "Church-State" remained the working model for both popes and emperors and continued to bring tension and confusion. Questions remained even for those who accepted the Church's supremacy within society. For example, to what extent could popes dictate the internal workings of a given kingdom? Could the Church establish its own set of laws for clergy that were independent of royal or imperial law? Was it appropriate for popes to excommunicate, that is cut off from the Church's community, those who challenged its authority in the temporal sphere? Decades of protracted struggle between temporal rulers and popes still lay ahead.

CHAPTER 26

Islam's Golden Age

The caliph al-Ma'mun took a deep interest in the sciences of the ancients and was keen to test their accuracy. Having read in their works that the circumference of the globe is twenty-four thousand miles . . . [he] wished to test the truth of this assertion and asked the Banu Musa what they thought. They replied that this was certainly the case and the caliph then said, "I wish you to use the methods described by the ancients so that we can see whether it is accurate or not."

Ibn Khallikan,
Deaths of Eminent Men and History of the Sons of the Epoch[1]

The caliph's request was no simple matter. In order to test the ancient Greek theory about the globe, three scholars known as the Banu Musa ("sons of Musa") first located a flat area and took measurements of a specific star's location. They drove a pole into the ground at the spot of their calculation, attached a rope to it, and then walked due north as best as they were able. Whenever the rope gave out, they drove another stake into the ground, attached another rope, and repeated the process. They did this until the measurement of the star they were observing had moved one degree on the horizon. They measured the distance they had walked—approximately 66 and ⅔ miles—and then repeated the exercise by walking to the south from their original site. Once again, they noted that the star moved one degree when they had journeyed approximately 66 and ⅔ miles. This distance they associated with one degree of a circle and therefore multiplied 66 and ⅔ miles by 360 to calculate the globe's circumference. The caliph asked them to repeat the entire experiment at a second location in order to confirm their findings. Their second calculation mirrored the first, and al-Ma'mun admitted that the ancients were right in

1 Ibn Khallikan, *Deaths of Eminent Men and History of the Sons of the Epoch* quoted in Hugh Kennedy, *When Baghdad Ruled the World* (New York: Da Capo, 2005), 258–9.

their reckoning. Strikingly, the final estimate provided by the Banu Musa was within 5 percent of the modern-day value of 24,901 miles.

This episode captures the spirit of the **Islamic Golden Age** (c. 762–c. 1258), which flourished even as Charlemagne and his successors were still laying the

The **Mosque-Cathedral of Córdoba**. Built by the Umayyad ruler Abd ar-Rahman I c. 785 in Córdoba, Spain. It is emblematic of the artistic achievements of the Islamic Golden Age. The hypostyle prayer hall is famous due to its columns with distinctive striped arches. ("Hypostyle" is an architectural term indicating that a hall has a roof supported by columns.) The *mihrab*, a niche indicating the direction of prayer towards Mecca, was added by al-Hakam II c. 971. The mosque became a cathedral in 1236 but did not undergo significant architectural alterations until 1523, when a Renaissance cathedral nave and transept were added in the middle of the complex. The building today is known as the Cathedral of Our Lady of the Assumption. It is a UNESCO World Heritage Site.

foundations of medieval Europe. Thanks to the Umayyad conquests, the Muslim elite had inherited a treasure trove of learning from Byzantium, Persia, and elsewhere and used their wealth to fund scholars as they translated and studied the wisdom of the ancients. These intellectuals both valued previous achievements and wanted to ascertain for themselves the validity of their claims. The resulting legacy of translation, experiment, and scholarship enriched Islamic society. Furthermore, the 'Abbasids of Baghdad and the Umayyads of Spain acted as conduits of knowledge for Christian Europe. Europe reaped still richer intellectual gains after the First Crusade brought the two cultures into closer contact. Indeed, the crusade's success was intimately tied to the events within the 'Abbasid caliphate, for the centuries of Islam's Golden Age involved more than research and study. Intrigue and strife were also at work, undermining the political stability of the Muslim world and laying the groundwork for its permanent fragmentation.

The Foundations of 'Abbasid Glory

We concluded chapter 21 by discussing the 'Abbasid Revolution and how that movement brought an end to the Umayyad caliphate in 750. The Umayyads had successfully established their realm across three continents, but their treatment of those they conquered aroused resentment. Muhammad had envisioned Islam as a universal religion that was destined to spread throughout the earth. In contrast, Umayyad rulers treated *mawalis*, non-Arab converts to Islam, as second-class members of society. They also frequently excluded former Byzantine and Persian administrators from the highest levels of authority even though these same bureaucrats had the most experience in governing. For the Umayyads, political power, like Islam itself, was best reserved for Arabs.

The 'Abbasids capitalized on the widespread dissatisfaction and rallied Shi'ites and *mawalis* to their cause. However, their success in dislodging the Umayyads from power did not immediately confirm their own right to rule. In fact, the rhetoric that they were restoring Muhammad's family to leadership was a double-edged sword. Many thought that 'Ali's family had the better claim, and 'Abbasid descent from Muhammad's uncle 'Abbas was as much a liability as it was an asset. 'Abbas had never converted to Islam, and devout Muslims assumed that he was in Hell for his nonbelief. The 'Abbasids needed to move decisively if they were to secure their position. Fortunately for their family, the second 'Abbasid caliph, Abu Ja'far, better known as the "Victorious" or **al-Mansur** (r. 754–775), both skillfully removed the chief threats to the dynasty's stability and laid the foundations for its future grandeur.

Al-Mansur combined piety and simplicity with cunning and ruthlessness. He embraced a caliph's religious responsibilities as successor to the Prophet Muhammad:

each Friday he publicly led the prayers and preached, even developing a reputation for eloquence. Furthermore, unlike later 'Abbasid rulers who surrounded themselves with pleasures and remained aloof from those they ruled, al-Mansur lived frugally and without ostentation. At the same time, al-Mansur was relentless in removing any obstacle to his authority. These threats included both an uncle who challenged him and the powerful general Abu Muslim. The former questioned al-Mansur's right to rule, and in response he was imprisoned and ultimately executed. The message was clear to other members of the 'Abbasid family: they must support the caliph or suffer the consequences. Meanwhile, Abu Muslim's victories had been instrumental in bringing about the 'Abbasids' rise to power, but these very successes made him a potential rival in al-Mansur's eyes. The caliph murdered him in cold blood and then bribed the officers of Abu Muslim's army to avoid any unrest among the soldiers.

The caliph also effectively convinced many descendants of 'Ali to remain loyal by bringing them to court and providing for their wants. Nonetheless, such tactics did not persuade everyone. 'Ali's great-great-grandson, Muhammad the Pure Soul (718–762), was convinced that God would bless his cause and began a rebellion in Medina in 762. As his epithet suggests, Muhammad was known for his religious fervor. He even selected Medina as the center of his rebellion for its spiritual significance rather than for any strategic advantage. Unfortunately for Muhammad the Pure Soul, his prayers did not ensure victory; al-Mansur swiftly crushed the rebellion and soon displayed his enemy's head on a silver platter.

Muhammad's rebellion proved to be the last serious threat to al-Mansur's authority, and the caliph's remaining years saw him devote his attention to state-building. His most significant decision in this regard was to designate a new city as his capital. Just as the Umayyads' move from Medina to Damascus indicated that their ambitions extended beyond Arabia, so, too, al-Mansur's decision to transfer his capital to Mesopotamia signified his desire to incorporate the Persian world more fully into the caliphate. The site he chose was along the western bank of the Tigris River and near the ruins of Ctesiphon, the former capital of the Sassanid Empire. In 762, labor began on Madinat as-Salam, the City of Peace. Four years later, the initial work had been completed. This included a circular wall that surrounded the heart of the city, which became known as the Round City. At the Round City's center were a mosque and the caliph's palace, fitting emblems of the caliph's combined spiritual and political authority. Though "City of Peace" remained the official title for the Round City, many still used the name of the small village, Baghdad, that had originally occupied the site to describe the expanding urban area as a whole.

Baghdad was destined to become one of the most famous cities in history. Historians estimate that its medieval population eventually swelled to over one million, making it the largest city in the world, at that time. Its buildings and palaces spanned the Tigris, and bridges of boats tied together connected the eastern bank with al-Mansur's original foundation. The river, far from being an inconvenient obstacle, was the cause for much of Baghdad's growth. The Tigris not only provided a continual and sufficient water supply to the urban area but also facilitated trade and travel both to the north and south. Goods from Asia, Africa, and Europe flowed into the city, and the wealth of the 'Abbasid capital became legendary. Already, delegations connected al-Mansur's court with that of the emperors of Tang China. In 765, he also received the ambassadors of Pepin III the Short; three years later, al-Mansur's representatives arrived in France. (These friendly relations continued into the ninth century with al-Mansur's grandson Harun and Charlemagne.)

Moreover, Baghdad represented the establishment of the 'Abbasid bureaucracy. Unlike his Umayyad predecessors, al-Mansur gladly incorporated non-Arabs into the highest levels of power. At the very top were the viziers. This office evolved from its original secretarial role under the Umayyads into a powerful position second only to the caliph. Viziers advised 'Abbasid rulers and served as the head of the civil bureaucracy. Educated administrators oversaw the caliphate's finances and maintained the necessary infrastructure for its governance. Interestingly, in contrast to the imperial Church system that was taking root in Western Europe, the caliphs predominately relied on secular officials to supervise the administration rather than religious figures.

While viziers and other officials could become fantastically wealthy, political prominence was not without its dangers. The 'Abbasid court was a place of intrigue, and a given family's or individual's success aroused suspicion and jealousy. The Burmakid family was the most famous early example of success and downfall. These Persian aristocrats came from modern-day Afghanistan and converted from Buddhism to Islam. During the 'Abbasid Revolution, they were prominent supporters of the 'Abbasids, and the head of their family became an important adviser to al-Mansur. This man's son, Yahya Ibn Khalid (d. c. 803), was one of the most powerful men in the 'Abbasid world for a number of years, for he was the personal friend and adviser to the caliph **Harun al-Rashid** (r. 786–809). Future generations looked to Yahya as the model counselor and vizier, and his patronage of the arts and translation efforts helped set in motion the intellectual achievements of Islam's Golden Age. And yet, none of his accomplishments could save him from sudden disaster. We do not know precisely what triggered the fall of the powerful Burmakid family, but in 803 Harun imprisoned his former friends and even executed one of Yahya's sons, despite the fact that this son and Harun had been close companions. Some historians speculate that the Burmakids were conspiring with

Shi'ites, while others suggest that Harun wished to rule on his own without further advice from Yahya. Whatever the reason, the Burmakids' fall was an example to future viziers that, regardless of past success and wealth, their well-being depended on the whim of their caliph.

Harun al-Rashid as well as his ill-fated Burmakid friend were immortalized in the collection of stories commonly known in English as *Tales of Arabian Nights*. Harun's historical importance, however, goes beyond 'Abbasid literature or even his treatment of the Burmakids. His reign both continued the flowering of intellectual endeavors (discussed below) and set in motion events that would undermine the 'Abbasids' long-term stability. Harun himself represents an important transition in the role of the caliph in 'Abbasid society. Though he made the pilgrimage to Mecca multiple times during his life and participated in the *jihad* against Byzantium, he apparently neglected his grandfather's practice of public preaching each Friday. Whereas al-Mansur had remained relatively available to Muslims, Harun withdrew into his harem and limited his public appearances. It was a precedent that future 'Abbasid caliphs would embrace.

More important still was Harun's decision to choose two of his sons as his heirs. The 'Abbasids never practiced exclusive succession by the firstborn son. The caliphs, with their multiple wives and concubines, typically had a number of sons whom they considered as potential heirs. Each of these contenders attracted support from ambitious individuals who hoped that their assistance would be richly rewarded if and when their chosen candidate became caliph. The result was that tensions and rivalries among factions accompanied each transition of power. Harun hoped to avoid this situation by appointing two sons as successors and dividing his territory among them. Harun compelled each son to sign a lengthy document detailing their respective privileges and obligations to each other, and he hung this record in the holy city of Mecca to signify the religious nature of their oaths. Tragically for his sons and for the dynasty in general, Harun's efforts to secure a smooth succession merely exacerbated the tensions.

Sibling rivalry quickly escalated after Harun's death. Each heir had his advisers who encouraged him to take actions to secure his own power and to undermine that of his half-brother. The critical moment came when the one son, al-Amin (r. 809–813), ordered the agreement hanging in Mecca to be brought to him so that he could personally tear it apart. Civil war broke out, and the forces of his half-brother **al-Ma'mun** (r. 813–833) eventually besieged Baghdad itself. From 812–813, Muslim soldiers fought against one another, laying waste to much of the City of Peace. In the end, al-Ma'mun was victorious, and his reign initiated one last period of glory before political decline set in.

A Flourishing of Learning

One of the most famous symbols of the Golden Age of Islam was the **House of Wisdom**. Harun had established it for his personal collection of manuscripts, but his son al-Ma'mun turned it into a public research center. It became the largest library of its era; scholars and students from China, Byzantium, and across the caliphate came to study there. Nor was its learning available solely to Muslims. Nestorian Christians, for example, contributed to 'Abbasid efforts to preserve what they had inherited from Greece and Rome. Generations earlier, members of the Church of the East had translated many Greek texts into Syriac, and now their descendants translated these manuscriptions into Arabic, the official language of the Muslim world and Western Civilization's predominant language of scholarship during this period. In fact, many texts unavailable to the monasteries of the Carolingian Renaissance nonetheless survive today thanks to the 'Abbasids' passion for learning. Their desire to expand their knowledge was so genuine that they once demanded an ancient Greek text on geography as part of a treaty with the Byzantine Empire.

The **House of Wisdom**. Illuminated miniature made c. 1237 by Yahya ibn Mahmūd al-Wāsitī. Currently "Ms. Arabe 5847 folio 5v" in the National Library of France, Paris, France. This image is from the *Maqamat al-Ḥariri*, a collection of 50 tales of adventures written by al-Ḥairi of Basra.

Medicine in particular became one of the most vibrant scholarly fields in 'Abbasid society. At one point, over eight hundred doctors were practicing medicine and conducting research in Baghdad alone. Their experiments and treatises explored the inner workings of the eye, the stomach, the heart, and the circulatory system. Again, the 'Abbasid willingness to embrace learning wherever it could be found was evident: Nestorian Christians frequently served as the private physicians for caliphs.

Other fields also thrived and combined the insights of different cultures. 'Abbasid society adapted paper-making technology from the Chinese, and the mathematician al-Khwarizmi (780–850) developed the study of algebra and revolutionized Western numbers by introducing the numeral system of earlier Indian mathematicians. (Europeans later called this system "Arabic numerals" since they learned of it through Muslims.) Other 'Abbasid mathematicians studied Euclid's *Elements* to develop the concept of square roots and to explore geometric properties in greater depth. In the realm of architecture, they developed a style that combined the large spaces prized by the Romans with the curves and elasticity characteristic of Persian designs. This architecture spread throughout Muslim-controlled areas of the Mediterranean and is best demonstrated by the mosques constructed during this period. On a more practical level, Muslim merchants and scholars publicized improvements in irrigation techniques and brought crops from one continent to another.

Muslim geographers created new and more accurate maps of the heavens and the earth. Refinements in astronomy brought about more accurate measurements of the months and hours that were necessary for the devout observance of the month of Ramadan and other holy days in Islam. In a similar fashion, Muslim cartographers became known for the (relative) accuracy of their maps. In 1154, the Christian king of Sicily contracted Muhammad al-Idrisi (1100–1165) to compose a map of the world. While this map shows the limits of 'Abbasid geographic knowledge, especially in the Indian Ocean region, it is nonetheless significant that a Christian king sought out a Muslim cartographer. Clearly, they were regarded as the best-informed of their era.

Nor were the 'Abbasids alone in their achievements. Further west, the Umayyad rulers of al-Andalus in modern-day Spain became renowned patrons of the arts and learning. The city of Córdoba was an especially important cultural center. At a time when most monasteries in Europe had perhaps 100 books, the palace library at Córdoba possessed somewhere between 400,000 and 500,000 volumes. Christians, such as the future pope Sylvester II (see chapter 24), studied in Spain and brought back as much learning as they could.

While Muslims did not generally study Latin or Greek literature, they were fascinated by Greek philosophy. Initially, Muslim philosophers were most interested in Plato. Al-Farabi (870–950) even attempted to construct an Islamic version of Plato's *Republic*. However, al-Farabi's greatest contribution to Western Civilization was his role in the preservation of Aristotle's philosophy, which had been all but lost to Western Europe. Gradually, Aristotle gained more attention, such as when the Persian philosopher Ibn Sina, better known in Europe as Avicenna (980–1037), used Aristotle to propose rational proofs for the existence of God.

Al-Farabi's attempts to gather and preserve the writings of Aristotle later inspired a Jewish philosopher, Moses Maimonides (1138–1204), to bring Aristotle's works from Egypt to Spain. There Aristotle gained his greatest Muslim disciple, Ibn Rushd, whose name was "Latinized" in Europe to **Averroes** (1126–1198). Averroes wrote over one hundred treatises during his life covering a broad range of topics, including medicine and law. His most important works were commentaries on Aristotle's philosophy. In these, he argued vigorously in favor of using human senses and reason as the basis for acquiring knowledge. His extensive and perceptive commentaries on

Aristotle's philosophy won the admiration of many medieval Christian intellectuals; Thomas Aquinas even praised him as "the Commentator."

Another fruit of the Golden Age was more specific to Islamic learning: the formation of four major schools of interpretation of ***Shari'a***. *Shari'a* is the body of religious law in Islam, and its importance to the people can be discerned from the term itself: *Shari'a* is Arabic for "watering place," a location of evident importance to those who live in the desert. Muhammad's combined religious and political authority made him a lawgiver, but it was challenging for subsequent generations to know precisely what principles should guide Islamic jurisprudence. The verses in the *Qur'an* that deal with legal affairs only provided an initial framework, so Muslim religious scholars, known as *ulama* ("persons of right knowledge"), needed to develop alternative foundations for Islamic law. They turned to the *hadith*, those accounts of Muhammad's conversations or sayings, and established principles for identifying which *hadith* were the most trustworthy. (This typically involved a given *hadith*'s *isnad*, or "support." The "support" was its chain of people who vouched for a given saying's authenticity. An *isnad* generally took the form of a phrase like "So-and-so heard from so-and-so who heard from so-and-so that the Prophet said . . . .") Given that different religious scholars held various individuals' testimonies in greater esteem than that of others, different interpretations and emphases arose. During the 'Abbasid Caliphate, these eventually coalesced into four principal legal schools of thought, known as *madhabs* (the Arabic term for an Islamic school of legal thought). Each *madhab* embraced a certain methodology of interpretation, which led to very different conclusions about aspects of Muslim life. The most important school in the 'Abbasid Caliphate was the Hanafi legal school. This remained influential for centuries, even becoming the preferred interpretation for the Ottoman Empire as well.

The Trials of the 'Abbasid Caliphate

Islam's Golden Age took place against a backdrop of political and religious tension. Whereas Christianity had spread slowly over the course of three centuries before it became politically influential, Muslim conquests had established Islam across three continents in only fifty years. Muslims rulers struggled to maintain standardized beliefs and practices across the vast territories of their realm and among the new converts.

Even under the Umayyad dynasty, many new Muslims retained Christian, Jewish, or Zoroastrian beliefs and practices after their conversion. These attitudes were considered heretical by many Muslim legal scholars. Just as debates arose in Christianity regarding, for example, the natures of Jesus, so, too, in Islam disagreements now arose about such concepts as free will and prophecy. Since caliphs possessed both spiritual and political authority, they considered heretical beliefs not only as offenses against religious orthodoxy but also as acts of treachery against the community and its ruler. The Persian term *zandaqa*, which was used by Muslims to denote heresy, not only conveyed the concept of religious error but also included the idea of opposition to public order.

The 'Abbasids' revolution had been successful, in part, because they claimed to safeguard Islamic orthodoxy. Now that they had replaced the Umayyads, they felt the need to demonstrate their status as champions of orthodoxy by suppressing Islamic heresies. For example, al-Mansur executed former Zoroastrians who held a dualist interpretation of Islam. They had proposed the existence of an evil god and an alternate version of the *Qur'an*. Al-Mansur's successor instituted a religious inquisition in 780 to investigate suspected dualists in Syria and Iraq. Those who refused to renounce beliefs considered heretical were put to death.

Just like the contemporary iconoclast emperors of Byzantium, Muslim rulers resorted to physical coercion to establish religious unity. Unlike the Byzantines, however, the caliphs' claim to such authority was rooted in Islamic teaching. As successors of Muhammad, they were both the generals of the armies of God's people and the spiritual leaders who led the prayers of the Muslim community. Their

AL-ANDALUS: LAND OF MEDIEVAL TOLERANCE?

Twentieth-century historians have interpreted the history of Muslim Spain, or al-Andalus, in distinct ways. For much of the century, many historians espoused a theory of "*Reconquista.*" This perspective emphasized the late medieval Christian view that Spanish history was defined by nearly eight centuries of struggle against Muslim invaders. This explanation also worked well within many modern historians' own context of the fight against Communism, both during the Spanish Civil War (1936–1939) and, later, during the Cold War.

This interpretation, however, did not withstand close scrutiny. During much of this eight-century period, Spanish Christian monarchs were just as likely to war against one another as they were to fight against Muslims, and alliances between Muslims and Christians were more common than a "*Reconquista*" reading suggested. Although Christian monarchs sometimes worked together to defeat a common Muslim foe, frequent Christian infighting belied a simplified historical interpretation that merely stressed Christian-versus-Muslim activity.

The reevaluation of the "*Reconquista*" model has led to another, very different interpretation of Iberian history. This emphasizes Muslim Spain as a land of tolerance and even as an early model for our modern society's religious pluralism. Historians who follow this interpretation highlight how prominent Jews served in high positions in Muslim governments. They also point to the apparent freedom and even careers that certain women enjoyed in Andalusian society.

Jewish communities did face less oppressive laws under Muslim rulers than they had under the previous Visigothic rulers, but they still encountered significant social limitations. Umayyad Spain's predominate *madhab* was the Maliki Madhab. This understanding of Islamic law emphasized social segregation for non-Muslims and even advocated separation from those Muslims who followed a different *madhab*'s interpretation of *Shari'a*. According to Maliki thought, Jews needed to wear distinctive clothing, and it was forbidden for a Muslim to greet a Jew or Christian first. (Christians were considered particularly polluted to the point that some Muslims argued that it was forbidden to accept water from them or to touch the ground where Christians had walked with bare feet.) Furthermore, Jewish prominence in the administration of Muslim Spain did not ensure their physical safety and sometimes aroused deep resentment. When, for example, the Jewish vizier Joseph Ibn Naghrela fell from favor in 1066, Muslims in Granada slaughtered thousands of Jews.

Regarding women in al-Andalus, while some did receive an education and develop careers as doctors, it is important to note these women were frequently slaves or came from the lowest levels of society. Women belonging to respected or elite families had severe restrictions placed upon their activities. In fact, in some circles, they were not allowed to visit other women more than once a week. When a man from outside their family came to their home, they were expected to be veiled and had to withdraw behind a curtain.

Of course, not every Muslim in Spain faithfully observed the precepts of the Maliki Madhab. However, its legal ideal of segregation contradicts the historiographical interpretation of Medieval Muslim Spain as a land of protomodern tolerance. Ultimately, both the *Reconquista* and the "religious pluralism" perspectives err by attempting to impose the values of the historian on the past. Our ideal should be to let previous generations' beliefs and worldview speak for themselves without seeking to find within them support for our own contemporary experiences and biases.

A Christian and a Muslim playing chess. Illuminated miniature made c. 1283. Currently "Libros de ajedrez, dados y tablas, folio 64r" in the Library of the Monastery of San Lorenzo de El Escorial, Madrid, Spain. This image is from *Libros de ajedrez, dados y tablas* ("Book of Games, Chess, Dice and Boards") compiled by Alfonso X of Castile. Scholars have pointed out that the tent and weapons signify a military context for the game and the arrangement of the chess pieces indicates that the Christian player will lose the game.

decisions theoretically defined Islamic law and teaching, even when these decisions contradicted the position of former caliphs.

Such a situation occurred early in 'Abbasid history. The caliph al-Ma'mun instituted a new inquisition to address the pressing debate among Muslims about the nature of the *Qur'an*. Traditional Muslims held that the *Qur'an* was God's word and therefore timeless and uncreated. To teach otherwise suggested to them that God could change. Other Muslims concluded that the *Qur'an* proceeded from God and that, therefore, God must have preexisted the *Qur'an*. Al-Ma'mun supported this second, rationalist position. His inquisition targeted the religious elite in Baghdad and forced them to disavow any belief in the uncreated nature of the *Qur'an*. Those who refused were beheaded. The majority of Muslims remained unshaken in their belief in an uncreated *Qur'an* despite this threat of death. The inquisition came to an end fifteen years later, having failed to uproot this popular belief. Its failure led later caliphs to side with the majority, and they condemned the rationalist position that the *Qur'an* had a created nature. Nonetheless, the damage to their spiritual prestige proved lasting. Future generations increasingly looked to Muslim scholars rather than to caliphs for religious leadership.

Moreover, the victory of the traditional position reaffirmed the absolute omnipotence of God, but with a particular Islamic interpretation. Muslim scholars argued that because God was all-powerful, His current actions were not limited by His previous actions or by any moral law. In fact, His actions could not be described or understood by human language or human relationships. What humanity could understand were His commands as revealed in the *Qur'an*. Such a position was a stark contrast to the Christian belief that God cannot contradict Himself and that humanity can know God (albeit imperfectly) through both revelation and human reason.

Sufism, a minority position within Islam, challenged this notion that humanity could have no knowledge of God outside the *Qur'an*. Sufis, whose name came from their garments of white wool (*suf* in Arabic), claimed that by entering into an ecstatic state, their souls experienced spiritual communion with God. They even honored their dead leaders as saints by venerating their tombs. Such practices were horrifying to conservative Muslim scholars. Venerating later Muslim leaders implied that Muhammad was not the final prophet who taught the fulness of revelation, and they believed that claims of spiritual union with God hinted at polytheism. Caliphs accordingly launched an inquisition against the Sufis. Most famously, a Sufi named Husayn Ibn Mansur al Hallaj (858–922) was convicted of heresy in 922. His hands and feet were cut off, and he was publicly exposed for a day after this disfigurement before finally being decapitated. His body was burned, and the ashes cast into the Tigris River to prevent his followers from honoring his memory.

The orthodox Islamic position regarding humanity's inability to know God also had ramifications for the intellectual achievements of the Golden Age. Aristotle's works proposed that men could both learn about God and themselves through reason and the knowledge they gained through their senses. Such a view was at obvious variance with the Islamic orthodoxy described above. As early as the tenth century, an 'Abbasid vizier attacked those who were translating Greek philosophical books into Arabic, declaring that Muslims did not need to study logic.

In 1091, the leader of the influential Ash'ari school of theology, al-Ghazali (1058–1111), published a work titled *The Incoherence of the Philosophers,* the culmination of a four-volume series of attacks on Muslim philosophers. In this text, he accused Avicenna and his disciples of being utterly irreligious and guilty of seventeen counts of heresy. Al-Ghazali specifically condemned them for trying to use reason to explain God's existence and attributes rather than relying on faith.

Averroes faced similar opposition. He wrote a response disputing al-Ghazali's claims, boldly titled *The Incoherence of the Incoherence*, in which he argued that Greek rational thought does not contradict Islam but that the *Qur'an* and Greek philosophy could point towards God in different ways. This claim was not well received. Averroes was summoned to the court of the ruler of al-Andalus where he was publicly insulted, cursed, and accused of heresy. He was then exiled, and his philosophical books were ordered to be burned. The subsequent persecution was severe, and opposition to studying Averroes's philosophy among Muslims would last for centuries.

The Decline of the Golden Age

Perhaps more troubling to the early 'Abbasid caliphs than these religious debates was their weak hold over the military. Many Muslim soldiers remained loyal to their local tribal leaders rather than to the caliphs. In the 830s, the caliph al-Mu'tasim (r. 833–842) decided that the solution was to buy slaves and train them as his soldiers. These slave-soldiers came primarily from the Turkish peoples who had recently settled on the eastern borders of the caliphate. Al-Mu'tasim believed that these slaves would be more loyal since, unlike Arab soldiers, they lacked family networks of support and had to rely on the caliph's good favor for everything.

Initially, this system was successful. The Turkish warriors were loyal to the caliph and maintained order among the Arab tribes. Eventually, however, the slave-soldiers realized their own power and began to fight for their own interests. They assassinated four caliphs in the next fifty years. In 946, one group of Turkish warriors, the Buyids, even seized Baghdad itself. While they did not claim the caliphate for themselves, they now effectively controlled the 'Abbasid dynasty.

Adding another layer of humiliation for the ʿAbbasids was the fact that the Buyids had embraced Shiʿism, a form of Islam the caliphs considered heretical. Shiʿite influence was on the rise throughout the caliphate during the tenth century, and in 909, Shiʿites seized control of Egypt. They established the **Fatimid dynasty** (909–1171) and claimed to be descended from Muhammad's daughter Fatima. Unlike the Buyids, the Fatimids hoped to establish a Shiʿite caliphate. By 976, they had seized Damascus and much of Syria. The Sunni inhabitants of these lands employed different Turkish warrior groups to protect them from the Fatimids. The Turkish mercenaries promptly carved out their own territories and fought with one another in addition to the Fatimids. The region became increasingly unstable.

Al-Azhar Mosque. Built by Caliph al-Muʿizz li-Din Allah in 970 in Cairo, Egypt. It was the first mosque constructed in Cairo, a newly built capital of the Fatimid caliphate following the Fatimid conquest of Egypt. The courtyard dates from the Fatimid period, but the minarets were added c. 1500.

The ʿAbbasids were "rescued" from the Buyids by another Turkish group, the Seljuks. The Seljuks had settled in modern-day Iran in the tenth century and had converted to Sunni Islam. Their power increased, and in 1055, their leader, Tughril (c. 990–1063), drove out the Buyids and seized Baghdad. Tughril appointed himself to the new office of ***sultan*** (Arabic for "authority" or "strength"). By claiming this title, Tughril did not present himself as a successor to Muhamad like the caliphs, but rather as a pious military leader charged by the caliphs with defending orthodox Islamic teaching from heretics like the Buyids and other enemies. It was Tughril's successor, Alp Arslan, who won the Battle of Manzikert against the Byzantines in 1071 and thus precipitated the events that led to the First Crusade.

The success of the First Crusade must be understood in light of this chronic political and religious fragmentation, which engulfed even the Seljuks in the years immediately before the crusade. Despite its advances in technology and education, the ʿAbbasid world was deteriorating. Though, in theory, the caliphs remained the political-religious leaders of the Islamic world, the rulers in Baghdad were predominately now mere figureheads whose lands their own generals and rival religious leaders divided among themselves.

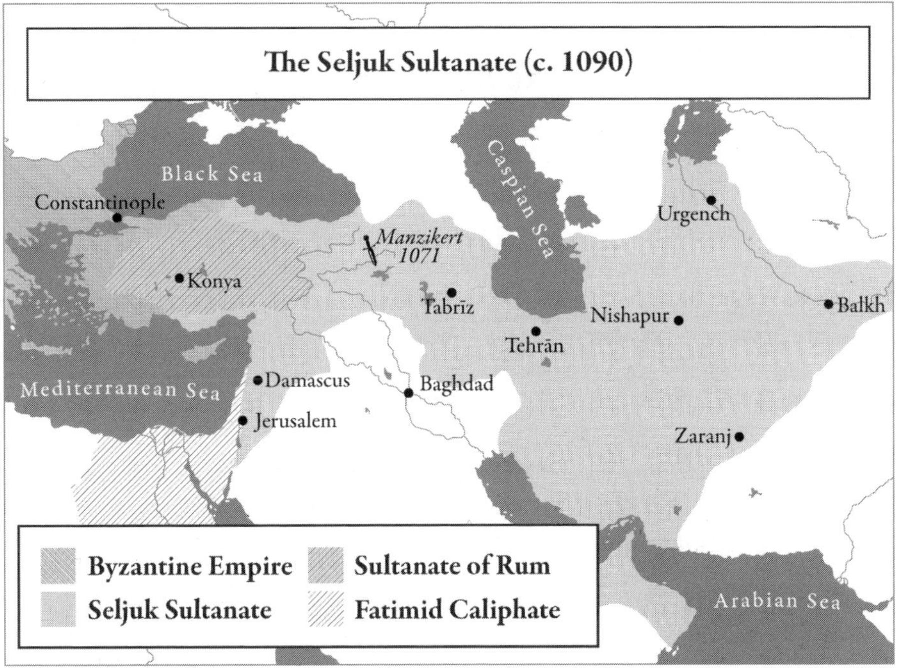

Conclusion

The political and religious conflicts that wracked the ʿAbbasid caliphate also posed an existential threat to the intellectual culture of Islam's Golden Age. While Sufis were targeted because of their mysticism, the prevailing religious culture was far more suspicious of any type of independent rational inquiry. The ʿAbbasid response to the question of God's omnipotence made speculative philosophy an attack on Islam. According to many Muslim *ulama*, any effort to uncover underlying rational principles that governed the universe was a blasphemous effort to understand and limit God's power.

Learning that directly supported the practice of Islam, such as the efforts to understand the movements of the stars so as to observe more accurately seasons of feasting and fasting, was approved. But other philosophical and scientific knowledge was considered dangerous by the caliphs and scholars of Islam. In contrast, many in Christian Europe eagerly embraced whatever knowledge came to them. Though there was resistance among some Christians to new ideas, it never amounted to the official persecution against philosophy that some caliphs and others encouraged. In fact, as we will see in the next unit, the torch of learning would ultimately pass to the universities of medieval Europe, which would debate, incorporate, and deepen the ancient wisdom whose preservation and spread was the lasting fruit of the Islamic Golden Age.

THE ASSASSINS

Shi'ism had its own different branches, including the Nizari Ismailis. These disagreed with the majority of Shi'ites regarding the proper succession of leadership after 'Ali and argued that a break had occurred in leadership at the seventh generation (c. 765). (They are therefore often known as "Sevener Shi'ites.") This small branch of Islam—a minority position within a minority—developed a military branch of warriors who became known as the Order of Assassins. In the twelfth century, these fighters held a series of fortifications in northern Syria and elsewhere. These Shi'ites terrorized opposing Muslims as well as Christians who settled in the area after the First Crusade. For nearly two centuries, assassins killed prominent leaders, including three caliphs and a king of Jerusalem. The head of their organization came to be known as "The Old Man of the Mountain," and, according to tradition, the title "assassin" has its origin in hashish, a narcotic that they apparently used before their murderous missions. The assassins continued to be a threat until the thirteenth century when the Mongols systematically destroyed their strongholds and either butchered the survivors or sold them into slavery.

Masyaf Castle. Located about 25 miles west of Hama, Syria. It became famous as the stronghold for the Order of Assassins during the days of Rashid ad-Din Sinan, the "Old Man of the Mountain" from 1162-1193.

UNIT VII
The Flowering of Christendom

CHAPTER 27

The Era of Eleanor of Aquitaine

Trees are known not by their leaves or their flowers, but by their fruits.

Eleanor of Aquitaine, *Letter to Pope Celestine III*

Eleanor of Aquitaine (c. 1122–1204) was born into an era of dramatic events. The First Crusade had ended in triumph, and the crusader states now granted European Christians access to the holy city of Jerusalem and other biblical sites. The end of the Investiture Controversy also promised a new beginning, and popes cautiously hoped that their authority in the Church was now beyond dispute. Yet, many challenges lay ahead. The monarchs and nobility of medieval Europe still sought to increase their power by subordinating the Church to their authority. Furthermore, the papal-imperial dispute entered a new stage that saw the emperor reassert a spiritual role in the life of Christendom.

Nonetheless, many of these nobles, kings, and emperors were also people of faith and acknowledged the Church's teachings to an extent hitherto unknown in European history. The ongoing Church reform fostered this religious worldview and helped to reduce the violence and turmoil of previous centuries. Furthermore, the increased stability of the twelfth century inspired medieval men and women to see law rather than physical might as an effective principle to guide society and limit abuses. Both temporal leaders and clergymen embraced a new, legal mindset that contributed to the flourishing of medieval European culture. While the leaves and even the flowers of these twelfth-century trees could be quite ugly, their fruit was rich indeed.

Crusader Queen of France

Eleanor was the eldest daughter and heir of the Duke of Aquitaine, one of the most powerful nobles in France. Her grandfather was the infamous William IX (1071–1126), and her childhood was shaped by the artistic refinement of his court. Poetry, troubadours, and scandal abounded in William's Aquitaine. When, for example, a bishop criticized William's openly adulterous relationship, William imprisoned him until the cleric died and then he joked that he had helped the bishop gain Heaven. His surviving poems frequently express his lust, and their crassness shocked his contemporaries. Nonetheless, it was William's Aquitaine that shaped the society of southern France and influenced its politics.

In contrast, the kings of West Frankia, or France as we will now consistently call it, were weak. Ever since the Viking raids of the ninth century, the authority of Carolingian kings had fragmented and then ended altogether when the last Carolingian king, Louis V the Do-Nothing, died without children. The new **Capetian dynasty** (987–1328) at first fared little better than its predecessors. Capetian kings could only uphold royal law in the so-called *Île de France* ("Island of France"), a small region basically composed of the cities of Paris and Orleans. So ineffective was royal prestige that it was unsafe even for the king to travel unguarded between the two cities. Nonetheless, the Capetians had one significant asset—their consistent ability to produce an heir. Though technically elected at the beginning, their dynasty successfully passed the crown from father to son until 1316 (at which point an uncle ascended the throne). These centuries of stable, orderly succession helped transform the French monarchy into a dominant power in medieval politics.

In the eleventh century, the Capetians were still attempting to establish their influence. Louis VI (r. 1108–1137) reinforced royal claims within the *Île de France*, but his greatest diplomatic success came shortly before his death when he arranged the marriage between the fifteen-year-old Eleanor of Aquitaine and his son Louis VII of France (r. 1137–1180). Louis's background could not have been more different from that of his bride. Originally it was his elder brother who was expected to reign, and Louis had prepared for a life in the Church. When his brother died prematurely, the devout and reserved Louis found himself thrust into the heart of French politics. For the cosmopolitan and worldly-wise Eleanor, Louis's piety was unbecoming. She once contemptuously declared that she expected her husband to be a king only to discover that she had married a monk.

Events in the Levant began to shape the course of Eleanor's life. Division among local Muslim rulers had been a key factor in the success of the First Crusade. These conditions persisted for several more decades and enabled the crusader states, such as the Latin Kingdom of Jerusalem, to develop feudal structures and learn to live side-by-side with their Muslim subjects. Many local Muslims actually preferred coexisting peacefully in the crusader states since they could observe their own religious law while avoiding the more severe Islamic government of the Turks. This situation changed in the 1120s when a new generation of Muslim rulers from northern Syria began to unite the surrounding areas and promote campaigns against the crusaders as acts of pious *jihad*.

The first of these leaders was a Turkish governor, or *atabeg*, named Zengi (r. 1127–1146). He was a determined leader and used fear to intimidate his soldiers and enemies alike. Warriors who fell out of line on the march were crucified, and he once executed those who had rebelled against him even after he swore on the *Qur'an* to accept their surrender. By 1144, Zengi was ready to attack the County of Edessa, the most vulnerable of the crusader states. After a four-month siege, he breached the city of Edessa on Christmas Eve and took its citadel two days later. Zengi died in 1146, but his example encouraged Muslim leaders in the region to unite against the crusaders.

The fall of Edessa shocked those Christians who had assumed that the cities captured by crusaders would never again fall into Muslim hands. Pope Eugenius III (r. 1145–1153) called on the knights and rulers of Europe to remember the glorious example of those who had fought in the First Crusade and to imitate them by taking the crusading vow. The ensuing campaign is known as the **Second Crusade** (1146–1148).[1]

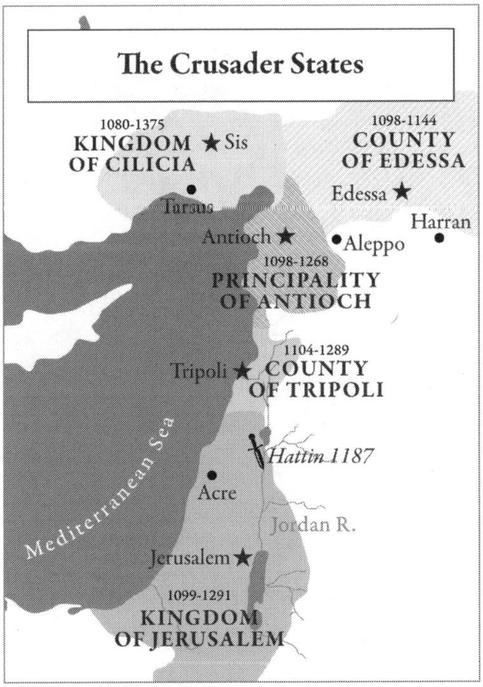

This crusade's most effective preacher was Western Europe's leading spiritual figure, **Bernard of Clairvaux** (1090–1153). Bernard belonged to the Cistercian Order, a new and vibrant branch of Benedictine monasticism. By the twelfth century, Cluny and its related monasteries had lost much

1 There were many crusade campaigns that are not reflected in the traditional numbering. These frequently happened in the years between the "numbered" crusades. Furthermore, while historians agree upon the naming for the "first" five crusades, consensus breaks down after the Fifth Crusade, and historians use different names to signify the same campaign.

of their reforming spirit. Costly donations became commonplace, and the abbey became less austere. Monks now performed little or no manual labor, sometimes merely touching a shovel to symbolize their fulfilment of the monastic rule's call to labor. The actual work was carried out by serfs attached to the abbey. Cluny's liturgies remained as elaborate and solemn as before, but medieval men and women increasingly sought a spirituality that also embraced the poverty and simplicity of the early Church.

During the eleventh century a number of monastic movements developed that emphasized lives of asceticism through silence, solitude, and poverty. The most rigorous of these new foundations was the Order of Carthusians, founded by Bruno of Cologne (c. 1030–1101). The first Carthusians lived high in the Alps, one of the most remote areas in all Western Europe. Unlike the Cluniac monks, they did not own farms and had to survive on the alms given them. They could go out to beg for sustenance but only after spending two days without food. Individual monks spent almost their entire lives in their cells, each of which had a small walled garden and a lavatory. They joined other monks for Matins and Lauds, Mass, and Vespers each day in the chapel and shared a meal as a community after Mass on Sundays. Otherwise, they spent their lives alone in prayer and contemplation.

Grande Chartreuse. Located in the mountains north of Grenoble, France. This has been the head monastery of the Carthusian Order since the days of St. Bruno.

The Cistercians promoted asceticism, too, but they emphasized greater community life and a more active ministry beyond the monastery walls. Their founder, Robert of Molesme (1029–1111), insisted that they would not employ peasants to work their lands like the monks of Cluny. Instead, their liturgies were shorter and simpler to allow time for monks to work and become self-sufficient. The Cistercians began constructing their first abbey on the feast of St. Benedict in 1098, in a wooded, swampy area known as Cîteaux in eastern France. They lived in humble wooden huts as they labored to clear the forests, grow crops, and build a monastery. The Cistercians refused to accept cultivated land whenever they founded another monastery, so many nobles willingly gave their communities territory commonly regarded as wasteland. By converting these lands into productive monastery farms, the Cistercians played an important role in supporting Europe's growing population by increasing the total acres under cultivation. Furthermore, Cistercian monks contributed to medieval agricultural practices by studying cow- and horse-breeding techniques as well as the effective use of watermills.

The main catalyst for the Cistercians' remarkable early growth was Bernard of Clairvaux. Bernard was born to a noble family, but he abandoned his status to join the young community at Cîteaux in 1112. He possessed a dominant—perhaps even domineering—personality, but his eloquence as a writer and preacher was spellbinding. In fact, thirty other young nobles joined him when he decided to become a monk. They were not the last he motivated to enter religious life.

His physical appearance reflected his life of self-denial, and his gaunt features were apparently so repellent to others that he was instructed to live in a separate cell and not in the common dorm. He vigorously denounced heretics and condemned corruption in the Church and at royal courts, but he also expressed deep tenderness when writing about the sacrificial love of Christ on the cross and the humble dedication of the Virgin Mary. He was the first to describe Jesus's mother as the "star of the sea" and the "mediatrix of all grace." The hymns *O Sacred Head Surrounded* and *Jesu Dulcis Memoria* are also attributed to Bernard.

Bernard's enthusiasm had swayed many young men to join the Cistercians, and Pope Eugenius—one of his former students—now turned to Bernard to preach the Second Crusade. As we discussed in chapter 25, the crusading vow involved a penitential character; Bernard saw this as a temporary adoption of the monastic vocation, which was in his eyes the surest route to Heaven. Knights throughout Western Europe flocked to the crusading banner when they heard his sermons. Eleanor and Louis were both inspired by Bernard's preaching and became the first monarchs to take the cross. Bernard also convinced the German Conrad III to join the crusade by pointing out all the good things he had received in his life and asking

THE KNIGHTS TEMPLAR

The Knights Templar was a military order which originated in the twelfth century when the French knight Hugh of Payn journeyed to Palestine with eight companions. They took the traditional monastic vows and an additional vow to defend pilgrims traveling to the Holy Sepulcher. The order was named for their headquarters, said to be the site of the Temple of Solomon. It received papal approval in 1128.

Bernard of Clairvaux was an enthusiastic supporter of the Templars. He helped write the rule for the order and saw participation in this company of fighting monks as a way for warriors to share in the spiritual riches of monastic life. The Templars followed the traditional monastic schedule of prayers, and those knights who were illiterate prayed a specified number of memorized prayers. The religious habit of the Templars was distinctive: a red cross on a white background.

The Templars provided the Latin Kingdom of Jerusalem with a loyal and well-trained strike force. On one occasion, a group of five hundred Templars led a force of five thousand crusaders to victory over a Muslim army that outnumbered them four to one. While the Templars had their rivals and enemies, no one questioned their bravery. They were not allowed to surrender unless the whole army had stopped fighting or to leave the battlefield unless every standard had fallen. Fleeing from the battle was grounds for expulsion from the order.

Aside from military duties, the Templars also served as the first bankers of Europe. They had established recruiting and training houses across Europe. Pilgrims could, for a small fee, deposit money at one of these local Templar houses. They received a receipt that then enabled them to access the same amount at any other Templar station along their route and in the Holy Land. This service made the Templar Order extremely wealthy, a development that would lead to tragedy in the years ahead.

what more Jesus must do to prompt Conrad to follow Him. Furthermore, Bernard labored extensively to protect Jewish communities from any repeat of the atrocities of the First Crusade, but, unfortunately, his efforts failed to protect everyone.

To the monk's bitter regret, the early promise of the Second Crusade never yielded its fruit. Both Louis's and Conrad's armies were severely weakened by attacks from Turkish forces as they crossed Anatolia. They received little help from the Byzantines, who viewed the crusade with suspicion. When the crusaders arrived in the Holy Land, their one attempted attack foolishly targeted one of the crusaders' few Muslim allies and was an abysmal failure. Eleanor openly disagreed with Louis's military strategy, and rumors spread that she was having an affair with her uncle, the urbane ruler of crusader Antioch. The Second Crusade ended with the crusader states in worse circumstances and Louis and Eleanor's marriage falling apart.

Bernard, like most other medieval Christians, was confused and disheartened by the failure of the Second Crusade. How could God have allowed such a holy enterprise to fail? He concluded that God was allowing His people to be defeated in order to foster in them a spirit of true repentance and a greater reliance on Him. Despite military failure, he emphasized that the campaign had benefited the souls of those crusaders who had confessed their sins and had died out of love for the Holy Land. Bernard's emphasis on the spiritual benefit to participants is crucial for understanding the medieval approach to crusading. While the crusaders earnestly desired to preserve Christian Jerusalem, many considered the salvation of the crusaders' souls a fundamental goal that could be achieved regardless of a campaign's success or failure.

Queen of England

After returning from the Second Crusade, Eleanor and Louis sought an annulment of their marriage. Eleanor had no respect for Louis, and Louis grew bitter because Eleanor had not given him a son. Pope Eugenius tried for three years to salvage the relationship. In the end, he consented to the opinion of four French archbishops that Louis and Eleanor were too closely related to marry due to the fact that they were third cousins once removed. The marriage was annulled. Eleanor's lands were returned to her, and Louis received custody of their two daughters.

It was dangerous for a lady with Eleanor's possessions to remain single for long. As she returned to her lands, two lords attempted to kidnap her and force her to marry them. Eleanor decided to propose marriage to Henry Plantagenet, Duke of Normandy and heir to the English throne. They were married in May 1152, eight weeks after Eleanor's annulment was granted. Ironically, Henry and Eleanor were also third cousins.

The rise and fall of Eleanor's marriages illustrates both improvement and lingering problems in the understanding of marriage among European nobility. On the one hand, many Church leaders no longer turned a blind eye when kings divorced their wives or publicly kept concubines as they had in the time of Charlemagne. On the other hand, some individuals expected that they should be able to dissolve their marriage vows for political or personal interests. These found an excuse for such behavior in the fact that many noble or royal couples could appeal to a common ancestor and thus claim that they were too closely related to their spouse for their marriage to have been valid. Of course, the bishop of the king or queen was responsible for informing them if they were too closely related to one another for marriage. Many times, however, they were either negligent or bowed to pressure from those who desired such unions for political reasons. The European nobility needed further persuasion that marriage was truly permanent and monogamous if they were not to view annulments as a convenient legal loophole to be abused.

Two years after Eleanor's marriage, her new husband became King **Henry II** (r. 1154–1189) of England. (Henry II Plantagenet should not be confused with the German Henrys whom we have studied in previous chapters.) Unlike Louis, Henry did not have a monk's disposition, and both his and Eleanor's fiery personalities led to heated arguments and a tumultuous marriage. Nonetheless, Eleanor bore Henry eight children, including five sons, thus securing his dynasty for another generation.

In addition, their marriage made Henry immensely powerful. After becoming king of England in 1154, he ruled not only England and Normandy but also Eleanor's Aquitaine and the French lands he had inherited from his father. Historians call Henry's network of territories the "Angevin Empire," after Henry's father, Geoffrey of Anjou. This "empire" was not a unified, centralized state but rather a collection of feudal communities that remained distinct entities. Nonetheless, Henry had access to their resources and was a far more powerful ruler than Louis VII, the feudal lord to whom he technically owed homage for these French territories as a vassal.

Henry inherited an English kingdom in disorder. His mother, Matilda, was the granddaughter of William the Conqueror and had inherited the throne in 1135. Her cousin Stephen contested the crown in a long and confusing civil war that was concluded by an agreement that Henry would inherit the throne after Stephen's death. This civil war had weakened the English monarchs' power over their kingdom, and English nobles constructed stone castles to establish their own independent authority over local regions.

Henry's priority was to restore stability and royal power. He set about demolishing the castles that had been built without royal authorization and gave lands to minor nobles to ensure their loyalty to the crown. A standard system of law, enforced equally throughout England by a panel of royal judges, also reasserted his royal power. This standardized royal law, which included the use of juries and the creation of a legal handbook, had an influence far beyond Henry's own ambitions. It is traditionally seen as the foundation of English Common Law, which shaped the legal system of the United States centuries later.

One area of English society remained outside Henry's legal control: the Church. Clergymen ran their own ecclesiastical courts, which oversaw situations that involved clerics. Henry desired to bring such cases under royal authority. When the archbishop of Canterbury, the most senior bishop in England, died in 1162, Henry saw his opportunity to secure the appointment of a successor who would agree with his agenda. He believed he had the ideal candidate in his chancellor **Thomas Becket** (1118–1170), a close friend whose extravagant lifestyle rivaled the king's. Henry

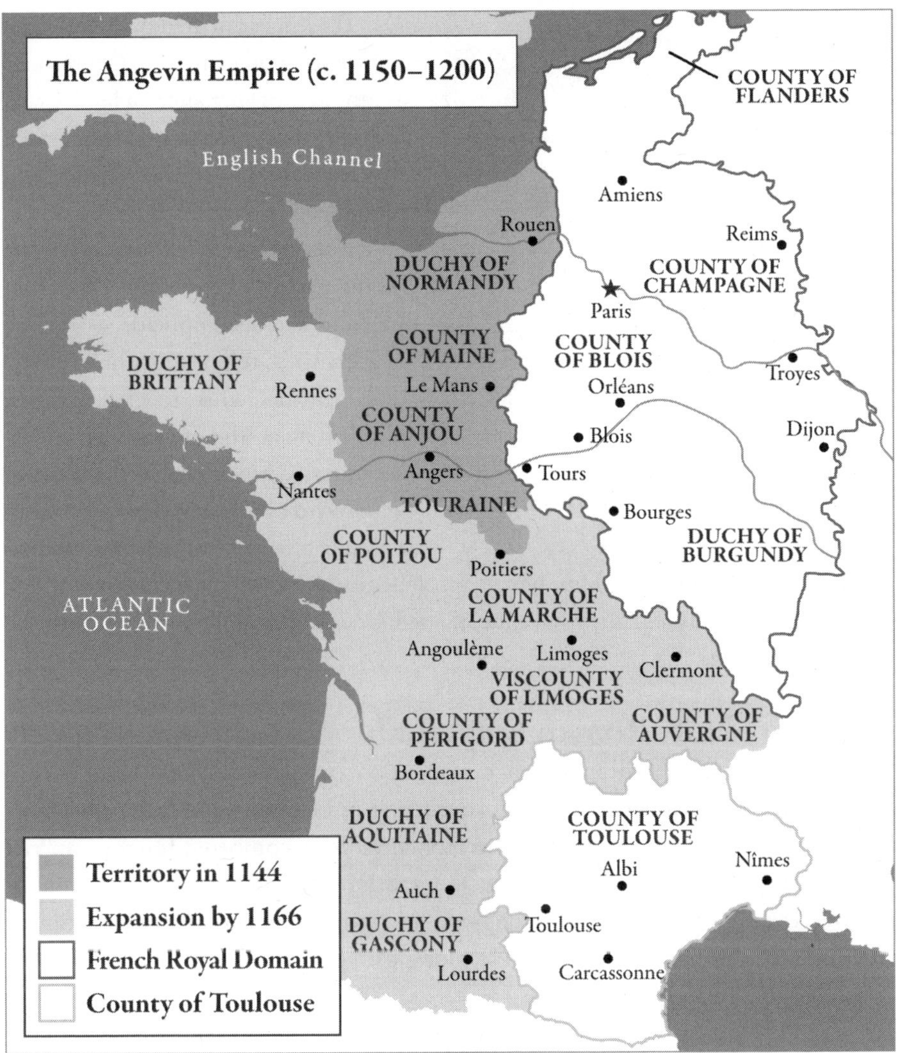

convinced the clergy to elect Becket, though Eleanor warned that Becket might not be as pliable as Henry hoped.

Indeed, upon receiving episcopal ordination, Becket began defending the liberty of the Church against Henry's reforms. Becket's apparent ingratitude infuriated Henry, and the two became bitter opponents. Eventually, four knights who hoped to win royal favor murdered Becket in his own cathedral in 1170. Christians were horrified by this act of sacrilege and many blamed Henry. Pilgrims soon came from across Europe to honor Becket as a martyr, and reports of miracles through his intercession spread.

Dispute of King Henry II and Thomas Becket. Illuminated miniature made c. 1307-1327 by Peter of Langtoft. Currently "Royal MS 20 A II, ff. 7v-8r" in the British Library, London, England. This image is from *The Chronicle of England*.

The king admitted guilt and himself went on pilgrimage to Canterbury as an act of penance. He allowed himself to be scourged, venerated the tomb of his former friend, and renounced his efforts to gain control of the ecclesiastical courts. For the moment, the liberty of the Church in England had been upheld.

Henry's reign remained unsettled. All his sons rebelled against him, often at the encouragement of Eleanor. By 1189, Henry was old and sick. When he heard that his youngest, and favorite, son had also joined the latest rebellion against him, he collapsed beneath the weight of his sorrow. He recovered consciousness one final time, made his last confession, and died with the Church's blessing.

The First "Holy Roman Emperor"

While rulers in England and France worked to establish effective control over their territories, a similar struggle was occurring in Germany and Italy. Two powerful noble families, the Welfs and the Hohenstaufens, competed for the imperial title. The first Hohenstaufen ruler was Conrad III (r. 1138–1152). Conrad never received the imperial crown from the pope, and so he remained merely the "king of the Romans" throughout his reign. He, along with Louis VII, set the precedent for monarchs to join a crusade.

Conrad's son was only six years old when Conrad died, and the dying king decided to designate his nephew **Frederick Barbarossa** (r. 1152–1190) as his heir. Though many of Frederick's ambitions met with failure, contemporaries and later generations considered Frederick one of the most politically adept and militarily accomplished rulers of the entire medieval period. He dreamed of restoring the empire to its ancient glory and encouraged a revival of the sixth-century Justinian Code across his lands. The reemphasis on Roman law promoted the imperial throne, for the Justinian Code described the emperor in quasi-religious terminology and assumed his authority in Church matters. This perspective encouraged pro-imperial political theorists to reject the suspicion towards temporal authority that Augustine had expressed in *The City of God*. Rather, they concluded that temporal government

Bust of Frederick I Barbarossa. Made of gilded bronze c. 1160. Currently in St. Johannes Evangelist Church in Cappenberg, Germany. Frederick's Italian nickname "Barbarossa" referenced his red beard.

was naturally good and therefore invested by God with great power.

Frederick took advantage of the conflicts raging among Italian city-states to secure his authority in northern Italy. These cities were technically vassals of the Roman Empire, and their local factions soon identified with one of the rival German families. The Ghibellines, as the Hohenstaufens were known in Italian, fought for the current imperial family, while the Guelfs allied themselves with the Welfs.

Pope Adrian IV (r. 1154–1159) welcomed Frederick's attempt to stabilize the region and agreed to crown Frederick emperor. However, two years after the coronation, Adrian's legate seemingly declared that the crown was a type of fief in a lord-vassal relationship where the pope was the lord and Fredrick was his vassal. Frederick rejected this claim of papal overlordship and insisted that the emperor held authority over Rome and the surrounding region. To emphasize this, Frederick began to use the adjective "holy" to describe the empire in his official documents. By claiming that he ruled not just the "Roman Empire" but the "**Holy Roman Empire**," Frederick was claiming that the empire was holy in itself and did not require papal blessing. It was a striking assertion of the temporal ruler's claim to be the true head of Christendom's "Church-State".

Adrian IV died in 1159. In the conclave that followed, the cardinals failed to decide on a single candidate. Most favored Alexander III (r. 1159–1181). Others supported Barbarossa's ally, who also claimed the papacy and took the name Victor IV (r. 1159–1164). Frederick cited the precedent of Charlemagne, Otto I, and Henry III and asserted the right to decide the election. He declared Victor to be the pope and forced clerics across his lands to swear oaths rejecting Alexander.

Louis VII and Henry II both offered limited support to Alexander, but their own rivalry as well as Henry's efforts to subordinate the Church in England undermined the effectiveness of their help. Rather, Alexander's primary political assistance came from the cities in northern Italy who were increasingly resentful of Frederick's influence in the region. Guided by Alexander, these Italians established an alliance known as the Lombard League. Their coalition confronted and routed the imperial army at the Battle of Legano in 1176.

The defeat forced Frederick to adopt diplomatic methods and agree to the Treaty of Venice in 1177. The emperor acknowledged Alexander as pope, begged his absolution, and recognized the independence of the Lombard League cities and the papacy. In return, Frederick secured permission for those clerics who had sided against Alexander to retain their positions.

With his authority now secured, Alexander summoned the Third Lateran Council in 1179. The canons of this ecumenical council were designed to eliminate clerical abuses, including charging fees for sacraments and pluralism, which was the practice of bishops and priests holding multiple sees or parishes to increase their personal revenue. They also strengthened the integrity of papal elections by requiring a two-thirds majority, rather than a simple majority, to win.

The texts of the Third Lateran Council demonstrate the rise of a legal mindset in the Church during this period. The Investiture Controversy and subsequent conflict with Frederick had emphasized to churchmen the need for an independent system of laws that would outline Church government. This universal canon law system was based on principles of Roman law and applied to the whole Church instead of a local region. Its emergence shaped subsequent Church government and encouraged popes to use legal principles to define the extent of their jurisdiction. Indeed, various canons gave legal justification for papal intervention wherever local authority was deemed neglectful. By promulgating a separate system of ecclesial laws, Church officials emphasized that the Church was not governed by temporal rulers; furthermore, those same temporal rulers were subject to the Church's law.

In contrast to the papacy's successful centralization, Frederick Barbarossa realized that strong rivals had used his campaigns in Italy to undermine the emperor's position in Germany itself. He was forced to confirm the feudal authority of German dukes in order to secure their loyalty. This action did enable him to defeat his primary rival, Henry the Lion of Saxony, but it came at tremendous cost: nobles now had petty realms that were effectively independent of imperial oversight. Even as the monarchs of England and France were consolidating power, the Holy Roman Empire was destined to remain feudal and fragmented.

Nonetheless, Frederick successfully arranged the marriage of his son Henry to the aunt of the Norman king of Sicily. This Norman kingdom included southern Italy and Sicily and had been established in 1130. It blended Byzantine, Arab, and Norman populations into a culturally rich society, and its official documents were issued in Arabic, Greek, and Latin. It even maintained separate judges who supervised the administration of Islamic law for the Muslim population and Roman law for Christians. The marriage alliance between the Norman and Germanic worlds would have significant consequences for Frederick's descendants.

The Third Crusade

While Christians in Europe enjoyed a brief truce from the struggle between spiritual and temporal authority, the crusader states experienced a series of military defeats that jeopardized their very existence. **Saladin** (1138–1193) was a brilliant general and a committed Muslim, who once declared that he was willing to sail across the whole earth to liberate it from anyone who would not submit to Islam. He had served as the vizier to the last caliph of the Shi'ite Fatimid dynasty before deposing that ruler in 1171. Saladin claimed the title of sultan, removed Shi'ites from positions of power, and pledged religious fidelity to the 'Abbasid caliphs in Baghdad. This action reunited the region under Sunni leadership and set the stage for Saladin's assault against the Kingdom of Jerusalem in 1187.

The crusader states were rapidly becoming their own worst enemies. The tragic rule of Baldwin IV the Leper King (r. 1174–1185) contributed to internal rivalries as local lords sought to control the throne after his death. Their antagonism was exacerbated when Saladin besieged the citadel of Tiberias, which at the time was commanded by the wife of the Count of Tripoli. Saladin used the mistrust among the crusader leaders to lure the crusader army out into the desert. There, his tactical skill and numerical superiority allowed him to surround the Christians at the Battle of Hattin. The overwhelming majority were either killed or captured. Saladin's forces also captured the relic of the True Cross and carried it in triumph to Saladin's capital in Damascus. Muslims celebrated its capture as evidence of Islam's superiority over Christianity.

The news of the defeat at Hattin sent shockwaves through Medieval Europe. Pope Urban III reportedly died of sorrow when he heard the news. His successor, Gregory VIII (r. 1187), immediately issued a call for all Christians to participate in a new crusade. Those who could not fight were to contribute spiritually through prayer and fasting.

Thus began what historians call the **Third Crusade** (1189–1192). This campaign is considered the high point of the crusading movement, and all the leading rulers of Europe took the crusading vow. (Only the Spanish kings, who were engaged in their own campaigns against Muslims, did not join.) Frederick Barbarossa was among the first monarchs to take the cross. Now a man of almost seventy, he ended his turbulent reign by making peace with the Italian cities, the German dukes, and the pope and dedicating his final campaign to the service of God. Leaving Constantinople and crossing Anatolia, Frederick made use of his experience fighting in these territories during the Second Crusade to achieve a series of impressive victories. Tragedy struck, however, when the aging emperor drowned while crossing a river, perhaps after suffering a heart attack. Most of his troops returned home to participate in the election of a new German ruler.

Even the kings of England and France put aside their long-standing feud to join the crusade. Henry II died before he could fulfil his vow, but his son Richard I (r. 1189–1199), known as Richard the Lionheart, took up the cross in his father's place and sailed to the Holy Land with the French king Philip II, also known as Philip Augustus. These two were uneasy allies. Richard was tall, extroverted, beloved by his men, and considered the leading soldier of the age. Such was his charisma that he remains one of England's most beloved kings—despite the fact that he spent only several months in England after becoming its king! Philip was perhaps the most adept politician of this period, but he was taciturn, sickly, and uninspiring.

The two kings bickered and quarreled throughout their travels together. During the siege of Acre, Richard's leadership was widely recognized as crucial to the crusaders' capture of the city. Even while sick, he arranged for two soldiers to carry him around the front lines in a litter, from which he fired a crossbow at the enemy soldiers. Philip was also sick and participated only sparingly in the siege. Once the city had fallen, he declared he had participated sufficiently in the crusade and returned home, leaving Richard to fight alone.

The remaining crusaders marched south along the coast towards Jerusalem. Saladin shadowed them with his army, trying to use his archers to lure them out of position, but Richard maintained tight discipline. Muslim authors were impressed that these soldiers could march all day in the heat of the sun while wearing metal armor and being peppered with arrows. Eventually, Saladin's subordinates panicked and demanded that the sultan confront Richard head-on. At the Battle of Arsuf, Richard wielded the might of the medieval cavalry charge with a dexterity displayed by few other commanders. The medieval knights, led by the king, shattered Saladin's lines, and the Muslim army fled in retreat.

Despite this success, Richard knew that his army did not have the resources to capture and hold Jerusalem. Moreover, he had received news that Philip Augustus had defied Church law by attacking Richard's lands in France even though he was on crusade. To make the situation even worse, Richard's younger brother John (r. 1199–1216) had usurped his throne in England. Richard therefore agreed to a three-year truce with Saladin that allowed Christian pilgrims to travel to Jerusalem and venerate the Holy Sepulcher.

Richard himself refused to go to Jerusalem, declaring that he had pledged to return the city to Christian hands and would not enter until he had done so. Yet,

Tomb Effigies of Eleanor of Aquitaine and Henry II. Made of carved marble c. 1204. Currently in Fontevraud Abbey in Anjou, France. Eleanor herself commissioned the effigies and chose to portray herself reading a Bible. Effigies of her son Richard the Lionheart and her daughter-in-law Isabelle, wife of King John of England, are located in the same hall. The Abbey was sacked during the French Revolution and the human remains were destroyed, but, remarkably, the original effigies survived. They remain among the best preserved effigies from this period.

his departure shortly after the truce broke his promise to remain in the Holy Land until the following Easter. Had he stayed as long as he initially said he would, the warrior-king would have been nearby when Saladin died unexpectedly several weeks before the holy day. Who can say what he might have done as Muslim unity fell apart once more? As it was, Richard's return journey only added to his troubles. Enemies in the Holy Roman Empire intercepted him en route, and Frederick Barbarossa's son held the crusader-king captive until the English delivered a vast amount of money for his ransom. Philip Augustus even attempted to convince the emperor to keep Richard captive permanently. When Richard finally secured his freedom, he returned a determined enemy to the French king who had so undermined his crusade and his kingdom.

Despite failing to reclaim Jerusalem, the Third Crusade demonstrated that crusader armies could still win victories in the Levant. It also showcased the success of the Church in shaping medieval culture. It was now an expectation that the most elite figures in society would risk their lives and dedicate their military abilities to the service of God's honor and the protection of the Holy Land.

Conclusion

The last decades of Eleanor's long life remained turbulent. Henry had effectively imprisoned her for her role in his sons' rebellions; for sixteen years she was under supervision, appearing only occasionally in public with Henry for form's sake. By 1202, all but two of her children were dead, and Eleanor became a nun at Fontevraud Abbey, which she had founded to support monastic reform. She dedicated her remaining days to prayer. They buried her next to her husband, Henry II, when she died two years later.

Eleanor's life epitomizes the culture of European nobles during the twelfth century. They were often quick to oppress the Church in their quest for power, yet they were also willing to sacrifice everything to fight for the Holy Land. They labored to establish systems of law that would establish accountability for all and promote a more just and stable society, but they willingly engaged in petty wars or betrayals for political gain. The European nobility of the twelfth century were flawed and inconsistent, but their sincere efforts contributed to the flowering of Christian culture in the generations that followed.

CHAPTER 28

The High Middle Ages

We, however, place the love of God and His honor, above our own and above the acquisition of many regions.

Richard the Lionheart[1]

This quote from Eleanor of Aquitaine's favorite son succinctly captures the spirit of the **High Middle Ages**. This period, which historians date from approximately the year 1000 to 1300, witnessed medieval Europeans build a culture of faith, beauty, and learning that was also increasingly economically successful. Monks still offered prayers to God, knights continued to fight for their lords, and peasants still tilled the fields, but other roles were also emerging. Merchants brought goods from faraway lands, artisans crafted beautiful buildings and practical tools, and scholars immersed themselves in ancient works and applied their wisdom to contemporary questions. In and among the steeples and marketplaces of medieval Europe, a new civilization flourished. This society was still an earthly community and was certainly not perfect. Nevertheless, it is accurate to say that the chief energies of this society—its building projects, its education, and even its ideals for warriors—were directed towards and motivated by the desire to give honor and glory to God.

1 Christopher Tyerman, *God's War: A New History of the Crusades* (Harvard: Belknap Press, 2006), 455.

The Medieval Economy

The strength of the Roman economy had been based on a simple land tax collected by the government. The empire had used its tax revenue to provide the stability and security that guaranteed lucrative, or profitable, trade throughout the Mediterranean and beyond. With the end of the Western Roman Empire in the fifth century, this system of commerce and taxation collapsed. Instead, barbarian kings maintained the loyalty of their warriors by allowing them to plunder treasure from the lands they conquered. The feudal system developed once the supply of treasure was exhausted. Warriors received land in return for their loyalty, and their serfs—whose peasant ancestors had first been tied to the land by Diocletian's reforms—farmed the land for them in exchange for the opportunity to keep some of the crops they cultivated. Most peasants were subsistence farmers who simply grew as much food as they could in order to feed themselves. They had no money or resources to acquire anything else.

Beginning in the late tenth century, the economic situation in Europe began to improve. The traumatic invasions of the preceding century had come to an end with the defeat of the Magyars at Lechfeld and the gradual conversion and assimilation of Viking Scandinavia. Greater peace contributed to economic prosperity. Crops and animals were less likely to be seized or destroyed by rampaging armies, and farmers were less likely to be summoned to war when they could ill afford to be spared from the fields.

Economic development was further enhanced by warmer temperatures during this period. Global temperatures tend to vary in slow fluctuations and have rarely remained static throughout history. The tenth century marked a period of warmer temperatures known as the **Medieval Warming Period**, which lasted for the next three and a half centuries. More lands were available to farm because more snow melted from higher places in the Alps during the spring and summer. As average temperatures increased, farmers across Europe were able to grow more food. (The temperatures were so warm that vineyards were cultivated in the north of England!) The average yield—the number of grains expected from planting a single seed—doubled from two to four, a significant increase for medieval society.

Medieval farmers capitalized on the stability and warmer temperatures. Farmers had previously grown a winter and summer crop, but now inventive landlords developed a system of cultivating three crops a year to increase the amount of food produced. Monks developed lighter plows that enabled their farmers to grow crops on more land. Monasteries and lay landlords drained marshland and reduced forests to increase the total area they were able to farm. More land under cultivation, more crops farmed on that land, and more productive crops all contributed to a surplus of food and a healthier and growing population.

By 1050, medieval Europe was developing an increasingly sophisticated economy. The lands of the nobles were now consistently producing more food than their households could consume. Markets emerged where this surplus was sold, and towns grew up around the sites of these markets. Many towns gradually grew into new cities that were protected by walls and were often situated near rivers to provide the best means of transportation. There was no urban planning or zoning, so the streets were narrow, haphazard in direction, and poorly drained. Waste, for example, was disposed of in an exposed gutter running down the middle of the street. Not only did this smell unpleasant but it also created a breeding ground for any number of diseases. This unsanitary situation did not stop these emerging urban centers from becoming vital hubs in medieval trade.

Many city-dwellers still kept gardens and raised a portion of their own food, but they were no longer forced to rely on a subsistence farming lifestyle. The supply of food from the countryside was reliable enough that they could instead dedicate themselves to developing trades. In this way, a market economy developed in which a wealthy elite lived in the cities and purchased the food, goods, and services they desired. An artisan class also lived on the food provided by the countryside and manufactured tools and luxury items. The revival of silver coins as a token of exchange facilitated these purchases. After the fall of Rome, farmers had simply bartered crops and services, but the reintroduction of currency in the tenth and eleventh centuries made it possible for artisans to sell their wares and buy food with the money they received.

The prices of this market economy were not shaped solely by supply and demand. Artisans belonged to **guilds** which regulated the number of goods members produced, the prices they could charge, and the hours they could work. These limits were imposed to protect their industry by ensuring high quality workmanship and by reducing competition that could lower prices. Apprentices lived in their mentor's household until they were accomplished enough to begin their own workshop. They received free food and lodging during their apprenticeship but worked without pay. Guilds were social and religious as well as business organizations; they buried and prayed for their deceased members and provided support for any widows or orphans left behind.

As the medieval economy expanded, cities became centers for long-distance trade that brought goods from outside the local community to sell in these population centers. The region of Italy was ideally positioned to play a central role in this expanding economy. Italian cities like Venice and Genoa were homes to merchants who carried out trade with North Africa and the Byzantine Empire. Crusader held

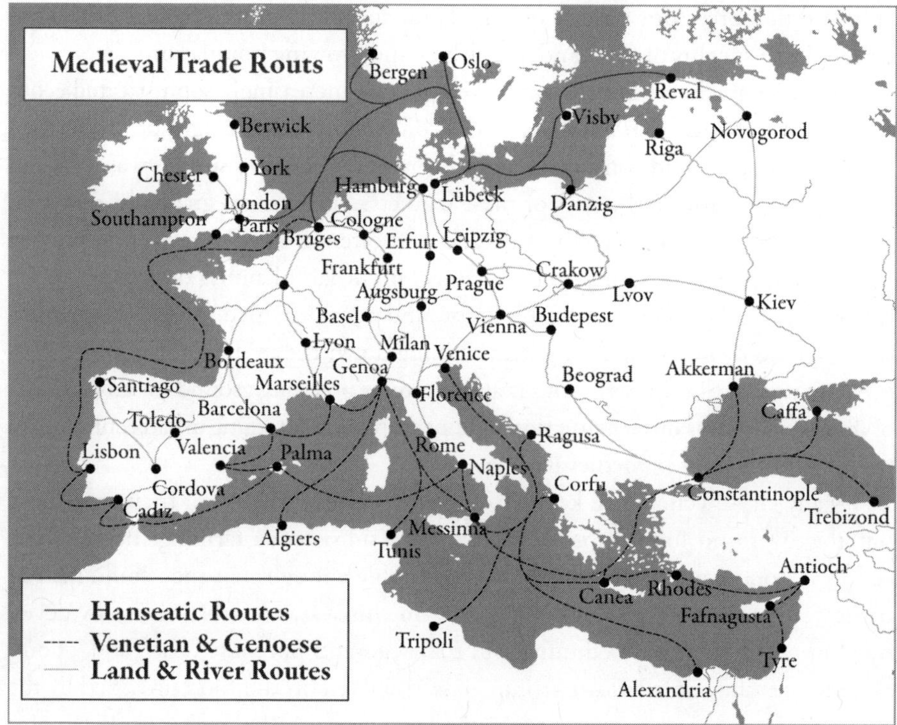

ports in Palestine also provided them with opportunities to trade for goods from West Asia and beyond. Merchants brought products from all these areas to their home cities in Italy, where they sold them at a profit to other merchants, who then brought them to market towns further inland. Some market towns developed into major economic centers that hosted fairs. These gatherings were important events and held at regular times. Merchants from across a region and beyond would gather for weeks at a time to exchange goods. A whole system of fairs blossomed in medieval Italy, England, and Flanders. The series of fairs in the County of Champagne were especially famous and well-attended.

Rivers were the most efficient means of transport, and many merchants used the Rhine River in particular as a means of bringing goods to central Europe. Other networks developed in northern Europe, where goods from England and Scandinavia were transported to the mainland. In this vibrant economic climate, many merchants and cities in Italy and the Netherlands and Belgium (where the Mediterranean and Baltic networks met via the Rhine river) became fabulously wealthy. By the end of the thirteenth century, Genoa was producing more wealth each year than the entire kingdom of France.

Gothic Architecture

Medieval men and women devoted a significant portion of their new wealth to the honor of God. This devotion was perhaps best demonstrated by the emergence of the Gothic architectural style and the construction of Gothic cathedrals.

Initially, medieval churches were built in imitation of the traditional Roman meeting hall, called a basilica. Bishops like Wilfrid (from chapter 22) promoted this style to encourage Christians across Europe to remember the shared Faith that linked them with ancient Rome and the teachings of the apostles. These buildings were built with heavy facades and rounded arches that emphasized the solemnity of the rites that took place inside.

In the mid-twelfth century, **Abbot Suger** (1081–1151), superior of a monastery in Paris and personal friend of Louis VII, pioneered a new style. This was given the name **Gothic** by later writers who despised medieval society and considered it barbaric, but this pejorative name does not detract from the unquestionable beauty of this architectural style. Gothic churches emphasized height and light—height in order to encourage clergy and laity to raise their minds to Heaven, and light because it was considered a fitting metaphor for God in the natural world, immaterial but warming and nurturing.

Abbot Suger was able to emphasize these characteristics because of recent technological advances in architecture. Architects had discovered that pointed arches displaced the weight resting on the opening more evenly than rounded ones and therefore allowed builders to construct larger windows that flooded the churches with light. These windows not only brought beauty but also served as tools to educate the largely illiterate population through their depictions of Bible stories or saints' lives. Similarly, the development of wall supports—known as flying buttresses—shifted the weight of the wall away from the building. These constructions enabled church builders to build taller walls that would not collapse in on themselves. Now they could build structures that seemed to reach into the sky, bridging the divide between Heaven and Christians still on earth.

Gothic cathedrals came to dominate the cultural and geographic landscapes of the new medieval cities. They were almost always the largest buildings in the city and frequently were built at the highest point. They represented incredible dedication and commitment of time, energy, and expense on the part of these communities. For example, the construction of Salisbury Cathedral in England required four thousand tons of lead, thirty-two thousand square feet of glass, and a central wooden beam that was eighty feet long. These projects typically involved great commitments of time and resources across generations, and many who invested their work and income to lay a church's foundations knew that they would not live to see its completion.

Cathedral of Our Lady of Chartres. Built c. 1194–1220 in Chartres, France. Located about 50 miles southwest of Paris, this cathedral epitomizes Gothic architecture with its pointed arches, soaring vaulted ceilings, stained glass windows and flying buttresses.

Just as Ancient Greek architecture embodied the Greeks' optimism that the universe was based on rational principles humans could understand, Gothic cathedrals reflected medieval confidence in their Christian faith. And yet, there was a striking difference in the symbolism. Whereas we could interpret the flat roofs of Greek temples to represent that society's underlying horizontal, or humanistic, perspective, the Gothic spires reaching to the sky indicated the medieval worldview that God was the ultimate source of this world's order and stability.

Medieval Learning

From the seventh to the tenth century, monasteries were the chief source of medieval learning. Monks and nuns were educated by means of ***lectio divina,*** focused reading of the Bible that combined prayer and meditation with the study of Sacred Scripture. This system of education had the ultimate goal of inspiring greater devotion either by the composition of theological, exegetical, or homiletic texts or through the expression of mystical experiences in music and poetry.

Beginning in the eleventh century, bishops across Western Europe began to promote intellectual activity by establishing schools attached to their cathedrals. The original purpose of these institutions was to train the choir and diocesan clergy for their tasks: singing, proclaiming the readings, managing episcopal accounts, and the like. The Cluniac reform movement further stimulated the growth of these schools by encouraging the education of clerics so that they could preach clearly and could understand and explain the reasoning behind canon law regulations. This reform-inspired curriculum concentrated on the ancient Greco-Roman program of study that included grammar, logic, and rhetoric. This was known as the *trivium*, or "place where three roads meet."

The reputation for academic excellence at some of the cathedral schools attracted many students who, thanks to the flourishing medieval economy, could travel to distant sites for study. The increased enrollment (and payments!) helped cathedral schools attract and retain expert faculty who could provide instruction in a broad range of subjects. Students began to attend such classes without any intention of becoming a religious or of serving as an administrator for the local bishop. By the end of the thirteenth century, cities that could accommodate these larger programs had establish charters that formed these schools into independent institutions dedicated to professional study; they had become Europe's first universities.

These universities no longer trained students only in theology, and they increasingly asserted their independence from the bishop and the cathedral school model. The faculty, or instructors, at universities fought fiercely to maintain the freedom to teach and develop ideas without diocesan oversight, instead pledging allegiance to the papacy, which provided less immediate supervision. Most universities gained accreditation from both the pope and the respective king and maintained this status even during periods of disagreement with one authority or another.

The structure of the medieval university in many ways mirrored the structure of the guilds that were developing in these cities at the same time. Each university offered a basic program of instruction in the traditional "seven liberal arts." This included the *trivium* as well as the *quadrivium*, that is, the subjects of astronomy, geometry, arithmetic, and music. Upon completing these studies, graduates received a Bachelor of Arts degree. They had now completed their apprenticeship and could apply for a license to teach. Graduates could also continue on to specialize in one of the higher disciplines: theology, law, or medicine. After completing this further course of study and defending their doctoral thesis, they were granted full status and voting rights among the university faculty, along with the credentials to teach at any medieval university. There were not many medieval universities, and so only the best students and faculty from across Europe participated in these programs.

A Course of Philosophy at the University of Paris. Illuminated miniature made c. 1330. Currently, "MS 3, f. 277r" in the Municipal Library of Castres, France. This image is from the *Grandes Chroniques de France*, a French history first compiled during the reign of Louis IX and subsequently updated by later monarchs to include later events. There are many copies available, and the illuminated miniatures in each manuscript vary considerably.

The oldest medieval university was in Bologna, in northern Italy. It was founded in 1088 and became most famous for its courses in canon and civil law. The University of Montpellier was located at an ancient spa town in southeast France and emphasized the study of medicine. The university of Paris, founded around 1150, was perhaps the most prestigious of all and famous for its courses in theology. The English universities of Oxford and Cambridge gained their reputations for scholarly excellence by promoting scientific research.

Who were the students who attended these universities, and what were their lives like? Almost all students were clerics, even if they had only taken minor orders and had no plans to become priests. They normally received some kind of initial sponsorship from their local priest or bishop but still had to find a clerical position with a stipend (perhaps as a sacristan or a lector at a parish) to support themselves when they arrived in the city. Although the universities had libraries and chapels, other buildings were uncommon. Students were expected to find their own lodging and food. Professors were expected to host classes in their houses or rent an area in which to accommodate the students. Professors also had to negotiate the fees for the course with each student. As young men with few or no dependents and little responsibilities beyond their own studies, students were typically the most

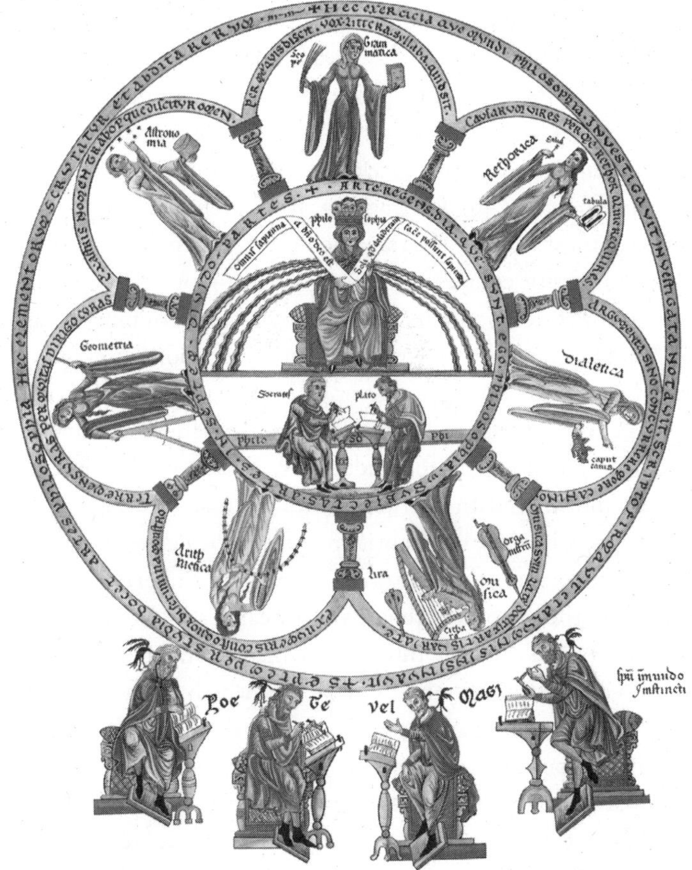

Philosophy and the Seven Liberal Arts. Original diagram made c. 1180 by Herrad of Landsberg. This image is a copy made in 1818 by Christian Maurice Engelhardt. Currently, "Zwölf Kupfertafeln zu [Chr. M. Engelhardts] Herrad von Landsperg *Hortus deliciarum*, Tafel VIII" in the Heidelberg University Library, Heidelberg, Germany. This diagram is from the *Hortus deliciarum* ("Garden of Delights"), a massive compendium made by the abbess of Hohenburg Abbey and currently in the Alsatian Library of Crédit Mutuel, Strasbourg, France. In this image, Philosophy sits as queen in the center circle, with Socrates and Plato seated at desks beneath her. Surrounding them are the seven liberal arts (beginning at the top and moving clockwise): grammar, rhetoric, dialectic, music, arithmetic, geometry, and astronomy.

raucous demographic of medieval society. Other inhabitants of the city frequently complained about their riotous parties, and violence sometimes broke out between students and their neighbors. Such conflicts were all the more bitter since students were technically clerics and thus under canon law rather than civil law. Secular officials could not prosecute crimes committed by disorderly or violent students, which encouraged the disreputable among them to engage in lawless behavior.

Another consequence that arose from the students' clerical status was the exclusion of women from university education. Whereas the monastic schools of previous centuries had educated both young men and women, women could not become clerics and so were prohibited by canon law from attending medieval universities. Convents did continue to provide educational opportunities, and some elite women, such as Heloïse du Paraclet (c. 1100–1164), excelled in studies under private tutors. Even so, there was a growing attitude among medieval thinkers that women were incapable of higher learning. This prejudice limited the academic opportunities for most women and remained influential for centuries.

Medieval university courses were significantly more rigorous than those of most modern universities. Students could choose from a number of different professors who were teaching the same subject and often audited several classes at the beginning of the term to find an instructor with whom they developed a productive relationship. The student's day began at five or six in the morning with the praying of the Divine Office, a requirement for students because they were clerics. Most classes were held in the morning, with instruction and discussion conducted in Latin. The teacher would typically read aloud a brief passage from a great book of the past and then spend the remainder of the lesson explaining all the previous interpretations of this passage and their various strengths and weaknesses. In this fashion, the class made its way slowly and carefully through the main text. After attending Mass, the professor would hold an afternoon drill session in which the students discussed and were quizzed on the morning's material. They were required to be able to argue and explain the different positions the professor had expounded. Students also frequently attended debates and discussions among different faculty members.

The emphasis of this text-based teaching technique coincided with the rise of **scholasticism**. This philosophy of education took its name from the Latin word for school ("*schola*") and emphasized the detailed study of great texts by using logic, establishing categories, creating definitions, and organizing content.

Furthermore, Scholastics, or "Schoolmen," desired to learn about the world around them using their natural reason. They were willing and even eager to study the writings from ancient authors, including those of non-Christians, as the foundation for their work. This led them to explore the works of Aristotle and his philosophy of logic. Most of Aristotle's works had been lost in Western Europe after the fall of the Western Roman Empire, but medieval thinkers were able to gain access to copies of these texts, which had been preserved in the Byzantine Empire and the Islamic world, especially in al-Andalus. These and other similar ancient texts and commentaries formed the core of the study material at medieval universities.

For monks trained through *lectio divina*, this new approach seemed dangerous, if not impious. Monastic thinkers and reformers, such as Peter Damian and Bernard of Clairvaux, wrote against scholasticism, particularly since its emphasis on logic seemingly diverged from the primarily devotional goal of monastic study. The works of two prominent eleventh-century thinkers, Berengar of Tours (d. 1088) and Roscelin (d. c. 1125), helped inspire monastic critique. These writings were condemned for their rationalistic conclusions about the Holy Eucharist and the Trinity, which reinforced suspicion that the use of pagan philosophers by Christians could inspire erroneous interpretations of the Faith.

Despite these condemnations, scholastic methods became increasingly influential. For example, though Bernard of Clairvaux warned against the theological works of Peter Abelard (c. 1079–1142), Abelard's important work on logic, *Sic et Non* ("Yes and No"), remained popular. This text compared opposing statements from Church Fathers about theological topics and left it to the reader to discern how best to reconcile them. This early scholastic writing formed the foundation for future intellectual achievements, such as those of Thomas Aquinas. Other theologians, such as Anselm of Canterbury (c. 1033–1109), accepted the use of logic and reason to organize information but urged caution about a widespread application of these methods to every Church teaching. They held that some doctrines were mysteries that demanded the respect of belief, and that to try to explain them using human terminology was irreverent and inaccurate.

Among twelfth-century intellectuals, **Peter Lombard** (c. 1096–1160) was most successful in demonstrating that scholastic techniques could be applied to theology while avoiding heretical positions. In 1152, he completed his most famous work, the *Book of Sentences*. In it, Peter used the skills of the *trivium* to organize a vast collection of texts from Sacred Scripture, the Church Fathers, and contemporary thinkers. Furthermore, his presentation of the different topics of theology avoided the repetitions, inconsistencies, and digressions of previous works. This book was widely accepted and remained the standard theological textbook for the next three centuries. The adoption of Peter's book signaled the acceptance of scholasticism and its methods by medieval universities.

The scholastic method of education had many strengths. Students learned a common core of essential texts in detail, and this foundation provided them with a common vocabulary and background for further discussions. The scholastic emphasis on logic and oral debate also gave scholastics the ability to approach the new sources they were encountering from the Greek and Islamic worlds critically and creatively.

THE LEGEND OF ROBIN HOOD

The legends associated with Robin Hood tell the stories of popular resistance to abuses of power in medieval society. According to the legend, Robin was a yeoman, someone who was not a noble but who owned his own land. A local noble, Sir Guy of Gisborne, and the Sheriff of Nottingham, governor of one of these new medieval towns, took advantage of Richard the Lionheart's absence on crusade to declare Robin an outlaw and seize his lands.

In medieval society, an outlaw was someone who had been indicted as a criminal and then had failed to come to court to stand trial and receive punishment. It was declared that such people no longer enjoyed the protections of the law until they were caught or faced justice. Members of society could steal from outlaws or even kill them, and they would not have to face criminal charges themselves. The life of an outlaw was therefore extremely harsh, and the declaration of outlawry was one of the severest punishments of the time.

According to the legend, however, Robin Hood's outlawry was not harsh. Rather, he lived a life of daring adventures and rambunctious comradeship with his band of "merry men," living under an oak tree hidden deep in Sherwood Forest where they could easily evade their pursuers. They were famous for their skills in fighting against their enemies, using swords, staves, and most especially the longbow. They were said to care for the needs of the oppressed poor by stealing from those who made themselves rich by unjust means.

The legend of Robin Hood has captivated audiences for centuries, but the questions of whether Robin was real and, if so, who he was, continue to vex historians. There is no evidence to prove or disprove conclusively the existence of the Robin Hood of Sherwood Forest. The name "Robin Hood," for example, is found in court documents dated as early as 1261. This is not as early as the time of Richard the Lionheart, but it is almost within living memory. However, these references to "Robin Hood" imply a variety of individuals with that name, so it is hard to say with confidence that any one in particular is *the* Robin Hood.

The earliest mention of the tales of Robin Hood as a famous outlaw dates from the late 1300s. The following century developed a number of different collections of tales about Robin Hood, and some accounts suggest that Robin Hood lived during the late 1200s–about a century after King Richard the Lionheart–or that he lived in a different part of England. It may be that these collections of tales combined various myths and legends associated with separate outlaws who lived at different times and places across Medieval England.

Chivalry and Medieval Literature

We introduced the concept of **chivalry** in chapter 25's insert on the Peace and Truce of God movements. At its core, the chivalric code was an appeal to the mounted warrior's sense of nobility and justice. It acknowledged knights' prowess on the battlefield and emphasized their station in life, but then used that very praise to demand conduct that restricted acts of violence and encouraged the protection of the innocent and defenseless. The insert emphasizes how Church reformers used the liturgical year and religious rituals to establish a spiritual dimension to this knightly code. While these were very important, they were not the only sources of inspiration for the aspiring chivalric knight. Medieval vernacular literature also played a role in developing the concept of chivalry. ("Vernacular" means that it was written in the spoken language of the people rather than a scholarly language like Latin.)

Two literary genres were particularly influential in developing the chivalric ethos. The first was the ***chanson de geste*** ("song of heroic deeds"). This was predominately associated with northern France and emphasized knights' martial valor. Some scholars believe that these epic stories were primarily intended to introduce young boys to acts of heroism so that they would imitate such bravery on their own future battlefields. Regardless of whether that theory is fully accurate, these epic songs evidently enjoyed much popularity among the aristocracy.

The Song of Roland provides us with a good introduction to the typical *chanson*'s content and themes. Our earliest manuscript dates from the mid-twelfth century, but the song itself is undoubtedly older. The story's semi-historical setting is the reign of Charlemagne, specifically during a seven-year campaign he is waging against the Muslims of Spain. The Muslim ruler treacherously offers to surrender and convert to Christianity but then attacks Charlemagne's rearguard as the Franks withdraw. These soldiers are under the command of Count Roland, and he has the choice of blowing his horn to summon reinforcements or making an attempt to fight off the Muslims without additional aid and thus win more glory. His pride gets the better of him, and he refuses to sound his horn until it is too late. When Charlemagne arrives, he finds Roland and all his companions slaughtered. More fighting follows until Charlemagne's enemies submit and Roland is avenged. The story concludes with the angel Gabriel summoning the Frankish king to yet another campaign.

On the one hand, this epic song is straightforward to the point of being simplistic. Muslims are bad, Christian knights are good. Roland and his companions (including a warrior-bishop!) are brave and laugh boldly as they split the skulls of their enemies. On the other hand, the story offers a fascinating literary interpretation of feudal relationships and the nature of chivalric piety. One instance that highlights both themes comes as Roland prepares to die. He wishes to destroy his blade lest that sword be used by a Muslim. Each time he tries to break it against a rock, he speaks about a different aspect of his role as vassal to Charlemagne. He finally realizes that he cannot break the sword because of the holy relics that are embedded in its hilt. This moment serves as a catalyst for Roland's humble confession before his death shortly thereafter.

The juxtaposition of pride and humility, glory and defeat make *The Song of Roland* more thought-provoking than one would initially guess. Is the audience expected to celebrate Roland's decision not to blow the horn and thus earn great glory? Or should we condemn his pride as his wise friend Oliver does? Even the story's infrequent references to women invite greater analysis. True, we do not learn that Roland has a fiancée until the very end. Yet this does not mean that women are completely unimportant to the world of the *chansons de geste*. After all, it is the conversion of a Muslim queen that signals the great triumph at the story's conclusion.

The brief roles played by women in this epic tale contrast dramatically with the second literary genre that influenced the development of chivalry. These works are commonly grouped together under the heading of "**courtly love,**" but this phrase was invented by nineteenth-century Romantics rather than by medieval audiences. These works place women and interpersonal drama at the forefront of their stories. It is not surprising, therefore, that aristocratic ladies, like Eleanor of Aquitaine, promoted these works and patronized the troubadours, or minstrels, who composed and recited them. They also read *romances*, a designation roughly akin to our "novel." Despite the modern connotation of the word "romance," these did not always revolve around love stories.

Nonetheless, tales of courtly love often involved situations of forbidden love and love at first sight. A common protagonist is a knight who falls in love with his lord's wife. This leads to an impossible state of affairs since he constantly tries to please her while knowing that he can never marry her. The great virtue for these tales is not battlefield heroics but courtesy. This involved respect for women, a willingness to sacrifice for the good of others, and a generally civilized demeanor. Many of these stories celebrate how the protagonist overcomes temptation and serves his lady sinlessly by transcending his passion and living a life of denial. Other poems, such as those composed by William IX of Aquitaine, were less idealized and told of adulteries and broken marriages.

The most famous example of the "courtly love" genre is probably that of King Arthur, his loyal knight Lancelot, and Lancelot's love for Arthur's wife, Guinevere. Lancelot once asks his lady how he can serve her and, on a whim, she tells him to

Herr Bernger von Horheim and Herr Walther von Klingen. Illuminated miniatures made c. 1310–1350. Currently "Cod. Pal. germ. 848, folios 178r and 52r" in the Heidelberg University Library, Heidelberg, Germany. These two images are from the *Codex Manesse*, also known as *Große Heidelberger Liederhandschrif* ("Great Heidelberg Songbook"), a collection of German sung poetry with a portrait of each poet followed by the text of his poems. Bernger von Horheim was a poet who wrote predominately about courtly love. Walther von Klingen, meanwhile, is shown here as the victor of a joust.

perform as poorly as possible at a tournament. What follows is an amusing story of the land's greatest knight purposefully failing at every combat, but behind the humor is the recognition of the influence women can wield in society. Not all Arthurian stories are as innocent, and the breakdown of Arthur's kingdom begins with the forbidden love between his wife and his best friend.

Through the literature of *chansons de geste* and courtly love, chivalry came to have a spiritual, heroic, and even "romantic" character. Knights were expected to be pious and devout, heroic and glorious in battle, and genteel and even subservient to women. These ideals, of course, were *ideals*, and many knights failed in one way or another to live up to chivalric expectations. Nonetheless, chivalry helped channel the violence of previous ages and turned mere warriors into knights of bravery and culture. For example, loosely controlled fights between groups of combatants transformed into highly organized medieval tournaments, which involved many rules designed to protect the participants and to ensure fair fighting. What was more, the knights now had the opportunity to showcase their individual prowess through jousting and other events that took place before admiring lords and ladies. It was now not only physical strength that mattered; a knight must also demonstrate his courtesy and decorum before the lady of his devotion.

Conclusion

The achievements of the High Middle Ages helped to shape the future of Western Civilization. The beauty of Gothic architecture survives today in the many medieval cathedrals that have been preserved and in later churches that imitated them. All these buildings are testaments to the medieval desire to lift one's mind and heart toward Heaven. Medieval intellectual life laid the foundations for the future expansion of Western influence as scholars examined the writings of both ancient pagans and Muslims in order to uncover truths about the world. Meanwhile, medieval traders who journeyed to foreign areas and discovered the achievements of other cultures stimulated further curiosity and exploration even as they promoted economic prosperity at home. The development of a knightly code of life helped reduce acts of violence and gave birth to new literary expressions that continue to fascinate and entertain even modern audiences. In the next chapter, we resume our narrative and explore the life of one of the most powerful individuals in the medieval era—Pope Innocent III.

CHAPTER 29

Plenitudo Potestatis

Who then is the faithful and wise servant,
whom his master has set over his household,
to give them their food at the proper time?

Matthew 24:45

Popes had claimed to hold the ***plenitudo potestatis*** (Latin for "fullness of power") since Leo I in the fifth century, but **Innocent III** (r. 1198–1216) asserted this authority more broadly and directly than any of his predecessors. This became apparent in a sermon he delivered on the occasion of his consecration as pope. Though only thirty-seven years old, Innocent used this excerpt from the Gospel of Matthew to explain his calling as he understood it to be "the faithful and wise servant" charged with governing and ministering to the household of the Church.

To Innocent, this role meant that he exercised ultimate authority over Christendom's "Church-State" in nearly every detail. The rise of canon law in the twelfth century had encouraged further centralization of Church government, and Innocent used this development to proclaim that the pope proactively governed the entire Church. Previously, individual bishops had typically enjoyed relative independence and freedom to govern their dioceses. Now, Innocent invoked his authority to intervene in their dioceses on a more regular basis.

Innocent also emphasized the papacy's "fullness of power" in the area of temporal government. Because the conduct of nobles, kings, and emperors shaped the spiritual lives of those under them, Innocent asserted not only the right to discipline those rulers whose actions endangered their subjects' immortal souls but also the

Innocent III. Fresco c. 1210. Currently in the Monastery of Sacro Speco in Subiaco, Italy. Sacro Speco was the cave where St. Benedict had lived when he first withdrew from Rome to pursue a monastic life. In 1203, Innocent III issued a papal bull making the monastic community at Sacro Speco a priory, which significantly increased its revenue.

right to intervene if he believed an unworthy candidate was about to gain power. Despite his genuine intentions for good, Innocent's expansive understanding of papal power set the stage for the catastrophic conflict between popes and emperors, which we will discuss in future chapters.

The Fourth Crusade

The restoration of the Holy Land was the cause dearest to Innocent's heart, and he called for a new campaign to Jerusalem in the first year of his pontificate. He saw crusading as an opportunity not only to liberate the holy places where Jesus had walked but also as a powerful source of purification that would inspire many Christians to do penance for their sins. Richard the Lionheart was the obvious candidate to lead this latest endeavor, but he died in 1199 fighting against rebels in his lands in France. Fortunately for Innocent, enthusiasm for the effort caught fire when several prominent French nobles combined chivalry and crusade by dramatically taking the crusading vow while at a tournament. By 1200, Innocent's crusade, known today as the **Fourth Crusade** (1202–1204), had come alive. Massive crowds flocked to hear preachers proclaim the crusade, and many influential knights and nobles—though no monarchs—took the vow.

Innocent and his advisors decided that the crusade would travel to Palestine by sea. This avoided any risk of repeating the fighting in Anatolia that had doomed the Second Crusade and would enable the army to arrive at its full strength close to Jerusalem. Crusade leaders, therefore, negotiated a contract with the merchant city-state of Venice to build a fleet to transport their soldiers.

According to tradition, Venice was established on March 25, 421, when refugees from the declining Western Roman Empire withdrew to islands off the northwestern coast of Italy. In the centuries that followed, Venice developed a complex relationship with Byzantium. On the one hand, Venetians had been loyal subjects to the emperors and had received the right from the iconoclast Emperor Leo III to have their own *dux* or governor. (This designation later evolved into the Venetian title *doge*.) On the other hand, the Venetians asserted their own independence in later

Effigy of Richard I the Lionheart. Made of stone c. 1199. Currently in the Cathedral of Rouen, France. This effigy contained the embalmed heart of Richard I until it was exhumed in 1838. The rest of his body was interred in a different effigy commissioned by his mother Eleanor of Aquitaine at Fontevraud Abbey. His remains were destroyed during the French Revolution.

centuries and even attacked imperial territories if they felt it was in their financial interests to do so. The city-state was wealthy, had numerous connections and resources, and was an obvious candidate both to supply the crusaders with vessels and to transport them safely to the eastern Mediterranean. Nonetheless, as its sometimes-violent relationship with the Byzantine Empire revealed, it could be ruthless in the pursuit of its own success.

It was while negotiating with Venice that the crusade's leaders made their first and greatest error. Misjudging preachers' reports of overwhelming enthusiasm, those responsible for the contract drastically overestimated the number of the assembling crusader forces. They consequently overestimated the size of the fleet required by these soldiers. The Venetian *doge* agreed to the contract but ordered the entire population to suspend their businesses for a year in order to fulfill the obligation of building such a large fleet.

When the crusaders arrived in Venice in 1202, their combined army numbered only eleven thousand, a third of the size anticipated by both the crusade's leaders and the Venetians. Because there were fewer soldiers to pay for their passage, the crusaders could offer the Venetians only half of the agreed amount. The Venetians felt that accepting this settlement would condemn their citizens to poverty, but they also did not wish to impede or anger the crusading army camped in their city. By way of a solution, they proposed that the crusaders should capture the Christian city of Zara, which had rebelled against Venetian authority, in the hopes that the plunder acquired there would satisfy their remaining debt. Innocent, who was following reports of the crusade closely from Rome, was outraged when he heard that the crusaders were going to attack fellow Christians in Zara. He wrote letters threatening the crusaders with excommunication, but the crusade leaders hid these from the rank-and-file soldiers and went forward with the plan to capture the city. The Zarans placed crosses on the outside of the city walls to remind the crusaders that they were attacking a Christian city, but to no avail. Zara fell, the crusaders were excommunicated, and, ironically, they still owed money to the Venetians because the plunder they obtained was still insufficient to pay their entire debt.

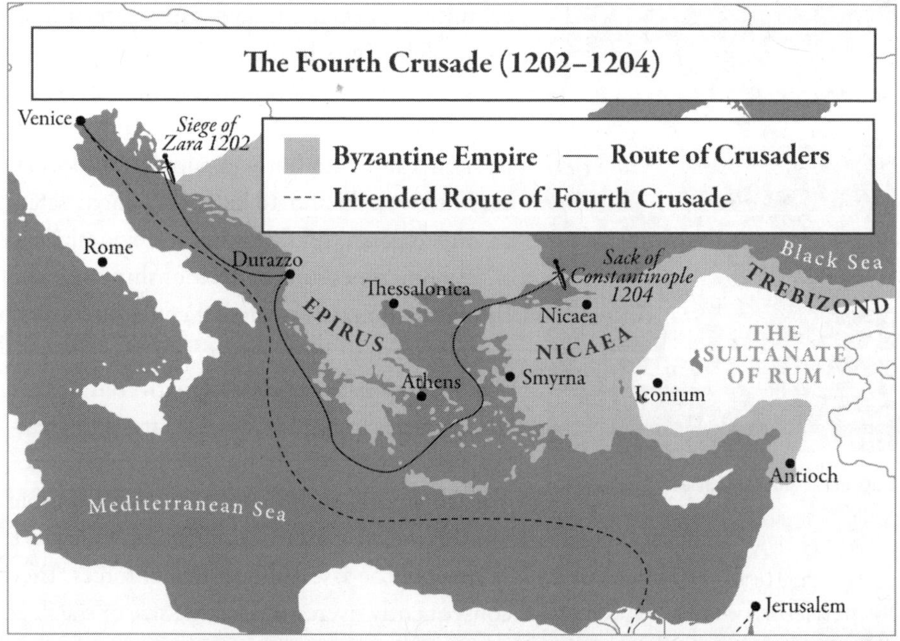

At this juncture, a young man named Alexius (1182–1204) presented himself to the crusaders as the heir to the Byzantine throne. Alexius, along with his father the emperor, had been deposed in one of the many coups that rocked the Byzantine Empire during this period. He promised the crusaders that if they brought him to Constantinople, the Byzantine citizens would rise up and restore him to power. Once established on the throne as Alexius IV, he would satisfy their debts and provide troops and support for the crusaders' campaign in Palestine.

Once again, Innocent wrote letters to the crusade leaders advising against this plan. He did not believe that Alexius could deliver what he promised. In contrast, the crusade's leaders convinced themselves that their own model of feudal relationships between lords and vassals could be applied to Byzantium. From this perspective, the Byzantines would see themselves as obligated to fight to restore Alexius and his father to the throne. They did not realize that the Western European feudal system with its oaths of fidelity was a foreign concept to Byzantines.

The crusader army arrived at Constantinople in 1203 and attacked the city. The defenders, safely ensconced behind Constantinople's massive fortifications, easily repelled their assault. Despite the failure of the attack, the ruling emperor decided to steal most of the empire's treasury and flee the city. Faced with no other acceptable leader, the Byzantines peacefully welcomed Alexius into the city as the new emperor.

Alexius's reign was short-lived. The treasury was empty, so he began raiding tombs and melting down altar ornaments to pay his debt to the crusaders. After two months of such outrages, a Byzantine coup deposed him and strangled him. When the crusader army heard that the Byzantines had murdered Alexius, their frustration reached a breaking point. It was now 1204, they were still in debt, stranded hundreds of miles from their destination, and their liege lord had been killed. In desperation, they attacked the city of Constantinople, hoping to avenge Alexius, repay the Venetians, and finally fulfill their crusading vows.

The walls of Constantinople would have enabled even a small force to repel the crusaders, but the Byzantine soldiers showed no interest in defending their city. They assumed that Boniface of Montferrat, a crusade leader who was distantly related to Alexius through marriage, would peacefully claim the throne. Soon after the assault began, the defenders left the walls and allowed the crusaders to enter. The peaceful transfer of power never happened. Instead, the crusaders unleashed all their fury on the unsuspecting city. For three days, they ransacked houses and even churches, profaning altars and stealing relics. The Byzantine inhabitants became refugees in their own city as crusaders stole their possessions and preyed upon women and the defenseless. Many ancient and valuable works of art and devotion were seized or destroyed and thus lost forever. It is impossible to calculate the damage sustained by this ancient Christian city, which had long preserved some of the richest treasures of Western Civilization.

The Fourth Crusade, which began with so much enthusiasm, became infamous in the history of the crusades. Some historians have argued that the Venetians plotted to use the crusading army to destroy a commercial rival and bring about the Byzantine Empire's final decline. They stress Venice's prior tensions with Byzantium and also interpret the looting of the city as evidence that crusaders joined these expeditions to acquire wealth rather than for any spiritual motive.

Triumphal Quadriga. Made of bronze c. 100–200(?). Currently in St. Mark's Basilica in Venice, Italy. A quadriga is a chariot drawn by four horses. Historians are uncertain of the original location of these statues or in what century they were made. They were displayed at the Hippodrome of Constantinople from the fourth century until the Fourth Crusade when they were looted and taken back to Venice. The collars around their necks were added to hide where the crusaders had cut off the horses' heads for transport.

More recent commentaries have pointed out that the Venetians had no reason to destroy their most important trading partner. These historians argue that the diversion to Constantinople was due to a series of unforeseen missteps, the most important of which was a failure to estimate accurately the size of the crusading force. They suggest that the fall of the city was predominantly a result of the division and dysfunction within the Byzantine Empire, which allowed the comparatively small and bedraggled crusader force to capture one of the most heavily fortified cities in the world.

Innocent was appalled when he heard the news of the sack and condemned it in the strongest terms. As he struggled to understand how God would bring good out of this evil, he concluded that Divine Providence intended to end the Great Schism and reunite Constantinople with Rome. He approved the creation of a feudal crusader state, the Latin Empire of Constantinople, and installed a Venetian cleric as the Latin Patriarch of Constantinople. In theory, the schism between the Eastern and Western Churches was ended since the patriarch of Constantinople was now in communion with Rome. In reality, the brutality of the sack of Constantinople and the creation of a separate Church hierarchy of Latin Rite priests and bishops hardened the divisions between the two Churches. The memory of the sack of their holy city by the pope's army created bitterness and resentment among Greek Christians towards the papacy and the Latin Church that persists even to this day.

Papal Influence in Germany and Italy

In coming to terms with the failure of the Fourth Crusade, Innocent reached similar conclusions to those of Bernard of Clairvaux following the Second Crusade. The campaign had failed because of Christian sinfulness. God would not favor His people and lead their armies to victory until they renounced their errors and returned to faithful observance of Church teaching. Bernard could only encourage others to repent, but Innocent claimed both the spiritual authority and the political power to bring about this reform.

Innocent shared the view of the Cluniac reformers that the Church must remain independent of temporal control in order to avoid compromise or corruption from political influence. Furthermore, he was convinced that the surest way to guarantee Church independence was for the papacy to possess its own territories with their accompanying military and natural resources. Thus, Innocent began his reforms by securing his rule over the regions of central Italy under his immediate political authority—areas known collectively as the Papal States—and thereby cementing his political independence.

He took advantage of the confusion then engulfing the German Empire, which he viewed as the chief rival of the papacy in the region. The Holy Roman Emperor Henry VI (r. 1191–1197) had fulfilled the goals of his father, Frederick Barbarossa, when he received not only the title of emperor but also, through his marriage, the kingdom of Sicily. This combination of inheritances gave Henry the power to reassert traditional imperial claims to overlordship of the cities of northern Italy as well as seizing some papal lands near Rome. The emperor died suddenly in 1197, leaving behind both his three-year-old son, Frederick II, and a power vacuum in the Holy Roman Empire. When young Frederick's mother died the following year, Innocent took control of the situation. He established himself as Frederick's guardian and declared that the Kingdom of Sicily was a fief of the papacy. This gave Innocent authority to choose the king of Sicily and to require that king to swear homage to the pope as his lord.

Aside from securing control of the Papal States, Innocent's goal was to ensure that the German territories to the north and Sicily to the south were never united under a single ruler or dynasty. His fear was that if this were to happen, the ruling family would then surround and control the Church. The pope hoped to divide power between the Welf family and their rivals, the Hohenstaufen dynasty of Frederick Barbarossa. He therefore supported the rights of his ward, Frederick, in Sicily but opposed the efforts of Frederick's uncle Philip of Swabia (1177–1208) to become king of the Romans in Germany. (Remember that German rulers first became king of the Romans and then had to receive the imperial crown from the pope in order to become emperor.) Innocent instead encouraged the powerful dukes who elected the German ruler to choose Otto IV of Brunswick (r. 1198–1218). Philip retorted that the election was the decision of the German people alone. Civil war broke out and continued until Philip's assassination in 1208.

Many in the eleventh century had considered it a revolutionary act when Gregory VII deposed Henry IV. At that time, the pope had intervened to declare that feudal obligations to a certain ruler were no longer obligatory. A century and a half later, Innocent was now asserting that he had the additional right to select the German people's ruler. He argued that, though the German princes had the authority to elect their king, this right had been given to them by the pope when Leo III crowned Charlemagne emperor. Thus, Innocent's "fullness of power" allowed him, as the head of the "Church-State," to determine who held temporal rule. For Innocent, the care of souls mandated that he intervene wherever he thought it was necessary. Unfortunately, it was becoming all too easy to blur the line between moral necessity and temporal expediency.

Papal Influence in France and England

Innocent's use of the *plenitudo potestatis* was more clearly justified in situations involving the sanctity of marriage. Church leaders had struggled to compel the Frankish kings and their nobles to accept the Church's discipline and teachings on marriage for five hundred years. Boniface felt that he must avoid raising the issue in order to maintain Charles Martel's support for his missions to the Germans. Clerics ruled by Charlemagne seem to have turned a blind eye to the emperor's scandalous array of concubines. Even as late as the reign of Eleanor of Aquitaine, the French bishops allowed the nobility to misuse the process of annulment to marry again when it served their political or private interests. Innocent finally succeeded in insisting that even kings must follow the laws of the Church.

Philip Augustus (r. 1180–1223), the French king who briefly joined Richard the Lionheart on the Third Crusade, had married the Danish princess Ingeborg in 1193. The king rejected his bride almost immediately after the marriage, allegedly on account of her bad breath, and began living with a noblewoman from Bavaria. When Philip refused Innocent's demands to put away his mistress and return to his wife, the pope placed the French kingdom under interdict.

Interdict was among the most severe penalties the Church could impose. With the exception of a handful of high holy days like Easter, Pentecost, and Christmas, no public liturgies were permitted in lands under interdict. The bells of the great cathedrals that marked the hours of prayer were silent, and the doors of the churches were barred shut. Even the sacraments were administered only to those in danger of death. For medieval Christians, the suspension of the Church's daily and weekly liturgies was the most serious punishment they could endure. Their desire for the grace of the sacraments could impel their rulers to acknowledge the authority of the Vicar of Christ, a papal title that Innocent emphasized more than his predecessors. After a year, even Philip, skilled politician though he was, yielded to this pressure and acknowledged Ingeborg as his wife.

Innocent's actions marked a significant development within the Church as well. Interdict had previously been considered a penalty exercised by local bishops. Now the pope had wielded this power directly to discipline a high-profile sinner. The independence and geographical remoteness of the Holy See enabled Innocent to act without fear of reprisals and further centralized ecclesiastical authority in the hands of the popes.

In England, too, Innocent exercised his spiritual authority to subjugate the ruler and compel him to accept the teachings of the Church. After Richard the Lionheart's death, he was succeeded by his brother John (r. 1199–1216), the youngest child of Henry II and Eleanor of Aquitaine. He was able and intelligent but had been spoiled by his father, who favored him above John's brothers. His rule was characterized by dishonesty, laziness, and tyranny. He seized the property of his subjects to enrich himself and taxed others relentlessly to support his extravagant lifestyle at court and his ill-fated military campaigns.

One of John's first notable crimes was to abduct a lady engaged to marry someone else and force her to marry him as a means of gaining her lands in southern France. When her fiancé protested, Philip Augustus summoned John, who still technically held his lands in France as a vassal of the French king, to appear at his court to answer these charges. John refused, and Philip happily used this pretext to make war on his lands. John was a capable general but did not have the discipline to conduct a sustained campaign. After four years of fighting, the French king had gained control of almost all the lands of the English kings in France. The so-called "Angevin Empire" of Henry II was severely reduced.

In 1205, John became engaged in a dispute with Innocent over the next archbishop of Canterbury. The man who held this office was the primate, or senior bishop, in the kingdom, and the diocese controlled vast amounts of wealth and land. John was especially anxious to secure the position for one of his supporters in order to increase royal revenue. When the monks of the cathedral elected a successor, John refused to confirm him and instead attempted to impose his own candidate. Innocent rejected both men and consecrated as archbishop a scholar from the University of Paris, where Innocent had studied. (Innocent's choice, Stephen Langton, is responsible for our current chapter divisions in the Bible.) John was outraged. He saw Innocent's claim to select bishops for his kingdom without any input from the king or the local clergy as a radical overreach of papal power and refused to allow the archbishop to set foot in the kingdom. Innocent responded by placing the kingdom of England under interdict and later excommunicated John.

John still refused to relent. Priests were imprisoned and tortured to try to force them to break the interdict. The king also attempted to take advantage of the interdict to seize the lands of the clergy who upheld the pope's instructions. In 1213, Innocent authorized Philip Augustus to invade England and install a new king. Faced with an invasion by an army backed by the pope, John's support quickly unraveled, and he agreed to submit to the pope in order to retain his throne. He then plotted his revenge against Philip. John formed an alliance with the Holy Roman Emperor Otto IV and invaded southern France from his lands in Aquitaine while Otto attacked from the northeast. This campaign was another failure. John's attack was quickly bogged down by his unpopularity among his nobles, who refused to fight for him. To the north, Philip comprehensively defeated Otto at the **Battle of Bouvines** in 1214.

This battle is considered one of the most important of the medieval era. It demonstrated the significant increase of French royal power that had been achieved by the leadership of Philip Augustus. By defeating the rulers of both England and Germany, he reestablished the independence and strength of the French kingdom. The Capetian kings, who had been dominated or simply ignored by their barons for many centuries, were now positioned to take on a new role as the most powerful rulers of Europe.

Another significant consequence of the Battle of Bouvines was the drafting and signing of the **Magna Carta** in 1215. Following his disastrous war in France, John's vassals were no longer willing to accept his oppressive rule. They rebelled and demanded that he sign an agreement or charter that guaranteed the rights and freedoms of the Church and of his subjects. The Magna Carta expressly stipulated that the Church must remain independent of royal interference and coercion. It also stated that royal subjects had a right to swift justice and could not be imprisoned indefinitely without charges proved in court. Finally, it limited the king's authority to tax his subjects without the consent of the nobles.

The Magna Carta was revised several times in the years that followed. Innocent himself rejected the initial draft because it did not sufficiently acknowledge the papal *plenitudo potestatis* over the whole kingdom. The main ideas of the document nevertheless remained the same, and it was seen as the written enshrinement of the

Magna Carta. Ink on parchment 1215. Currently "Cotton MS Augustus II.106" in the British Library in London, England.

fundamental liberties of English subjects. It is important to note that the Magna Carta was focused on establishing the limits of the monarch's powers, not eliminating the monarchy itself or creating a society based on individual rights. In contrast to modern assumptions that democracy is the only form of government that adequately restricts government power, this document demonstrates that medieval kings had to rule in collaboration with their subjects, who could and did act as effective restraints on their power. Those kings who tried to override these constraints faced sustained opposition and even rebellion.

Papal Influence in Spain

As discussed in chapter 26, one of the surviving members of the Umayyad dynasty escaped the 'Abbasid Revolution by fleeing to Spain, or al-Andalus as it was known to Muslims. There he established another Umayyad state, with its capital in Córdoba. The Muslims controlled the majority of Spain for the next three centuries. There were a few small Christian kingdoms in northern Spain, but they were weakened through their frequent wars against each other. In 997, the renowned Umayyad general **Almanzor** (938–1002) even sacked and burned the holy shrine of Compostela in the northwest. Christian Spain seemed once again on the verge of destruction. However, the Umayyad Caliphate collapsed in civil war about thirty years later, and al-Andalus splintered into dozens of petty states known as *taifas* (Arabic for "band" or "faction"). These *taifa* states no longer posed a significant threat to the Christian kingdoms which, when united, could defeat these smaller Muslim principalities.

In 1085, Alfonso VI of Castile (r. 1065–1109) obtained a great victory by capturing the city of Toledo. The ancient capital city of the Visigothic kings was once again in Christian hands. This success encouraged additional attempts to gain Muslim territories. Fearing the complete Christian conquest of Spain, Muslim *taifa* leaders appealed to the Berber rulers of the Almoravid Empire in northwest Africa for aid. The Almoravids were fervent Muslims and fierce warriors who not only wanted to defeat the Christians but also desired to restore Spain to a more rigorous adherence to Islam. They met Alfonso's army at the Battle of Sagrajas in 1086 and, under the command of Yusuf Ibn Tashfin (r. 1061–1106), drove the Christians from the field. Alfonso himself was wounded and more than half the Christian army was lost. The Almoravids allegedly loaded the bodies of the dead Christians onto carts and sent them throughout al-Andalus as a testimony of their victory. They also demanded the submission from the *taifas'* inhabitants to their rigorist rule. Yet Muslim losses had also been substantial, and the Christian Spaniards, while defeated, did not surrender Toledo or any of their other conquests.

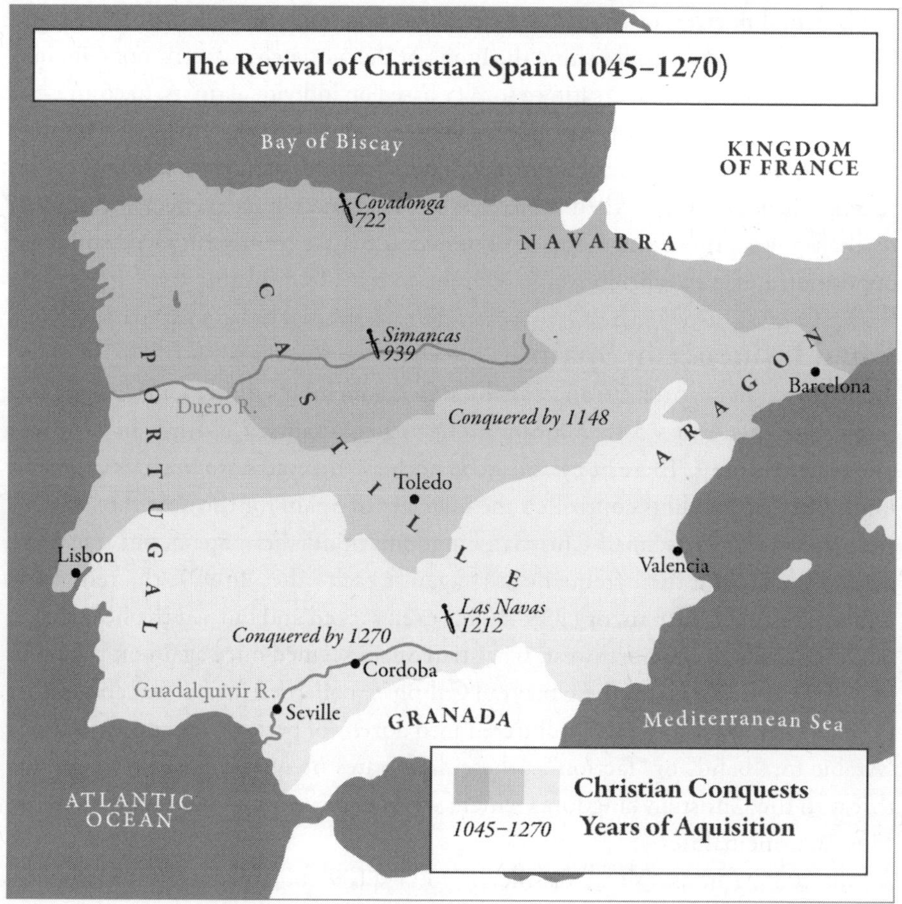

The borders between the kingdoms did not shift greatly until the Second Crusade. At that time, the king of Portugal convinced crusaders on their way to Palestine from England, Belgium, and Normandy to help him and his army take the city of Lisbon. Italian crusaders also helped capture cities along the eastern coast of Spain. These campaigns were the main military successes of the Second Crusade. They also encouraged Spaniards to see their efforts to restore Christian Spain as part of the broader crusading movement and helped give birth in later generations to the idea of the "*reconquista*" or "reconquest" of Spain. This historical perspective stressed that there was a continual struggle between Christians and Muslims in Spain ever since the days of the initial Muslim conquest in 711. It conveniently overlooked the many times when previous Spanish Christian kings had allied with Muslims to fight their fellow Christians and instead presented a simplified narrative that sought to inspire greater solidarity among medieval Spaniards against a common foe. As the insert on

PAPAL CARE FOR THE POOR

Today, many associate Innocent III with the unprecedented expansion of papal temporal authority. Many modern readers are disquieted by the political influence of the Medieval Church and see figures like Innocent as predominantly driven by secular motives and a desire for power. While we have focused mostly on Innocent's interactions with political rulers during this chapter, it is important to remember that Innocent saw his overarching mission as profoundly pastoral.

Although he considered himself the pastor to the whole Church, Innocent did not forget the special and immediate responsibility of the popes to care for the people of Rome and especially for the poor. He washed, fed, and cared for twelve poor men every Sunday in imitation of Christ. Poor children were encouraged to attend papal meals and could even eat from the pope's table when the meal was ended. He was also famous for providing dowries for poor virgins so that they could marry.

Innocent was aware that the growing medieval towns required new, large hospitals. The Hospitallers, another military order like the Templars, had provided an early model through their hospital for pilgrims at Jerusalem. Here they cared for over two thousand sick male and female pilgrims every year. These inpatients received comfortable beds, meat, and wine, luxuries many of them would never have experienced at home as peasants.

In 1204, Innocent founded his own hospital of Santo Spirito in Sassia near the Vatican. He explained that this institution should be a center for exercising the virtues of hospitality, since those who exercised the corporal works of mercy would be especially rewarded on the Day of Judgment. Here the hungry were fed, the poor clothed, and the sick received care. Those in danger of death could make their confessions, and all could hear the Divine Office and the preaching of the Gospel.

Innocent was especially concerned for the children of the poor. Pregnant women in poverty were cared for at the hospital free of charge, and any baby in danger of abandonment could be placed in a small rotating box set in the wall by the entrance to the hospital. When the box was turned, the child was safely deposited on a small mattress in the care of the hospital warden. Innocent wrote that, in caring for these children, the hospital, like Abraham and Lot, would host angels (see Gn 18–19).

Innocent's care for those most in need reflected a further aspect of how the Church helped guide and civilize medieval Europe. Innocent's political power and influence may have made kings tremble, but his exercise of political power must be understood within the broader context of his sense of pastoral responsibility for all Christians, especially his love and concern for the poor.

al-Andalus in chapter 26 indicates, this historiographical interpretation remained influential for many generations.

By 1151, the Christian rulers of Aragon, Castile, León, Barcelona, and Portugal were confident enough to sign the Treaty of Tudellen, which preemptively established how they would divide the territories of al-Andalus between them once all of Spain was restored to Christian rule. The most powerful party in the treaty was Alfonso VIII of Castile (r. 1158–1214), who had married a daughter of Henry II and Eleanor of Aquitaine. Alfonso's preeminence was resented by the other Christian kings of Spain, especially Alfonso IX of León (r. 1188–1230), whom we will discuss more in chapter 31.

Unfortunately for the Christian kings, their plan collapsed when a new North African Muslim dynasty arrived in Spain. The **Almohads** were a group of Berbers from the Atlas Mountains led by Ibn Tumart (1077–1130). While making the pilgrimage to Mecca, he experienced a powerful religious conversion. When he returned home, he began to practice Islam with great zeal and austerity, accusing the Almoravids of falling prey to the corrupting influence of material goods. Beginning in 1120, the Almohads began attacking the Almoravids, and by 1163, they had established their own Almohad Caliphate in the former Almoravid lands of North Africa and Spain. In 1194, the Almohads launched an invasion of Christian Spain. Alfonso VIII suffered a devastating defeat at the Battle of Alarcos one year later. It was said that the Almohad holy men proclaimed the call to evening prayer while standing in the battlefield atop piles of Christian skulls. The Almohads reclaimed all the land south of Toledo but did not attempt to capture the city itself. Instead, they provided money and troops to Alfonso's rivals and encouraged the Christians to destroy each other.

Innocent responded to this distressing situation by forcing the Christian kings of Aragon and León to make peace and ally with Alfonso VIII. Those who refused he threatened with excommunication. Innocent also recruited additional soldiers from as far away as France and Austria, promising that those who aided the Spanish armies would receive the same indulgence as crusaders who travelled to the Holy Land. The pope led a series of penitential processions through the streets of Rome to beg God's aid for the campaign, and there are reports of similar devotions elsewhere across Europe.

When the Almohads responded to Alfonso's raids with a full-scale invasion in 1212, the Christians kings finally united. The armies of the Almohad caliph thought that they were camped on an impregnable plateau, but a local shepherd showed the Christians how to reach the high ground unopposed. When the battle began, Peter II of Aragon defeated one of the flanks before Alfonso VIII broke through

Monument at Las Navas de Tolosa. Sculpted in stone by Antonio González Orea and Manuel Millán López c. 1881 in Jaén, Spain. The figures depicted are Lord Diego López II de Haro of Castile, Archbishop Rodrigo Jiménez de Rada of Toledo, King Peter II of Aragon, King Alfonso VIII of Castile, and King Sancho VII of Navarre. The darker figure in front of them, pointing ahead, is the shepherd who showed them the path through the mountains.

the center of the Muslim line. The Almohads were forced to flee. The **Battle of Las Navas de Tolosa** was a stunning victory that shocked even the victorious Spaniards. It ended the power of the Almohads and exposed the southern peninsula to Christian conquest. From this point onwards, whenever they were united, the Christians held the upper hand in conflicts against the Muslims in Spain.

Conclusion

Innocent was overjoyed to receive a triumphant letter about the victory from Alfonso VIII. He gathered a crowd in Rome and read the letter to them. He reminded them that their own spiritual participation had played a role in the victory but emphasized that this triumph was due above all to the power of God. After the bitter disappointment of the Fourth Crusade, the victory at Las Navas de Tolosa was a sweet success for a united Christian society whose members could fight and pray to defend each other under the leadership of the pope.

Innocent saw victory in Spain as a sign that God was pleased by his efforts to unite and reform the rulers of Europe under papal leadership. He had skillfully wielded that authority to compel earthly princes to obey and respect the Church's leadership of society. As the next chapter discusses, Innocent's efforts to reform medieval society also succeeded thanks to the new religious communities he fostered. In some respects, it was a glorious moment in Western Civilization.

Nonetheless, troubles loomed on the horizon. Innocent's "fullness of power" had effectively reduced the religious pretensions of royal authority, but it also created a confusing and dangerous precedent. The kings might not be king-priests, but the pope was becoming a priest-king whose claims seemingly erased any meaningful jurisdiction for royal authority. Historians refer to a "papal monarchy," and the popes of the thirteenth century increasingly ruled as kings who used both spiritual and military force against royal competitors. By the end of the century, even pious kings had misgivings when popes intervened in temporal matters. The impious simply rebelled.

Ironically, it was Innocent who empowered the most infamous opponent of papal authority in the High Middle Ages. In 1215, he withdrew his support from the Holy Roman Emperor Otto IV and instead promoted his former ward Frederick II as the next king of the Romans. Soon Frederick would rule both Germany and Sicily, thus bringing about the very situation Innocent had sought to avoid. The ensuing conflict grievously destabilized both the papacy and the empire.

CHAPTER 30

The Mendicants

When he [Jesus] chose some of the indispensable witnesses to his holy preaching and to his glorious manner of living for the salvation of the human race, he surely did not choose rich merchants but poor fishermen.

Anonymous, *Sacred Exchange between St. Francis and Lady Poverty*[1]

This early Franciscan source described a dialogue between Francis of Assisi and the figure of Lady Poverty. In it, Lady Poverty expressed her dismay that Christians have been corrupted by wealth and allowed greedy, lazy, and selfish desires to stifle their efforts to follow Christ. Lady Poverty explained that only those who renounced their worldly possessions can possess the Kingdom of Heaven. These sentiments were typical of the poverty movement that emerged in the late twelfth and early thirteenth centuries. Against the backdrop of medieval economic success, many of the laity became anxious that these new riches were preventing their society from following the teachings of the Gospels. They were especially concerned to see the leaders of the Church enjoying luxuries, social prestige, and political power that seemed a far cry from the lives of Jesus's apostles. Had Christ really intended that the successors of his disciples should live in palaces and spend much of their time attending court and managing property?

A growing number of medieval laity thought not. They began to form their own movements to preach moral conversion and a renewed fidelity to the teachings of the Gospel. They became beggars, or **mendicants**, living without homes and relying on

1 Regis J. Armstrong, ed. *Francis of Assisi: Early Documents*, vol. 1 (NY: New City Press, 2002), 535–536.

the charity of others for their food in order to focus solely on following the Gospel in its fullness. These groups faced a great challenge: to reform the Church while remaining faithful to her teachings and obedient to her (often worldly) leaders. The different groups we examine in this chapter met with varying degrees of success in their efforts to reclaim apostolic poverty and reinvigorate the Church.

Waldensians and Humiliati

The earliest mendicant group was founded by a merchant named **Waldes** (1140–1218). Around 1173, Waldes experienced a dramatic religious conversion when he heard a minstrel recounting the life of St. Alexius, a fourth-century monk who gave up his possessions and even his family to imitate Jesus's poverty. Waldes abandoned his career and threw his money in the streets. He arranged for his wife and daughters to enter a convent and took up a new life that emphasized poverty and simplicity. He vowed to possess neither gold nor silver and to eat only what others gave him. A number of followers soon joined him. They dressed in simple woolen garments and preached that all should renounce wealth and embrace repentance.

It is important to remember that laity were not allowed to preach publicly without the permission of their bishop, who was supposed to ascertain whether they had the necessary theological training to interpret Scripture correctly. Waldes's bishop refused to give him and his followers permission to preach. When they disobeyed him, he expelled them from his diocese. At the Third Lateran Council in 1179 (see chapter 27), Waldes and his followers approached Pope Alexander III and asked him to approve their way of life. Alexander encouraged them to continue their lives of poverty but insisted that they must receive permission from the local bishop in order to preach. The Waldensians refused to obey this command and continued to preach publicly. This situation led the pope to condemn the movement in 1184. He cited Paul's words to the Romans—"And how can men preach unless they are sent?" (Rom 10:15)—as evidence against the Waldensians.

The Waldensians' disobedience implied a rejection of the clergy's authority to regulate liturgical roles, but that was only the first step. As disobedience degenerated into heresy, they began to produce their own translations of the Bible and to reject the need for clergy to celebrate the sacraments. All, including women, were told they could celebrate Mass, provided that they wore sandals while doing so as a symbol of their adherence to the poverty of the apostles. The Waldensians were effectively forming a separate church, which soon fragmented into multiple communities. These groups never gained many members, but they did survive numerous attempts to root them out throughout the later medieval period. Waldensian communities remain even until today, and their members typically see themselves as representing the first wave of the Protestant Reformation, though scholars debate the accuracy of this connection.

The **Humiliati** ("humble ones") were another mendicant group that formed in northern Italy for similar reasons to the Waldensians, but they maintained a stronger relationship with the Church. They formed family communities desiring to live in poverty, do penance, and earn their food by simple manual labor rather than begging. Like the Waldensians, they sought permission to preach from the pope, but he directed them to respect the authority of their local bishops in this matter. While some rejected this command, others remained obedient to the Church, received permission to preach, and continued to live in poverty in their own communities. Still others joined religious orders that promoted similarly simple lifestyles and that had recently received formal approval from the Church. (We will discuss these later in this chapter.)

Some academic critics have interpreted the Church's response to the Waldensians as evidence that medieval popes and bishops cared more about retaining power than about following the Gospel and ministering to souls. They claim that the hierarchy suppressed these groups because their emphasis on poverty and simplicity drew attention to the bishops' own luxury and materialism. Further, they argue that the bishops' condemnation of the biblical translations of the Waldensians shows that they would rather control Sacred Scripture and protect their authority than make the Bible available to all.

Regarding the first charge, it is likely correct that some corrupt bishops feared that the Waldensians and Humiliati would draw an unwelcome spotlight on their abuses, but it is also true that pious bishops were likewise hesitant to grant the laity the freedom to preach. This reluctance was not because they disagreed with the ideals of these groups but because the laity's lack of formal theological education could cause them to lead others into error. Pope Alexander, for example, did not immediately suppress the Waldensians, as he presumably would have if he saw their lifestyle as a critique of his own. The fact that the Waldensians insisted on the immediate right to preach publicly regardless of whether they received permission demonstrated their conviction that their proposed reforms were more important than the Church's existing hierarchy. It was this disobedience, not their desire to follow literally the Gospel's call to give up their possessions, that led to their suppression.

Regarding the second charge, Church leaders were not categorically opposed to translations of the Bible into vernacular languages. Innocent III even wrote that the laity's desire to understand Sacred Scripture should be encouraged. Nonetheless, he condemned those biblical translations that were produced by those who lacked the necessary training or who had already shown that they were opposed to Church teaching. Bishops and theologians were concerned that unskilled translations and interpretations of difficult passages in the Bible by those without instruction in Latin, Greek, or theology would lead to confusion and error. The Waldensians' increasingly divergent beliefs based on their own translations of Scripture demonstrate that this concern was not groundless or based in clerical prejudice. (Some later Waldensians, for example, apparently believed that the individual's soul was a part of the Holy Spirit and that any good man was therefore divine and a "son of God" in whom the Incarnation—with all of the events of Jesus's life—was repeated.) Instead, popes and bishops accurately understood the challenges of interpreting the Bible and insisted that efforts to do so be guided by the education and principles provided by the Church.

The Albigensians

As we discussed briefly in chapter 16, Augustine had converted from a dualistic religion known as Manichaeanism. This religion taught that a good god had created the spiritual realm and an evil god had created everything material. The Manicheans disappeared soon after the fall of Rome but seemingly reemerged in the Byzantine Empire in the eleventh century led by a man named Basil the Bogomil (d. c. 1111). Their ideas appear to have migrated westward through Europe and took root in the region of Albi in southern France. Those who adopted these beliefs called themselves the "Good Men" or "Good Women" but were more popularly referred to as **Albigensians** or Cathari (the "pure ones").

The Albigensians believed that the good god had created human souls but that they were then imprisoned in their bodies by the evil deity. They denied the Incarnation, claiming that Christ was an angel who had merely appeared to take on human form and to suffer death. They taught that humans must escape the power of the devil by rejecting the body and anything physical or material. Albigensians also abandoned the sacraments of the Church as demonic because they made use of tangible matter such as water, oil, bread, and wine. They especially rejected marriage because it represented a commitment to physical union. Pregnant women were considered possessed by the devil and were shunned and despised.

The main way the Albigensians taught that their followers could be saved was by receiving a rite called the ***consolamentum***, during which one of the leaders of the religion, known as the *perfecti,* laid their hands upon the recipient. This ceremony was said to break the power of the devil over the recipient, but the newly cleansed was now obliged to observe perpetual continence and abstain from all food derived from animal reproduction, such as meat or dairy. If they failed to follow these requirements, the saving power of the *consolamentum* was broken and they were once again enslaved by the material universe of the devil. Some believers slowly starved themselves to death in order to die in the "state of grace" of the *consolamentum.* Suicide came to be regarded as a heroic act.

Why would anyone want to join such a religion? Most people in southern France who were sympathetic to the Albigensians had no plans to adopt its strict standards. Instead, they tried to live a simple life that rejected material luxuries and intended to receive the *consolamentum* and its promised salvation immediately before they died. They admired the example of the *perfecti* whose regular preaching and lives of humble abstinence seemed to reflect the teachings of the Gospel. The *perfecti* also donated the wealth that was given to them by patronizing the businesses of their followers. Thus, it became economically advantageous for many local inhabitants to adopt Albigensian beliefs. By the early thirteenth century, the Albigensian religion was spreading more thoroughly throughout the region.

Ever since the conversion of Constantine, the Church had expected Christian rulers to be involved in eradicating heretics from their lands. (Even Augustine, who had written with such caution about the temporal order, had ultimately enlisted imperial aid in suppressing the rigorist Donatists in North Africa.) Since heresy threatened people's faith and the salvation of their souls, it was considered a capital crime punishable by death as early as the Code of Justinian. In the case of the Albigensians, southern France was under the rule of the counts of Toulouse, who had struggled to control their territories. The current count, Raymond VI (r. 1194–1222), was also sympathetic to Albigensianism. For Innocent III, the spread of the Albigensians was a sign of the spiritual failings of medieval society that had contributed to the failure of the Fourth Crusade. He saw it as his duty to supervise the uprooting of this heresy and began urging Raymond to suppress the heretics. Raymond delayed.

Pope Innocent III excommunicating the Albigensians (left), **Massacre against the Albigensians by the crusaders** (right). Illuminated miniature made c. 1332–1350. Currently "Royal 16 G VI f. 374v" in the British Library, London, England. This image is from the *Chronicle of St. Denis*, a Latin history of the French monarchs compiled at the Abbey of St. Denis during the 13–15th centuries. It became a source for the French history, *Grandes Chroniques de France*.

Innocent began sending legates into the region to preach against the heretics. In 1208, one of the papal legates boldly condemned Raymond's failure to suppress Albigensianism and was found brutally murdered the next day. Most people concluded that Raymond had ordered or allowed the murder. He denied any involvement, but he was also not sorry that it had happened. Innocent saw the murder as a direct attack against the Church. He wrote a letter to the nobles of France denouncing Raymond as a murderer and calling on them to march on his lands and defend the Church. Most significantly, he awarded any who did so the same indulgence granted to those who joined a crusade to the Holy Land.

The **Albigensian Crusade** (1209–1229) that followed was the first crusade called to purify a Christian territory from heresy. It lasted twenty years and was notorious for the acts of cruelty committed by both sides. It began with the brutal victory at Béziers, a city whose population was known to include Albigensians. When it fell, the crusaders put everyone to the sword, even the priests who stood before their cathedral's altar, and burned down the city. These actions were so shocking that

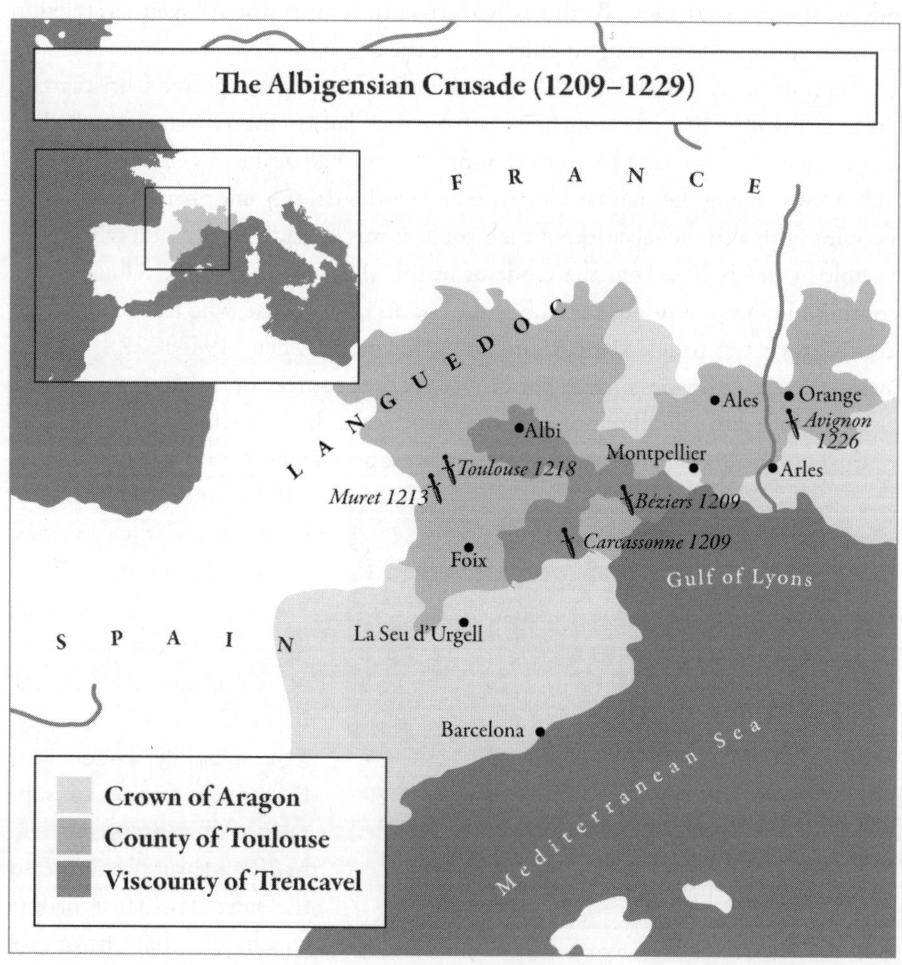

THE DISAPPEARING ALBIGENSIANS

One modern school of historical interpretation argues that the Albigensian religion was a papal invention. Scholars, such as R. I. Moore, claim that there was a desire for poverty and some slightly eccentric local religious practices among Christians in southern France. The leaders of these practices, who lived far more exemplary lives than those of the bishops, were respected by the local people, and the Church hierarchy was jealous of this esteem. Popes feared that, if these expressions of Christianity were not halted, they would undermine the authority of the bishops and the papacy. Church leaders therefore invented Albigensian beliefs and accused the rulers in southern France of professing them in order to justify a crusade in the region. Papal inquisitors then followed to eradicate these rivals to papal and episcopal authority. This theory concludes that other political rulers supported the actions of the Church hierarchy out of fear that a future crusade might target their own lands and authority.

Before addressing the specific problems with these claims, it is important to recognize that this is an example of a very common accusation made against Catholics and any other traditional religious group. The argument is based on the idea that many men and women who practice religion, especially those who lead religious communities, are primarily driven by a desire to exercise power over others and to control society. In this view, religious ceremonies and rituals are simply means for duping and manipulating others in an effort to maintain power over them. The idea that power is the primary driving motivation for actions has become more popular in modern times. It has led some scholars to adopt a hermeneutic, a lens or principle of interpretation, centered on power, which biases their interpretation of events and leads to erroneous conclusions.

While there have always been individuals who cunningly use religion as a tool to gain power, many people practice their religion because of their sincere belief that it honors and pleases God. In the case of medieval society, we know that such piety was especially widespread. The sacraments and liturgies of the Church were the chief way that medieval Christians interacted with God, so they thought about them deeply and paid them close attention. The records of the papal inquisition show that even miniscule changes to devotions and religious practices were heavily scrutinized. Medieval men and women did not join the Albigensian religion by accident. They were well aware that those who rejected the traditional sacraments of the Church in favor of the *consolamentum* were embracing a different creed.

Furthermore, newer evidence has emerged that describes debates between local bishops and Albigensian *perfecti* on specific doctrinal points. If the Albigensian heresy were a papal invention, the *perfecti* could have easily denied holding its doctrines, and there would not have been a debate. Even skeptical scholars find this evidence convincing, and support for the theory that Albigensianism was invented by the Church has declined in recent years.

Expulsion of Cathari from Carcassonne. Illuminated miniature made c. 1415. Currently "Ms. Cotton Nero E II Pt2, f20 verso" in the British Library, London, England. This image is from the *Grandes Chroniques de France*, a French history first compiled during the reign of Louis IX and subsequently updated by later monarchs to include later events. There are many copies available and the illuminated miniatures in each manuscript vary considerably.

many of the towns opened their gates to the crusade lest they suffer the same fate. The second target was the city of Carcassonne. This town submitted after a two-week siege. The crusaders did not massacre this population, but the people were expelled from the city and forbidden to bring any of their belongings with them. Contemporary accounts describe the inhabitants as departing either naked or with only their innermost garments. With two major centers of heresy defeated, it seemed as though the campaign would quickly complete its mission.

The crusade's march to success became bogged down due to two different factors. The first was the nature of its crusading vow. Whereas the crusades to the Holy Land had an obvious destination in Jerusalem, the Albigensian Crusade did not have an identifiable location to be visited. Rather, a specific duration of time was set to indicate when one's crusading vow had been fulfilled. Forty days was the typical period of time, and the number of the crusade's participants swelled in the spring and summer when people took the vow. Most victories occurred during these months of the year. Once the fall and winter approached, the number of soldiers taking (or renewing) their crusading vow dwindled, and the gains of the previous spring and summer were now vulnerable to counterattack.

The second difficulty confronting the Albigensian Crusade was its ambiguous nature. Its goal was to eradicate heresy in the region, but this quickly became intertwined with the feudal relationships that defined the politics of this area. Some of the nobility, such as Count Raymond of Toulouse, at least indirectly promoted Albigensianism. Others held aloof from the religious situation but still resented the crusade and resisted it as an invasion. Such was the attitude of Peter II of Aragon (r. 1196–1213). This ally of Alfonso VIII and hero of the recent Battle of Las Navas de Tolosa was lord over several territories targeted by the crusade. Peter wrote to

Innocent III to complain of the crusade's excesses, but the pope was convinced that Raymond of Toulouse needed to be defeated before the heresy could be ended. When Peter refused to participate and even prepared to defend his territories from the crusaders, Innocent threatened him with excommunication. In 1213, one year after his victory for Christendom in Spain, Peter II died fighting to protect his lands against the Albigensian Crusade.

The crusade dragged on for years, and the ebb and flow of its conquests, rebellions, and counterassaults make for discouraging reading. Its most significant results were to weaken the counts of Toulouse and to allow the Capetian kings of France to establish royal control over the region. Nonetheless, pockets of Albigensianism persisted and widespread popular conversion had yet to take place.

The Dominicans and Franciscans

The most famous preacher against the Albigensians was **Dominic of Caleruega** (1170–1221), a Spanish cleric who journeyed to Rome in 1204 seeking the pope's permission to travel to the Holy Land and convert Muslims. Innocent instead commissioned him to preach against the Albigensians in France. Dominic established his own Order of Preachers, later known as the Dominicans. These were not traditional monks but rather "friars," a term that meant "brother" and which indicated that they were mendicants who begged for their food rather than living in self-sufficient communities like the Benedictines. They prayed a shortened version of the Office together and were expected to spend most of their days actively preaching the Gospel in the world. They lived out the poverty of the Gospel by owning nothing themselves, eating only one meal a day for half the year, and perpetually abstaining from meat. They also fully embraced the academic life of medieval universities and received an education in logic, rhetoric, and Scripture that would enable them to debate, and hopefully convert, heretics. Dominic recognized that these preachers would require profound spiritual support and established communities of contemplative nuns who prayed for their guidance and success. According to tradition, he also promoted devotion to the Virgin Mary through the recitation of the Rosary.

The order grew rapidly, and soon there were thousands of friars. The Order of Preachers provided an opportunity for men and women to embrace poverty while still remaining faithful to the hierarchy of the Church. Their charism was fundamentally consistent with Innocent's efforts to reinvigorate the Church, and Innocent granted them the freedom to preach anywhere without requiring the approval of the local bishop. This decision dovetailed with Innocent's other actions that tended to centralize decision-making into the hands of the pope alone and that reduced

Francis of Assisi. Fresco c. 1223-1224. Currently in the Monastery of Sacro Speco in Subiaco, Italy. This is the oldest known portrait of St. Francis and was painted during his time as a pilgrim at Subiaco in 1223-1224. The image is unique because Francis does not have the stigmata or a halo.

the effective authority and independence of individual bishops. With this papal support, the preaching friars helped strengthen the faith of many who might otherwise have been attracted to the Albigensians or other erroneous movements.

Another mendicant movement that emerged during the twelfth century was the Order of Friars Minor. Their founder, **Francis of Assisi** (1181–1226), showed little interest in pursuing a life of poverty in his early years. His father was one of the new class of merchants who had become wealthy through buying and selling silk. His parents indulged Francis, and he lived an extravagant lifestyle. He was better educated than previous generations, loved music and social gatherings, and dreamed of becoming a knight or a troubadour, one of the travelling poets or minstrels associated with "courtly love" who performed at the courts of kings and barons.

In 1205, Francis joined a crusade launched by Innocent III against a political rival in southern Italy. Francis's father proudly bought his son the best armor and weapons available, eager to show that he and his son were now equals with the nobles and their sons. While travelling with the expedition, Francis suffered a spiritual crisis. He returned to Assisi—to the shame of his father—and then made a pilgrimage to Rome. When he returned, he renounced all worldly possessions and dedicated himself to rebuilding the nearby churches. He endured the scorn of the community and the embarrassment of his parents, especially his father who had hoped to see his family take its place among the leading families of the city. Wearing only a poor tunic, Francis travelled the countryside preaching that all should do penance and reform their lives. Francis's preaching and commitment were inspiring, and many flocked to join him. His followers were officially known as the Order of the Lesser Brothers or "Minorites," though the term "Franciscans" became the most popular way to reference the community.

Confirmation of the Rule by Innocent III. Fresco by Giotto c. 1296–1304. Currently in the Upper Basilica of San Francesco d'Assisi in Assisi, Italy. The scene is part of the Life of St. Francis, a cycle of 28 frescoes based on the biography of St. Francis by St. Bonaventure.

The first friars travelled to Rome to seek papal approval for their community in 1209. Innocent was clearly moved by the experience of meeting Francis. He granted them the privilege to preach anywhere throughout Western Europe. Francis also founded communities of contemplative nuns led by his great friend, Clare of Assisi (1194–1253), to support the work of the friars through their prayers and sacrifices from the convent. The Franciscans experienced even more explosive growth than the Dominicans. By 1220, there were around five thousand Franciscan friars. Such numbers required some form of organization and planning, but Francis had little interest in the administrative tasks required for an order of this size. He retired to the hills above Assisi to live a life of prayer and contemplation until his death in 1226. Nonetheless, there was a fundamental tension between Francis's ideal of simple trust in God and the necessity of maintaining order and proper behavior among so many followers. Future Franciscan leaders would have to find a road between the founder's idealism and the temptation to mere administrative pragmatism.

Although Francis renounced the idea of the life of a court troubadour, he kept his love of musical composition. His most famous work, the *Canticle of the Sun*, is considered one of the first works of literature written in Italian. This effusive hymn praises God for the wonders of creation. The verses emphasize that God made and sustains the riches of nature as a means of teaching all men to know and love Him, Who became incarnate in this world to save them. Francis was also famous for honoring the Incarnation by starting the tradition of a Christmas manger scene. This love of the Incarnation was a particularly effective response to the errors of Albigensianism which were so prevalent at that time.

Today, Francis is a universally beloved and frequently mischaracterized figure. Many accounts depict him as a modern free spirit who wished to love God in nature and who rejected the political power and ritual of the institutional Church. However, Francis was no medieval hippie. Such a depiction obscures Francis's faithfulness and devotion to the hierarchy of the Church and traditional Catholic practices and teachings. Francis and his followers were famous for their loyalty to the pope and papal authority, a fact that set them apart from the earlier Waldensians despite other similarities. Like the Dominicans, their lives demonstrated that it was possible to embrace radical poverty without rebelling against the Church. Francis loved the Holy Land and ardently desired the recovery of Jerusalem and the conversion of Muslims. He even briefly accompanied the Fifth Crusade (which we will discuss in the next chapter) in an unsuccessful effort to convert the Muslim leader and publicly prayed for the crusaders while the army was fighting.

Perhaps most importantly, Francis's devotional life was deeply rooted in the sacraments of the Church. He was at the forefront of the movement to increase devotion to the Holy Eucharist. He was one of the leading voices demanding that the faithful should kneel in the presence of the Holy Eucharist and that bowing showed insufficient devotion. He also insisted on the production and maintenance of the finest altar linens and church buildings to serve as resting places for God incarnate in the Blessed Sacrament. For the poor man of Assisi, no expense was too great to honor his Eucharistic Lord.

The Fourth Lateran Council

In what turned out to be the last years of his pontificate, Innocent organized an ecumenical council to establish a program of reform and sacramental renewal for the entire Church. After two years of preparation, the **Fourth Lateran Council** convened in November 1215 with over four hundred bishops and more than eight hundred abbots, priors, and lay dignitaries present. Unlike previous councils, in which there were often heated debates, here the seventy decrees composed by the pope and his staff were simply read aloud and approved.

The decrees of the council were numerous and varied in nature from the theological to the political and social. The doctrine of transubstantiation was defined as a dogma that all Christians must believe. ("Transubstantiation" is the term used to describe what happens at the consecration during Mass, namely, that the bread and wine are converted into the body, blood, soul, and divinity of Jesus, leaving behind only the appearance of bread and wine.) The council also required the faithful to confess their sins and receive the Holy Eucharist at least once each year. In addition, the clergy were forbidden from participating in trade or practicing extravagant lifestyles. Other pronouncements laid out plans for a new crusade with details of how to recruit soldiers and how to fund the expedition to avoid the problems of the Fourth Crusade. The council also mandated that Jews wear special clothing so that they could easily be identified both to protect them from violence and to isolate them. (The Council pointed out that Moses had instructed the Jews to wear distinctive clothing and therefore the council fathers did not see this measure as necessarily oppressive.) Jews were exempted from some religious and social obligations, but they were not permitted to hold certain offices or marry Christians. Finally, the council called for an end to the Albigensian Crusade and instead promoted other measures for suppressing heresy which would become the basis of the Papal Inquisition.

An **inquisition** is a legal investigation in which religious leaders find, convert, or suppress individual heretics using state authority. While this open intermingling of religious and political authority may seem unsettling to modern readers, it is important to remember that the medieval worldview saw society as a unity between Church and State. Heresy undermined Christendom by introducing new religious beliefs that both jeopardized souls and threatened the stability of the "Church-State" hierarchy. Thus, it made sense, from the medieval perspective, that both clergy and political officials would be involved. After all, Charlemagne's *missi dominici* had set the precedent for this cooperation between the religious and temporal authorities. On a practical level, it also made sense to include priests in these decisions since political officials typically lacked theological expertise and relied on the religious inquisitors to determine who was and who was not a heretic.

The first medieval inquisitions were in the eleventh and twelfth centuries; these were local diocesan investigations known as episcopal inquisitions. Pope Innocent III brought these under greater papal oversight by sending papal legates to assist bishops in their examinations. These joint efforts were known as legatine inquisitions. (It was the murder of one such papal legate that precipitated the Albigensian Crusade.) The Fourth Lateran Council increased the pope's role even further by establishing papal inquisitions. These were gradually implemented during the later papacies of Honorius III and Gregory IX. These pontiffs entrusted the Dominicans with the administration of the inquisitions in southern France against the Albigensians.

The papal inquisitors traveled from town to town, showing their credentials to the magistrates and then issuing proclamations. The proclamations instructed Catholics to denounce any heretics they knew who lived in the community and gave heretics a set time to confess and abjure their errors. Those who were accused were allowed a lawyer to defend them, a new development that would eventually become a right in modern justice systems. The accused could also provide a list of those they considered their personal enemies, and the inquisitors would reject any accusations made by these individuals.

A summons to answer questions from the inquisitors would certainly have been a frightening experience. Sometimes the innocent were accused of heresy by their political enemies or those who superstitiously blamed them for sickness or poor harvests. Nonetheless, the papal inquisition had more external oversight than any other court systems at that time and served to prevent the informal mob lynching of alleged heretics that were otherwise prevalent. While some inquisitors abused their power, the papacy removed, excommunicated, or even imprisoned inquisitors who violated the approved code of conduct. Ultimately, the inquisition succeeded where the force of arms had failed, and Albigensianism faded away over the course of the thirteenth century.

Conclusion

The Fourth Lateran Council was one of the greatest achievements of Innocent III's influential pontificate, a sign of his success in centralizing the government of the Church under the leadership of the papacy. Innocent died less than a year after the council ended, but the reforms he initiated lasted far into the future. The Dominican and Franciscan friars were invaluable agents for implementing the sacramental renewal proposed by the council. In the years that followed, they traveled throughout Europe preaching repentance, hearing confessions, and bringing the sacraments to thousands. They were a source of orthodox preaching whose approved status and loyalty to the papacy enabled them to spread a consistent message of reform throughout Christendom.

The spread of the mendicants was a powerful and authentic response to the desire within society to embrace poverty during this period. The mendicant friars were a constant witness both that reform was possible and that those who wished to embrace poverty did not have to reject the authority of the Church and the reception of her sacraments. For the merchants who had become wealthy as a result of the growing medieval economy, the mendicants offered an important opportunity to sanctify their lives and even their money by giving to the friars who begged at their doors. In this way, merchants could honor the virtue of poverty and place their newfound riches in the service of the Gospel.

CHAPTER 31

Scourges and Saints

If our Lord send you any prosperity, either health of body or other thing, you ought to thank Him humbly for it, and you ought be careful that you are not worse for it either through pride or anything else, for it is a very great sin to fight against our Lord with His gifts.

Louis IX, Letter to His Son[1]

Louis IX was renowned for his humility and piety. He saw his authority, as this letter to his son reveals, as a gift from God that had to be used for His glory and the good of those entrusted to Louis's care. His reign in France, as well as that of his cousin Ferdinand III in Spain, rank among the great triumphs of medieval Europe. Both these monarchs demonstrated in their personal lives that kings could pursue the temporal interests of their kingdoms without compromising their adherence to their Christian faith. What was more, this era also witnessed the lives of two towering intellectual figures, Thomas Aquinas and Bonaventure, whose contributions to philosophy and theology are still studied and celebrated today. Yet, amidst this flourishing of the thirteenth-century, trouble was brewing both within and without. From within, Frederick II Hohenstaufen became a chronic enemy of the papacy and challenged its vision of a Europe guided by papal authority. From without, Mongol invasions initiated by Genghis Khan devastated

1 David O'Connell, *The Teachings of Saint Louis: A Critical Text* (Chapel Hill: University of North Carolina Press, 1972), 46–49.

Central Europe[2] and redirected the history of both Europe and Asia. These disparate figures highlight the triumphs achieved by Christendom during the High Middle Ages and the challenges that menaced its future.

Genghis Khan

For centuries the Mongolian tribes had inhabited the East Asian steppe as nomads. They grazed their flocks and herds and lived in tents lined with fur, burning animal droppings to stay warm. They raided the borderlands of China from time to time, but they were usually occupied waging their own feuds against one another. Survival was difficult, and the Mongols lacked a central leader who could unite them. This situation began to change during the Medieval Warming Period. A more plentiful food supply enabled more children to survive to adulthood and caused their population to increase rapidly.

Around 1162, a boy named Temüjin was born to one of the leading tribal families. His father died when he was young, and for a time he was a social outcast. Nonetheless, Temüjin eventually became a skillful leader. He expanded his army by inviting brave warriors he defeated to join his own forces. These new allies could even advance to high rank since Temüjin rewarded talent rather than birth. He steadily strengthened his position in Mongol society until, in 1206, he achieved an unprecedented feat by uniting all the Mongol tribes under his rule. He was now the "universal ruler" or **Genghis Khan** (r. 1206–1227).

Emperor Taizu (Genghis Khan). Paint and ink on silk c. 1278. Currently in the National Palace Museum in Taipei, Taiwan. The portrait is from the "Album of Yuan Emperor Portraits."

In 1207, he took his formidable army south into China. After several successful campaigns, he captured and sacked the city of Beijing in 1215. Sources described mountains of bones

2 In previous chapters we have followed the Roman model of dividing Europe into a two halves, that is Western and Eastern Europe. However, by the end of the High Middle Ages, Germanic and Slavic influences had created a third region within Europe, Central Europe. This term typically includes modern-day Germany, Switzerland, Poland, Czechia, Slovakia, Austria, and Hungary. We will explore this region and its characteristics in greater detail in volume II.

THE MONGOL ARMY

The Mongol army was one of the most brilliant military machines in history and was critical to the success of Genghis Khan and his descendants. It was entirely meritocratic, meaning that promotion was based on merit or ability rather than family connections. The soldiers all had opportunities for reward and promotion and were therefore exceptionally loyal.

The Mongol army was highly mobile. They travelled with herds of cattle running alongside them. These animals served as their food supply, which reduced the need to halt and forage while on the march. Mongol soldiers also had access to multiple horses and changed mounts frequently during a day in order to ride at high speed. Their swiftness enabled them to arrive before their opponents had gathered their forces or prepared a defense. Like the Parthians centuries earlier, the Mongols fought primarily as horse archers, riding towards the enemy while firing their bows and then wheeling away and returning to their lines while still firing over their shoulders. They frequently cut down their enemies' armies before their opponents could even come to grips with them.

Some have proposed that Mongol strategy was drawn from their traditional hunting practices. Whereas hunting in Europe typically involved targeting a single prey, the Mongols were said to have surrounded a given area, driven every animal to the center of this area, and then killed as many animals as they could. This practice reflects the efficiency, teamwork, and ruthlessness displayed by the Mongol armies during this period of conquest. In battle, the Mongols typically replicated this effort to surround their prey, but they left one route open for escape. This gave them two advantages. First, it gave their enemies an apparent opportunity to escape and weakened the resolve of those who were already terrified to stay and fight. Secondly, it channeled the flight of those who abandoned the battlefield and made it easier for Mongol horsemen to attack the fleeing enemy after they had routed those who had remained.

The Mongols were also proficient in technological and psychological warfare. They used gunpowder and other advanced weapons developed by the Chinese to conduct sieges effectively. Whenever the Mongols entered a new territory, they offered the inhabitants the opportunity to accept their rule peacefully. If this offer was rejected, the Mongols would advance on the city, beating enormous drums that had to be carried by four men. We are told that when the inhabitants heard the throb of these drums, they would almost go mad with fear. The Mongols would then sack the city with particular thoroughness, killing every living thing they found, even dogs and cats. It is no surprise that terrifying reports of these merciless and seemingly unstoppable warriors spread rapidly across Europe and Asia.

piled alongside the streets and outside the city following the Mongols' victory. Genghis Khan seems to have intended to lead his army to further Chinese conquests, but news of rebellion at home led him to return to Mongolia. He pursued the rebels

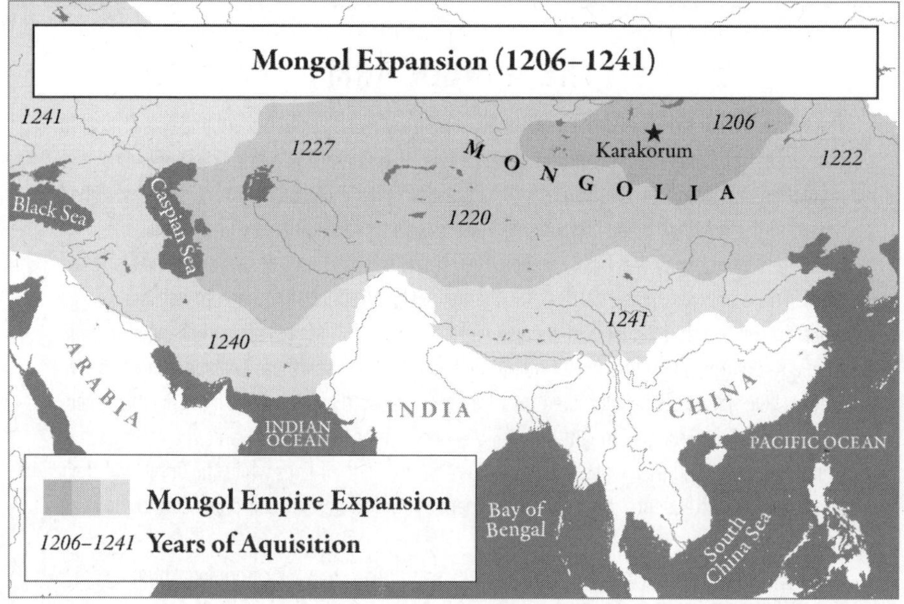

west until he reached the lands of the Muslim Khwarazmian Empire (modern-day Afghanistan and Central Asia). Recognizing the wealth of this domain, the warlord initially proposed a commercial partnership, demonstrating Mongol interests were not limited to conquest but also included the acquisition of wealth through trade. When the rulers rejected this offer, he unleashed a campaign of terror across the region. Countless men, women, and children were killed or enslaved as Mongol soldiers destroyed their towns and cities. The region has never recovered its previous prosperity even until today. It is said that after taking a particular city, Genghis Khan ordered its elites to congregate in its mosque. There he declared to them that if they had avoided sin, their God would not have sent him to punish them.

Genghis Khan was not the only person who thought that God was using him. Christians in Europe and in the crusader states rejoiced at the news that someone was defeating Muslim armies to the east. Active imaginations combined these reports with traditions about Thomas the Apostle in India as well as a legendary figure known as "Prester (or Elder) John." Already in the previous century, people had spread rumors—probably based on garbled accounts of the Nestorian Church of the East—that there was a Christian king, fabulously wealthy and descended from one of the three Magi recorded in the Gospel of Matthew. This king was supposedly attempting to join the crusades and aid their cause. Many thirteenth-century Christians believed that the Mongol khan was a descendant of Prester John, and ambassadors from Western Europe journeyed eastward hoping to establish contact with this Christian kingdom.

Their hopes were bitterly disappointed. After their conquest of Central Asia, the Mongols did indeed move further west, but they brought terror rather than aid to Europe. They defeated the Bulgars and some Russians in the Caucasus (modern-day Armenia, Azerbaijan, Georgia, and southern Russia). Only Genghis Khan's death in 1227 slowed the onslaught. (His body was returned to Mongolia, and according to tradition, the burial party was ordered to kill every living thing they saw as they journeyed to his final resting place so that nothing would know where he was buried.) Genghis Khan's third son, Ogedei (r. 1229–1241), succeeded him, and the advance continued. The Mongols sacked the city of Kiev in 1237 and soon defeated other Russian principalities. In 1241, they defeated the Hungarians at the Battle of Mohi. Historians estimate that as much as half the Hungarian population was killed by the Mongol invaders. Poland, Croatia, Austria, and even Germany suffered additional devastating raids.

All Europe seemed to be at the Mongols' mercy. There was no obvious force capable of resisting the invasion, and Church leaders offered the crusading indulgence to anyone who would fight to defend the eastern borders of Christendom. Relief came when Ogedei died unexpectedly in 1241. Although Mongol bands would continue to raid Central Europe periodically in the decades to come, they never returned with the same strength or conducted a full invasion of Europe. Nonetheless, the Mongol conquests shaped world history. As discussed in the next chapter, their campaigns to the south had profound ramifications for Islam. Also, as we will see in volume II, Mongol rule will transform China and the developing Russian society.

Frederick II and his eagle. Illuminated miniature made c. 1250. Currently "Pal. lat 1071, fol. 1v" in the Vatican Library, Vatican City. This image is from *De Arte Venandi Cum Avibus* ("The Art of Hunting with Birds"), a book on falconry written by Fredrick II himself.

Frederick II Hohenstaufen

We introduced **Frederick II Hohenstaufen** (r. 1212–1250) in chapter 29 as the young ward of Pope Innocent III. Frederick was destined to rule the kingdom of Sicily, and he came to love the exotic and complex culture of his realm. The various Arab, Greek, and Norman traditions fascinated him, and he learned to speak Italian, German, Latin, Hebrew, Arabic, and other languages. In addition, he founded the first government-funded university, located in Naples, and also wrote a detailed study about falconry that combined his personal observations with his knowledge of Aristotelian philosophy. His contemporaries were amazed by the variety of his interests and called him *stupor mundi* ("the wonder of the world"). As if to add to the mystique, he kept a menagerie of giraffes, cheetahs, lynxes, leopards, and elephants.

In 1211, Innocent III abandoned his former support for the Holy Roman Emperor Otto IV. Otto had invaded southern Italy, and in response Innocent now championed the election of Frederick II as the king of the Romans. Though he helped Frederick receive that crown in 1215, Innocent disliked this arrangement because the area under the papal political control was now surrounded by Fredrick's realms to the north (the Holy Roman Empire) and to the south (the Kingdom of Sicily). Innocent's one comfort was that Frederick had promised to join the new crusade which the pope would proclaim at the Fourth Lateran Council later that same year.

This **Fifth Crusade** (1217–1221) began with the departure of groups from Hungary, Austria, and Germany. The main body of crusaders decided first to conquer territory in Egypt so that they would have a secure base in the region from which they could launch their campaign to recover the Holy Land. Richard the Lionheart had considered such an approach but had been unable to enact it during the Third Crusade. Now conditions in Egypt seemed particularly favorable to this strategy. Saladin had died in 1193. His three nephews divided his empire among themselves and soon fell into an almost constant state of war and intrigue against one another. Frederick, however, was distracted by a civil war with Otto IV in Germany and delayed his departure for the crusade.

Damietta was the crusaders' first important target in Egypt. This port city controlled access from the Nile to the Mediterranean Sea. After a long and difficult siege, they finally captured the city in 1219 thanks to their construction of an innovative floating, rotating siege machine. The crusaders could now prevent Egyptian export of goods for trade and could use the city as a base to reinforce Frederick's imperial army. Unfortunately, the crusade had stalled by 1221. Though Frederick had been formally crowned Holy Roman Emperor, he had still not left to join the crusade.

When the crusaders finally marched south to continue their campaign, their decision was motivated, in part, by the reports of an eastern king who was moving against the Muslims. The crusaders knew little of Genghis Khan or his ambitions; they assumed that this eastern king must be a descendant of Prester John and took comfort in the thought that soon Christian armies from the east and the west would work together against the spread of Islam. There were even rumors that a Muslim prophecy foretold as much by declaring that Islam would end during a year when

Easter fell on April 3. The next year, 1222, was such a year, and the Christian army left Damietta confident in their coming victory. Their hopes evaporated when al-Kamil (r. 1218–1238), the Muslim ruler of Egypt, used his superior knowledge of the Nile to flood the Christians' march. They had no choice but to surrender and abandon Damietta. The Fifth Crusade had seemed to be on the verge of great success, only to end as yet another failed attempt to regain the Holy Land.

Much of the blame for this failure was directed toward Frederick, who claimed he was still securing his lands and never joined the crusade. By 1227, it had been twelve years, and the emperor still showed no sign of crusading. The new pope, Gregory IX (r. 1227–1241), lost patience and excommunicated him for failing to uphold his vow. In a move that demonstrated the breakdown of papal-imperial relations, Frederick left with an army for Palestine the following year. Gregory condemned Frederick's crusade as a mockery of the crusading movement since the emperor was excommunicated and could receive no spiritual benefit. Frederick did not care. Instead, he negotiated a treaty with al-Kamil that permitted Frederick to enter Jerusalem and be crowned as its king. In return, Frederick would not challenge continued Muslim control of many holy sites such as the Temple Mount. He also destroyed Jerusalem's fortifications, leaving it defenseless against any future Muslim attack. The patriarch of Jerusalem, who resided at the remaining Christian stronghold of Acre, boycotted Frederick's coronation and placed Jerusalem under interdict. For him and many others, the imperial campaign insulted crusading piety by using Jerusalem to promote Frederick's interests rather than honoring and protecting the holy city. Frederick and his army left soon afterwards.

Some modern commentators have presented Frederick's campaign as an enlightened, diplomatic alternative to the crusades. After all, had he not achieved the goal of returning Jerusalem to Christian rule through peaceful negotiation while the crusaders' violent methods had failed? This evaluation ignores that Frederick's diplomacy yielded more than he gained. The Christians still did not have control over the region or even over various holy sites. Frederick's agreement to dismantle Jerusalem's defenses even made it less likely that Christian control would be reestablished, as became apparent when a Muslim army sacked the city less than twenty years later. It was likely that he himself did not view his crusade as a lasting success but rather as an opportunity to score a point against papal criticisms.

During Frederick's time in Jerusalem, the rivalry between the popes and the emperors entered a new and more bitter phase. Gregory IX began attacking Frederick's lands in Italy, hoping to strengthen the papal territory at the expense of the empire. Frederick responded by employing Muslim mercenaries from Sicily to fight in his armies, claiming that he had been unjustly excommunicated and therefore forced to rely on non-Christian troops. The presence of Muslims in an army that was attacking the city of Rome terrified Church leaders, who went so far as to claim that Frederick was an anti-Christ. Pope Gregory IX died in 1241, and the new pope, Innocent IV (r. 1243–1254), fled from Rome to Lyons in southeastern France out of fear of Frederick's forces.

In 1245, Innocent called an ecumenical council to meet in Lyons. The pope opened the gathering by preaching a sermon in which he lamented the five wounds afflicting the Church: lukewarmness and corruption among clergy and laity, the Great Schism between the Greek and Latin Churches, the attacks of the Mongols, the recent Muslim sack of Jerusalem, and Frederick's persecution of the Church and the papacy. Innocent declared Frederick not only excommunicated but deposed from his throne. He demanded that no Hohenstaufen ever again be chosen to rule the Germans and tried to rally support for another emperor. However, a number of princes, even those renowned for their piety like Louis IX of France, had tired of papal involvement in German politics and refused to back Innocent's candidate.

Innocent IV persisted in his determination to eradicate the threat posed by Frederick even as Frederick fought to retain his control in Italy and Sicily. The emperor established a universal written law enforced by a central bureaucracy of government employees who were directly loyal to himself. These measures increased and solidified imperial authority in Sicily, but Frederick's focus on the south led to an erosion of imperial authority in Germany. He made numerous concessions to the German dukes to prevent them from siding with his rivals. For example, he allowed them to pass their lands to their heirs without requiring the heirs to swear service to the emperor. He also gave up imperial authority to tax these lands. These decisions contributed to the decentralization that had already taken root during the reign of Frederick II's grandfather, Frederick Barbarossa. Thanks to the concessions from both Fredericks, Germany remained a fragmented collection of largely independent feudal states instead of a centralized kingdom under a single leader. Future medieval emperors would no longer exercise the significant influence in European politics that their eleventh, twelfth, and thirteenth-century predecessors had wielded. In Italy, the northern city-states allied with one or the other party according to their own immediate interests. Eventually, most of them turned against Frederick and defeated him, crushing his hopes of securing his authority throughout the peninsula.

Frederick's last years witnessed a number of disappointments, but he died peacefully in December of 1250. Among the items listed in his will were the return of lands seized from the papacy and the liberation of prisoners. Always a figure of contradiction, he was buried by his Muslim bodyguard while wearing the habit of a Cistercian monk with a red crusader's cross draped over his shoulder.

Louis IX and Ferdinand III

The resolution of the Albigensian Crusade gave the Capetian kings control of the contested lands in southern France. Even as Germany fragmented, France was becoming more centralized. Furthermore, French royal authority expanded both politically and spiritually under the leadership of the pious Louis IX. His example and prompt canonization reenforced the quasi-religious character of the French monarchy that had existed since the days of Clovis and Charlemagne. As we will see in the next chapter, future kings were quick to exploit this prestige.

Blanche of Castile Instructing King Louis IX of France. Illuminated miniature made c. 1227–1234. Currently "MS M.240 folio 8r" in the Morgan Library and Museum, New York.

Philip Augustus was succeeded by his son, Louis VIII (r. 1223–1226). When this king died unexpectedly, his twelve-year-old son, **Louis IX** (r. 1226–1270), became king. Louis's mother was Blanche of Castile (1188–1252), a daughter of Alfonso VIII, the victor of the Battle of Las Navas de Tolosa. Blanche oversaw Louis's instruction in Latin, rhetoric, the military sciences, and government. Her most enduring lesson, however, was that she would rather see her son die than commit a mortal sin. Louis took his mother's instruction to heart and recognized that he had the opportunity, even the responsibility, to use the resources God had placed at his disposal to liberate Jerusalem.

In 1249, he left his mother as regent of his kingdom while he led a crusading expedition. This campaign, often called "the First Crusade of Louis IX," followed the path of the Fifth Crusade to Egypt. It enjoyed initial success, but, just as before, the crusaders were defeated as they tried to navigate the Nile. Louis endured a brief period of captivity before he was ransomed, and then spent four years in the Holy Land. While his army could not successfully retake Jerusalem, he helped support the few remaining cities in the region that were still under crusader control. One important effect of Louis's crusade was the destabilization and collapse of Saladin's Ayyubid dynasty in Egypt. They were replaced by the Mamluks, a dynasty of Turkish slave-warriors from Central Asia.

When Louis returned to France, he engaged in a comprehensive social reform, hoping that by building a more just kingdom he would win God's favor for his armies. For example, he replaced superstitious practices, such as the ancient Germanic custom of trials by combat, with a jury system. This and similar reforms enabled the French monarchy to centralize power and control their nobles. He funded the construction of hospitals throughout the kingdom to serve lepers and the poor. Louis also promoted laws against blasphemy and sought to convert heretics and Jews. The latter efforts led to the famous Disputation of Paris in 1240. This debate focused on anti-Christian statements in the Jewish *Talmud* and resulted in book burnings of the *Talmud* for its derogatory statements about Jesus. (This decision to destroy copies of the *Talmud* was overturned several years later.) Louis's effort to purge his kingdom of whatever he deemed offensive to God also included his own activities. He lived a penitential life and fed beggars at his table himself. In addition, he built the beautiful chapel of Sainte-Chapelle to hold relics from Jesus's passion, such as the crown of thorns.

While Louis obeyed the pope in most matters, he also resisted when he believed that the pope was abusing his authority. On the one hand, he refused to fight against Frederick and continued to treat him as emperor even after the pope had declared him excommunicated and deposed. He also refused to let his son accept rule over the Kingdom of Sicily since, in Louis's view, Frederick's descendants had a just claim to rule it. On the other hand, Louis also took steps to defend the papacy against Frederick's aggression, most notably when Frederick planned to attack the pope, who had fled to the city of Lyons. These positions might seem contradictory, but Louis saw everything through the lens of crusade and sought to end the prolonged fighting between emperor and pope so that the crusading endeavor could achieve success.

This perspective also explains why, even though he was now in his mid-fifties, Louis attempted another crusade in 1270. This time the campaign traveled to the North African coastal city of Tunis in the hope of converting the local Muslim ruler and forming an alliance to fight the Mamluks. The expedition was a military failure. The conversion and alliance did not occur, and the army was ravaged by disease. Louis himself fell sick and died, lying on a bed of ashes, uttering the word "Jerusalem."

Louis's prominent piety provided the Church with an opportunity to refine medieval notions of holiness and how kings and subjects could live out their vocations. It is important to note that the French king was canonized as a confessor of the Faith rather than as a martyr. For all the rhetoric used by popes, preachers, and crusaders regarding "holy war," the Church avoided formally linking crusade with automatic martyrdom, a decision that highlighted the differences between Christian and Islamic understandings of warfare and its role in the spiritual life.

Louis's exemplary piety and Christian kingship were mirrored by that of his cousin Ferdinand III of Castile. The cousins were related through a messy sequence of relationships. Ferdinand's father, Alfonso IX of León, had married his first cousin, later had this union annulled, and then married Berengaria (1180–1246). She was the sister of Blanche of Castile and daughter of Alfonso VIII. She also was Alfonso IX's first cousin once removed, and Innocent III condemned their relationship as unlawful. The couple continued to live together until their son **Ferdinand III** (r. 1217–1252) was five years old. At this point, Berengaria returned to Castile. When her brother died unexpectedly in 1217, she became queen of Castile but gave the throne to the teenage Ferdinand. Alfonso IX of León resented the power of Castile, and Ferdinand soon faced an invasion led by his father. Not only did the young king defeat Alfonso but he even gained the throne of León when his father died twelve years later. Ferdinand was now master of a powerful kingdom with substantial resources. Like Louis, he believed he had an obligation to use these resources to advance Christianity, but he fought his crusade closer to home.

Paired statues of Beatrix of Swabia and Ferdinand III of Castile. Stone sculptures made c. 13th century. Currently in the Cathedral of Saint Mary of Burgos in Burgos, Spain. Beatrix of Swabia was the fourth daughter of Philip of Swabia (see Ch. 29); her cousin, Frederick II Hohenstaufen, arranged her marriage to Ferdinand III. The wedding took place on November 30, 1219 in the Burgos cathedral.

In 1228, Ferdinand announced the crusade to re-Christianize Spain to the Cortes, the council of Spanish nobles who advised the king. The Almohad Empire had collapsed after their defeat at the Battle of Las Navas de Tolosa, and Muslim Spain was once again divided into small principalities. Ferdinand worked in collaboration with James I of Aragon (r. 1213–1276), ruler of Spain's second great Christian kingdom, to capture most of al-Andalus. Their determination to succeed inspired those Christians under Muslim rule to support them even at great risk. For example, in 1236, the Christian population of Córdoba seized control of part of the former capital of Umayyad Spain. They had lived under Islamic rule for five hundred years, but they believed Ferdinand would finally deliver them. Ferdinand was surprised when he heard of this development but immediately rode to Córdoba through a winter storm with only a hundred knights. This provided enough support for the insurgents until the remainder of his army arrived to secure the rest of the city.

For twenty years, Ferdinand fought to gain more of Spain for Christianity than any previous monarch. Some historians consider him to be the most successful crusader in history. Nonetheless, Ferdinand was not simply a warrior. He was a committed proponent of medieval education and founded the first Spanish university in Salamanca. When he died in 1252, Ferdinand was buried in the cathedral of Seville. The inscription on his tomb was written in Arabic, Latin, Hebrew, and Spanish, an indication of Ferdinand's support for Spain's cosmopolitan society. His tomb also expressed Christian confidence. Previous generations would never have risked burying their king so close to the remaining Muslim territory of Granada, but Ferdinand's descendants were convinced that Muslim forces would not recover the lands their crusader-king had claimed for Christendom.

Mendicant University Saints

The mendicant orders grew rapidly in the thirteenth century. Their influence was particularly visible in the context of the medieval university. The Dominicans had been founded with the express intention of providing the Church with educated preachers. They quickly gravitated towards the universities, where they became prominent figures as both students and professors. Their dedication to poverty and learning inspired **Thomas Aquinas** (c. 1225–1274) to join the Dominicans in 1243 despite the opposition of his family.

The Apotheosis of Thomas Aquinas. Fresco by Andrea di Bonaiuto c. 1366. Currently in the Church of Santa Maria Novella in Florence, Italy. This church is one of the best known in Florence.

Thomas's intellectual abilities were soon recognized, and he was sent to the University of Paris. He studied there under another brilliant Dominican scholar, Albert the Great (c. 1200–1280). Albert was a prolific scholar who wrote works on a vast array of subjects, including philosophy, theology, geography, biology, and astronomy. His many achievements revealed the ability of the scholastic method of education to equip scholars with the intellectual foundation necessary to examine a wide range of topics and sources.

Albert and Thomas both engaged in the chief philosophical debate of the era concerning the philosophy of Plato and Aristotle. Medieval philosophers and theologians were especially impressed by Averroes's commentaries on Aristotle. Averroes, as we discussed in chapter 26, argued that reason and human senses were the basis for acquiring knowledge and was persecuted as a blasphemer by Islamic theologians because of these opinions. At the University of Paris, one school of thought, led by Siger of Brabant (1240–1280), fiercely defended the positions of Aristotle and his Muslim commentator. Some of these scholastics even adopted heretical positions, denying the existence of a first man and the immortality of the human soul. They argued that philosophy and reason were superior to faith. These claims seemingly confirmed the concerns of medieval Platonic philosophers that Aristotle's philosophy was incompatible with Christian theology.

Thomas and Albert were among the most prominent of those who successfully demonstrated that faith and reason are compatible. Knowledge gained through reason supports truths believed by faith, but reason does not supersede or overwrite faith. Furthermore, Thomas remained well aware that his arguments in no way confined or restricted the majesty of God to the limits of human understanding. Towards the end of his life, he went so far as to declare that all he had written was but straw in comparison with the reality of God.

Thomas's contribution to medieval spirituality extended beyond his theological and philosophical writings. In 1264, Thomas composed the texts for the newly established feast of Corpus Christi. His hymns like *O Salutaris Hostia* and *Tantum Ergo* beautifully blend his theological insights with profound reverence for the Eucharistic mystery. They still play a prominent role in the life of the Church today and showcase the medieval world's success in harnessing the greatest intellects in their society to serve the worship of God.

Unlike the Dominicans, who were founded to serve as intellectual preachers, the Franciscans were unsure after Francis's death how best to follow his example regarding education. One group, known as the Conventuals, argued that the order should own land and buildings in cities so that the friars could both receive an education and live a life of preaching the Gospel. Another branch of the Franciscans, the Spirituals, vehemently opposed this. They were willing to forego studies in order to live out more explicitly the poverty modeled by Francis.

The division between the two parties became so embittered that the order was in danger of tearing itself apart. In this turmoil, a friar named **Bonaventure** (1221–1274) was elected the Minister General, or superior, of the Franciscans in 1257.

Bonaventure acted decisively to save the Minorites. He disciplined the most extreme voices among both the Conventuals and the Spirituals and implemented guidelines that clarified how to live out their Rule. Bonaventure cited a letter from Francis permitting his friars to teach theology within the order and argued that this permission, as well as their mission to preach, required education. This decision meant that the friars needed books and other possessions while pursuing their studies. The question was how to live out their vocation to poverty and preaching while simultaneously sanctifying the intellect through their studies. Bonaventure's solution was ingenious: the order's convents and properties were placed in the hands of the papacy so that the friars could continue to use these buildings without owning them. Later generations honored him as a second founder of the Franciscans because of the success of his reforms in restoring unity to the order. Thanks to his encouragement, Franciscans became prominent teachers and scholars in medieval university life.

Bonaventure was himself a renowned academic, bishop, and cardinal. His many works remain influential, including his scriptural commentaries and his *Itinerarium mentis in Deum* (*The Mind's Road to God*). Bonaventure incorporated both Platonic and Aristotelian themes into his work and became, alongside Thomas Aquinas, one of the most important theologians of his era.

Conclusion

For all its turmoil, the thirteenth century gave the Church an impressive array of saints. Louis IX was canonized in 1297, just twenty-seven years after his death. Thomas Aquinas was canonized not long after in 1323. Ferdinand III and Bonaventure would eventually follow in 1671 and 1482, respectively. Each of these holy men embraced the opportunities they were given to promote love for God and neighbor. Even Frederick II, who is unlikely to be canonized, understood that fighting on crusade, promoting piety and learning, and caring for the poor were the rubric by which his reign would be evaluated.

In 1272, Pope Gregory X summoned a new council to meet at Lyons. This Second Council of Lyons was attended by representatives from all the Christian kingdoms of Western Europe. The council aimed to accomplish medieval Christendom's two greatest dreams: the restoration of the Holy Land and the reunification of the Catholic and Orthodox Churches. Thomas Aquinas was invited to participate in the council, but he died on the way. Bonaventure became its leading theologian and worked tirelessly to heal the schism until his death in the midst of the council. Neither witnessed the council's triumphant end or the ultimate failure of its goals.

CHAPTER 32

Papal Overreach and the Fading of the High Middle Ages

If the terrestrial power err, it will be judged by the spiritual power; but if a minor spiritual power err, it will be judged by a superior spiritual power; but if the highest power of all err, it can be judged only by God and not by man. This authority, however, although it has been given to man and is exercised by man is not human but rather divine, granted to Peter by a divine word and reaffirmed to his successors.

Boniface VIII, *Unam Sanctam*[1]

Pope Boniface VIII wrote these words in 1302 while engaged in a dispute with the French king. The matter of disagreement was whether secular rulers had the authority to tax clergy, but the pope's statements about his authority went far beyond this particular issue. Indeed, Boniface's papal bull *Unam Sanctam* emphasized earlier pronouncements that popes were answerable to God alone; no worldly or spiritual power could dare to judge a pope. Indeed, the popes alone, as leaders of the medieval "Church-State," determined the best interests of the souls assigned to their care. Only they could judge, approve, and remove anyone who held spiritual or temporal office within Christendom. Inasmuch as almost any political decision or disagreement could be framed as a potential moral danger, Boniface claimed essentially unlimited power to influence temporal affairs.

Boniface's declaration was the culmination of the efforts of popes such as Gregory VII, Alexander III, and Innocent III to centralize, define, and strengthen the authority of the papacy, but the popes' consistent involvement in temporal affairs undermined the effectiveness of that authority. By the end of the thirteenth

1 Boniface VIII, "Unam Sanctam," in *The Crisis of Church and State 1050-1300*, ed. Brian Tierney (Toronto: University of Toronto Press, 1988), 188–189.

century, many saw papal interventions as motivated by temporal, rather than spiritual, concerns. Despite the assertions in *Unam Sanctam*, respect for the papacy and its claim to leadership had eroded. The medieval struggle between the emperors and the popes had entered its climatic act. Its conclusion pointed to the rise of royal power and the concurrent breakdown of the High Middle Ages.

Charles of Anjou and the Fall of the Hohenstaufens

Ideally, the popes and the German emperors were supposed to work together as partners to strengthen Christendom, but ever since the Investiture Controversy their relationship was more frequently characterized by rivalry. As we saw in the previous chapter, the conflict between Pope Gregory IX and Frederick II escalated this rivalry into a bitter feud. Innocent IV had deposed Frederick at the First Council of Lyons and vowed that the papacy would never consent to another emperor or ruler of Sicily from the Hohenstaufen dynasty.

When Frederick II died in 1250, his empire was weak. Many of the German dukes had taken advantage of the emperor's absence in Italy to assert their independence from imperial control. For his part, Frederick's son Manfred (r. 1258–1266) pursued the imperial dream of uniting Italy under his rule. He defeated the papal army in 1254 and achieved a spectacular victory over the city of Florence at the Battle of Montaperti in 1260.

Manfred's successes forced the new pope, the Frenchman Urban IV (r. 1261–1264), to flee Rome. Though he had previously served as the Latin Patriarch of Jerusalem, Urban was not a cardinal when he was elected pope. His selection signified the growing French influence at the papal court, and it was natural that he looked to his native France for aid as Manfred advanced in Italy. Urban made an alliance with the youngest brother of Louis IX, **Charles of Anjou** (1226–1285). Charles was a charismatic soldier and a ruthless, opportunistic politician. He

Coronation of Charles of Anjou. Illuminated miniature made c. 1375-1377. Currently "Gallica 2813 folio 294r" in the National Library of France, Paris, France. This image is from the *Grandes Chroniques de France*, a French history first compiled during the reign of Louis IX and subsequently updated by later monarchs to include later events. There are many copies available, and the illuminated miniatures in each manuscript vary considerably.

had originally been educated for a career in the Church, but he instead married the wealthy heiress of the duchy of Provence and remained on the lookout for further opportunities to advance his power.

In 1263, Urban and Charles agreed that Charles would come to Italy to fight against Manfred for the crown of Sicily. Urban considered Manfred an enemy of the Church and proclaimed a crusade against him, offering an indulgence for all who fought with Charles or financially supported his army. Charles arrived in Rome in 1265. The new pope, Clement IV (r. 1265–1268), was another Frenchman and crowned him as king of Sicily. At the Battle of Benevento in 1266, Charles annihilated Manfred's army, and Manfred himself perished. Two years later, Charles beheaded Frederick II's teenage grandson Conradin (1250–1268) when Conradin attempted to reclaim the throne. This action both secured Charles's conquests and ended the male line of the Hohenstaufen dynasty.

German emperors, and the Hohenstaufens in particular, had been the frequent antagonists of popes for nearly two hundred years. With Charles's victories in Italy, the papacy had emerged as the final winner of their contest to lead the medieval "Church-State," but this victory came at significant cost for those involved. In particular, the people of Central Europe failed to develop a powerful, unified kingdom. The subsequent emperors in Germany struggled to control their vassals who, thanks to Frederick II's concessions, were effectively independent agents. This lack of central authority contributed to the destabilization of the region and to the wars and religious turmoil of the coming centuries. The papacy, too, paid a high price for its victory. Not only had popes come to act more like political rulers than spiritual shepherds, but they would also soon discover that French royalty could be just as dangerous to papal independence as German emperors.

Michael VIII and the Second Council of Lyons

Charles's ambition and thirst for further adventure remained unquenched. Unfortunately for him, his new opponent, the Byzantine Emperor **Michael VIII** (r. 1261–1282), was an even more resourceful politician. After the conquest of Constantinople during the Fourth Crusade, the crusaders established the Latin Empire of Constantinople and continued to rule the city. Most Byzantines never accepted the legitimacy of these Latin emperors, and they established several rival successor states from the remaining Byzantine territory. Each of these desired to become the dominant Byzantine power after the events of 1204, but the largest and best positioned was the Empire of Nicaea. Not only was this state geographically close to Constantinople, but it also had a series of talented rulers who provided relative stability.

Michael VIII Palaiologos. Illuminated miniature made c. 14th century. Currently in "Cod. graec. 442 scan 390" in the Bavarian State Library, Munich, Germany. This image is from the Historia by Georgius Pachymeres.

In 1259, the ambitious Michael Palaeologus became regent for and then co-emperor with the eight-year-old John IV (r. 1258–1261). Michael's rise to such prominence was not surprising for those who knew his political cunning. Already in 1253, the ruler of Nicaea suspected that Michael was plotting to seize the throne. The accused was told to prove his innocence through trial by ordeal. This ancient practice typically involved some dangerous experience or deed that was supposed to confirm your blamelessness if you survived unscathed. (Pope Innocent III at the Fourth Lateran Council had forbidden Latin priests from supporting these "judgments.") In Michael's case, he had to hold a red-hot iron without injury to demonstrate that God was proclaiming his innocence. He gladly agreed to submit to the trial—provided that a nearby bishop handed him the iron with his bare hands. After all, Michael argued, the bishop was surely innocent of rebellion. The ordeal never took place.

Michael's rise to power was rocky. At one point, he fled to the Seljuk Turks and served as one of their mercenary captains. Even after he became co-emperor, he was unsure of his position until he had blinded the eleven-year-old John and sent him to live out his life in a monastery. Nonetheless, he was a skillful—if unscrupulous—leader and not only defeated a crusader army but also captured Constantinople by tricking the garrison into leaving the city. Most Byzantines promptly accepted him as their emperor.

The fall of the Latin Empire of Constantinople required a papal response. The popes had previously claimed that the capture of Constantinople and the installation of a Latin patriarch had ended the Great Schism between the Catholics and the Orthodox. Now the Byzantines had driven out the Latin patriarch and restored a Church that was separate from Rome. The popes could no longer pretend that the schism was ended; they needed to take concrete action to address it. Charles of

Anjou saw an opportunity to invade the Byzantine Empire, defeat Michael, capture Constantinople, and make himself emperor—all with papal support. Michael was in grave peril because he also faced Turkish attacks on his eastern border. In desperation, Michael opened negotiations with Pope Gregory X (r. 1271–1276), pledging to a reconciliation of the schism. He hoped that, if this union were achieved, the pope would not sanction Charles's invasion.

For the present, Michael's strategy was successful. Gregory suspended his approval of Charles's campaign and convened the **Second Council of Lyons** in 1274. He hoped to end the schism and plan a united crusade to recover Jerusalem. The council seemed to be a great success. It proclaimed a new German emperor and laid out the steps for launching a new crusade. Most dramatically, the Byzantine delegation declared its willingness to accept the *Filioque* clause. The *Filioque* was triumphantly chanted three times at the council's concluding Mass, and the schism was officially ended. This moment might be said to mark the apex of medieval papal prestige. The pope had secured acceptance of his leadership by the Greeks, approved the election of the German emperor, and summoned Christendom to a crusade.

Yet, as we have seen before, the implementation of a council was often very different and less successful than the decrees of the council itself. Seventy years after the sack of Constantinople, the Byzantine clergy and laity were not willing to reconcile with the papacy and accept papal theology. They indignantly refused to accept the *Filioque* or union with Rome. Michael carried out a brutal campaign of repression in an effort to compel his subjects to accept this union, but this only strengthened their resistance to it. Whether Michael genuinely believed in this reconciliation or pursued it for purely political reasons, he knew that without it Charles might gain papal approval to invade Byzantium at any time.

The Sicilian Vespers

Charles indeed began preparing for war with the blessing of the latest French pope, Martin IV (r. 1281–1285). In response, Michael conspired with the Spanish king Peter III of Aragon (r. 1276–1285) to encourage a rebellion against Charles in Sicily. The Sicilians resented the French occupation and the high rates of taxation Charles had levied to fund his campaigns. At the signal of the bells ringing for Vespers on Easter Monday, 1282, they rose up and drove the French out of Sicily. This rebellion, known as the **Sicilian Vespers**, caught Charles by surprise. He hurriedly organized an army in southern Italy and prepared to cross into Sicily to restore his rule.

At this point, Peter III intervened. He was married to a Hohenstaufen (a daughter of Manfred) and claimed the right to rescue his wife's imperial inheritance from French usurpation. Conveniently, he had just finished constructing a powerful

Voyage of Peter III of Aragon landing in Sicily. Illuminated miniature made c. 14th century. Currently "Ms. Chig.L.VIII.296 f. 127r" in the Vatican Apostolic Library, Vatican City. This image is from the Nuova Cronica by Giovanni Villani. The king and his wife are shown in the upper boat pointing out where to land.

new fleet which "happened" to be sailing off the coast of Sicily at the time of the rebellion. Peter landed and was acclaimed king of Sicily. The Aragonese troops and Sicilian rebels successfully resisted the French attack. The subsequent War of the Sicilian Vespers continued for twenty years and eventually resulted in Aragonese rule in Sicily and French control of Naples and southern Italy.

In attacking Charles, Peter and the Aragonese had made another enemy—the papal see. Over the previous decades, popes had become increasingly tied to French interests and dependent on support from the French crown and Charles of Anjou's kingdom to the south. At the urging of Charles of Anjou, Martin IV responded to the Sicilian Vespers by excommunicating Peter III and calling for a crusade against him on the grounds that he was attacking the papacy. This crusade became known as the **Aragonese Crusade** (1284–1285). The French king at this time was Philip III (r. 1270–1285), the second son of Louis IX. Philip lacked the wisdom his father had displayed in avoiding the popes' political conflicts, but he was mindful of his father's exhortations to be loyal to the papacy. Under pressure from his uncle

Charles and desiring to obey the pope's call to crusade, he led an army into Spain to attack Aragon in 1285. The campaign was a disaster. Philip's army was struck with dysentery and forced to retreat. The king himself contracted the disease and died. He was succeeded by his sixteen-year-old son **Philip IV** (r. 1285–1314), who would rule with a grim determination to resist the papal influence that had brought about the death of his father.

The Aragonese Crusade damaged papal authority broadly across Europe. While some Christian rulers had been skeptical of the popes' previous campaigns against the Hohenstaufen, they understood that the emperors were attacking the Papal States in Italy and that the popes called these crusades to defend themselves. The Aragonese Crusade, in contrast, was widely viewed as an overt abuse of papal power. The popes were seen as using their spiritual authority to call crusades as a proactive political maneuver rather than a defensive measure. European monarchs and nobles became resistant to crusading and less receptive to papal instructions and leadership.

On his deathbed in 1282, Michael VIII is said to have gloated that he had engineered the defeat of Charles of Anjou in Sicily and saved the Byzantine Empire from invasion. Yet despite Michael's efforts, the Byzantine Empire did not recover its former strength. Michael's son, Andronicus II (r. 1282–1332), was deposed by his own son Andronicus III (r. 1332–1341), and when Andronicus III died in 1341, a disastrous civil war raged for six years. During the war, one Byzantine faction shortsightedly employed a group of Muslim warriors called the Ottoman Turks as their mercenaries. The Ottomans used this opportunity to secure territories in Greece as well as Anatolia. Constantinople was soon surrounded.

Baghdad and the Rise of the Mamluks

The rise of the Ottoman Turks was part of a series of events that transformed the Muslim world in western Asia during the second half of the thirteenth century. The catalyst for these changes was the arrival of the Mongols. While the death of Ogedei Khan in 1241 spared much of Europe from further Mongol attacks, the same was not true for the lands held by the 'Abbasid Caliphate to the south.

In 1258, the army of Ogedei's successor, Möngke Khan (r. 1251–1259), arrived outside the city of Baghdad and demanded its surrender. Baghdad at this time was still technically governed by the 'Abbasid caliphs. As discussed in chapter 26, the 'Abbasid caliphs no longer possessed effective rule over their vast empire, but they were still recognized by Sunni Muslims as the successors of Muhammad and figures of religious authority. The city of Baghdad, with its wealth and legacy of learning and influence, was the last great symbol of the caliphate and the Muslim unity it represented. The Mongols swept it all away after a siege of twelve days.

The **Sack of Baghdad** was one of the most traumatic events in Islamic history. The Mongols seized the caliph and most likely killed him by rolling him up in a carpet and then trampling him with their horses. This ended the line of caliphs permanently. Even to this day, Sunni Muslims (who comprise over 80 percent of the Muslim world), do not recognize anyone as the undisputed successor of Muhammad

Sack of Baghdad. Illuminated miniature made c. 1430-1434. Currently "Supplément persan 1113 fol. 180-181" in the National Library of France, Paris, France. This image is from the *Jami al-tarawikh* ("Compendium of Chronicles") by Rashid al-Din. It was produced by the Mongol Ilkhanate as a history of events from China and Europe in order to situate the cultural heritage of the Mongols.

and leader of their community. The Mongols also destroyed the House of Wisdom. Historical accounts claim that so many books were thrown into the Euphrates that the river turned black from the ink. With the destruction of this library, Islam's intellectual leadership in the world was literally washed away. Finally, the Mongols destroyed the infrastructure that had supported the city, such as the canal systems that irrigated the surrounding fields. They killed so many inhabitants that the population did not have the strength to rebuild these structures. Mesopotamia, which had been a center of civilization since the dawn of history, faded into obscurity.

The Ottoman Turks rose to power in the chaos and upheaval that followed the Mongol invasion. They had been a relatively minor group among the Turkish populations that settled in Anatolia after the Battle of Manzikert. When their overlord was defeated by the Mongols, they took advantage of the subsequent power vacuum to establish themselves as one of the leading forces in the region. They saw themselves as *gazis*, or warriors for Islam, and would play a central role in the next stage of Islamic history.

The Mongols remained undefeated, and their advance continued. Now they encountered the Mamluk rulers of Egypt. These Turkish slave-warriors had overthrown their masters and taken control of Egypt during the aftermath of Louis IX's First Crusade. In 1260, the Mongols sent the Mamluks an embassy with their customary demand for submission. The Mamluks boldly killed the emissaries and prepared for war. Fortunately for the Mamluks, Möngke Khan had recently died, and the Mongols were divided as to whether they should continue their campaign or return to Mongolia to conduct the election of a new khan. In the end, a large part of their army returned to Mongolia. When the Mamluks realized that the Mongols were weakened, they advanced into Palestine to confront them. The two armies met at the Battle of Ain Jalut. The Mamluks successfully encircled the Mongol force and defeated them, thus ensuring future Mamluk (and Muslim) dominance of Egypt and southwestern Asia.

Mamluk dominance was bad news for the crusaders who still held the remaining cities of the Latin Kingdom of Jerusalem along the coast of Palestine. Despite the Muslim capture of Jerusalem a hundred years before, they had defended this handful of cities successfully with the help of reinforcements from Europe. Now the Mamluk sultan Baybars (r. 1260–1277) desired to emphasize his leadership of the Islamic world by uniting the region and removing these last Christian outposts. In 1266, he attacked the city of Antioch without offering it the customary choice to surrender peacefully. When the city fell, his army carried out the most vicious massacre perpetrated by either Christians or Muslims in the entire history of the crusades. Baybars boasted of the acts of brutality and blasphemy carried out by his soldiers, but even Muslim chroniclers, who typically celebrated Muslim victories, were scandalized by the wanton slaughter.

Unfortunately, the destruction of Antioch did not result in significant European aid for the Latin Kingdom. Gregory X had helped Charles of Anjou gain the title of king of Jerusalem in 1277, hoping that he would lead the crusade proposed by the Second Council of Lyons. However, Charles was preoccupied with his rivalry against Byzantium and, after the Sicilian Vespers, with the affairs in Italy itself. His death in 1285 ended the hope of a major European ruler leading a crusade to help the Latin Kingdom. In 1291, a new Mamluk sultan began a campaign against Acre, the last city in crusader hands. He assembled an enormous army, reportedly as many as one hundred thousand men and one hundred siege engines. Although

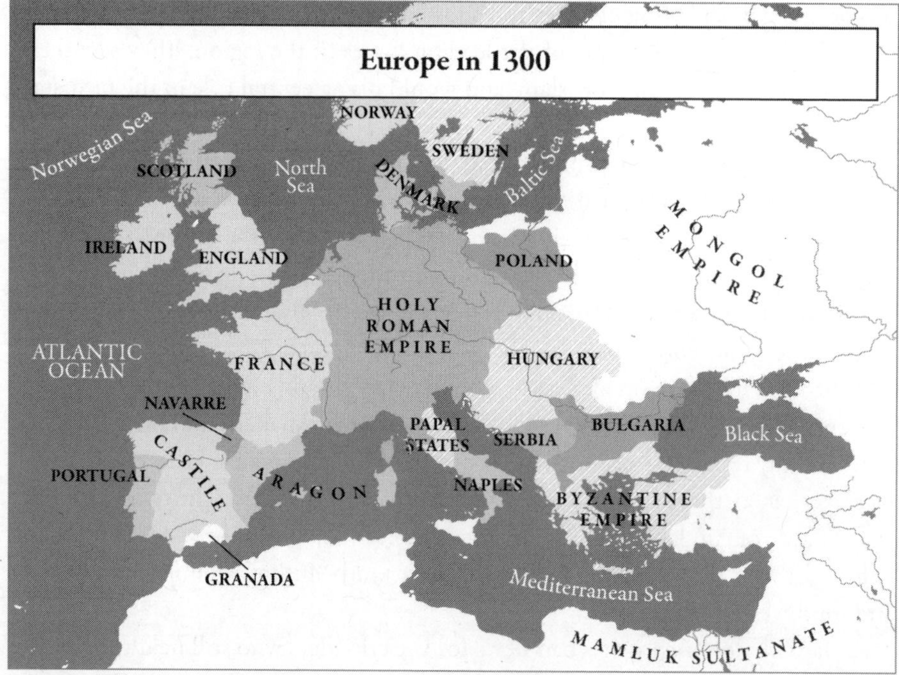

the military orders sent every knight available, the crusaders were still outnumbered seven to one. After six weeks, the Mamluks breached the walls and captured the city. Some knights fled from the harbor on ships; others fought to the death. This final defeat of the Latin Kingdom of Jerusalem marked the end of the crusader presence in the Levant.

The Mongol conquests had dramatically reshaped the Islamic world. The immediate effect was to move the Muslim center of power and influence westward from Baghdad to Egypt. This shift led to the construction of a Mamluk Empire that was too powerful for crusaders to resist. No Christian monarch in Europe had any enthusiasm to launch yet another doomed effort to fight for Jerusalem's liberation. The era of crusades in Palestine—one of the most prominent characteristics of the High Middle Ages—had drawn to its close.

Papal Crisis

The papacy's failure to galvanize a crusade in response to the Mamluk threat was, in part, because its own stability and authority were in a state of crisis. For over two years, from 1292 to 1294, the papacy lay vacant. The cardinals' inability to elect another pontiff arose primarily because powerful Roman nobles refused to accept any candidate who might help a rival family. After over a century of dynamic papal leadership, the Church suddenly found itself leaderless. Eventually, the cardinals received a letter from Pietro Angelerio, a hermit with a reputation for sanctity. This letter warned them that they would suffer divine judgment if they did not swiftly elect a successor to St. Peter. The cardinals, in what they probably believed was an inspired choice, elected Pietro himself as the next pope. Despite his protests, Pietro assumed the papal office in 1294 and took the name Celestine V (r. 1294).

Celestine's pontificate was a disaster. He had no administrative experience and accidentally appointed several candidates to hold the same office. He also went on solitary retreat for long periods of time. His attempts to guide the Church were unduly influenced by the self-serving advice of Charles II (r. 1285–1309), the son of Charles of Anjou and king in Naples. Charles II, unsurprisingly, wanted war with Sicily, and Celestine V helped fund his proposed campaign by granting him Church revenue from England, France, and the Holy Roman Empire. Many felt that the Church was teetering towards disaster.

After five months, Celestine abdicated with the support of Cardinal Gaetani, who replaced him as **Boniface VIII** (r. 1294–1303). Fearing that his enemies would set Celestine up as an antipope, Boniface imprisoned Celestine in a castle where he died less than a year later.

Boniface VIII. Illuminated miniature made c. 1312. Currently "MS Vat.lat. 2463 fol. 1r" in the Vatican Apostolic Library, Vatican City. This image is from the *Thesaurus corporalis praelatorum ecclesiae Dei et magnatum fidelium* ("The corporeal treasure of the prelates of the Church of God and of the magnates of the faithful") by Galvano da Levanto. The scene shows Galvano da Levanto presenting his writings to Pope Boniface VIII.

The new pope was determined to reassert papal authority over the Christian "Church-State." This agenda placed him in conflict with Philip IV the Fair, the most powerful monarch in Europe. Philip had not forgotten how his father had unwisely participated in the Argonese Crusade, and he was committed to minimalizing any papal influence in his kingdom. Their clash, as noted in our chapter introduction, arose over the issue of taxation. At this time, rulers could tax the Church only to help fund crusades, but Philip had been taxing the Church in order to support his war with England. When Boniface objected, Philip responded by refusing to allow any money raised from Church lands to leave his kingdom. This action, especially if adopted by other kingdoms, would severely diminish the revenues popes received from across Europe while increasing the wealth of each individual kingdom. It also threatened to establish an independent Church in France since Philip's actions could be interpreted as reasserting temporal rulers' authority over the clergy.

Boniface counteracted in an equally dramatic manner. In 1302, he promulgated the papal bull, or decree, *Unam Sanctam* (quoted at the head of this chapter). In this, he reasserted the papacy's role as head of Christendom's society by insinuating that those who resisted the pope's *plenitudo potestatis* were actively rejecting the will of God. This was because the papacy possessed both the ultimate spiritual and temporal authority. Boniface supported this claim by appealing to the so-called "**doctrine of two swords.**" This theory had its roots in the writings of Pope Gelasius I, who had taught that there were two distinct powers, the spiritual and the temporal (see insert on Papal Leadership in chapter 23). Of the two, the spiritual held the greater authority because it dealt with matters of salvation. Papal reformers of the eleventh century adopted this idea and compared the two swords in Luke's Gospel (see Luke 22:38) with the spiritual and temporal spheres of authority. They argued that God had entrusted both to the papacy. Boniface embraced this exegesis and even walked in procession holding two swords to represent the fullness of his power. For proponents of this understanding of papal power, *all* authority—including royal and even episcopal—derived from God through the pope.[2] Furthermore, Boniface formally proclaimed in *Unam Sanctam* that membership in the Church, including

---

2 During the Second Vatican Council (1962–1965), the Church clarified her teaching regarding the source of episcopal authority. *Lumen Gentium* §27 reaffirmed that all bishops are vicars of Christ within their own dioceses and that their "power, which they exercise personally in the name of Christ, is proper, ordinary and immediate, although its exercise is ultimately controlled by the supreme authority of the Church and can be confined within certain limits should the usefulness of the Church and the faithful require that." Thus, though the pope has authority to regulate the *jurisdiction* of a given bishop, the bishop's spiritual authority in itself does *not* derive from the pope but rather from Christ Himself: "The pastoral charge, that is, the permanent and daily care of their sheep, is entrusted to them fully; nor are they to be regarded as vicars of the Roman Pontiff; for they exercise the power which they possess in their own right and are called in the truest sense of the term prelates of the people whom they govern."

submission to the pope, was absolutely necessary for salvation. This last claim was not unique to Boniface—indeed many theologians had taught this throughout the centuries—but its pronouncement now deliberately implied that submission to the pope required support for his political agenda.

It can be difficult for modern Catholics to understand the claims of *Unam Sanctam* and its ramifications for the Faith. It is important to note that its teaching that one must belong to the Church, that is, the Body of Christ, in order to be saved is infallible, as is its corollary that one needs to recognize and acknowledge the unifying role of the pope. Nonetheless, Boniface's claims regarding the papacy's authority over the political sphere pertain to his historical context and are not formally tied to the document's teachings on faith and morals. Unfortunately, as Catholic historian Philip Hughes notes, Boniface closely associated his solemn affirmation of a perennial teaching of the Church—namely, that Christ's flock has but one shepherd and sheepfold—with a contemporary political theory that has never been a formal part of the Church's belief.[3] (Indeed, later theologians would nuance medieval assumptions by emphasizing that the papacy's authority over the political sphere was, at most, indirect.[4]) Royal apologists were already challenging papal claims to political oversight, and that dispute compromised the efficacy of *Unam Sanctam*'s spiritual teaching. It became all the easier to reject even the popes' claims

3 Philip Hughes, *A History of the Church*, Vol. III (New York: Sheed & Ward, 1947), 105–7.

4 St. Robert Bellarmine (1542–1621), for example, taught that the pope's *plenitudo potestatis* included only an indirect authority over temporal rulers and should be understood as "full" only in relation to the authority of bishops. Popes did not, Bellarmine argued, have absolute authority over the Church in the same sense that Christ has. Rather, the papacy has been entrusted by Jesus to preserve the Church's teachings, which it does by safeguarding what has been handed down through the ages. Interestingly, though Bellarmine denied that a council could sit in judgment against a pope, he argued that military force could be used to stop a pope from actively harming the Church. Such positions are especially striking since Bellarmine is typically considered an outstanding proponent of papal power. Nonetheless, Bellarmine went so far as to state: "In order to resist and defend oneself no authority is required.... Therefore, as it is lawful to resist the Pope, if he assaulted a man's person, so it is lawful to resist him, if he assaulted souls, or *troubled the state* (turbanti rempublicam), and much more if he strove to destroy the Church. It is lawful, I say, to resist him, by not doing what he commands, and hindering the execution of his will." (*De Rom. Pont.* 2.29 quoted in John Henry Cardinal Newman, "A Letter Addressed to His Grace, the Duke of Norfolk" in John Henry Cardinal Newman, *Conscience, Consensus, and the Development of Doctrine* [New York: Image Books, 1992], 446; italics in original). Bellarmine's teaching that the papacy had only an "indirect" power in temporal matters was ill received by the current pope, Sixtus V (r. 1585–1590), who considered placing the offending text, found in the first volume of Bellarmine's *De Controversiis*, on the Index of Forbidden Books. Fortunately, a new pope reversed that situation and permitted Bellarmine's treatise to be published.

St. John Henry Newman (1801–1890) provides us with another example of someone who broke with the medieval theory of the pope's authority in temporal matters. His "A Letter Addressed to His Grace, the Duke of Norfolk" argued that the political authority comes from God, not the pope, and he rejects the notion that a Catholic owes the papacy an "Absolute Obedience." In matters when the pope's and a political leader's commands conflict (assuming that neither is ordering something that obviously contradicts the Faith), he declares that we must try to decide the merits of the specific case and, ultimately, rely on our own judgment and conscience. (See Newman, "A Letter," 442–447).

to spiritual leadership when such statements were apparently tied to what many saw as a corrupt ambition for *political* mastery.

Thus, Boniface's overreaching statements proved to be the catalyst that resulted in a fatal blow to papal leadership of medieval society, for Philip responded to this threat with the most obvious tool available: the sword. In 1303, the king sent a trusted deputy and a band of mercenary soldiers to teach the pope the limits of his authority. The troops broke into the papal residence and imprisoned him without food or water for the next three days. Under pressure from the local inhabitants, they eventually released the pope, but this treatment had deeply shaken Boniface, and he died less than a month later. The papal conclave that was convened to elect his successor was conducted in an atmosphere of shock and fear of Philip's troops. The new pope, Benedict XI (r. 1303–1304), hastily released Philip from the excommunication that Boniface had imposed, but this pontiff died less than a year later.

The next conclave was influenced by the French king and elected the archbishop of Bordeaux, Philip's personal friend. He chose the name Clement V (r. 1305–1314) and was crowned as pope in Lyons. He quickly appointed nine new French cardinals, all approved by Philip. Five years later, Philip convinced Clement to move his papal residence from Rome to the imperial city of Avignon, which was surrounded by French territory.

With these actions, Philip appeared to gain control of the papacy. Outside of France, the popes were increasingly seen as puppets of the French monarchy, and their instructions were more frequently ignored. As we will see in volume II, for the next seventy years, the popes were chosen by a body of cardinals dominated by French members who were approved by the king. The popes no longer wielded their authority as the successors of St. Peter from the tomb of the apostle but instead resided near royal territory and under the threat of the French army. Their greatest ally had become their most successful foe.

Conclusion

The end of crusading and of papal leadership in medieval society, combined with the decline of Byzantium and the Islamic caliphate, signaled the close of the High Middle Ages. After a period of such striking cultural flourishing, it is worthwhile to pause and consider how this had come to pass. The Mongol attack had brought about an end to the last traces of 'Abbasid authority in the Muslim world and gave rise to the Ottoman Turks, who would ultimately overthrow the Byzantine Empire. Meanwhile, the papal-imperial contest to determine who would lead the medieval "Church-State" upset the delicate medieval balance between spiritual and temporal power.

As we have mentioned repeatedly, there were no distinct concepts of "Church" and "State" in medieval Christendom. Instead, there was a sense of unity between the two spheres so that, ideally, what we term today "Church" and "State" cooperated together for the spiritual and physical good of society. There is much to recommend this worldview. Spiritual realities were not confined to Sunday morning Mass or private devotion in one's home; rather, the practice of Christianity extended to corporate and public life. Society as a whole, not just its individual members, was expected to give glory to God. It is not a coincidence that the medieval era fostered so many saints and has left behind so many rich treasures in religious art, music, and scholarship.

Nonetheless, the same vision that enriched Christendom also included its fatal weakness. The interconnection of temporal and religious authority pitted political rulers and popes against one another in a devastating duel for leadership. Once the papacy had gained the upper hand, the temptation to confuse moral necessity and temporal advantage took hold. This tendency was exacerbated by the complex relationships inherent in feudal society as well as papal political rule in central Italy. Popes launched crusades seemingly more for their own political benefit than for any spiritual need and could appeal to their true spiritual power and responsibility as an opportunity, or excuse, to intervene whenever a king pursued a policy the reigning pope did not like. The more frequently the popes emphasized this authority in politics, the more pious Christians had misgivings. Furthermore, a growing awareness of royal authority encouraged monarchs' resistance to ecclesiastical intrusions into their realms. Even Louis IX refused to follow the pope's lead during much of the war with Frederick II.

And yet, papal fears were real. The emperors were not merely fighting for political independence; their ambition included spiritual leadership, too. We have only to remember the 'Abbasid Caliphate in chapter 26 to imagine what medieval Christianity would have undergone if the emperors had successfully subordinated the papacy to their control. Imperial rulers would likely have dictated doctrine based on their own political agenda rather than from theological insight and a desire for objective truth. The triumphs of the medieval papacy—such as its defense of the marriage bond and its continual efforts at reform—would probably not have taken place.

The thirteenth-century papacy found itself in an impossible situation. It seemed as though the only way to overcome the threat of imperial control was to become ever more invested in medieval politics. Yet, this activity opened up both charges of spiritual corruption and the possibility that another power, like France, would simply replace the Holy Roman Empire as a dominating influence. Indeed, a new age of powerful kings was dawning, where the popes were now not leaders but subjects and even captives.

JUDAISM IN MEDIEVAL EUROPE

One other narrative that needs to be addressed before we bring this volume to a close is the history of Judaism. The Jewish communities in medieval Europe can be divided into two groups based on their locations: the *Sephardim* lived in Spain and Portugal, while the *Ashkenazim* were located in Central Europe. (The terms "Sephardic" and "Ashkenazi" derived from two Biblical place names which the Jews mistakenly associated with Spain and Germany respectively.) As we have seen in chapter 26, the Sephardic Jews usually prospered under the Umayyad Caliphate, though dangers could also accompany those in prominent positions. Once Umayyad rule collapsed, the Jews suffered a devastating persecution under the Almohads, and many fled to the Christian kingdoms of northern Spain in the twelfth century.

The *Ashkenazim* in Central Europe likewise experienced dangers and uncertainties. Charlemagne had initially encouraged Jewish merchants to migrate northward into Frankish territory and even welcomed prominent Jews at his court. Their commerce helped the economy and resulted in the establishment of Jewish communities in France, Germany, and elsewhere. Despite Charlemagne's support, Frankish law clearly treated Jews as second-class subjects. In the following centuries, Jews were typically excluded from feudal networks and forced to give up their land and migrate into towns. As towns developed into cities, Jews found themselves cut off from both public office and guild membership due to their religion. Many turned to moneylending, an occupation that was considered sinful by Christians on account of its association with the biblical prohibition against usury (the charging of interest on loans). Jewish moneylenders thrived in the developing medieval economy and became the bankers of Europe.

The financial success of the Jews and later rumors that Jews used Christian blood in their Passover rituals likely inspired much of the violence against Ashkenazi communities during the crusades. The first four crusades all witnessed horrifying assaults against Jewish people. Church leaders sought to protect the Jews and commanded that attacks and forced baptisms cease. The popes were largely successful in protecting the Jewish communities in Rome, but episcopal efforts elsewhere were largely ignored. Kings such as Henry II and Louis VII were more successful than individual bishops because they used royal authority to protect Jews in their kingdoms. In the kingdom of Sicily, Jews even received equal rights with the rest of the population. Nonetheless, Jewish security was dependent upon the goodwill of the monarch, and that could swiftly change. Some later rulers were motivated by greed and used the Jews' vulnerable condition to extort money from them or exile them and seize their property.

In the early thirteenth century, a debate arose within Judaism regarding the Talmud. As we have seen, debates arose in both Islam and Christianity when Aristotle was introduced, and Judaism was no different. The great Jewish scholar and leader Moses ben Maimon—better known as Maimonides (1138-1204)—inadvertently caused dissent among Jewish rabbis with his writings. His *Mishneh Torah* was accused of reducing the Talmud's importance, while his *Guide for the*

Perplexed attempted to reconcile Aristotelian philosophy with Jewish belief. Rabbis, particularly in southern France, denounced Maimonides and even appealed to Christian authorities to destroy his writings as dangerous. This was a mistake. The Jewish communities of southern France had already suffered during the Albigensian Crusade and now the additional attention brought more difficulties. It is during this era that famous debates took place between Dominicans and rabbis and that Louis IX burned the Talmud as blasphemous.

Efforts by thirteenth-century popes to shield Jewish communities largely failed. Even Innocent III was unable to check anti-Jewish sentiment, and the popes' decreasing influence only lessened the effectiveness of their protection. By 1300, France, England, Spain, and Germany had expelled their Jewish communities, promulgated harsh laws against them, or renewed acts of murder and violence. Motivation for these acts was a combination of the royal desire to amass wealth by seizing it from otherwise defenseless Jews, rumors and suspicion that Jews participated in various secret acts of violence against Christians, particularly Christian children, and a general fear that Jewish communities compromised the unity and stability of a given kingdom or region. This cycle of mistrust, misunderstanding, and resentment would, unfortunately, continue in the centuries ahead.

Conclusion

Ought not Christ to have suffered these things
and so to enter into his glory?

Luke 24:26[1]

The exchange between Jesus and two disciples on the road to Emmaus is one of the most poignant episodes in the Gospels. We can imagine the sense of defeat and even despair that these two must have felt as they slowly walked away from Jerusalem. Their journey took them from the site of Jesus's death to an encounter with the resurrected Savior, and this road to Emmaus is a fitting symbol of our own pilgrimage. We travel between the era of Jesus's ascension into Heaven and that of His triumphant return. Through faith we know that He came to save us and established His Church to continue His mission until the end of the world. However, like the two disciples, we can become dismayed at the apparent defeats that have often characterized the Church's endeavors. We await His second coming when all will be clear, and we will understand how God's Providence oversaw every facet of history.

At the moment, we are still on the road, and the temptation to discouragement can be strong. This conclusion, therefore, seems an appropriate time to revisit the claim we made in the introduction to this volume that the study of history can deepen our appreciation for the four marks of the Church. It may seem odd, now that we are at the end of this first book, to continue to assert that history helps us

1 Translation from the ESV:CE.

understand how the Church is *one*, *holy*, *catholic*, and *apostolic*. After all, there are many individuals, events, and tragedies in the history of Western Civilization that would seem to undermine each of these qualities. Yet if we remember that the four marks of the Church are both her identity *and* her mission, we can start to understand history's role in our Catholic formation. We begin by considering the marks as the Church's identity.

The *oneness* of the Church seems particularly vulnerable to historical critique. How can we claim that the Church is one when there have been two major schisms within its first millennium? What are we as Catholic historians to do with the deep divisions that cut across the centuries? Two important observations help us understand how the Church has preserved her unity. First, the Church's doctrine has remained one despite the schisms and heresies that have threatened her teachings. While later insights might refine previous declarations—for example, how the Council of Constantinople added to the Nicene Creed—these alterations did not contradict the earlier content of the teaching. This continuity, this oneness of belief, unites us with Catholics from every single era in our past and joins us with the generations to come.

The second point addresses the reality of the schisms. There is no denying that theological divisions exist among Christians. However, it is equally important to note that many of these separations were exacerbated by cultural differences and political ambitions. We can think back to the rivalry between the "schools" of Antioch and Alexandria or the Great Schism between Catholicism and Orthodoxy and reflect on the differing cultural practices and expectations that created a sense of mistrust that then led to the rejection of different theological positions, such as the *Filioque* clause. This cultural influence does not make a schism any less real or tragic, but it does highlight how it is the human element of the Church, not the Church's teaching as such, that often perpetuates these disputes.

This divine-human nature of the Church must also be remembered when we consider the Church's claim to be *holy*. The Church has never asserted that her members are the source of her holiness. (We can easily think of counterexamples to disprove this.) Rather, God alone is holy, and it is Jesus, as the Head of the Church, Who bestows holiness on His bride. The Church's sacraments, her liturgies, and her saints are the manifestation of this quality. Holiness—that is, the divine life of Christ shining through us—can take many forms. It can imitate Christ when He forcefully rejected the Pharisees' traditions, or it can be revealed in His apparent failure as He hung dying upon the Cross. For example, St. Cyril of Alexandria used incredibly harsh words to condemn heresy, whereas St. Louis IX spent his reign preparing for a victory in the Holy Land but died in defeat instead. It is important that we do not

Walking to Emmaus by Robert Zund. Oil on canvas c. 1877. Currently in the St. Gallen Museum of Art in St. Gallen, Switzerland.

allow our limited understanding of what holiness looks like to blind us to the many, often unobserved and surprising, manifestations of God's sanctity throughout the Church's history.

The third mark of the Church is her *catholicity*. The Church is not bound by a given political entity or ethnicity or culture. Selfless missionaries like SS. Patrick, Boniface, Cyril, and Methodius have demonstrated this time and again. The Church's call is for everyone. This holds true even in terms of intellectual development. It can be easy to become confused and concerned when we read about different ecumenical councils and the fine points of theology that are being debated. Those details *are* important and help us to understand our Faith and to articulate and defend our beliefs. Nonetheless, not every person needs to have a PhD in theology or philosophy to be incorporated into Christ's Mystical Body. This was the error of the Gnostics. They wanted secret knowledge that only a few could learn, but the Catholic Church opens her doors to both the learned and the unschooled.

Finally, we turn to the Church's *apostolic* nature. Many have looked at the power and wealth of the medieval papacy and dismissed it as an unholy mockery of the poor apostles who had nothing except the Gospel. Innocent III's *plenitudo potestatis* seems a far cry from the humility and weakness of SS. Peter and Paul. History can help us here by allowing us to understand the historical context of different eras in Church history. Jesus foretold that His Church was like a mustard seed that would grow into the largest of the garden plants (see Mt 13:32). This parable implies significant changes in structure and appearance. The apostles may never have ruled central Italy, but later generations of leaders, such as Gregory I, found themselves in situations where it was necessary to be both a spiritual and temporal authority. While we can debate the prudence or even morality of certain decisions made by medieval popes, we should also acknowledge that without some form of (political) independence, the popes' ability to teach and reprove would have been severely limited by the ambitions and military force of temporal rulers.

Furthermore, the Church's apostolic succession shines brightly throughout the centuries. Her leadership passes without fail from one generation to the next and will do so until the end of time. And yet, there can be a temptation to identify the Church (or at least much of her glory) with one particular era in the past. Many, for example, tend to idealize the High Middle Ages or the Early Church. It can be easy to think only of the victories and to forget the real struggles and shortcomings that each individual era has faced. When we consider the time of the apostles themselves, for example, we should celebrate the spread of the Gospel through eyewitness testimony and heroic martyrdoms, but we should also realize that there were bitter disputes, internal corruption, and external threats. Apostolic succession guarantees Church leadership, but the challenges presented by fallen human nature still remain. As Catholic historians, our task is to learn from each era's failings and to appreciate its successes, all the while remembering that its specific historical context can never be repeated.

This awareness of context is closely tied to empathy, one of the virtues we mentioned in our introduction. It can be tempting to judge the past (for good or ill) based on our knowledge of today. We know, for example, that Iconoclasm is a heresy condemned by the Church, but for many at that time the issue was not clear-cut. Through empathy, we can understand how someone, for example, might in good conscience take the side of Henry IV against St. Gregory VII. Do not the very human failings of even the great saints give us courage and hope? Does not the sheer messiness of history arouse empathy so that we take to heart the message from Christ to judge not (see Mt 7:1-3)? Empathy can also provide us some comfort regarding our own era and its confusions. Just as previous generations endured decades of hardships and trouble, so, too, can we. Eventually, clarity will come to the debates of today just as, through God's grace, it came to the disputes of the past.

Maybe not all these considerations will be entirely convincing, but we must remember that the living out of the four marks of the Church is also each generation's mission. As we have emphasized throughout this book, the Church is both divine and human. Her divinity comes from the fact that she was founded by Jesus and is, as St. Paul teaches us, His body (see 1 Cor 12:12–27). The Church, therefore, participates in the holiness of her Founder and Head. And yet, her members remain human and liable to imperfection and sin as long as they continue their sojourn on earth. We have seen this human frailty time and again seemingly bring catastrophe.

And yet, these human shortcomings also bring us hope. If the Church were solely of human origin, we could rightly expect her to have collapsed in ruin under the corrupt leadership of the Early Medieval popes or to have officially perverted her message due to political pressure and worse at the hands of temporal rulers. Instead, the Church has weathered these tremendous storms in her past; against all human expectation, she has risen again each time she seemed to have been on the verge of ruin. Archbishop Fulton Sheen once declared on his television show that the Church was not just another temporal institution that exists for some length of time, however long. She is constantly dying and returning to life: "And there comes the defeat, the seeming decay, we are put in the grave, and then we rise again."[2]

Therein lies our confidence. We do not place our trust in some model society or culture, no matter how good it may appear. Even the holiest saints and rulers cannot bring about Heaven on earth. Our confidence is in the resurrected Christ, Who shares His victory over death and sin with His Church. Our mission remains to live out the four marks of the Church in our own lives and, to the best of our ability, in our general society.

This perspective should fill us with hope and patience. Hope, because we know that God has never abandoned His people. Neither the darkness of the Babylonian Captivity nor the failings of the Church's own leaders can overcome His solicitude. Patience, because we await His timing as we continue on our pilgrimage. It is beyond the historian's discipline to claim to know the inner workings of God's Providence, but we trust as people of faith that He uses all of history to further His glory. Consequently, we use our knowledge of history to inform our decisions and to prepare us for the inevitable limitations of our successes as we strive to live out the four marks in our daily choices.

---

2 Fulton Sheen quoted in Joseph Pronechen, "Archbishop Sheen's Warning of a Crisis in Christendom" *National Catholic Register*, May 8, 2023, https://www.ncregister.com/blog/archbishop-sheen-s-warning-of-a-crisis-in-christendom. The authors would like to thank Fr. Deacon James Smith of the Eparchy of Passaic, NJ for bringing this quote to our attention.

We encourage you to keep these thoughts in mind as you approach the second volume of *Pilgrimage*. As we will see, new challenges will rock Western society and the Church to their very foundations. New ideologies will call into question the heart of Christian teachings, and the powerful "State-God" will arise to demand humanity's worship. And if we feel discouraged about the continual struggles confronting the Church, we need only remember that Christ is walking beside us and teaching us along our journey—just as He did while walking to Emmaus. He says to us, "Ought not Christ's Church to suffer these things and so to enter into His glory?"

RECOMMENDED READING

Note: Many ancient primary sources have mature content. The secondary sources are some of the works whose insights the authors consulted for the present volume. Nonetheless, their conclusions may not be reflected in the interpretation presented in *Pilgrimage*.

Unit I

Primary Sources

The Epic of Gilgamesh.
The Book of Exodus.
1 & 2 Samuel and *1 & 2 Kings [1–4 Kings].*
Herodotus. *The Histories* (Book II).

Secondary Sources

Bergsma, John and Brant Pitre. *A Catholic Introduction to the Bible: The Old Testament.*
Dawson, Christopher. *Dynamics of World History.*
Dean, Maximilian Mary. *A Primer on the Absolute Primacy of Christ: Blessed John Duns Scotus and the Franciscan Thesis.*
Kitchen, K. A. *On the Reliability of the Old Testament.*
Janzen, Mark D., ed. *Five Views on the Exodus: Historicity, Chronology, and Theological Implications.*
Murphy, Dennis J., *The Church and the Bible: Official Documents of the Catholic Church*
Rohl, David. *Exodus: Myth or History?*
Shaw, Ian, ed. *The Oxford History of Ancient Egypt.*
Van de Mieroop, Marc. *A History of the Ancient Near East.* 3rd ed.
Wilkinson, Richard H. *The Complete Gods and Goddesses of Ancient Egypt.*

Unit II

Primary Sources

Aristotle. *Politics.*
Herodotus. *Histories.*
Hesiod. *Works and Days.*
Homer. *The Iliad.*
Plato. *The Republic.*
Thucydides. *History of the Peloponnesian War.*

Secondary Sources

Barr, Stringfellow. *The Will of Zeus.*
Dodge, Theodore A. *Alexander.*
Hornblower, Simon. *The Greek World: 479–323 BC.*
Rahl, Paul. *The Spartan Regime.*
Sealey, Raphael. *A History of the Greek City States: 700–338 BC.*

Unit III

Primary Sources

Appian. *The Civil Wars.*
Livy. *From the Founding of the City.*
Tacitus. *The Annals of Imperial Rome & The Histories.*

Secondary Sources

Barr, Stringfellow. *The Mask of Jove.*
Chadwick, Henry. *The Early Church.*
Goldsworthy, Adrian. *The Complete Roman Army.*
Goodman, Martin. *Rome and Jerusalem: The Clash of Ancient Civilizations.*
Hughes, Philip. *A History of the Church.*
Levick, Barbara. *Augustus: Image and Substance.*
Pitre, Brant. *The Case for Jesus: The Biblical and Historical Evidence for Christ*
Salmon, E. T. *The Rise of Roman Italy.*
Wilken, Robert Louis. *The Christians as the Romans Saw Them.*

Unit IV

Primary Sources

Augustine of Hippo. *City of God.*
Benedict of Nursia. *The Rule.*
Eusebius of Caesarea. *The Church History.*

Secondary Sources

Brown, Peter. *The World of Late Antiquity.*
Chadwick, Henry. *East and West: The Making of a Rift in the Church.*
Davis, Leo Donald. *The First Seven Ecumenical Councils.*
Dawson, Christopher. *Religion and the Rise of Western Culture.*
Goldsworthy, Adrian. *How Rome Fell: Death of a Superpower.*
Halsall, Guy. *Barbarian Migrations and the Roman West, 376–568.*
Jones, A. H. M. *The Decline of the Ancient World.*
Pelikan, Jaroslav. *The Christian Tradition, Vol. 1: The Emergence of the Catholic Tradition* (100–600).
Wilken, Robert Louis. *The First Thousand Years.*
Wilken, Robert Louis. *The Spirit of Early Christian Thought.*

Unit V

Primary Sources

Bede the Venerable. *Ecclesiastical History of the English People.*
Gregory the Great. *The Pastoral Rule.*
Gregory of Tours. *History of the Franks.*
Procopius. *History of the Wars.*
The Qur'an.

Secondary Sources

Berkey, Jonathan. *The Formation of Islam.*
Hillenbrand, Carole. *Introduction to Islam: Beliefs and Practices in Historical Perspective.*
Kennedy, Hugh. *The Prophet and the Age of the Caliphates.*
Markus, Robert. *Gregory the Great and His World.*
Oakley, Francis. *Empty Bottles of Gentilism: Kingship and the Divine in Late Antiquity and the Early Middle Ages.*
Richard, Jeffrey. *Consul of God.*
Treadgold, Warren. *A Concise History of Byzantium.*

Unit VI

Primary Sources

Einhard. *The Life of Charlemagne.*

John of Damascus. *Three Treatises on the Divine Images.*

Tierney, Brian. *The Crisis of Church and State with Selected Documents: 1050–1300.*

Secondary Sources

Dawson, Christopher. *The Formation of Christendom.*

Dawson, Christopher. *Religion and the Rise of Western Culture.*

Duffy, Eamon. *Saints and Sinners: A History of the Popes.* 4th ed.

Hillenbrand, Carol. *The Crusades: Islamic Perspectives.*

Leclercq, Jean. *The Love of Learning and the Desire for God.*

Pelikan, Jaroslav. *The Christian Tradition, Vol. 2: The Spirit of Eastern Christendom (600–1700).*

Riley-Smith, Jonathan. *What Were the Crusades?* 4th ed.

Southern, Robert. *The Making of the Middle Ages.*

Unit VII

Primary Sources

Francis of Assisi, *Canticle of the Sun.*

Hamilton, Bernard. *The Medieval Inquisition.*

Jean de Joinville, *The Life of St. Louis.*

The Song of Roland.

Secondary Sources

Ames, Christine Caldwell. *Medieval Heresies: Christianity, Judaism, and Islam.*

Haskins, Charles. *The Renaissance of the Twelfth Century.*

Jordan, William. *Europe in the High Middle Ages.*

Lawrence, Charles. *Medieval Monasticism.*

Little, Lester. *Religious Poverty and the Profit Economy in Medieval Europe.*

Madden, Thomas. *The Concise History of the Crusades.* 3rd ed.

Prudlo, Donald. *Thomas Aquinas: A Historical, Theological, and Environmental Portrait.*

Thompson, Augustine. *Cities of God.*

Thompson, Augustine. *Saint Francis: A New Biography.*

INDEX

B

C

D

E

F

G

J

K

L

M

N

O

P

Q

R

S

IMAGE CREDITS

P. 4 *The Venerable Bede translating the Gospel*, illustration from 'Hutchinson's Story of the British Nation', c.1920. Artist: Penrose, James Doyle (1862–1932). Photo credit: The Stapleton Collection / Bridgeman Images

P. 7 *Annunciation*, circa 1644, Artist: Philippe de Champagne (1602–1674), Collection: Ferens Art Gallery, https://en.m.wikipedia.org/wiki/File:Philippe_de_Champaigne_-_Annunciation_-_WGA04705.jpg, Source/Photographer: Web Gallery of Art, License: [Public Domain], via Wikimedia Commons

P. 12 Christopher Dawson, https://commons.wikimedia.org/wiki/File:Christopher_Dawson.jpg, Author: Levan Ramishvili, Source: https://www.flickr.com/photos/levanrami/51414620320/in/album-72157719755653166/, License: [Public Domain], via Wikimedia Commons

P. 15 Neolithic rock art, over 7,000 years old. Cave of Beasts, Egypt, https://commons.wikimedia.org/wiki/File:Bestias11.JPG, Author: Clemens Schmillen, Source: File:Bestias11.JPG, License: (CC BY-SA 3.0) https://creativecommons.org/licenses/by-sa/3.0/deed.en

P. 17 *The Creation of Adam*, circa 1511, Artist: Michelangelo (1475–1564), Collection: Part of Sistine Chapel ceiling, https://commons.wikimedia.org/wiki/File:Michelangelo_-_Creation_of_Adam_(cropped).jpg, License: [Public Domain], via Wikimedia Commons

P. 19 Göbekli Tepe, Şanlıurfa, https://commons.wikimedia.org/wiki/File:Göbekli_Tepe,_Urfa.jpg, Source/Author: Teomancimit, License: (CC BY-SA 3.0) https://creativecommons.org/licenses/by-sa/3.0/deed.en

P. 23 Dwelling foundations discovered in Tel Al-Sultan in the city of Jericho, https://commons.wikimedia.org/wiki/File:Jerycho8.jpg, Source/Author: A. Sobkowski, License: [Public Domain], via Wikimedia Commons

P. 34 Bronze head of a king of the Old Akkadian dynasty, most likely representing either Naram-Sin or Sargon of Akkad. Unearthed in Nineveh (now in Iraq). In the National Museum of Iraq, Baghdad, https://commons.wikimedia.org/wiki/File:Sargon_of_Akkad_(1936).jpg, Source: Mallowan (1936) "The Bronze Head of the Akkadian Period From Nineveh", Iraq Vol. 3(1) pp. 104–110, Author: unknown, License: [Public Domain], via Wikimedia Commons

P. 35 *Victory Stele of Naram-Sin*, https://commons.wikimedia.org/wiki/File:Victory_stele_of_Naram_Sin_9064.jpg, Collection: Louvre Museum, Source/Author: Rama, License: (CC BY-SA 3.0) https://creativecommons.org/licenses/by-sa/3.0/deed.en

P. 36 Sumerian king list, https://commons.wikimedia.org/wiki/File:Weld-Blundell_Prism_with_transcription_by_Stephen_Herbert_Langdon_(1876-1937).jpg, Source/Author: unknown, License: [Public Domain], via Wikimedia Commons

P. 43 The Nile River and delta as seen from space by the MODIS sensor on the Terra satellite, Date: 5 February 2003, https://commons.wikimedia.org/wiki/File:Nile_River_and_delta_from_orbit.jpg, Source: http://visibleearth.nasa.gov/view_rec.php?id=4927 [1] Author: Jacques Descloitres, MODIS Rapid Response Team, NASA/sh, License: [Public Domain], via Wikimedia Commons

P. 47 The great pyramid of Giza, https://commons.wikimedia.org/wiki/File:Kheops-Pyramid.jpg, Source/Author: Nina, Photographer: Nina Aldin Thune, Attribution: Nina at the Norwegian bokmål language Wikipedia, License: (CC BY-SA 3.0) https://creativecommons.org/licenses/by-sa/3.0/deed.en

P. 48 Great Sphinx of Giza, Egypt, https://commons.wikimedia.org/wiki/File:Great_Sphinx_of_Giza_-_20080716a.jpg, Source/Author: w:es:Usuario:Barcex, License: (CC BY-SA 3.0 DEED) hhttps://creativecommons.org/licenses/by-sa/3.0/deed.en

P. 53 Statuette of Akhenaten and Nefertiti after 1345 BC. AD (after the year 9 of the reign) Painted limestone, https://commons.wikimedia.org/wiki/File:Akhénaton_et_Néfertiti_(Musée_du_Louvre)_(8736520486).jpg, Source: Akhénaton et Néfertiti (Musée du Louvre), Author: Jean-Pierre Dalbéra from Paris, France, License: (CC BY 2.0) https://creativecommons.org/licenses/by/2.0/deed.en

P. 55 Fragment of a wall with hieroglyphs from the tomb of Seti I (reign c.1294 or 1290—1279 BC), https://commons.wikimedia.org/wiki/File:Hieroglyphs_from_the_tomb_of_Seti_I.jpg, Source: The British Museum (http://www.egyptarchive.co.uk/html/british_museum_29.html (Jon Bodsworth)—https://www.egypt archive.co.uk/), Author: unknown Egyptian scribe, License: (Copyrighted free use) via https://commons.wikimedia.org/wiki/Template:Copyrighted_free_use, transferred from Egypt Archive: https://www.egyptarchive.co.uk/

P. 56 Stele of Intef and Shenetsetji: Harvard University—Boston Museum of Fine Arts Expedition. Photo by Mary Reidy.

P. 61 *Stele of Hammurabi*, Collection: Louvre Museum, Date: between circa 1793 and circa 1751 BC, https://commons.wikimedia.org/wiki/File:P1050763_Louvre_code_Hammurabi_face_rwk.JPG, Source/Author: Mbzt, License: (CC BY 3.0) https://creativecommons.org/licenses/by/3.0/deed.en

P. 61 *Stele of Hammurabi*, (Close up), Collection: Louvre Museum, Date: between circa 1793 and circa 1751 BC, https://commons.wikimedia.org/wiki/File:F0182_Louvre_Code_Hammourabi_Bas-relief_Sb8_rwk.jpg, Source/Author: Mbzt, License: (CC BY 3.0) https://creativecommons.org/licenses/by/3.0/deed.en

P. 65 The Meneptah stele, including inscription. Wellcome Collection. Attribution 4.0 International (CC BY 4.0). https://en.wikipedia.org/wiki/File:The_Merneptah_stele,_including_inscription._Wellcome_M0008443.jpg, Primary Source: Wellcome Collection. Wikimedia Commons Source/Photographer: https://wellcomeimages.org/indexplus/obf_images/ad/ec/0691b39ca5b688b666b4d2bb4614.jpg, Gallery: https://wellcomeimages.org/indexplus/image/M0008443.html, Wellcome Collectiongallery (2018-04-05): https://wellcomecollection.org/works/j5duevqb, License: (CC BY 4.0) https://creative commons.org/licenses/by/4.0/deed.en

P. 73 Relief detail of King Ashurbanipal hunting a lion on horseback, North Palace, Nineveh, 645–635 BC, British Museum, https://commons.wikimedia.org/wiki/File:Relief_detail_of_King_Ashurbanipal_hunting_a_lion_on_horseback,_North_Palace,_Nineveh,_645%E2%80%93635_BC,_Exhibition_I_am_Ashurbanipal_king_of_the_world,_king_of_Assyria,_British_Museum_(45972457881).jpg, Source: Relief detail of King Ashurbanipal hunting a lion on horseback, North Palace, Nineveh, 645–635 BC, Exhibition: I am Ashurbanipal king of the world, king of Assyria, British Museum, Author: Carole Raddato from FRANKFURT, Germany, License: (CC BY-SA 2.0) https://creativecommons.org/licenses/by-sa/2.0/deed.en

P. 74 Lamassu from the Palace of Sargon II, winged bull with human head, https://commons.wikimedia.org/wiki/File:Human-headed_Winged_Bulls_Gate_Khorsabad_-_Louvre_02a.jpg, Source/Author: Vania Teofilo, License: (CC BY-SA 3.0) https://creativecommons.org/licenses/by-sa/3.0/deed.en

P. 77 The genealogy of the kings of Israel and Judah, https://commons.wikimedia.org/wiki/File:Genealogy_of_the_kings_of_Israel_and_Judah.svg, Source: Genealogy_of_the_kings_of_Israel_and_Judah.png, Author: Genealogy_of_the_kings_of_Israel_and_Judah.png: User: Mr. Absurd, derivative work: Jon C (talk), License: [Public Domain], via Wikimedia Commons

P. 81 1930s reconstruction of the Ishtar Gate completed using original bricks from c. 575 BC, Pergamon Museum, Berlin, Germany. Photo credit: © Zev Radovan / Bridgeman Images

P. 82 Clay tablet. The Akkadian cuneiform inscription lists certain rations and mentions the name of Jeconiah (Jehoiachin), King of Judah (in modern-day Israel), and the Babylonian captivity, https://commons.wikimedia.org/wiki/File:Clay_tablet._The_Akkadian_cuneiform_inscription_lists_certain_rations_and_mentions_the_name_of_Jeconiah_(Jehoiachin),_King_of_Judah_and_the_Babylonian_captivity._From_Babylon,_Iraq._C._580_BCE._Vorderasiatisches_Museum,_Berlin.jpg, Source/Author: Osama Shukir Muhammed Amin FRCP(Glasg), License: (CC BY-SA 4.0) https://creativecommons.org/licenses/by-sa/4.0/

P. 84 Clay tablet with two columns of inscription. Astronomical treatise, tablet 1 of the series Mul-Apin, https://commons.wikimedia.org/wiki/File:MulApin-British Museum.jpg, Source: British Museum https://www.britishmuseum.org/collection/image/152339001 Author: British Museum, License: (CC BY-SA 4.0) https://creativecommons.org/licenses/by-sa/4.0/

P. 86 Front of the Cyrus Cylinder, Location: British Museum, https://commons.wikimedia.org/wiki/File:Cyrus_Cylinder_front.jpg, Source/Author: Prioryman, License: (CC BY-SA 3.0) https://creativecommons.org/licenses/by-sa/3.0/deed.en

P. 88 Gate of All Nations, Persepolis—Iran, https://commons.wikimedia.org/wiki/File:20101229_Gates_of_the_nations_Persepolis_Iran.jpg, Source/Author: User: Ggia, License: (CC BY-SA 3.0) https://creativecommons.org/licenses/by-sa/3.0/deed.en

P. 95 Palace of Minos North Portico in Knossos, Crete, Greece, https://commons.wikimedia.org/wiki/File:Knossos_-_North_Portico_02.jpg, Source/Author: Bernard Gagnon, License: (CC BY-SA 3.0) https://creativecommons.org/licenses/by-sa/ 3.0/deed.en

P. 95 Palace of Minos North Entrance and the Dolphin Fresco, Knossos, Source/Author: C messier, License: (CC BY-SA 4.0) https://creativecommons.org/licenses/by-sa/4.0/deed.en

P. 96 Archaeological Museum in Herakleion. Minoan clay bottle showing an Octopus (1500 B.C.), https://commons.wikimedia.org/wiki/File:AMI_-_Oktopusvase.jpg, Source/Author: Wolfgang Sauber, License: (CC BY-SA 3.0) https://creativecommons.org/licenses/by-sa/3.0/deed.en

P. 96 National Archaeological Museum of Athens: Golden cup from tholos tomb at Dendra, https://commons.wikimedia.org/wiki/File:Dendra_Findings_4.JPG, Source/Author: Schuppi, License: (CC BY-SA 3.0) https://creativecommons.org/licenses/by-sa/3.0/deed.en

P.99 Lion Gate—Mycenae by Joy of Museums, for information, see www.joyof museums .com,https://commons.wikimedia.org/wiki/File:Lion_Gate_-_Mycenae_by_Joy _of_Museums.jpg, Source/Author: Joyofmuseums, License: (CC BY-SA 4.0) https: //creativecommons.org/licenses/by-sa/4.0/deed.en

P. 99 Lions Gate detail in Mycenae, https://commons.wikimedia.org/wiki/File:Lions _Gate_detail.JPG, Source/Author: Orlovic, License: (CC BY-SA 4.0) https: //creativecommons.org/licenses/by-sa/4.0/deed.en

P. 104 Peplos Kore, circa 530 BC, Collection: Acropolis Museum, https://commons .wikimedia.org/wiki/File:ACMA_679_Kore_1.JPG, Source/Photographer: Marsyas, 06.04.2007, License: (CC BY-SA 2.5) https://creativecommons.org/licenses/by -sa/2.5/deed.en

P. 106 Mykonos vase (Archaeological Museum of Mykonos, Inv. 2240). Decorated pithos found at Mykonos, Greece depicting one of the earliest known renditions of the Trojan Horse, Date 670 BCE, https://commons.wikimedia.org/wiki/File: Mykonos_vase .jpg, Source: https://www.flickr.com/photos/travel lingrunes/2949254926/, Author: Travelling Runes, License: (CC BY-SA 2.0) https://creativecommons.org/licenses /by-sa/2.0/deed.en

P. 112 Lycurgus marble bas-relief, https://commons.wikimedia.org/wiki/File:Lycurgus _bas-relief_in_the_U.S._House_of_Representatives_chamber.jpg, Source: https: //www.aoc.gov/art/relief-portrait- plaques- lawgivers/lycurgus, Author: Sculpture by C. Paul Jennewein; Photo by the Architect of the Capitol, License: [Public Domain], via Wikimedia Commons

P. 113 A statue of a spartan soldier, https://commons.wikimedia.org/wiki/File:Helmed _Hoplite_Sparta.JPG, Source: First uploaded on Wikipedia de: (14. Jun 2004 19:06), own picture, Author: de:Benutzer:Ticinese, License: GFDL, (CC BY-SA 3.0) https://creativecommons.org/licenses/by-sa/3.0/deed.en

P. 115 Ancient Roman busts from the Farnese Collection, now in Naples, https://commons .wikimedia.org/wiki/File:Ignoto,_c.d._solone,_replica_del_90_dc_ca_da_orig ._greco_del_110_ac._ca,_6143.JPG, Source/Author: Sailko, License: (CC BY-SA 3.0) https://creativecommons.org/licenses/by-sa/3.0/deed.en

P. 117 These ostraka from 482 BC were recovered from a well near the Acropolis, Collection: Museum of the Ancient Agora, https://commons.wikimedia.org/wiki /File:Athen_Stoa_Ostrakismos_2.jpg, Source/Photographer: Self-photographed by Xocolatl, 3 March 2008, License: [Public Domain], via Wikimedia Commons

P. 117 Ostrakon from 482 BC was recovered from a well near the Acropolis, Collection: MuseumoftheAncientAgora,https://commons.wikimedia.org/wiki/File:AGMA_Ostrakon_Thémistocle_1.jpg,Source/Photographer:Self-photographedbyMarsyas, December 2005, License: (CC BY-SA 2.5) https://creativecommons.org/licenses/by-sa/2.5/deed.en

P. 121 Corner of the Apadana Darius the Great inscription, https://commons.wikimedia.org/wiki/File:Corner_of_the_Apadana_Darius_the_Great_inscription.jpg, Source: Persepolis Books, Photo by Erich Schmidt, License: (CC BY-SA 3.0) https://creative commons.org/licenses/by-sa/3.0/deed.en

P. 126 Parthenon temple in Acropolis Hill in Athens, Greece shot in blue hour with the moon rising above the sky, © PNIKOL, Shutterstock.com

P. 127 The temple of Apollo (the centre of the Delphi oracle and Pythia) dated to the 4th century BC., https://commons.wikimedia.org/wiki/File:Delfi_Apollons_tempel.jpg, Source/Author: Helen Simonsson, License: (CC BY-SA 3.0) https://creativecommons.org/licenses/by-sa/3.0/deed.en

P. 128 Trireme panoramic view in Athens, ancient greek ship, © LeaDigszammal, Shutterstock.com

P. 129 Statue of the King of Sparta, https://commons.wikimedia.org/wiki/File:Leonidas.jpg, Source/Author: Andtsi10, License: (CC BY-SA 4.0) https://creativecommons.org/licenses/by-sa/4.0/deed.en

P. 129 View of the Thermopylae pass at the area of the Phocian Wall, https://commons.wikimedia.org/wiki/File:Thermopylae_ancient_coastline_large.jpg, Source/Author: Fkerasar, License: GFDL, (CC BY-SA 3.0) https://creativecom mons.org/licenses/by-sa/3.0/deed.en

P. 133 Allegory of the cave illustration, © delcarmat, Shutterstock.com

P. 136 Gold death-mask known as the "Mask of Agamemnon", Collection: National Archaeological Museum of Athens, https://en.wikipedia.org/wiki/File:MaskOfAgamemnon.jpg, Author/Photographer: Xuan Che, License: (CC BY 2.0) https://creativecommons.org/licenses/by/2.0/deed.en

P. 147 Alexander Mosaic (detail), House of the Faun, Pompeii, Source: extracted from The Guardian (DEA/G Nimatallah/De Agostini/Getty Images), https://commons.wikimedia.org/wiki/File:Alexander_the_Great_mosaic_(cropped).jpg, Author: unknown, License: [Public Domain], via Wikimedia Commons

P. 147 Alexander Mosaic, House of the Faun, Pompeii, https://commons.wikimedia.org/wiki/File:Battle_of_Issus_mosaic_-_Museo_Archeologico_Nazionale_-_Naples_2013-05-16_16-25-06_BW.jpg, Source: Self-photographed by Berthold Werner, Naples National Archaeological Museum, May 2013, Author: unknown, License: [Public Domain], via Wikimedia Commons, (CC BY-SA 3.0) https://creativecommons.org/licenses/by-sa/3.0/deed.en

P. 148 Portrait of Alexander the Great. From Alexandria, Egypt, Collection: Ny Carlsberg Glyptotek, Artist: unknown, https://commons.wikimedia.org/wiki/File:Alexander_the_Great_Ny_Carlsberg_Glyptotek_IN574_n1.jpg, License: [Public Domain], via Wikimedia Commons, Photograph Source/Author: Marie-Lan Nguyen, (CC BY 4.0) https://creativecommons.org/licenses/by/4.0/deed.en

P. 150 Roman amphitheatre (amphitheater) in Pergamum (Pergamon), Turkey, © Kattiya. L, Shutterstock.com

P. 151 Buddha Shakyamuni Meditating in the Indrashala Cave (top) and Buddha Dipankara (bottom), https://commons.wikimedia.org/wiki/File:Buddha_Shakyamuni_Meditating_in_the_Indrashala_Cave_(top)_and_Buddha_Dipankara_(bottom).jpg, Source/Author: Art Institute Chicago, License: [Public Domain], via Wikimedia Commons

P. 153 Grave Naiskos of an Enthroned Woman with an Attendant, Artist/Maker: unknown, Date: about 100 B.C., Collection: Getty Villa, Gallery 111, The Hellenistic World, License: [Public Domain], via https://creativecommons.org/publicdomain/zero/1.0/

P. 162 The Capitoline She-Wolf with figures of Romulus and Remus, c.1484–96 (bronze), Etruscan, (5th century BC), Musei Capitolini, Rome, Italy, Photo credit: © Bridgeman Images

P. 163 Coin from the reign of Nero, https://commons.wikimedia.org/wiki/File:Nero_Sestertius_65_90020174.jpg, Source: http://www.cngcoins.com/Coin.aspx?CoinID=163662, Author: Classical Numismatic Group, Attribution: Classical Numismatic Group, Inc. http://www.cngcoins.com, License: (CC BY-SA 2.5) https://creativecommons.org/licenses/by-sa/2.5/deed.en

P. 164 Liver of Piacenza, Mantik, https://commons.wikimedia.org/wiki/File:Foie_de_Plaisance.jpg, Source/Author: Shonagon, License: [Public Domain] https://creativecommons.org/publicdomain/zero/1.0/deed.en

P. 166 Togatus Barberini sculpture, https://commons.wikimedia.org/wiki/File:Togato_Barberini.jpg, Source/Author: Carlo Dell'Orto, (CC BY-SA 4.0) https://creativecommons.org/licenses/by-sa/4.0/deed.en

P. 171 Shaded relief map of Europe and Africa, © AridOcean, Shutterstock.com

P. 179 View of the Roman Forum from the Capitoline Museums in Rome, https://commons.wikimedia.org/wiki/File:Foro_Romano_Musei_Capitolini_Roma.jpg, Source: Author/Photo by Wolfgang Moroder, Author: unknown, License: Multi-license with GFDL and Creative Commons (CC BY-SA 3.0) https://creativecommons.org/licenses/by-sa/3.0/deed.en

P. 182 Bronze eagle shaped plaque—aquila, https://commons.wikimedia.org/wiki/File:Bronze_eagle_shaped_plaque_-_aquila_(51234150144).jpg, Source: Bronze eagle shaped plaque—aquila Author: TimeTravelRome, License: (CC BY 2.0) https://creativecommons.org/licenses/by/2.0/deed.en

P. 183 Arch of Constantine, https://commons.wikimedia.org/wiki/File:KonstantinsbogenAttika.jpg, Source/Author: Rabax63, License: (CC BY-SA 4.0) https://creativecommons.org/licenses/by-sa/4.0/deed.en

P. 187 *Augustus of Prima Porta*, Artist: unknown, Collection: Vatican Museums, https://commons.wikimedia.org/wiki/File:Statue-Augustus.jpg, License: [Public Domain], via Wikimedia Commons, Author/Photographer: Till Niermann, License: (CC BY-SA 3.0) https://creativecommons.org/licenses/by-sa/3.0/deed.en

P. 187 Torso of the *Augustus of Prima Porta* statue, https://commons.wikimedia.org/wiki/File:Return_of_the_Roman_military_standards.jpg, Source/Author: Sailko, License: (CC BY-SA 3.0) https://creativecommons.org/licenses/by-sa/3.0/deed.en

P. 189 Ornate pair of gladiator shin guards, https://commons.wikimedia.org/wiki/File:Ornate_pair_of_gladiator_shin_guards_depicting_a_procession_of_Bacchus_from_the_gladiator_barracks_in_Pompeii_01.jpg, Source/Author: Mary Harrsch, License: (CC BY-SA 4.0) https://creativecommons.org/licenses/by-sa /4.0/deed.en

P. 190 Altar of Augustan Peace built around 10 B.C. in its new museum, https://commons.wikimedia.org/wiki/File:Ara_Pacis_Augustae.jpg, Source: Flickr: Ara Pacis Augustae, Author: teldridge+keldridge, License: (CC BY 2.0) https://creativecommons.org/licenses/by/2.0/deed.en

P. 190 Panel of Tellus, Ara Pacis, Rome, https://commons.wikimedia.org/wiki/File:Panel_of_Tellus,_Ara_Pacis,_Rome.jpg, Source: Flickr: Panel of Tellus, Ara Pacis, Rome, Author: Andy Hay, License: (CC BY 2.0) https://creativecommons.org/licenses/by/2.0/deed.en

P. 197 The Western Wall, https://commons.wikimedia.org/wiki/File:Westernwall2.jpg, Source/Author: Golasso, (CC BY-SA 4.0) https://creative commons.org/licenses/by-sa/4.0/

P. 199 Group 4 Denarius (18 AD – 35 AD) of Tiberius (Roman emperor (Emperor 14 AD – 37 AD), also sometimes referred to as a Tribute Penny, https://commons.wikimedia.org/wiki/File:Emperor_Tiberius_Denarius_-_Tribute_Penny.jpg, Source/Author: Photograph, DrusMAX, License: (CC BY-SA 3.0) https://creativecommons.org/licenses/by-sa/3.0/deed.en

P. 201 *Ecce Homo*, circa 1860 and circa 1880, Artist: Antonio Ciseri (1821–1891), Collection: MASI Lugano, https://commons.wikimedia.org/wiki/File:Ecce_homo_by_Antonio_Ciseri_(1).jpg, Source/Photographer: http://www.most-famous-paintings.org/Ecce-Homo-large.html, License: [Public Domain], via Wikimedia Commons

P. 207 The Arch of Titus in the Forum Romanum, https://commons.wikimedia.org/wiki/File:Arch_of_Titus_viewpoint.jpg, Source: Arch of Titus, Author: Sebastian Bergmann from Siegburg, Germany, License: (CC BY-SA 2.0) https://creativecommons.org/licenses/by-sa/2.0/deed.en

P. 207 The Arch of Titus, Upper Via Sacra, Rome, https://commons.wikimedia.org/wiki/File:The_Arch_of_Titus,_Upper_Via_Sacra,_Rome_(31862188061).jpg, Source: The Arch of Titus, Upper Via Sacra, Rome, Author: Carole Raddato from Frankfurt, Germany, License: (CC BY-SA 2.0) https://creativecommons.org/licenses/by-sa/2.0/deed.en

P. 211 Portrait of Nero. Marble, Roman artwork, 1st century CE, https://commons.wikimedia.org/wiki/File:Nero_Palatino_Inv618.jpg, Source/Author: Jastrow, License: [Public Domain], via Wikimedia Commons

P. 213 Rome Colosseum © chriscasey, Shutterstock.com

P. 215 Castle and bridge of the Holy Angel, Rome, Italy, © Mistervlad, Shutterstock.com

P. 217 Early Christian inscription with the Greek letters "ΙΧΘΥΣ" carved into marble in the ruins of the ancient Greek city of Ephesus at Turkey, https://commons.wikimedia.org/wiki/File:Ephesus_IchthysCrop.jpg, Source: Rotated and cropped from Commons image Image:Ephesus Ichthys.jpg, Author: User:Mufunyo, License: GDFL, (CC BY-SA 3.0) https://creativecommons.org/licenses/by-sa/3.0/deed.en

P. 219 Mithras sacrificing the Bull (100-200 AD), https://commons.wikimedia.org/wiki/File:Mithra_sacrifiant_le_Taureau-005.JPG, Source/Author: Serge Ottaviani, License: (CC BY-SA 3.0) https://creativecommons.org/licenses/by-sa/3.0/deed.en

P. 228 Kerch Missorium representing the Late Roman emperor Constantius II, https://commons.wikimedia.org/wiki/File:Missorium_Kerch.jpg, Source: Materials about archeology of Russia, 1892, Author: de Castelli, License: [Public Domain], via Wikimedia Commons

P. 228 Monogramme of Christ on a plaque of a sarcophagus, 4th-century CE, https://commons.wikimedia.org/wiki/File:Chrisme_Colosseum_Rome_Italy.jpg, Source/Author: Jebulon, License: [Public Domain], https://creativecommons.org/public domain/zero/1.0/deed.en

P. 229 Marcus Aurelius statue, Rome, Italy, Photo credit: © Bridgeman Images

P. 233 *Severan Tondo,* circa 200, Collection: Antikensammlung Berlin, https://commons .wikimedia.org/wiki/File:Portrait_of_family_of_Septimius_Severus_-_Altes_Museum_-_Berlin_-_Germany_2017.jpg, License: [Public Domain], via Wikimedia Commons, Source/Photographer: Self-photographed by Jbribeiro1, 25 July 2017, Attribution: © José Luiz Bernardes Ribeiro / CC BY-SA 4.0, https://creativecommons.org/licenses/by-sa/4.0/deed.en

P. 235 A Roman libellus, a certificate that the owner had sacrificed to the Gods, Date: 250 AD, https://commons.wikimedia.org/wiki/File:Libellus_scroll.jpg, Source: [http://www.romanity.oodegr.com/christianity.html, Η ΕΠΙΚ ΡΑΤΗΣΗ ΤΟΥ ΧΡΙΣΤΙΑΝΙΣΜΟΥ ΣΤΗΝ ΑΥΤΟΚΡΑΤΟΡΙΑ], Author: unknown, License: [Public Domain], via Wikimedia Commons

P. 238 *Portrait of the Four Tetrarchs*, Date: 290s, Collection: Piazza San Marco, https://commons.wikimedia.org/wiki/File:Venice_–_The_Tetrarchs_03.jpg, Source/Author: Nino Barbieri (talk · contribs), License: (CC BY-SA 3.0) https://creativecommons.org/licenses/by-sa/3.0/deed.en

P. 241 Wall-painting of martyred saints, https://commons.wikimedia.org/wiki/File:Wall_painting_of_martyred_saints,_Ananias,_Azarias,_and_Misael_from_the_town_of_Samalut_with_Saints_Damian_and_Cosmas._Stucco._6th_century_CE._From_Wadi_Sarga,_Egypt._British_Museum.jpg, Source/Author: Osama Shukir Muhammed Amin FRCP(Glasg), License: (CC BY-SA 4.0) https://creativecommons.org/licenses/by-sa/4.0/deed.en

P. 246 Constantine's head at Capitoline, https://commons.wikimedia.org/wiki/File:Constantine%27s_head_at_capitoline_-_Flickr_-_cking.jpg, Source: https://www.flickr.com/photos/spotsgot/3362379/Author: Camille King from Toronto, Canada, License: (CC BY-SA 2.0) https://creativecommons.org/licenses/by-sa/2.0/deed.en

P. 247 Solidus (Coin) Portraying Emperor Constantine I. Source: Art Istitute of Chicago: Arts of the Ancient Mediterranean and Byzantium, Gallery 153. Ancient Roman, Antioch. Struck 324 CE-325 CE, Gold. Gift of Martin A. Ryerson, Reference # 1922.4903. Public Domain Designation, Creative Commons Zero (CC0).

P. 248 Church of the Holy Sepulchre, https://commons.wikimedia.org/wiki/File: Church_of_the_Holy_Sepulchre_by_Gerd_Eichmann_(cropped).jpg, Source: File:Jerusalem-Grabeskirche-14-vom_Erloeserkirchturm-2010-gje.jp, Author: Gerd Eichmann, License: (CC BY-SA 4.0) https://creativecommons.org/licenses /by-sa/4.0/deed.en

P. 256 Ancient Egyptian Obelisk of Theodosius in Istanbul, Turkey © Sergii Figurnyi, Shutterstock.com

P. 260 *The Favourites of the Emperor Honorius*, (1883), Artist: John Williams Waterhouse, Collection: Art Gallery of South Australia, Adelaide, https://commons.wikimedia .org/wiki/File:John_Williams_Waterhouse_-_The_Favourites_of_the_Emperor _Honorius_(1883).jpg, Source: https://www.agsa.sa.gov.au/collection-publications /collection/works/the-favourites-of-the-emperor-honorius/25266/, Author: John William Waterhouse, License: [Public Domain], via Wikimedia Commons

P. 267 A high quality reconstruction of the Anglo Saxon helmet from Sutton Hoo, Photo credit: National Trust Photographic Library/Angus Wainwright / Bridgeman Images

P. 271 Theodoric the Great in the Basilica of Sant'Apollinare Nuovo, https://commons .wikimedia.org/wiki/File:Estimated_image_of_Theodoric_the_Great_in_the _Basilica_of_Sant%27Apollinare_Nuovo._Ravenna,_Italy.jpg, Source/Author: Ввласенко, License: (CC BY-SA 3.0) https://creativecommons.org/licenses/by-sa /3.0/deed.en

P. 273 Basilica of Sant'Apollinare in Classe, https://commons.wikimedia.org/wiki /File:O015015_Basilica_di_Sant%27Apollinare_in_Classe_-_Ravenna-.jpg, Source/Author: Vanni Lazzari, License: (CC BY-SA 4.0) https://creativecommons .org/licenses/by-sa/4.0/deed.en

P. 273 Ceiling mosaic of Arian Baptistry. Built in 5-6 century A.D. by Ostrogothic King Theodoric the Great in Ravenna, Italy. Mosaics are depicting the baptism of Jesus by Saint John the Baptist with procession of the Apostles around, https: //commons.wikimedia.org/wiki/File:Arian_Baptistry_ceiling_mosaic _-_Ravenna.jpg, Source/Author: Petar Milošević, License: (CC BY-SA 4.0 DEED) https://creativecommons.org/licenses/by-sa/4.0/deed.en

P. 274 Ivory binding plate, Reims, last quarter of the 9th century, Musée de Picardie in Amiens, https://commons.wikimedia.org/wiki/File:Musée_Picardie_Médiéval_01.jpg, Source/Author: Vassil, License: [Public Domain], via Wikimedia Commons

P. 279 Monte Cassino Abbey 2019, https://commons.wikimedia.org/wiki/File:Monte _Cassino_Abbey_2019_02.jpg, Source/Author: DonGatley, License: [Public Domain], (CC0 1.0) https://creativecommons.org/publicdomain/zero/1.0/deed.en

P. 285 Relics Collection—Residenz—Munich—Germany, https://commons.wikimedia.org/wiki/File:Relic_of_St._John_Chrysostom_-_Relics_Collection_-_Residenz_-_Munich_-_Germany_2017.jpg, Source/Author: José Luiz, © José Luiz Bernardes Ribeiro, License: (CC BY-SA 4.0) https://creativecommons.org/licenses/by-sa/4.0/deed.en

P. 286 John Rylands Library Papyrus 470, https://commons.wikimedia.org/wiki/File:Hypo_ten_sen_eusplanchnian_(papyros).jpg, Source: https://www.omhksea.org/wp-content/uploads/2011/08/theotokos-prayer.jpg, Author: unknown, License: [Public Domain], via Wikimedia Commons

P. 289 13th-century icon of the Great Panagia (*Our Lady of the Sign*) from the Saviour Minster in Yaroslavl, Russia, https://commons.wikimedia.org/wiki/File:Oranta.jpg, Source: https://belygorod.ru/img2/Ikona/Used/ 065SLBOGO2.jpg, https://www.icon-art.info/masterpiece.php?mst_id=170, Author: unknown, License: [Public Domain], via Wikimedia Commons

P. 295 Diagram depicting the major divisions within Christianity, https://commons.wikimedia.org/wiki/File:Major_Divisions_Within_Christianity.png, Source/Author: Noah Howard, License: (CC BY-SA 4.0) https://creativecommons.org/licenses/by-sa/ 4.0/deed.en

P. 302 Empress Theodora with her court of two ministers and seven women, c.547 AD, (mosaic), Byzantine School, (6th century), San Vitale, Ravenna, Italy, Photo credit: © Bridgeman Images

P. 303 Barberini diptych. Constantinople, Late Roman Theodosian style, Collection: Louvre Museum, Peiresc Collection; Barberini Collection; purchase, 1899, https://commons.wikimedia.org/wiki/File:Diptych_Barberini_Louvre_OA9063_whole.jpg, Source/Photographer: Marie-Lan Nguyen, License: [Public Domain], via Wikimedia Commons

P. 304 Emperor Justinian I and his retinue of officials, guards and clergy, c.547 AD (mosaic), Byzantine School, (6th century), San Vitale, Ravenna, Italy, Photo credit: © Bridgeman Images

P. 307 Hagia Sophia, https://commons.wikimedia.org/wiki/File:Hagia_Sophia_Mars_2013.jpg, Source/Author: Arild Vågen, License: (CC BY-SA 3.0) https://creativecommons.org/licenses/by-sa/3.0/deed.en

P. 307 Hagia Sophia I, https://commons.wikimedia.org/wiki/File:Interior_of_Hagia_Sophia.jpg, Source: https://www.flickr.com/photos/dstrelau/6745869403/, uploaded by Randam, Author: Dean Strelau, License: (CC BY 2.0) https://creativecommons.org/licenses/by/2.0/deed.en

P. 307 Frescoes of the Cathedral of Saint Sophia in Istanbul, https://commons.wikimedia.org/wiki/File:Interior_of_Hagia_Sophia_125.jpg, Source/Author: Vyacheslav Bukharov, License: (CC BY-SA 4.0) https://creativecommons.org/licenses/by-sa/4.0/deed.en

P. 314 Jewelled cross of Heraclius, https://commons.wikimedia.org/wiki/File: Greek_treasures_in_the_Church_of_the_Holy_Sepulchre._Jewelled_cross_of_Heraclius._Given_to_the_Holy_Sepulchre_by_this_Emperor_in_628_A.D._LOC_matpc.02495_(cropped).jpg, Source: Library of Congress, Catalog: https://www.loc.gov/pictures/collection/matpc/item/mpc2004004816/PP, Original url: https://hdl.loc.gov/loc.pnp/matpc.02495, Author: Matson Collection, License: This image is available from the United States Library of Congress's Prints and Photographs division under the digital ID matpc.02495, License: [Public Domain], via Wikimedia Commons

P. 315 Herakleios, Silver, Hexagram, Constantinople, circa 615-625 (BZC.2015.015), © Dumbarton Oaks, Coins and Seals Collection, Washington, DC.

P. 322 An inscription in Tihamah dating back to the 6th century in the Christian Era, documenting the expedition of Abraha the Abyssinian and the Companions of the Elephant, on their way to Makkah to demolish the Ka'bah, https://commons.wikimedia.org/wiki/File:Abrahalfil.jpg, Source: http://nadialarab.com/?page_id=4679, Author: nadialarab, License: (CC BY-SA 4.0) https://creativecommons.org/licenses/by-sa/4.0/deed.en

P. 324 Grotte Hira, Mecca, Source: http://en.wikipedia.org/wiki/Image:Cave_Hira.jpg, Author: User Nazli, License: [Public Domain], via Wikimedia Commons

P. 325 Muslim Pilgrims at The Ka'ba in The Great Mosque of Mecca, Saudi Arabia, during Hajj, © ali_z, Shutterstock.com

P. 329 The Ka'ba, Great Mosque of Mecca, Saudi Arabia, https://commons.wikimedia.org/wiki/File:The_Ka%27ba,_Great_Mosque_of_Mecca,_Saudi_Arabia_(4).jpg, Source: https://www.flickr.com/photos/43714545@N06/50702603023/, Author/Photographer: Richard Mortel, License: (CC BY 2.0) https://creativecommons.org/licenses/by/2.0/deed.en

P. 335 Yarmuk valley and Hejaz railway bridge Jisr el-Hawi, Source/Author: Bukvoed, https://commons.wikimedia.org/wiki/File:Jisr-el-Hawi-KY-946.jpg, License: (CC BY 4.0 DEED) https://creativecommons.org/licenses/by/4.0/deed.en

P. 337 Umar medallion in Hagia Sophia, Source: https://commons.wikimedia.org/wiki/File:Hagia_Sopia_6163502494_(cropped).jpg, Author: William Neuheisel from DC, US [cropped by Fazoffic], License: (CC BY 2.0 DEED) https://creativecommons.org/licenses/by/2.0/deed.en

P. 337 Uthman medallion in Hagia Sophia, Source: https://commons.wikimedia.org/wiki/File:Ayasofya_13_(cropped).JPG, Author: Vikiçizer, License: (CC BY-SA 4.0 DEED) https://creativecommons.org/licenses/by-sa/4.0/deed.en

P. 337 Ali medallion in Hagia Sophia, Source: https://commons.wikimedia.org/wiki/File:Istanbul_-_Santa_Sofia_-_Medalló_(cropped).JPG, Author: Josep Renalias, License: (CC BY-SA 3.0 DEED) https://creativecommons.org/licenses/by-sa/3.0/deed.en

P. 338 Imam Ali Mosque—Shrine of: 1st Shia Imam—Ali ibn Abi Talib; Prophet Adam; Prophet Nuh, (Najaf, Iraq) Source: https://commons.wikimedia.org/wiki/File:ImamAliMosqueNajafIraq.JPG, Author: Toushiro, License: [Public Domain], via Wikimedia Commons

P. 342 Crown of Recceswinth, Source: https://commons.wikimedia.org/wiki/File:Corona_de_(29049230050).jpg, Author: Ángel M. Felicísimo from Mérida, España, License: (CC BY 2.0 DEED) https://creativecommons.org/licenses/by/2.0/deed.en

P. 346 Damascus, Syria: The courtyard of the 8th-century Umayyad Mosque. The Umayyad Mosque, located in the old city of Damascus, is one of the largest and oldest mosques in the world. It is considered by some Muslims to be the fourth-holiest place in Islam, Source: https://commons.wikimedia.org/wiki/File:Syria,_Damascus,_The_Umayyad_Mosque.jpg, Author: Vyacheslav Argenberg, Attribution: © Vyacheslav Argenberg / http://www.vascoplanet.com / License: (CC BY 4.0 DEED) https://creativecommons.org/licenses/by/4.0/deed.en

P. 352 Caelian Hill, Rome, seen from Aventine Hill. Circus Maximus in the foreground, Source: https://en.m.wikipedia.org/wiki/File:Caelian_Hill_from_Aventine_Hill.jpg, Author: Jensens, License: [Public Domain], via Wikimedia Commons

P. 353 Pope Gregorius I dictating the gregorian chants, Date: Circa 1000, https://commons.wikimedia.org/wiki/File:Gregory_I_-_Antiphonary_of_Hartker_of_Sankt_Gallen.jpg, Source: Antiphonary of Hartker of the monastery of Saint Gall (Cod. Sang. 390, p. 13) https://www.e-codices.unifr.ch/en/csg/0390/13/0/Sequence-1324, Author: Hartker of Sankt-Gallen, License: [Public Domain], via Wikimedia Commons

P. 357 Iona Abbey, https://commons.wikimedia.org/wiki/File:Iona_Abbey_(45322644484).jpg, Source: https://www.flickr.com/photos/16801915@N06/ 45322644484/, Author: Reading Tom from Reading, UK, License: (CC BY 2.0 DEED) https://creativecommons.org/licenses/by/2.0/deed.en

P. 359 Page with Chi Rho monogram from the Gospel of Matthew in the Lindisfarne Gospels, Date: AD 700. https://commons.wikimedia.org/wiki/File: LindisfarneChiRiho_(cropped).jpg, Source: Lindisfarne Gospels, c 700 AD, Author: Eadfrith, License: [Public Domain], via Wikimedia Commons

P. 362 Church of Sant'Agnese fuori le mura, on via Nomentana, in Rome, inside view, https://commons.wikimedia.org/wiki/File:RomaSAgneseInterno01.jpg, Source /Author: MM, License: (CC BY-SA 3.0 DEED) https://creativecommons.org/licenses/by-sa/3.0/deed.en

P. 362 Sant'Agnese outside the walls—Rome, https://commons.wikimedia.org/wiki/File: Pope_Honorius_I_-_Apse_mosaic_-_Sant%27Agnese_fuori_le_mura_-_Rome_2016.jpg, Source/Author: José Luiz, © José Luiz Bernardes Ribeiro, License: (CC BY-SA 4.0), https://creativecommons.org/licenses/by-sa/4.0/

P. 371 Chludov Psalter (Moscow State Historical Museum MS. D.129), folio 67r, c. 850–875, 19.5 x 15 cm, https://commons.wikimedia.org/wiki/File:Crucifixion_with_iconoclasts,_Chludov_Psalter,_folio_67r.jpg, Source: Chludov Psalter, State Historical Museum, Moscow, Author: Unknown, License: [Public Domain], via Wikimedia Commons

P. 372 Image of Hagia Eirene church in Istanbul, next to Topkapi Palace, https://commons.wikimedia.org/wiki/File:Hagia_Eirene_Constantinople_2007.jpg, Source/Author: Gryffindor, License: [Public Domain], via Wikimedia Commons

P. 377 The Bust of Charlemagne is a reliquary from around 1350 which is said to contain the top part of Charlemagne's skull, https://commons.wikimedia.org/wiki/File: Bust_of_Charlemagne.png, Source/Author: Florian B. Gutsch, License: (CC BY-SA 4.0 DEED) https://creativecommons.org/licenses/by-sa/4.0/deed.en

P. 378 Page of text (folio 160v) from a Carolingian Gospel Book (British Library, MS Add. 11848), written in Carolingian minuscule. — The text is Luke 23:14–26, https://en.m.wikipedia.org/wiki/File:Minuscule_caroline.jpg, Source: http://www.bl.uk/catalogues/illuminatedmanuscripts/record.asp, Author: Unknown, License: [Public Domain], via Wikimedia Commons

P. 379 Solidus with Irene and Constantine VI. (BZC.1960.125.36), © Dumbarton Oaks, Coins and Seals Collection, Washington, DC.

P. 380 Aachener Dom, Karlsthron, https://commons.wikimedia.org/wiki/File:Aachener_Dom_BW_2016-07-09_13-49-15.jpg, Source/Author: Berthold Werner, License: (CC BY-SA 3.0 DEED) https://creativecommons.org/licenses/by-sa/3.0/deed.en

P. 386 Charles the Bald welcomes monks from Tours who bring the Vivian Bible which includes this miniature. Bibliothèque Nationale, Paris, Date: 9th century, https://commons.wikimedia.org/wiki/File:KarlII_monks.jpg, Source: Dr. Uwe K. Paschke: Weltgeschichte—Von der Urzeit bis zur Gegenwart, Karl Müller Verlag, Author: Count Vivien, License: [Public Domain], via Wikimedia Commons

P. 387 English: Carolingian warrior on a war horse (8th–10th century) with lance, round shield, chainmail and spangenhelm, https://commons.wikimedia.org/wiki/File:Carolingian_Warrior.jpg, Source/Author: ACBahn, License: (CC BY-SA 3.0 DEED) https://creativecommons.org/licenses/by-sa/3.0/deed.en

P. 391 Picture stone from Tjängvide, Alskog Parish, Gotland, Sweden, https://en.wikipedia.org/wiki/File:Tjängvide.jpg, Source/Author: Berig, (CC BY-SA 4.0 DEED) https://creativecommons.org/licenses/by-sa/4.0/

P. 394 An illustration of a Motte & Bailey Castle. The Keep is loosely based on Rochester and Hedingham, https://commons.wikimedia.org/wiki/File:Motte_%26_Bailey.png, Source/Author: Lordoftheloch, License: [Public Domain], via Wikimedia Commons

P. 397 The Imperial Crown, https://commons.wikimedia.org/wiki/File:Weltliche_Schatzkammer_Wien_(190)2.JPG, Source/Author: MyName (Gryffindor) CS vBibra, License: [Public Domain], via Wikimedia Commons

P. 400 Pope Formosus and Stephen VI"—The "Cadaver Synod", Artist: Jean-Paul Laurens (1838–1921), Date: 1870, Collection: Nantes Museum of Arts, https://commons.wikimedia.org/wiki/File:Jean_Paul_Laurens_Le_Pape_Formose_et_Etienne_VI_1870.jpg, Source/Photographer: Musée des Beaux-Arts, Nantes, License: [Public Domain], via Wikimedia Commons

P. 402 Cluny Abbey, https://commons.wikimedia.org/wiki/File:Clocher_abbaye_cluny_2.JPG, Author: TL, License: [Public Domain], via Wikimedia Commons

P. 404 The Crowning of Otto II (955–983) and Theophano (958–991) from a plaque binding, c.982-983 (ivory), Byzantine, (10th century), Musee National du Moyen Age et des Thermes de Cluny, Paris, Photo credit: © Bridgeman Images

P. 409 Canute the Great, c.995–1035 and Emma of Normandy, c. 985–1052. Illuminated manuscript, Liber Vitae, 1031, Stowe Ms 944, folio 6, The British Library, Source: Scanned from the book The National Portrait Gallery History of the Kings and Queens of England by David Williamson, Author: https://commons.wikimedia.org/wiki/File:Canute_and_Ælfgifu.png, License: [Public Domain], via Wikimedia Commons

P. 410 Panel from the Bayeux Tapestry—this one depicts Bishop Odo of Bayeux, Duke William, and Count Robert of Mortain, https://commons.wikimedia.org/wiki/File:Bayeuxtapestryodowilliamrobert.jpg, Source: Lucien Musset's The Bayeux Tapestry ISBN 9781843831631, Author: 12th century, License: [Public Domain], via Wikimedia Commons

P. 410 Bayeux Tapestry—Scene 57: the death of King Harold at the Battle of Hastings, https://commons.wikimedia.org/wiki/File:Bayeux_Tapestry_scene57_Harold_death.jpg, Source/Author: Myrabella, License: [Public Domain], via Wikimedia Commons

P. 417 Hugh of Cluny, Holy Roman Emperor Henry IV, and Matilda of Tuscany, https://commons.wikimedia.org/wiki/File:Hugo-v-cluny_heinrich-iv_mathilde-v-tuszien_cod-vat-lat-4922_1115ad.jpg, Date: circa 1115, Source: Cod. Vat. lat. 4922, fol. 49r (completed in 1115 AD), Author: Unknown, License: [Public Domain], via Wikimedia Commons

P. 421 Crusader Graffiti in the Church of the Holy Sepulchre, https://commons.wikimedia.org/wiki/File:Crusader_Graffiti_in_the_Church_of_the_holy_supulchure_Jerusalem_Victor_2011_-1-21.jpg, Source/Author: Victorgrigas, License: (CC BY-SA 3.0 DEED) https://creativecommons.org/licenses/by-sa/3.0/deed.en

P. 424 Regensburg-Prüfening (Upper Palatinate). Saint George abbey church (1130)-Romanesque frescos: Holy Roman Emperor Henry V, https://commons.wikimedia.org/wiki/File:Prüfening_Klosterkirche_-_Romanische_Fresken_3a_König_Heinrich_V_(cropped).jpg, Source/Author: Wolfgang Sauber, License: (CC BY-SA 4.0 DEED) https://creativecommons.org/licenses/by-sa/4.0/deed.en

P. 425 Wormser Dom, View of the West (Westchor), https://commons.wikimedia.org/wiki/File:Wormser_Dom_Westchor_Westtürme.jpg, Source/Author: AndreasThum, (CC BY-SA 3.0 DEED) https://creativecommons.org/licenses/by-sa/3.0/deed.en

P. 428 The Mezquita of Córdoba seen from the air, (Córdoba, Spain), https://commons.wikimedia.org/wiki/File:Mezquita_de_Córdoba_desde_el_aire_(Córdoba,_España).jpg, Source: https://commons.wikimedia.org/wiki/Category:Flickr, Author: Toni Castillo Quero, License: (CC BY-SA 2.0 DEED) https://creativecommons.org/licenses/by-sa/2.0/deed.en

P. 428 Great Mosque of Cordoba, interior, 8th–10th centuries (38). "The effect of two sets of arches is mesmerizing, especially so because the white stone arches are banded with red brick" — Witold Rybczynski, The Story of Architecture, 2022, https://commons.wikimedia.org/wiki/File:Great_Mosque_of_Cordoba,_interior,_8th_-_10th_centuries_(38)_(29721130342).jpg, Source: Great Mosque of Cordoba, interior, 8th–10th centuries (38), Author: Richard Mortel from Riyadh, Saudi Arabia, License: (CC BY 2.0 DEED) https://creativecommons.org/licenses/by/2.0/deed.en

P. 428 Mihrab of Mosque of Córdoba, Spain, https://commons.wikimedia.org/wiki/File:Mihrab_-_Mosque_of_Córdoba.jpg, Source: https://www.flickr.com/photos/21479883@N05/2722889806, Author: Michael Cohen, License: (CC BY 2.0 DEED) https://creativecommons.org/licenses/by/2.0/deed.en

P. 433 Manuscript with depiction by Yahya ibn Vaseti found in the Maqama of Hariri located at the Bibliotheque Nationale de France. Image depicts a library with pupils in it, https://commons.wikimedia.org/wiki/File:Maqamat_hariri.jpg, Source/Author: Zereshk, License: [Public Domain], via Wikimedia Commons

P. 437 Christian And Moor Playing Chess. Libros de juegosd'Alphonse X le sage fol. 64r., Date: between circa 1251 and circa 1283, https://commons.wikimedia.org/wiki/File:ChristianAndMuslimPlayingChess.JPG, Source: Middle Ages painting. Reproduced in Lebedel, "Les Croisades, origines et consequences", p. 108, Author: Unknown, License: [Public Domain], via Wikimedia Commons

P. 440 Al-Azhar Mosque, Cairo: The courtyard of the mosque, dating to the Fatimid period. Above, the minarets date from the Mamluk period, https://commons.wikimedia.org/wiki/File:Al-Azhar_(inside)_2006.jpg, Source/Author: Tentoila, License: [Public Domain], via Wikimedia Commons

P. 442 Masyaf Castle, https://commons.wikimedia.org/wiki/File:The_Masyaf_Castle.jpg, Source/Author: Hatem keylani, License: (CC BY-SA 4.0 DEED) https://creativecommons.org/licenses/by-sa/4.0/deed.en

P. 448 Monastery of the Grande Chartreuse, in Saint-Pierre-de-Chartreuse (Isère, Rhône-Alpes, France), https://commons.wikimedia.org/wiki/File:La_Grande_Chartreuse.JPG, Source/Author: Floriel, License: (CC BY-SA 3.0 DEED) https://creativecommons.org/licenses/by-sa/3.0/deed.en

P. 454 St. Thomas Becket faces King Henry II in a dispute; Henry II and Thomas Becket. This is taken from 'Peter of Langtoft, Chronicle of England' which was probably written and pictures added during the reign of Edward II (1307-1327), https://commons.wikimedia.org/wiki/File:BecketHenryII.jpg, Date: between 1307 and 1327, Source: http://www.traditioninaction.org/SOD/SODimages3/108_Becket

HenryII.jpg; original held in British Library, Royal 20 A II folio, Author: Peter of Langtoft, License: [Public Domain], via Wikimedia Commons

P. 455 Bust of Friedrich I., "Barbarossa", gilded bronze, ca. 1160, https://commons.wikimedia.org/wiki/File:Friedrich_I._Barbarossa.jpg, Source/Author: Montecappio, License: (CC BY 3.0 DEED) https://creativecommons.org/licenses/by/3.0/deed.en

P. 459 Our Lady church of Fontevraud abbey, in Fontevraud-l'Abbaye (Maine-et-Loire, France): effigies of Eleanor of Aquitaine and Henry II of England, https://commons.wikimedia.org/wiki/File:Fontevraud-l%27Abbaye_-_abbaye_royale,_abbatiale,_int%C3%A9rieur_25.jpg Source/Author: Fab5669, License: (CC BY-SA 4.0 DEED) https://creativecommons.org/licenses/by-sa/ 4.0/deed.en

P. 466 Chartres Cathedral, High Gothic—view from south-east, https://commons.wikimedia.org/wiki/File:Notre_Dame_de_Chartres.jpg, Source/Author: Olvr, License: (CC BY-SA 3.0 DEED) https://creativecommons.org/licenses/by-sa/3.0/deed.en

P. 466 The choir of Chartres Cathedral, https://commons.wikimedia.org/wiki/File:Chartres_Cathedral_(19165875583).jpg, Source: Chartres Cathedral, Author: Joe deSousa, License: [Public Domain], (CC0 1.0 DEED) https://creativecommons.org/publicdomain/zero/1.0/deed.en

P. 466 Stained glass window. Chartres, France. South transept, Cathedral of Our Lady of Chartres, Rose Window, Mary, Jesus, and Apostles, c.1225–30, https://commons.wikimedia.org/wiki/File:Rose_Window_and_other_windows_at_Cathedral_of_Our_Lady_of_Chartres.jpg, Source: https://www.flickr.com/photos/hunky_punk/14318311949/, Author: Spencer Means from New York City, USA, License: (CC BY-SA 2.0 DEED) https://creativecommons.org/licenses/by-sa/2.0/deed.en

P. 468 Grandes chroniques de France, https://en.m.wikipedia.org/wiki/File:Philo_mediev.jpg, Source: Castres, bibliothèque municipale, ms. 3, f. 277r, Author: Unknown, License: [Public Domain], via Wikimedia Commons

P. 469 Philosophy and the Seven Liberal Arts, by Herrad of Landsberg, circa 1180, https://commons.wikimedia.org/wiki/File:Hortus_Deliciarum,_Die_Philosophie_mit_den_sieben_freien_Künsten.JPG, Source: Hortus deliciarum, Author: Herrad of Landsberg (1125–1195), License: [Public Domain], via Wikimedia Commons

P. 475 Codex Manesse, UB Heidelberg, Cod. Pal. germ. 848, fol. 52r: Walther von Klingen, Date: between 1305 and 1315, https://en.wikipedia.org/wiki/File:Codex_Manesse_052r_Walther_von_Klingen.jpg, Source: http://digi.ub.uni-heidelberg.de/diglit/cpg848/0099, Author: Master of the Codex Manesse (fl. circa 1306–circa 1377), License: [Public Domain], via Wikimedia Commons

P. 475 Copy of miniature 178r from the Manesse codex, titled: Herr Bergner von Horheim, https://commons.wikimedia.org/wiki/File:Guillem_de_Cabestany.jpg, Source/Author: Engruna, License: [Public Domain], via Wikimedia Commons

P. 478 "The Pope Innocent III"—fresco mid 13th century—Monastery of Sacro Speco of Saint Benedict—Subiaco (Rome), https://commons.wikimedia.org/wiki/File:Pope_Innocent_III_(Monastery_of_Subiaco).jpg, Source: https://www.flickr.com/photos/70125105@N06/27634903650/, Author: Carlo Raso, License: [Public Domain], via Wikimedia Commons

P. 479 Detail of the recumbent figure of Richard the Lionheart, https://commons.wikimedia.org/wiki/File:Gisant_Richard_Cœur_de_Lion3.JPG, Source/Author: Giogo, License: (CC BY-SA 3.0 DEED) https://creativecommons.org/licenses/by-sa/3.0/deed.en

P. 481 St Mark's Horses, https://commons.wikimedia.org/wiki/File:St_Mark%27s_Horses_(51350878771).jpg, Source: https://www.flickr.com/photos/nanpalmero/51350878771/, Author: Nan Palmero from San Antonio, TX, USA, License: (CC BY 2.0 DEED) https://creativecommons.org/licenses/by/2.0/deed.en

P. 486 The Magna Carta (originally known as the Charter of Liberties) of 1215, written in iron gall ink on parchment in medieval Latin, using standard abbreviations of the period, authenticated with the Great Seal of King John. The original wax seal was lost over the centuries, One of four known surviving 1215 exemplars of Magna Carta, https://en.wikipedia.org/wiki/File:Magna_Carta_(British_Library_Cotton_MS_Augustus_II.106).jpg, Source: British Library, Author: Original authors were the barons and King John of England. Uploaded by Earthsound, License: [Public Domain], via Wikimedia Commons

P. 491 Monument at Las Navas de Tolosa in Spain remembering Battle of same name in La Carolina (province of Jaén, Spain), https://commons.wikimedia.org/wiki/File:NavasDeTolosaMonument.jpg, Source/Author: SuspirodelMoro, License: (CC BY 3.0 DEED) https://creativecommons.org/licenses/by/3.0/deed.en

P. 497 Pope Innocentius III excommunicating the Albigensians (left), Massacre against the Albigensians by the crusaders (right) (British Library, Royal 16 G VI f. 374v), Date: 14th Century (after 1332, before 1350), https://commons.wikimedia.org/wiki/File:Albigensian_Crusade_01.jpg, Source: http://www.bl.uk/catalogues/illuminatedmanuscripts/ILLUMIN.ASP?Size=mid&IllID=43733, Author: Chroniques de Saint-Denis, License: [Public Domain], via Wikimedia Commons

P. 500 Expulsion of the inhabitants from Carcassone in 1209. Image taken from Grandes Chroniques de France, Date: circa 1415, Artist: Workshop of Master of Boucicaut (–1425), Medium: illumination on parchment, Collection: British Library, https:

//commons.wikimedia.org/wiki/File:Cathars_expelled.JPG, Source/Photography: Grandes Chroniques de France, BL Cotton MS Nero E II, License: [Public Domain], via Wikimedia Commons

P. 502 Top part of the oldest portrait of St. Francis, a mural painting in the sacred grotto "St. Benedict's Cave" in Subiaco, https://commons.wikimedia.org/wiki/File:StFrancis_part.jpg, Source: https://commons.wikimedia.org/wiki/File:StFrancis_part.jpg, Author: Parzi, License: [Public Domain], via Wikimedia Commons

P. 503 Confirmation of the Rule by Innocentius III, Date: 1295, Artist: Giotto (1266–1337), Medium: fresco, Collection: Upper Basilica of San Francesco d'Assisi, https://commons.wikimedia.org/wiki/File:Giotto_-_Legend_of_St_Francis_-_-07-_-_Confirmation_of_the_Rule.jpg, Source/Photographer: Giotto di Bondone, License: [Public Domain], via Wiki media Commons

P. 508 Taizu, better known as Genghis Khan, Yuan dynasty, Collection: National Palace Museum, https://commons.wikimedia.org/wiki/File:YuanEmperorAlbumGenghisPortrait.jpg, Reference: https://painting.npm.gov.tw/Painting_Page.aspx?dep=P&PaintingId=15475, Source/Photographer: Digitized by National Palace Museum; file is directly from Shuge, License: [Public Domain], via Wikimedia Commons

P. 511 Frederick II and his falcon. From his book De arte venandi cum avibus (The art of hunting with birds). From a manuscript in Biblioteca Vaticana, Pal. lat 1071, fol. 1), late 13th century, https://commons.wikimedia.org/wiki/File:Frederick_II_and_eagle.jpg, Date: 1240s, Source: http://www.fh-augsburg.de/~harsch/Chronologia/Lspost13/FridericusII/fri_arsp.html, Author: Unknown, License: [Public Domain], via Wikimedia Commons

P. 515 Moralized Bible of Toledo, known as the Saint-Louis Bible, dedication scene, Date: circa 1220–1230, Medium: illumination on parchment, Collection: The Morgan Library & Museum, https://commons.wikimedia.org/wiki/File: Blanche_of_Castile_and_King_Louis_IX_of_France;_Author_Dictating_to_a_Scribe_-_Google_Art_Project.jpg, Source/Photographer: RAEUHtEGAy7O3Q at Google Cultural Institute, License: [Public Domain], via Wikimedia Commons

P. 517 King Ferdinand and his wife, https://commons.wikimedia.org/wiki/File: Ferdinand_III_%26_Beatriz_of_Swabia.jpg Beatriz, Source/Author: dalv89, License: (CC BY-SA 4.0 DEED) https://creativecommons.org/licenses/by-sa/4.0/deed.en

P. 518 Triumph of St. Thomas Aquinas, "Doctor Angelicus", with saints and angels, Andrea di Bonaiuto, 1366. Basilica of Santa Maria Novella, fresco, https://commons.wikimedia.org/wiki/File:Andrea_di_Bonaiuto._Santa_Maria_Novella_1366-7_fresco_0001.jpg, Source: Self-scanned, Author: Andrea di Bonaiuto (14th century), License: [Public Domain], via Wikimedia Commons

P. 522 Coronation of Charles of Anjou, Date: 14th Century, https://commons.wikimedia.org/wiki/File:KorunovaceKarlazAnjou.jpg, Source: Gallica Digital Library, Author: Anonymous, License: [Public Domain], via Wikimedia Commons

P. 524 Michael VIII Palaiologos. Miniature from the manuscript of Pachymeres' Historia, 14th century. Munich, Bayerische Staatsbibliothek, Date: 14th century, https://commons.wikimedia.org/wiki/File:Michael_VIII_Palaiologos.jpg, Source: Bayerische Staatsbibliothek (Munich), Author: unknown Byzantine illuminator, License: [Public Domain], via Wikimedia Commons

P. 526 Journey of Peter III of Aragon towards Trapani (Sicily), Date: 14th Century, https://commons.wikimedia.org/wiki/File:Nuova_cronica._f.127r.jpg, Source: Biblioteca Apostòlica Vaticana, Author: Giovanni Villani, License: [Public Domain], via Wikimedia Commons

P. 528 Mongols besieging Baghdad in 1258, Date: circa 1430–1434, https://commons.wikimedia.org/wiki/File:Bagdad1258.jpg, Source: Rashid al-Din's Jami al-tarawikh; Bibliothèque nationale de France, Département des Manuscrits, Division orientale, Supplément persan 1113, fol. 180v-181, Author: Sayf al-vâhidî et al, License: [Public Domain], via Wikimedia Commons

P. 531 MS Vat.lat. 2463, fol. 1r, top, showing Galvano da Levanto presenting his writings to Pope Boniface VIII, https://en.wikipedia.org/wiki/File:Vat.lat.2463,_f._1r,_top.png, Source: https://digi.vatlib.it/view/MSS_Vat.lat.2463, License: [Public Domain], via Wikimedia Commons

P. 541 The Walk to Emmaus, c.1877 (oil on canvas) Artist: Zund, Robert (1827–1909) / Swiss, Photo credit: © Christie's Images/Bridgeman Images